Methods of Environmental Impact Assessment
Third edition

**Edited by Peter Morris
and Riki Therivel**

Routledge
Taylor & Francis Group

LONDON AND NEW YORK

First edition published 1995 by UCL Press

Second edition published 2001 by Spon Press

Third edition published 2009
by Routledge
2 Park Square, Milton Park, Abingdon, Oxon OX14 4RN

Simultaneously published in the USA and Canada
by Routledge
270 Madison Avenue, New York, NY 10016, USA

Reprinted 2010

Routledge is an imprint of the Taylor & Francis Group,
an informa business

© 2009 Peter Morris and Riki Therivel for selection and editorial
matter; individual chapters, the contributors

Typeset in Goudy by Graphicraft Limited, Hong Kong
Printed and bound by CPI Antony Rowe, Chippenham, Wilts

British Library Cataloguing in Publication Data
A catalogue record for this book is available from the British Library

Library of Congress Cataloging in Publication Data
Methods of environmental impact assessment / edited by Peter Morris
and Riki Therivel.
    p. cm. – (The natural and built environment series)
    Includes bibliographical references.
    1. Environmental impact analysis–Great Britain.   2. Environmental
impact analysis–European Union countries.   I. Morris, Peter, 1934–
II. Therivel, Riki, 1960–
    TD194.68.G7M48 2009
    333.71′4–dc22   2008032569

ISBN10: 0-415-44174-9 (hbk)
ISBN10: 0-415-44175-7 (pbk)
ISBN10: 0-203-89290-9 (ebk)

ISBN13: 978-0-415-44174-2 (hbk)
ISBN13: 978-0-415-44175-9 (pbk)
ISBN13: 978-0-203-89290-9 (ebk)

For Angie and Tim, again?

Contents

Contributors to this edition

Andrew Brookes is a Divisional Director at Jacobs Engineering UK Ltd.

Andrew Chadwick is a Research Associate at the Impacts Assessment Unit in the School of the Built Environment, Oxford Brookes University.

Richard Cottle is a Principal Environmental Scientist at Royal Haskoning, Exeter, UK.

Hannah Dalton is a Principal Consultant at Gifford, UK.

Roy Emberton is a Technical Director of Environment Development Planning at Gifford, UK.

Chris Fry is Director in Environmental Policy at AEA, UK.

John Glasson is Professor Emeritus in Environmental Planning, Co-Director of the Impact Assessment Unit, and Founding Director of the Oxford Institute for Sustainable Development – all at Oxford Brookes University.

Kevin Hawkins is a Technical Director at WSP Environmental Ltd, London.

Martin Hodson was a Principal Lecturer (now Visiting Researcher) in Environmental Biology in the School of Life Sciences, Oxford Brookes University.

Sian John is a Director of the UK Environment team for Royal Haskoning, Peterborough, UK.

Sally-Beth Kelday is a Senior Environmental Scientist at Jacobs Engineering UK Ltd.

Rebecca Knight is an Associate at Land Use Consultants, UK.

Peter Morris was a Principal Lecturer (now retired) in Ecology in the School of Biological and Molecular Sciences, Oxford Brookes University.

Agustin Rodriguez-Bachiller is an Associate Lecturer, partly retired, in Quantitative Methods in Planning and GIS in the School of the Built Environment, Oxford Brookes University.

Chris Stapleton is Managing Director of Bell Cornwell Environmental, UK.

Riki Therivel is a partner of Levett-Therivel sustainability consultants, and a visiting professor at the School of the Built Environment, Oxford Brookes University.

David Walker is a Technical Director of Environment Development Planning at Gifford, UK.

Graham Wood is a Reader in Environmental Assessment and Management in the School of the Built Environment, Oxford Brookes University.

Preface and acknowledgements

The idea of a book on methods of environmental impact assessment arose during the writing of the first edition of *Introduction to Environmental Impact Assessment* (Glasson *et al.* 1994). We realised that very few books existed on how EIA should be carried out for specific environmental components such as air, flora and fauna, or socio-economics, and that none was written for the UK/EU context. Since then, *Introduction* has gone through a second and third edition, and the second edition of *Methods* has become more dated than we would like. Together with the third edition of *Introduction*, this book aims to provide a comprehensive coverage of the theory and practice of EIA in the UK and EU twenty years after the implementation of the European EIA Directive.

This book is aimed at people who organise, review and make decisions about EIA; at environmental planners and managers; at students taking first degrees in planning, ecology, geography and related subjects with an EIA content; and at postgraduate students taking courses in EIA or environmental management. It explains what the major concerns of the EIA component specialists are, how data on each environmental component are collected, what standards and regulations apply, how impacts are predicted, what mitigation measures can be used to minimise or eliminate impacts, what some of the limitations of these methods are, and where further information can be obtained. It does not aim to make specialists out of its readers; to do so would require at least one book per environmental component. Instead it aims to foster better communication between experts, a better understanding of how EIAs are carried out, and hopefully better EIA-related decisions.

Like its sister volume, this book emphasises best practice – what ideally should happen – as well as minimal regulatory requirements. EIA is a constantly evolving and improving process. If the trends of the last two decades continue, today's EIA best practice will be tomorrow's minimal regulatory requirement.

The basis of this book is a unit on Oxford Brookes University's MSc course in Environmental Assessment and Management. The unit is taught by a range of university staff and outside specialists who have practical expertise in EIA. The chapters in this edition, like those of the previous two editions, were written by people who teach (or have taught) on the course plus additional outside experts. We are very grateful to the authors of this edition for their excellent contributions. We are also grateful to the authors who contributed to previous editions of the book, but were unable to take part in this edition – and who gave permission for the new authors to modify and update the relevant chapters rather than writing them from scratch. That these chapters are based on the previous authors' contributions is acknowledged by citing them.

We are also grateful to:

- Land Use Consultants, Natural England and Ordnance Survey for permission to use Figure 6.1. Reproduced by permission of Ordnance Survey on behalf of HMSO. © Crown copyright 2008. All rights reserved. Ordnance Survey Licence number 100045659. The figure was produced in ESRI ArcMap 9.2 taking into account the curvature of the earth. The results of the study are for information only and do not reflect or represent Natural England's views on a barrage.
- Land Use Consultants and npower renewables limited for permission to use Figure 6.2. The figure is based on 3D OS Landform Panorama Digital Terrain Map, 1:50,000 scale. Copyright for the figure is with npower renewables limited.
- Land Use Consultants, Cascade Consulting, Lewin Fryer and Partners, and Gwynedd Council for permission to use Figure 6.4. The map is based on Ordnance Survey data and is redrawn from an OS base map 1:1250 scale. Reproduced by permission of Ordnance Survey on behalf of HMSO. © Crown copyright 2008. All rights reserved. Ordnance Survey Licence number 100045659.
- Roger Barrowcliffe (Environmental Resources Management, London) who provided Figures 8.1 and 8.2.
- ESRI UK for permission to use Figure 14.1.
- Derek Whitely and Rob Woodward (both of Oxford Brookes University) for the line drawings.

Although every effort has been made to ensure accuracy throughout the book, the authors cannot accept responsibility for any consequences of actions taken as a result of advice or opinions given. In addition, the contributors wish to make clear that any views expressed are their own and not necessarily those of their employers.

Reference

Glasson J, R Therivel and A Chadwick 1994. *An introduction to environmental impact assessment*. London: UCL Press.

Part I

Methods for environmental components

1 Introduction

Riki Therivel and Peter Morris

1.1 EIA and the aims of the book

This book aims to improve practice of environmental impact assessment (EIA) by providing information about how EIAs are, and should be, carried out. Although it focuses on the UK context in its discussion of policies and standards, the principles it discusses apply universally, as do many of the assessment methods it describes. This introductory chapter (a) summarises the current status of EIA, and the legislative background in the UK and EU, (b) explains the book's structure, and (c) considers some trends in EIA methods.

Formal EIA can be defined as "the whole process whereby information about the environmental effects of a project is collected, assessed and taken into account in reaching a decision on whether the project should go ahead or not" (DCLG 2006a). It can also be defined more simply as "an assessment of the impacts of a planned activity on the environment" (UNECE 1991). In addition to the decision on whether a project should proceed, an EIA will consider aspects such as **project options/alternatives** and mitigation measures that should be implemented if the development is allowed. The findings of an EIA are presented in a document called an Environmental Statement or (as in this book) **Environmental Impact Statement** (EIS). The overall EIA process is explained and discussed in this book's "sister volume", *Introduction to Environmental Impact Assessment* (Glasson *et al.* 2005).

EIAs involve individual assessments of aspects of the environment (e.g. population, landscape, heritage, air, climate, soil, water, fauna, flora) likely to be significantly affected by a proposed project. This book focuses on assessment methods (practical techniques) used in the part of the EIA process concerned with analysing a development's impacts on these **environmental components**.

1.2 The EIA process

1.2.1 Introduction

The main EIA procedures that will be followed in the assessment of any environmental component are summarised in **Figure 1.1**. The figure assumes that the

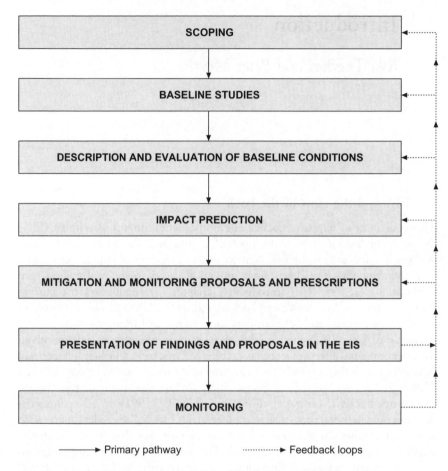

The model illustrates the stepwise nature of EIA, but also the requirement for continuous reappraisal and adjustment (as indicated by the feedback loops).

Figure 1.1 Procedures in the assessment of an environmental component for an EIA.

developer has conducted feasibility studies, and that *screening* has already been carried out – and these assumptions are made in the chapters. Screening is discussed in Glasson *et al.* (2005).

1.2.2 Scoping and baseline studies

Scoping is an essential first step in the assessment of a component. The main aims are:

- to identify at an early stage (when the project design is relatively amenable to modification) what key *receptors*, impacts and project alternatives

to consider, what methodologies to use, and whom to consult. UK government policy also advocates an appraisal-led design process, and various
documents (e.g. MAFF 2000) provide guidance on identifying the **preferred
option** from an environmental perspective;

- to ensure that resources and time are focused on important impacts and
  receptors;
- to establish early communication between the developer, consultants, statutory
  consultees and other interest groups who can provide advice and information;
- to warn the developer of any constraints which may pose problems if not
  discovered until later in the EIA process.

The scoping exercise should provide a ground plan for subsequent steps by
making a preliminary assessment of:

- the project's **potential impacts** on component receptors, estimated from the
  project description (including its size, construction requirements, operational
  features and secondary developments such as access roads) and the nature
  of components and receptors;
- the **impact area/zone** within which impacts are likely occur, estimated from
  the impact types and the nature of the surrounding area and environmental components, e.g. impacts on air or water may occur at considerable
  distances from the project site;
- possible **mitigation measures**;
- the need and potential for **monitoring**;
- the **methods and levels of study** needed to obtain reliable baseline information that can be used to evaluate the baseline conditions, make accurate
  impact predictions, and formulate adequate mitigation measures and monitoring procedures. The selection of methods should involve consideration of:

  - the impact and receptor variables on which the studies will focus, and
    the accuracy and precision needed for each;
  - the most appropriate methods for collecting, analysing and presenting
    information;
  - the resource requirements and timing considerations, especially for
    field surveys;
  - constraints such as the time and resources available.

Some commonly used aids in EIA are outlined in **Table 1.1**. Two of these, checklists and scorecards, are useful scoping tools, particularly for tasks such as
identifying key impacts and receptors, and selecting appropriate consultees and
interest groups. The findings of the scoping exercise should be documented in
a **scoping report** that is made available to the developer, participating consultants and consultees. However, lack of detailed information at the scoping stage
means that scoping estimates and decisions should be reassessed in the light of
baseline information gained as the EIA progresses.

Table 1.1 Commonly used aids in EIA

Method	Attributes
Checklists	Useful, especially in scoping, for identifying key impacts and ensuring that they are not overlooked. Can include information such as data requirements, study options, questions to be answered, and statutory thresholds – but are not generally suitable for detailed analysis. Can have various uses, e.g. (a) to identify impacts and cause–effect links between impact sources (plotted along one axis) and impacts (plotted along the other axis); (b) to link features such as magnitude and extent (e.g. localised or extensive, short or long term); and (c) to derive estimated impact significances from assessed receptor values and impact magnitudes (e.g. see Table 11.8).
Scorecards	Provide a simple, transparent method for comparing and ranking "subjects" such as receptors or impact factors. Scores for several criteria can be assigned to each subject; and various scales can be used, although summation is only possible if the same scale applies to all criteria (**Table 1.2**). The method can be used for assessing the relative importance of "subjects" in various contexts including scoping (e.g. identifying key receptors), impact prediction, project options appraisal, and integration of component assessments. However: (a) it does not assist in determining if criteria overlap/ interact or should be given different weightings; and (b) unless based on quantitative data, the scores are subjective, and experts with differing viewpoints may assign different scores for a given criterion.
Flowcharts and networks	Can be useful for identifying cause–effect links/pathways: between impact sources; between sources and impacts; and between primary and secondary impacts. However, they cannot quantify the magnitudes of impacts or of their effects.
Mathematical/ statistical models	Are based on mathematical or statistical functions which are applied to calculate deterministic or probabilistic quantitative values from numerical input data. They range from simple formulae to sophisticated models that incorporate many variables. They need adequate/reliable data, can be expensive, and may not be suitable for "off the peg" use.
Maps	Are often essential. They can indicate features such as impact areas/zones, and locations and extents of receptor sites and/or features within these. Overlay maps can combine and integrate two or three "layers", e.g. for different impacts and/or environmental components or receptors.
GIS (Chapter 14)	Can be very valuable (a) as a sophisticated mapping tool that can relate a number of different variables by spatially referencing (overlaying) datasets, and (b) in conjunction with an external tool (such as an expert system or simulation model) as a means of analysing quantitative data and modelling outcomes.

Table 1.2 A hypothetical scorecard to compare and rank four subjects in relation to four criteria assessed by means of different scales

	Criterion 1 (% scale)	Criterion 2 (1–10 scale)	Criterion 3 (0–5 scale)	Criterion 4 (+/– scale)	Sum (if applicable)	Rank (if possible)
Subject 1	15	5	5	+		2
Subject 2	40	3	2	0		3
Subject 3	60	6	4	++		1
Subject 4	10	4	1	–		4

Baseline studies form the backbone of component assessments. It is only when they provide sound information on the socio-economic or environmental systems in the impact area that valid impact predictions can be made, and effective mitigation and monitoring programmes formulated.

The distinction between baseline studies and scoping is not clear cut because (a) consultation should be ongoing, and (b) scoping includes gathering information, much of which is effectively baseline material that can at least form the starting point for more detailed studies. In both stages, it is usually possible to compile some of the required information, by means of a **desk study**. A thorough search should be made because (a) gathering existing information is generally less expensive and time-consuming than obtaining new data, and (b) it is pointless to undertake new work that merely duplicates information that already exists. However

- Scoping will usually require brief site visits (e.g. for reconnaissance or to confirm features identified on maps) – perhaps including walkover surveys. Such initial visits are best undertaken by several members of the EIA and design team, so that relationships between components can be identified.
- In most cases, existing baseline data will be inadequate or out of date, and it will be necessary to obtain new information by some form of **field survey**.

The **description and evaluation of baseline conditions** should include:

- a clear presentation of methods and results;
- indications of limitations and uncertainties, e.g. in relation to data accuracy and completeness;
- an assessment of the value of key receptors and their sensitivity to impacts.

1.2.3 Impact prediction

Impact prediction is fundamental to EIA, and the likely impacts of a project should be considered for all environmental components. In order to predict the impacts of a development it is also necessary to consider changes in the baseline conditions that may occur in its absence (a) prior to its initiation, which can be several years after production of the EIS, and (b) during its projected lifetime. These can be assessed in relation to the current baseline conditions and information on past, present and predicted conditions and trends. Most of the relevant information will have to be sought through the desk study although comparison of field survey data with previous data can help to elucidate recent trends. Box 7.1 gives sources of historical information.

According to the EIA legislation (§1.3) impact prediction should include assessment of

- **Direct/primary impacts** – that are a direct result of a development.
- **Indirect/secondary impacts** – that may be "knock on" effects of (and in the same location as) direct impacts, but are often produced in other locations and/or as a result of a complex pathway.
- **Cumulative impacts** – that accrue over time and space from a number of developments or activities, and to which a new project may contribute. In *"appropriate assessment"* (under the Habitats Directive), these are called "in combination" impacts.

An additional possibility is **impact interactions** – between different impacts of a project, or between these and impacts of other projects – that result in one or more additional impacts, e.g. $(A + B) \rightarrow C$. For instance, the interaction of population and air pollution may cause health effects.

All impacts may be: **positive** (beneficial) or **negative** (adverse); **short-**, **medium-**, or **long-term**; **reversible** or **irreversible**; and **permanent** or **temporary**.

Ideally, impact prediction requires:

- a good understanding of the nature of the proposed project, including project design, construction activities and timing;
- knowledge of the outcomes of similar projects and EIAs, including the effectiveness of mitigation measures;
- knowledge of past, existing or approved projects which may cause interactive or cumulative impacts with the project being assessed;
- predictions of the project's impacts on other environmental components that may interact with that under study;
- adequate information about the relevant receptors, and knowledge of how these may respond to environmental changes/disturbances.

Methods of impact prediction vary both between and within EIA components. For example, the assessment of impact **magnitude** (severity) may be qualitative or quantitative. Qualitative assessments usually employ ratings such as *neutral, slight, moderate, large* – applied to both negative and positive impacts. They are typically used where quantitative assessments are difficult or impossible, for instance in landscape, archaeological and ecological assessment. Quantitative assessments involve the measurement or calculation of numerical values, e.g. of the level of a *pollutant* in relation to a statutory threshold value.

Standard techniques that can be used to aid impact prediction in assessments of most environmental components are reviewed in Glasson *et al.* (2005) and briefly summarised in Table 1.1.

It is also important to assess **impact significance**, which is the "product" of an impact's magnitude and the value, sensitivity/fragility and recoverability of the relevant receptor(s). It therefore requires an evaluation of these receptor attributes – which should have been carried out in the baseline evaluation.

Impact prediction is often poorly addressed, perhaps because it is the most difficult step in EIA. Direct impacts are usually relatively easy to identify, but accurate prediction of indirect and **cumulative impacts** can be much more problematic. Guidance on assessing these (and impact interactions) is provided in CEAA (1999) and EC (1999).

Whatever methods are employed, impact prediction is not an exact science. There are bound to be uncertainties (that can sometimes be expressed as ranges) which should be clearly stated in the EIS.

1.2.4 Mitigation

Mitigation measures aim to avoid, minimise, remedy or compensate (in that sequence) for the predicted adverse impacts of the project. They can include:

* selection of alternative production techniques, and/or locations or alignments (of linear projects);
* modification of the methods and timing of construction;
* modification of design features, including site boundaries and features, e.g. landscaping;
* minimisation of operational impacts (e.g. pollution and waste);
* specific measures, perhaps outside the development site, to minimise particular impacts;
* measures to compensate for losses, e.g. of amenity or habitat features.

Much of the environmental damage caused by developments occurs during the **construction phase**, and a problem is that construction is usually contracted to a construction company who will not have participated in the EIA process, and over whom the developer may have little control (Wathern 1999). Consequently, there is a need to provide a Construction Environmental Management Plan, ideally as part of an overall project Environmental Management Plan (see §1.5). In addition, because project specifications frequently change between publication of the EIS and the start or completion of construction (often for unforeseeable reasons) developers sometimes employ site environmental managers to ensure (a) that such modifications take account of environmental considerations, and (b) that construction phase mitigation measures are carried out.

Different mitigation measures will be needed in relation to specific impacts on different environmental components and receptors. The EIS should provide detailed prescriptions for proposed measures for each impact, indicate how they would actually be put in place, and propose how they might be modified if unforeseen post-project impacts arise. A primary consideration is the likely significance of post-mitigation **residual impacts**, and care is needed to ensure that a mitigation measure does not generate new impacts, perhaps on receptors in other environmental components.

Best practice dictates that the *precautionary principle* (advocated in EU and UK environmental policy) should be applied, i.e. that mitigation should be based on the possibility of a significant impact even though there may not be conclusive evidence that it will occur. Similarly, on the basis of the EU principles that preventive action is preferable to remedial measures, and that environmental damage should be rectified at source (see §1.3) the best mitigation measures should involve modifications to the project rather than containment or repair at receptor sites, or compensatory measures such as habitat creation – which should normally be considered only as a last resort (see §11.8.4).

In addition to mitigation, government guidelines suggest that opportunities for **environmental enhancement** (improvement of current environmental conditions and features) should be sought in EIA. For instance, this is one of the duties of the Environment Agency, especially in relation to coastal and flood defences (Defra 2005).

1.2.5 Presentation of findings and proposals in the EIS

The information presented in the EIS must be clear and, at least in the non-technical summary, should be in a form that can be understood by "non-experts" without compromising its integrity. It should also be "transparent", e.g. in relation to limitations and uncertainties. Presentation methods vary between components, but can include the use of maps, graphs/charts, tables and photographs.

The EIS must be an integrated document, and this will necessitate assessing the component in relation to others, e.g. to evaluate its relative importance, and ensure that potential conflicts of interest have been addressed (see §1.5).

1.2.6 Monitoring

Monitoring can be defined as the continuous assessment of environmental or socio-economic variables by the systematic collection of specific data in space and time. It can be strictly continuous, e.g. using recording instruments, but more commonly involves periodic repeat data collection, usually by the same or similar methods as in baseline surveys. Monitoring in EIA can include

- **Baseline monitoring** – which may be carried out over seasons or years to quantify ranges of natural variation and/or directions and rates of change, that are relevant to impact prediction and mitigation. This can avoid the frequent criticism that baseline studies are only "snapshots" in time. However, time constraints in EIA usually preclude lengthy survey programmes, and assessments of long-term trends normally have to rely on existing data.

- **Compliance monitoring** – which aims to check that specific conditions and standards are met, e.g. in relation to emissions of pollutants.
- **Impact and mitigation monitoring** – which aims to compare predicted and actual (residual) impacts, and hence to determine the effectiveness of mitigation measures.

Unless otherwise specified, "monitoring" in EIA normally refers to impact and mitigation monitoring, which is also sometimes called auditing. There is often considerable uncertainty associated with impacts and mitigation measures, and it is responsible best practice to undertake monitoring during both the construction and post-development phases of a project. Monitoring is essential to learn from both successes and failures. For example:

- It is the only mechanism for comparing predicted and actual impacts, and hence of checking whether mitigation measures have been put in place, testing their effectiveness, and evaluating the efficiency of the project management programme;
- If mitigation measures are amenable to modification, it should still be possible to reduce residual impacts identified during monitoring (feedback loop in Figure 1.1);
- It can provide information about responses of particular receptors to impacts;
- It is the only means of EIA/EIS evaluation and of identifying mistakes that may be rectified in future EIAs. For example, it will provide information that can be used to assess the adequacy of survey and predictive methods, and how they may be improved. Thus, a principal aim of monitoring should be to contribute to a cumulative database that can facilitate the improvement of future EIAs (Clark 1996).

Three requirements are essential for successful monitoring: (a) baseline data that are good enough to detect residual impacts; (b) funding to carry out the monitoring survey work; and (c) sufficient contingency funds to enable modifications to mitigation measures to be made, or faults to be rectified, if necessary.

Monitoring is not strictly part of the EIA process, is not statutory in the UK, and can be expensive. Consequently, in spite of government guidance that it should be undertaken (e.g. Defra 2005) lack of monitoring is a serious deficiency in current EIA practice (SNH 2005).

1.3 The current status of EIA

Since the first EIA system was established in the USA in 1970, EIA systems have been set up worldwide and have become a powerful environmental safeguard in the project planning process. In Europe, EU Directives 85/337/EEC, 97/11/EC and 2003/35/EC (EC 1985, 1997, 2003) set the legal basis for individual member states' EIA regulations. More than 300 EISs are currently prepared annually in the UK alone.

Several important internationally-accepted principles underlie the recent rapid growth in EIA and *strategic environmental assessment* (SEA) (see §1.6). The World Commission on Environment and Development espoused the principle of **sustainable development** in its report of 1987 (WCED 1987), and this was further elucidated at the UN Conference on Environment and Development (UNCED 1992) – the "Rio Earth Summit". EIA is an example of this evolving worldwide emphasis on preventive, holistic approaches to environmental protection and promotion of sustainable development (see Chapter 16).

EU Directives 85/337/EEC and 97/11/EC require that, for a specified list of project types (Annex I of Directive 97/11), EIA *must* be carried out. EIA *may* be carried out for projects in another list (Annex II), depending on the characteristics and location of the project, and the characteristics of the potential impacts (Annex III). The required contents of the EIS are given in Annex IV. These are:

1. Description of the project, including in particular:

    -   a description of the physical characteristics of the whole project and the land-use requirements during the construction and operational phases;
    -   a description of the main characteristics of the production processes, for instance, nature and quantity of the materials used;
    -   an estimate, by type and quantity, of expected residues and emissions resulting from the operation of the proposed project.

2. An outline of the main alternatives studied by the developer and an indication of the main reasons for this choice, taking into account the environmental effects.

3. A description of the aspects of the environment likely to be significantly affected by the proposed project including, in particular, population, fauna and flora, soil, water, air and climate, material assets (including the architectural and archaeological heritage), landscape and the inter-relationship between the above factors.

4. A description of the likely significant effects of the proposed project on the environment resulting from:

    -   the existence of the project;
    -   the use of natural resources;
    -   the emission of pollutants, the creation of nuisances and the elimination of waste; and
    -   the description by the developer of the forecasting methods used to assess the effects on the environment.

5. A description of the measures envisaged to prevent, reduce and where possible offset any significant adverse effects on the environment.

6. A non-technical summary of the information provided under the above headings.

7. An indication of any difficulties (technical deficiencies or lack of know-how) encountered by the developer in compiling the required information.

Directive 97/11/EC (EC 1997), which became operational on 14 March 1999, expanded the requirements of Directive 85/337/EEC by:

• requiring EIA for a wider range of projects, and upgrading of some Annex II projects to Annex I status;
• giving criteria (including the concept of **"sensitive environments"** and a list of specified types of sensitive environments) for choosing which Annex II projects require EIA;
• strengthening the procedural requirements concerning transboundary impacts (where pollution from one country affects another country);
• requiring developers to include an outline of the main alternatives that they studied and explain the reasons for the final choice between alternatives;
• allowing developers to request an opinion from the **competent authority** on the scope of an EIA;
• requiring competent authorities to make public the main reasons on which project decisions are based and the main mitigation measures required.

The *Public Participation Directive* 2003/35/EC (EC 2003) aims to contribute to the implementation of the obligations arising under the Aarhus Convention, by improving public participation and providing for access to justice through EIA. It provides more detailed requirements for how the public and other Member States should be informed about EIA. It also sets new requirements that allow members of the public with a sufficient interest or whose rights have been impaired through a planning decision to have access to a legal review procedure.

In the UK, EIA Directives are implemented by about 40 regulations – mainly Statutory Instruments (SIs). The core regulations are the *Town and Country Planning (Environmental Impact Assessment) (England and Wales) Regulations 1999* (HMSO 1999) and the equivalent regulations in Scotland (SE 1999a). The requirements of each regulation differ slightly, but all are essentially variants of the core regulations. Schedules 3 and 4 of the regulations are particularly relevant to this book.

English government guidance on the EIA procedures is given in ODPM (2000). Guidance on the preparation of EISs is given in DoE (1995), DETR (1999) and two consultation documents DCLG (2006a, 2006b). Information about legal issues related to EIA is at DCLG (undated). Scottish guidance is given by SE (1999b) and SNH (2005). EU guidance on EIA is available at http://ec.europa.eu/environment/eia/home.htm. EIA procedures are further discussed in Glasson *et al.* (2005), which also presents a wide range of further literature on the topic.

EIA is also being carried out informally in situations where it is not mandatory, but where developers feel that its structured approach would help in project management or in speeding up the planning process (Hughes & Wood 1996). Moreover, authorities such as the Environment Agency frequently produce or require informal **environmental appraisals** for projects not requiring statutory EIA. The principles and procedures described in this book also apply to such informal assessments.

In addition to the specific EIA legislation, a wide range of legislation affects the assessment of individual environmental components, key examples of which are referred to in the relevant chapters of this book.

1.4 Book structure

The book is divided into two main parts.

Part I discusses EIA methods for a range of environmental components. **Table 1.3** shows how the chapters correspond to the components itemised for particular attention in the EU and UK legislation. The book includes some components not specifically listed in the regulations but often discussed in practice, namely noise, transport, geology and geomorphology. Chapters 2 and 3 deal with socio-economic impacts. Chapters 4–7 deal with impacts that are partly socio-economic and partly physical: noise; landscape; transport; and heritage. "Physical" environmental components are covered as follows: air and climate in Chapter 8; soils, geology and geomorphology in Chapter 9 (which also covers impacts on agriculture); and water in Chapter 10. "Flora and fauna" is covered in Chapter 11 in terms of the ecology of terrestrial and freshwater ecosystems; but because of the particular importance of coastal geomorphology and its close relationship with coastal ecology, these two components are considered together in Chapter 12.

All of these chapters are all similar in structure; each includes the main EIA steps for the assessment of an environmental component (as outlined in §1.2). The main chapter sections are:

Table 1.3 The book's coverage of the environmental components listed in Annex IV of Directive 97/11/EC and Schedule 4 of the UK regulations

Environmental component	Chapter number and title
Population	2. Economic impacts 3. Social impacts 4. Noise 5. Transport
Landscape	6. Landscape
Material assets and the cultural heritage	2. Economic impacts 3. Social impacts 7. Heritage
Air, climatic factors	8. Air quality and climate
Soil	9. Soils, geology and geomorphology
Water	10. Water
Fauna and flora	11. Ecology 12. Coastal ecology and geomorphology

- introduction;
- definitions and concepts;
- legislative background and interest groups;
- scoping and baseline studies;
- impact prediction;
- mitigation;
- monitoring.

Part II of the book considers some "cross-cutting" EIA methods: risk assessment and management in Chapter 13; GIS in Chapter 14; Quality of Life Capital in Chapter 15; and sustainability appraisal in Chapter 16. These techniques can often be applied to, and/or facilitate integration between, the environmental components discussed in the first part. These chapters are necessarily somewhat different and individual in structure.

There are four **Appendices**: Appendix A lists acronyms, internet addresses, chemical symbols and quantitative units used in the text. Appendix B lists (and outlines the roles of) UK environment, conservation and heritage organisations; and Appendices C and D supplement the ecological information given in Chapters 11 and 12. Lastly, there is an extensive **Glossary** which is referred to in the chapters and appendices by highlighting the relevant terms in bold italics.

The subjects covered cannot all be discussed in depth in a book of this size. Each chapter aims to provide an overview of the subject. However: (a) the subjects are large and complex, so only brief mention can be made of many aspects including specific methods; and (b) the wide range of subjects covered by the different chapters means that a reader is likely to be familiar with some but not others. These problems are addressed in three ways.

1. Each chapter's "concepts and definitions" section provides some background information for the benefit of readers who have little or no knowledge of the subject.
2. Terms that will not be familiar to some readers are defined in the glossary rather than within chapters. This reduces repetition in different chapters, which is also why the glossary contains some references.
3. The chapters aim to act as springboards for further reading by making frequent reference to other published material in which additional information is available.

1.5 Integration of component assessments

Although the chapters in this book are presented as separate entities, in practice the individual environmental component assessments should be integrated, and be part of the wider process of project planning. Clearly, an EIA must involve a **team of experts** on the various components, and in many cases on different aspects of a given component. As indicated in Figure 1.1, close coordination is needed to avoid duplication of effort, while ensuring that important aspects are not omitted. This is particularly important for inter-related components such as soils, geology, air, water and ecology. In addition, the EIS must be an integrated document in which relationships between components are clearly explained. The use of GIS (Chapter 14) can facilitate the integration and comparison of data on different components.

It follows that there must be an **EIA coordinator** who will ensure that (a) cross-component consultation is carried out throughout the EIA process, and (b) appraisals are conducted to consider aspects such as components' relative importances, the relative significance of different impacts, interactions between impacts, possible conflicts of interest, and distributional effects. For example:

- One sector of the community, or part of the impact area, may be particularly affected by multiple developments, or by the concentration of a project's impacts. For instance, lower socio-economic groups are more likely to suffer from traffic accidents, air pollution and noise (Lucas and Simpson 2000). Identification of the groups/areas most strongly affected can be facilitated by use of GIS or simply by a table listing receptors (e.g. particular socio-economic groups, sensitive sites) on one axis, and the main impacts of a project on the other axis. A more equitable distribution of impacts may then be sought, or strongly affected groups may be compensated in some way.
- It is important to ensure that mitigation measures proposed for different environmental components are consistent with those for other components, and do not themselves cause negative impacts. For instance, tree plantings which reduce visual impacts could have beneficial side-effects for noise, but could intrude on archaeological remains.

An initial assessment of the relative importance of environmental components can be made by means of a scorecard, in which each component is entered as a "subject" (Tables 1.1 and 1.2). More sophisticated appraisals can include the use of scenarios and **sensitivity analysis** of the effects (on an appraisal) of varying the projected values of important variables. Another useful tool is the use of an *audit trail*, which can be particularly beneficial if further EIA analysis is needed because the project changes substantially between the time when it is approved and when it is built. Ideally, final assessment should result in the preparation of a list of proposed planning conditions/obligations and an *Environmental Management Plan* (EMP) for the proposed development, to be included in the EIS or presented in a separate document (Brew and Lee 1996).

1.6 The broader context and the future of EIA methods

Projects are not planned, built, operated and decommissioned in isolation, but within regional, national and international processes of change which include other projects, programmes, plans and policies. The aim of assessing cumulative impacts (§1.2.3) is to take these into account as far as possible in relation to a single development project. However, some projects are so inextricably related to other projects, or their impacts are so clearly linked, that a joint EIA of these projects should be carried out. For instance if a gas-fired power station requires the construction of a new pipeline and gas reception/processing facility to receive the gas, and transmission lines to carry the resulting electricity, these projects should be considered together in an EIA, despite the fact that each requires EIA under different regulations.

Other projects are "growth-inducing", i.e. necessary precursors to other projects. For instance a new motorway may, directly or indirectly, trigger the construction of motorway service stations, hypermarkets or new towns; or the infrastructure provided for one project may make a site more attractive, or may present economies of scale, for further development. Although it is probably not feasible to consider induced impacts in detail in an EIA, the EIA should at least acknowledge the possibility of these further developments.

The broadening of EIA's remit to encompass other projects may allow trade-offs to be made between impacts and between projects. For instance, an environmentally beneficial **"shadow project"** may be proposed to compensate for the negative impacts of a development project. An example of this is the "creation" of a new waterfowl feeding ground on coastal grassland as compensation for the loss of tidal mudflat feeding grounds caused by the Cardiff Bay Barrage. However, shadow projects need to be treated with caution. For instance, it can be argued that the provision of a coastal grassland area does not effectively compensate for the loss of tidal mudflats because it is a different habitat supporting different wildlife communities. Compensatory like-for-like creation of valuable habitats is generally much more difficult (see §11.8.4).

Project EIAs also need to be set in the context of **strategic environmental assessment** (SEA) of sectoral or spatial policies, plans and programmes. SEAs can, in theory, reduce the time and cost of EIA, and even eliminate the need for certain types of EIA (Bass 1998), although not much evidence of this currently exists. SEA can also provide background information about the local policy context, baseline environmental conditions, and existing environmental problems in the project area. It has been required in Europe since 2004 as a result of the "SEA Directive" (EC 2001). The UK Government has published guidance on how to carry out SEAs (ODPM 2005).

EIA and SEA should be, and are increasingly being, linked to other related techniques. For example:

- Project design is increasingly being influenced by environmental concerns. There is increasing awareness of the need to minimise resource use in building construction and use, and greater application of techniques such as passive solar heating, photovoltaics and greywater recycling, and of innovative construction methods such as straw bale and earth-sheltered housing and self-build schemes. Tighter building regulations, and the Code for Sustainable Homes and BREEAM (see Chapter 16) are contributing to this.
- *Appropriate assessment* (or Habitats Regulations Assessment) is required where a project may have a significant "in combination" impact on the integrity of a European or Ramsar site (see Table D.1). Appropriate assessment of

projects has been carried out for more than 20 years in response to the Habitats Directive (EC 1992), but appropriate assessment of plans in the UK was only triggered by a European Court of Justice (2005) ruling. Appropriate assessment of plans is identifying wider scale and more diffuse impacts than appropriate assessments of projects alone, for instance the impacts of diffuse air pollution or recreational disturbance on sensitive sites and species. This is likely to affect future appropriate assessments and EIS of projects.

- There is increasing use of environmental risk assessment (ERA) and risk management (Chapter 13). This also employs statistical modelling, and techniques such as **event tree analysis** (§13.4.1) which is a form of flowchart analysis. ERA is particularly relevant to the prediction of impacts from accidents, and is embodied, for example, in the *Control of Major Accident Hazards (COMAH) Regulations* (SI 1999/743) which implement the EU COMAH Directive 96/82/EC on the control of major accident hazards involving dangerous substances (see HSE and EA/SEPA 1999).

- The Quality of Life Capital approach (CC *et al.* 1997) discussed in Chapter 15, can be used to develop management plans for areas of various sizes, based on an analysis of the benefits and disbenefits that they provide: it is likely to provide a particularly useful early input to the project design process.

- Integrated pollution prevention and control (IPPC) legislation and techniques bring together analyses of the impacts of new developments on air, water and soils.

- Village/community mapping exercises can help to identify features that are particularly valued by local residents.

- Life cycle analyses can help to identify the impacts of buildings from the production of the materials used to build them through to their ultimate dismantling and disposal.

- At the global level, environmental policy is experiencing a general move away from a narrow emphasis on the protection of current environmental resources, and towards a broader promotion of sustainability, although this is not without its critics (see Chapter 16). Sustainability checklists can be used by development control officers to ensure that all developments – not just those for which EIA is required – minimise their environmental impacts.

New tools, techniques and approaches are being developed which complement and support the EIA process. For example:

- Mapping software and geographical information systems (GIS) (Chapter 14) now allow much more effective analysis and presentation of information than in the past;

- There is a rapid expansion in the range and availability of information databases, including remote sensed data and other digital data suitable for GIS;

- The internet now provides ready access to a wealth of information, including legislation, other publications, databases and software;

- In ecology and landscape analysis, although legislation and government guidelines still focus on protecting designated areas, there is a shift from "save the best and leave the rest" to consideration of the "wider countryside" and characterisation of areas, with the aim of promoting their uniqueness and joint diversity (CC & EN 1998, Defra 2007);
- More emphasis is being placed on environmental enhancement, not just mitigation of negative impacts;
- Although monitoring is still not mandatory, it is being encouraged in government guidelines;
- Evolving approaches to public participation – particularly in developing Sustainable Community Strategies and in community mapping exercises – allow local residents' views to be better understood and taken into consideration in EIA.

Finally, concern about wider distributional impacts – for instance about whether some countries are "importing" sustainability at the cost of making environmental conditions in other countries unsustainable – is likely to lead to more evolved forms of public participation and political negotiations, and ultimately to a more equitable approach to development and the environment.

References

Bass R 1998. *Quantifying the environmental impacts of land use plans*. Paper presented at the International Association of Impact Assessment annual conference. Christchurch, New Zealand.

Brew D and N Lee 1996. The role of environmental management plans in the EIA process. *EIA Newsletter (12)*, Manchester University EIA centre.

CC (Countryside Commission), English Heritage, English Nature and Environment Agency 1997. *Environmental capital: a new approach – what matters and why*, prepared by CAG Consultants and Land Use Consultants. Cheltenham, Glos: CC.

CC and EN (Countryside Commission and English Nature) 1998. *The character of England: landscape, wildlife and natural features*. Cheltenham, Glos: CC.

CEAA (Canadian Environmental Assessment Agency) 1999. *Cumulative effects assessment practitioners guide*, Hull, Quebec: CEAA, www.ceaa-acee.gc.ca/013/0001/0004/index_e.htm.

Clark BD 1996. *Monitoring and auditing in environmental assessment – improving the process*. London: IAE and EARA Joint Annual Conference.

DCLG (Department for Communities and Local Government) 2006a. *Environmental impact assessment: a guide to good practice and procedures: a consultation paper*, London: DCLG, www.communities.gov.uk/archived/publications/planningandbuilding/environmental-impactassessment.

DCLG 2006b. *Amended circular on environmental impact assessment: a consultation paper*. www.communities.gov.uk/archived/publications/planningandbuilding/amendedcircular.

DCLG (undated) Note on environmental impact assessment directive for local planning authorities, www.communities.gov.uk/planningandbuilding/planning/sustainability-environmental/environmentalimpactassessment/noteenvironmental/.

Defra (Department for Environment Food and Rural Affairs) 2005. *New high level targets for flood and coastal erosion risk management.* London: Defra, www.defra.gov.uk/environ/fcd/hltarget/default.htm.

Defra 2007. *Conserving biodiversity – the UK approach.* PB12772. London: Defra, www.defra.gov.uk/wildlife-countryside/pdfs/biodiversity/ConBioUK-Oct2007.pdf.

DETR 1999. *Circular 2/99, Environmental impact assessment.* London: HMSO, www.communities.gov.uk/publications/planningandbuilding/circularenvironmentalimpact.

DoE (Department of the Environment) 1995. *Preparation of environmental statements for planning projects that require environmental assessment: a good practice guide.* London: HMSO, www.tsoshop.co.uk/bookstore.asp.

EC (European Commission) 1985. Council Directive 85/337/EEC on the assessment of the effects of certain private and public projects on the environment. *Official Journal of the European Communities* L 175/40. Brussels: European Commission, http://ec.europa.eu/environment/eia/full-legal-text/85337.htm.

EC 1992. Council Directive 92/43/EEC on the conservation of natural habitats and of wild fauna and flora. *Official Journal L 206, 22/07/1992 P. 0007 – 0050* (http://eur-lex.europa.eu/LexUriServ/LexUriServ.do?uri=CELEX:31992L0043:EN:HTML).

EC 1997. Council Directive 97/11/EC amending Directive 85/337/EEC on the assessment of the effects of certain public and private projects on the environment. *Official Journal of the European Commission*, No. L073/5-21. Brussels: EC, http://ec.europa.eu/environment/eia/full-legal-text/9711.htm.

EC 1999. *Guidelines for the assessment of indirect and cumulative impacts as well as impact interactions.* Brussels: EC, http://ec.europa.eu/environment/eia/eia-support.htm.

EC 2001. Directive 2001/42/EC on the assessment of the effects of certain plans and programmes on the environment (The SEA Directive). Brussels: EC, http://eur-lex.europa.eu/LexUriServ/LexUriServ.do?uri=OJ:L:2001:197:0030:0037:EN:PDF.

EC 2003. Directive 2003/35/EC of the European Parliament and of the Council of 26 May 2003 providing for public participation in respect of the drawing up of certain plans and programmes relating to the environment and amending with regard to public participation and access to justice Council Directives 85/337/EEC and 96/61/EC. *Official Journal L156/17.* Brussels: EC, www.cefic.be/Files/Publications/4.pdf.

European Court of Justice 2005. Commission of the European Communities vs. United Kingdom of Great Britain and Northern Ireland Case C-6/04, http://eur-lex.europa.eu/LexUriServ/LexUriServ.do?uri=OJ:C:2005:315:0005:0006:EN:PDF.

Glasson J, R Therivel and A Chadwick 2005. *Introduction to environmental impact assessment*, 3rd edn. London: Taylor & Francis.

HMSO 1999. *The Town and Country Planning (Environmental Impact Assessment) (England and Wales) Regulations 1999, SI 1999 No 293.* London: HMSO, www.opsi.gov.uk/si/si1999/19990293.htm.

HSE (Health and Safety Executive) and EA/SEPA 1999. *Guidance on the environmental risk assessment aspects of COMAH safety reports*, www.environment-agency.gov.uk/commondata/acrobat/Comah.pdf.

Hughes J and C Wood 1996. Formal and informal environmental assessment reports: their role in UK planning decisions. *Land Use Policy* 13(2), 101–113.

Lucas K and R Simpson 2000. *Transport and accessibility: the perspectives of disadvantaged communities.* Research paper for the Joseph Rowntree Foundation. London: Transport Studies Unit, University of Westminster.

MAFF (Ministry of Agriculture Fisheries and Food) 2000. *Flood and coastal defence project appraisal guidance: environmental appraisal (FCDPAG5).* London: MAFF, www.defra.gov.uk/environ/fcd/pubs/pagn/fcdpag5.pdf.

ODPM (Office of the Deputy Prime Minister) 2000. *Environmental impact assessment: guide to procedures*. London: ODPM, www.communities.gov.uk/documents/planningandbuilding/pdf/157989.

ODPM 2005. *A practical guide to the Strategic Environmental Assessment Directive*. www.communities.gov.uk/publications/planningandbuilding/practicalguidesea.

SE (Scottish Executive) 1999a. *The Environmental Impact Assessment (Scotland) Regulations 1999, Circular 15/1999*. Edinburgh: Scottish Executive, www.scotland.gov.uk/library2/doc04/eia-00.htm.

SE 1999b. *Planning Advice Note (PAN) 58 – Environmental impact assessment*. Edinburgh: Scottish Executive, www.scotland.gov.uk/library/pan/pan58-00.htm.

SNH (Scottish Natural Heritage) 2005. *Environmental assessment handbook: guidance on the Environmental Impact Assessment proces*, Edinburgh: SNH, www.snh.org.uk/publications/on-line/heritagemanagement/EIA/.

UNCED 1992. *United Nations Conference on Environment and Development* (UNCED), Rio de Janeiro, 3–14 June 1992. www.un.org/geninfo/bp/enviro.html.

UNECE (United Nations Economic Commission for Europe) 1991. *Policies and systems of environmental impact assessment*. Geneva: UNECE.

Wathern P 1999. Ecological impact assessment. In *Handbook of environmental impact assessment*, Vol. 1, J Petts (ed.), 327–346. Oxford: Blackwell Science.

WCED (World Commission on Environment and Development) 1987. *Our common future*. Oxford: Oxford University Press.

2 Socio-economic impacts 1: overview and economic impacts

John Glasson

2.1 Introduction

Major projects have a wide range of impacts on a locality – including bio-physical and socio-economic – and the trade-off between such impacts is often crucial in decision making. Major projects may offer a tempting solution to an area's, especially a rural area's, economic problems, which however may have to be offset against more negative impacts such as pressure on local services and social upheaval, in addition to possible damage to the physical environment. Socio-economic impacts can be very significant for particular projects and the analyst ignores them at his/her peril. Nevertheless they have often had a low profile in EIA although there is a growing awareness of their importance in decision making.

This chapter begins with an initial overview of socio-economic impacts of projects/developments, which explains the nature of such impacts. Economic impacts, including the direct employment impacts and the wider, indirect impacts, on a local and regional economy are then discussed in more detail. The chapter dovetails with Chapter 3, which focuses on related impacts such as changes in population levels and associated effects on the social infrastructure including accommodation and services. Several of the methods discussed straddle the two chapters and will be cross-referenced to minimise duplication. Chapters 2 and 3 draw in particular on the work of the Impacts Assessment Unit (IAU) in the School of Planning at Oxford Brookes University, which has undertaken many research and consultancy studies on the socio-economic impacts of major projects.

2.2 Definitions and concepts: socio-economic impacts

2.2.1 Origins and definitions

Socio-economic impact assessment (SIA) developed in the 1970s and 1980s mainly in relation to the assessment of the impacts of major resource development projects, such as nuclear power stations in the US, hydro-electric schemes in Canada and the UK's North Sea oil- and gas-related developments. The growing interest in socio-economic impacts, partly stimulated by the introduction of the US *National Environmental Policy Act* of 1969 and subsequent amendments of 1977, generated some important studies and publications, including the works of Wolf (1974), Lang and Armour (1981), Finsterbusch (1980, 1985), and Carley and Bustelo (1984). It also led to considerable debate on the nature and role of SIA. Some authors refer to social impact assessment; others refer to socio-economic impact assessment. Some see SIA as an integral part of EIA, providing the essential "human elements" complement to the often narrow bio-physical focus of many EISs . . . "from the perspective of the social impact agenda, this meant: valuing people 'as much as fish' . . ." (Bronfman 1991). Others see SIA as a separate field of study, a separate process, and some authors raise the legitimate concern that SIA as an integral part of EIA runs the risk of marginal-isation and superficial treatment. Chapters 2 and 3 of this text, focus on the wider definition of socio-economic impacts, *within* the EIA process.

Wolf (1974), one of the pioneers of SIA, adopted the wide-ranging definition of SIA as "the estimating and appraising of the conditions of a society organ-ised and changed by the large scale application of high technology". Bowles (1981) has a similarly broad definition: "the systematic advanced appraisal of the impacts on the day to day quality of life of people and communities when the environment is affected by development or policy change". A more light-hearted, but often relevant approach to definition can be typified as the "grab bag" (Carley and Bustelo 1984) or "Heineken" approach – with SIA including all those vitally important, but often intangible impacts which other methods cannot reach.

More recently a major study by the Interorganisational Committee on Guidelines and Principles for Social Impact Assessment (1994) defined social impacts as "the consequences to human populations of any public or private actions that alter the ways in which people live, work, play, relate to one another, organ-ise to meet their needs, and generally cope as members of society."[1] Social impacts are the "people impacts" of development actions. Social impact assessments focus on the human dimension of environments, and seek to identify the impacts on people, and who benefits and who loses. SIA can help to ensure that the needs and voices of diverse groups and people in a community are taken into account.

2.2.2 Socio-economic impacts in practice: the poor relation?

The early recognition, by some analysts, of the importance of socio-economic impacts in the EIA process and in the resultant EISs, has been partly reflected in legislation. The definition of the environment, as included in the 1979 US CEQ regulations addresses biophysical components and socio-economic factors and characteristics. The EU Directive 85/337/EEC (EC 1985), outlined in §1.3, requires a description of possible impacts on human beings. Furthermore the UK government produced guidance which suggests that "certain aspects of a project including numbers employed and where they will come from should be con-sidered within an environmental statement" (DoE 1989). The 1999 Town and Country Planning (EIA/England and Wales) Regulations required "a description of the environment likely to be significantly affected by the development, including, in particular, population, fauna, flora, soil, water, air, climatic factors, material assets, including the architectural heritage, landscape and the inter-relationship between the above factors" (Glasson *et al.* 2005). Yet despite some legislative impetus, the consideration of social and economic impacts has continued to be the poor relation in EIA and in EISs (Glasson and Heaney 1993, Burdge 2002, Chadwick 2002).

There may be several reasons for this which can be summed up by the general perceptions that:

- socio-economic impacts seldom occur;
- when they do they are covered elsewhere in the planning and development process;
- their inclusion can be used to downplay biophysical impacts;
- they are invariably negative; *and*
- they cannot easily be quantified.

However, socio-economic effects do occur in relation to most developments; they are often positive; and their inclusion in a single document facilitates a more balanced view of the range of impacts (and of tradeoffs) and provides greater transparency of process. The view that certain types of socio-economic impacts are difficult to quantify is not necessarily a reason for their complete exclusion from EIA (Newton 1995). Socio-economic impacts are important because the economic fortunes and lifestyles and values of people are important.

In an early review of the coverage of socio-economic impacts in EISs produced in the UK between 1988 and 1992, Glasson and Heaney (1993) showed that from a sample of 110 EISs, only 43 per cent had considered socio-economic impacts at all. Coverage was better than (a low) average for power station, mixed development and mineral extraction projects. Within those EISs which included socio-economic impacts, there was more emphasis on economic impacts (particularly direct employment impacts) than social impacts. Both operational and construction stages of projects were considered, although with more emphasis on the former. The geographical level of analysis was primarily local, with only very limited coverage of the wider regional scale and no consideration of impacts at the national level. There was very limited use of techniques; where they were included they were primarily economic or employment **multipliers**. Quality was also generally unsatisfactory; only 36 per cent of EISs that considered socio-economic impacts were considered to deal with the economic impacts adequately or better. For social impacts, the figure was only 15 per cent.

In a subsequent follow-up study, Chadwick identified some improvement in the position, revealing that 81 per cent of the 110 EISs studied included some consideration of social and economic effects –

> However, coverage of such impacts tends to be very brief, with only one or two pages devoted to socio-economic issues in the majority of EISs examined. As a result, treatment of impacts is often superficial, with limited baseline

data and little discussion of prediction methods or relevant supporting material. Quantification of socio-economic effects is also rarely attempted, other than for certain direct employment effects.

(Chadwick 2002)

Box 2.1 *Importance of social impacts in EIA*

To quote UNEP (1996):

> There is often a direct link between social and subsequent biophysical impacts. For example, a project in a rural area can result in the in-migration of a large labour force, often with families, into an area with low population density. This increase in population can result in adverse biophysical impacts, unless the required supporting social and physical infrastructure is provided at the correct time and place.
>
> Additionally, direct environmental impacts can cause social changes, which, in turn, can result in significant environmental impacts. For example, clearing of vegetation from a riverbank in Kenya, to assist construction and operation of a dam, eliminated local tsetse fly habitats. This meant that local people and their livestock could move into the area and settle in new villages. The people exploited the newly available resources in an unsustainable way, by significantly reducing wildlife populations and the numbers of trees and other wood species which were used as fuel wood. A purely "environmental" EIA might have missed this consequence because the social impacts of actions associated with dam construction would not have been investigated.
>
> The close relationship between social and environmental systems, make it imperative that social impacts are identified, predicted and evaluated in conjunction with biophysical impacts. It is best if social scientists with experience of assessing social impacts are employed as team members under the overall direction of a team or study leader who has an understanding of the links between social and biophysical impacts.

And the World Bank (1991):

> Social analysis in EA is not expected to be a complete sociological study nor a cost-benefit analysis of the project. Of the many social impacts that might occur, EA is concerned primarily with those relating to environmental resources and the informed participation of affected groups.
>
> Social assessment for EA purposes focus on how various groups of people affected by a project allocate, regulate and defend access to the environmental resources upon which they depend for their livelihood. In projects involving indigenous people or people dependent on fragile ecosystems, social assessment is particularly important because of the close relationship between the way of life of a group of people and the resources they exploit. Projects with involuntary resettlement, new land settlement and induced development also introduce changes in the relationships between local people and their use of environmental resources.

Socio-economic impacts merit a higher profile. A United Nations study of EIA practice in a range of countries advocated a number of changes in the EIA process and in the EIS documentation (UNECE 1991). These included giving greater emphasis to socio-economic impacts in EIA. **Box 2.1** highlights the important links between social and biophysical impacts with particular reference to developing countries. It also cautions against over-ambitious SIA. In a different context, in a survey of academics on the effectiveness of the US *National Environmental Policy Act*, Canter and Clark (1997) drew out five priorities for the future, one of which was the need for better integration of biophysical and socio-economic factors and characteristics. For the UK, Chadwick (2002) argues for explicit recognition by all EIA stakeholders (developers, consultants, competent authorities) for inclusion of socio-economic impact as an impact category; for further quantification; and for improved guidance on the assessment of the range of such impacts. A starting point in raising the SIA profile is to clarify the various dimensions of socio-economic impacts.

2.2.3 The scope of socio-economic impacts

A consideration of socio-economic impacts needs to clarify the type, duration, spatial extent and distribution of impacts; that is, the analyst needs to ask the questions: what to include; over what period of time; over what area; and impacting whom?

An overview of **what to include** is outlined in **Table 2.1**. There is usually a functional relationship between impacts. Direct economic impacts have wider indirect economic impacts. Thus direct employment of a project will generate expenditure on local services (e.g. for petrol, food and drink). The ratio of local to non-local labour on a project is often a key determinant of many subsequent impacts. A project with a high proportion of in-migrant labour will have greater implications for the demography of the locality. There will be an increase in population, which may also include an influx of dependants of the additional employees. The demographic changes will work through into the housing market and will impact on other local conditions and associated services and infrastructure (for example, on health and education), with implications for both the public and private sector (see **Figure 2.1**). The area of health impacts has been a particular growth area within the wider socio-economic field, to the extent that it has generated its own Health Impact Assessment (HIA) process often running in parallel to EIA (Taylor and Quigley 2002).

In some cases, population changes themselves may be initiators of the causal chain of impacts; new small settlements (often primarily for commuters) would fit into this category. Development actions may also have socio-cultural impacts. A new settlement of 15,000 people may have implications for the lifestyles in a rural, small-village-based environment. The introduction of a major project, with a construction stage involving the employment of several thousand people over several years, may be viewed as a serious threat to the quality of life of a locality. Social problems may be associated with such development, which may

Table 2.1 What to include? – types of socio-economic impacts

1. **Direct economic:**
    - local – non-local employment;
    - characteristics of employment (e.g. skill group);
    - labour supply and training;
    - wage levels.
2. **Indirect/wider economic/expenditure:**
    - employees' retail expenditure;
    - linked suppliers to main development;
    - labour market pressures;
    - wider multiplier effects;
    - effects on development potential of area.
3. **Demographic:**
    - changes in population size; temporary and permanent;
    - changes in other population characteristics (e.g. family size, income levels, socio-economic groups);
    - settlement patterns.
4. **Housing:**
    - various housing tenure types;
    - public and private;
    - house prices;
    - homelessness and other housing problems.
5. **Other local services:**
    - public and private sector;
    - educational services;
    - health services; social support;
    - others (e.g. police, fire, recreation, transport);
    - local finances.
6. **Socio-cultural:**
    - lifestyles/quality of life;
    - gender issues; family structure;
    - social problems (e.g. crime, illness, divorce);
    - community stress and conflict; integration, cohesion and alienation;
    - community character or image.
7. **Distributional effects:**
    - effects on specific groups in society (by virtue of gender, age, ethnicity, location etc.).

generate considerable community stress and conflict. In practice, such socio-cultural impacts are usually poorly covered in EISs, being regarded as more intangible and difficult to assess.

The question of **what period of time** to consider in SIA raises, in particular, the often substantial differences between impacts in the construction and operational stages of a project. Major utilities (such as power stations and reservoirs) and other infrastructure projects, such as roads, may have high levels of construction employment but much lower levels of operational employment. In contrast, manufacturing and service industry projects often have shorter construction periods with lower levels of employment, but with considerable employment levels over projects which may extend for several decades. The clo-

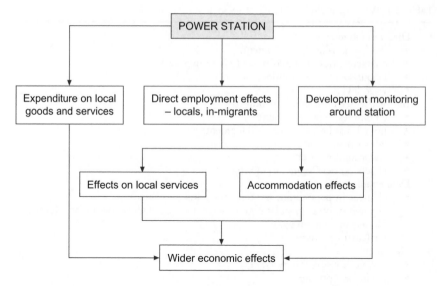

Figure 2.1 Example of linkages between socio-economic impacts for a power station project.

sure of a project may also have significant socio-economic impacts; unfortunately these are rarely covered in the initial assessment. Socio-economic impacts should be considered for all stages of the life of a development. Interestingly, nuclear reactor decommissioning did become a project requiring mandatory environmental assessment under Directive 97/11/EC (EC 1997). Subsequent EISs of decommissioning projects have increasingly included a socio-economic dimension, and the overall Strategy for the UK Nuclear Decommissioning Authority gives coverage to socio-economic issues and to stakeholders (NDA 2006). Even within stages, it may be necessary to identify sub-stages, for example peak construction employment, to highlight the extremes of impacts which may flow from a project. Only through monitoring can predictions be updated over the life of the project under consideration.

What area to cover in SIA raises the often contentious issue of where to draw the boundaries around impacts. Boundaries may be determined by several factors. They may be influenced by estimates of the impact zone. Thus, for the construction stage of a major project, a sub-regional or regional boundary may be taken, reflecting the fact that construction workers are willing to travel long distances daily for short-term, well-paid employment. On the other hand, permanent employees of an operational development are likely to locate much nearer to their work. Other determinants of the geographical area of study may include the availability of data (e.g. for counties and districts in the UK), and policy issues (e.g. providing spatial impact data related to the areas of responsibility of the key decision makers involved in a project). Different socio-economic impacts will often necessitate the use of different geographical areas, reflecting some of the determinants already discussed. As noted earlier, EISs in practice have focused on local areas. This may provide a very partial picture; economic impacts often have wider regional, and occasionally national and international implications.

Box 2.2 Examples of social differences which may be environmentally significant

Communities are composed of diverse groups of people, including, but not restricted to the intended beneficiaries of a development project. Organised social groups hold territory, divide labour and distribute resources. Social assessment in EA disaggregates the affected population into social groups which may be affected in different ways, to different degrees and in different locations. Important social differences which may be environmentally significant include ethnic or tribal affiliation, occupation, socio-economic status, age and gender.

Ethnic/Tribal groups. A project area may include a range of different ethnic or tribal groups whose competition for environmental resources can become a source of conflict. Ethnicity can have important environmental implications. For example, a resettlement authority may inadvertently create competition for scarce resources if it grants land to new settlers while ignoring customary rights to that land by indigenous tribal groups.

Occupational groups. A project area may also include people with a wide array of occupations who may have diverse and perhaps competing interests in using environmental resources. Farmers require fertile land and water, herders require grazing lands, and artisans may require forest products such as wood to produce goods. A project may provide benefits to one group while negatively affecting another. For example while construction of dams and reservoirs for irrigation and power clearly benefits farmers with irrigation, they may adversely affect rural populations engaged in other activities living downstream of the dam.

Socio-economic stratification. The population in the project area will also vary according to the land and capital that they control. Some will be landless poor, others will be wealthy landowners, tenant farmers or middlemen entrepreneurs. Disaggregating the population by economic status is important because access to capital and land can result in different responses to project benefits. For example, tree crop development may benefit wealthy farmers, but displace the livestock of poor farmers to more marginal areas.

Age and gender. A social assessment should include identification of project impacts on different individuals within households. Old people may be more adversely affected by resettlement than young people. Men, women and children play different economic roles, have different access to resources, and projects may have different impacts on them as a result. For example, a project that changes access to resources in fragile ecosystems may have unanticipated impacts on local women who use those resources for income or domestic purposes.

Source: World Bank (1991).

The question of **who will be affected** is of crucial importance in EIA, but is very rarely addressed in EISs. The distributional effects of development impacts do not fall evenly on communities; there are usually winners and losers. For example a new tourism development in a historic city in the UK may benefit visitors to the city and tourism entrepreneurs, but may generate considerable pressures on a variety of services used by the local population. Distributional effects can be analysed by reference to geographical areas and/or to groups involved (for example local and non-local; age groups; socio-economic groups; employment groups).

SIA should also pay particular attention to vulnerable sections of the population being studied – the elderly, the poor, and minority or ethnically distinctive groups – and to areas which may have particular value to certain groups in terms of cultural or religious beliefs. In this context, an interesting development in the USA, after long campaigning by black and ethnic groups, was the Clinton *Executive order on federal actions to address environmental justice in minority populations and low income populations* (White House 1994). Under this Order, each federal agency must analyse the environmental effects, including human health, economic and social effects, of federal actions, including effects on minority and low-income communities, when such analysis is required under NEPA. The focus is on "environmental justice", a component of the broader field of SIA; it is concerned with "fair treatment", meaning that "minority and low income groups should not bear a disproportionate share of the negative environmental impacts of government actions" (Bass 1998). Bass provides an example of a proposal for a nuclear enrichment centre in Louisiana (US) which was refused a licence on the basis that "racial and economic discrimination played an unacceptable role in the project's planning". Similarly, but from the wider perspective of the World Bank (1991), **Box 2.2** provides some examples of the key social differences which may be environmentally significant.

There are of course many other dimensions to impacts besides the areas discussed here, including adverse and beneficial, reversible and irreversible, quantitative and qualitative, and actual and perceived impacts (see Glasson *et al.* 2005). All are relevant in SIA. The distinction between actual and perceived impacts raises the distinction between more "objective" and more "subjective" assessments of impacts. The impacts of a development perceived by residents of a locality may be significant in determining local responses to a project. They can constitute an important source of information to be considered alongside more "objective" predictions of impacts.

2.3 Baseline studies: direct and indirect economic impacts

2.3.1 Understanding the project/development action

Socio-economic impacts are the outcome of the interaction between the characteristics of the project/development action and the characteristics of the "host" environment. As a starting point, the analyst must assemble baseline information on both sets of characteristics.

The assembling of relevant information on the characteristics of the project would appear to be one of the more straightforward steps in the process. However projects have many characteristics and for some, relevant data may be limited. In socio-economic terms, what is important is the capital investment of the project and its associated human resources for the key stages of the project life cycle. The essential components of the project can be assembled as a flow diagram (see Chapter 9 of Rodriguez-Bachiller and Glasson 2004). The drafting of a **direct employment labour curve** is a vital initial source of information (see **Figure 2.2**). This shows the anticipated employment requirements of the project. To be of maximum use it should include a number of dimensions, including in particular the duration and categories of employment. The labour curve should indicate the anticipated labour requirements for each stage in the project life cycle.

For the purposes of prediction and further analysis, there may be a focus on certain key points in the life cycle. For example, an SIA of peak construction employment could reveal the maximum impact on a community; an analysis of impacts at full operational employment would provide a guide to many continuing and long-term impacts. The labour curve should also indicate requirements by employment or skill category. These may be subdivided in various ways according to the nature of employment in the project concerned, but often involve a distinction between managerial and technical staff, clerical and administrative staff and project operatives. For a construction project, there may be a further significant distinction in the operatives category between civil works operatives. A finer disaggregation still would focus on the particular trades or skills involved, including levels of skills (e.g. skilled/semi-skilled/unskilled) and types of skills (e.g. steel erector, carpenter, electrician).

Projects also have associated **employment policies** which may influence the labour requirements in a variety of ways. For example, the use/type of shift working and the approach to training of labour may be very significant in determining the scope for local employment. An indication of likely wage levels could be helpful in determining wider economic impacts into the local retail economy. An indication of the main developer's attitude/policy to sub-contracting can also be helpful in determining the wider economic impacts for the local and regional manufacturing and producer services industries.

It is to be hoped that the initial brief from the developer will provide a good starting point on labour requirements and associated policies. But this is not always the case, particularly where the project is a "one-off" and the developer cannot draw on comparative experience from within the firm involved. In such cases the analyst may be able to draw on EISs of comparative studies. However many major projects are at the forefront of technology and there may be few national, or even international, comparators available. For instance, the EIA for the London Gateway bridge – which would link two deprived areas of London across the River Thames – emphasised the employment benefits to local residents of being able to cross the river more easily (Transport for London 2004). Opponents of the bridge instead argued that increased access to jobs

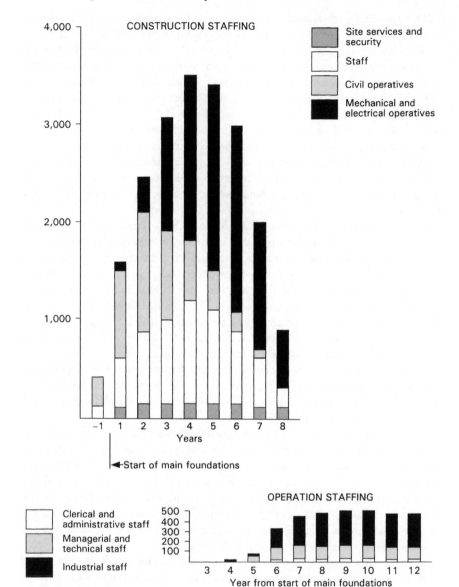

Figure 2.2 Labour requirements for a project disaggregated in time and by employment category.

alone would not improve local residents' employment prospects without associated training and support. There were no obviously relevant UK comparators to support either side's arguments.

There may be genuine uncertainty on the relative merits of different designs for a project, and this may necessitate the assessment of the socio-economic impacts of various possibilities. For example, an assessment by the IAU at Oxford in 1987 for the Hinkley Point C power station proposal, considered the socio-economic impacts for both pressurised water reactor and advanced gas-cooled reactor designs (Glasson *et al.* 1987). Twenty years later (2007–2009), work on assessment for a possible new generation of UK nuclear power stations has initially had to contend with the implications of four alternative power station reactor types.

Projects also have a tendency to change their characteristics through the planning and development process and these may have significant socio-economic implications. For example, the discovery during the early stages of project construction of major foundation problems may necessitate a much greater input of civil works operatives. Major projects also tend to have a substantial number of contractors, and it may be difficult to forecast accurately without knowledge of such sub-contractors, and indeed of the main contractor. Such uncertainties reinforce the necessity of regular monitoring of project characteristics throughout project planning and development.

2.3.2 Establishing the economic environment baseline

Defining the **"host" economic environment area** depends to some extent on the nature of the project. Some projects may have significant national or even international employment implications. The construction of the Channel Tunnel had wide ranging inter-regional economic impacts in the UK, bringing considerable benefits to areas well beyond Kent and the South East region of England, for example to the West Midlands (Vickerman 1987). Many projects have regional or sub-regional economic impacts, and almost all have local economic impacts. As noted in §2.2, it can be useful to make a distinction between the anticipated construction and operational daily commuting zones for a project. The former is invariably much larger in geographical area than the latter, possibly extending up to 90 minutes one-way daily commuting time from the project. For these areas, and for the wider region and nation as appropriate, it is necessary to assemble data on current and anticipated labour market characteristics, including size of labour force, employment structure, unemployment and vacancies, skills and training provision.

The **size of the labour force** provides a first guide to the ability of a locality to service a development. Information is needed on the economically active workforce (i.e. those males and females in the 16 to retirement age bands). This then needs disaggregation into industrial and/or occupational groups to provide a guide to the economic activities and employment types in the study area(s). An industrial disaggregation would identify for example, those in agriculture, types of manufacturing and services. In the UK, the *Standard Industrial Classification* (SIC) provides a template of categories (**Table 2.2**). An occupational disaggregation indicates particular skill groups (**Table 2.3**). Data on unemployment and vacancies provides indicators of the pressure in the labour market and the availability of various labour groups. It should be disaggregated by length of

Table 2.2 UK broad Standard Industrial Classification (SIC) since 2007 (ONS 2007)

Section	Description
A	Agriculture, Forestry and Fishing
B	Mining and quarrying
C	Manufacturing
D	Electricity, gas, steam and air-conditioning supply
E	Water supply, sewerage, waste management and remediation activities
F	Construction
G	Wholesale and retail trade; repair of motor vehicles and motorcycles
H	Accommodation and food service activities
I	Transportation and storage
J	Information and communication
K	Financial and insurance activities
L	Real estate activities
M	Professional, scientific and technical activities
N	Administrative and support service activities
O	Public administration and defence; compulsory social security
P	Education
Q	Human health and social work activities
R	Arts, entertainment and recreation
S	Other service activities
T	Activities of households as employers; undifferentiated goods- and services-producing activities of households for own use
U	Activities of extraterritorial organisations and bodies

Table 2.3 UK Standard Occupational Classification (SOC) since 2000

1	Managers and senior officials
2	Professional occupations
3	Associate professional and technical occupations
4	Administrative and secretarial occupations
5	Skilled trades occupations
6	Personal service occupations
7	Sales and customer service occupations
8	Process, plant and machine operatives
9	Elementary occupations

Source: ONS (2000).

unemployment, as well as by skill category and location. Data should also be collected on the provision of training facilities in an area. Such facilities may be employed to enhance the quality of labour supply.

In the UK, the provision of labour market data comes from various, and changing, sources. The national Department for Work and Pensions is a primary source, and a guide to available data is provided in **Table 2.4**. The National Online Manpower Information Service (NOMIS) computerised database is a particularly useful source of employment and unemployment data at various geographical levels. Department of Employment regions may also provide useful annual

Table 2.4 Major UK Government employment data sources

Economic & Labour Market Review (ELMR) (www.statistics.gov.uk/elmr) – replaced Labour Market Trends (incorporating Employment Gazette) in January 2007. Published monthly (as an online and print journal) this is the major source on employment. At the regional level there is (a) monthly information on employment, redundancies, vacancies, unemployment and Regional Development Grants, and (b) annual information on number of employees (age/sex/SIC), activity rates, seasonal unemployment and new employment data. Breakdowns by travel-to-work areas, Assisted Areas and Parliamentary constituencies are also available. There are also occasional labour force projections (male/female/total) by region. Previous editions of Labour Market Trends will continue to be available online.

Annual Survey of Hours and Earnings (ASHE) (www.statistics.gov.uk/STATBASE/ Product.asp?vlnk=13101) – replaced the New Earnings Survey (NES) in 2004. It is a sample survey of the earnings of employees in Great Britain at April each year, and provides information on the levels, distribution and make-up of earnings of employees in industries, occupations, regions and age groups, and on the collective agreements which cover them.

Labour Market Statistics (www.statistics.gov.uk/statbase/Product.asp?vlnk=1944) – provides a commentary, including tables and charts, on current labour market trends and the implications for training, employment, unemployment, and includes special features on particular labour market topics. It includes some regional data.

National Online Manpower Information System (NOMIS) (www.nomisweb.co.uk) – provides labour market and related population data for local areas from a variety of sources including the Labour Force Survey (LFS), claimant count, Annual Business Inquiry (ABI), Annual Survey of Hours and Earnings (ASHE), and the 1981, 1991 and 2001 and Censuses of Population. The data are from official government sources (mostly National Statistics). NOMIS includes the latest published figures and time series data, in some cases dating back to the 1970s. Data is freely available but access to ABI data requires special permission for which there is a fee.

---

and more regular reviews of the employment situation in their region. A basic geographical area for the Department of Work and Pensions data is the Travel to Work Area (TTWA). Another important UK source of data is the Census of Population. The results of the 2001 census include information on the economic activity, workplace and transport to work of the population. The statutory Local Plans (and subsequent Local Development Frameworks) and current Structure Plans for the area under consideration also provide valuable employment data; this may be complemented by data in statutory Regional Spatial Strategies (RSSs) produced by Regional Assemblies (e.g. SEERA 2006) and by Regional Economic Strategies (RESs) produced by Regional Development Agencies. Most regions now also have Regional Observatories which are valuable sources for socio-economic information.

In some areas, the sources noted may be enhanced by various one-off studies, including for example skills audits which seek to establish the current and latent skills provision of an area. In the UK, a network of Local Skills Councils provides a useful contact, particularly on training information. Predictably, the various data sources do not use the same geographical bases; in particular the discrepancy between TTWAs and local authority areas can cause problems for the analyst. The latter should also be aware of the influence of "softer" data – for example, information on possible developments in other major projects in a locality which may have labour market implications for the project under consideration. Data on other "host" area economic characteristics – such as wage levels, characteristics of the retail economy and of local businesses – may be more limited, although many local authorities do now produce very useful business directories, and some information may be available in the sustainability appraisals/strategic environmental assessments for their Local Development Documents.

Local economic impacts may also be influenced by the policy stance(s) of the host area. For many localities the possibility of employment and local trade gains from a project may be the only perceived benefits. There may be a desire to maximise such gains and to limit the **leakage** of multiplier benefits (see §2.5). This may result in an authority taking a policy stance on the percentage of "local" labour to be employed on a project. For example, in an extreme case, Gwynedd County Council negotiated, through the use of an Act of Parliament, a very high percentage of local labour for the construction of the Wylfa nuclear power station on Anglesey. A local position may also be taken on the provision of training facilities. There may be concern about the possible local employment "boom–bust" scenario associated with some major projects, which may of course bring caution into the setting of high local employment ratios.

2.3.3 Clarifying the issues

Consideration of **project and "host" environment characteristics** can help to clarify key issues. Denzin (1970) and Grady et al. (1987) remind us that issue specification should be rooted in several sources, and they advocate the use of the philosophy of **"triangulation"**: for data (the use of a variety of data sources), for investigators (the use of different sets of researchers), for theory (the use of multiple perspectives to interpret a single set of data) and for methods (the use of multiple methods). Thus, the use of quantitative published and semi-published data, as outlined, should be complemented by the use of key informant interviews, working groups (e.g. of developer, local planning officers, councillors, and representatives of interest groups) and possibly focus groups and public meetings.

While many direct and indirect employment impacts will be specific to the case in hand, the following key questions tend to be raised in most cases:

- What proportions of project construction and operation jobs are likely to be filled by local workers, as compared to in-migrants, and what are the likely origins of the in-migrant workers?
- What is likely to be the magnitude of the secondary (indirect and induced) employment resulting from project development? What proportions of these jobs will be filled by local workers?

- How will local businesses be affected by rapid growth resulting from a major project? For example, will development provide opportunities for expansion or will local firms experience difficulty competing with new chain stores and in attracting and retaining quality workers?

(Murdock *et al.* 1986)

2.4 Impact prediction: direct employment impacts

2.4.1 *The nature of prediction*

Prediction of socio-economic impacts is an inexact exercise. Ideally the prediction of the direct employment impacts on an area would be based on information relating to the recruitment policies of the companies involved in the development, and on individuals' decisions in response to the new employment opportunities. In the absence of firm data on these and related factors, predictions need to be based on a series of assumptions related to the characteristics of the development and of the locality. These could for example include the following:

the labour requirement curves for construction and operation will be as provided by the client; local recruitment will be encouraged by the developer with a target of 50%; employment on the new project will be attractive to the local workforce by virtue of the comparatively high wages offered.

Predictive approaches may use **extrapolative methods**, drawing on trends in past and present data. In this respect, use can be made of comparative situations and the study of the direct employment impacts of similar projects. Unfortunately the limited monitoring of impacts of project outcomes reduces the value of this source, and primary surveys may be needed to obtain such information. Predictive approaches may also use **normative methods**. Such methods work backwards from desired outcomes to assess whether the project, in its environmental context, is adequate to achieve them. For example, the desired direct employment outcome from the construction stage of a major project may be "X" per cent local employment.

Underpinning all prediction methods should be some clarification of the **cause–effect relationships** between the variables involved. **Figure 2.3** provides a simplified flow diagram for the local socio-economic impacts of a power station development. Prediction of the local (and regional as appropriate) labour recruitment ratios is the key step in the process. Non-local workers are, by definition, not based in the study area. Their in-migration for the duration of a project will have a wider range of secondary demographic, accommodation, services and socio-cultural impacts (as discussed in Chapter 3). The wider economic impacts, on for example local retail activity, will be discussed further in this chapter. The key determinants of the local recruitment ratios are the labour requirements of the project, the conditions in the local economy, and relevant local

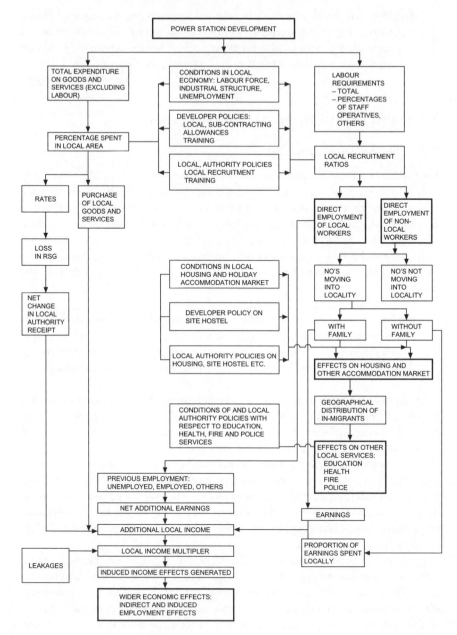

Figure 2.3 A cause–effect diagram for the local socio-economic impacts of a power station proposal.
Source: Glasson *et al.* (1987).

Note: RS = Rate Support Grant

authority and developer policies on topics such as training, local recruitment and travel allowances. It is possible to quantify some of the cause–effect relationships, and various **economic impact models**, derived from the multiplier concept, can be used for predictive purposes. These are discussed further in §2.5.

Whatever prediction method is used, there will be a degree of **uncertainty** attached to the predicted impacts. Such uncertainty can be partly handled by the application of probability factors to predictions, by sensitivity analysis, and by the inclusion of ranges in the predictions (see Glasson *et al.* 2005, Chapters 5 and 9).

2.4.2 *Predicting local (and regional) direct employment impacts*

Disaggregation into project stages, geographical areas and employment categories is the key to improving the accuracy of predictions. For example the construction stage of major projects will usually involve an amalgam of professional/managerial staff, administrative/secretarial staff, local services staff (e.g. catering, security) and a wide range of operatives in a variety of skill categories. Most projects will involve civil-works operatives (e.g. plant operators, drivers), and most will also include some mechanical and electrical activity (e.g. electricians, engineers). For each employment category there is a labour market, with relevant supply and demand characteristics. Guidance on the mix of local/non-local employment for each category can be obtained from comparative studies and from the best estimates of the participants in the process (e.g. from the developer, from the local employment office). Hopefully, but in practice not often, guidance will be informed by the monitoring of direct employment impacts in practice.

As a normal rule, the more specialist the staff, the longer the training needed to achieve the expertise, the more likely that the employee will not come from the immediate locality of the project. Specialist professional staff and managerial staff are likely to be brought in from outside the study area; they may be transferred from other sites, seconded from headquarters or recruited on the national or international market. Only a small percentage may be recruited from the local market, which may simply just not have the expertise available in the numbers necessary. On the other hand, local services staff (e.g. security, cleaning, catering), and to a slightly lesser extent secretarial and administrative staff, may be much more plentiful in most local labour markets, and the local percentage employed on the project may be quite high, and in some cases very high. Other skill categories will vary in terms of local potential according to the degree of skill and training needed. There may be an abundance of general labourers, but a considerable shortage of coded welders.

Comparative analysis of the disaggregated employment categories is likely to produce broad bands for the level of local recruitment. These can then be refined with reference to the conditions applicable to the particular project and locality under consideration. For example, high levels of unemployment in particular skill categories in the locality may boost local recruitment in those categories. Normative methods may also come into play. The developer may

Table 2.5 Example of predicted employment of local and non-local labour for the construction stage of a major project

	Total labour requirements	Local labour		Non-local labour	
		%	range	%	range
Site services, security and clerical staff	300	90	250–290	10	10–50
Professional, supervisory and managerial staff	430	15	50–80	85	350–380
Civil operatives	500	55	250–300	45	200–250
Mechanical and electrical operatives	1520	40	550–670	60	850–970
Total	2750	44	1100–1340	56	1410–1650

Local labour: Employees already in residence in the Construction Daily Commuting Zone before being recruited on site. *Non-local labour*: All other employees.

introduce training programmes, skills audits and apprenticeships to boost the supply of local skills (see Glasson 2005). **Table 2.5** provides an example of the sort of estimates which may be derived. While the predictions may still use ranges, a prediction from the disaggregated analysis is much more robust than taking employment as a homogenous category.

A further level of **micro-analysis** would be to predict the employment impacts for particular localities within the study area, and for particular groups, such as the unemployed. A further level of **macro-analysis**, used in some EISs, would include an estimate of the total person days of employment per year generated by the project (e.g. 10,000 employment days in 2010).

2.5 Impact prediction: wider economic impacts

2.5.1 The range of wider economic impacts

In addition to the direct local (and/or regional) employment effects, major projects have a range of **secondary** or **indirect impacts**. The workforce, which may be very substantial (and well paid) in some stages of a project, can generate considerable retail expenditure in a locality, on a whole range of goods and services. This may be a considerable boost for the local retail economy; for example, IAU studies of the impact of power station developments suggest that retail turnover in adjacent medium and small towns may be boosted by at least 10 per cent (Glasson and Chadwick 1988–1997). The projects themselves require supplies ranging from components from local engineering firms, to provisions for the canteen. These can also boost the local economy.

Such demands create employment, or sustain employment, additional to that directly created by the project. As will be discussed in Chapter 3, the additional workforce may demand other services locally (e.g. health, education), and housing, which may generate additional construction. These demands will create additional employment. Training programmes associated with a project may bring other economic benefits in terms of a general upgrading of the skills. Overall, the net effect may be considerably larger than the original direct injection of jobs and income into a locality, and such wider economic impacts are invariably regarded as beneficial.

However, there can be **wider economic costs**. Existing firms may fear the competition for labour which may result from a new project. They may lose skilled labour to high wage projects. There may be inflationary pressures on the housing market and on other local services. Major projects may be a catalyst for other development in an area. A road or bridge can improve accessibility and increase the economic potential of areas. But major projects may also cast a shadow over an area in terms of alternative developments. For example, large military projects, nuclear power stations, mineral extraction projects and others, may have a deterrent impact on other activities, such as tourism – although the construction stage and the operation of many projects can be tourism attractions in themselves, especially when aided by good interpretation and visitor centre facilities.

2.5.2 Measuring wider economic impacts: the multiplier approach

The analysis of the wider economic effects of introducing a major new source of income and employment into a local economy can be carried out using a number of different techniques (Brownrigg 1971, Glasson 1992, Lewis 1988, McNicholl 1981). The three methods most frequently used are (a) the economic base multiplier model, (b) the input–output model, and (c) the Keynesian multiplier, although it should be added that the percentage of EISs including such studies is still small.

The **economic base multiplier** is founded on a division of local (and/or regional) economies into basic and non-basic activities. Basic activities (local/regional supportive activities) are seen as the "motors" of the economy; they are primarily oriented to markets external to the area. Non-basic activities (regional dependent activities) support the population associated with the basic activities, and are primarily locally oriented services (e.g. retail services). The ratio of basic to non-basic activities, usually measured in employment terms, is used for prediction purposes. Thus an "X" increase in basic employment may generate a "Y" increase in non-basic employment. The model has the advantages, and disadvantages, of simplicity (Glasson 1992).

Input–output models provide a much more sophisticated approach. An input–output table is a balancing matrix of financial transactions between industries or sectors. Adapted from national input–output tables, regional or local tables can provide a detailed and disaggregated guide to the wider economic impacts resulting from changes in one industry or sector. However, unless an up-to-date table exists for the area under study, the start-up costs are normally too great for most EIA exercises. Batey *et al.* (1993) provide an interesting example of the use of input–output analysis to assess the socio-economic impacts of an airport development.

For several reasons – primarily related to the availability of appropriate data at a local level – the **Keynesian multiplier approach** has been used in several studies and is discussed in further detail here. The basic theory underlying the Keynesian multiplier is simple: "a money injection into an economic system, whether national or regional, will cause an increase in the level of income in that system by some multiple of the original injection" (Brownrigg 1974). Mathematically this can be represented at its most simple as:

$$Y_r = K_r J \tag{1}$$

where: Y_r is the change in the level of income in region r
         J is the initial income injection (or multiplicand)
         K_r is the regional income multiplier

If the initial injection of money is passed on intact at each round, the multiplier effect would be infinite. The £X million initial injection would provide £X million extra income to workers, which in turn would generate an extra income of £X million for local suppliers, who would then spend it, and so on ad infinitum. But the multiplier is not infinite because there are a number of obvious leakages at each stage of the multiplier process. Five important leakages are:

s the proportion of additional income saved (and therefore not spent locally);
t_d the proportion of additional income paid in direct taxation and National Insurance contributions;
M   the proportion of additional income spent on imported goods and services;
U   the marginal transfer benefit/income ratio (representing the relative change in transfer payments, such as unemployment benefits, which result from the rise in local income and employment);
t_i the proportion of additional consumption expenditure on local goods which goes on indirect taxation (e.g. VAT).

The multiplier can therefore be formulated as follows:

$$K_r = \frac{1}{1 - (1 - s)(1 - t_d - u)(1 - m)(1 - t_i)} \tag{2}$$

Substituting (2) into (1) then gives:

$$Y_r = \frac{1}{1 - (1 - s)(1 - t_d - u)(1 - m)(1 - t_i)} J \tag{3}$$

Thus, when applied to the multiplicand J, the multiplier K_r gives the accumulated wider economic impacts for the area under consideration, as in equation (3). The Keynesian multiplier can be calculated in income or employment terms. The various leakages normally reduce the value of local and regional multipliers in practice to between 1.1 and 1.8; in other words, for each £1 brought in directly by the project, an extra £0.10–0.80 is produced indirectly. The size of the import leakage is a major determinant, since the bigger the leakage, the smaller the multiplier. Leakages increase as the size of the study area declines, and decrease as the study area becomes more isolated. Thus, of the UK regions, Scotland has the highest regional multiplier (Steele 1969). Local (county and district level multipliers) normally vary between 1.1 and approximately 1.4.

Keynesian multiplier studies have been used particularly extensively in **tourism impact studies** (Fletcher and Archer 1991, Eadington and Redman 1991, Beeston 2003), and more recently in the assessment of the impact of higher education on local and regional economies. Universities can have very significant local economic impacts. The direct employment associated with them is the most obvious of these impacts, and universities are often among the largest single employers in their local labour markets. A CVCP study (1994) lists some 20 published university local economic impact studies. Such work has been undertaken by universities, reflecting a desire to demonstrate their local economic significance (Lincoln *et al.* 1993). Lawton Smith brings together a collection of studies on "Universities and Local Economic Development" in a special edition of the *Local Economy* journal (Lawton Smith 2003). In an article on the widening local and regional development impacts of the modern universities, Glasson (2003) shows that two medium-sized universities (Oxford Brookes and Sunderland) each generated local expenditure of approximately £100 million per year, and over 2,000 (FTE) local jobs, making them major employers in their respective cities. In addition they can contribute to development of the knowledge economy through technology transfer and spinoffs, and to sustainable development through their policies for the built environment and for community development.

In practice, EIA studies will probably limit such analyses to gross estimates of the wider economic impacts at perhaps the peak construction and full operation stages. But it is possible to disaggregate also with reference to the various employee groups. A study of the predicted local socio-economic impacts of the construction and operation of the proposed Hinkley Point C nuclear power station illustrated the variations, with higher multipliers associated with in-migrants with families (1.3–1.5) than with unaccompanied in-migrants (1.05–1.11) (Glasson *et al.* 1988). The Keynesian multiplier model, with modifications as appropriate, is well suited to the assessment of the wider economic impacts of projects. But it can only be as good as the information sources on which it is based to construct both the multiplicand and the multiplier. Predictive studies of proposed developments are more problematic in this respect than studies of existing developments, although knowledge of the latter can inform prediction.

2.5.3 Assessing significance

Socio-economic impacts, including the direct employment and wider economic impacts, do not have recognised standards. There are no easily applicable "state of local society" standards against which the predicted impacts of a development

Table 2.6 Assessing the local significance of socio-economic impacts: extracts from a nuclear power station decommissioning project

Type of impact	Negligible impact	Slight impact	Moderate impact	Major impact
Demographic impacts				
Change in local population level	No measurable change in local population level	Change in local population of less than + or – 1%	Change in local population of + or – 1–2%	Change in local population of more than + or – 2%
Direct and indirect employment impacts				
Change in site (direct) employment levels	Change of less than + or – 10% on baseline site employment levels	Change of + or – 10–20% on baseline site employment levels	Change of + or – 20–50% on baseline site employment levels	Change of more than + or – 50% on baseline site employment levels
Change in employment level in local economy	No measurable change in employment levels in the local economy	Change of less than + or – 1% on baseline employment levels in the local economy	Change of + or – 1–2% on baseline employment levels in the local economy	Change of more than + or – 2% on baseline employment levels in local economy
Change in unemployment level in local economy	Change of less than + or – 2% in claimant unemployment level	Change of + or – 2–5% in claimant unemployment level	Change of + or – 5–10% in claimant unemployment level	Change of more than + or – 10% in claimant unemployment level
Local expenditure and wider economic impacts				
Change in levels of local expenditure by site employees	Change of less than + or – 10% on baseline levels of local expenditure	Change of + or – 10–20% on baseline levels of local expenditure	Change of + or – 20–50% on baseline levels of local expenditure	Change of more than + or – 50% on baseline levels of local expenditure

Source: BNFL (2002).

can be assessed. While a reduction in local unemployment may be regarded as positive, and an increase in local crime as negative, there are no absolute standards. Views on the significance of economic impacts, such as the proportion and types of local employment on a project, are often political and arbitrary. Nevertheless it is sometimes possible to identify what might be termed **threshold or step changes** in the socio-economic profile of an area. For example, it may be possible to identify predicted impacts which threaten to swamp the local labour market, and which may produce a "boom–bust" scenario. It may also be possible to identify likely high levels of leakage of anticipated benefits out of a locality, which may be equally unacceptable. It is valuable if the practitioner can identify possible criteria used in the analysis for a range of levels of impacts, which at least provides the basis for informed debate. **Table 2.6** provides some examples from a decommissioning of a nuclear power station project. It must be stressed that this is an imprecise exercise.

In the assessment of significance, the analyst should be aware of the philosophy of **"triangulation"** noted earlier. Multiple perspectives on significance can be gleaned from many sources, including the local press, which can be very powerful as an opinion former, other key local opinion formers (including local councillors and officials), surveys of the population in the host locality, and public meetings. All can help to assess the significance, perceived and actual, of various socio-economic impacts. A very simple analysis might measure the column-centimetres of local newspaper coverage of certain issues in the planning stage of the project; a survey of local people might seek to calculate simple measures of agreement (MoA) with certain statements relating to economic impacts. MoA is defined as the number of respondents who agree with the statement, minus the number who disagree, divided by the total numbers of respondents. Thus, a MoA of 1 denotes full agreement; −1 denotes complete disagreement.

2.6 Mitigation and enhancement

Many predicted economic impacts are normally beneficial and encouraged by the local decision makers. However some may be disputed. There may be concern about some of the issues already noted, such as the poaching of labour from local firms, the swamping of the local labour market, or the shadow effect on other potential development. In such cases, there may be attempts to build in formal and/or informal controls, such as "no poaching agreements". The fear of the "boom–bust" scenario may lead to requirements for a compensatory "assisted area" package for other employment with the demise of employment associated with the project in hand (Rodriguez-Bachiller and Glasson 2004). A number of studies of post-redundancy employment experiences have been undertaken in the UK. Some relate to traditional industries such as coal-mining, shipbuilding and steel (Hinde 1994, Turner and Gregory 1995). A number of studies have been associated with the restructuring of the defence and aerospace sectors (Bishop and Gripaios 1993). There have also been studies of the end of construction programmes (Armstrong *et al.* 1998, Glasson and Chadwick 1997). An interesting study on the disputed costs and benefits of UK airport expansion, in this case the planned expansion of Stansted Airport, is provided by Ross and Young (2007). The study focuses in particular on the economic leakage out of the UK associated with an airport so closely tied to the budget airline/mass-tourism market. In this case the protagonists' proposed mitigation measure is to "Stop Stansted Expansion".

However in general the focus for economic impacts is more on measures to **enhance benefits**. When positive impacts are identified there should be a concern to ensure that they do happen and do not become diluted. The potential local employment benefits of a project can be encouraged through appropriate skills training programmes for local people. Targets for the proportion of local recruitment may be set. Various measures, such as project open days for potential local suppliers and a register of local suppliers, may help to encourage local links and to reduce the leakage of wider economic impacts outside the locality. For example, the UK Olympic Development Authority announced in 2008 the setting up of a website (www.competefor.com/london2012business/login.jsp) to bring contract opportunities for the London 2012 Olympics to the attention of possible suppliers.

2.7 Monitoring

Previous stages in the EIA process should be designed with monitoring in mind. **Key indicators** for monitoring direct employment impacts include: levels and types of employment, by local and non-local sources and by previous employment status; trends in local and regional unemployment rates; and the output of training programmes. All these indicators should be disaggregated to allow analysis by employment/skill category. Relevant data sources include developer/ contractor returns, monthly unemployment statistics, and training programme data; these can be supplemented by direct survey information. Key indicators of the wider economic impacts include: trends in retail turnover, the fortunes of local companies and development trends in the locality. Some guidance on such indicators may be gleaned from published data. The project developer may also provide information on the distribution of sub-contracts, but surveys of, for example, workforce expenditure, and the linkages of local firms with a project, may be necessary to gain the necessary information for useful monitoring.

Monitoring is currently not mandatory for EIA in the UK. The omission was recognised in the review of the EU EIA Directive, and the EC is a strong advocate, but despite good practice in some EU Member States (e.g. the Netherlands) others are more defensive and reactive. As such, there are few comprehensive studies to draw on. The work of the IAU at Oxford on monitoring the local socio-economic impacts of the construction of Sizewell B (Glasson 2005) provides one of the few documented examples of a longitudinal study of socioeconomic impacts in practice. It shows the significance of direct employment and wider economic impacts for the local economy. At peak over 2,000 local jobs were provided, but with a clear emphasis on the less skilled jobs. Local skills have been upgraded through a major training programme, and while some local companies have experienced recruitment difficulties as a result of Sizewell B, the impact did not appear to be too significant. A group of about 30 to 40 mainly small local companies have benefited substantially from contracts with the project. Although the actual level of project employment was higher than predicted, many of the predictions made at the time of the public inquiry have stood the test of time, and the key socio-economic condition of encouraging the use of local labour has been fulfilled. The study also showed the project management advantages of monitoring, with issues being highlighted by such monitoring being quickly managed for the benefit of the project and the local community.

2.8 Conclusions

Socio-economic impacts are important in the EIA process. They have traditionally been limited to no more than one EIS chapter, and often a small late chapter, if they have been included at all. Our placing of such impacts early in this text, and in two chapters, emphasises our concern to indicate their importance in a comprehensive EIA. Our focus is on the incorporation of such impacts within an EIA process rather than as separate SIA (or even SIA and HIA) assessments (see Ahmad 2004).

The discussion has outlined the broad characteristics of such impacts and discussed economic impacts in more detail, with a particular focus on approaches to establishing the information baseline and to prediction. Some predictive methods can become complex. This may be appropriate for major studies; for smaller studies, some of the simpler methods may be more appropriate. The non-local/local employment ratio associated with a project has been identified as a key determinant of many subsequent socio-economic effects.

Notes

1. The Interorganisational Guidance and Principles have had a bumpy ride since their inception in 1994. In 2003 there was a dividing of the ways between a US-oriented version and a more international-oriented version. The US version differs little from 1994, relating closely to regulatory requirements and with a focus on assessment in advance of development actions. In contrast, the international version argues that SIA should not necessarily be tied to a regulatory context, should not just be "in advance" (but should be more participative and ongoing), and should "consider how to ensure the achievement of the intended positive consequences or goals of development as well as preventing unintended negative outcomes" (Vanclay 2003).
2. The encouragement of a particular local employment percentage has, for a number of years, been influenced in the EU by the free labour market regulations which require major projects to advertise for labour on an EU-wide basis.

References

Ahmad B 2004. Integrating health into impact assessment: challenges and opportunities. *Impact Assessment and Project Appraisal* **22**(1), 2–4.

Armstrong HW, M Ingham and D Riley 1988. *The effect of the Heysham 2 power station on the Lancaster and Morecambe economy.* Lancaster: Department of Economics, Lancaster University.

Bass R 1998. Evaluating environmental justice under the National Environmental Policy Act. *EIA Review* **18**, 83–92.

Batey P, M Maddenand G Scholefield 1993. Socio-economic impact assessment of large-scale projects using input-output analysis: a case study of an airport. *Regional Studies* **27**(3), 179–192

Beeston S 2003. *An economic analysis of rail trails in Victoria, Australia.* Bendigo, VIC: La Trobe University.

Bishop P and P Gripaios 1993. Defence in a peripheral region: The case of Devon and Cornwall. *Local Economy* **8**, 43–56.

BNFL (British Nuclear Fuels Limited) 2002. *Environmental statement in support of application to decommission Hinkley Point A nuclear power station.* Magnox Electric/BNFL.

Bowles RT 1981. *Social impact assessment in small communities.* Toronto: Butterworth.

Bronfman LM 1991. Setting the social impact agenda: an organisational perspective. *Environmental Impact Assessment Review* **11**, 69–79.

Brownrigg M 1971. The regional income multiplier: an attempt to complete the model. *Scottish Journal of Political Economy* **18**.

Brownrigg M 1974. *A study of economic impact: the Stirling University.* Scottish Academic Press.

Burdge R 2002. Why is social impact assessment the orphan of the assessment process? *Impact Assessment and Project Appraisal* **20**(1), 3–9.

Canter L and R Clark 1997. NEPA effectiveness – a survey of academics. *Environmental Impact Assessment Review* **71**, 313–328.

Carley MJ and ES Bustelo 1984. *Social impact assessment and monitoring: a guide to the literature.* Boulder, CO: Westview Press.

Chadwick A 2002. Socio-economic impacts: are they still the poor relations in UK Environmental Statements? *Journal of Environmental Planning and Management* **45**(1), 3–24.

CVCP (Committee of Vice-chancellors and Principals) 1994. *Universities and communities.* A report by CURDS, London: University of Newcastle for CVCP.

Denzin NK 1970. *Sociological methods: a source book.* Chicago: Aldine Publishing Company.

DoE (Department of the Environment) 1989. *Environmental assessment: a guide to the procedures.* London: HMSO.

Eadington W and M Redman 1991. Economics and tourism. *Annals of Tourism Research,* 41–56.

EC (European Commission) 1985. Council Directive on the assessment of the effects of certain private and public projects on the environment (85/337/EEC). *Official Journal of the European Communities* L **175/40**, 5 July 1985, Brussels: European Commission.

EC 1997. Council Directive 97/11/EC amending Directive 85/337/EEC on the assessment of the effects of certain public and private projects on the environment. Brussels: *Official Journal of the European Commission* No. L073/5-21, www.europa.eu.int/comm/environment/eia.

Finsterbusch K 1980. *Understanding social impacts: assessing the effects of public projects.* Beverley Hills, CA: Sage Publications.

Finsterbusch K 1985. State of the art in social impact assessment. *Environment and Behaviour* **17**(2), 193–221.

Fletcher J and B Archer 1991. The development and application of multiplier analysis. In *Progress in Tourism*, Vol. 3. C Cooper (ed.), 28–47. London: Belhaven Press.

Glasson J 1992. *An introduction to regional planning*. London: UCL Press.

Glasson J 2003. The widening local and regional development impacts of the modern universities. *Local Economy* 18(1), 21–37.

Glasson J 2005. Better monitoring for better impact management: the local socio-economic effects of constructing Sizewell B nuclear power station. *Impact Assessment and Project Appraisal* 23(3), 1–12.

Glasson J and A Chadwick 1988–1997. *The local socio-economic impacts of the Sizewell 'B' PWR construction project*. Impacts Assessment Unit, Oxford Brookes University.

Glasson J and A Chadwick 1997. Life after Sizewell B: post-redundancy experiences of locally recruited construction employees. *Town Planning Review* 68(3), 325–345.

Glasson J and D Heaney 1993. Socio-economic impacts: the poor relations in British EISs. *Journal of Environmental Planning and Management* 36(3), 335–343.

Glasson J et al. 1982. *A comparison of the social and economic effects of power stations on their localities*. Oxford: Oxford Polytechnic Power Station Impacts Team.

Glasson J, MJ Elson, D van der Wee and B Barrett 1987. *The socio-economic impact of the proposed Hinkley Point 'C' power station*. Oxford: Oxford Polytechnic Power Station Impacts Team.

Glasson J, D van der Wee and B Barrett 1988. A local income and employment multiplier analysis of a proposed nuclear power station development at Hinkley Point in Somerset. *Urban Studies* 25, 248–261.

Glasson J, R Therivel and A Chadwick 2005. *Introduction to environmental impact assessment*, 3rd edn. London: Routledge.

Grady S, R Braid, J Bradbury and C Kerley 1987. Socio-economic assessment of plant closure: three case studies of large manufacturing facilities. *Environmental Impact Assessment and Review* 26, 151–165.

Hinde K 1994. Labour market experiences following plant closure: the case of Sunderland's shipyard workers. *Regional Studies* 28, 713–724.

Interorganisational Committee on Guidelines and Principles for Social Impact Assessment 1994. Guidelines and principles for social impact assessment. *Impact Assessment* 12 (summer), 107–152.

Lang R and A Armour 1981. *The assessment and review of social impacts*. Ottawa: Federal Environmental Assessment and Review Office.

Lawton Smith H 2003. Guest Editor: Special Edition of *Local Economy* journal on "Universities and Local Economic Development" 18(1).

Lewis JA 1988. Economic impact analysis: a UK literature survey and bibliography. *Progress in Planning* 30(3), 161–209.

Lincoln I, D Stone and A Walker 1993. *The impact of higher education institutes on their local economy: a review of studies and assessment methods*. Report by NERU. London: University of Northumbria for CVCP.

McNicholl IH 1981. Estimating regional industry multipliers: alternative techniques. *Town Planning Review* 55(1), 80–88.

Murdock SH, FL Leistritz and RR Hamm 1986. The state of socio-economic impact analysis in the USA: limitations and opportunities for alternative futures. *Journal of Environmental Management* 23, 99–117.

Newton JA 1995. The integration of socio-economic impacts in EIA and project appraisal. MSc dissertation. Manchester: UMIST.

NDA (Nuclear Decommissioning Authority) 2006. *NDA Strategy*. London: NDA, www.nda.gov.uk/strategy/.

ONS (Office for National Statistics) 2000. *Standard Occupational Classification 2000*. London:ONS, www.statistics.gov.uk/methods_quality/ns_sec/downloads/SOC2000.doc.

ONS 2007. *The 2007 revision of the UK Standard Industrial Classification of Economic Activities*. London: ONS, www.statistics.gov.uk/methods_quality/sic/operation2007.asp.

Rodriguez-Bachiller A and J Glasson 2004. *Expert systems and geographical information systems for EIA*. London: Taylor & Francis.

Ross B and M Young (2007) Proof of evidence on behalf of Stop Stansted Expansion: economic impacts (www.stopstanstedexpansion.com).

SEERA (South East of England Regional Assembly) 2006. *The south east plan*. Guildford, Surrey: SEERA.

Steele DB 1969. *Regional multipliers in Britain*. Oxford Economic Papers, **19**.

Taylor L and R Quigley 2002. *Health impact assessment: a review of reviews*. London: Health Development Agency.

Transport for London (2004) Thames Gateway Bridge: Regeneration Statement. London: Transport for London.

Turner R and M Gregory 1995. Life after the pit: the post-redundancy experiences of mineworkers. *Local Economy* **10**, 149–162.

UNECE (United Nations Economic Commission for Europe) 1991. *Policies and systems of environmental impact assessment*. Geneva: UNECE.

UNEP (United Nations Environment Programme) 1996. *Environmental impact assessment: issues, trends and practice*. Stevenage: SMI Distribution.

Vanclay F 2003. Principles for social impact assessment: A critical comparison between international and US documents. *EIA Review* **26**, 3–14.

Vickerman R 1987. Channel Tunnel: consequences for regional growth and development. *Regional Studies* **21**(3), 187–197.

White House 1994. *Memorandum from President Clinton to all heads of all departments and agencies on an executive order on federal actions to address environmental injustice in minority populations and low income populations*. Washington, DC: White House.

Wolf CP (ed.) 1974. *Social impact assessment*. Washington, DC: Environmental Design Research Association.

World Bank 1991. *Environmental assessment sourcebook*, Vol. 1, Chapter 3, *World Bank technical paper No. 139*. Washington, DC: World Bank.

3 Socio-economic impacts 2: social impacts

Andrew Chadwick

3.1 Introduction

Chapter 2 discussed how the workforce involved in the construction and operation of any major project is likely to be drawn partly from local sources (within daily commuting distance of the project site) and partly from further afield. Those employees recruited from beyond daily commuting distance can be expected to move into the locality, either temporarily during construction or permanently during operation. Some of these employees will bring families into the area. In-migrant employees and their families will exert a number of impacts on their host localities:

- They will result in an increase in the **population** of the area and possibly in changes to the age and gender profile of the local population.
- They will require **accommodation** within reasonable commuting distance of the project site.
- They will place additional demands on a range of **local services**, including schools, health and recreational facilities, police and emergency services.
- They may have **other social impacts**, such as changes in the local crime rate or in the social mix of the area's population.

3.2 Baseline studies

3.2.1 Demography – *establishing the existing baseline*

The geographical extent of social impacts, i.e. the **impact area**, will depend largely on the residential location of in-migrant workers and their families. In-migrant employees can be expected to move into accommodation within reasonable commuting distance of the project site, although the definition of what constitutes a reasonable distance will depend on the project stage (construction or operation), as well as local settlement patterns and the local transport network. Monitoring data from similar projects elsewhere should indicate the likely extent of daily commuting and thus the likely boundaries of the impact area. These boundaries can be defined in various ways, for example in terms of a fixed distance or radius from the project site or, more usually, in terms of administrative or political areas such as local authority districts (LADs), health authority areas or school catchment areas.

The demographic impact of any development will depend on the project-related changes in population in relation to the existing population size and structure in the impact area. It is therefore necessary to establish the existing population baseline in the impact area (i.e. size and age/gender profile). The most useful source of population data in the UK, particularly for small geographical areas, is the *Census of population*. This is carried out once every ten years, most recently in 2001. Since all households are included in the census, reliable information is available at all geographical levels, from census output areas (typically covering 125 households) upwards. Census data is published by the Office for National Statistics (ONS) for England & Wales, the General Register Office for Scotland (GROS), and the Northern Ireland Statistics & Research Agency (NISRA). The data can be accessed at the websites of these organisations, and also from the NOMIS website (see list of websites at the end of the chapter for details).

The great strengths of the census are its comprehensiveness and the availability of data for small or user-defined geographic areas. Its main weakness is that it is only undertaken once every ten years. Given the delay in the processing and publication of results, the latest data are sometimes more than a decade out of date. Between censuses, it is therefore necessary to consult other sources to obtain a more up-to-date picture of population size and structure in the impact area. The most often used of these sources are the official *mid-year population estimates*, published annually by ONS, GROS and NISRA. In addition, most local authorities produce their own population estimates, both for the authority as a whole and its constituent parts (i.e. wards or parishes). These estimates tend to be derived by using proxy measures of population change since the latest census, such as changes in the electoral roll or doctors' registrations. A number of commercial market analysis companies also produce census-based population estimates for small geographic areas.

3.2.2 Projecting the demographic baseline forward

The data sources outlined above allow the existing population baseline in the impact area to be established. But it may also be desirable to project this baseline forward, ideally to the expected times of peak construction and full operational activity for the proposed development. A number of data sources are available to guide this process. Sub-national population projections are published by ONS, the Welsh Assembly Government, GROS and NISRA. The projections cover a 25-year period and are available at local authority district level. Population projections and forecasts are often also produced by local authorities themselves. These are used by authorities as inputs to their land use planning work and to estimates of future service requirements (e.g. school places). Projections are usually available for LADs and in some cases are disaggregated to ward or parish level.

These various sources have **limitations** as means of projecting forward the population baseline for relatively small geographical areas. Projections for smaller areas (e.g. LADs) tend to be less reliable than those for larger areas (e.g. counties or regions). This is because net migration is usually a more important determinant of population change for smaller areas; and migration flows are much more difficult to predict than the number of births and deaths. The sources also differ in the extent to which they simply project forward past trends in an unmodified way. For example, ONS stresses that its population projections are not "forecasts", in that they take no account of the potential effects of changes in local planning policies (ONS 2006). These are often designed to counteract past trends, for example to slow down the rate of population and housing growth in an area. Local authority forecasts are much more likely to incorporate such anticipated policy effects and may therefore be preferable, although of course the intended policy effects may not materialise in practice.

3.2.3 Accommodation – Establishing the existing baseline

The 2001 census, as well as providing population data, is also a useful source of data on the **housing stock** in small geographical areas. The census provides a breakdown of the housing stock in an area, according to its tenure (i.e. whether it is owner occupied, privately rented, rented with a job or business, or rented from a housing association or local authority). The amount of vacant accommodation is identified, as is accommodation which is not used as a main residence – this includes second homes, which can account for a sizeable proportion of the housing stock in some rural areas.

All of this information, although providing a very detailed picture of the available housing stock, relates to the position at the time of the latest census and will therefore need to be updated. Annual estimates of the dwelling stock at local authority district level in England are produced by the Department for Communities and Local Government. Similar data can be accessed for the rest of the UK from the relevant devolved administrations (see list of websites at the end of the chapter for further details). This information, perhaps supplemented by more detailed development control data from local authorities themselves, should allow any significant changes in the overall size of the housing stock since the latest census to be estimated. Up-to-date house price data for areas in England and Wales is published by the Land Registry.

During the construction stage of any development, some **in-migrant employees** are likely to move into bed and breakfast establishments, hotels, caravans or other types of tourist accommodation. It is therefore necessary to establish how much of such accommodation is available in the impact area, and if possible to determine typical occupancy levels. Any unoccupied accommodation (e.g. outside the peak tourist season) could be used by in-migrant employees without affecting the availability of accommodation for other existing users. Regional tourist boards, local authorities and tourist information centres all maintain databases or lists of accommodation establishments within their areas of jurisdiction. Details of each individual establishment are often available, including the location, number of rooms and charges/tariffs. A detailed picture of the existing stock of accommodation can therefore be obtained. When combining lists prepared by different organisations for the same geographical area, care should be taken to avoid the double-counting of establishments.

3.2.4 Projecting the accommodation baseline forward

Non-project related changes in the local housing stock can be estimated most easily by using simple **trend projection methods**. These are typically based on the assumption that recent rates of growth in the number of dwellings will continue for the foreseeable future. Information on changes in the dwelling stock at local authority district level is published annually by the Department for Communities and Local Government (for England), and by the devolved administrations in the rest of the UK. Such methods, although easily applied, are rather crude, in that they take no account of possible changes in the state of the national economy (which may affect housebuilding rates) or in local rates of population and household growth; they also fail to allow for the influence of local planning policies on the scale and location of new housebuilding.

An alternative approach would be to use estimates of future population and household growth in the area to predict the likely demand for new houses. *Local authority population and household forecasts* are likely to be particularly relevant. High and low estimates of household growth are usually made by local authorities, using different assumptions about net migration, employment and household formation. Of course, the anticipated increase in the number of households in an area may not be met by an equivalent increase in the housing stock. This is because local planning policies may be intended to meet only part of the projected increase in households. The extent, phasing and location of new housebuilding envisaged by local planning authorities is indicated by the *housing allocations in approved structure plans and adopted local plans* (currently being replaced by local development frameworks).

Likely changes in the stock of tourist and other temporary accommodation are difficult to predict, although regional tourist boards and local authorities may be able to indicate the scale of any significant additional provision, either already under construction or with outstanding planning permission.

3.2.5 Local services

In-migrant employees and their families will place demands on a wide range of services provided by local authorities, health authorities and other public bodies. In the space available, it is not possible to discuss each of these service areas in detail. The bulk of this section therefore examines one service area – **local education services** – as an example of how the existing service baseline might be established and projected forward. Other service areas are briefly discussed at the end of the section.

The **number and type of schools** within the impact area can be obtained directly from local education authorities (LEAs) (for LEA-maintained schools and colleges), or from websites such as Edubase (which allows users to identify all educational establishments within fixed distances of a specified location). Edubase also provides information on the existing number of pupils on school rolls and the total available capacity (in permanent and temporary accommodation), for each individual school. This information can be used to determine the extent to which the available capacity in LEA schools is currently being utilised, across the authority as a whole and for individual schools.

Information on significant **planned changes in school capacity** due to the closure, amalgamation or enlargement of existing schools and the opening of new schools should be obtained from the LEA concerned. All LEAs also produce forecasts of future pupil numbers, both for the authority as a whole and for individual schools. These are derived in some cases from the authority's own population and household projections, and should incorporate the effects of anticipated non-project in-migration. These data sources will allow any significant anticipated changes in pupil numbers and the utilisation of capacity within the impact area to be identified.

Information on **other public services,** such as recreation, police, fire and social services, should be obtained directly from the relevant local authority department. For **health services,** local primary and acute care NHS trusts will be able to provide a wide range of data on existing medical, dental and pharmacy services, as well as hospital facilities in the impact area.

3.3 Impact prediction

3.3.1 Population changes

Changes in population caused by a major project can include both direct and indirect increases. The **direct increase** will consist of in-migrant employees and any other family members brought into the locality. A number of separate estimates are therefore required to determine the population changes directly due to the project: (a) the total number of employees moving into the impact area, during both the construction and operational stages of the development; (b) the proportion of these in-migrant employees bringing other family members; and (c) the characteristics of these families (i.e. their size and age structure).

The total number of employees moving into the impact area

Chapter 2 has outlined the methods available for predicting the mix of local and in-migrant employees associated with the construction and operation of major projects. *During the construction stage,* the build up in the number of in-migrant workers will reflect the build up of the construction workforce and changes in the local labour percentage. At the end of the construction stage, most in-migrant workers will move out of the impact area and return to their original address or another construction project elsewhere. However, a small proportion may establish local ties, especially during a lengthy construction project, and may decide to remain in the area. A construction project spanning several years may therefore result in a small permanent increase in the local population. *During operation*, the main flow of in-migrant employees will usually occur at a relatively early stage, with subsequent in-migration limited to that caused by the normal turnover of employees.

The proportion of in-migrant employees bringing their family

During the construction stage, only a minority of in-migrant employees – mainly those on long-term contracts – are likely to bring their family into the area. The precise proportion will depend on various factors:

- the length of the construction programme (for projects lasting only a few months, it is likely to be negligible; for projects spanning several years, the proportion may reach at least 10–20 per cent);
- the location and accessibility of the project site, which will determine the relative merits of weekly commuting and family relocation;
- conditions in the national and local housing markets (a depressed national housing market or sharp inter-regional house price differentials may discourage house and family relocation);
- the availability of suitable family accommodation, schools and other amenities in the locality.

During the operational stage, the vast majority of in-migrant employees will relocate permanently to the area, although there may be some initial delay while suitable accommodation is found and existing properties are sold. Those employees with partners or children can be expected to bring them into the area (with the exception of a small number of weekly commuters). The precise proportion of employees with families will depend on the age and gender profile of the in-migrant workforce. For example, a younger workforce might be expected to contain a higher proportion of single, unattached employees who will not bring families into the area.

The characteristics of in-migrant families

Once the likely number of in-migrant families has been determined, it is necessary to estimate the average size and broad age structure of these families. The usual approach to estimating the size of in-migrant families is to use detailed census data on household headship. The census shows the average size of households of different types, classified according to the age, gender and marital status of the head of household. Therefore, if it was considered likely that most in-migrant families would contain a married, male head of household, aged 20–59 years, the average size of this type of household – either nationally or in the impact area – could be calculated. For projects with a younger anticipated workforce, the average size of households with married male heads aged, say 20–44 years, could be calculated instead. This method assumes that the household characteristics at the time of the latest census will remain largely unchanged; it also requires some knowledge (or guesswork) about the age and gender profile of the in-migrant workforce.

Let us assume that the method outlined above suggests that each in-migrant family will contain an average of 3.2 persons. It could then be assumed that each of these families would consist of two adults of working age (the in-migrant employee and partner) and an average of 1.2 other family members – mainly dependent children up to 18 years old, but also including a small proportion of "adult" children (over 18 years old) still living with their parents and perhaps some elderly relatives. The precise proportion of adult children and elderly relatives should ideally be derived from monitoring data, but – in the absence of such information – a rough guestimate may be required. Information on the age structure of the 0–18-year-old population is available from a number of sources, and this can be used as the basis of predictions of the ages of dependent children brought into the area. The current age breakdown of 0–18-year-olds is provided by the 2001 census, the latest mid-year population estimates and local authority population estimates. The projected future age breakdown of this group can be obtained from the various population projections and forecasts outlined in §3.2.2. The census also provides an age breakdown of children (and others) moving into particular areas during the 12 months prior to the census date.

The precise age distribution of dependent children will of course depend on the age profile of their parents. For example, a younger workforce will tend to have a higher proportion of pre-school children than might be suggested by the data sources above, whereas an older workforce may have higher proportions of secondary school children. Some fine-tuning of the age distribution revealed by the data sources above may therefore be required, to take account of the expected age profile of the project workforce. The age breakdown of the workforce should ideally be estimated by obtaining information on the age of employees on similar projects elsewhere. Such information should be readily available to the project developer (for operation) or its contractors (for construction).

As well as the direct population increase due to the arrival of in-migrant project employees and families, the development may give rise to **indirect population impacts**. These impacts can arise in two main ways. First, some locally recruited project employees will leave local employers to take up jobs on the project. This will result in local job vacancies, some of which may be filled by in-migrants. Indirect employment may also be created in local industries supplying or servicing the project, or in the provision of project-related infrastructure. Again, some of these jobs may be taken by in-migrant employees. The scale of the resulting additional in-migration is very difficult to estimate, but its possible existence should at least be acknowledged (see Clark *et al.* 1981, for some possible estimation methods). A second source of indirect impacts arises from the fact that some locally recruited project employees might have migrated out of the impact area if the project had not gone ahead, especially if alternative job opportunities locally were limited. The project may therefore lead to a reduction in out-migration from the area. Again, the extent of any such reduction is difficult to predict. It is likely to be significant only in areas experiencing static or declining population, net out-migration and limited or declining employment opportunities.

3.3.2 The significance of population changes

The significance of project-related population changes will depend on three main factors: (a) the existing population size and structure in the impact area (i.e. the population baseline); (b) the geographical distribution of the in-migrant population; and (c) the timing of the population changes. Put simply, if in-migrants are few relative to the existing population and have a similar age and gender profile, are distributed over a wide area and do not all arrive at once, then the impacts are unlikely to be significant. The first step in assessing significance is therefore to **express the estimated project-related population increase as a percentage of the baseline population** in the impact area. The predicted age structure of in-migrants should be compared with the baseline age structure, and any significant differences outlined.

The next step is to estimate the likely **geographical distribution of in-migrants**. Population changes may be quite localised, rather than being evenly distributed throughout the impact area. However, in the absence of information from monitoring studies, the precise distribution of in-migrants is difficult to predict. The simplest approach would be to assume that the number of employees moving into a particular settlement would be a positive function of that settlement's size and a negative function of its distance from the project site. In practice, the predictions derived from this type of model would need to be modified to allow for the characteristics of the particular locality. These could include the expected location of future housebuilding in the impact area; differences in the availability and price of various types of housing; and the attractiveness of each settlement in terms of schools and other facilities and general environment. **The timing of the arrival of in-migrant employees** and the associated population changes will largely follow the expected build up in the project workforce. However, during the construction stage, most in-migrant families are likely to arrive in the early stages, given that families will tend to be brought by those employees on long-term contracts for the duration of the project.

The nature and significance of population impacts will change as the project progresses through the various stages of its life cycle. In-migrant employees and their families will become older. In addition, during the operational stage – which may span several decades – there may be some natural increase from the original in-migrant population. These changes can be estimated by using a simple "cohort survival" method, applying age-specific birth and death rates to the original population. Some allowance may also need to be made for the turnover of employees on the project. As older employees retire, they will tend to be replaced by younger employees, with younger families. This process will counteract, but not completely reverse, the tendency for the in-migrant population to become older.

3.3.3 Accommodation requirements

The total amount of accommodation required will be determined by the size of the **in-migrant workforce** and the extent to which accommodation is shared. Methods to estimate the total number of in-migrant employees were outlined in Chapter 2. Sharing of accommodation is likely to be minimal among the permanent **operational workforce**, since most in-migrant employees will be accompanied by their families. However, there may be a limited amount of sharing among younger, single employees, especially in rented accommodation. During the **construction stage**, sharing may be much more significant, especially among those employees using rented, caravan and perhaps B&B accommodation. Estimates of the likely extent of sharing should be incorporated into any predictions of the demand for accommodation by the construction workforce. Otherwise, the amount of accommodation required is likely to be over-estimated, perhaps significantly. Published monitoring studies of recent construction projects, although limited in number in the UK, may provide an indication of the likely extent of sharing (e.g. see Glasson and Chadwick 1995).

The type and location of accommodation required will also differ in the operational and construction phases. The vast majority of in-migrant **operational employees** are likely to relocate permanently to the impact area. Most will wish to purchase a property in the area, although a small proportion may prefer private rented accommodation. This latter group will include younger, single employees and a small number of weekly commuters not relocating their family. There may also be some demand for social rented accommodation, from local authorities and housing associations. The likely mix between owner occupied, private and social rented accommodation requirements can be roughly estimated by using census data – the census provides information on the tenure of all households moving address during the 12 months prior to the census date. Separate tenure patterns can be identified for different types of move (e.g. moves within the same LAD, inter-county or inter-regional moves). This information is also available for different age groups, according to the age of the head of household. These data could perhaps be combined with the expected age profile of the operational workforce, to produce estimates of the likely tenure patterns of in-migrant households.

Predicting the likely **mix of accommodation used by in-migrant construction workers** is a more complicated exercise. A wider range of accommodation is likely to be suitable, including B&B, caravan and other types of tourist accommodation. A further complication is that, for larger construction projects, the developer may decide to provide accommodation specifically for the workforce. The extent of such provision will have important implications for the take up of other types of accommodation. Because the local supply of different types of accommodation and the extent of developer provision will vary from one locality and project to another, the precise mix of accommodation used can vary considerably from project to project. Monitoring data, even if they are available, may therefore provide only a rough indication of the likely take up of each type of accommodation.

In the absence of developer provision, the vast majority of in-migrant construction workers are likely to use private rented, B&B/lodgings or caravan accommodation. The use of each type of accommodation can be roughly estimated by drawing on the available monitoring data from other construction projects, adjusted to allow for the particular supply characteristics in the impact area, i.e. the amount of each type of accommodation available, its location, cost and existing occupancy levels (see §3.2.3). For example, if the local supply of tourist accommodation is very limited, concentrated in highly priced hotels at some distance from the project site and is usually fully occupied, the proportion of employees using such accommodation is likely to be relatively low.

Some construction workers may wish to purchase properties in the locality. The number is likely to be minimal during construction projects lasting only a few months, but may be more significant (at least 10 per cent) in cases where construction activity spans several years. The proportion of in-migrant employees buying properties will be closely linked to the proportion bringing families into the impact area. However, since some families will prefer to use rented accommodation, the number of owner occupied properties required is likely to be lower than the total number of in-migrant families.

In certain cases, the project developer may decide to make specific accommodation provision for the construction workforce. This may involve negotiations with the local planning authority over the provision of additional caravan sites or the expansion of existing sites. In other cases, the developer may wish to provide purpose-built hostel accommodation, located on or adjacent to the construction site. This typically consists of single bedrooms and associated catering, recreational and other facilities. To the extent that such provision is made, the proportion of in-migrant employees using other types of accommodation will be lower than would otherwise have been the case.

It may be helpful to provide estimates of the demand for different types of accommodation in various alternative scenarios, e.g. without any hostel or additional caravan provision, with a small hostel or with a larger hostel. Such estimates will themselves help to clarify the need for such developer provision. The precise geographical distribution of the accommodation taken up by in-migrant employees is difficult to predict: §3.3.2 outlined a possible approach.

3.3.4 The significance of accommodation requirements

The project-related demand for local accommodation is likely to result in a net change in the amount of accommodation available in the impact area. On the one hand, the availability of accommodation will be reduced by the take up of local accommodation by project employees and their families. This accommodation would otherwise have been available to local residents and non-project in-migrants. On the other hand, to the extent that project-related demands are met by the release of unoccupied or under-occupied accommodation and/or the bringing forward of speculative house building development, the amount of accommodation available locally will be higher than would otherwise have been the case. The balance between these two types of change will represent the net change due to the project. This should then be expressed as a percentage of the existing (or projected) stock of accommodation in the impact area. Similar calculations can be made for each separate type of accommodation and for particular settlements or areas within the impact area.

In extreme cases, the net decline in the availability of accommodation due to the project may be such that the project-related and non-project demands for accommodation may outstrip the available local supply. Assessment of such pressures requires projections of the following:

- the likely project-related demand for accommodation (as outlined earlier in the section);
- the likely non-project demand for accommodation by local residents and non-project in-migrants (derived from the projected growth in population and households, as outlined in §3.2.2 and §3.2.4);
- likely changes in the local supply of accommodation, including project-induced changes, such as the release of unoccupied and under-occupied accommodation and the bringing forward of speculative development.

Cases in which the project results in a shortfall in the local supply of accommodation are likely to require the consideration of mitigation measures. However, in practice, pressure on one locality is likely to be relieved by the diversion of demand (both project and non-project) into adjacent localities. Unless seen as undesirable, this may eliminate the need for mitigation measures.

3.3.5 The demand for local services

In-migrant employees and their families will place demands on a wide range of services provided by local authorities and other public bodies. The demand for these services will largely reflect the age and gender distribution of the in-migrant population (see §3.3.1). For example, in the case of **health and personal social services**, the number of young children and elderly people will be a critical determinant of demand. In such cases, rough estimates of likely demand can be obtained by combining the predicted age and gender profile of the in-migrant population with age and gender-specific data on visiting rates to or by doctors, health visitors or social workers. The latter can be obtained from local and health authorities.

In the case of **education services**, demand also clearly depends on the age structure of the in-migrant population, since provision must be made for all children between the ages of 5 and 16. However, there are complications, given that this provision can be made either by the state or the independent sector and that some children below and above compulsory school age may also require school or college places. The remainder of this section provides an example of the calculations involved in estimating the number of additional state sector primary and secondary school places likely to be required locally in response to an influx of project employees.

Predicting the demand for additional local school places requires separate estimates of:

- the total number of children aged 0–18 years brought into the impact area by in-migrant employees (see §3.3.1);
- the proportion of these children below compulsory school age (0–4 years), aged 5–16 and above school-leaving age (see §3.3.1);
- the proportion of 5–16-year-olds attending independent (private sector) schools.

The proportion of pupils attending independent schools can be calculated for individual local authority areas, and is also published at national level by the Department for Children, Schools and Families (for England, and by the relevant devolved administrations covering the rest of the UK). These national proportions could be assumed to apply to the children brought into the area, again assuming no changes in the relative importance of the state and independent sectors before the project gets underway. The estimated number of pupils attending independent schools could then be subtracted from the total school place requirement to show the number of places required in local state sector schools.

The demand for additional school places is unlikely to be evenly distributed throughout the impact area. The extent to which demand is geographically concentrated or dispersed will determine the total number of schools affected and the likelihood of strains on educational provision in individual schools. The distribution of school place requirements will largely reflect the place of residence of in-migrant families. Unfortunately, the latter is difficult to predict in the absence of relevant monitoring data: §3.3.2 outlined a possible approach to prediction, but it may be helpful to present a series of estimates based on different assumptions about the concentration or dispersal of in-migrant families.

3.3.6 *The significance of demands on local services*

An important indicator of the significance of local service impacts is the extent to which **capacity thresholds** are exceeded as a result of the demands arising from the in-migrant population. Let us consider the example of the demand for local school places. If the current accommodation capacity in a school is expected to be almost fully utilised in the absence of the project, and pupil/teacher ratios are already high, then even a small project-induced increase in pupil numbers may create a need for additional classrooms and/or extra teaching staff. In the absence of such additional provision, the result may be overcrowding and an unacceptable increase in class sizes. By contrast, a large increase in pupil numbers in a school with a considerable amount of under-utilised capacity and low pupil/teacher ratios may be much less significant. Increases in pupil numbers in such schools may still be important, even if they do not put the available capacity under pressure. Class sizes will be larger than would otherwise have been the case, and additional staff time may need to be devoted to individual assessments of incoming pupils. Assessment of significance therefore requires information not only on the likely project-related increase in demand, but also the existing (and projected) utilisation of service capacity.

In certain circumstances, additional service demands may be seen as beneficial. For example, an influx of pupils into a small rural primary school with declining pupil numbers may help to safeguard the future of the school, either in the short term (during construction) or in the medium to long term (during operation). The nature and significance of local service impacts will change as the project progresses through its various stages. The in-migrant population, including children, will tend to become older, with the result that the type of services demanded will tend to change over time. For example, there will tend to be a shift away from nursery and primary school demand towards secondary school demand. This tendency will be counterbalanced to some extent by the turnover of employees (bringing new, younger, families into the area) and by births in the original in-migrant families.

3.3.7 Other social impacts

Other social impacts can be wide-ranging and may include:

- increased crime levels locally, particularly during the construction stage, associated with an influx of young (typically) male itinerant employees into the impact area;
- changes in the occupational and socio-economic mix of the population; and
- linked to the above, problems in the integration of incoming employees and families into the local community and community activities. There may be a clash of lifestyles or expectations between incomers and the existing host community.

An extensive literature concerned with the assessment of such social and cultural impacts is available, much of it written from a North American perspective. Further details are provided in §3.6. Prediction of such impacts is difficult, but is likely to require at least a comparison of the predicted age, gender and occupational profile of in-migrants with that of the existing population in the impact area. The latter can be determined largely by reference to census data, as outlined in §3.2.1. Monitoring studies may be helpful in indicating the likely scale of certain impacts (e.g. see Glasson and Chadwick (1995) for an assessment of the impact of a major construction project on local crime levels).

3.4 Mitigation

A number of approaches to the mitigation of **demographic impacts** are available. The most basic would be to encourage the maximum recruitment of labour from within daily commuting distance of the project site, thereby reducing the number of employees and families moving into the impact area. Possible methods to encourage the use of local labour by developers and contractors were discussed in Chapter 2. In addition, during the construction stage, developer policies on travel, accommodation and relocation allowances might be used to influence the relative attractiveness of daily and weekly commuting versus relocation. Such policies might lead to some reduction in the proportion of in-migrant employees relocating and bringing families into the area.

The mitigation of local **accommodation impacts** is likely to involve attempts either to provide additional accommodation for the workforce or to encourage the use of unoccupied or under-occupied accommodation in the impact area. Encouragement of the sharing of accommodation would also be a useful mitigation measure, but it is uncertain how this could be carried out in practice. The provision of accommodation specifically for the workforce, in the form of purpose-built hostel or additional caravan accommodation, has already been discussed in §3.3.3. The success of such provision as a mitigation measure will depend on its attractiveness in relation to the alternatives available locally, in terms of location, facilities and cost. The release of unoccupied accommodation is rather more difficult to influence. During construction, one approach might involve the placing of advertisements in the local press requesting those willing to provide workforce accommodation to contact the developer. This may alert potential providers of accommodation to the opportunities presented by the project. In some circumstances, it may be considered desirable to encourage the use of local B&B and other tourist accommodation (e.g. to boost occupancy levels outside a short tourist season). This could be achieved by the compilation of a directory of local accommodation establishments by the developer, and its use by contractors and individuals seeking accommodation in the area.

Impacts on **local services** can be partially mitigated by the direct provision of certain facilities by the developer. Examples might include a medical centre and fire-fighting equipment and staff located on the project site, as well as recreational facilities for the workforce. Developer funding of additional local authority provision necessitated by the project is also likely to be requested. Funding of local community projects may also be offered as partial compensation for the adverse impacts of the project. The voluntary provision of community benefit funding by developers is widespread with certain types of project (e.g. for renewable energy schemes in Scotland, see for example Highland Council 2003).

3.5 Monitoring

Existing monitoring of demographic and social impacts is limited, other than for large-scale energy and resource development projects. Ideally, such monitoring should consist of three key elements. The first of these is the establishment of **administrative systems to ensure a regular flow of information on key parameters**, including at the very least the total numbers directly employed on the project and the mix of local and in-migrant employees. During most construction projects, the developer is likely to request this type of information from the contractors on site as a routine part of project management, for example to monitor earnings levels, bonuses and allowances across the construction site. The provision of such information can be made a contractual requirement. Existing monitoring systems can therefore often be used with only minimal modifications. For most projects, information on the operational workforce should be directly available to the developer via its own personnel records. However, this will not be the case for certain developments, such as business parks or retail projects, where several employers occupy the floorspace provided by the developer. In such cases, the developer (or perhaps the local authority) may wish to establish data collection systems covering all occupants, with the submission of information being requested on a regular basis.

The systems described above will, at best, only indicate the total number of employees moving into the impact area. Information on the number of these employees bringing families, the characteristics of these families, the type and location of accommodation taken up and the use of local services, can only be obtained directly from the workforce itself. The second component of any monitoring system must therefore be a **periodic survey of the project workforce**. This is likely to involve interviewing a sample of the workforce, with care taken to ensure a representative coverage of all types of employees. Such surveys can also be used to obtain information on other issues, such as workforce expenditure and journey to work patterns. Survey work of this type might be repeated on an annual basis, at least during the initial stages of the development.

The final element in any monitoring system should be the **monitoring of various social and economic trends within the impact area**. This can range from regular monitoring of house prices or rent levels, the amount of housebuilding, occupancy levels in local B&B and other accommodation, school rolls, doctors' list sizes or crime levels. Such trends should be compared with those in suitable control areas, including the wider region or sub-region; comparison with national trends may also be appropriate. In addition, periodic surveys of local service providers (e.g. headteachers or doctors) may provide a useful source of monitoring data.

3.6 Sources of further information

Useful data sources in the assessment of economic and social impacts include **census data** and a range of other **official statistics** published by government departments and agencies. These are particularly useful when assembling baseline data for the assessment. In the UK, relevant guidance on the use of official statistics in baseline assessment work includes ODPM (2004, 2006). Further information is also available from the websites listed at the end of this chapter.

Government guidance on the assessment of socio-economic impacts is rather limited at present, although a number of examples can be found in North America, Australia and New Zealand, as well as in international aid agencies. Examples include ADB (1991, 1994), CEPA (1994), Lang and Armour (1981), ODA (1995), SIAWG (1995) and USAID (1993). Other useful guidance can be found in ICGPS (1995) and Shell International Exploration and Production (1996).

A number of **general texts** on EIA include some discussion of socio-economic impacts and their assessment. Examples include Barrow (1997), Canter (1995), Clark *et al.* (1981), Colombo (1992), Erickson (1994), Petts and Eduljee (1994), and Vanclay and Bronstein (1995). The incorporation of socio-economic impacts into EIA is also discussed in Bond (1995), Burdge (2002), Chadwick (2002), Dale and Lane (1995), Dale *et al.* (1997), Glasson and Heaney (1993), Kirkpatrick and Lee (1997), Kolhoff (1996), Newton (1995) and Pellizzoni (1992).

Specialist texts on socio-economic and social impact assessment, mainly written from a North American perspective, include Barrow (2000), Becker (1997), Becker and Vanclay (2002), Branch *et al.* (1984), Burdge (1994, 2004a, 2004b), Canter *et al.* (1985), Finterbusch *et al.* (1983, 1990), Halstead *et al.* (1984), Lang and Armour (1981), Leistritz and Murdoch (1981), Maurice and Fleischman (1983), Taylor *et al.* (2004), and Wildman and Baxter (1985). Other useful references include Becker (1995), Burdge (2003a, 2003b), Burdge and Vanclay (1995), Leistritz (1994), Leistritz *et al.* (1994) and Vanclay (2002).

Specific impact or development types, or aspects of socio-economic assessment have also generated a considerable literature. For example, the socio-economic impacts of **major projects**, mainly in relation to large-scale energy and resource development projects, are discussed in Buchan and Rivers (1990), Chadwick and Glasson (1999), Cocklin and Kelly (1992), Denver Research Institute (1982), Egre and Senecal (2003), Gilmore *et al.* (1980), Glasson and Chadwick (1995), Hill *et al.* (1998), and Leistritz and Maki (1981). In a related area, the social impacts of rapid **"boomtown" development**, largely in a North American context, are discussed in England and Albrecht (1984), Freudenburg (1984), and Thompson and Bryant (1992). The social impact of **tourism development** is another area highlighted in the literature. Examples include Beekhuis (1981), and Shera and Matsuoka (1992). **Uncertainty** in relation to the prediction of social impacts is discussed in Marx (2002).

The **monitoring** or follow-up of socio-economic impacts is examined in Bisset and Tomlinson (1988), Chadwick and Glasson (1999), Denver Research Institute (1982), Gilmore *et al.* (1980), Glasson (1994, 2005), Lavallee and Pierre (2005), Petajajarvi (2005), Storey and Jones (2003), and Storey and Noble (2005). More general reviews of the field of socio-economic and social impact assessment can be found in Burdge (1987), Burdge and Vanclay (1996), Finterbusch (1995), Freudenburg (1986), Lane (1997), Lockie (2001), McDonald (1990), Murdoch *et al.* (1986), Rickson *et al.* (1990), and Wildman (1990).

A number of publications provide an overview of experience with socio-economic impact assessment in **specific countries**. UK and European experience is discussed in Chadwick (2002), Glasson and Heaney (1993), Juslen (1995), Newton (1995), Pellizzoni (1992) and Pinhero and Pires (1991). US and Canadian practice is reviewed in Denq and Altenhofel (1997), Finterbusch (1995), Gagnon (1995), Haque (1996), Lang and Armour (1981), Lavallee and Pierre (2005), Maurice and Fleischman (1983), and Murdoch *et al.* (1986). The development of socio-economic impact assessment in Australia and New Zealand is reflected in an extensive literature. Examples include Beckwith (1994), Buchan and Rivers

(1990), CEPA (1994), Cocklin and Kelly (1992), Dale and Lane (1995), Dale *et al.* (1997), Howitt (1989), Lane (1997), Rivers and Buchan (1995), Seebohm (1997), SIAWG (1995) and Taylor *et al.* (2003).

Social impact assessment in **developing countries**, and for projects financed by international aid agencies, is discussed in ADB (1991, 1994), Burdge (1990), Derman and Whiteford (1985), Henry (1990), Finterbusch *et al.* (1990), Francis and Jacobs (1997), Fu-Keung Ip (1990), Jiggins (1995), ODA (1995), du Pisani and Sandham (2006), Ramanathan and Geetha (1998), Rickson *et al.* (1990), Suprapto (1990), and USAID (1993).

The following **useful websites** provide guidance on and access to a wide range of statistics relevant to baseline assessment for social impacts with UK-based projects.

Audit Commission (Area Profiles) – www.areaprofiles.audit-commission.gov.uk
Data for Neighbourhood Renewal – www.data4nr.net
Department for Communities and Local Government – www.communities.gov.uk
Department for Children, Schools and Families – www.dcsf.gov.uk
Edubase – www.edubase.co.uk
Floor Targets Interactive – www.fti.neighbourhood.gov.uk
Home Office (Crime Statistics) – www.crimestatistics.org.uk
Land Registry – www.landreg.gov.uk
National Health Service (NHS) – www.nhs.uk
National Online Manpower Information System (NOMIS) – www.nomisweb.co.uk
Neighbourhood Statistics – www.neighbourhood.statistics.gov.uk
Northern Ireland Neighbourhood Information Service (NINIS) – www.ninis.nisra. gov.uk
Northern Ireland Statistics and Research Agency (NISRA) – www.nisra.gov.uk
Office for National Statistics (ONS) – www.statistics.gov.uk
Scottish Government – www.scotland.gov.uk/Topics/Statistics
Scottish Neighbourhood Statistics – www.sns.gov.uk
Welsh Assembly Government (Statistical Directorate) – http://wales.gov.uk/topics/ statistics

References

ADB (Asian Development Bank) 1991. *Guidelines for social analysis of development projects*. Manila: ADB.

ADB 1994. *Handbook for incorporation of social dimensions in projects*. Manila: Social Development Unit, ADB.

Barrow CJ 1997. *Environmental and social impact assessment: an introduction*. London: Arnold.

Barrow CJ 2000. *Social impact assessment: an introduction*. London: Arnold.

Becker HA 1995. Demographic impact assessment. In *Environmental and social impact assessment*, F Vanclay and DA Bronstein (eds), 141–151. Chichester: Wiley.

Becker HA 1997. *Social impact assessment: method and experience in Europe, North America and developing world*. London: UCL Press.

Becker HA and F Vanclay (eds) 2002. *The international handbook of social impact assessment*. Cheltenham, Glos: Edward Elgar.

Beckwith JA 1994. Social impact assessment in Western Australia at a crossroads. *Impact Assessment* **12**(2), 199–213.

Beekhuis JV 1981. Tourism in the Caribbean: impacts on the economic, social and natural environment. *Ambio* **X**(6), 325–331.

Bisset R and P Tomlinson 1988. Monitoring and auditing of impacts. In *Environmental impact assessment: theory and practice*, P Wathern (ed.), 117–128. London: Unwin Hyman.

Bond AJ 1995. Integrating socio-economic impact assessment into EIA. *Environmental Assessment* **3**(4), 125–127.

Branch K, DA Hooper, J Thompson and JC Creighton 1984. *Guide to social impact assessment: a framework for assessing social change*. Boulder, CO: Westview Press.

Buchan D and MJ Rivers 1990. Social impact assessment: development and application in New Zealand. *Impact Assessment Bulletin* **8**(4), 97–105.

Burdge RJ 1987. Social impact assessment and the planning process. *Environmental Impact Assessment Review* **7**(2), 141–150.

Burdge RJ 1990. The benefits of social impact assessment in third world development. *Environmental Impact Assessment Review* **10**(1–2), 123–134.

Burdge RJ 1994. *A conceptual approach to social impact assessment*. Middleton, WI: Social Ecology Press.

Burdge RJ 2002. Why is social impact assessment the orphan of the assessment process? *Impact Assessment and Project Appraisal* **20**(1), 3–9.

Burdge RJ 2003a. The practice of social impact assessment – background. *Impact Assessment and Project Appraisal* **21**(2), 84–88.

Burdge RJ 2003b. Benefiting from the practice of social impact assessment. *Impact Assessment and Project Appraisal* **21**(3), 225–229.

Burdge RJ 2004a. *A community guide to social impact assessment: 3rd edition*. Middleton, WI: Social Ecology Press.

Burdge RJ 2004b. *The concepts, process and methods of social impact assessment*. Middleton, WI: Social Ecology Press.

Burdge RJ and F Vanclay 1995. Social impact assessment. In *Environmental and social impact assessment*, F Vanclay and DA Bronstein (eds), 31–65. Chichester: Wiley.

Burdge RJ and F Vanclay 1996. Social impact assessment: a contribution to the state-of-the-art series. *Impact Assessment* **14**(1), 59–86.

Canter LW (ed.) 1995. *Environmental impact assessment*, 2nd edn. New York: McGraw Hill.

Canter LW, B Atkinson and FL Leistritz 1985. *Impact of growth: a guide for socio-economic impact assessment and planning*. Chelsea, MI: Lewis Publishers.

CEPA (Commonwealth Environmental Protection Agency) 1994. *Social impact assessment*. Barton, ACT, Australia: CEPA.

Chadwick A 2002. Socio-economic impacts: are they still the poor relations in UK environmental statements? *Journal of Environmental Planning and Management* **45**(1), 3–24.

Chadwick A and J Glasson 1999. Auditing the socio-economic impacts of a major construction project: the case of Sizewell B nuclear power station. *Journal of Environmental Planning and Management* **42**(6), 811–836.

Clark BD, K Chapman, R Bissett, P Wathern and M Barrett 1981. *A manual for the assessment of major development proposals*. London: HMSO.

Cocklin C and B Kelly 1992. Large-scale energy projects in New Zealand: whither social impact assessment? *Geoforum* **23**(1), 41–60.

Colombo AG (ed.) 1992. *Environmental impact assessment*. Dordrecht, The Netherlands: Kluwer Academic Publishers.

Dale AP and MB Lane 1995. Queensland's Social Impact Assessment Unit: its origins and prospects. *Queensland Planner* **35**(3), 5–10.

Dale AP, P Chapman and ML McDonald 1997. Social impact assessment in Queensland: why practice lags behind legislative opportunity. *Impact Assessment* **15**(2), 159–179.

Denq F and J Altenhofel 1997. Social impact assessments conducted by federal agencies. *Impact Assessment* **15**(3), 209–231.

Denver Research Institute 1982. *Socio-economic impacts of power plants.* EPRI EA-2228. Palo Alto, CA: Electric Power Research Institute.

Derman W and S Whiteford (eds) 1985. *Social impact analysis and development planning in the third world.* Boulder, CO: Westview Press.

Egre D and P Senecal 2003. Social impact assessments of large dams throughout the world: lessons learned over two decades. *Impact Assessment and Project Appraisal* **21**(3), 215–224.

England JL and SL Albrecht 1984. Boomtowns and social disruption. *Rural Sociology* **49**, 230–246.

Erickson PA 1994. *A practical guide to environmental impact assessment.* London: Academic Press.

Finterbusch K 1995. In praise of SIA – a personal review of the field of social impact assessment: feasibility, justification, history, methods, issues. *Impact Assessment* **13**(3), 229–252.

Finterbusch K, LJ Ingersol and LG Llewellyn (eds) 1990. *Methods for social impact analysis in developing countries.* Boulder, CO: Westview Press.

Finterbusch K, LG Llewellyn and CP Wolf (eds) 1983. *Social impact assessment methods.* Beverley Hills, CA: Sage.

Francis P and S Jacobs 1997. Institutionalizing social analysis at the World Bank. *Environmental Impact Assessment Review* **19**, 341–357.

Freudenburg WR 1984. Differential impacts of rapid community growth. *American Sociological Review* **49**, 697–705.

Freudenburg WR 1986. Social impact assessment. *Annual Review of Sociology* **12**, 451–478.

Fu-Keung Ip D 1990. Difficulties in implementing social impact assessment in China: methodological considerations. *Environmental Impact Assessment Review* **10**(1–2), 113–122.

Gagnon C 1995. Social impact assessment in Quebec: issues and perspectives for sustainable community development. *Impact Assessment* **13**(3), 272–288.

Gilmore JS, DM Hammond, JM Uhlmann, KD Moore, DC Coddington 1980. The impacts of power plant construction: a retrospective analysis. *Environmental Impact Assessment Review* **1**, 417–420.

Glasson J 1994. Life after the decision: the importance of monitoring in EIA. *Built Environment* **20**(4), 309–320.

Glasson J 2005. Better monitoring for better impact management: the local socio-economic impacts of constructing Sizewell B nuclear power station. *Impact Assessment and Project Appraisal* **23**(3), 215–226.

Glasson J and A Chadwick 1995. *The local socio-economic impacts of the Sizewell B PWR power station construction project, 1987–1995: summary report.* Report to Nuclear Electric plc. Oxford: School of Planning, Oxford Brookes University.

Glasson J and D Heaney 1993. Socio-economic impacts: the poor relations in British environmental impact statements. *Journal of Environmental Planning and Management* **36**(3), 335–343.

Halstead JN, RA Chase, SH Murdoch and FL Leistritz 1984. *Socio-economic impact management*. Boulder, CO: Westview Press.

Haque EE 1996. The integration of regional economic impact assessment with social impact assessment: the case of water improvement service projects in rural Manitoba, Canada. *Impact Assessment* **14**(4), 343–369.

Henry R 1990. Implementing social impact assessment in developing countries: a comparative approach to the structural problem. *Environmental Impact Assessment Review* **10**(1–2), 91–101.

Highland Council 2003. *Community benefit in relation to renewable energy proposals – guidance note*. Inverness, Scotland: The Highland Council.

Hill AE, CL Seyfrit and MJE Danner 1998. Oil development and social change in the Shetland Islands 1971–1991. *Impact Assessment and Project Appraisal* **16**(1), 15–25.

Howitt R 1989. Social impact assessment and resource development: issues from the Australian experience. *Australian Geographer* **20**(2), 153–166.

ICGPS (Interorganisational Committee on Guidelines and Principles for Social Impact Assessment) 1995. Guidelines and principles for social impact assessment. *Environmental Impact Assessment Review* **15**(1), 11–43.

Jiggins J 1995. Development impact assessment: impact assessment of aid projects in non-western countries. In *Environmental and social impact assessment*, F Vanclay and DA Bronstein (eds), 265–281. Chichester: Wiley.

Juslen J 1995. Social impact assessment: a look at Finnish experiences. *Project Appraisal* **10**(3), 163–170.

Kirkpatrick C and N Lee (eds) 1997. *Sustainable development in a developing world: integrating socio-economic appraisal and environmental assessment*. Cheltenham, Glos: Edward Elgar.

Kolhoff AJ 1996. Integrating gender assessment study into environmental impact assessment. *Project Appraisal* **11**(4), 261–266.

Lane M 1997. Social impact assessment: strategies for improving practice. *Australian Planner* **34**(2), 100–102.

Lang R and A Armour 1981. *The assessment and review of social impacts*. Ottawa: Federal Environmental Assessment and Review Office.

Lavallee L and A Pierre 2005. Social impact follow-up in Quebec, Canada: 25 years of EIA practice. *Impact Assessment and Project Appraisal* **23**(3), 241–245.

Leistritz FL 1994. Economic and fiscal impact assessment. *Impact Assessment* **12**(3), 305–318.

Leistritz FL and KC Maki 1981. *Socio-economic effects of large-scale resource development projects in rural areas: the case of McLean County, North Dakota*. Fargo, ND: Department of Agricultural Economics, North Dakota State University.

Leistritz FL and H Murdoch 1981. *The socio-economic impact of resource development: methods of assessment*. Boulder, CO: Westview Press.

Leistritz FL, RC Coon and RR Hamm 1994. A microcomputer model for assessing socioeconomic impacts of development projects. *Impact Assessment* **12**(4), 373–384.

Lockie S 2001. Social impact assessment in review: setting the agenda for impact assessment in the 21st century. *Impact Assessment and Project Appraisal* **19**(4), 277–287.

McDonald GT 1990. Regional economic and social impact assessment. *Environmental Impact Assessment Review* **10**(1/2), 25–36.

Marx A 2002. Uncertainty and social impacts: a case study of a Belgian village. *Environmental Impact Assessment Review* **22**(1), 79–96.

Maurice EV and WA Fleischman (eds) 1983. *Sociology and social impact analysis in federal resource management agencies*. Washington, DC: US Department of Agriculture, Forest Service.

Murdoch SH, FL Leistritz and RR Hamm 1986. The state of socioeconomic impact analysis in the United States of America: limitations and opportunities for alternative futures. *Journal of Environmental Management* **23**, 99–117.

Newton JA 1995. The integration of socio-economic impacts in environmental impact assessment and project appraisal. MSc dissertation, University of Manchester (UMIST) (mimeo).

ODA (Overseas Development Administration) 1995. *A guide to social analysis for projects in developing countries*. London: HMSO.

ODPM (Office of the Deputy Prime Minister) 2004. *Creating, using and updating a neighbourhood baseline*. London: ODPM.

ODPM 2006. *Research Report 21 – Data provision for neighbourhood renewal: final report*. London: ODPM.

ONS (Office for National Statistics) 2006. *2004-based subnational population projections for England – methodology guide*. London: ONS.

Pellizzoni L 1992. Sociological aspects of EIA. In *Environmental impact assessment*, AG Colombo (ed.), 313–334. Dordrecht, The Netherlands: Kluwer Academic Publishers.

Petajajarvi R 2005. Follow-up of socio-economic aspects in a road project in Finland. *Impact Assessment and Project Appraisal* **23**(3), 234–240.

Petts J and G Eduljee 1994. *Environmental impact assessment for waste treatment and disposal facilities*. Chichester: John Wiley & Sons.

Pinhero P and AR Pires 1991. Social impact analysis in environmental impact assessment: a Portuguese case study. *Project Appraisal* **6**(1), 2.

Pisani du JA and LA Sandham 2006. Assessing the performance of social impact assessment in the EIA context: A case study of South Africa. *Environmental Impact Assessment Review* **26**(8), 707–724.

Ramanathan R and S Geetha 1998. Socio-economic impact assessment of industrial projects in India. *Impact Assessment and Project Appraisal* **16**(1), 27–31.

Rickson RE, T Hundloe, GT McDonald and RJ Burdge (eds) 1990. Special issue: Social impact of development: putting theory and methods into practice. *Environmental Impact Assessment Review* **10**(1–2).

Rivers MJ and D Buchan 1995. Social assessment and consultation: New Zealand cases. *Project Appraisal* **10**(3), 181–188.

Seebohm K 1997. Guiding principles for the practice of social assessment in the Australian water industry. *Impact Assessment* **15**(3), 233–251.

Shell International Exploration and Production 1996. *Social impact assessment – HSE manual*. The Hague: Shell.

Shera W and J Matsuoka 1992. Evaluating the impact of resort development on an Hawaiian island: implications for social impact assessment policy and procedures. *Environmental Impact Assessment Review* **12**(4), 349–362.

SIAWG (Social Impact Assessment Working Group) 1995. *Social impact assessment in New Zealand: a practical approach*. Wellington: Town and Country Planning Directorate, Ministry of Works.

Storey K and P Jones 2003. Social impact assessment, impact management and follow-up: a case study of the construction of the Hibernia offshore platform. *Impact Assessment and Project Appraisal* **21**(2), 99–107.

Storey K and B Noble 2005. Socio-economic effects monitoring: towards improvements informed by biophysical effects monitoring. *Impact Assessment and Project Appraisal* **23**(3), 210–214.

Suprapto RA 1990. Social impact assessment and environmental planning: the Indonesian experience. *Impact Assessment Bulletin* **8**(1–2), 25–28.

Taylor CN, BC Hobson and CG Goodrich 2004. *Social assessment: theory, process and techniques: 3rd edition*. Middleton, WI: Social Ecology Press.

Taylor N, W McClintock and B Buckenham 2003. Social impacts of out-of-centre shopping centres on town centres: a New Zealand case study. *Impact Assessment and Project Appraisal* **21**(2), 147–153.

Thompson JG and D Bryant 1992. Fiscal impact in a western boomtown: unmet expectations. *Impact Assessment* **10**(3).

USAID (US Agency for International Development) 1993. *Handbook No. 3: project assistance (Appendix 3F – social soundness analysis)*. Washington, DC: USAID.

Vanclay F 2002. Conceptualising social impacts. *Environmental Impact Assessment Review* **22**(3), 183–211.

Vanclay F and DA Bronstein (eds) 1995. *Environmental and social impact assessment*. New York: John Wiley & Sons.

Wildman P 1990. Methodological and social policy issues in SIA. *Environmental Impact Assessment Review* **10**(1–2), 69–79.

Wildman PH and GB Baxter 1985. *The social assessment handbook: how to assess and evaluate the social impact of resource development on local communities*. Sydney: Social Impact Publications.

4 Noise

Riki Therivel
(based on Therivel and Breslin 2001)

4.1 Introduction

Virtually all development projects have noise impacts. Noise during construction may be due to such activities as land clearance, piling, and the transport of materials to and from the site. During operation noise levels may decrease for some forms of developments such as science parks or new towns, but may remain high or even increase for developments such as new roads or industrial processes. Demolition is a further cause of noise. As a result, despite the fact that Directives 85/337 and 97/11 (§1.4) do not require noise to be analysed, the EIAs for most projects do consider noise.

Noise is a major and growing form of **pollution**. It can interfere with communication, increase stress and annoyance, cause anger at the intrusion of privacy, and disturb sleep, leading to lack of concentration, irritability and reduced efficiency. It can contribute to stress-related health problems such as high blood pressure. Prolonged exposure to high noise levels can cause deafness or partial hearing loss. Noise can also affect property values and community atmosphere.

A recent MORI (2008) poll found that 63 per cent of respondents were bothered by one or more sources of noise, with noise from cars and motorbikes being most commonly cited; and 10 per cent of respondents suffered "a great deal or a fair amount". The Building Research Establishment (BRE 2002) found that more than half of the homes in England and Wales were exposed to noise levels over the standards recommended by the World Health Organization: roughly 87 per cent of respondents were affected by traffic noise, 41 per cent by aircraft noise, 12 per cent by train noise, and 8 per cent by construction noise. In Europe, 57 million people are annoyed by road traffic noise, 42 per cent of them seriously; and the social costs of traffic noise in Europe amount to at least €40 billion per year (CE Delft 2007).

Although most EIAs – and this chapter – are limited to the impact of noise on people, noise may also affect animals and in certain (highly unusual) cases EIAs will need to include specialist studies on these impacts. Although noise is linked to vibration, this chapter deals only with noise; most EIAs do not cover vibration. It should be noted, however, that for some studies (particularly major railway projects and/or projects involving substantial demolition or piling) vibration effects can be significant and a full vibration assessment must be carried out. In the UK the principal vibration standards to be considered are British Standards 6472 and 7385 (BSI 1992, 1993).

4.2 Definitions and concepts

4.2.1 Definitions

Noise is unwanted sound. This definition holds within it one of the core aspects of noise impact assessment: namely it deals with peoples subjective responses ("unwanted") to an objective reality ("sound"). The physical level of noise does not clearly correspond to the level of annoyance it causes (think about your v. your parents' reaction to your favourite CD), yet it is the annoyance caused by noise that is important in EIA. Noise impact assessment revolves around the concept of quantifying and "objectifying" people's personal responses. The following definitions and concepts all relate to this issue.

Sound consists of pressure variations detectable by the human ear. These pressure variations have two characteristics, frequency and amplitude. Sound **frequency** refers to how quickly the air vibrates, or how close the sound waves are to each other (in cycles per second, or Hertz (Hz)). For example, the sound from a transformer has a wavelength of about 3.5m, and hums at a frequency of 100Hz; a television line emits waves of about 0.03m, and whistles at about 10,000Hz or 10kHz. Frequency is subjectively felt as the **pitch** of the sound. Broadly, the lowest frequency audible to humans is 18Hz, and the highest is 18,000Hz. For convenience of analysis, the audible frequency spectrum is often divided into standard octave bands of 32, 63, 125, 250, 500, 1k, 2k, 4k and 8kHz.

Sound **amplitude** refers to the amount of pressure exerted by the air, which is often pictured as the height of the sound waves. Amplitude is described in units of pressure per unit area, microPascals (μPa). The amplitude is sometimes converted to sound **power**, in picowatts (10^{-12} watts), or sound intensity (in 10^{-12} watts/m^2). Sound intensity is subjectively felt as the **loudness** of sound. However, none of these measures are easy to use because of the vast range which they cover (see **Table 4.1**). As a result, a logarithmic scale of **decibels** (dB) is used. A sound level in decibels is given by

$$L = 10 \log_{10}(P/p)^2 \text{ dB},$$

where P is the amplitude of pressure fluctuations, and p is 20μPa, which is considered to be the lowest audible sound. The sound level can also be described as

$$L = 10 \log_{10}(I/i) \text{ dB},$$

where I is the sound intensity and i is 10^{-12} watts/m^2, or by

$$L = 10 \log_{10}(W/w) \text{ dB},$$

Table 4.1 Sound pressure, intensity and level

Sound pressure (μPa)	Sound power (10^{-12} watt) or intensity level (10^{-12} watt/m^2)	Sound level (dB)	Example
200,000,000	100,000,000,000,000	140	threshold of pain
	10,000,000,000,000	130	riveting on steel plate
20,000,000	1,000,000,000,000	120	pneumatic drill
	100,000,000,000	110	loud car horn at 1m
2,000,000	10,000,000,000	100	alarm clock at 1m
	1,000,000,000	90	inside underground train
200,000	100,000,000	80	inside bus
	10,000,000	70	street-corner traffic
20,000	1,000,000	60	conversational speech
	100,000	50	business office
2,000	10,000	40	living room
	1,000	30	bedroom at night
200	100	20	broadcasting studio
	10	10	normal breathing
20	1	0	threshold of hearing

where W is the sound power, and w is 10^{-12} watts. The range of audible sound is generally from 0dB to 140dB, as is shown in **Table 4.1**.

Because of the logarithmic nature of the decibel scale, a doubling of the power or intensity of a sound, for instance adding up two identical sounds, generally leads to an increase of 3dB, not a doubling of the decibel rating. For example two lorries, each at 75dB, together produce 78dB. Multiplying the sound power by ten (e.g. ten lorries) leads to an increase of 10dB. **Figure 4.1** shows how the dB increase can be calculated if one noise source is added to another. **Box 4.1** shows two examples of these principles.

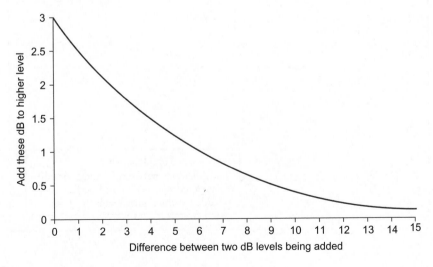

Figure 4.1 Adding two sources of sound.

Box 4.1 Adding sound levels: examples

Adding sources with different levels
Assume three sources with sound levels of 59dB, 55dB and 61dB. Start with two of these, e.g. 59 and 55dB. Take the higher: 59. Calculate the difference between the two levels being added: 59–55=4. Figure 4.1 shows that about 1.4dB needs to be added to the higher level: 59+1.4=60.4. To add the third level, repeat the process using 60.4 (i.e. 55+59) and 61. The total of all three is about 63.7dB.

   The same procedure could be carried out with a different combination of the three levels. For instance, start with 61 and 59. The difference is 2. Figure 4.1 shows that about 2dB need to be added to the higher figure: 61+2=63. Repeating the process with 63 and 55 gives about 63.7dB.

Adding ten equal levels
Assume that all of ten sound levels are at 50dB. Remember that two equal sound levels added together equal one level plus 3dB (as in the far left of Figure 4.1). Start from top left:

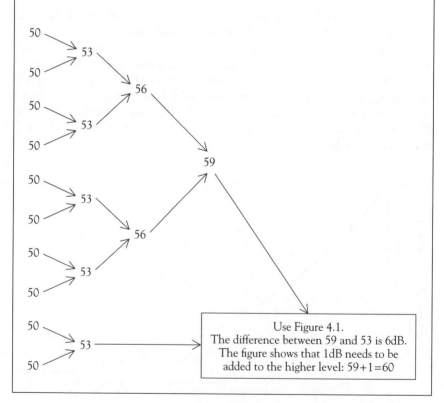

Use Figure 4.1.
The difference between 59 and 53 is 6dB.
The figure shows that 1dB needs to be added to the higher level: 59+1=60

Subjectively, a change of 3dB is generally held to be barely detectable by the human ear under normal listening circumstances, providing that the change in sound pressure level is not accompanied by some change in the character of the sound[1]. A change of 10dB is broadly perceived as a doubling/halving of loudness. Consequently, the logarithmic decibel scale, in addition to simplifying the necessary manipulation of a very large range of sound pressures/intensities, is conveniently related to the human perception of loudness.

The human ear is more sensitive to some frequencies than to others (think of fingernails on a blackboard). It is most sensitive to the 1kHz, 2kHz and 4kHz octaves, and much less sensitive at the lower audible frequencies. For instance, tests of human perception of noise have shown that a 70dB sound at 4kHz sounds as loud as a 1kHz sound of about 75dB, and a 70dB sound at 63Hz sounds as loud as a 1kHz sound of about 45dB. Since most sound analyses, including those in EIA, are concerned with the loudness experienced by people rather than the actual physical magnitude of the sound, an **A-weighting curve** is used to give a single figure index which takes account of the varying sensitivity of the human ear; this is shown at **Figure 4.2**. Most sound measuring instruments incorporate circuits which carry out this weighting automatically, and all EIA results should be A-weighted (dB(A)). Other weightings exist, but are rarely used.

Noise levels are rarely steady: they rise and fall with the types of activity taking place in the area. Time-varying noise levels can be described in a number of ways. The principal measurement index for environmental noise is the **equivalent continuous noise level**, LA_{eq}.

The LA_{eq} is a notional steady noise level which, over a given time, would provide the same energy as the time-varying noise: it is calculated by averaging all of the sound pressure/power/intensity measurements, and converting that average into the dB scale. Most environmental noise meters read this index directly.

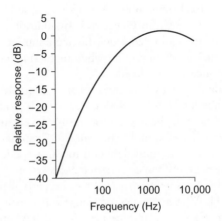

Figure 4.2 A-weighting curve.

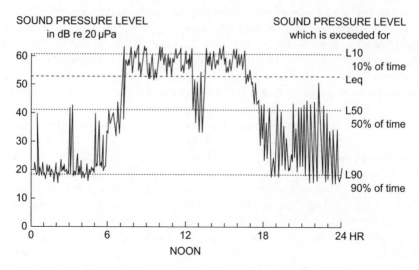

Figure 4.3 Sound levels exceeded for stated percentage of the measurement period.

LA_{eq} has the dual advantages that it: takes into account both the energy and duration of noise events; and is a reasonable indicator of likely subjective response to noise from a wide range of different noise sources.

In the UK, in addition to LA_{eq}, statistical indices are used as the basis of some types of noise assessment. LA_{90}, the dB(A) level which is exceeded for 90% of the time, is used to indicate the noise levels during quieter periods, or the **background noise**. Industrial noise, or noise from stationary plant, is often assessed against the background noise level (BS 4142). LA_{10}, the dB(A) level which is exceeded for 10% of the time and which is representative of the noisier sounds, is used as the basis of road traffic noise assessment in the UK.[2] Note that in all cases, $L_{10} \geq L_{eq} \geq L_{90}$, as shown in **Figure 4.3**. In addition to LA_{eq} and the statistical indices it can be useful to consider the maximum noise level, the LA_{max}. The LA_{max} can be particularly important when night-time noise and the potential for sleep disturbance is considered.

Many noise standards specify the length of time over which noise should be measured. For instance the Noise Insulation Regulations 1975 are based on measures of $dBLA_{10}$ (18 hours); the average of the L_{10} levels, in dB(A), measured in each hour between 6am and midnight. Mineral Planning Guidance note 11 refers to $dBLA_{eq}$ (1 hour), the equivalent continuous noise level, in dB(A), during one hour of a weekday. When considering noise criteria which are expressed in terms of LA_{eq}, the measurement period can be particularly important. The slow passage of an HGV at a distance of 10m, for instance, may give rise to a 12-second LA_{eq} of 75dB(A), a 5-minute LA_{eq} of 61dB(A) and a 1-hour LA_{eq} of 50dB(A).

4.2.2 Factors influencing noise impacts

The principal physical factors which influence how much effect a sound will have upon a potentially affected receptor are the **level of the sound** being assessed and the **level of other sounds** which also affect the receptor. For instance, people in rural environments would expect lower sound levels than those in a busy city centre. This interplay of location and noise is not often seen in noise standards, though the OECD (1996) recommends different noise levels for urban, suburban and rural areas. The level of sound being assessed is determined by several factors.

First, as one gets further away from a source of sound in the environment, the level of noise from the source decreases. The principal factor contributing to this is probably **geometric dispersion of energy**. As one gets further away from a sound source, the sound power from the source is spread over a larger and larger area (think of the way that ripples diminish from a stone thrown into a pond). The rate at which this happens is between 3dB per doubling of distance for very big sources (such as major roads) and 6dB per doubling of distance for comparatively small sources (for instance an individual small piece of machinery). It is because of this principle that noise fades rapidly near a noise source, but slowly far from it (it is why, for instance, motorways can be heard over such long distances).

The next most important factor in governing noise levels at a distance from a source is **whether the propagation path from the noise source to the receiver is obstructed**. If there is a large building, a substantial wall or fence, or a topographic feature which obscures the line of sight, this can reduce noise levels by, typically, a further 5–15dB(A). The amount of attenuation (reduction) depends upon the geometry of the situation and the frequency characteristics of the noise source. Trees, unfortunately, do not generally act as effective barriers.

If the sound is travelling over a reasonable distance (generally hundreds rather than tens of metres), the **type of ground** over which it is passing can have a substantial influence on the noise level at the receiver. If the sound is passing at a reasonably low physical level over soft ground (grassland, crops, trees, etc.) there will be an additional attenuation to that due to geometric dispersion. It should be noted, however, that only soft ground attenuation or barrier attenuation (i.e. not both) should generally be included in calculations.

Beyond these simplest physical characteristics it may be necessary to consider other physical characteristics of the sound being assessed. In particular it may be important to consider whether the sound is **impulsive** (it contains distinct clatters and thumps), **tonal** (whine, scream, hum) or whether it contains **information content** (such as speech or music). Other physical effects which may have to be considered, if detailed noise calculations are to be carried out, could include reflection and meteorological effects.

Probably the most important aspect of reflection that needs to be considered is whether the propagation model being used calculates **free-field** (at least 3.5m from reflective surfaces other than the ground) or **facade** (1m from the facade of the potentially affected receptor). PPG 24 suggests a facade value is 3dB higher than the free-field level determined for the same location, and the DoT/WO's (1988) *Calculation of road traffic noise* suggests a 2.5dB differential. In reality, facade effects vary from source to source and depending on whether the soundfield is directional or diffuse. Whether calculation or measurement results are free-field or facade is critical, however, as the differentials that have to be assumed are considerable. Other reflection effects occur where hard surfaces act as acoustic mirrors, increasing the sound pressure level or intensity (not the power) of a source. This may need to be considered where detailed calculations are being carried out.

Meteorological effects generally only need to be considered where calculations are being made over large distances (upwards of 100m or so). Wind speed and direction can affect noise levels. A gentle positive wind (the wind blowing from the noise source to the receptor) slightly increases noise levels compared with calm conditions, but a negative wind has a larger effect (i.e. it reduces noise levels more than a positive wind increases them). Some propagation models have a positive wind component allowance built into them, others allow the modelling of noise levels under different meteorological conditions. Clearly, as distances increase from a noise source, the degree of certainty to which noise levels can be estimated rapidly diminishes. Where large distances are involved, and noise level estimates are critical (as they can be for power stations or large petrochemical plants for instance) it is essential that the conditions for which any noise predictions are expected to hold are clearly defined.

4.3 Legislative background and interest groups

Noise is controlled in three ways: by controlling overall noise levels, setting limits on the emission of noise, and keeping people and noise apart. The local authority environmental health officer's view will be sought by the planning authority when an application is received. He/she will be able to identify issues of particular concern and advise on the most appropriate regulations and guidance for appraising a given development project, so the developer should discuss plans with him/her prior to submission.

The overarching regulations and guidance that apply to most developments are the *Control of Pollution Act 1974*, the *Environmental Protection Act 1990*, the EC (2002) Environmental Noise Directive, and *Planning Policy Guidance Note 24: Planning and Noise* (PPG24) (ODPM 1994). Under the Control of Pollution Act a local authority can control noise from construction sites and designate noise abatement zones in which specified types of development may not exceed specified noise levels. The Environmental Protection Act makes statutory nuisances, including noise from a premise which is prejudicial to health or a nuisance, subject to control by the local authority. The Environmental Noise Directive requires European Member Stages to map noise in densely populated areas and from major transport projects; and to introduce plans to manage noise where necessary and prevent specified quiet areas from getting noisier.

Table 4.2 Noise exposure categories from *Planning Policy Guidance Note 24*

Noise source		A	B	C	D
road traffic	07:00–23:00	>55dB(A)	55–63	63–72	>72
	23:00–07:00	<45dB(A)	45–57	57–66	>66
rail traffic	07:00–23:00	<55dB(A)	55–66	66–74	>74
	23:00–07:00	<45dB(A)	45–59	59–66	>66
air traffic	07:00–23:00	<57dB(A)	57–66	66–72	>72
	23:00–07:00	<48dB(A)	48–57	57–66	>66
mixed sources	07:00–23:00	<55dB(A)	55–63	63–72	>72
	23:00–07:00	<45dB(A)	45–57	57–66	>66

Notes

A: Noise need not be considered as determining factor in planning application.

B: Noise should be taken into account when determining planning applications and, where appropriate, conditions imposed to ensure an adequate degree of protection against noise.

C: Planning permission should not normally be granted. If it is, conditions should be imposed to ensure a commensurate degree of protection against noise.

D: Planning permission should normally be refused.

PPG24 gives guidance to local authorities in England and Wales on how to minimise noise impacts. It discusses issues to be considered when applications for noisy and noise-sensitive developments are made, advises on the use of planning conditions to minimise noise, and proposes noise exposure categories for new residential development (see **Table 4.2**). The World Health Organization (WHO 1999) has also devised guideline levels for community noise (**Table 4.3**). The local planning authority may require a Section 106 obligation concerning noise to be agreed before granting planning permission.

Further legislation and guidance applies to specific types of developments: the key ones are reviewed at **Table 4.4**. A longer discussion can be found in e.g. Hughes *et al.* (2002) or Smith *et al.* (1996). Other relevant legislation includes the *Public Health Act 1961, Health and Safety at Work etc. Act 1974, Motor Vehicles (Construction and Use) Regulations 1978, Road Traffic Regulation Act 1984, Civil Aviation Act 1982, Local Government (Miscellaneous Provisions) Act 1982, Town and Country Planning Act 1990, Town and Country Planning (Scotland) Act 1972*, BS8233 on sound insulation and noise reduction for buildings, local authority byelaws, and building regulations which require houses and flats to be built to prescribed noise insulation standards. Various EC Directives control noise from vehicles, aircraft and construction plant. Individuals may resort to common law if they suffer annoyance from noise; this generally involves proving the existence of a private nuisance, namely an unlawful interference with their land, their use and enjoyment of their land, or some right enjoyed by them over the land or connected with it.

Understanding of noise and its impacts is still developing. For instance, a key point of contention of the recent discussions about a third runway at Heathrow

Table 4.3 World Health Organization guidelines for community noise

Specific environment	Critical health effect(s)	LAeq (dB)	Time base (hours)	LAmax, fast (dB)
Outdoor living area	Serious annoyance, daytime and evening	55	16	–
	Moderate annoyance, daytime and evening	50	16	–
Dwelling, indoors	Speech intelligibility and moderate annoyance, daytime and evening	35	16	–
Inside bedrooms	Sleep disturbance, night-time	30	8	45
Outside bedrooms	Sleep disturbance, window open (outdoor values)	45	8	60
School class rooms and pre-schools, indoors	Speech intelligibility, disturbance of information extraction, message communication	35	during class	–
Pre-school bedrooms, indoors	Sleep disturbance	30	sleeping time	45
School, playground outdoor	Annoyance (external source)	55	during play	–
Hospital, ward rooms, indoors	Sleep disturbance, night-time	30	8	40
	Sleep disturbance, daytime and evenings	30	16	–
Hospitals, treatment rooms, indoors	Interference with rest and recovery	#1		
Industrial, commercial, shopping and traffic areas, indoors and outdoors	Hearing impairment	70	24	110
Ceremonies, festivals and entertainment events	Hearing impairment (patrons: <5 times/year)	100	4	110
Public addresses, indoors and outdoors	Hearing impairment	85	1	110
Music through headphones/earphones	Hearing impairment (free-field value)	85 (#4)	1	110
Impulse sounds from toys, fireworks, firearms	Hearing impairment (adults)	–	–	140 #2
	Hearing impairment (children)	–	–	120 #2
Outdoors in parkland and conservation areas		#3		

Notes
#1: As low as possible.
#2: Peak sound pressure (not LAmax, fast), measured 100mm from the ear.
#3: Existing quiet outdoor areas should be preserved and the ratio of intruding noise to natural background sound should be kept low.
#4: Under headphones, adapted to free-field values.

Table 4.4 Noise regulations, standards and guidelines

Type of project	Key regulations, standards and guidelines	Comments
Road	Land Compensation Act 1973	Allows people whose enjoyment of their property has been reduced by public works to be compensated, and allows regulations to be enacted to determine when compensation is due. To date only the Noise Insulation Regulations 1975 have been introduced, which apply to new highways.
	Noise Insulation Regulations 1975 (SI 1975/1763) Noise Insulation (Amendment Regulations) 1988 Memorandum on the Noise Insulation (Scotland) Regulations *Calculation of road traffic noise* (DoT/WO 1988)	The regulations and amendments require highway authorities to provide noise insulation for residential properties if they are (a) within 300m from a new or altered highway, (b) not subject to compulsory purchase, demolition or clearance, (c) not already receiving a grant for noise insulation works, (d) subject to 18-hour L_{10} noise levels over 67.5dB(A), (e) subject to an increase of at least 1dB(A) over the existing noise level, and (f) on a new road which contributes at least 1dB(A) to the final noise level.
		Gives procedures for predicting noise in areas where noise is dominated by traffic noise; this can be extrapolated to distances of up to 300m from the road. Calculations incorporate information about traffic volume, vehicle speeds, the percentage of HGVs, the road gradient, road surface, and distance from source to receiver. This procedure must be used for the Noise Insulation Regulations.
	Design manual for roads and bridges (DMRB) Vol. 11 (DoT 1993) *Transport analysis guidance* (TAG) (DfT 2008)	Gives procedures for assessing the impact of road schemes where traffic increases or decreases of 25% or more (about 1dB(A)) are expected in the year the scheme opens. Provides a framework for assessing the impacts of road scheme options, using the DMRB methods (see Chapter 5).
Airport	*BS5727 Method for describing aircraft noise heard on the ground:* 1979 Civil Aviation Act 1982	Provides methods for measuring, analysing and describing aircraft noise. Allows airports to fine noisy aircraft, and allows an action for nuisance caused by aircraft.
Railway	*Noise Insulation (Railways and Other Guided Transport Systems) Regulations* 1996	Provides for noise insulation related to railways, tramways or guided transport.
Industrial	*BS4142 Rating industrial noise affecting mixed residential and industrial areas:* 1990	Provides methods for determining the increase in noise levels from new buildings and plant, and the likelihood of this increase causing complaints (based on background and predicted noise levels).
Mineral workings, construction and other open sites	Mineral Planning Guidance note 11, *The control of noise at surface mineral workings* (DoE 1993) *Noise Emission in the Environment by Equipment for Use Outdoors (Amendment) Regulations 2005* (DTI 2006) *BS5228 Noise control on construction and open sites:* 1984/1992	Gives guidance for determining background noise at proposed surface minerals workings, predicting and assessing their noise impacts, and ensuring that these impacts are kept within acceptable limits. Sets product standards for equipment for use outdoors, e.g. vibratory plates, loaders, mobile cranes. Presents indices for noise from opencast coal extraction, piling operations, and similar works, and gives guidance on how such noise can be measured, assessed and controlled.

Airport has been what noise metric to use: the Department for Transport (DfT 2007) used 57dBAL$_{eq}$ as an indicator for the onset of significant noise annoyance, whilst another study (MVA Consultancy *et al.* 2007) suggested that there is no noise level at which there is an onset of significant annoyance, so every flight triggers some annoyance.

4.4 Scoping and baseline studies ✓

The EIA scoping stage identifies relevant potential noise sources, the people and resources likely to be affected by the proposed development's noise (the receivers), and noise monitoring locations. The baseline studies involve identifying existing information on noise levels, carrying out additional noise measurements at appropriate locations where necessary, and considering future changes in baseline conditions. These stages – which are interlinked and do not necessarily happen consecutively – are discussed below.

The project details should be analysed and **each potential source of noise impact identified**. Both on-site and off-site sources should be considered and (where appropriate) both the construction and operational stages. Each source of impact should be considered and a judgement made with regard to (a) carrying out further detailed assessment; (b) carrying out further but less detailed assessment; or (c) discarding the source of impact from the main EIA stage on the grounds that any resultant effects are highly unlikely to be significant. The reasoning for the ranking of sources of impact should be made explicit. This process enables the EIA proper to be concentrate on assessing noise from the sources of impact most likely to give rise to significant effects.

Ultimately the effects of noise are dictated by the characteristics of the **potentially affected receptors**. Various maps can help to identify noise receptors in the area, but this should be confirmed by a site survey. The people affected by a development are not only local residents but also people working nearby, users of public places such as parks and footpaths, and users of other outdoor areas such as private playing fields and fishing lakes. EIAs should identify any potentially particularly noise-sensitive receivers such as schools, hospitals and recording studios.

Sites for monitoring are normally determined in consultation with the environmental health officer, and possibly also with the local community. Where there are only a limited number of receivers, monitoring will normally be carried out for all of them. However where there are many receivers, for instance along a proposed road or rail line, representative receivers will need to be identified. Particularly noise sensitive receivers are normally all monitored. A systematic approach is required, splitting potentially affected receivers into residential, non-residential and noise sensitive, and non-residential and not noise sensitive. Clearly the latter (e.g. factories and other industrial premises) can be scoped out. Noise-sensitive non-residential receivers may need a further degree of sub-classification (a major broadcast studio may be potentially more sensitive than a shopping centre for instance). It is advisable, however, to treat residential receivers uniformly. Although individual sensitivities to noise vary enormously, the aim of the assessment should be to evaluate the likely response of "normal" communities.

Because noise is primarily a local impact, only **limited existing information** can be obtained from desktop studies, and virtually all EIAs rely on noise measurements carried out at the site. Information about the wider area may be gleaned from the strategic noise maps prepared in response to the Environmental Noise Directive; and the CPRE (2006) "tranquillity maps", which combine information about landscape (lack of urban development, low flying aircraft etc.) and lack of noise. Local authority environmental audits may include noise data, but are unlikely to be site-specific.

Measurement of ambient noise is normally achieved by carrying out measurements at the potentially most affected noise-sensitive receptors. Every effort should be made to carry out measurements at the times when the new source will be operating and with typical ambient conditions (normal prevailing winds, no rain, dry roads and during normal weekdays and weekends as appropriate). If under particular conditions (e.g. a specific wind direction) higher background levels commonly occur, these are also recorded. For some projects (wind farms for instance) it may be appropriate to carry out assessments for a range of climatic conditions; care should be taken, however, to exclude the effects of atypical climatic conditions, such as temperature inversions. The noise survey may also record the quietest conditions which typically occur in an area (e.g. on a quiet Sunday morning). This is because the biggest increase in noise caused by a proposed development will be in comparison with these quiet conditions.

Sound measuring equipment is portable and battery-powered, and usually consists of (a) a microphone which converts changes in ambient pressure into an electrical quantity (usually voltage), (b) a sound level meter which amplifies the voltage signals, averages them, and converts them to dB, (c) an analyser which records noise descriptors (e.g. L_{eq}, L_{10}) over a period of time, and (d) a reference sound source against which to calibrate the equipment. Several of these will normally be incorporated into the same piece of machinery. The sound level meter will have different types of settings, corresponding to different ways of averaging voltage; slow (over 1 sec.), fast (0.125 sec.), and sometimes peak and impulse. A windshield should always be used for environmental noise measurements.

The precise procedures for measuring sound, for instance the length of time of measurement, location of equipment, and measurement levels are sometimes specified in the relevant regulations or guidelines (see §4.3). It is generally advisable to agree the noise-monitoring regime with the relevant environmental health officer, who will have a good understanding of local conditions and any particular "hot spots". A typical survey strategy may include a limited number of positions where long-term (24 hours or more) unattended measurement positions are carried out, plus several positions where shorter term (15 minutes or more) attended sample measurements are carried out.

Broadly, noise measurements involve:

- taking note of the equipment used, including manufacturer and type;
- taking note of the date, weather conditions, wind speed, and wind direction;
- calibrating the sound meter and microphone;
- setting up the microphone at the appropriate site (check relevant guide-lines/legislation for details);
- noting the precise location where measurements are taken (e.g. on a map or using grid references);
- taking measurements using the criteria from the relevant guidelines (e.g. continuous for 24 hours, or for 1 hour; using fast weightings for traffic or slow for construction noise);
- noting start and finish times, identifying the principal influences on the noise environment (particularly the major influences on the LA_{eq}, LA_{90} and LA_{max}) during the measurement period, and any other factors (e.g. whether the equipment was attended or not) which could affect the measurements; and
- checking the calibrations.

Table 4.5 gives an example of baseline noise data. Generally an EIA includes such data, a description of how they were collected, and a map showing the location of the measurement points. Where noise monitoring is carried out during construction and operation, the same measurement points will generally be used.

A final stage of scoping and baseline studies is to *consider whether baseline noise levels are likely to change in the future in the absence of the proposed development.* For instance, if a development is proposed near an industrial complex that is currently under construction, then the future baseline is likely to change. In some cases the future baseline may be established through calculations, particularly intensification of a route corridor where the level of noise from the existing traffic can be readily calculated.

Table 4.5 Example of baseline sound data

Date	Start of period	Sound levels, in dB(A)					Comments
		L_{90}	L_{50}	L_{10}	L_{Amax}	L_{eq}	
1 April	1500	56	57	60	62	58	mostly traffic noise
	2200	46	49	53	55	50	traffic, dog barking
2 April	0720	55	57	59	61	57	traffic, birdsong

Notes
The most important things to be noted are generally:
- principal influence on LA_{eq};
- principal influence on LA_{90};
- whether the samples can be considered representative.

4.5 Impact prediction ✓

The aim of noise prediction in EIA is to identify the changes in noise levels which may occur, both in the short and long terms, as a result of the development; and the significance of these factors.

Predicting noise levels is a complex process which incorporates a wide range of variables, including:

- existing and likely future baseline noise levels;
- the type of equipment, both mobile and fixed, used at the site (see BS5228 for indicative sound levels from mobile plant; **Table 4.6** gives examples of typical sound levels from construction equipment);
- the duration of various stages of construction and operation;
- the time of day when the equipment is used;
- the actions of the site operator;
- the location of the receivers and their sensitivity to noise;
- the topography of the area, including the main forms of land use and any natural sound barriers;
- meteorological conditions in the area.

These will affect the amount and type of sound coming from the site (e.g. type of equipment, duration of workings), how that sound travels (e.g. distance between source and receptor, topography, meteorology), and the response of the receptors (e.g. timing of workings, sensitivity to noise).

Essentially noise level prediction involves predicting the sound power level at the source; predicting the sound level at each monitoring site (which represents certain receivers) using corrections for factors such as distance, screening and ground attenuation; and adding the new sound levels to the ambient levels. **Table 4.7** shows an example. Where a development project has multiple sound sources that are close together, they will normally be considered together as one source (by adding their levels using Figure 4.1). Where multiple sound sources are not close together, each source's sound level at each receiver is calculated, and these sound levels are then added together (again using Figure 4.1) for each receiver: **Box 4.2** gives a very basic example to illustrate these principles.

Table 4.6 Examples of typical sound levels from construction equipment (BS5228)

Type of equipment	Sound level, in dB(A), at 7m
unsilenced pile-driver	110
unsilenced truck scraper, grader	94
unsilenced pneumatic drill	90
unsilenced compressor	85
concrete breaker	85
crane	85
unsilenced generator	82
sound-reduced compressor	70

Table 4.7 Example of noise predictions

receiver no.	noise source	distance (m)	sound power level at source (dB(A))	distance correction (dB(A))	screening attenuation (dB(A))*	soft ground attenuation (dB(A))*	predicted Leq at receiver (dB(A))	ambient noise levels (LAeq)	increase in noise (dB(A)Leq)
1	loading operations	470	110	−61.4	−5	0	43.6	52.4	0.6
2		335	110	−58.5	0	−8.2	43.3	42.9	3.2
3		135	110	−50.6	0	0	59.4	60.1	2.6

Note
* Either screening/barrier or soft ground attenuation is valid for a given site, not both.

Box 4.2 Noise predictions for dispersed multiple sound sources

Assume that a receiver will be affected by sound from three dispersed sources:

- Source A emits 95dB at 1m, and is 64m from the receiver;
- Source B emits 97dB at 1m, and is 128m from the receiver;
- Source C emits at 109dB at 1m, and is 256m from the receiver.

Take the basic principle from §4.2.2 that a doubling of distance reduces sound by 6dB: −6dB at 2m, −12dB at 4m. . . . −36dB at 64m, −42dB at 128m, −48dB at 256m (N.B. in practice, this reduction will depend on many other factors so the principle should be used as a broad rule of thumb only). The additional sound at the receiver will thus be 59dB from source A (95dB to start with, minus 36dB because it is 64m away), 55dB from source B, and 61dB from source C. The total additional sound at the receiver will be 59+55+61dB: Box 4.1 shows that this is about 63.7dB.

Detailed procedures for predicting sound levels from different types of development, and different stages of development (construction, operation, decommissioning) are specified in many of the regulations listed in §4.3. The procedures are too cumbersome and diverse to discuss in detail here; they are often set up as computer models. The reader is referred to the relevant regulations and standards for further information. It may be necessary to carry out noise monitoring at a similar existing activity or development in order to predict the effects of a proposal.

The **significance** of changes in noise levels generally depends on the number of people affected, and how badly they are affected. The latter is the difference between the current ambient sound levels at the receivers, and the predicted future sound levels (i.e. ambient plus additional new sound). Considerable, but not unchallenged, consensus exists about the significance of noise impacts. A change of 3dB is barely detectable whereas a change of 10dB corresponds subjectively to a doubling or halving of loudness; **Table 4.8** suggests possible significance criteria. The World Health Organization suggests that daytime outdoor noise levels should be below $50dBLA_{eq}$ to prevent significant community annoyance, but in cases where there are other reasons to be in an area, like good schools, people may tolerate up to $55dBLA_{eq}$ (WHO 1988). PPG24 implies that $55dB LA_{eq}$ may be considered a general environmental health goal (see Table 4.3).

Within this overall framework, however, variations exist. An increase in noise in an area already subjected to high noise levels may be more significant than a similar increase in an area with lower noise levels. The same level of noise at a noise sensitive location will be more significant than that at a less sensitive location. If the new source is a road and the area is already dominated by road traffic noise, then it is unlikely that the subjective response will be dramatically greater than any calculated change in noise levels would suggest. A new industrial source, however, could be tonal or impulsive or a new specialist commercial source (say, perhaps, a cinema complex or a night-club) may give rise to appreciable levels of low frequency noise. In these instances, a description of the impact in terms of change or absolute levels of A-weighted sound pressure

Table 4.8 Example of noise significance criteria (adapted from Arup Environmental 1993)

Criterion	Construction noise	Traffic noise
Severe adverse	Noise above traffic noise insulation thresholds for >8 weeks; insulation or permanent rehousing required	>15dB increase
Major adverse	Noise above traffic noise insulation thresholds for <8 weeks; insulation or temporary rehousing required	10–15dB increase
Moderate adverse	Noise above ambient levels for >8 weeks, but below traffic noise insulation thresholds	5–10dB increase
Minor adverse	Noise above ambient levels for <8 weeks, but below traffic noise insulation thresholds	3–5dB increase
None	Noise at or below ambient levels	<3dB increase

levels may not be an adequate indicator to allow potential effects to be assessed, and more detailed descriptions will be necessary.

4.6 Mitigation

Mitigation will be necessary if the noise from the proposed development is likely to exceed the levels recommended in the relevant standards (see §4.3). However, it may be useful to implement noise mitigation measures even if standards are met, to prevent annoyance and complaints and as part of best practice procedures. The best noise mitigation is that which is integrated into the project design: the siting of machinery and buildings, choice of equipment, and landscaping to reduce noise are all easiest, cheapest and most effective if they are designed in rather than pasted on near the end.

For a new potentially "noisy" project, mitigation of noise is best carried out at the source, before the noise has escaped. Failing this, barriers and the siting of buildings can be used to separate noise sources from potentially affected noise-sensitive locations. As a last resort, noise can be controlled at the receiver's end through the provision of, say, secondary glazing or other noise insulation measures.

Control of noise at the source can take a number of forms. First, the equipment used or the modes of operation can be changed to produce less noise. For instance, rotating or impacting machines can be based on anti-vibration mountings. Internal combustion engines must be fitted with silencers. Airplanes can be throttled back after a certain point at take-off, to reduce their noise. Traffic can be managed to produce a smooth flow instead of a noisier stop-and-start flow, and use of quieter road surfacing materials can significantly reduce tyre noise. Well-maintained equipment is generally quieter than poorly-maintained equipment.

Second, the source can be sensitively located. It can be located (further) away from the receivers, so that noise is reduced over distance. A buffer zone of undeveloped land can be left between a noisy development and a residential area. The development can be designed so that its noisier components are shielded by quieter components; for instance housing can be shielded from a factory's noise by retail units. Natural or artificially-constructed topography or landscaping can be used to screen the source.

The source can be enclosed to insulate or absorb the sound. Sound insulation reflects sound back inside an enclosure or barrier, so that sound outside the enclosure is reduced. However, merely enclosing the source is not the optimum solution, since the noise reverberates within the enclosure, and effectively increases the strength of the enclosed sound. Providing sound absorption within the enclosure avoids this happening. Sound absorption occurs where the enclosure or barrier absorbs the sound, converting it into heat. Most enclosures are constructed of both insulating and absorbing materials.

Details of requirements for noise enclosures and their effectiveness are very complex and require specialist knowledge. The reader is referred to the relevant standards and to textbooks on noise control (e.g. Crocker 2007 or Smith *et al.*

1996). However, some general points can be made here. Methods of measuring sound insulation usually distinguish between airborne sound (noise) and structural sound (vibration), and any reference to insulation should distinguish between them. Broadly, the ability of a panel to resist the transmission of energy from one side of a panel to the other, or its transmission loss, will depend on (a) the mass of the panel (more mass = more transmission loss), (b) whether it is layered or not, with or without discontinuities between the layers, (c) whether it includes sound absorbing material, and (d) whether it has any holes or apertures.

Acoustic fencing or other screens, either at the source or at the receiver, can also reduce noise by up to 15dB. The effectiveness of screens depend on their height and width (larger is better), their location with respect to the source or receiver (closer is better), their form (wrapped around the source or receiver is better), their transmission loss, their position with respect to other reflecting surfaces, the area's reflectivity, and whether they have any holes or apertures.

Noise screens can consist of topographical features or tree plantings as well as of artificial materials. For instance, earth mounds (bunds) are often built alongside roads to absorb and reflect traffic noise away from nearby buildings. Thick areas (≥30m) of dense trees and underbrush may reduce noise by up to 3–4dB at low frequencies and 10–12dB at high frequencies; although thinner tree belts have little actual effect on noise, the visual barrier they form can make people think that noise levels have been reduced. A mixture of deciduous and coniferous trees will give maximum noise reduction in the summer, and some reduction in the winter when the deciduous trees' leaves have fallen. It must be remembered that saplings take time to mature, and are unlikely to reduce noise for several years after planting.

Control of noise at the receiver's end is often similar to that at the source. Good site planning can minimise the impact of noise; for instance in a house by a busy road the more noise-sensitive rooms (e.g. bedroom, living room) can be shielded from the road noise by the less noise-sensitive rooms (e.g. kitchen, bathroom). A screen can be erected to reflect sound away from the receiver, for instance an acoustical screen between a highway and house. The equivalent of a noise enclosure can be achieved by soundproofing a house using double-glazed windows. The *Land Compensation Act 1973* requires highway authorities to insulate houses affected by noise over a certain level.

4.7 Monitoring

Any conditions imposed as part of a project's planning permission are enforceable, including conditions related to noise. These can apply not only to noise levels (e.g. during construction, operation; during the day, night), but also to noise monitoring to be conducted by the developer (e.g. distance from the site boundary, frequency). If no planning conditions are set, local environmental health officers can still monitor noise from a site, for instance in response to local residents' complaints, to determine whether it is a statutory nuisance.

There are at present no requirements to compare any noise monitoring data with the noise predictions made in EIAs. A best practice EIA could propose not only noise-related planning conditions, but also a noise monitoring programme, and relate its findings to the EIA to improve future noise prediction methodologies. The sites and noise-measurement techniques used in carrying out baseline noise surveys should be such that comparable monitoring data can later be collected. However, given the current lack of legislative requirements for monitoring, this is unlikely to occur.

4.8 Conclusion

This has only been a brief introduction to a very technically-complex topic. Noise prediction requires expert input, and probably computer models. Reader are strongly urged to familiarise themselves with the relevant regulations and standards (see §4.3) as well as standard texts on acoustics and noise control.

Note

1. This fundamental principle, however, is currently the subject of debate. For instance the *Design Guide for Roads and Bridges* (DoT 1993) asserts that abrupt changes as small as 1dB in road traffic noise, for instance, can bring appreciable benefits or disbenefits. However long-term significant effects are unlikely from changes of less than 3dB (DETR 1997).

References

Arup Environmental 1993. *Redhill Aerodrome environmental statement*. London: Ove Arup & Partners.

BRE (Building Research Establishment) 2002. *The national noise incidence study (England and Wales) 2000*. www.defra.gov.uk/environment/noise/research/nis0001/pdf/nis_report.pdf; and *The national noise incidence study 2000/2001* (including Scotland and N. Ireland), Watford, Herts: BRE, www.bre.co.uk/page.jsp?id=438.

BSI (British Standards Institute) 1992. *British Standard guide to evaluation of exposure to vibration in buildings (1Hz–80Hz)*. BS 6472. London: BSI.

BSI 1993. *Evaluation and measurement for vibration in buildings. Part 2. Guide to damage levels from groundborne vibration*. BS 7385: Part 2. London: BSI.

CE Delft 2007. *Traffic noise reduction in Europe: Health effects, social costs and technical and policy options to reduce road and rail traffic noise*. Delft, The Netherlands: CE Delft, www.transportenvironment.org/Publications/prep_hand_out/lid:495.

CPRE (Campaign to Protect Rural England) 2006. *Tranquillity*, www.cpre.org.uk/campaigns/landscape/tranquillity.

Crocker MJ (ed.) 2007. *Handbook of noise and vibration control*, Hoboken, NJ: John Wiley & Sons.

DETR (Department of Environment, Transport and the Regions) 1997. *Digest of environmental statistics 1997*, London: The Stationery Office.

DfT 2007. *Adding Capacity at Heathrow Airport – Consultation document*. London: DfT, www.dft.gov.uk/consultations/closed/heathrowconsultation/consultationdocument/.

DfT (Department for Transport) 2008. *Transport Analysis Guidance* (TAG): *Noise, TAG Unit 3.3.2*. London: DfT TAG website (WebTAG), www.webtag.org.uk/webdocuments/ 3_Expert/3_Environment_Objective/3.3.2.htm.

DoE (Department of the Environment) 1993. *Mineral planning guidance note 11: The control of noise at surface mineral workings*. London: HMSO.

DoT (Department of Transport) 1993. *Design manual for roads and bridges (DMRB)*, Vol. 11: *Environmental assessment*, Section 3, Part 7: *Traffic noise and vibration*. London: Highways Agency, www.standardsforhighways.co.uk/dmrb/vol11/section3.htm.

DoT/WO (Department of Transport, Welsh Office) 1988. *Calculation of road traffic noise*. London: HMSO.

DTI (Department of Trade and Industry) 2006. *Noise emission in the environment by equipment for use outdoors (amendment) regulations 2005*, www.opsi.gov.uk/si/si2005/ 20053525.htm.

EC (European Commission) 2002. Directive 2002/49/EC of the European Parliament and of the Council of 25 June 2002 relating to the assessment and management of environmental noise. *Official Journal L189*, http://ec.europa.eu/environment/noise/ directive.htm.

Hughes D, T Jewell, J Lowther, N Parpworth and P de Prez 2002. *Environmental law*, 4th edn, Oxford: Oxford University Press.

MORI 2008. *National noise survey 2008, Research for Environmental Protection UK*, www.environmental-protection.org.uk/assets/library/documents/National_Noise_Survey_ 2008.pdf.

MVA Consultancy in association with John Bates Services, Ian Flindell and RPS 2007. *Attitudes to noise from aviation sources in England*, report to Department for Transport, www.dft.gov.uk/pgr/aviation/environmentalissues/Anase/.

ODPM (Office of the Deputy Prime Minister) 1994. *Planning Policy Guidance Note 24: Planning and Noise (PPG24)*, London: TSO, www.communities.gov.uk/publications/ planningandbuilding/ppg24.

OECD (Organisation for Economic Co-Operation and Development) 1996. *Pollution prevention and control: environmental criteria for sustainable transport*. Paris: OECD.

Smith BJ, RJ Peters and S Owen 1996. *Acoustics and noise control*, 2nd edn, London: Longman.

Therivel R and M Breslin 2001. Chapter 4 in *Methods of environmental impact assessment*, 2nd edn, P Morris and R Therivel (eds), London: Spon Press.

WHO (World Health Organization) 1988. *Environmental criteria 12: noise*. Geneva: WHO.

WHO 1999. *Guidelines for community noise*. Geneva: WHO, www.who.int/docstore/peh/ noise/guidelines2.html.

5 Transport

Chris Fry and Riki Therivel
(based on Richardson and Callaghan 2001)

5.1 Introduction

Transport is increasingly seen as a key factor in the design, approval and likely success of prospective new developments. Developments require good access for their residents, employees and customers, as well as good servicing arrangements. This affects the surrounding transport network, which in turn affects the delivery of sustainable planning policies.

Both new transport projects and the transport activities associated with non-transport projects can lead to other indirect impacts, including noise and vibration, air pollution, impacts on biodiversity, community severance, visual intrusion, accidents and economic regeneration. In turn, management of these impacts may require management of the development's transport impacts. The nature and location of the development, and any proposed transport provision, will determine the nature of trips to and from the site, as well as the potential for achieving a modal shift through increased walking, cycling and use of public transport. As such, although neither the EIA Directive nor its implementing legislation in the UK specifically mentions the need to assess transport impacts, it is clear that, in order to assess a project's environmental impacts properly, its transport impacts must be considered.

Two methodologies used by transport planners are of particular interest to EIA practitioners: transport assessments which evaluate the impacts of proposed non-transport projects on the transport network; and the *Transport analysis guidance* (TAG) (DfT 2008) which appraises the environmental impacts of transport investment proposals.

5.2 Definitions and concepts

Over the past 20 years, the emphasis in transport planning has changed from improvement of mobility to improvement of accessibility. The earlier focus on **mobility** – ease of movement – was linked to "predict and provide" planning practices which considered future transport demand based in part on past trends, and aimed to provide the transport infrastructure needed to fulfil this demand. This led to a strong focus on the provision of road (and to a lesser extent other forms of transport) infrastructure.

However an influential report of 1994 concluded that new infrastructure can generate new traffic as well as catering to existing needs, especially where high levels of congestion are preventing people from making as many journeys as they would ideally wish (SACTRA 1994). In other words, it concluded that we cannot build our way out of congestion.

The government's current focus is firmly on improving **accessibility** – the "ease of reaching". This can include ease of access to the transport system, ease of access to facilities, ease of participation in activities and delivery of goods, and the possibility of having an alternative way of accessing services even if this is used only rarely (like when the car when breaks down). Accessibility can be improved by, for instance, careful siting of housing vis-à-vis employment and other land uses to reduce the need to travel, promotion of walking and cycling, use of information technology to substitute for physical journeys, and efficient use of the existing transport infrastructure. Since 1997 the Government's Roads Programme has also been dramatically cut. That said, in practice, most transport assessments still focus heavily on road infrastructure, although this emphasis is slowly changing.

Several **modes of transport** are associated with new developments: vehicular traffic, heavy and light rail, cycling and walking. Vehicular traffic can be further subdivided into private cars and taxis, vans, goods vehicles, buses and motorcycles. The different modes have different impacts, and the government aims to promote a **modal shift** from private vehicles to walking, cycling and public transport.

Each existing road link, road junction, or link on a public transport network has a finite **capacity**: a maximum number of vehicles or passengers that it can nominally accommodate. As traffic levels approach and then exceed capacity, congestion, queuing and overcrowding occur. Public transport services may have licences that do not permit them to exceed their capacity.

It is possible to describe a stream of traffic on a length of road at a particular time with reference to:

- highway link capacity;
- junction capacity (which is often more restricted than highway link capacity);
- driver delay/queuing time at junctions;
- speed;
- turning movements;
- number of accidents or accident rate;
- proportion of heavy goods vehicles;
- number of bus movements;
- pedestrian and cycle flows;
- location and type of on street car parking;
- the nature of frontage land uses (Hughes 1994).

On the rail network, pertinent factors are:

- line capacity (single or dual);
- station capacity (stairwells, platform width etc.);
- platform length;

- rolling stock passenger capacity;
- frequency of service and station wait time;
- junction capacity and signalling;
- lay over capacity;
- proportion of freight trains;
- proportion of stopping and non-stopping services;
- speed.

Different types of trips will have different impacts. **New trips** are those that did not occur anywhere else on the transport network prior to the development. **Pass-by trips** are made as part of another journey such as stopping off on the way home from work. **Diverted trips** are similar to pass-by trips, but involve a longer diversion from the existing route to the site. **Linked trips** are trips with multiple destinations. **Transferred trips** are trips that are already being made, and that would be transferred to the proposed development (DCLG/DfT 2007). For example, a new housing development which generates 1,000 new trips per day will have very different transport impacts compared to a new shopping centre which also generates 1,000 trips per day but where most of these trips may be transferred or pass-by.

The most significant traffic problems on a given route are likely to occur at times of **peak traffic flow**. These are typically weekday morning and evenings, but could be different, for instance near major distribution centres or airports, or on weekends in tourist areas. It is at times of peak flow that the worst congestion occurs on roads, public transport capacity is most likely breached, and any unusual event (e.g. an accident) has the greatest repercussions. One of the government's transport priorities is to make best use of existing transport infrastructure. This includes supporting projects whose peak traffic flow does not coincide with peak flows on the surrounding transport network.

Finally, new transport developments can cause **community severance**. They can essentially cut a community in two if they are difficult to cross – for instance a busy road or a railway line protected by fencing.

5.3 Legislative background

The government's approach to transport reflects the complexity of the subject matter and the public's ambivalence towards it: we want to be able to easily access goods and services, and are aware that the economy relies heavily on good transport links, but don't want to live near roads, airports or railway lines, or be subject to their noise, air pollution and safety problems.

The government's recent Eddington Transport Study (Eddington 2006) highlights the critical importance of transport infrastructure to the economy and suggests that the transport infrastructure should be significantly improved:

> the performance of the UK's transport networks will be a crucial enabler of
> sustained productivity and competitiveness: a 5 per cent reduction in travel
> time for all business travel on the roads could generate around £2.5 billion

of cost savings – some 0.2 per cent of GDP. Good transport systems support the productivity of urban areas, supporting deep and productive labour markets, and allowing businesses to reap the benefits of agglomeration. Transport corridors are the arteries of domestic and international trade, boosting the competitiveness of the UK economy.

On the other hand, in the wake of the SACTRA report,

> Government policy is no longer to attempt to cater for unrestrained road traffic growth. . . . Developers can no longer expect that all the traffic they might produce will be allowed without restraint. This would lead to ever-increasing congestion, which poses a threat to economic growth and the environment.
>
> (DfT 2007a)

Government tries to reconcile these issues through its policies and guidance on transport and planning.

5.3.1 Transport policy and guidance

The Transport White Paper, *The Future of Transport* (DfT 2004a) establishes a transport strategy to 2030 which aims to maximise the benefits of all modes of transport while minimising their negative impacts. The strategy promotes investment in transport infrastructure and services, better management of the transport sector and network, and "planning ahead" (e.g. considering road pricing). It seeks to balance the need to travel with the need to improve quality of life, and particularly to improve air quality and reduce greenhouse gas emissions.

The Labour Government has gradually changed its policies towards road traffic over the last ten years. The early and ground-breaking *Road Traffic Reduction Act 1997* required local traffic authorities to assess existing levels of traffic, forecast expected traffic growth, and set targets for reducing the level or rate of growth of traffic. However the government's first report on national road traffic reduction targets (DfT 2005a) recommended that it would be better to focus on outcomes such as improved air quality and road safety rather than on traffic targets *per se*; and parallel draft guidance to local authorities (DfT 2005b) allows local authorities to not set targets if they consider them to be "inappropriate".

Managing our roads (DfT 2003a), the government's key strategy for managing the UK road network to about 2030, aims to promote alternatives to travel and particularly to travel by car, tackle congestion, make best use of existing transport infrastructure, promote new transport management technology (for instance "real time" information on travel conditions), and consider road pricing. *The Traffic Management Act 2004* requires local transport authorities in England to enable the road network to work efficiently without unnecessary delay to those travelling on it.

Much of Labour government policy on rail transport has attempted to deal with the repercussions of the privatisation of the railway system in 1994 by the previous Conservative government. After considerable problems with the privatisation process culminating in the Hatfield train crash of 2000, the government White Paper *The future of rail* (DfT 2004b) essentially re-nationalised the rail lines, although not the rail operating companies. The White Paper *Delivering a sustainable railway* (DfT 2007b) discusses future government investment in railways, plans to improve rail reliability and increase capacity, rail station modernisation and an improved fare system, and the need to reduce the carbon footprint of railway travel.

The *Air transport white paper* (DfT 2003b) set out a framework for expanding airport capacity to about 2030, taking into account environmental concerns. It responded to predictions that air travel will roughly treble between 2000 and 2030. It specified what growth can be expected at each of the main airports in the UK, although relevant development proposals still need to be taken through the planning process. It recommended that the owners of 30 main airports prepare Airport Master Plans.

Modern Ports: A UK policy (DfT 2000) stressed the importance of ports to the UK's economy and aimed to support their effective management and, where appropriate, expansion. However, in contrast to the Air Transport White Paper, it made no recommendations on the location and scale of shipping growth. A recent interim review of the policy (DfT 2007c) recommended that the policy should not be substantially changed, although port owners were also encouraged to prepare master plans.

The *Planning Bill* would, *inter alia*, lead to Government preparing National Policy Statements for nationally significant projects, and decisions on such projects being made by an Infrastructure Planning Commission, taking relevant National Policy Statements into account. Nationally significant projects would include large-scale highway-related developments, construction of railways, and construction or expansion of airports, harbour facilities, or rail freight interchanges.

A key guidance document for assessing the impacts of transport projects is the *Design manual for roads and bridges (DMRB)*, Vol. 11 (Highways Agency *et al.* 1993). This sets out the procedures and methodologies for assessing the environmental impacts of proposed road schemes including new roads, road widening and junction improvements. It can also be used as a starting point for assessing other linear transport schemes such as railways. However, it is less useful for assessing the transport impacts of other development projects because it focuses on just a single mode of transport (trunk road schemes).

The *Transport analysis guidance* (TAG) (DfT 2008) is the Department for Transport's appraisal tool for transport investment decisions. It incorporates the *New approach to appraisal* (NATA) (DETR 1998) which began as a tool for road scheme assessment, but has subsequently been modified to inform decisions about all transport modes and (to an extent) strategic as well as project level decisions. It tests proposals against five overarching objectives:

- to protect the built and natural *environment*;
- to improve *safety*;

- to support sustainable *economic* activity and get good value for money;
- to improve *access* to facilities for those without a car and to reduce severance;
- to ensure that all decisions are taken in the context of the Government's *integrated* transport policy (DfT 2008).

Use of TAG is a requirement for all transport projects/studies that require government approval. It is also seen as a best practice guide for projects/studies that do not require government approval.

5.3.2 Planning policy and guidance

Government has also set a framework of policies and guidance which aims to locate and design developments so as to reduce the need to travel and encourage modal shift. Developments are expected to be located in areas that are accessible by walking, cycling and public transport; and to be accompanied by complementary transport infrastructure and measures such as car parking restrictions, increased provision for pedestrians and cyclists, traffic management measures, and contributions to public transport improvements.

Planning Policy Guidance Note 13: Transport (PPG13) (DETR 2001) aims to integrate planning and transport at the national, regional, strategic and local level in order to reduce the need to travel, especially by car, and promote accessibility to jobs and services by public transport, walking and cycling. The guidance also recognises the role of walking and cycling in reducing air pollution. PPG13 requires transport assessments to be submitted alongside applications for major developments: these identify what measures will be taken to promote alternatives to the car, deal with the anticipated transport impacts of the development, and improve accessibility and safety for all modes of travel. Government has published guidance on the contents and preparation of transport assessments (DCLG/DfT 2007). This is a key guidance document for people carrying out transport studies as part of EIA.

Planning Policy Statement 6: Planning for town centres (PPS6) (DCLG 2005) promotes a sequential approach to locating large-scale developments. Developments should first be steered towards city/town centre sites; only where there are no appropriate central locations should edge-of-centre and then out-of-centre sites be considered. This test is designed to prevent urban sprawl and reduce the need to travel. PPS6 also notes that developments should be accessible by a choice of means of transport.

Local authorities can use Sections 106 and 278 of the *Town and Country Planning Act 1990* to secure developer contributions to ameliorate adverse impacts of developments, including funding for transport infrastructure and accessibility improvements to ameliorate traffic impacts. Section 106 negotiations have moved away from developers traditionally providing for highway improvements and are now more actively used to help improve public transport and other "softer" modes. The transport assessments prepared under PPG13 are often key documents used in Section 106 negotiations between local authorities and developers. For example, a transport assessment may identify a development requirement to improve the access to the site, through the building of a new access road, the improvement of a junction, or by introducing new or expanded public transport services.

5.3.3 Other policies and guidance

Local authorities are responsible for developing Air Quality Strategies designed to meet the Government's national objectives on air quality (see Chapter 8). Where these objectives are likely to be exceeded – typically due to nitrogen oxide emissions from transport – an action plan must be drawn up detailing how poor air quality will be improved.

Local authorities' social exclusion strategies aim to deal with the specific needs of vulnerable groups such as the long-term unemployed. Many of these groups depend on an efficient public transport system. As such, social exclusion strategies often consider transport issues.

5.4 Interest groups and sources of information

The *Town and Country Planning Act 1990* (as amended by the Planning and Compensation Act 1991 [Town and Country Planning (Scotland) Act 1972] and the Local Government Act 1972 [Local Government (Scotland) Act 1973]) requires planning authorities to consult the relevant highway authority if a proposed development involves access to a highway or is likely to increase traffic movements on the local highway network. For motorways and other trunk roads, the Highway Authority is the Secretary of State for Transport. For other classified roads the local authority, which may be the county council or a unitary authority, is regarded as the local highway authority. County councils and unitary authorities are responsible for developing and monitoring Local Transport Plans that set out a five-year transport planning framework. They are also are responsible for meeting the targets set in their road traffic reduction reports.

Information regarding traffic flows is generally held by local authorities. They may collect their own data as part of the process of preparing their Local Transport Plans. They may also possess information on pedestrian and cycling flows, and bus and rail services in their area. Some authorities possess traffic or multi-modal transport models which simulate the transport network in the area and that can be used to forecast future scenarios relating to traffic growth or future developments.

The Department for Transport (DfT) undertakes a national traffic census every three years, which includes surveys of traffic flows on major roads (both trunk and principal roads). The DfT also holds additional information from:

- national traffic surveys;
- trunk road network management;
- appraising infrastructure movements;
- research and monitoring studies.

TAG guidance is published via the Government's web-based transport analysis guidance WebTAG (DfT 2008). The equivalent appraisal systems that apply to transport investment decisions in Scotland and Wales are the *Scottish Transport Appraisal Guidance* (Transport Scotland 2008) and the *Welsh Transport Planning and Appraisal Guidance* (WelTAG 2008).

Non statutory interest groups with an interest in – and often strong opinions on – transport issues include local authorities' Local Strategic Partnerships and non-government organisations such as Campaign for Better Transport, the Aviation Environment Federation, the Campaign to Protect Rural England, Friends of the Earth and local community groups.

5.5 Scoping and baseline studies

This section first discusses the transport baseline and then the environmental baseline associated with the transport system. The former applies primarily to non-transport projects; the latter to the primary/direct impacts of transport projects and the secondary/indirect impacts of non-transport projects.

5.5.1 Transport baseline

Guidance on transport assessment (DCLG/DfT 2007) provides key guidance on how the transport baseline of a project can be described. It recommends that the following information should be collated:

Information about the existing site:

- a plan that shows the proposed development site in relation to the surrounding area and transport system;
- the permitted and existing use of the site;
- a detailed description of the existing land uses in the vicinity of the site, including development plan allocations or potential future uses in the case of undeveloped sites;
- existing site access layout and access constraints, where appropriate;
- air quality and noise problems in or near the site, for instance whether the site is in or near an Air Quality Management Area;
- carbon emissions data for the site, broken down by mode;
- any abnormal load uses of the current site.

Baseline transport data:

- the number of person-trips generated by the existing site for each mode or, where the site is vacant or partially vacant, the person-trips that might realistically be generated by any extant planning permission or permitted uses;
- existing public transport facilities (including provision/frequency of services and location of bus stops, train stations, park and ride facilities etc.) in the study area and, if available, the current level of usage of these services;

- capacity of the public transport network;
- parking facilities available in the vicinity of the site and their capacity;
- existing pedestrian and cycle facilities in the vicinity of the site, and their capacity;
- pedestrian and cyclist movements in the vicinity of the site;
- the road network in the vicinity of the site and its capacity;
- current traffic flows on links and junctions within the study area;
- the critical links and junctions on the highway network, with calibrated capacity tests to reflect existing conditions;
- current peak periods on the adjacent road network;
- daily traffic flow data to and from the site;
- the current personal injury accident record for the study area for the last three to five years, and critical locations on the road network with accident levels that are higher than the local average;
- planned transport improvements in the study area.

This data should include recent traffic counts, broken down into HGVs, cars/vans, abnormal loads, pedestrians and cyclists on given road lengths; turning counts at junctions; queue length surveys at signal junctions; and journey time surveys. The traffic data should reflect normal conditions on the transport network near the site, as well as unusual conditions such as holiday periods. **Figure 5.1** shows a simple example of how some of this data may be presented.

Typically transport assessments, including the baseline description, consider weekday morning and evening peak times for the adjacent transport system; weekday morning and evening peak times for the proposed development; an off-peak period selected to allow assessment of the greatest change resulting from the proposed development; and the weekend peak period if the development is expected to generate significant trips during the weekend or if the transport system suffers more congestions on weekends than weekdays. Seasonal variations are also considered.

The future baseline without the development is then determined, using local traffic forecasting models such as TEMPRO, or where appropriate the National Road Traffic Forecast (DCLG/DfT 2007). Broadly this involves changing (usually increasing) the baseline levels to reflect likely future activity on the transport network. This change can be significant, say a 1–2 per cent increase per year. The analysis period – the future years for which impact predictions are carried out – should reflect the trip generation characteristics of the proposed development and the conditions on the transport system. It should include the construction and operation stages, and where appropriate the decommissioning stage of the development.

5.5.2 Environmental baseline

Changes to the transport system will have follow-on impacts on the environment, safety, the economy, accessibility, and the implementation of other policies.

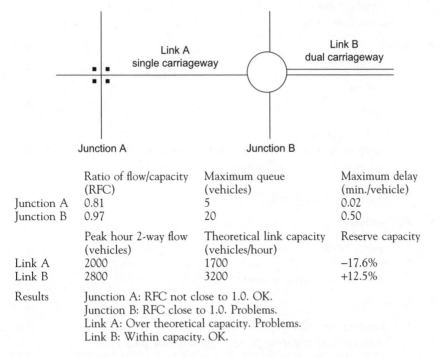

	Ratio of flow/capacity (RFC)	Maximum queue (vehicles)	Maximum delay (min./vehicle)
Junction A	0.81	5	0.02
Junction B	0.97	20	0.50

	Peak hour 2-way flow (vehicles)	Theoretical link capacity (vehicles/hour)	Reserve capacity
Link A	2000	1700	−17.6%
Link B	2800	3200	+12.5%

Results	Junction A: RFC not close to 1.0. OK.
	Junction B: RFC close to 1.0. Problems.
	Link A: Over theoretical capacity. Problems.
	Link B: Within capacity. OK.

Figure 5.1 Example of baseline traffic flows on a road network (based on Hughes 1994).

These will be direct impacts in the case of new transport projects, and indirect impacts where a non-transport development leads to changes to the transport system. The methods of collecting data on these environmental impacts will vary by subject area, and in many cases are described in other chapters.

Volume 11 of the *Design manual for roads and bridges* (Highways Agency *et al.* 1993) provides information on how this can be done for road projects, and some of its principles can be extended to other types of transport projects.

The five overarching objectives of TAG give rise to the following sub-objectives or criteria:

- **Environment**
    - *   noise
    - *   local air quality
    - *   greenhouse gases
    - *   landscape
    - *   townscape
    - *   biodiversity
    - *   heritage or historic resources
    - *   water environment

* physical fitness
* journey ambience

- **Safety**

  * accidents
  * security

- **Economy**

  * public accounts
  * transport economic efficiency for business users and transport providers
  * transport economic efficiency for consumer users
  * reliability
  * wider economic impacts

- **Accessibility**

  * option values
  * severance
  * access to the transport system

- **Integration**

  * transport interchange
  * integration of transport policy with land-use policy
  * integration of transport policy with other Government policies

All transport schemes must be assessed regarding their impact on these object-ives. Some of the baseline data is quite TAG-specific and relates to the TAG appraisal methods (see §5.6.2).

5.6 Impact prediction and evaluation

Again, this section first discusses transport impacts and then the environmental impacts of transport.

5.6.1 Transport impacts

Assessment of a development's transport impacts involves predicting the num-ber and mode of trips that will result from the development (trip generation); determining the likely origin and destination of these trips (trip distribution); determining the routes affected by these trips (trip assignment); and assessing the impact of the traffic changes on these routes (impact assessment). Again, the *Guidance on transport assessment* (DCLG/DfT 2007) provides key guidance for this stage.

Predicting the transport impact of a development first requires information about the proposed development:

- a site plan showing site location, layout and use;
- proposed land uses;
- site area and scale (e.g. number of residential units, gross floor area of the development);
- a weekly profile of hours of operation, including weekends and seasonal variations if appropriate;
- proposed access arrangements for all modes: locations and links to the existing transport infrastructure;
- proposed servicing arrangements: routes and facilities for service vehicles;
- traffic generated by the site construction works, including any abnormal loads resulting from decommissioning of the present development, and construction and use of the proposed development;
- proposed parking arrangements: number of spaces, parking layout, ratio of operational to non-operational spaces, overspill parking, disabled parking, motorcycle and cycle parking, methods of car park operation;
- development phasing where applicable (DCLG/DfT 2007).

Trip generation

Determining trip generation involves estimating, by mode, the number of trips that the development is likely to generate. Tools for this include databases, first principles, comparisons with other similar existing developments in similar areas, and complex traffic models.

Databases are probably the most widely used, and most accepted, way of predicting the number of trips generated by a development proposal. The most widely accepted database is TRICS (Trip Rate Information Computer System), which provides trip information based on a range of developments contained within the database. Trip information relates to gross floor area, location and use class, number of employees etc. The information supplied by this database primarily relates to car borne trips.

The **first principles method** involves making predictions based on a number of assumptions. Some may be based on survey data but where this does not exist, best judgement can be used. Assumptions may include average car occupancy or the percentage of long distance travellers versus local ones. First principles as a method for predicting trips and modal choice is not commonly accepted by local authorities; it may be used for developments that do not have a high trip attraction or are unique. This method can be difficult to quantify.

Comparisons with similar developments are often undertaken where databases do not provide sufficient information relating to specific use classes, or locations or modal shifts. This is the simplest method of trip assessment and it may be prudent to survey more than one similar site in order to assess a range of data. This method can be used to survey in more detail specifics relating to modal shift, car occupancy, cycle flows and pedestrian activity etc.

It is also possible to assess the number of trips and modal split of a development using a **traffic model**. The most widely used traffic models are SATURN and TRIPS which can be used to assess the traffic effects of major developments, as well as calculating trip distribution and assignment. However, these models are unlikely to be accurate for many land-use types.

A proposed development's traffic impacts can vary significantly depending on whether the trips that it generates are new, pass-by, linked, diverted or transferred (see §5.2). It may be helpful to determine what kinds of trips will be generated, and to adjust the overall trip generation figures accordingly.

The public transport accessibility level of the site, the level of car parking, and complementary measures to encourage public transport (e.g. bus lanes or bus priority measures) can all affect modal choice and trip numbers: the trip generation predictions may need to be reduced to take these factors into account (DCLG/DfT 2007). It is also becoming more accepted that car parking at development sites can be limited, to help restrict the number of car borne trips and encourage visitors to the site to use public transport facilities. However, although the TRICS database provides public transport service information for some sites, there is no database that specifically relates to public transport trips. This makes it difficult to establish the number and mode of future trips. It is often better to obtain information based on similar sites in the same area as the development proposal.

Trip distribution

Determining trip distribution involves determining where people who travel to the proposed site come from and go to. This will be affected by where the main centres of population are, their location with respect to the highway network, and their public transport accessibility. A catchment area for the transport assessment should be agreed early in the EIA process, and this should cover all centres of population from where a significant proportion of visitors to the proposed development could come.

Trip distribution can be carried out using:

- prior knowledge of the catchment area, e.g. knowledge of the destinations of employees;
- information about current traffic patterns in the area;
- travel time isochrones (maps showing areas that can be reached from the site in a given time, by mode) to assess journey times;
- gravity models which takes into account the population size of two places and the distance between them: "gravity" (the likelihood that people from A will be willing to travel to B) decreases as the distance between A and B increases, but increases as the size of B increases;
- sophisticated computer models such as SATURN and TRIPS.

Trip assignment

Based on the information about trip generation and trip distribution, trips can be "assigned" to the road network. This involves identifying the route likely to be taken from each origin to each destination. The end result of this stage is a series of maps of the transport network showing predicted traffic levels at each link and junction, in specified future years, both with and without the development.

Trip assignment can be done using a range of techniques, from crude guess-work based on knowledge of the local highway network, to sophisticated computer modelling such as SATURN and TRIPS. These models provide the most robust way of assigning traffic based on a representation of the transport network connected to a database. The models assign the trips in the database to the network according to a set of parameters describing the optimum route. They also allow the assignment of future trips on the network taking into account year-on-year growth in traffic and changes on the network.

Impact assessment

The above information allows the transport impacts of the proposed development to be assessed. This includes changes in traffic flow, junction delays, capacity of public transport and the road infrastructure, and the impact of road delays on public transport. Junction capacities can be tested using software such as PICADY, ARCADY, OSCADY, LINSIG or TRANSYT, which assesses priority junctions, roundabouts or signals respectively.

The significance of a project's transport impacts, cumulatively with existing traffic and likely future traffic growth, relates to:

- the total number and mode of trips the project generates, in different hours, days and years;
- the percentage by which it would increase flows on the traffic network, particularly during peak times for the project and for the network;
- whether the trips cause road link, junction or transport infrastructure capacities to be reached or exceeded (particularly during peak times);
- the type and timing of the trips: for instance, a given number of HGV journeys during the night will affect local residents more than a similar number of car journeys during the day.

This may identify the need for mitigation measures to deal with these problems, for instance in the form of junction improvements, bus lanes, bus priority, cycling facilities or pedestrian crossing facilities. These would be integrated into the proposed development; transport impacts would be predicted again; and residual transport impacts would be identified.

The residual transport impacts (as well as other components of the proposed project) are likely to affect the environment, safety, economy, accessibility and integration. This is discussed at §5.6.2. It may also be appropriate to assess how transport changes will affect specific groups, for instance children, the elderly, disabled people, and public transport operators.

5.6.2 Environmental impacts

Transport-related environmental impacts can be assessed using techniques from the *Transport analysis guidance* (TAG) (DfT 2008) and the *Design manual for roads and bridges*, Vol. 11 (Highways Agency *et al.* 1993). **Box 5.1** summarises the TAG appraisal methods for the environmental objectives (noise, local air quality, greenhouse gas emissions, landscape, townscape, biodiversity, heritage, water, physical fitness and journey ambience). In the case of the appraisal of landscape, townscape, biodiversity, heritage and water, the methods are based on the Quality of Life Capital approach (see Chapter 15). There are two key aspects of this approach that complement and strengthen EIA methods:

1. the environmental **features** (attributes) on which the appraisal is focused (**Box 5.2**);
2. the **indicators** (criteria) that are used to evaluate the significance of impacts (**Box 5.3**).

Box 5.1 TAG assessment methods for the main environmental objectives

Noise impacts will depend on the time of day, flow, and type of traffic. The TAG noise assessment involves two steps and builds on guidance in DMRB 11.3.7 for road schemes. The first step is based on the concept of noise annoyance and involves calculating the difference in the estimated population who would be annoyed by noise – i.e. experiencing changes of greater than 3dB(A). The population annoyed under the "with scheme" and "without scheme" scenarios are compared. The second step is based on the effect of noise on house prices. This involves calculating the present value of households' willingness to pay to avoid transport related noise for each scenario. A noise spreadsheet is used to automate this monetary valuation.

   Local air quality is assessed using the methodology for predicting air quality from traffic flow provided in DMRB 11.3.1. As indicators, TAG uses the objectives for NO_2 and PM_{10} of the UK Air Quality Strategy (AQS) (see §8.2.3). To assess compliance with the NAQS for the "do minimum" and the proposed option, the difference in roadside PM_{10} and NO_2 levels in the opening year is calculated using predicted traffic flows for each option. The number of properties within each of the following bands is ascertained: road centre to 50m beyond road centre; 50–100m from the road centre; 100–150m from the road centre; and 150–200m from the road centre. A series of factors are then added to each band against which the number of properties is multiplied. This reflects the diminishing impact of adverse air quality as one retreats from the roadside.

Box 5.1 (continued)

Transport schemes can also have air pollution impacts beyond the local situation, most notably acidification, excess nitrogen deposition, and generation of tropospheric ozone. In most areas of the country the potential to affect air quality on a regional basis will be limited but if it is likely to be an issue, a regional air quality assessment should be carried out to determine the change in emissions of nitrogen oxides.

Greenhouse gas emissions are assessed by predicting CO_2 levels from the expected additional number of vehicle-km induced by each option. Monetary values are then calculated per tonne of carbon released into the atmosphere using the estimated "Social Cost of Carbon".

Landscape is assessed uses Natural England's countryside character and quality of life capital approach (see Chapter 15) to describe the baseline or character of the landscape and then evaluate the impact on it. The approach is:

* describe sequentially the characteristic features of the countryside;
* appraise environmental capital – using a set of indicators (see Box 5.3);
* describe how the proposed scheme impacts on the landscape features, including effects on its distinctive quality and substantial local diversity; and
* produce an overall assessment score on a seven point scale.

A similar approach is followed for the **townscape** assessment.

Biodiversity is assessed in terms of the nature conservation value of the features listed in Box 5.2 (primarily in sites) and the project's impacts on them using the indicators listed in Box 5.3. A four-stage approach is used which is similar to the landscape assessment. Further details of the appraisal are given in §11.7.3.

Heritage is assessed using the same four stage approach. The heritage components are characterised using the features identified in Box 5.2 and the impacts are evaluated based on the indicators listed on Box 5.3.

Water is assessed in terms of water quality and land drainage/flood risk (see §10.8.5 for further details). A four-stage approach is followed:

* review the activities proposed and the potential impacts identified;
* appraise the importance of the water environment within the study area;
* appraise the potential impacts of the proposal on the important attributes; and
* final assessment score.

Box 5.4 summarises the appraisal methods for the remaining TAG components (safety, economy, accessibility, and integration). For each objective, one or more worksheets are completed which set out the procedure used for predicting and evaluating the impacts. A written comment is also recorded against each appraisal, from which the summary assessment score is determined.

Box 5.2 Examples of TAG environmental features (attributes)

Landscape
- **Pattern** – relationship between topography, elevation and degree of enclosure of landscape.
- **Tranquillity** – degree of remoteness, isolation, lack of intrusion of built environment.
- **Cultural** – Distinctive local views, traditional field patterns, building styles, materials and archaeological remains.
- **Landcover** – all types of land use in the area.
- **Summary of character** – summarises and pulls together the relationships between the features.

Biodiversity (and earth heritage) (see also §11.7.3)
- **Habitats**.
- **Species and species groups**.
- **Natural (geological) features** (including earth heritage sites).

Heritage
- **Form** – physical form of the site.
- **Survival** – the extent to which the original fabric of the building remains.
- **Condition** – includes the appearance and present management of the site.
- **Complexity** – the diversity and the relationships of the elements that make up the site.
- **Context** – the setting within the immediate surroundings.

Water (see also §10.8.5)
- **Water quality and supply.**
- **Ecological value.**
- **Land drainage and flood defence.**

Box 5.3 Examples of TAG environmental indicators for evaluating the significance of impacts

Landscape
- **Description** – of the existing landscape, before the scheme is constructed.
- **Scale it matters** – the policy level scale at which this feature matters; for example, international, national, regional or local.
- **Importance** – the reasons why this feature is important, such as reasons for a designation.
- **Rarity** – the relative abundance of the feature or its trend in relation to a target feature.

Box 5.3 *(continued)*

- **Substitutability** – whether the feature is replaceable within a given time period, e.g. 100 years.[1]
- **Impact** – the impact of the scheme on the feature, using the seven point text scale.

Biodiversity (see also §11.7.3)
- **Site location.**
- **Site designation** – statutory and non statuary designation.
- **Habitat type or species group** – e.g. dry heath, birds, invertebrates.
- **Scale** (of importance) – international, national, regional or local.
- **Importance** – e.g. reasons for designation.
- **Rarity** – trend in relation to targets.
- **Substitution possibilities** – e.g. potential for relocation or recreation.[2]
- **Impact** – assessment of the impact of the scheme, using the seven-point text scale.

Heritage
- **Scale it matters** – the policy level scale at which this feature matters; for example, international, national, regional or local.
- **Significance** – in terms of designations and other information, which can suggest levels of importance for the site.
- **Rarity** – including aspects such as representativeness and fragility/vulnerability of other existing examples.
- **Impact** – assessment of the impacts (physical, visual and cumulative) of the scheme, using the seven-point text scale.

Water (see also §10.8.5)
- **Water quality indicators** – general quality assessment (GQA) of the water chemistry, EU Freshwater Fish Directive, water abstraction points, groundwater vulnerability, location of wells/boreholes.
- **Land drainage/flood defence indicators** – floodplain, watercourses, river corridors, flood risk.
- **Impact** – risk-based negative impacts (five-point scale) which are reassessed in relation to mitigation measures.

1. The concept of *substitutability* can be controversial as it allows valued landscape features/areas to be developed as long as "there is suitable land available locally to recreate the features being lost". Comments from relevant authorities, statutory bodies, organisations and local residents are also important. A preliminary judgement can be made using the following questions:

   - does the development affect the locally distinctive pattern of landscape elements?
   - how intrusive would the scheme be on the field of view and visual amenity?
   - can the landscape accommodate further change?

2. Substitution of biodiversity features is also controversial because ecological systems are very difficult to recreate (see §11.8.3 and §11.8.4) – and it should normally be considered only as a last resort.

Box 5.4 *Outline of the appraisal methods for the safety, economy, accessibility and integration objectives (based on DfT 2008)*

SAFETY

It has been common practice for some time in the UK to place monetary values on casualties and accidents of differing severity, and to include these within a cost/benefit analysis. These values include the direct costs of accidents, such as loss of output, hospital, police and insurance costs, and damage to property and, more controversially, an allowance for the pain, grief and suffering incurred. However, in some cases there is concern with the direct safety performance of the system, it is therefore helpful to estimate accident numbers directly as well.

The personal security of travellers and their property increases with the provision of surveillance, design features which reduce the opportunities for attackers to surprise travellers, and facilities for making emergency calls. The security of car users increases when the instances when they are required to stop or travel very slowly are reduced, vehicles can be parked in safety, and facilities for making emergency calls are provided.

ECONOMY

Congestion and unreliability of journeys add to the costs of business, undermining competitiveness particularly in towns and cities where traffic is worst. The cost to the British economy is estimated to run into billions of pounds every year and is rising. The economic impacts of transport schemes are appraised using cost/benefit analysis, where the benefits of a scheme are balanced against its costs. The calculation of the costs includes an assessment of impacts of a scheme on pedestrians, cyclists and other road users, with a monetary value applied to these impacts.

ACCESSIBILITY

Appraisal of accessibility considers how well people in different locations, and with differing availability of transport, can reach different types of facility:

- ease of access to the transport system itself in terms of, for example, the proportion of homes within x minutes of a bus stop or the proportion of buses which may be boarded by a wheelchair user;
- ease of access to facilities, with the emphasis being on the provision of the facilities necessary to meet people's needs within certain minimum travel times, distances or costs;
- the value which people place on having an option available which they might use only under unusual circumstances – "option value"; and the value people place on simply the existence of an alternative which they have no real intention of using – "existence value";
- ease of participation in activities (for personal travel) or delivery of goods to their final destination (for goods travel), provided by the interaction of the transport system, the geographical pattern of economic activities, and the pattern of land use as a whole.

Box 5.4 (*continued*)

Community severance is appraised by calculating how non-motorised modes of transport, especially walking, are affected by the scheme. Both the extent of the severance in time and the numbers of people affected are used in assessing the significance of the impact

INTEGRATION

Appraisal of integration focuses on:

- integration within and between different types of transport, so that each contributes its full potential and people can move easily between them;
- integration with the environment, so that the transport choices available support a better environment;
- integration with land-use planning, at national, regional and local level, so that transport and planning work together to support more sustainable travel choices and reduce the need for travel; and
- integration with policies for education, health and wealth creation, so that transport helps make a fairer, more inclusive society.

The TAG process concludes by compiling all of this information into one Appraisal Summary Table (AST) (see **Table 5.1**). It may be appropriate to include an AST or a similar summary in the EIS. The AST contains three columns for evaluating the significance of the predicted impacts. The first column is qualitative, and allows a textual description of the impact. The next column is quantitative: it uses numbers to measure the scale of the impacts. The final column is the summary assessment and uses a monetary scale, quantitative indicators, or a seven-point scale of the impacts (large, moderate, or small negative/adverse; neutral; and small, moderate, or large positive/beneficial).

The AST is accompanied by appraisal of the achievement of local and regional objectives; effectiveness of problem solving; and supporting analyses that cover distribution and equity, affordability and financial sustainability, and practicality and public acceptability. Again, much of this information may usefully be included in an EIS.

5.7 Mitigation measures

Traditionally, the transport impacts of development were considered to be primarily mobility-related. Mitigation measures thus involved off-site highway works to reduce driver delay (e.g. junction improvements), pedestrian and cyclist delay (e.g. improved crossing facilities), or accidents (e.g. traffic calming).

In the light of current government and local policies, mitigation measures have become more focused on reducing the need to travel, improving accessibility,

Table 5.1 TAG appraisal summary table (AST)

Option	Description		Problems	Present value of costs (PVCs) to public accounts £m	
OBJECTIVE	SUB-OBJECTIVE		QUALITATIVE IMPACTS	QUANTITATIVE ASSESSMENT	ASSESSMENT
ENVIRONMENT	Noise				Net population win/lose,
					Net present value £m
	Local air quality				Concentrations weighted
	Greenhouse gases				for exposure tonnes of CO_2
	Landscape				Score
	Townscape				Score
	Heritage of historic resources				Score
	Biodiversity				Score
	Water environment				Score
	Physical fitness				Score
	Journey ambience				Score
SAFETY	Accidents				PVB £m
	Security				Score
ECONOMY	Public accounts			Central and local government PVCs	PVC £m
	Transport economic efficiency:			Users Present Value of Benefits (PVB),	PVB £m
	business users and transport providers			Transport Providers PVB, Other PVB	
	Transport economic efficiency:			Users PVB	PVB £m
	consumers				
	Reliability				Score
	Wider economic impacts				Score
ACCESSIBILITY	Option values				PVB £m
	Severance				Score
	Access to the transport system				Score
INTEGRATION	Transport interchange				Score
	Land-use policy				Score
	Other government policies				Score

providing transport alternatives and addressing environmental issues. Mitigation measures for the transport impacts of non-transport developments thus include public transport improvements, reductions in car parking, travel plans, improved pedestrian and cycling facilities, and traffic management measures together with contributions towards more strategic transport measures such as park-and-ride. These measures are summarised at **Table 5.2**.

Mitigation measures for the environmental impacts of transport infrastructure relate primarily to reducing noise, air and water pollution and visual intrusion; improving lighting; enhancing wildlife and ecology, amenity and recreation; and promoting the sustainable use of natural resources. These measures are summarised at **Table 5.3**.

It has now become standard practice with transport assessment to prepare a travel plan, normally at the request of the local authority. This plan identifies measures for encouraging the modal shift of employees or visitors from the private car to public transport, cycling and walking. These measures can range from the provision of showers and changing facilities to bike loans and season bus tickets. This, together with restrictions in car parking provision, has been successful at a number of development sites in achieving a modal shift. Under PPG13, the production of a travel plan may be a planning requirement for a new development that is likely to generate significant traffic. The development of a travel plan may be a mitigation measure proposed in the EIA. Where travel plans already exist, they may suggest other mitigation measures that can be included in the EIA.

5.8 Monitoring

Monitoring of the transport impacts of specific developments is useful but often neglected. Where a developer has prepared a travel plan, monitoring of its success is an important requirement, but where no such plans have been prepared, development-specific transport monitoring is rare.

Monitoring of transport projects is identified as part of the TAG appraisal process but little guidance is provided on monitoring the environmental sub-objectives. However, monitoring is a mandatory part of Strategic Environmental Assessment of plans and programmes and may therefore lead to monitoring of the environmental performance of transport projects. This requirement is reflected in TAG Unit 2.11.

Local authorities are required to monitor transport against indicators (and possibly targets) set by their road traffic reduction reports and as part of their Local Transport Plan annual progress reports. Transport models need to be kept up to date, and require periodic surveys of bus service frequency and traffic levels to obtain realistic figures. Consequently, relevant information may already be collected that could be used to monitor the impacts of the development.

5.9 Conclusions

Transport planning exists in, and reflects, a rapidly changing policy arena. The sustainability agenda encourages land use planning and transport planning to

Table 5.2 Mitigation measures: transport impacts of non-transport developments (adapted from BRF 1999)

Main factor	Examples of project-level mitigation measures	Examples of more strategic measures involving or affecting more than one development project
Car parking	• Reduce car parking. • Travel plan.	• One parking area used for multiple purposes (e.g. to service office during the week, church or recreation ground on the weekend). • Tight maximum parking standards. • Parking controls/charging.
Highway capacity	• Travel plan. • Reduce the number and length of trips. • Promote pass-by, linked, diverted or transferred rather than new trips. • Promote car sharing/pooling. • Managed access from the development onto the highway network. • Support for public transport. • Improved road junctions, road widening, new roads etc.	• Improved public transport (see below). • Demand management, e.g. congestion charging. • Other traffic control measures over a wide area, e.g. Intelligent Transport Systems. • High-occupancy vehicle lanes. • Advanced signal systems. • Provision of new or expanded roads.
Pedestrians	• Travel plan. • Direct and desirable pedestrian routes, including crossing facilities. • Traffic calming, e.g. humps, reduced carriageway size. • Environmental and public realm improvements, e.g. wider pavements. • Good lighting. • CCTV.	• Well-located facilities vis-à-vis homes and employment sites. • Reduced traffic speeds, e.g. Home Zones. • Pedestrianisation.
Cycling	• Direct and desirable cycling routes, including crossing facilities. • Provision of cycle paths and/or lanes. • Restrictions on car parking. • Traffic calming. • Secure parking. • Changing facilities.	• Strategic cycling network.
Public transport	• Developer contributions towards strategic measures.	• Bus lanes and bus priority improvements (e.g. bus-operated traffic lights). • Real time bus information. • Upgrading of facilities. • Introduction of new bus routes. • Improved frequency of buses. • Park-and-ride. • Provision of more frequent/ improved/extended public transport.

Table 5.3 Mitigation measures: environmental impacts of transport infrastructure (adapted from BRF 1999)

Main factor	Examples of project-level mitigation measures

Noise pollution	• Noise barriers:
	    • reflective barriers;
	    • absorbent barriers;
	    • vegetative barriers.
	• Road surfacing:
	    • porous asphalt;
	    • "whisper" concrete;
	    • thin surfacing.
	• Traffic management, e.g. humps, chicanes, speed limits
	• Engineering solutions:
	    • cuttings;
	    • cut & cover;
	    • optimum junction design.

Air pollution	• Measures to reduce/improve traffic flow • Pedestrian priority • Speed restrictions
Water pollution	• Improved runoff • Pollution interceptors • Careful choice of car park surfaces
Visual intrusion	• Integration of transport infrastructure with development • Promotion/restriction of views • Promotion of gateways
Improved lighting	• Improvement of lighting while avoiding light pollution
Species and habitats	• Locate transport infrastructure to avoid habitat • "Green bridges": badger and toad tunnels etc. • Provision of new habitats at edge of roads, railway lines etc.
Amenity and recreation	• Support for walking, cycling and public transport (see Table 5.2) • Improved facilities for disabled people • Traffic signage • Enhanced environment • Reduce community severance through, e.g., crossings, tunnels, bridges

coordinate so as to reduce the need to travel. Developments must seek to achieve a modal shift. Methods to assess transport impacts reflect this changing agenda and seek to influence developments in a sustainable manner. These methods increasingly aim to provide a level playing field for different modes, and an integrated assessment process for different types of impacts.

The effectiveness of both transport assessment and TAG depends on the way they are used, the proponents' intentions, and the stage in the development process at which they are used. TAG is designed to be flexible: it can be used at the strategic or feasibility stages, before detailed design, using subjective judgement; more quantitative information can be completed at the later detailed design stage. This two-tier approach should enable environmental consideration to be incorporated into the decision making process at an earlier stage and thus have a greater influence on the outcome.

References

BRF (British Roads Federation) 1999. *Old roads to green roads*. London: BRF.

DCLG (Department for Communities and Local Government) 2005. *Planning Policy Statement 6. Planning for town centres* (PPS6). London: DCLG, www.communities.gov.uk/publications/planningandbuilding/pps6.

DCLG/DfT (Communities and Local Government/Department for Transport) 2007. *Guidance on transport assessment*. London: DCLG/DfT, www.dft.gov.uk/162259/165237/202657/guidanceontapdf.

DETR (Department of the Environment, Transport and the Regions) 1998. *Guidance on the New Approach to Appraisal*. London: DETR.

DETR 2001. *Planning Policy Guidance Note 13. Transport*. London: DETR, www.communities.gov.uk/documents/planningandbuilding/pdf/155634.pdf.

DfT (Department for Transport) 2000. *Modern ports: a UK policy*. London: DfT, www.dft.gov.uk/pgr/shippingports/ports/modern/modernportsaukpolicy.

DfT 2003a. *Managing our roads*. London: DfT, www.dft.gov.uk/pgr/roads/network/policy/managingourroadsprintver.pdf.

DfT 2003b. *The future of air transport*, www.dft.gov.uk/about/strategy/whitepapers/air/.

DfT 2004a. *The future of transport*, www.dft.gov.uk/about/strategy/whitepapers/fot/.

DfT 2004b. *The future of rail*, www.dft.gov.uk/about/strategy/whitepapers/rail/.

DfT 2005a. *Tackling congestion and pollution: the government's first report*, www.dft.gov.uk/pgr/roads/tpm/congestionresearch/tacklingcongestionandpolluti4028?page=2#a1001.

DfT 2005b. *Road Traffic Reduction Act 1997: draft guidance to local traffic authorities*, www.dft.gov.uk/pgr/roads/tpm/congestionresearch/roadtrafficreductionact1997d4027.

DfT 2007a. *Circular 2/07: Planning and the strategic road network*. London: DfT, www.dft.gov.uk/162259/165237/circular207planningsrnpdf.

DfT 2007b. *Delivering a sustainable railway*. London: DfT, www.dft.gov.uk/about/strategy/whitepapers/whitepapercm7176/whitepapersustainablerailway1.

DfT 2007c. *Ports policy review interim report*. London: DfT, www.dft.gov.uk/pgr/shippingports/ports/portspolicyreview/.

DfT 2008. *Transport analysis guidance* (TAG). London: DfT TAG website (WebTAG), www.webtag.org.uk.

Eddington, Sir Rod 2006. *The Eddington transport study*, www.dft.gov.uk/162259/187604/206711/executivesummary.

Highways Agency, Scottish Office, Welsh Office & Department of the Environment Northern Ireland 1993. *Design manual for roads and bridges (DMRB)*, Vol. 11: *Environmental assessment.* (Sections updated periodically). London: Highways Agency, www.standardsforhighways.co.uk/dmrb/vol11/index.htm.

Hughes A 1994. *Traffic.* In *Methods of environmental impact assessment*, P Morris and R Therivel (eds), 64–77. London: UCL Press.

Richardson J and G Callaghan 2001. Transport. Ch. 5 in *Methods of Environmental Impact Assessment*, 2nd edn., P Morris and R Therivel (eds). London: Spon Press.

SACTRA (Standing Advisory Committee on Trunk Road Assessment) 1994. *Trunk roads and the generation of traffic.* London: HMSO.

Transport Scotland 2008. *Scottish transport appraisal guidance* (STAG), www.transportscotland.gov.uk/stag/home.

WAG (Welsh Assembly Government) 2008. *Wel-TAG – Welsh transport planning and appraisal guidance*(WelTAG), http://wales.gov.uk/topics/transport/publications/weltag/?lang=en.

6 Landscape and visual

Rebecca Knight
(based on Therivel and Goodey 2001)

6.1 Introduction

> The landscape . . . is an important part of the quality of life for people everywhere:
> in urban areas and in the countryside, in degraded areas as well as in areas of
> high quality, in areas recognised as being of outstanding beauty as well as every-
> day areas.
>
> (Preamble to *The European Landscape Convention*, Florence,
> 20 October 2000, COE 2000).

While progressive change is welcomed, projects may result in effects on landscape character or quality, and on views experienced and valued by the local
population. The need to incorporate landscape considerations into decision making has grown in importance as the Government's emphasis on sustainable development has increased (CA/SNH 2002a).

The European EIA Directives and UK regulations require an EIA to identify,
describe and assess the direct and indirect effects of a project on the population,
the landscape, and the inter-relationship between the two. However, neither
the Directive nor the regulations prescribe any particular methodology for the
assessment of these effects. Landscape and visual effects are probably the most
subjective elements addressed by EIA and it is therefore crucial that there is
clarity in assessment methods, and consistency in terminology used. The main
source of guidance is the Landscape Institute and Institute of Environmental
Management and Assessment's *Guidelines for landscape and visual impact assessment* (LI/IEMA 2002). The terminology used in this chapter is consistent with
these guidelines; thus "impact assessment" refers to the process of landscape or
visual assessment, while "effect" refers to a change resulting from a development.

Landscape and visual effects, are closely related. **Landscape effects** describe
"changes in the landscape, its character and quality" and are assessed as an effect
on an environmental resource, while **visual effects** describe the "appearance of
these changes and the resulting effect on visual amenity" and are assessed as one
of the inter-related effects on population (LI/IEMA 2002).

This chapter aims to address the major concerns of the landscape specialist
by defining concepts, indicating what standards and regulations apply, describing

how landscape and visual data are collected and how landscape and visual effects are predicted, highlighting potential mitigation measures that can be employed, and pointing out the limitations of methods for landscape and visual impact assessment (LVIA). It also points to sources of further information where relevant.

6.2 Definitions and concepts

6.2.1 Landscape

The European Landscape Convention defines landscape as "a zone or area as perceived by local people or visitors, whose visual features and character are the result of the action of natural and/or cultural (that is, human) factors". This definition reflects the idea that landscapes evolve through time, as a result of being acted upon by natural forces and human beings. It also underlines that a landscape forms a whole, whose natural and cultural components are taken together, not separately (COE 2000).

The former Countryside Agency (now Natural England) and Scottish Natural Heritage describe landscape as the relationship between people and place, providing the setting for our day-to-day lives. They suggest that "landscape" does not just refer to special, designated landscapes and does not only apply to the countryside:

> Landscape can mean a small patch of urban wasteland as much as a mountain range, an urban park as much as an expanse of lowland plain. It results from the way that different components of our environment – both natural (the influences of geology, soils, climate, flora and fauna) and cultural (the historic and current impact of land use, settlement, enclosure and other human interventions) – interact together and are perceived by us.
>
> (CA/SNH 2002a)

The following factors contribute to the landscape:

- natural factors: geology, landform, air and climate, soils, flora and fauna;
- cultural/social factors: land use, settlement, enclosure;
- aesthetic and perceptual factors: colour, texture, pattern, form, sounds, smells, touch/feel, preferences, associations, memories.

Natural and cultural factors can be more accurately and objectively described than aesthetic and perceptual factors.

6.2.2 Landscape quality and landscape character

Up until the 1980s, the consideration of landscape in land use planning focused on landscape quality, or what makes one area "better" than another. This process was described as landscape evaluation (CA/SNH 2002a). Designated areas were often protected at the expense of the rest, so that non-designated were often targeted by developers. Another problem with this approach was that the concept of landscape beauty is not timeless and is dependent on fashion and taste, so that today's judgement could be tomorrow's mistake. An emphasis on designations is now considered insufficient in EIA.

Box 6.1 Approaches to Landscape Character Assessment across the UK

England: The Character of England map, jointly published in England by the former Countryside Commission and English Nature (CC/EN 1996), provides a national framework for more detailed assessments by local authorities and others. This map identifies 159 character areas, defined in terms of their landscape, sense of place, wildlife and natural features. The key natural and cultural characteristics of each character area are presented as eight volumes of Countryside Character descriptions, published by the former Countryside Agency (CA 1998–1999).

This framework has more recently been strengthened by the development of a national landscape typology by the former Countryside Agency in collaboration with English Nature and English Heritage, and with support from Defra (CA 2002). The landscape typology has been derived by map analysis of the main physical, biological and cultural factors that determine landscape character using GIS manipulation of digital data sets.

A large number of county and district authorities have undertaken more local landscape character assessments of their areas. The former Countryside Agency developed a database of landscape character assessments undertaken across England which is currently being managed by the Landscape Character Network (2008).

Scotland: Unlike the CA's top-down approach to characterisation, SNH used a bottom-up approach in partnership with local planning authorities and other stakeholders. SNH's approach comprised 29 regional studies, each describing, mapping and analysing key landscape characteristics, and identifying forces of change affecting the landscape. The types across the 29 studies were then grouped up into higher order types –106 Level 2 types and 52 Level 3 types – to provide a strategic framework for Scotland (CA/SNH 2002b).

Wales: The Countryside Council of Wales (CCW) developed a GIS-based Landscape Assessment and the Decision Making Process (LANDMAP) for informing policies and decision making (CCW 2001). This is used by Welsh Planning Authorities to inform countryside policy and to develop strategies for development or protection of the countryside. Currently the CCW is producing a landscape character map of Wales that will identify a number of character areas to underpin the Wales Spatial Plan and Environment Strategy. These character areas will form a framework for the more detailed LANDMAP Aspect local areas.

Northern Ireland: The Environment and Heritage Service (EHS) in association with the Planning Service, commissioned a survey which resulted in the identification of 130 distinct character areas. Landscape character assessments were published for each district as part of the Northern Ireland Landscape Character Assessment Series (DOE 1999). Maps and profiles of these character areas are now available at www.ehsni.gov.uk/landscape/country_landscape.htm.

In the 1980s there was a shift away from this approach of "preserve the best and leave the rest", and landscape assessment evolved as a means of identifying what makes one area "different" or "distinct" from another. This approach was pioneered by the former Countryside Commission (subsequently the Countryside Agency, and now Natural England) and acknowledges the character of individual landscapes, the diversity of all landscapes, and the benefits and services that landscapes provide.

Landscape character is now a central concept in landscape assessment. It can be defined as "a distinct, recognizable and consistent pattern of elements in the landscape that makes one landscape different from another, rather than better or worse" (CA/SNH 2002a). Particular combinations of geology, landform, soils, vegetation, landuse, field patterns and human settlement create character. This approach changes the emphasis from landscape as "scenery" to landscape as "environment". Understanding the landscape character of an area therefore involves systematic investigation of these various factors.

A key aspect of landscape character assessment is the distinction between the relatively value-free process of **characterisation**, and the subsequent **evaluation**, or making of judgements that are based on knowledge of landscape character. Approaches to landscape character assessment across the UK are outlined in **Box 6.1**.

Although separate national landscape characterisation programmes were carried out in England, Scotland, Wales and Northern Ireland, the strong parallels of approaches in England and Scotland led to their joint working in producing guidance on the preparation and use of landscape character assessments. This now well-established guidance (CA/SNH 2002a) is accompanied by a series of Topic Papers on specific subjects related to landscape character assessment.

6.2.3 Landscape quality and landscape value

Concepts of landscape quality and landscape value differ from landscape character. Landscape quality can be defined as "judgements about the physical state of the landscape, and about its intactness from visual, functional, and ecological perspectives" (CA/SNH 2002a). It also reflects the state of repair of individual elements of the landscape, and may be described in terms of landscape condition.

People value the landscape for many different reasons. Whether we value certain landscapes for their distinctiveness, or for other reasons, is a separate issue from landscape character. Landscape value is concerned with the relative value that is attached to different landscapes (CA/SNH 2002a). This is often recognised through landscape designation. However, a landscape without any formal designation may also be valued by society, for example for its perceptual aspects (such as tranquillity or wildness), cultural associations, its functional role, or other conservation issues.

6.2.4 Tranquillity and wild land

The CPRE have carried out a nationwide survey to understand what tranquillity means to people, and then used a Geographical Information Systems (GIS) model to create a map showing how likely each locality was to make people feel tranquil (CPRE 2005). The tranquillity data is based on features considered to positively contribute to tranquillity (deemed to be openness of the landscape, perceived naturalness of the landscape, rivers in the landscape, areas of low noise and visibility of the sea) and negative features that are considered to detract from tranquillity (deemed to be presence of other people, visibility of roads, general signs of overt human impact, visibility of urban development, road, train and urban area noise, night time light pollution, aircraft noise and military training noise). This map may assist in describing the more intangible elements of the landscape, although it should be noted that the information provided by the mapping is limited to the criteria chosen to define tranquillity and the way in which these criteria have been applied.

In Scotland, "wild land" is described, in National Planning Policy Guideline 14, as "uninhabited and often relatively inaccessible countryside where the influence of human activity on the character and quality of the environment has been minimal" (SNH 1999). SNH have mapped remote areas and preliminary areas of search for wild land. The purpose of the maps is not to delimit wild land, but to act as a starting point for review of where the main resource of wild land is most likely to be found. They are accompanied by Policy Statement No. 02/03 *Wildness in Scotland's countryside* (SNH 2003).

6.2.5 Landscape receptors

In landscape and visual impact assessment landscape receptors comprise the individual landscape elements that make up the landscape (for example trees, woodlands, hedgerows, and built elements), landscape character types and/or areas, and designated landscapes. Effects on these receptors are assessed as part of landscape and visual impact assessment.

6.2.6 Visual amenity and visual receptors

Visual amenity can be defined as "the value of a particular area or view in terms of what is seen" (LI/IEMA 2002). In landscape and visual impact assessment effects on views and visual amenity are assessed. The visual receptors comprise viewpoints and the people who experience views from these viewpoints.

6.3 Legislative background and interest groups

For some EIA topics, potential effects can be assessed against measurable, technical international or national guidelines or legislative standards. However, the assessment of potential effects on landscape and visual amenity is more complex, involving a combination of objective and subjective judgements. The legislation that is relevant to landscape and visual impact assessment relates specifically to landscape designations.

6.3.1 *Legislation and landscape quality designations*

Natural England, Scottish Natural Heritage and the Countryside Council for Wales have the remit to protect and improve the landscape, and to provide new and improved opportunities for access to the countryside.

The European Landscape Convention (COE 2000) is aimed at the protection, management and planning of all landscapes and aims to ensure that the importance of landscape is recognised as a whole, rather than according to special areas. It came into force on 1 March 2004, and is the first international agreement to address landscape issues, providing a framework for legislation in the UK.

National Parks are recognised for their outstanding landscape quality and recreational potential – they are the most spectacular and valued landscapes in Britain. National Parks in England and Wales are designated under the *National Parks and Access to the Countryside Act 1949*. Legislation to create National Parks in Scotland was passed by the Scottish Parliament in August 2000, the *National Parks (Scotland) Act 2000*, and National Parks were established in Loch Lomond and The Trossachs in 2002 and in the Cairngorms in 2003.

Also designated under the National Parks and Access to the Countryside Act 1949 are **Areas of Outstanding Natural Beauty** (AONB) in England and Wales, recognised for their outstanding landscape quality and scenic beauty. Since 2000, the *Countryside and Rights of Way Act 2000* (CROW) raised the profile of AONBs and made it obligatory for local authorities and conservation boards to produce new AONB Management Plans. The Scottish equivalent of an AONB is a National Scenic Area (NSA). There is currently no formal statutory basis for creating NSAs, although the Scottish Executive still proposes to legislate on this.

Non-statutory landscape designations carry less weight than statutory designations. Relevant non-statutory designations include:

- more than 1,000km of Heritage Coasts which are defined by agreement between the relevant maritime local authorities and Natural England;
- World Heritage Sites such as the Ironbridge Gorge industrial archaeology complex in Shropshire;
- National Trails such as the Pennine Way and Ridgeway; and
- local landscape designations, often known as Areas of Great Landscape Value, or Special Landscape Areas.

Green Belt is a planning designation, rather than a landscape quality designation. However, the reasons for designation of areas of Green Belt are often linked to landscape character, particularly in terms of "sense of openness". It may be relevant for the landscape and visual impact assessment of a proposal within an area of Green Belt to address any potential impact on "sense of openness" to help inform potential impacts on this planning designation.

There is sometimes an overlap between cultural and landscape chapters of EIAs concerning certain cultural heritage designations, such as Parks and Gardens of Special Historic Interest, Conservation Areas, Scheduled Ancient Monuments and Listed Buildings. It is critical that there is a distinction between which aspects of these designations are covered in which chapter – this is often brought to light by studying the reason for the designation. For example, if the landscape setting or views from the park or garden as well as its historic importance are both listed as reasons for its designation, it might be appropriate that the land-scape and visual chapter addresses potential impacts of the proposed develop-ment on views from, and the setting of, historic parks and gardens, while the cultural heritage chapter addresses the potential impact on the inherent historic importance of the park or garden.

6.3.2 Interest groups

Although landscape and visual impact assessment is the responsibility of the devel-oper, the opinions of the regulatory authority, relevant statutory consultees, and other interest groups such as conservation bodies and local residents should be taken into account. Interest groups are likely to comprise:

- Natural England, Scottish Natural Heritage, Countryside Council for Wales, Environment and Heritage Service Northern Ireland (as relevant);
- local planning authority, including landscape officers;
- local residents.

6.3.3 Planning policy

In England, Planning Policy Guidance notes (PPGs) and their replacements Planning Policy Statements (PPSs) explain statutory provisions and provide guid-ance on planning policy and the operation of the planning system. The main PPGs/PPSs relevant to landscape and visual impact assessment are PPG15, PPS7 and PPS22.

PPG15: *Planning and the historic environment* (DoE 1994a) is relevant in rela-tion to historic parks and gardens, stating that local planning authorities should protect registered parks and gardens in preparing development plans and in deter-mining planning applications. The effect of proposed development on a registered park or garden or its setting is a material consideration in the determination of a planning application.

PPS7: *Sustainable development in rural areas* (ODPM 2004a) draws attention to the Government's objectives for rural areas. Among these are promoting

> good quality, sustainable development that respects and, where possible, enhances local distinctiveness and the intrinsic qualities of the countryside;

and continued protection of the open countryside for the benefit of all, with the highest level of protection for our most valued landscapes and environmental resources.

PPS22: *Renewable energy* (ODPM 2004b) recommends the use of landscape character to aid decision making with landscape character assessment used at a regional level to inform planning for renewables. It states that schemes should be assessed using objective descriptive material and analysis wherever possible even though the final decision on the visual and landscape effects will be, to some extent, one made by professional judgement. The Companion Guide to PPS22 (ODPM 2004c) offers practical advice to planners, regional and local decision-makers and other stakeholders as to how the policies of PPS22 can be implemented on the ground.

In Scotland, Scottish Planning Policies (SPPs) provide statements of Scottish Executive policy on nationally important land use and other planning matters. SPPs are gradually replacing existing National Planning Policy Guidelines (NPPGs). The main SPPs/NPPGs relevant to landscape and visual impact assessment are: *NPPG13 – Coastal planning* (1997); *NPPG14 – Natural heritage* (1999); *NPPG18 – Planning and the historic environment* (1999); *SPP1 – The planning system* (2002); *SPP6 – Renewable energy developments* (2007); *SPP15 – Planning for rural development* (2005), *SPP17 – Planning for Transport* (2005); and *SPP20 – Role of architecture and design* (SE 2005). In addition, Circulars provide statements of Scottish Executive policy and contain guidance on policy implementation through legislative or procedural change, and Planning Advice Notes (PANs) provide advice on good practice. All SPPs/NPPGs and PANs can be found at www.scotland.gov.uk/planning.

In Wales, current land use planning policy is contained in "Planning Policy Wales" (March 2002), which provides the strategic policy framework for the effective preparation of local planning authorities' development plans. This is supplemented by 20 topic-based Technical Advice Notes (Wales) (TANs). The main TANs relevant to landscape and visual impact assessment include: *TAN 6 – Agricultural and rural development* (2000); *TAN 8 – Renewable energy* (2005); *TAN 10 – Tree preservation orders* (1997); *TAN 12 – Design* (2002); *TAN 14 – Coastal planning* (1998); *TAN 18 – Transport* (2007); and *TAN 19 – Telecommunications* (2002). All the above documents can be found at http://new.wales.gov.uk/topics/planning/?lang=en.

In Northern Ireland the Regional Development Strategy "Shaping Our Future" offers strategic planning guidance for Northern Ireland up to the year 2025. This is accompanied by Planning Policy Statements (PPSs), which set out policies on land use and other planning matters and apply to the whole of Northern Ireland. The main PPSs relevant to landscape and visual impact assessment include: *PPS1 – General principles* (1998); *Draft PPS14 – Sustainable development in the countryside* (2007); and *Draft PPS18 – Renewable energy* (2007). In addition, non-statutory planning guidance supplements such as Development Control Advice Notes (DCANs) provide guidance in particular areas, for example DCAN 10 provides guidance on Environmental Impact Assessment. All the above documents can be fund at www.planningni.gov.uk/AreaPlans_Policy/APP.htm.

Regional and local planning guidance will also be relevant as context for the LVIA.

6.3.4 Guidance for landscape character assessment, and landscape and visual impact assessment

Landscape assessment: a Countryside Commission approach (CC 1987) was an early guide to landscape assessment, which advised on the approach, practical methods and applications of landscape assessment. *Landscape assessment principles and practice* (CCS 1991) established practical guidelines for landscape assessment, focusing particularly on assessing Scottish landscapes for designation. *Landscape assessment guidance* (CC 1993) updated the earlier documents, and became the basis for landscape character assessments in the UK and abroad. However, only the most recent guidance reflects the now accepted version of landscape character assessment discussed in §6.2.2. The current accepted guidance on landscape character assessment is the *Landscape character assessment guidance for England and Scotland* (CA/SNH 2002a).

Table 6.1 summarises guidance on landscape and visual impact assessment.

6.4 Baseline studies

In EIA, baseline studies establish the parameters and structure for subsequent impact assessment. They need to be extensive and rigorous, establish a digestible account of the area and project concerned, and highlight specific details that will require later investigation. They should include a clear statement of purpose, initial consideration of the full range of landscape and visual receptors, application of a comprehensive and tested methodology, and clear communication in terms which can be understood and discussed by the wider community. It is also necessary to investigate and record the landscape's likely evolution without the development.

6.4.1 Establishing the study area – the ZTV

The project area to be assessed should contain all of the likely significant effects of a proposal on any component of the landscape and visual resource. The term **Zone of Theoretical Visibility** (ZTV) is used to describe the area over which a development can theoretically be seen, and is usually computer generated using Computer Aided Design (CAD) or a Geographic Information System (GIS), based on a digital terrain model (see §14.2.3). This is also sometimes known as a Zone of Visual Influence, or a Visual Envelope Map. The results of a ZTV are usually presented on an Ordnance Survey map base. **Figure 6.1** shows an example of a ZTV for a potential Severn Barrage, produced in ESRI ArcMap 9.2 taking into account the curvature of the earth. The image was produced by

Table 6.1 Guidance for landscape and visual impact assessment

Guidance	When to use it
Guidelines for landscape and visual impact assessment (LI/IEMA 2002)	This is the most general guidance for landscape and visual impact assessment. It contains good practice guidance as well as case studies.
Advice Note 01/04 *Use of photography and photomontage in landscape and visual assessment* (LI 2004)	This guidance should be used if photomontages or visualisations are being prepared to accompany an LVIA.
Design manual for roads and bridges, Vol. 11, *Landscape effects* (DoT 1993)	Although old, this document contains some useful guidance. It should be referred to when assessing a road or bridge scheme.
Transport analysis guidance (TAG) (DfT 2003)	This is the latest advice on transport analysis from the DfT. It includes landscape and townscape sub-objectives. It should be referred to when dealing with transport schemes.
Guidelines on the environmental impacts of windfarms and small scale hydroelectric schemes (SNH 2001)	This guidance should be consulted when assessing windfarms and small-scale hydroelectric schemes.
Visual assessment of windfarms best practice (University of Newcastle 2002)	This guidance should be consulted when assessing windfarm schemes.
Visual representation of windfarms, good practice guidance (SNH 2006)	This guidance should be consulted when assessing windfarm schemes – provides best practice on producing and presenting ZTVs and visualisations such as photomontages.
Guidance: cumulative effect of windfarms, version 2 (SNH 2005)	This guidance should be consulted when assessing the cumulative effects of windfarm schemes.
Guidance on the assessment of the impact of offshore wind farms: seascape and visual impact report (DTI 2005)	This guidance should be consulted when assessing the effects of offshore windfarms, as well as other offshore developments.
An assessment of the sensitivity and capacity of the Scottish seascape in relation to offshore windfarms (Scott *et al.* 2005)	'This guidance should be consulted when assessing the potential effects of offshore windfarms'.
Guide to best practice in seascape assessment (Hill *et al.* 2001)	'This guidance should be consulted when undertaking seascape assessment as part of the baseline for offshore schemes'.

Land Use Consultants on behalf of Natural England and is reproduced here with kind permission of Land Use Consultants and Natural England. The results of the study are for information only and do not reflect or represent Natural England's views on a barrage.

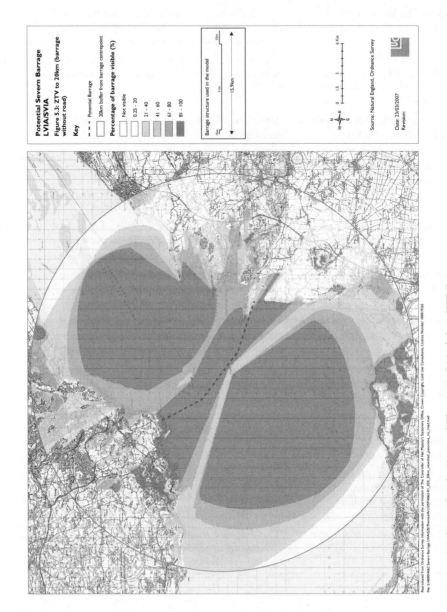

Figure 6.1 Example of a Zone of Theoretical Visibility (ZTV). Reproduced by permission of Ordnance Survey on behalf of HMSO. © Crown copyright 2008. All rights reserved. Ordnance Survey Licence number 100045659.

ZTVs usually show theoretical visibility, based on a "bare ground" terrain model. Actual visibility is often considerably reduced by screening features such as buildings and vegetation. In undulating landscapes it is likely that landform will define the limit of the ZTV; but in flat, open landscapes the ZTV could theoretically extend as far as the curvature of the earth allows. In reality, of course, the extent of visibility will depend on atmospheric conditions and how far the human eye can "see". The extent of visibility will also depend on the size and prominence of the development being considered. The extent of the ZTV should be agreed with the Local Planning Authority, particularly in the case of tall structures such as wind turbines. As a general guide:

- for a wind farm in a remote area in Scotland, it may be necessary to run the ZTV to 30km or beyond;
- 10–20km is usually sufficient for an industrial chimney stack, an industrial building or bridge;
- in urban environments it may not be necessary to consider such distances since buildings are likely to limit the extent of visibility.

In addition, it may be necessary to undertake some visibility studies of existing developments in the same type of landscape to determine the extent of visibility of such features.

Visual significance limits, and how the discernible level of detail of a landscape diminishes with distance, have been investigated further by Hill *et al.* (2001). More information on ZTV generation can be found in LI/IEMA (2002) and SNH (2006).

6.4.2 Landscape baseline

The key aim of the landscape baseline is to identify, describe and evaluate the existing landscape of the site and surrounding area including the individual landscape elements and characteristics that make up the landscape, and how these combine to create landscape character. Landscape designations can be an indicator of the recognised value of a landscape, and the location of landscape designations should be presented, clearly outlining the reasons for their designation.

Desk studies provide the starting point for a landscape assessment. Some useful sources of desktop information are listed below (from LI/IEMA 2002):

- ordnance survey maps;
- national planning policy guidance;
- development plan documents and supplementary planning documents;
- informal planning documents such as countryside strategies and landscape character assessments;
- geology, soils and land use maps, hydrological survey (see Chapters 9 and 10);
- vertical aerial photographs;
- information on landscape designations;

- National Park and AONB management plans;
- data on conservation interests (see Chapters 11 and 12);
- common land and rights of way maps;
- Meteorological Office data;
- site plans including topographical survey, tree condition surveys etc.

These will provide initial information on:

- landscape elements;
- landscape character;
- designated areas;
- other special values and interests.

The **field survey** provides an opportunity to check desk-based information in the field, to gather information on potential landscape receptors and analyse the value or importance of these. As well as addressing landscape character, the description of the landscape should address landscape condition and landscape value.

The **Quality of Life Capital Approach** (see Chapter 15) can also be used as a means of evaluating landscape value. This may include asking a series of questions:

- What benefit does the landscape in each character area provide? Examples include tranquillity, cultural heritage, sense of place, and land cover (e.g. agriculture, semi-natural habitats).
- To whom does the benefit matter, at what scale, and how important is it?
- How rare is the benefit – is there enough of it?
- How could the benefit be substituted?

Baseline mapping should show the location of the development in relation to landscape character areas and landscape designations. Photographs are also useful to illustrate the baseline landscape (including individual landscape elements and landscape character). The results of the baseline evaluation should be presented in a clear and structured way. More guidance on presentation is contained in (LI/IEMA 2002).

6.4.3 Visual baseline

The key aim of the visual baseline is to identify existing visual amenity, and to identify visual receptors, i.e. representative viewpoints and key sensitive viewers.

Desk studies provide the starting point for a visual assessment. Some useful sources of desktop information include the ZTV and OS maps. These will provide initial information on potential receptors and allow the assessor to identify potential representative viewpoints for assessment, as well as highlight potential sensitive visual receptors.

The **field survey** provides an opportunity to test the ZTV, fine-tuning it by considering ground level screening where appropriate. The field survey also provides the opportunity to confirm representative viewpoints in the field, and identify the key sensitive receptors, recording their existing visual amenity.

Representative viewpoints form the basis for the assessment of the potential effect of the proposal on views (LI/IEMA 2002). All viewpoints should be agreed with the Local Planning Authority. The selection of representative viewpoints should:

- have a reasonably high potential number of viewers or be of particular importance to the viewers affected;
- provide a representative range of viewing distances (i.e. short-, medium- and long-range views);
- include the nearest residents and the clearest viewpoints of the site;
- represent a range of viewing experiences (i.e. static views, for example from residential properties, and points along sequential views, for example from roads and footpaths); *and*
- consider any important cultural associations, for example if a site has been painted from a particular point.

Baseline mapping should show the location of representative viewpoints. In addition, photographs should be used to illustrate the existing visual amenity in and around the site, as well as the views from the representative viewpoints.

6.5 Impact prediction

6.5.1 *Overview*

Successful landscape/visual impact assessment involves effectively communicated predictions of the nature, likelihood and significance of changes that may occur as a result of the proposed development, and the incorporation of good project design from the beginning.

6.5.2 *Good project design*

The project's location, dimensions (especially vertical), materials, colour, reflectivity, visible emissions, access routes, traffic volumes and construction programme will all need to be described in the EIS. Good project design and landscape/visual mitigation should be planned in at the start of the project including:

- use of landscape issues as a criterion in the selection of the project site or process (e.g. landfill v. incineration);
- careful siting of major structures, access routes and parking, materials storage etc. in relation to visual receptors, ridgelines/valleys etc.;
- sensitive choice of site levels;
- attention to the density, mix, height and massing of buildings;

- retention of special landscape features and provision of visual/ecological buffer zones;
- consideration of microclimates and the solar aspect of buildings;
- attention to materials used and details such as openings and balconies;
- careful design of open spaces including plantings and fencing; *and*
- enhancement through new wildlife habitats, restoration of derelict land, and the provision of public open space and/or beautiful new landscapes (Barton *et al.* 1995, Hankinson 1999).

Landscape design also has a part to play in other aspects of project design. For instance, it may need to be integrated with water holding facilities, acoustic fencing, or bunding. Turner (1998) suggests other innovative examples of "environmental impact design", including provision of wild food, new footpaths, and conservation farming as part of an integrated approach to project/landscape design. *Circular 5/94 Planning out crime* (DoE 1994b) explains how safety issues can be incorporated in project design.

6.5.3 Landscape impact assessment

The landscape impact assessment should describe the likely nature and scale of changes to landscape receptors (i.e. landscape elements, landscape character types and/or areas and designated landscapes). It is also important to consider how the baseline landscape would change without the development.

First it is necessary to determine **landscape sensitivity**, or the degree to which a particular landscape can accommodate the type of change predicted. The evaluation of the sensitivity of each landscape element should reflect "its quality, value, contribution to landscape character, and the degree to which the particular element or characteristic can be replaced or substituted" (LI/IEMA 2002). Landscape character sensitivity may be recorded in an existing landscape character assessment, or it may be necessary for the assessor to judge landscape sensitivity using techniques set out in *Techniques and criteria for judging capacity and sensitivity* (CA/SNH 2004). In the case of designated landscapes, sensitivity may be determined by considering the characteristics of the area, the reasons for the designation and the policy importance of the designation. The sensitivity and value of landscape receptors are necessarily derived from subjective judgements.

Next it is necessary to assess the **scale, or magnitude, of change** to landscape elements, landscape character types and/or areas and designated landscapes. The changes are likely to vary between different project stages (e.g. construction and operation, or phases of mineral extraction), and between seasons. Where the project involves night-time lighting, this will also need to be considered. The predictions should discuss the duration and timing of impacts, and impacts with and without mitigation.

It is often useful to rank the scale of change into a series of levels, based on the scale or degree of change to the landscape receptor. The LI/IEMA (2002) guidance suggests the categories shown in **Table 6.2**.

Table 6.2 Definition of magnitude of impact on landscape

Magnitude of impact on landscape components/character	Definition
High	An obvious change in landscape components, character and quality of the landscape.
Medium	Discernible but not obvious changes to landscape components, character and quality of the landscape.
Low	Minor change in components, character and quality of the landscape.
No change	No change in landscape components, character and quality of the landscape.

6.5.3 Visual impact assessment

The visual impact assessment should describe the likely nature and scale of changes in views resulting from the development, and the changes in the visual amenity of the visual receptors (LI/IEMA 2002). It is also important to consider how views would change without the development.

Viewpoint sensitivity should be established first. The sensitivity of a viewpoint is dependent upon (LI/IEMA 2002):

- the location and context of the viewpoint;
- the expectations and occupation/activity of the receptor;
- the importance of the view (which may be determined with respect to: its popularity or numbers of people affected; its appearance in guidebooks, on tourist maps, and in the facilities provided for its enjoyment; and references to it in literature or art).

There is an argument that it is not possible for us, as assessors, to predict an individual's interest in their view (and therefore their sensitivity to visual change). Landscape and visual effects can attract emotive public responses, for example from visitors or residents, which should be distinguished from the professional's judgement. Whether visual receptors are identified as representative viewpoints or individual viewers, it is important that the assessor remains objective (LI/IEMA 2002).

In terms of the **scale, or magnitude, of change** to views and visual amenity, the change may be described by reference to (interpreted from LI/IEMA 2002):

- the scale of change in the view with respect to loss or addition of features in the view and changes in its composition;
- the degree of contrast or integration of any new features;
- the duration and nature of the effect;
- the angle of view;

Table 6.3 Definition of magnitude of visual impact

Magnitude of visual impact	Definition
High	The development has a defining influence on the view and becomes a key focus in the view.
Medium	The development is clearly visible in the view and forms an important but not defining element of the view.
Low	The development is visible, but forms a minor element of the view.
No change	The development is not visible.

- the distance of the viewpoint from the proposed development;
- the extent of the area over which changes would be visible.

It is often useful to rank the scale of change into a series of levels. An example is presented at **Table 6.3**.

6.5.4 Illustrating visual effects

Photomontages and other forms of visualisation can be used to illustrate visual effects. Photomontages are illustrations that aim to represent an observer's view of a proposed development. *Visual representations of windfarms: good practice guidance* (SNH 2006) stresses that

> visualisations, whether they are hand drawn sketches, photographs or photomontages can never exactly match what is experienced in the field. Rather, their purpose is either to present technical information on a development that will aid the assessment of impacts on site, or to otherwise provide an image that illustrates the likely nature of these impacts.

For example, photographs do not accurately represent what is seen by the human eye because the human eye can distinguish elements by using a contrast range of about 1,000 shades between black and white, whereas a picture of the same view taken with a camera and shown on a computer screen will use only about 100 shades. This range of contrast is reduced to as low as 12 shades when printed on paper (SNH 2006).

Methods and guidance for the production of photomontages are contained in LI (2004), LI/IEMA (2002) and SNH (2006). The guidance gives detailed advice on issues such as field of view, appropriate camera focal lengths, and presentation of images in EIA.

The **field of view** is used to describe the height and width of a view as represented by an image, expressed as an angle in degrees. Although a human has a horizontal field of view of about 200°, only a small part of this will be in focus at any one time (6–10°) (SNH 2005). In terms of **focal length**, a 50mm focal length lens on a 35mm film camera is considered to be a good compromise (LI/IEMA 2002), balancing detail with field of view. In the **presentation** of photomontages, the size of paper required to illustrate visualisations will depend on the field of view of the photograph, the required image height, how many images are required to fit on each sheet, and the viewing distance of the paper.

Past convention has been to present visualisations in the EIS as a triple arrangement comprising a photograph of the existing view at the top of the page, a corresponding wireline diagram in the middle of the page, and the photomontage at the bottom of the page (see **Figure 6.2**). However, SNH (2006) guidance requires photomontages of windfarms to be at comfortable "viewing distance" (viewing distance is the distance at which the image should be viewed to provide a representation of the "real life view"). SNH recommend a viewing distance of at least 300mm and it may be necessary to produce photomontages on paper larger than A3, or to provide larger images on separate A3 pages to meet these good practice recommendations.

Technology is moving forward all the time and new tools and techniques are being introduced, such as video montage, animation and virtual reality. Video montages are expensive to produce and are rarely used, but animated photomontages are becoming more popular in schemes involving moving features, such as wind turbines.

6.5.5 Significance of effects

The severity (or significance) of effect depends on both the magnitude of change (impact) and the sensitivity of the receptor. A higher level of significance is generally attached to large-scale impacts on sensitive or high-value receptors. There are no quantitative criteria for assessing the significance of landscape/visual effects, and the appraisal is normally carried out using professional judgement. **Figure 6.3** represents the process by which the significance of effects is determined.

The levels of significance are used to standardise the results of the assessment. Usually, any major/substantial or moderate effect is considered to be significant for the purposes of the EIA, although this is not set out in any guidance and levels of significance are determined for each project by the landscape assessor. In order to comply with the Regulations the assessor should highlight those effects that are permanent and those that are temporary (including seasonal). It is worth noting that effects arising from construction are not always temporary and effects arising from the operational stage are not always permanent.

6.5.6 Assessing cumulative effects

The EU Directive on EIA (Directive 97/11/EC on the assessment of the effects of certain public and private projects on the environment) requires an analysis of cumulative effects. Cumulative effects can be defined as:

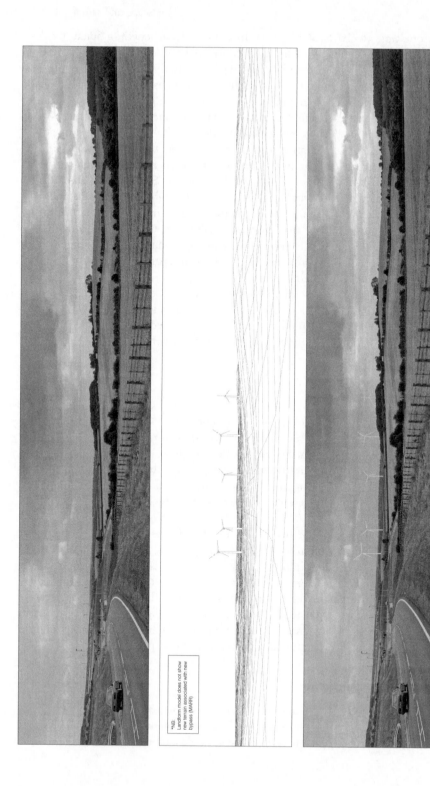

Figure 6.2 Example of a triple arrangement photomontage.
This photomontage is copyright of npower renewables limited and is reproduced here with kind permission of npower renewables limited and Land Use Consultants.

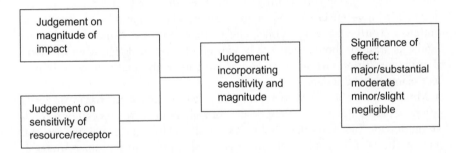

Figure 6.3 Determination of significance of effects.

landscape and visual effects [that] result from additional changes to the landscape or visual amenity caused by the proposed development in conjunction with other developments (associated with or separate to it), or actions that occurred in the past, present or are likely to occur in the foreseeable future.

(LI/IEMA 2002)

A cumulative effect may occur when developments are seen in combination when standing at a viewpoint and looking in one direction, or in succession when standing at a viewpoint and looking in different directions. A cumulative effect may also occur as a sequential experience, when moving through the landscape. Cumulative effects may also be perceived gradually, developing over time.

Cumulative landscape and visual assessment (CLVIA) should identify significant effects which are the result of introducing the development into the landscape in combination with other existing developments and developments not yet present. Although both CLVIA and LVIA look at the effects of a proposed development on views and landscape character of the surrounding area, there is a difference in the condition of the baseline on which the assessment is carried out. For LVIA, the baseline is the existing landscape – this is a relatively fixed baseline that is clearly and easily defined. For CLVIA, the baseline is to some extent uncertain, and is partially speculative. This is because other developments considered may include not only those already existing in the landscape, but also those subject to planning applications, whose outcomes are not yet determined.

Methodologies for cumulative landscape and visual impact assessment are currently still being developed. Brief guidance on the assessment of cumulative effects is provided in LI/IEMA (2002); more detailed guidance, specifically focussing on the cumulative assessment of windfarms is given in ODPM (2004c), and SNH (2005).

6.6 Mitigation and enhancement

The purpose of mitigation is to avoid, reduce and where possible remedy or offset, significant negative (adverse) effects on the environment arising from the proposed development (LI/IEMA 2002). As discussed earlier, good project design is a more effective, and often cheaper, way to minimise negative and optimise positive landscape/visual effects than post-hoc "landscaping". The landscape assessor should therefore be part of a landscape design team to ensure that the mitigation measures are designed as part of an iterative process of project planning and design.

Mitigation may be described as primary mitigation (measures that intrinsically comprise part of the development design through an iterative process) or secondary mitigation (measures designed to specifically address the remaining residual adverse effects of the final development proposals). There are four main strategies for mitigation – avoidance, reduction, remediation and compensation (LI/IEMA 2002). Some common mitigation measures include:

- sensitive location and siting;
- site layout;
- choice of site level;
- appropriate form, materials and design of any built structures;
- lighting;
- ground modelling;
- planting;
- use of camouflage or disguise.

Figure 6.4 shows an example of a landscape mitigation plan produced by Land Use Consultants as part of an assessment of a proposed marina. This image is reproduced with kind permission of Land Use Consultants, Cascade Consulting, Lewin Fryer and Partners, and Gwynedd Council.

It is good practice to consider **landscape enhancement** in addition to landscape mitigation. Landscape enhancement is an opportunity for the development to contribute positively to the landscape and may include enhancing landscape quality and character through meeting landscape management objectives for the area, restoring historic landscapes, restoring habitats or features, or reclaiming derelict land.

6.7 Monitoring

Monitoring is gradually being recognised as an essential element in environmental management and EIA, particularly where initial predictions of landscape effects and/or the effectiveness of proposed mitigation measures are uncertain. Monitoring procedures may be enforced through planning conditions to monitor whether the predicted effects occur and whether any unforeseen effects arise; and to ensure mitigation measures are implemented and that they are effective in avoiding or reducing the predicted adverse effects. Monitoring also provides a learning experience, which may feed directly into other projects, or provide feedback on the success of assessment techniques. The developer and regulatory authority have a joint responsibility for monitoring and should both benefit from

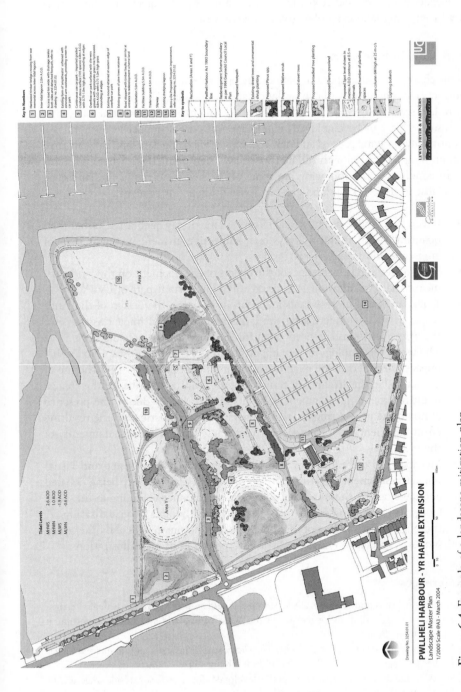

the experience – the developer by ensuring a successful project, and the authority by ensuring landscape objectives are achieved.

6.8 Concluding issues

This chapter has attempted to define concepts relevant to landscape and visual impact assessment, describe how landscape and visual data are collected and how landscape and visual effects are predicted, and highlight potential mitigation measures that can be employed. Landscape and visual impact assessment is a continually evolving process and new techniques are being developed all the time. Limitations associated with the methods have been pointed out where relevant.

In conclusion, the following are some of the key concerns of the landscape specialist in undertaking landscape and visual impact assessment.

- Given that landscape and visual effects are inevitably qualitative, rather than quantitative, there must always be a **subjective element** in the analysis of landscape and visual effects.
- The greater public awareness of the effects of development on the landscape means that **consultation** is an increasingly important part of LVIA.
- Since landscape professionals are often involved in the design of the landscape, as well as undertaking the landscape and visual impact assessment, the assessment must proceed as an **integral part of the scheme design**.
- The use of **terminology** is very important in the field of landscape and visual impact assessment. One example of commonly confused terms is the use of impact and effect. In simplest terms, "impact" may be described as the change resulting from a development (e.g. blocking of a view due to the presence of hoardings at construction) and "effect" may be described as the resulting effect experienced by the receptor (e.g. the effect on the visual amenity of the viewer).
- Methods and techniques for undertaking **cumulative landscape and visual impact assessment** are still relatively new, and are currently being debated and developed – there is likely to be further guidance emerging in this area.
- Continued development is to be expected in the area of **visualisation**. A thorough understanding of the limitations of photomontages and other techniques is crucial to ensure realistic interpretation of such illustrations.

References

Barton H, G Davis and R Guise 1995. *Sustainable settlements: a guide for planners, designers and developers*. Luton: University of the West of England and Local Government Management Board.

CA (Countryside Agency) 1998–1999. *The character of England's natural and man-made landscape*. Regional Guides, Vols 1–8. Cheltenham, Glos: Countryside Agency.

CA 2002. *Landscape typology (England)*, developed for the Countryside Agency by Steven Warnock, in conjunction with the Living Landscape Project and Entec Ltd., www.magic.gov.uk/datadoc/metadata.asp?dataset=31.

CA/SNH (Countryside Agency and Scottish Natural Heritage) 2002a. *Landscape character assessment guidance for England and Scotland*. CAX 84. Countryside Agency, Cheltenham, Glos, www.countryside.gov.uk/LAR/Landscape/CC/landscape/LCATopicPaper.asp.

CA/SNH 2002b. *Landscape character assessment guidance for England and Scotland. Topic Paper 1: Recent practice and the evolution of landscape character assessment*, www.countryside.gov.uk/LAR/Landscape/CC/landscape/LCATopicPaper.asp.

CA/SNH 2004. *Landscape character assessment guidance for England and Scotland – Topic Paper 6: Techniques and criteria for judging capacity and sensitivity*, www.countryside.gov.uk/LAR/Landscape/CC/landscape/LCATopicPaper.asp.

CC (Countryside Commission) 1987. *Landscape assessment: a Countryside Commission approach* (CCP 18). Cheltenham, Glos: Countryside Commission.

CC 1993. *Landscape assessment guidance*, CCP423. Cheltenham, Glos: Countryside Commission.

CC/EN (Countryside Agency and English Nature) 1996. *The character of England – landscape, wildlife and natural features* (Map/Leaflet). CCX 41. Cheltenham, Glos: Countryside Commission.

CCS (Countryside Commission for Scotland) 1991. *Landscape assessment principles and practice*, Edinburgh: CCS.

CCW (Countryside Council for Wales) 2001, updated 2003. *LANDMAP Information System Manual*, http://landmap.ccw.gov.uk/files/CCW_FinalPDFEng%5B1%5D.pdf.

COE (Council of Europe) 2000. *The European Landscape Convention*, Florence, 20 October, www.coe.int/t/dg4/cultureheritage/Conventions/Landscape/default_en.asp.

CPRE (Campaign to Protect Rural England) 2005. *Mapping tranquillity*. www.cpre.org.uk/library/results/tranquillity.

DfT (Department for Transport) 2003. *Transport Analysis Guidance (TAG)*, www.webtag.org.uk/webdocuments/3_Expert/3_Environment_Objective/index.htm.

DoE (Department of the Environment) 1994a. *Planning Policy Guidance 15 (PPG15): Planning and the historic environment* London: HMSO, www.communities.gov.uk/publications/planningandbuilding/planningpolicyguidance8.

DoE 1994b. *Circular 5/94 Planning out crime*. London: HMSO.

DOE (Northern Ireland) 1999. *Northern Ireland landscape character assessment series*. Belfast: DOE, www.ehsni.gov.uk/landscape/country_landscape.htm.

DoT (Department of Transport, now DfT) 1993. *Design manual for roads and bridges (DMRB)*, Vol. 11: *Environmental assessment*, Section 3, Part 5: *Landscape effects*. London: HMSO, www.standardsforhighways.co.uk/dmrb/vol11/section3/11s3p05.pdf.

DTI (Department of Trade and Industry) 2005. *Guidance on the assessment of the impact of offshore wind farms: seascape and visual impact report*. London: DTI, www.berr.gov.uk/files/file22852.pdf.

Hankinson M 1999. Landscape and visual impact assessment. In *Handbook of environmental impact assessment*, Vol. 1. J Petts (ed.), Ch. 16. Oxford: Blackwell Science.

Hill M, J Briggs, P Minto, D Bagnall, K Foley and A Williams 2001. *Guide to best practice in seascape assessment*. Maritime Ireland/Wales INTERREG 1994–1999, https://marine.ie/NR/rdonlyres/683C8CD0-3367-4704-8542-D3091607C9C2/0/interreg5_1.pdf.

Landscape Character Network 2008. *Database*, www.landscapecharacter.org.uk/db/index.html.

LI (Landscape Institute) 2004. *Use of photography and photomontage in landscape and visual assessment*, Advice Note 01/04. London: Landscape Institute.

LI/IEMA (Landscape Institute and Institute of Environmental Management and Assessment) 2002. *Guidelines for landscape and visual impact assessment*, 2nd edn. London: Spon Press.

ODPM (Office of the Deputy Prime Minister) 2004a. *Planning Policy Statement 7 (PPS7): Sustainable development in rural areas*. London: ODPM, www.communities.gov.uk/documents/planningandbuilding/pdf/147402.

ODPM 2004b. *Planning Policy Statement 22 (PPS22): Renewable energy* www.communities.gov.uk/documents/planningandbuilding/pdf/147444.

ODPM 2004c. *Planning for renewable energy: a companion guide to PPS22*, www.communities.gov.uk/documents/planningandbuilding/pdf/147447.

Scott KE, C Anderson, H Dunsford, JF Benson and R MacFarlane 2005. *An assessment of the sensitivity and capacity of the Scottish seascape in relation to offshore windfarms*, Scottish Natural Heritage Commissioned Report No. 103 (ROAME No. F03AA06), www.snh.org.uk/pdfs/publications/commissioned_reports/F03AA06.pdf.

SNH (Scottish Natural Heritage) 1999. *National Planning Policy Guidance 14:Natural Heritage*. Edinburgh: SNH, www.scotland.gov.uk/Publications/1999/01/nppg14.

SNH 2001. *Guidelines on the environmental impacts of windfarms and small scale hydroelectric schemes*: SNH Natural Heritage Management Series. Edinburgh: SNH, www.snh.org.uk/pubs/results.asp?o=title&c=-1&id=108.

SNH 2003. *Policy Statement No. 02/03 Wildness in Scotland's countryside*. Edinburgh: SNH, www.snh.org.uk/strategy/pd02c.asp.

SNH 2005. *Guidance: Cumulative effects of windfarms*. Edinburgh: SNH, www.snh.org.uk/pdfs/strategy/Cumulativeeffectsonwindfarms.pdf.

SNH 2006. *Visual representation of windfarms: good practice guidance*. Edinburgh: SNH, www.snh.org.uk/pdfs/publications/heritagemanagement/Visual%20Representation%20of%20windfarms%20-%20excerpt.pdf.

Therivel R and B Goodey 2001. Landscape. In *Methods of Environmental Impact Assessment*, 2nd edn. Morris P and R Therivel (eds), 105–121. London: Spon Press.

Turner T 1998. *Landscape planning and environmental impact design*, 2nd edn. London: UCL Press.

University of Newcastle 2002. *Visual assessment of windfarms: best practice*, Scottish Natural Heritage Commissioned Report F01AA303A, www.snh.org.uk/pdfs/publications/commissioned_reports/f01aa303a.pdf.

7 Heritage

Riki Therivel
(based on Grover and Therivel 2001)

7.1 Introduction

Europe has known some 500,000 years of human activity and settlement, from the earliest hunter-gatherers to the present day. As a result, almost all sites on mainland Britain have had previous human occupation and are therefore of potential historical interest. The study of archaeological and other historical resources is important to (a) fulfil an innate curiosity about the past, since the origins and development, lifestyles, economy and industry of previous generations can be traced and understood through archaeological remains; (b) contribute to the sense of tradition and culture; and (c) promote a sense of national identity.

Archaeology is a vital component of recreation, since many people enjoy visiting archaeological sites and studying archaeological remains. It contributes to education; archaeological study is used as a basis for integrating the teaching of a number of other subjects, and can promote an understanding of the role of the past and its relevance to today's society. Britain's historic heritage is also important to the tourism industry. It attracts visitors from all over the world and, if well interpreted and presented it can be an important financial asset.

However, archaeological and other historical remains are a fragile and finite resource that needs to be carefully managed and conserved, and are therefore one of the many elements that need to be addressed in any EIA. On most sites these remains are not important enough to affect development, but a site's historical and cultural interest is always monitored by planning authorities, and EIAs should show that it has been considered.

7.2 Definitions and concepts

7.2.1 Overview

The EIA Directive requires EISs to identify, describe and assess a proposed project's impacts on "material assets and the cultural heritage", and their interaction with other factors such as landscape and fauna and flora, but what exactly this means remains open to interpretation. The UK government's good practice guidance on EIA recommends that an EIS should describe the "effects of the development on buildings, the architectural and historic heritage, archaeological features, and other human artefacts" (DCLG 2006). The general requirement to consider such aspects ensures that an EIA is comprehensive and that issues of strong local feeling or wider social and cultural heritage are considered. Some EIAs have interpreted material assets very widely, including e.g. agriculture, forestry plantations, recreation and amenity, utilities and other services, communications, rights of way, and potential future resources. However, here material and cultural assets together are taken to be:

- archaeological remains, both above and below ground, i.e. buried remains and standing buildings;
- historic buildings and sites (including listed buildings, cemeteries and burial grounds, parks, gardens, village greens, bridges and canals);
- historic areas (including towns and villages in whole or in part – often designated as conservation areas);
- other structures of architectural or historic merit; and
- historic landscapes.

In practice, there is no precise distinction between archaeology and other aspects of the historic environment. For instance English Heritage (EH), which is responsible for the major archaeological sites in England, is alternatively known as the Historic Buildings and Monuments Commission. Academic historians are concerned with the past on the basis of written evidence (in the UK, effectively from Roman times), while archaeologists use a much wider range of evidence and therefore may go back to the earliest human occupation (in the UK, perhaps 500,000 years ago to the Second World War). The legislation covering the historic environment is (at the time of writing) a patchwork of regulations and guidance, which draws an arbitrary distinction between archaeology and ancient monuments on the one hand, and other aspects of the historic built environment such as listed buildings and conservation areas on the other. This chapter broadly follows the current legislative distinction, so each section discusses first archaeology and then historic buildings and sites. The historic landscape is discussed where appropriate. However this distinction is not always clear in practice and may not be applicable to all EIAs. Architectural and historic merit is also addressed in Chapter 6 on landscape.

7.2.2 Archaeology

The range of archaeological evidence reflects the diversity of human experience; the need for water, food and shelter, the use of changing technologies, and the religious, cultural and political needs of society. The physical remains of human activity and endeavour are known as the archaeological resource. These remains range in size and complexity from individual objects used and discarded, to settlements. They include many details in the landscape which itself is the product of human use and adaptation of the natural environment. The physical evidence may survive as earthworks such as burial mounds, hillforts, field banks and lynchets (a type of earth bank). They can also survive as structures such as buildings, canals, bridges and roads.

However, the majority of the archaeological resource is smaller and often hidden below ground, surviving as features such as pits, postholes, gullies and ditches cut into the subsoil. Very often the evidence is in the form of artefacts, like coins, pottery sherds, stone tools and metal objects. Archaeological remains lie below many of the buildings and streets of British cities and towns. Over 600,000 archaeological sites are presently known in the UK, or about 200 per parish. The archaeological record is the sum of present archaeological knowledge, i.e. that part of the archaeological resource which has been identified to date. **Table 7.1** summarises the principal archaeological periods and likely remains from these periods.

The rich pattern of archaeological remains that can be seen today is the result of the impact of successive generations on the remains left by previous generations. This process involves a degree of damage and destruction, which is an inevitable part of the evolution of the archaeological record. However the current threat to the archaeological resource is more significant than in the past due to the technological changes and the rapid increase in development that has occurred particularly since the Second World War. Today the archaeological record is more likely to be deleted than altered or added to. Land which

Table 7.1 Principal archaeological periods and likely remains (based on HA 2007a)

Period	Dates	Likely remains
Prehistoric	earliest Palaeolithic (~500,000 BC) to 43 AD	from early rock shelters and stone artefacts to the circles, barrows, Celtic field patterns, farmsteads, villages and hillforts of the Late Iron Age
Roman	43 AD to 410 AD	native and immigrant farms, Roman towns and cities, military forts, roads
Medieval	5th–16th centuries	origins of most modern towns (e.g. postholes from wooden buildings, masonry), Norman castles, deserted villages, ridge and furrow agriculture
Post-medieval	late 16th to early 18th centuries	Civil War constructions, beginnings of industrial-scale extraction and manufacture, country houses and their parks and gardens
Industrial	mid-18th century onwards	buildings and infrastructure linked with industrialisation, industrial relics
Post-industrial	World Wars	defences, e.g. pillboxes

has been marginal since prehistory has, with the use of modern machinery and chemicals, become viable for arable farming, with the resultant damage by ploughing and soil erosion. The increase in road building, housing and industrial developments and the need for materials for their construction continually depletes the archaeological resource. Already in some areas, post-war gravel extraction has been so extensive that the ability to understand the evolution of the landscape has been badly reduced. As a result of high land prices in towns, there is now a prevalence of deep basementing, below-ground carparks and substantial foundations to support high buildings. In some historic centres only a small proportion of the archaeological resource remains intact.

The significance of archaeological finds is derived both from the nature of the finds themselves in their contexts and from the interpretation archaeologists are able to put on them given contemporary understanding. While the ability to learn about the past is based on the investigation and interpretation of archaeological remains, this investigation often results in the destruction of the archaeological resource being studied. Archaeological excavation aims to dismantle remains to their constituent parts in order to understand the processes by which they were formed (see §7.4.1). This work is closely documented, with all the elements drawn and photographed and the objects which are found removed and conserved. Although this enables future study and reinterpretation of the results, the site cannot actually be reconstructed. However archaeology is an evolving study and is constantly harnessing new technologies, techniques, procedures and theories. Preserving archaeological remains for future study is therefore important. Just as archaeologists today can learn substantially more from the archaeological resource than their counterparts of yesterday, so preserving a site in situ for future archaeologists will allow even more information to be gained. In addition the more visible sites that are used for tourism, recreation and education need to be preserved and conserved. While the preservation of all remains would be impractical, and would lead to the stagnation of archaeology, the case for the preservation of the archaeological resource must always be carefully considered.

7.2.3 Historic buildings and sites

Historic buildings form the most visible and tangible of all aspects of the historic environment. They are a finite resource and cannot undergo change without cultural loss. The careful appraisal of their history and condition, together with their protection through effective policies and careful professional practice, can lead to improved decisions concerning their conservation. Three main sources of judgement apply to changes to the character of buildings, deriving from the disciplines of archaeology, architecture and architectural history.

In practice **listed buildings** should be seen as part of the wider historic environment which also includes archaeological remains. Unfortunately judgements on changes affecting listed buildings have often tended to focus purely on visual character rather than on a deeper appreciation of the intrinsic value of inherited or historically important building fabric. This emphasis on architectural character has in the past tended to give rise to facadism and imitative architectural styles, often of mediocre quality. A greater understanding of the impact of intervention by developers and a wider appreciation of the concept of stewardship on the part of building owners and local authorities needs to be encouraged if the special architectural and historic interest is to be properly safeguarded.

As well as individual buildings, the visible historic environment can be defined in terms of areas. Important groups/ensembles of historic buildings, perhaps encompassing the core of a historic city or town, or indeed a whole settlement, are now recognised as important elements of the wider historic environment. Areas of special architectural or historic interest are frequently designated as **conservation areas**, and in many respects their management should be seen as analogous to that of historic buildings. Conservation areas come in many forms but are typically characterised by important groups of historic buildings (not necessarily listed) based around a historic street pattern often with important urban squares or green spaces containing features such as mature trees. In the UK, designated conservation areas account for some 4 per cent of the built environment.

7.2.4 Historic landscapes

A more recent trends has been to also describe, assess and place greater value on **historic landscapes**, since "the whole of the landscape, to varying degrees and in different ways, is an archaeological and historic artefact, the product of complex historic processes and past land uses" (DCLG 2007). Historic seascapes may be equally important, having been used as sites for fishing, transport and trade over centuries, as well as sometimes being the sites of wrecks (CCW 2007). Elements and features of historic landscapes can also be ecologically important, for instance traditional hay meadows, ancient woodlands and clawdds (stone-faced earth banks) and hedgerows (CCW 2007).

Listed buildings, conservation areas and historic landscapes provide valuable points of reference in a rapidly changing world as well as representing the familiar and cherished local scene. Together, they form a distinctive and finite part of the nation's cultural heritage. Development affecting this resource therefore needs careful management, and EIAs must include a full assessment of the particular value of the features in question.

7.3 Legislative background and interest groups

7.3.1 Archaeology

The principal legislation protecting the archaeological resource in England, Wales and Scotland is the *Ancient Monuments and Archaeological Areas Act 1979*. The equivalent legislation in Northern Ireland is the *Historic Monuments and Archaeological Object (NI) Order 1995*. In addition, the *Town and Country Planning Act 1990* and its Scottish equivalent (1997) affords protection to archaeological sites through the statutory planning process. The acts provides legislative protection to a selection of archaeological sites or monuments which have been identified as being of national importance and included within schedules maintained by the heritage agencies (see §7.3.5). These are consequently referred to as **Scheduled Ancient Monuments**. The *National Heritage Act 2002* expands the definition of ancient monuments to also include monuments under the seabed. English Heritage's Monuments Protection Programme reviews and evaluates England's archaeological resource, and recommends monuments that should be scheduled.

Any works to, or within, a Scheduled Ancient Monument likely to damage that monument require the prior consent of the Secretary of State; this consent is referred to as Scheduled Monuments Consent. Where consent is issued it is frequently subject to conditions to prevent damage or to limit damage to agreed levels and with appropriate archaeological recording. Unauthorised works which damage a Scheduled Ancient Monument are a criminal offence, and significant penalties exist. The act also protects the setting of such monuments.

The Town and Country Planning Acts enable local planning authorities (LPAs) to protect a wide range of archaeological remains through the planning process. Where development threatens to destroy remains, the authority can require appropriate investigation through a planning condition or legal agreement. In certain circumstances it can also secure the positive long-term management of sites. These provisions are usually expressed in the policies relating to archaeology within development plans.

The impact of development on archaeology has been recognised as a material consideration within the planning system for some time. Policy Guidance Note 16 *Archaeology and planning* (DoE 1990) describes how archaeological matters are to be dealt with in the English planning system. PPG 16 is therefore an extremely useful and important reference document and should be carefully considered when preparing an EIA. Broadly PPG 16 requires LPAs to acquire sufficient information to enable the full impact of a development to be considered. These powers had already been frequently used for the archaeological resource but were formalised by the EIA regulations. Accordingly, the manner in which archaeological considerations are already dealt with in the planning system is closely akin to the requirements of EIAs. PPG 16's equivalents in the other devolved administrations are:

- Wales: Welsh Office Circular 60/96 *Planning and the historic environment – archaeology*;
- Scotland: National Planning Policy Guidance 5: *Archaeology and planning*; and
- Northern Ireland: Planning Policy Statement 6: *Planning, archaeology and the built heritage.*

7.3.2 Historic buildings and sites

The principal legislation governing the protection of historic buildings and sites in England and Wales is the *Planning (Listed Buildings and Conservation Areas)*

Act 1990, part of which has been superseded by the DCLG's (2007) *Revisions to principles of selection for listed buildings*. Parallel legislation exists for other parts of the UK in the form of the *Planning (Listed Buildings and Conservation Areas) (Scotland) Act 1997* and the *Planning (Northern Ireland) Order 1991*. For England, further central government guidance is to be found in Planning Policy Guidance Note 15, *Planning and the historic environment* (PPG15) which describes Government policies for the identification and protection of historic buildings, conservation areas and other elements of the historic environment (DoE/ DCMS 1994). PPG 15's equivalents in the other devolved administrations are:

- Wales: Welsh Office Circular 61/96 *Planning and the historic environment – historic buildings and conservation areas*;
- Scotland: National Planning Policy Guidance 18: *Planning and the historic environment*; and Historic Scotland's extremely comprehensive *Memorandum of guidance on listed buildings and conservation areas 1998*; and
- Northern Ireland: Planning Policy Statement 6: *Planning, archaeology and the built heritage*.

Listed buildings

A listed building is one which has been included in a list compiled by central government as being of "special architectural or historic interest". Listed buildings are graded to indicate their relative importance: Grade I buildings are of exceptional or outstanding interest, Grade II* are particularly important and of more than special interest, and Grade II are of special interest and warrant every effort being made to preserve them. Slightly different grades apply to Scotland and Northern Ireland.

A developer cannot demolish, alter or extend any listed building in a way that affects its architectural or historic character unless listed building consent has been obtained from the LPA, and listed buildings must be taken into account when LPAs land-use planning decisions. A small team of specialist investigators from EH identifies buildings to be listed: this method echoes that earlier employed for compiling schedules under the Ancient Monuments Acts 1882. In England about 450,000 individual buildings are protected by listing, accounting for some 2 per cent of the building stock. EH's proposals are closely scrutinised by the Secretary of State before confirmation, and similar scrutiny is applied to proposals by the other UK heritage agencies. Theoretically, listing applies to the whole of a property's curtilage, including objects and structures fixed to the building, although a detailed evaluation is needed to make a judgement about those features that are of worthwhile architectural or historic significance.

In choosing buildings for the list, the Secretary of State applies the following statutory criteria: (a) architectural interest by virtue of design, decoration, craftsmanship, building type and technique (e.g. displaying technological innovation or virtuosity), and significant plan forms; and (b) historic interest e.g.

illustrating important aspects of the nation's social, economic, cultural or military history; or close historical association with nationally important people or events. The building's "group value" may also be considered, where buildings comprise an important architectural or historic unity or a fine example of planning (e.g. squares, terraces or model villages). Similar, but slightly differing principles have been established in other parts of the UK.

In turn, "interest" can relate to the building's age and rarity, aesthetic merits, selectivity, and national interest. It does not take into account the building's state of repair. In terms of **age and rarity**, the heritage agencies list:

- all buildings built before 1700 which survive in anything like their original condition;
- most buildings between 1700 and 1840, though selection is necessary;
- after 1840 only buildings of definite quality and character;
- less than 30 years old, only buildings of exceptional quality under threat.

Aesthetic merits refer to the appearance of a building – its intrinsic architectural merit and any group value, as well as aspects not obviously related to external visual quality such as technological innovation or whether it illustrates particular aspects of social or economic history. **Selectivity** refers to the fact that a building may be listed primarily because it represents a particular historical type, so as to ensure that examples of such a type are preserved. Only the most representative or significant examples of the type are likely to be listed. Buildings may also be listed because of their **national interest**: they may not be the strongest architectural specimens, but they may illustrate important distinctive local or regional traditions or localised industries; for instance, shoemaking in Northamptonshire (DCLG 2007).

LPAs are responsible for determining the majority of proposals affecting listed buildings. Decisions are made in accordance with national legislation, statutory local policy and in the context of central government guidance. However, there is considerable variation in the strength and quality of the protection afforded to listed buildings over the nation as a whole. Consequently, EIAs need to consider the policies of county and district councils as well as national legislation.

If an LPA considers a non-listed building to be of special architectural or historic interest and in danger of demolition or significant alteration, it can serve a Building Preservation Notice, which effectively lists the building for six months; this allows the Secretary of State to determine whether the building should be included in the statutory list or not. This is however an infrequently used power since compensation is payable in the event of the Notice not being upheld by the Secretary of State.

Conservation areas

According to the Planning (Listed Buildings and Conservation Areas) Act 1990 and parallel legislation outside England, conservation areas are sections of land or buildings designated by LPAs as being "of special architectural or historic interest, the character or appearance of which it is desirable to preserve or enhance". LPAs must have regard to conservation areas when exercising their planning functions, and conservation area consent must be obtained from the LPA before a building within a conservation area can be demolished. The legislation and associated guidance encourages the involvement of local communities through conservation area advisory committees.

Conservation areas have proved to be a popular and positive element of town planning since the passing of the original enabling legislation in 1967. There are now over 8,000 conservation areas in England. It is the quality and interest of whole areas rather than individual buildings that is the prime concern of conservation areas. There is no standard specification for conservation areas. DoE Circular 8/87 has been superseded by PPG15, but it did contain some useful guidance which is still of relevance in defining conservation areas:

> [They] will naturally be of many different kinds. They may be large or small, from whole town centres to squares, terraces and smaller groups of buildings. They will often be centred on listed buildings, but not always. Pleasant groups of other buildings, open spaces, trees, an historic street pattern, a village green or features of historic or archaeological interest may also contribute to the special character of an area.
>
> (DoE 1987)

There is no specific national legislation addressing the **World Heritage Sites** promoted by the UNESCO Convention for the Protection of the World Cultural and Natural Heritage; their protection lies in the importance given to them within the planning process and through policies relating to the development plans.

7.3.3 Historic landscapes

EH maintains a *Register of parks and gardens of special historic interest in England*, namely sites which are regarded as an essential part of the nation's heritage. The register grades parks and gardens from Grade I of exceptional interest, to Grade II of special interest. These sites are not afforded statutory protection, but are protected by recognition of their importance through the planning system, and policies relating to them in development plans. Historic Scotland and Scottish Natural Heritage compile a similar *Inventory of gardens and designed landscapes in Scotland*, and the Environment and Heritage Services compiles the *Register of parks, gardens and demesnes of special historical interest for Northern Ireland*.

The historic landscapes of England are considered as part of the Countryside Character Map (CA 1998–1999) and English Heritage's *Atlas of rural settlement in England* (Roberts and Wrathmell 2000). English Heritage also piloted five historic seascapes in 2004–2007, and is currently (2008) in the process of devising a methodology for characterising historic seascapes. Cadw has compiled a Wales-wide *Register of landscapes of outstanding historic interest,* as well as registers of landscapes, parks and gardens of special historic interest for several Welsh counties. It has also produced guidance on how these can be used in the planning and development process (Cadw 2007): landscapes on the registers are a material consideration in planning in Wales.

7.3.4 White Paper on Heritage Protection

The recent White Paper on *Heritage Protection for the 21st Century* (DCMS/ WAG, 2007) aimed to counter some of the complexities and inconsistencies due to the multiple different forms of legislation and guidance discussed above. It recommended that a unified legislative framework for heritage protection be developed, that removes the current distinctions between the designation and management of buildings and archaeological remains, and between the urban and rural heritage; and that a single system of national designation and consents be developed to reflect this. It also aimed to maximise opportunities for inclusion and involvement in heritage protection, and to put the historic environment at the heart of the planning system.

A Heritage Protection Bill which implements the findings of the White Paper is in the draft legislative programme for 2008/09. It would streamline the planning consent process, with a new heritage asset consent replacing listed building consent and scheduled monument consent, and conservation area consent merged with planning permission.

7.3.5 Interest groups and sources of information

The heritage agencies are English Heritage (EH) in England, Cadw in Wales, Historic Scotland (HS) in Scotland and the Environment and Heritage Service (EHS) in Northern Ireland (see Appendix B). They advise the Secretaries of State on Scheduled Ancient Monuments and other archaeological, historical and heritage matters; compile and maintain the lists of Scheduled Ancient Monuments and listed buildings; and administer the most important sites. HS and EHS also fulfil many of the roles of the local authority archaeologists.

In respect of sites of known or potential archaeological interest the local authority archaeologist, or the equivalent officer in unitary authorities, should be involved early in the EIA process. They advise on the care of archaeological sites, maintain *Historic environment records* (see §7.4.1), screen planning applications for archaeological impacts, and make recommendations to the planning committee. They will be able to make a rapid initial assessment (see §7.4.1) and suggest professional contacts (e.g. members of the Institute of Field Archaeologists with local knowledge and experience) if further specialist knowledge is required. In England each county has its own archaeologist, as do most unitary authorities and some district councils. In London the role of the local authority archaeologists is fulfilled by EH. In many local authorities the Museum Service works closely with the local authority archaeologists.

In respect of listed buildings and conservation areas the local conservation officers should be involved early in the EIA process. They have specific detailed knowledge of historic buildings and conservation areas within their jurisdiction and are usually the principal advisers to the local planning committee in relation to proposals likely to have an impact on the historic environment. Most local authorities now have at least one conservation officer and some have small specialist teams.

In many areas local history or amenity societies have detailed local knowledge and take active interest in anything that affects their area. Local planning authorities must consult the national amenity societies when the demolition of a listed building is proposed. In practice, the societies are also consulted when more ordinary changes are proposed, as their expertise is substantial and unique. The advisory societies are the Ancient Monuments Society, the Society for the Protection of Ancient Buildings (SPAB), the Georgian Group, the Victorian Society, the Council for British Archaeology (CBA), and the Twentieth Century Society. Local amenity societies are more ephemeral; planning authorities maintain lists of societies in their localities which they consult over changes to listed buildings. The archaeologists' professional body is the Institute of Field Archaeologists (IFA); they publish lists of their members and their specialisations. The equivalent body for conservation officers and their counterparts in English Heritage, Cadw and Historic Scotland is the Institute of Historic Building Conservation (IHBC). The internet addresses of the above organisations are given in Appendix A.

7.4 Scoping and baseline studies

7.4.1 Archaeology

The aim of a baseline study is to identify and describe the nature, location and extent, period(s) and importance of the archaeological resources likely to be affected by the development. The resulting report should include:

- a summary of the archaeological context;
- an inventory of archaeological assets found both at the site and in the wider area likely to be affected by the development;
- an evaluation of these assets;
- an informed expectation of potential assets to be found in further investigation or likely to be at risk from development. Past construction activities which might have already destroyed archaeological resources should be noted;
- a map of the project area showing the location of these assets;
- a note of any inherent difficulties which may limit the study's usefulness (e.g. problems of access).

A number of sequential stages of data gathering can be identified. However not all stages would be necessary for every EIA.

Rapid appraisal

Rapid appraisal of the archaeological resource involves the collation and review of existing and easily accessible data. This will certainly include a review of the local **Historic Environment Records** (HER) (see Box 7.1) and consultation with the local authority archaeologists. It may also include a site visit. This appraisal will enable a preliminary view of the likely nature and scale of the archaeological constraint. It may in itself be sufficient to meet the aims of the EIA, or may identify the need for subsequent stages of data gathering.

HERs are the main source of archaeological information in England. Each HER is a local archaeological database containing information about the known archaeological sites and finds in each Local Authority. It has a statutory locus in that it is referred to within the General Permitted Development Order 1995; certain types of permitted development, such as mineral extraction, require permission where they affect an archaeological site registered on the HER. The HER information is gathered from a number of sources and in a variety of ways, from detailed surveys to chance finds. As a result there is considerable variance in the reliability of the data and the interpretation that can be placed upon it. It is often not very intelligible to non-archaeologists (and is not in fact a public document) and may need professional interpretation to assess the significance or potential of archaeological sites. The local authority archaeologists will usually be familiar with the nature and shortfalls of the data being considered, and will be able to advise on the appropriate interpretation of the archaeological data. It is important to note that the interpretation of archaeological data is rarely straightforward.

While the HER is a comprehensive statement of the archaeological resource as currently known, it is not a definitive statement: new archaeological information becomes available all the time. Therefore the sites on the record represent only a part of the actual archaeological resource and many archaeological sites remain as yet unlocated. This has two major implications for compiling an EIA. First, as the HER only reflects current knowledge, there may be other important archaeological remains as yet unlocated that may be affected by a proposal. Second, if considerable time elapses between when the HER is consulted and when that information is used, additional evidence may become available in the meantime. These unknown sites are nonetheless a material consideration and therefore should be addressed when considering a development proposal. This is recognised in PPG 16:

> Where early discussions with local planning authorities or the developer's own research indicate that important archaeological remains may exist, it is reasonable for the planning authority to request the prospective developer to arrange for an archaeological field evaluation to be carried out before any decision on the planing application is taken. This sort of evaluation is quite distinct from full archaeological excavations. It is normally a rapid and inexpensive operation, involving ground survey and small-scale trial

trenching, but it should be carried out by a professionally qualified archaeological organisation or archaeologist. . . . Evaluations of this kind help to define the character and extent of the archaeological remains that exist in the area of a proposed development, and thus indicate the weight which ought to be attached to their preservation. They also provide information useful for identifying potential options for minimising or avoiding damage. On this basis, an informed and reasonable planning decision can be taken.

Local planning authorities can expect developers to provide the results of such assessments and evaluations as part of their application for sites where there is good reason to believe there are remains of archaeological importance. If developers are not prepared to do so voluntarily, the planning authority may wish to consider whether it would be appropriate to direct the application to supply further information under the provisions of Regulation 4 of the Town and Country Planning (Applications) Regulations 1988 and if necessary authorities will need to consider refusing permission for proposals which are inadequately documented. In some circumstances a formal Environmental Assessment may be necessary.

(DoE 1990)

The local authority archaeologists both maintain the HER and are therefore a source of initial data, and advise the local planning authority and are therefore an initial source of advice. They will also be able to advise on the scope and content of the archaeological elements of the EIA. They are extremely knowledgeable about the archaeological potential of sites in their areas, and are also usually very realistic about development pressures. The local authority archaeologists will be anxious to ensure that the archaeological content of an EIA has been properly addressed, and will generally be happy to supply both data and advice. A charge may be made to cover the costs incurred in supplying data. As the local authority archaeologists usually advise the local planning authority regarding the acceptability of these elements it is important to be aware of their opinions at an early stage. Where failure to consult results in additional archaeological concerns being raised, there is the potential for uncertainty, delay and additional costs which will negate the benefits of having carried out the EIA. An English Heritage survey of local authority archaeologists (EH 2003) showed that roughly 3 per cent of planning applications that the archaeologists reviewed via HERs were found to have potentially significant implications and required more in-depth archaeological assessment.

Where a development is likely to affect a Scheduled Ancient Monument or its setting, the relevant heritage agency should be consulted and Scheduled Monument Consent may be required. The need to obtain this consent is independent of the planning process and unless identified early could introduce substantial delay or even compromise the development altogether. Furthermore, where a development is likely to affect a monument of national importance which, although not scheduled, may be considered for scheduling in due course, it is advisable to seek the advice and opinion of the relevant agency.

Desk-based assessment

A desk-based assessment should identify and collate as much existing information as possible and frequently requires some original research. Information may be retrieved from a number of sources (**Box 7.1**), but the HER is usually the most useful starting point.

Box 7.1 Sources of historical information in the UK

Information on ancient monuments and listed buildings is available at from three main sources.

1. Lists of Scheduled Ancient Monuments and listed buildings are held by the heritage agencies.
2. A much wider range of information about the historic heritage is held in the:
    *   National Monuments Record (NMR), by English Heritage (EH), www.english-heritage.org.uk/;
    *   National Monuments Record of Scotland (NMRS), by the Royal Commission on the Ancient and Historical Monuments of Scotland (RCAHMS), www.rcahms.gov.uk/;
    *   National Monuments Record of Wales (NMRW), by the Royal Commission on the Ancient and Historical Monuments of Wales (RCAHMW), www.rcahmw.gov.uk/; *and*
    *   Monuments and Buildings Record (MBR), by the Northern Ireland Environment and Heritage Service (EHS), www.ehsni.gov.uk/.
3. Local authority archaeologists hold a wide range of information about the historic heritage in their Historic Environment Record (HER). This was traditionally called the Sites and Monuments Record (SMR). However, because of the trend for considering a wider range of historic aspects (e.g. historic landscape) than simply sites and monuments, many authorities are renaming SMRs as HERs. HERs are increasingly available on the internet from: CARN (www.rcahmw.gov.uk/HI/ENG/Search+Records/CARN/) in Wales; Pastmap (http://jura.rcahms.gov.uk/PASTMAP/start.jsp) in Scotland; *and* ADS (Archaeology Data Service) (http://ads.ahds.ac.uk/) and Heritage Gateway (www.heritagegateway.org.uk/gateway) in England.

Information is also available from the Association of Local Government Archaeological Officers (www.algao.org.uk/), National Trust (www.nationaltrust.org.uk/), National Trust for Scotland (www.nts.org.uk/), and local history and archaeology societies.

Old maps exist for most areas, and are available at local record offices, some local libraries, and online at www.old-maps.co.uk/. Digitised maps dating from 1843 are also available from OS, (www.ordnancesurvey.co.uk/), e.g. 1:10,000, 1:2500 scales. Tithe, estate and enclosure act maps may be available, but the information these provide is limited and often unreliable.

Photographs of, and information about, many buildings that were on EH's List of Buildings of Special Architectural and Historic Interest in 2001 can be found at www.imagesofengland.org.uk.

Box 7.1 (*continued*)

Early **aerial photographs** are available in the records held by EH, EHS, RCAHMS, and RCAHMW. For example, EH holds RAF photographs from 1940 (including the 1946–1948 national survey) and OS photographs from 1952. Usually, oblique photographs are available for open-access viewing at the relevant offices, and vertical photographs can be viewed by appointment.

General historical information is available from local authority records offices, local libraries, museums, history societies, and the National Archives (www.nationalarchives.gov.uk/). EH publish annual landscape investigations of chosen heritage sites. Other sources of local information can include parish records and newspaper articles. Trade directories are available for most urban areas, and can provide historical information about commercial activities. Local history society books and pamphlets may contain similar information.

Local authority planning records frequently go back to the early 1940s, and the county records office will often be able to identify previously archived planning records. However, partly because of changes past to authorities and their boundaries, many records may be unavailable or difficult to find.

Aerial photographs are an important source of data. Earthworks are often more easily recognised and interpreted from the air than from the ground. Buried archaeological remains can also be traced from the air in certain circumstances. The buried remains can affect the growing crop. For instance a buried wall or road surface may retard crop growth, or in a dry year create a parch mark. A buried pit or ditch may promote crop growth. The patterns that result can be interpreted as archaeological features or sites. Different soil colours may also reveal archaeological sites. Aerial photographs may be found in national, local authority, and possibly private collections. The record office may contain historic maps or plans and other documents relating to the land, and it may be possible to find other data not yet assimilated into the HER. The Victoria County Histories and Local Archaeological Societies may have additional information.

Desk assessment is usually undertaken at an early stage in project planning, so there may be an issue of commercial sensitivity. If so, it may be reasonable to use the local authority archaeologist and the Victoria County Histories, but not to approach the voluntary societies until later.

Field survey

A wide range of field survey techniques are available, including geo-physical techniques, fieldwalking, augering, test-pitting, machine trench digging and earthwork surveys. These are described below. Not all of these techniques will be applicable in all circumstances. Some can act as useful preliminaries to other techniques. A phased approach to field survey is often the most sensible and cost effective, so it is common to use a suite of techniques as the proposal develops:

perhaps starting with a rapid appraisal and then a desk assessment in the earliest stages, then fieldwalking before the actual site is proposed, and machine trenching afterwards. When considering the appropriateness of the various techniques, consultation with the local authority archaeologists may be valuable.

The local authority archaeologists usually produce a brief or specification for the work when a field survey is being undertaken through the planning process. A brief is an initial statement regarding the aims and scope of the archaeological work required, identifying certain working standards. It would form the basis of any specification produced, which should be referred back to the local authority archaeologists to ensure that all matters in the brief have been properly addressed. Alternatively the local authority archaeologists may issue a full specification which sets out in detail the works required in the field survey and would be sufficient to enable the project to be implemented and progress to be monitored.

The local authority archaeologists may also wish to make arrangements for monitoring the field survey to ensure that works are carried out to professional standards and to any specification that has been issued. This has benefits both for the archaeological resource and for the developer, who may have no independent means to monitor the value of the work being undertaken. It also enables the local authority archaeologists to keep up to date with any archaeological sites that are discovered during the fieldwork. Some local authority archaeologists charge for monitoring.

Geophysical techniques can be used to investigate some characteristics and properties of the ground that may be altered by previous land uses. The principal techniques used are resistivity and magnetometer surveys, although others are also available. Resistivity surveys measure the ground's resistance to the progress of an electrical current. Measuring increases and decreases in the resistance can indicate the nature and location of buried features. Magnetometer surveys measure the magnetic properties of the soil and can be used to identify locations of past human activity, particularly those that involved burning or heating.

Geophysical techniques can only be applied in suitable site conditions and an experienced geophysical operator should visit the site to assess their feasibility. Where they are appropriate, geophysical techniques have an advantage over many of other field techniques in that they do not damage the archaeological resource. Because of this they are particularly appropriate for Scheduled Ancient Monuments, although Scheduled Monument Consent or a licence may still have to be obtained before surveys can be undertaken.

Although the results of geophysical techniques can sometimes be ambiguous, these techniques often successfully identify the location and extent of archaeological sites and can give some idea of their nature. The results can therefore help to focus subsequent stages of field survey to maximise data recovery. However geophysical techniques are unlikely to provide sufficient information on their own, are not universally applicable, and are often expensive.

Fieldwalking, also known as surface artefact collection, is confined to ploughed fields. A plough breaks and turns over the surface soil. In ploughed fields there is a tendency for buried material to be brought to the surface, and where the plough intrudes into a buried archaeological site this will include archaeo-logical artefacts. Rigorous collection and plotting of this material will enable the location, date, and extent of certain types of archaeological site to be described. The archaeological material collected can be anything that reflects human act-ivity, like pottery sherds, worked stone, coins, building material and even stone that is not local to the area and may have been imported.

The local authority archaeologists will be able to suggest a field-walking strategy that ensures that the data gathered will be comparable to other field-walking data already on the HER. The area being studied is divided up by a grid, usually based on the national grid. Artefacts are then collected from along the lines of one axis of the grid, usually the north-south axis, and stored and recorded according to where on the grid they were recovered. The size of the grid thus determines the size of the collection units, and the precision of the results. A survey on a large grid will be rapid but will represent a small sample of the available artefacts. A survey on a small grid will be more time-consuming but the results will be based on a larger sample. The size of the grid is usually deter-mined with reference to the sorts of archaeological sites that are anticipated. For instance a smaller grid would be required to locate small Mesolithic camps than a Roman villa. In general, grid spacing is about 20m or 25m.

Where a site has already been located, intensive fieldwalking, called total collection, can be used to determine spatial distributions across the site. Total collection involves laying out a small grid across the site, perhaps 5m × 5m, and collecting all the artefacts within each grid square.

Fieldwalking is a relatively rapid and inexpensive technique that can be applied over large areas. However the results can be ambiguous or misleading. Where a site is located by fieldwalking it is by definition being damaged. It is hard to judge from fieldwalking results alone how intact the site is, or whether it solely survives as artefacts trapped in the ploughed soil. A site surviving intact below the ploughed soil will not be represented on the surface. Certain periods do not produce artefacts which are likely to survive the ploughing action. The results of fieldwalking therefore need to be qualified by some understanding of the relationship between the depth of ploughing and the depth of the archaeology.

Augering is most frequently used in river valleys where alluvial, colluvial or peat deposits have masked the original land surface and where slightly higher ground in a wet environment may have acted as a focus for human activity. By recording the soil sequence from auger holes located over a wide area, the under-lying and hidden subsurface topography can be mapped and the archaeological potential of the area can be inferred. Augering alone is unlikely to confirm the presence or absence of archaeological deposits, but can clarify the archaeolo-gical potential and so focus subsequent stages of survey. It can also be used to clarify the nature of features located by geophysical techniques, and in certain areas to assess the potential for the preservation of palaeoenvironmental data.

Test pitting involves the hand excavation of an array of small pits of a pre-determined size. It provides a clear picture of the nature of the soil structure and the upper layers of the underlying geology. As with fieldwalking, the spacing and array of test pits usually reflect assumptions about the expected archaeological resource. Test pits can be varied in size and array in order to meet the requirements of the survey. They are usually 1m × 1m, or 1m × 0.5m for ease of excavation. The soil from test pits is often sieved through a wire mesh of a set size to ensure consistent artefact recovery, enabling a rigorous statement to be made regarding the number, type and depth of artefacts. Analysis of the different artefact recovery rates over an area gives an indication of the date, location and extent of archaeological sites. Test pitting is often used instead of field-walking where the land is pasture rather than arable, and in woodland where machine trenching may not be possible.

Machine trenching employs trenches, usually cut with a toothless ditching bucket, laid out in a pattern across the site. The trench pattern will attempt to maximise information retrieval, possibly on the basis of existing data such as aerial photographs, fieldwalking or geophysical results. The extent of trenching required is usually an agreed sample of the land. The size of the sample is commonly around 2 per cent, depending on local circumstances. When archaeological deposits are encountered excavation continues by hand. The excavation is controlled by a supervising archaeologist at all times. Machine trenching quickly locates features cut into the subsoil but, where large amounts of earth are rapidly removed, there is limited opportunity to collect artefacts and the rate of artefact retrieval is low. Higher rates of retrieval can be achieved by hand-digging parts of the trench, equivalent to a test pit, and the use of metal detectors.

Trenching is very disruptive and intervenes directly into the archaeological levels. This has the advantage of producing unambiguous information but is potentially damaging to archaeological remains one might otherwise wish to protect. It is also not always possible to get a machine onto a site.

Earthwork surveys can be used for archaeological sites that are visible as earth-works such as banks, ditches, burial mounds, and sites of deserted or shrunken settlements. Sites that survive as earthworks are generally more intact than other sites. Ploughing can degrade earthworks, and the success of earthwork surveys is limited in fields which have been arable for a long time; generally, such land is more productively scanned from aerial photographs. Pasture can have visible earthworks surviving. When they are obviously visible they will often have been recorded by the ordnance survey or the HER. They can also be identified through aerial photographs. Woodland, particularly ancient woodland, holds the greatest potential for producing previously unrecorded earthworks. The sites will often be obscured from the air by trees and on the ground by undergrowth, so it is best to undertake the survey during the winter or early spring.

The nature of the earthwork survey will depend on the aims of the evaluation. The survey can vary from sketch plotting the earthworks onto an OS map, through two-dimensional surveys such as plane table surveys, to a three dimensional survey producing an accurate contour or hachure plan.

Finds are recovered artefacts. Some of the these may be subject to the laws of treasure trove; specifically all discoveries of gold or silver should be reported to the coroner, who will consider whether the items were hidden with a view to being retrieved at a later date. If this is concluded to be the case, the state may retain any of these items, paying the landowner the market value. In all other situations the artefacts are the property of the landowner. It is usually recommended that they are donated to a local authority museum, so that they can be stored in appropriate conditions and made available for future study. All finds of human bone, from any period, have to be reported to the coroner.

The developer's responsibilities arising from the destruction of the archaeological resource often continue beyond excavation. If finds are donated to the appropriate local authority museum, it is likely that the planning authority will consider the developer to have met these responsibilities. If the developer wishes to make alternative arrangements, they may need to demonstrate that this alternative is appropriate. Some museums make a charge for accepting the long-term responsibility of storing archaeological material.

Some problems with field surveys

Access to the site will not be a problem where the developer already owns the land, although there may be problems where the project has off-site implications, e.g. as a result of **dewatering**. For projects such as road schemes a field survey may not be possible until the route is finally selected and the land acquired. This is undesirably late because it does not allow a route to be chosen which would preserve important remains in situ.

The project timetable may constrain the fieldwork options. Fieldwalking is not possible in a standing crop, and can only be done after the fields are ploughed. Similarly crop patterns show best in a well-grown crop and should be photographed just before the harvest.

The cost of archaeological surveys depends upon the extent and nature of the survey and the techniques employed. Surveys are frequently labour intensive and some elements can be expensive. Where the developer is liable to pay compensation to the landowner for damage arising from the evaluation, the scale of compensation will depend upon the techniques used. However the costs should be seen against the background of the cost resulting from unexpected delay to the progress of the planning application or indeed the progress of the development if significant archaeological deposits are located at a late stage in the process.

7.4.2 Historic buildings and sites

Although listed buildings account for only some 2 per cent of the UK's building stock, they are a fragile and valuable resource. Only a full assessment of a listed building's inherited character at the outset will allow well-informed judgements to be made about the significance of a proposed development's impacts. Both owners/developers and LPAs have their respective roles to play in such assessments.

An initial review of the listed building register will identify any **listed buildings** likely to be affected by a proposed development. Listed buildings will also normally be identified on the HER. If such buildings are identified, a baseline survey will be necessary, involving an audit of the buildings' special architectural and historic interest. Such a survey consists of a detailed archival search of local history libraries and other social and property record depositories. The written product should contain an evaluation of the building's particular architectural and historic significance supported by plans, sections and elevations, together with a photographic survey and diagrammatic analysis of the buildings' evolution over time. This information is evaluated in terms of the relative importance of the building's component parts. This survey involves specialised work and should be undertaken only by those with a qualification in historic or architectural conservation.

Baseline studies for **conservation areas** have a wider remit than those for listed buildings. An initial survey will identify characteristics of significance, including archaeological features of interest (whether buried remains or standing structures), all listed buildings with an indication of their property curtilages, building age, and geological, topographical or landscape features. Those townscape features that constitute the area's special architectural and historic interest then need to be appraised, including vernacular characteristics, indigenous building materials, spatial characteristics, sections of group coherence or special townscape value, and long-distance views within, outside or across the conservation area that are of importance in the perception of its inherited character.

The problems and policies that affect the present or future well-being of the area also need to be appraised. This consists of a statement of problems that adversely affect the physical amenity of the area (e.g. traffic intrusion, noise, visual intrusion, architectural disfigurements, decay of historic fabric etc.), the position with respect to present and future district-wide policies for preservation and enhancement, evaluations of specific problem sites, and opportunities for area-wide enhancements and improvements, including vehicular and pedestrian movement. An increasing number of LPAs have undertaken comprehensive character appraisals of conservation areas but coverage nationwide is very uneven.

7.5 Impact prediction

7.5.1 Archaeology

Prediction of archaeological impacts involves three unknowns: what the archaeological remains are (discussed in §7.4.1), what the proposed development's impacts would be, and how significant the impacts would be. Identification of impacts must include both direct and indirect impacts. The **direct impacts** are often clear, and usually involve the removal of archaeological materials. Some of the direct impacts may not be immediately obvious, when they result from secondary operations such as drainage and landscaping works associated with the development. A development's **indirect impacts** are often more difficult to define. For example dewatering associated with a development may lead to the destruction of some types of archaeological deposits on adjacent undisturbed sites which had previously survived due to waterlogging. A residential development may increase recreational pressure on a nearby earthwork or affect the visual setting of an adjacent archaeological site. Positive impacts are often indirect, e.g. when a road scheme relieves congestion in a historic town centre.

The **significance** of a development's impacts depends on a number of factors linked to the interpretation archaeologists are able to put on finds given contemporary understanding. When assessing whether an ancient monument is of national importance, and thus whether it should be scheduled, the Secretary of State refers to eight "scheduling criteria":

- period – the degree to which a monument characterises a particular period;
- rarity – the scarcity or otherwise of surviving examples of the monument;
- documentation – the significance of the monument may be enhanced by records, either of previous investigations or contemporary to the remains;
- group value – the significance of the monument may be enhanced by its association with related contemporary or non-contemporary monuments;
- condition – the condition or survival of the monument's archaeological potential;
- fragility – the resilience or otherwise of a monument to unsympathetic treatment;
- diversity – the combinations and quality of features related to the monument;
- potential – where the nature of the monument cannot be specified but where its existence and importance are likely.

These criteria are further described in Annex 4 of PPG16 (DoE 1990). They can be used to help establish the importance not only of ancient monuments but also of other archaeological remains.

Lambrick (1993) suggests that cultural impacts can be evaluated in terms of who is affected. He lists the resources: archaeological remains, palaeoenvironmental deposits, historic buildings and structures, historic landscape and townscape elements, sites of historical events or with historical associations, and the overall historical integrity of the landscape. He then gives a list of human receptors who may be affected by impacts on these resources: owners and occupiers of historic properties and monuments; visitors to sites and buildings specifically open to the public; local communities; the general public as regards general enjoyment of historic places through informal public access; and individuals or groups with special interest in the historic environment, including academic archaeologists. He then suggests:

Perhaps the best means of considering [significance] is to say that an effect is significant if it makes an appreciable difference to the present or future opportunity for people [receptors, as defined above] to understand and appreciate the historic environment [resources] of the area and its wider context.

(Lambrick 1993)

Impact significance may also be considered in geographic terms. The DMRB (HA 2007a) suggests four categories of importance for archaeological remains, namely (a) sites of national importance, usually Scheduled Ancient Monuments or monuments in the process of being scheduled as such; (b) sites of regional or local importance; (c) sites of district or local importance; and (d) sites which are too badly damaged to justify their inclusion in another category.

7.5.2 Historic buildings and sites

A proposed development action can directly affect a **listed building** in a variety of ways, ranging from the minor to the extensive:

- repairs of minor elements using replacement materials;
- changes to the interiors of buildings, where decorations or other architectural features may enrich the understanding of the building's interest;
- modifications to individual elements of the building which form a significant part of its character;
- new extensions;
- partial demolitions;
- complete demolitions;
- severance of part of a property from other parts (for instance, a house from its gardens or outbuildings).

Indirect impacts to listed buildings include noise and disturbance from nearby developments leading to a loss of amenity, and air pollution which can lead to deterioration of buildings and damage to garden and park vegetation. Nearby developments can cause visual intrusion and change the building's original land-scape setting.

Direct impacts on conservation areas from the private sector are most commonly related to proposals for development, whether new-build or refurbishment. Extensive damage can also be created by permitted development for which special directions under Article IV of the General Permitted Development Order are needed. Public sector developments such as those by highway authorities or utility companies can affect conservation areas without reference to conservation area policies; these may be brought under the control of the Town and Country Planning Acts by specific directions under Article IV of the General Permitted Development Order. A conservation area can be directly affected through the loss of buildings, through **cumulative impacts** resulting in a general deterioration in the setting of the buildings, or through severance. Development can also result in the neglect of a building or site, resulting in its deterioration or destruction. More generally, development can alter or destroy open spaces and change the character of historic districts.

Any proposed development constitutes a potential intrusion into an acknow-ledged heritage object. Building owners, as much as government agencies and professional advisors, play a curatorial role in the building's conservation and should be involved in predicting the impacts of the proposed development. As such, impact prediction is best undertaken as a dialogue between the owner or developer and the local authority, which respectively represent the private and the public aspects of curatorial influence. The developer determines the extent of change that is expected, and thus the utilization of the property and its financial value. The local authority makes a judgement about the extent of architectural and historic change that can be allowed, taking into account national and local policies and standards. The outcome may take the form of agreement, compromise or disagreement. This evaluation constitutes a special negotiation over and above that needed for normal building refurbishment. The LPA classes such a dialogue as an exploratory meeting. Agreement between the two parties at this stage can constitute an agreement for the later stages of design.

The **significance** of any impacts will depend on the significance of the building or site affected as well as on the magnitude of the impact. Assessing a development's impacts on a listed building involves judgements on architectural and aesthetic factors, as well as purely physical alterations to fabric. It is possible to amplify these quantitatively according to the type of impact involved. Section 7.3.2 summarised the grading systems used for listed buildings and parks and gardens, which provide an initial indication of relative importance. However no such gradings exist for conservation areas or historic landscapes.

Applications for **listed building consent** should be made for any change that would affect the character of a listed building, and for planning permission to undertake development of the land. In England PPG15 gives clear guidance to LPAs and owners on the approach that should be adopted in respect of proposals affecting listed buildings. Applicants are expected to justify their proposals, and provide the LPA with enough information to enable them to assess the likely impact of their proposals on the special architectural or historic interest of the building and on its setting. UK legislation empowers an authority to seek any particulars it considers to be necessary to ensure that it has a full understanding of the impact of the proposal on the character of the building in question. In reality practice varies between authorities, some demanding impact assessments or justification statements, while others require less rigorous information. However in general increasingly detailed assessments are being called for.

An application is often a way of confirming the earlier evaluation, and for determining the full historical significance of a building and its physical condition, and the implication of any changes to the building fabric. These surveys should be undertaken only by those who are qualified in historic or architectural conservation. Most old buildings do not meet regulatory requirements governing modern building construction, but this does not necessarily make them unsafe. It takes training and experience to make judgements about their conditions which obviate the destruction of the building's character. Detailed application for full planning permission and listed building consent can only be made with confidence once the initial surveys and evaluations have been successfully concluded.

7.6 Mitigation and enhancement

7.6.1 *Archaeology*

Having identified the nature of the archaeological resource and considered the development's impact upon it, a number of mitigation strategies may be recommended. For the majority of development proposals, no further archaeological activity is required because no archaeological resource has been identified, or there is no significant impact on any archaeological resource, or the scale or nature of the impact or the nature of the archaeological resource does not warrant further action.

An **archaeological watching brief** may be carried out during the relevant stages of development. These stages are likely to be earth moving, topsoil stripping, and the digging of foundations and services. The watching brief should enable any archaeological evidence encountered to be recorded, and removed if appropriate. It may be accepted that this will not cause unreasonable delay to the progress of the development; if some delay is considered likely, the circumstances which would warrant a delay should be described and agreed upon in advance.

In some circumstances the need for development may override the case for preserving an archaeological site. In this case the site should not be thoughtlessly destroyed, and the LPA may satisfy itself that appropriate provision has been made (DoE 1990). This will involve archaeological **site-excavation** prior to the development. The developer's responsibilities also include post-excavation (e.g. the long-term storage of the excavated material and the appropriate dissemination of the results). Depending on the nature and extent of the remains, excavation, post-excavation and publication can be expensive and time-consuming.

Preservation in situ means leaving the archaeological site undisturbed. This is the only mitigation measure which wholly meets the EIA Directive's principle of preventing environmental harm at source, and is usually the preferred action from the archaeological perspective. The LPA may require preservation in situ if the archaeological remains are important, or the developer may choose to preserve in situ if mitigation requirements are too expensive. Preservation in situ can be achieved in several ways. The development can be avoided altogether, or, if the archaeological constraint has been identified sufficiently early, by site or option selection. A common solution is to preserve the site within the design of the development, for example as an area of open or recreational space. The LPA may attach a fencing condition to the planning permission to prevent inadvertent damage during construction work. This secures the erection of a fence around a stipulated area and prohibits work within that area. Provision may also be made for positive management of the archaeology to secure its long-term future from any indirect impact of the development. Preservation in situ can be achieved within the construction of a development. For instance the less structurally demanding elements of a development, such as car parking, can be built on raised levels or rafted foundations above the archaeological deposits. While these options are feasible they can cause technical or engineering problems such as shrinkage of buried material as it dries out.

It may be possible to preserve the majority of an archaeological site by agreeing an acceptable level of destruction. For instance a low-density pile foundation may be acceptable where the pile has been designed to avoid the most significant deposits. Ultimately, preservation in situ may need to be achieved by abandoning elements of the development or indeed abandoning the development entirely. Where the importance of an archaeological site merits it, the LPA can refuse an application on archaeological grounds.

7.6.2 *Historic buildings and sites*

Mitigation measures in EIA should include policies to highlight and strengthen the historic building's or site's inherited and intrinsic qualities and special interest, as well as to preserve them:

> Refurbishment of historic buildings is a powerful stimulus to regeneration, particularly in disadvantaged areas. Major expenditure on historic buildings [can stimulate] wider investment in depressed economies. Repair of even modest historic buildings in key positions can instil confidence in a run-down area and generate a ripple effect of investment by other owners. There is ample evidence that people and businesses are attracted to invest in places of quality and character, and indeed to stay there rather than to move away.
>
> (Cadw 2003)

Preservation starts with the declaration of a listed building or conservation area: all subsequent actions should strengthen and reinforce architectural characteristics and retain historic interest. Without such intent, the intrinsic qualities of a listed building or a conservation area can be diluted and destroyed.

For **conservation areas**, unlike listed buildings, the legislation specifically allows their preservation to be accompanied by enhancement measures. Proposals for area-wide preservation and enhancement may consist of programmes of building maintenance and repair, and their implementation; programmes of building restorations involving the rectification of disfigurements and their implementation; programmes of face-lift enhancements; strategies for the enhancement of floorscape treatments and their integration into the design of public and private domains; strategies for building materials; and new infill building developments within clearly established building envelopes.

Proposals for the enhancement of conservation areas should be drawn up by LPAs and discussed at public meetings in the localities concerned. Such proposals may be compiled by local citizen groups with the advice and support of professionals qualified in architectural conservation or urban design, provided that the meetings at which proposals are presented are genuinely open to all local interests and involve elected representatives of the local authority. Where citizen groups take such initiatives, it still remains the province of the local authority to make formal adoptions of the proposals presented.

7.7 Monitoring

The prediction of archaeological impacts is not an exact science, and unexpected problems can arise. The chances of this happening are considerably reduced by a thorough evaluation, but some contingency should still be made for the unexpected. The planning authority has the power to revoke planning permission where an unexpected and overriding archaeological constraint warrants it. In this circumstance compensation would have to be paid. This can prove to be an expensive option and is one reason why local authorities are empowered to ensure, by field survey if necessary, that the full archaeological implications of the development have been properly identified prior to the determination of the application.

If unexpected archaeological remains are located, additional discussion between the developer and the local authority archaeologist will be needed. Where agreement cannot be reached, the relevant heritage agency may be able to arbitrate between the two parties. Where these unexpected remains warrant it, the Secretary of State may schedule them and the developer would then need consent to continue work. Developers can insure themselves against the risk of loss from encountering unexpected archaeological remains.

7.8 Conclusions

The historic environment is a specialist discipline, covering many different periods and types of remains. Historic Scotland (2003) have prepared a range of leaflets explaining different types of historic monuments (e.g. prehistoric settlements, wartime). EH's (2004) guidance *Scheduled monuments: a guide for owners and occupiers* gives advice on managing archaeological sites. Further reading on archaeological impacts includes EH (1991), Lambrick (1992), Morgan Evans (1985), Ralston and Thomas (1993), RICS (1982), and Roberts and Wrathmell (2002). In Ireland, the Heritage Council has published a range of useful guidance documents on the cultural heritage, including guidelines for developers on archaeology (HC 2000).

Few publications exist on listed buildings and conservation areas. The most generally readable treatment is by Ross (1996), who gives wide coverage to the rationale and evaluation of historic conservation in the UK. Mynors (1999) provide the most comprehensive coverage of the legal provisions affecting listed buildings, conservation areas and ancient monuments. PPG 15 provides the most detailed official guidance. Fielden's (1982) *Conservation of historic buildings* is a substantial reference volume, and several other publications on techniques of repair are provided by EH and the national amenity societies.

Relatively little guidance exists on how to assess and manage impacts on historic landscapes. The Highways Agency's useful guidance *Assessing the effects of road schemes on historic landscape character* (HA 2007b) recommends that historic landscape assessment should be carried out in parallel to landscape assessment, and that both should contribute to the development of landscape strategies for areas. Cadw have prepared guidance on managing the historic landscape (Cadw *et al.* 2007) and the coastal heritage (Cadw 1999).

In EIA, it is important to contact the local authority archaeologists in respect of archaeological sites, and the local conservation officer in respect of historic buildings and conservation areas as early as possible, since they are valuable sources of data and advice. Where consultation is left to a later stage, unexpected problems and delays are more likely to occur. The EIA should be carried out by specialists trained not only in survey and analysis techniques, but also in interpreting the data for the relevant period and type of remains. Specialist knowledge will be needed to interpret the relative importance of these results and suggest appropriate mitigation strategies. Using specialists in archaeology and/or historic or architectural conservation from the earliest stages of the EIA when the data-gathering programme is first being considered will ensure that the correct type and amount of data is obtained. The result of using inappropriately qualified staff may be that, after the EIA is completed, additional historical constraints may be identified, or additional information required, potentially introducing delay and so negating the benefits of carrying out the EIA.

Problems may arise where the developer gathers inadequate or inappropriate data for use in EIA. This frequently occurs as a result of cost-cutting on the data-gathering strategy. This can be a short-sighted saving when compared to the cost of delay to the progress of the application, or delay to the progress of the development.

References

CA (Countryside Agency) 1998–1999. *The character of England's natural and man-made landscape*. Regional Guides, Vols 1–8. Cheltenham, Glos: Countryside Agency.

Cadw (Historic environment service of the Welsh Assembly Government) 1999. *Coastal heritage*, www.cadw.wales.gov.uk/upload/resourcepool/Coastal%20Heritage9557.pdf.

Cadw 2003. *Review of the historic environment in Wales: a consultation document*, www.cadw.wales.gov.uk/default.asp?ID=201.

Cadw 2007. *Guide to good practice on using the register of landscapes of historic interest in Wales in the planning and development process*, www.cadw.wales.gov.uk/upload/resourcepool/Guide_to_Good_Practice_ENG7930.pdf.

Cadw, Welsh Assembly Government, CCW and the Welsh Archaeological Trusts 2007. *Caring for historic landscapes*, www.cadw.wales.gov.uk/default.asp?id=108.

CCW (Countryside Council for Wales) 2007. *SEA topic: Cultural heritage*. Prepared by C42. Bangor: CCW.

DCLG (Department for Communities and Local Government) 2006. *Environmental impact assessment: a guide to good practice and procedures*. London: DCLG, www.communities.gov.uk/documents/planningandbuilding/pdf/151087.

DCLG 2007. Circular 01/2007 *Revisions to the principles of selection for listing buildings*, www.communities.gov.uk/documents/planningandbuilding/pdf/324058.

DCMS/WAG (Department for Culture, Media and Sport and Welsh Assembly Government) 2007. Heritage Protection for the 21st Century, http://www.culture.gov.uk/images/consultations/hrp_whitepaper_doc1.pdf.

DoE (Department of the Environment) 1987. Circular 8/87: *Historic buildings and conservation areas – policy and procedures.* London: HMSO.

DoE 1990. *Planning Policy Guidance Note 16: Archaeology and planning.* London: HMSO, www.communities.gov.uk/publications/planningandbuilding/planningpolicyguidance9.

DoE/DCMS (Department for Culture, Media and Sport) 1994. Planning Policy Guidance Note 15: *Planning and the historic environment.* London: HMSO, www.communities.gov.uk/publications/planningandbuilding/planningpolicyguidance8.

EH (English Heritage) 1991. *Exploring our past – strategies for the archaeology of England.* London: English Heritage.

EH 2003. *Local authority archaeological services,* www.algao.org.uk/Publications/Docs/SurveySummary.pdf.

EH 2004. *Scheduled monuments: a guide for owners and occupiers.* London: English Heritage, www.english-heritage.org.uk/upload/pdf/scheduled_monuments_guide.pdf.

Fielden BM 1982. *Conservation of historic buildings.* London: Butterworth.

Grover P and R Therivel 2001. Archaeological and other material and cultural assets, Ch. 7 in Morris P and R Therivel, *Methods of environmental impact assessment.* London: Spon Press.

HA (Highways Agency) 2007a. *Design manual for roads and bridges (DMRB),* Vol. 11: *Environmental assessment,* Section 3, Part 2: *Cultural Heritage.* London: HA (Department for Transport), www.standardsforhighways.co.uk/dmrb/vol11/section3.htm.

HA 2007b. *Assessment the effect of road schemes on historic landscape character: draft for discussion.* London: HA, www.helm.org.uk/upload/pdf/Road-Schemes.pdf.

HC (Heritage Council) 2000. Archaeology and Development: *Guidelines for good practice for developers,* www.heritagecouncil.ie/publications/developers/.

Historic Scotland 2003. *Understanding monuments leaflet series,* www.historic-scotland.gov.uk/index/ancientmonuments/understandingmonuments.htm.

Lambrick GH 1992. The importance of the cultural heritage in a green world: towards the development of landscape integrity assessment. In *All natural things: archaeology and the green debate,* L Macinnes and CR Wickham-Jones (eds), 105–126. Oxford: Oxbow.

Lambrick GH 1993. Environmental assessment and the cultural heritage: principles and practice. In *Environmental assessment and archaeology,* I Ralston and R Thomas (eds), 9–19. Birmingham: Institute of Field Archaeologists.

Morgan Evans D 1985. The management of historic landscapes. In *Archaeology and nature conservation,* GH Lambrick (ed.), 89–94. Oxford: Department of External Studies, University of Oxford.

Mynors C 1999. *Listed buildings, conservation areas and monuments,* 3rd edn., London: Sweet and Maxwell.

Ralston I and R Thomas (eds) 1993. Environmental assessment and archaeology. *Occasional Paper 5,* Birmingham: Institute of Field Archaeologists.

RICS (Royal Institute of Chartered Surveyors) 1982. *Practitioners' companion to ancient monuments and archaeological areas act.* London: RICS.

Roberts BK and S Wrathmell 2000. *An atlas of rural settlement in England.* Swindon, Wilts: English Heritage.

Roberts BK and S Wrathmell 2002. *Region and place: a study of English rural settlement,* Swindon, Wilts: English Heritage.

Ross M 1996. *Planning and heritage: policy and procedures,* 2nd edn., London: E&FN Spon.

8 Air quality and climate

David Walker and Hannah Dalton
(based on Elsom 2001)

8.1 Introduction

8.1.1 Air and climate changes

A proposed development that will change the concentration of pollutants in the atmosphere, or alter the *weather* and *climate*, may result in effects on people, plants, animals, materials and buildings (Canter 1996, Colls 1997, Elsom 1992, Ortolano 1997, Turco 2002). These effects can occur at the local, regional or even global scale. Major developments, such as power stations, oil refineries, waste incinerators, chemical processing plants and roads, pose obvious potential pollution problems. In addition, even developments that emit little or no pollutants when completed and operating can create a local dust nuisance during the earth-moving and materials-handling operations of the construction stage, especially during dry weather conditions. Once completed, developments may give rise to additional vehicle emissions as people travel to them (e.g. edge-of-town shopping and leisure complexes). New roads will directly result in vehicle emissions, and some developments may cause emissions at other remote locations such as power stations.

Developments may give rise to both routine and non-routine pollutant emissions. For example, they may use one type of fuel for most of the time but on a few occasions have to switch to an alternative fuel. In the UK this can occur when an industrial plant intends to use an "interruptible" natural gas supply. This type of supply permits the supplier the right to cease supplying gas during peak periods of national demand, during which the plant has to switch to a standby fuel such as heavy fuel oil for up to 30 days a year. Whereas natural gas produces no emissions of sulphur dioxide (SO_2), fuel oil emits significant amounts depending upon its sulphur content. Another example of non-routine emissions to consider is the possibility of an accident at a proposed development that intends to store or process toxic chemicals or nuclear fuels giving rise to the risk of the release of hazardous substances.

As well as pollutants and dust, certain types of development may release odour to the atmosphere, causing a response among the local community. The nature of the response is likely to vary considerably depending upon the type of odour released – for instance a bakery is less likely to attract adverse comment than a development which releases strong odours, e.g. from waste processing activities. Any odour can be offensive if it is continuous and intrusive and therefore the potential effects of releases should be assessed carefully.

Finally, developments may cause a *perception* of releasing pollutants to the air when in they are actually not causing any significant releases at all – a typical example might be the release of steam from a vent stack which might cause concern to onlookers as well as resulting in a visual effect.

8.1.2 *Effects of air pollutants*

Air **pollutants** can affect the health of a person during inhalation and exhalation as the pollutants inflame, sensitise and even scar the airways and lungs. On reaching deep inside the lungs, they may enter the bloodstream, thus affecting organs other than the lung, and they can take up permanent residence in the body. In addition, some pollutants affect health through contact with the skin and through ingestion of contaminated foods and drinks. Pollutants affect health in varying degrees of severity, ranging from minor irritation through serious illness to premature death in extreme cases. They may produce immediate (acute) symptoms as well as longer term (chronic) effects. Health effects depend upon the type and amount of pollutants present, the duration of exposure, and the state of health, age and level of activity of the person exposed (Elsom 1996).

Pollution damage to plants and animals is caused by a combination of physical and chemical stresses that may affect the receptor's physiology. Pollutants can affect crops by causing leaf discoloration, reducing plant growth and yields, or by contaminating a crop, so making it unsafe to eat. Effects on terrestrial and aquatic ecosystems can occur locally or even regionally in the case of pollutants that contribute to **acid deposition**, especially in areas where the soils and lakes lack substances to neutralise or buffer the acidic inputs (see §9.6.2 & §10.3.4). Pollution problems for buildings can be short-term and reversible such as soiling by smoke (which can be removed by cleaning), whereas the effects of acid deposition can be cumulative and irreversible by causing erosion and crumbling of the stone.

8.1.3 *Effects of climate changes*

Weather and climate changes can occur locally when a development changes the characteristics of the area in terms of its radiation balance, surface friction and roughness, and moisture balance. Adverse microclimate changes include:

- alterations to the airflow around large structures such as office blocks, multi-storey car parks and shopping arcades, causing wind turbulence which affects the comfort and sometimes the safety of pedestrians;
- the addition of moisture from industrial cooling towers and large reservoirs, causing an increased frequency of fog or even icing on nearby roads;

- the reduction in sunlight for greenhouse crops lying beneath a persistent industrial pollution plume;
- the ponding of cold air behind physical barriers such as road and railway embankments, so increasing the incidence of frost which can damage agricultural and horticultural crops in those areas.

Macroclimatic changes can result from emissions of greenhouse gases (gases which are strong absorbers of outgoing terrestrial infra-red radiation) such as carbon dioxide (CO_2), methane (CH_4) and nitrous oxide (N_2O). These gases contribute to global warming, which is now a generally accepted trend. Because of the wide range of natural climatic variation through time, neither the significance of the human impact, nor the long-term effects of warming on global and regional climate changes can be predicted with any certainty. However, there is mounting evidence that warming is causing changes in the position and intensity of weather systems and consequent changes in regional wind, temperature and precipitation patterns.

Some regional climate changes may bring benefits, but others are likely to bring adverse impacts. Current predictions suggest that the UK may experience:

- slightly increased average rainfalls, especially in winter – resulting in increased river flows;
- increased average annual temperatures (possibly between 2° and 3.5°C by the 2080s), incidence of hot, dry spells in summer – resulting in increased drought risk;
- increased variability of rainfall, and a higher proportion of intense events (higher frequency of rainstorms) – resulting in greater risks of wind damage, erosion and flooding (see §10.6.7, §10.8.2, Defra 2005, Hulme *et al.* 2002, UKCIP 2008).

The changes are evidently already affecting wildlife, and are predicted have increasing impacts on biodiversity (see §11.1) and human health issues (DH 2001). Global warming is also causing global sea level to rise as a result of thermal expansion of seawater and melting of glaciers and polar ice sheets (Elsom 1992, Houghton 2004, Juniper 2007). This is of particular concern in coastal areas (see §12.1, §12.2.2, §12.3.2, and §12.5.2).

8.2 Legislative background and interest groups

8.2.1 Air quality guidelines and standards

Epidemiological studies of community groups and laboratory-based toxicological experiments using human volunteers provide assessments of the health effects of pollutants. Consideration of these findings has enabled various national and international organisations to identify levels of air pollution concentrations (*air quality standards*) which should not be exceeded if the health of people is not to be at risk. Research studies have enabled levels to be specified to protect ecosystems too. Sometimes these levels are advisory such as the World Health Organization (WHO) guideline values while others, such as the UK air quality objectives and the EU limit values, are mandatory, being backed by legislation. Concentrations are expressed either as mass of the substance per unit volume of air (e.g. micrograms per cubic metre, abbreviated to $\mu g/m^3$) or as volume of the substance to the volume of air (e.g. parts per million or parts per billion, abbreviated to ppm and ppb respectively). The units can be converted from one to another using conversion factors (published factors may vary slightly because they may be standardised to a different atmospheric pressure and temperature).

The WHO guideline values, initially issued in 1987 and subsequently revised (WHO 2000, 2005) are summarised in **Table 8.1**. They are based on the lowest concentration a pollutant has been shown to produce adverse health effects or the level at which no observed health effect has been demonstrated plus a margin of protection to safeguard sensitive groups within the population. Sensitive groups include people with asthma, those with pre-existing heart and lung diseases, the elderly, infants and pregnant women and their unborn babies. Such groups form one-fifth of the population in the UK (Elsom 1996). Some pollutants, notably carcinogenic pollutants such as arsenic, benzene, chromium, and polycyclic aromatic hydrocarbons (PAHs), have not been given a guideline value. Instead, exposure-effect information is provided, giving guidance to risk managers about the major health impact for short- and long-term exposure to various levels of this pollutant.

The WHO guideline values were considered by the UK and the EU when setting mandatory standards but unlike the WHO guideline values, which are based on health considerations alone, the EU limit values and UK objectives take into account the economic costs and technological feasibility of attainment. Given the costs and problems involved in attainment this explains why air quality standards vary nationally around the world and why they are not often as strict as the WHO guidelines (Murley 1995).

8.2.2 EU air quality limit values

From 1980 onwards, the EU began setting air quality standards in the form of mandatory health-based limit values and more stringent non-mandatory guide values to protect the environment. Guide values are intended to be long-term objectives which, when met, will protect vegetation as well as aesthetic aspects of the environment such as long-range visibility and soiling of buildings. More recently, as part of the European Community's Framework Directive on Ambient Air Quality Assessment and Management (96/62/EC), commonly referred to as the Air Quality Framework Directive, the EU has set limit values for a number of pollutants (EC 1996a). The values are specified in a series of Daughter Directives, with the first one being agreed in 1999 and covering SO_2, particulate matter (PM_{10} or $PM_{2.5}$), NO_2 and Pb (**Table 8.2**). Subsequent Daughter Directives refer to O_3, benzene and carbon monoxide (CO), polycyclic aromatic hydrocarbons (PAHs), cadmium, arsenic, nickel and mercury.

Table 8.1 World Health Organization air quality guideline values

Pollutant	Value	Averaging time
Carbon monoxide	$100mg/m^3$ $60mg/m^3$ $30mg/m^3$ $10mg/m^3$	15min 30min 1h 8h
Ozone	$120\mu g/m^3$	8h
Nitrogen dioxide	$200\mu g/m^3$ $40\mu g/m^3$	1h annual
Sulphur dioxide	$500\mu g/m^3$ $20\mu g/m^3$	10min 24h annual
$PM_{2.5}$ (Particulate matter – particle size <2.5μm)	$25\mu g/m^3$ $10\mu g/m^3$	24h annual
PM_{10} (Particulate matter – particle size 2.5μm – 10μm)	$50\mu g/m^3$ $20\mu g/m^3$	24h annual
Benzene	6×10^{-6} $(\mu g/m^3)^{-1}$	UR/lifetime*
Dichloromethane	$3mg/m^3$	24h
Formaldehyde	$0.1mg/m^3$	30min
PAHs**	8.7×10^{-5} $(ng/m^3)^{-1}$	UR/lifetime*
Styrene	$0.26mg/m^3$	1week
Tetrachloroethylene	$0.25mg/m^3$	24h
Toluene	$0.26mg/m^3$	1 week
Trichloethylene	4.3×10^{-7} $(\mu g/m^3)^{-1}$	UR/lifetime*
Arsenic	1.5×10^{-3} $(\mu g/m^3)^{-1}$	UR/lifetime*
Cadmium	$5ng/m^3$	annual
Chromium	0.04 $(\mu g/m^3)^{-1}$	UR/lifetime*
Lead	$0.5\mu g/m^3$	annual
Manganese	$0.15\mu g/m^3$	annual
Mercury	$1.0\mu g/m^3$	annual
Nickel	3.8×10^{-4} $(\mu g/m^3)^{-1}$	UR/lifetime*

Notes

* UR = excess risk of dying from cancer following lifetime exposure. Thus for benzene, 6 people in a population of 1 million will die as a result of a lifetime exposure of 1μg/m³; for PAHs 87 people in a population will die from cancer following lifetime exposure to 1ng/m³.

** Specifically benzo[a]pyrene

Pollutants for which no WHO guidelines were set, because of the lack of reliable evidence of risk or evidence of a "safe" level, included 1,3 butadiene, PCBs, PCDDs, PCDFs, fluoride and platinum.

Source: WHO (2000, 2005).

Table 8.2 EU air quality limit values for the protection of human health

Pollutant	Target date	Measuring period	Limit value
Lead	2005	annual	$0.5\mu g/m^3$
Nitrogen dioxide	2010	hourly annual	105ppb ($200\mu g/m^3$) ≤18 exceedances per year 21ppb ($40\mu g/m^3$)
PM_{10}	Stage 1 2005	daily annual	$50\mu g/m^3$ ≤35 exceedances per year $40\mu g/m^3$
	Stage 2 2010	daily annual	$50\mu g/m^3$ ≤7 exceedances per year $20\mu g/m^3$
$PM_{2.5}$	Concentration cap 2010	annual	$25\mu g/m^3$ There is also a human exposure reduction target of 20% on 2010 value to be achieved by 2020.
Sulphur dioxide	2005	hourly daily	132ppb ($350\mu g/m^3$) ≤24 exceedances per year 47ppb ($125\mu g/m^3$) ≤3 exceedances per year
Ozone	2010	8-hourly	$120\mu g/m^3$ ≤25 exceedances per year averaged over 3 years
Benzene	2010	annual	$5\mu g/m^3$
PAHs	2012	annual	$1ng/m^3$ (Benzo(a)pyrene)
Carbon monoxide	2005	Running 8-hour mean	$10mg/m^3$
Cadmiun	2012	annual	$5ng/m^3$
Arsenic	2012	annual	$6ng/m^3$
Nickel	2012	annual	$20ng/m^3$

8.2.3 UK air quality standards and objectives

Part IV of the *Environment Act 1995* established the UK *Air quality strategy* (AQS), which was first published in 1997, and subsequently updated in 2000 and 2007 (Defra 2007a) It specifies air quality standards and objectives for key pollutants. The standards are derived from reviews undertaken by the independent Air Quality Expert Group (AQEG) (see www.defra.gov.uk/environment/airquality/panels/ aqeg/index.htm). Air quality standards are not given statutory backing and there is no timescale of attainment attached to them. Instead, the Government considers the standards as reference points to be used for setting air quality objectives. These objectives represent the Government's judgement of achievable air

Table 8.3 UK National Air Quality Strategy objectives for the protection of human health

Pollutant	Concentration	Measuring period	Target date
PAHs	0.25ng/m^3 B[a]P	Annual mean	31/12/2010
Benzene	5μg/m^3 (England and Wales)	Annual mean	31/12/2010
	3.25μg/m^3 (Scotland)	Annual mean	31/12/2010
1, 3-butaiene	2.25μg/m^3	Running annual mean	31/12/2003
CO	10mg/m^3	Running 8-hour mean	31/12/2003
Pb	0.5μg/m^3	Annual mean	31/12/2004
	0.25μg/m^3	Annual mean	31/12/2008
NO$_2$*	200μg/m^3 (≤18 exceedances a year)	1-hour mean	31/12/2005
	40μg/m^3	Annual mean	31/12/2005
O$_3$	100μg/m^3 (≤10 exceedances a year)	8-hour mean	31/12/2005
PM$_{10}$	50μg/m^3 (≤35 exceedances a year)	24-hour mean	31/12/2010
	40μg/m^3	Annual mean	31/12/2010
PM$_{2.5}$	25μg/m^3 (except Scotland)	Annual mean	2020
	12μg/m^3 (Scotland)	Annual mean	2020
	15% reduction target (urban areas UK)	Annual mean	2010–2020
SO$_2$*	266μg/m^3 (≤35 exceedances a year)	15-minute mean	31/12/2005
	350μg/m^3 (≤24 exceedances a year)	1-hour mean	31/12/2004
	125μg/m^3 (≤3 exceedances a year)	24-hour mean	31/12/2004

Notes
* Objectives for annual means of 30μg/m^3 for nitrogen oxides and 20μg/m^3 for SO$_2$ are set for the protection of vegetation and ecosystems.

Source: Defra (2007a).

quality by specified target years between 2003 and 2020 on the evidence of costs and benefits and technical feasibility (Defra 2007b). For some pollutants the objective is identical to the standard but for others a specified number of occasions exceeding the standard is permitted (**Table 8.3**). The UK has also specified public information air quality bands, classifying pollution levels into four bands: low, moderate, high and very high. If high or very high bands are experienced or are forecast to occur the next day, health advice is issued, being directed especially at sensitive groups in the community.

8.2.4 Emission standards

Air quality standards refer to the levels of air pollution to which people are exposed. Another type of legislated standard is the **emission standard** which specifies the maximum amount or concentration of a pollutant which is allowed to be emitted from a given source. Emission standards are usually derived from consideration of the cost and effectiveness of the control technology available. The EU Directive on Integrated Pollution Prevention and Control (IPPC) (96/61/EC) was adopted in 1996 (EC 1996b). This was transposed into national legislation with the PPC Regulations for England and Wales (SI 2000/1973), Scotland (SSI2000/323) and Northern Ireland (SR 2003/46) which came into force in 2000 and 2003 (available at the OPSI website, www.opsi.gov.uk). Major developments such as power stations are classed as A1 activities and require authorisation by the Environment Agency (EA) in England and Wales. Less-polluting industrial plants and processes constitute A2 or Part B activities and are regulated by local authorities (district councils, borough and city councils, unitary authorities).

For specific types of pollution sources, the existence of an emission standard implies the type of operating process or pollution control equipment that should be employed (Guidance Notes are being issued by the EA). Details of emissions and emissions factors are available from the National Atmospheric Emissions Inventory at www.naei.org.uk/emissions/index.php which is part of the UK Air Quality Archive site (www.airquality.co.uk).

Under PPC, emission restrictions apply to air, land and water such that the *Best Avaialable Techniques* (BAT) must be adopted (see EA 2003). For example, it is not appropriate to adopt a mitigation measure which removes gaseous pollutants from an industrial stack by converting them to a sludge, if disposal of the sludge would create an even worse environmental problem in the form of landfill and/or water pollution. Furthermore, the emphasis of BAT is towards efficient and thoughtful process design and engineering to minimise the potential for emissions in the first place, rather than attempting to deal with them at the point of release (so called tail-pipe solutions), which is to be considered acceptable only when all other opportunities to reduce emissions throughout a process (e.g. through efficient combustion, choice of fuel-stock etc.) have been exhausted.

Emission limits for pollutants can apply nationally. For example, the UNECE *Second sulphur protocol* that was ratified by the UK in 1996 commits the Government to reducing SO_2 emissions by 80 per cent over the period 1980 to 2010. The UNECE *Protocol to abate acidification, eutrophication and ground-level ozone* agreed in December 1999 sets national ceilings for four acidifying, eutrophying and ozone-forming air pollutants: SO_2, NO_x, VOCs and NH_3 (see Table 8.4). Stricter national ceilings for these four pollutants for 2010 are set out in the EU Directive on national emission ceilings for certain atmospheric pollutants (2001/81/EC) which came into force in 2001 (EC 2001) and implemented in the National Emission Ceilings Regulations 2002 (available at www.opsi.gov.uk/si/si2002/20023118.htm).

8.2.5 Regulations for hazardous chemicals

In the case of a proposed development that involves materials that could be harmful to people in the event of an accident, the EIA should include an indication of the preventative measures to be adopted, so that such an occurrence is not likely to have a significant effect (ODPM 2000). Requirements were first included in the EU "Seveso" Directive of 1982 (82/501/EEC) which was imple-mented as a consequence of chemical accidents at Flixborough (UK) in 1974 and Seveso (Italy) in 1976. This was subsequently replaced by "Seveso II" the Council Directive on the Control of Major-accident Hazards Involving Dangerous Substances (96/82/EC) (EC 1996c). In the UK this Directive has been implemented through the *Control of Major Accident Hazards Regulations 1999 (COMAH)* (HSE 2008). Under the *Planning (Hazardous Substances) Act 1990*, the presence of a hazardous substance above a specified "controlled quantity" requires consent from the hazardous substances authority. Local authorities take accident risk into account when making development decisions. The above UK legislation (and amendments) is available at www.opsi.gov.uk.

8.2.6 Climate standards and regulations

There are few legislated standards with regard to climate. The United States introduced regulations to ensure that visibility is protected in pristine areas such as national parks and wilderness areas. Persistent and coherent pollution plumes from industrial plants during daylight hours are considered intrusive and objectionable and mitigation measures to minimise or eliminate the plume are required. Similarly, in the UK visible plumes are regulated because they may constitute a visual nuisance (see EA 2003).

At the global scale there are regulations concerning pollutants that contribute to global warming and those that cause stratospheric ozone depletion. In 1997 the UK and other nations agreed the Kyoto Protocol to the UN Framework Convention on Climate Change, which came into force on 16 February 2005. Industrialised nations agreed to an overall emission reduction of 5.2 per cent of 1990 levels by 2008–2012 for the three common greenhouse gases (CO_2, N_2O and CH_4) and the three halocarbon substitutes – hydrofluorocarbons (HFCs), perfluorocarbons (PFCs) and sulphur hexachloride (SF_6) (a base year of 1995 can be employed for the last three pollutants). The overall 5.2 per cent reduction is to be achieved by some nations taking larger cuts than others: the EU accepted a reduction of 8 per cent, the USA 7 per cent and Japan 6 per cent.

The EU reduction of 8 per cent is to be spread among its 15 Member States, and the UK will be required to reduce greenhouse gas emissions by 12.5 per cent. Further, the UK Climate Change Bill, published in 2007, sets a statutory target of reducing emissions by 60 per cent by 2050 and by 26–32 per cent by 2020 compared to 1990 levels (see Defra 2008). Consequently, a proposed develop-ment which will be a significant source of greenhouse gases will receive close scrutiny, and many local and regional planning policies now include tests of green-house gas emissions as part of the planning application process.

Pollutants that damage the ozone layer e.g. chlorofluorocarbons (CFCs) (which also contribute to global warming), methyl chloroform, carbon tetrachloride, hydrofluorocarbons (HCFCs) and methyl bromide, are subject to the *Montreal Protocol on substances that deplete the ozone layer* and its subsequent amendments (UNEP 2000). The Protocol requires the production and consumption of these pollutants to be reduced and eventually phased out completely.

8.2.7 *Air quality and climate indicators used in EIA*

Aspects of air and climate which need to be addressed in preparing an EIA are summarised by the UK guidelines (ODPM 2000) as (a) level and concentration of chemical emissions and their environmental effects, (b) particulate matter, (c) offensive odours, and (d) any other climatic effects. Depending upon the development project there is a wide range of atmospheric pollutants with which an EIA may need to be concerned (**Table 8.4**). The existence of the AQS objectives and EU limit values clearly indicate the need to consider SO_2, fine particulates, CO, NO_2, Pb, benzene, 1,3 butadiene, O_3, PAHs, cadmium, arsenic, nickel and mercury. In addition, many other health-threatening pollutants, some of which have been given WHO guideline values and others which have not, simply because of insufficient evidence to be able to define an appropriate safe level, should be considered. These latter pollutants include polychlorinated biphenyls (PCBs), dioxins (PCDDs), furans (PCDFs), toxic chemicals (e.g. ammonia, fluoride, chlorine) and toxic metals (e.g. chromium, manganese, platinum). Ionising radiation (radionuclides) released from certain medical facilities and nuclear power plants should be considered too. EA guidance (EA 2003) also suggests that global warming potential (e.g. in terms of greenhouse gas emissions) should be assessed.

Offensive odours could be a problem around proposed sewage treatment works, chemical plants, paint works, food processing factories and brick works. Odours often generate great annoyance when residents are subjected to them in their gardens and homes, and they may adversely affect health (e.g. ranging from discomfort, nausea and headaches through to severe respiratory illness).

Climate indicators include temperature, relative humidity, solar radiation, precipitation, wind speed and wind direction. All developments are likely to modify the microclimate to some extent, but in most cases the changes to local temperature, amount of sunlight and shade, and airflow are minor and not considered in EIA unless there are special reasons for doing so. Significant effects on sensitive environmental receptors could arise due to local changes in the frequency of weather extremes such as fog, frost, ice, precipitation and wind gusts.

8.3 Scoping and baseline studies

8.3.1 *Introduction*

Before the impact of a proposed development can be predicted, it is necessary to establish the current baseline conditions concerning air pollution and climate, and to establish whether they are likely to change in the future, irrespective of the planned development. Knowledge of baseline pollution conditions is essential because, even when a development is likely to add only small amounts of pollution to the area, it could lead to air quality standards being exceeded if air quality in the area is already poor or may become poor in the future. This requires obtaining measurements of the ambient levels of the pollutants of concern at one or more locations in the study area, so as to assess the amount of pollution present.

Table 8.4 Key air pollutants and their anthropogenic sources

Pollutant	Anthropogenic sources
Sulphur dioxide (SO_2)	Coal- and oil-fired power stations, industrial boilers, waste incinerators, domestic heating, diesel vehicles, metal smelters, paper manufacturing
Particulates (dust, smoke, PM_{10}, $PM_{2.5}$)	Coal- and oil-fired power stations, industrial boilers, waste incinerators, domestic heating, many industrial plants, diesel vehicles, construction, mining, quarrying, cement manufacturing
Nitrogen oxides (NO_x: NO, NO_2)	Coal-, oil- and gas-fired power stations, industrial boilers, waste incinerators, motor vehicles
Carbon monoxide (CO)	Motor vehicles, fuel combustion
Volatile organic compounds (VOCs) e.g. benzene	Petrol-engine vehicle exhausts, leakage at petrol stations, paint manufacturing
Toxic organic micropollutants (TOMPS) e.g. PAHs, PCBs, dioxins	Waste incinerators, coke production, coal combustion
Toxic metals e.g. lead (Pb), cadmium (Cd)	Vehicle exhausts (leaded petrol), metal processing, waste incinerators, oil and coal combustion, battery manufacturing, cement and fertiliser production
Toxic chemicals, e.g. chlorine (Cl), ammonia (NH_3), fluoride (F^-)	Chemical plants, metal processing, fertiliser manufacturing
Greenhouse gases, e.g. carbon dioxide (CO_2), methane (CH_4)	CO_2: fuel combustion, especially power stations; CH_4: coal mining, gas leakage, landfill sites
Ozone (O_3)	Secondary pollutant formed from VOCs and nitrogen oxides
Ionising radiation (radionuclides)	Nuclear reactors and waste storage, some medical facilities
Odours	Sewage treatment works, landfill sites, chemical plants, oil refineries, food processing, paintworks, brickworks, plastics manufacturing

8.3.2 *Pollution data availability*

Using information from current pollution monitors is the simplest and least expensive approach to obtaining current baseline pollution levels. There are various national monitoring networks collecting pollution data and many local authorities, universities and other organisations undertake short-term or long-term monitoring of pollutants. Pollution data from various national networks – funded and/or coordinated by Defra and the devolved administrations, and including the Automatic and Non-automatic Monitoring Networks – are available via the UK Air Quality Archive (AQA) website (www.airquality.co.uk). Pollution monitoring sites are classified and coded by type of location so, in the absence of a monitoring site in the vicinity of the proposed development, the data may be considered as indicative of what may be experienced at similar sites in other areas. The AQA website also holds national air quality data as does Defra's e-Digest of Environmental Statistics (www.defra.gov.uk/environment/statistics/index.htm).

Expert opinion obtained from environmental consultancies and universities can advise on the validity of using pollution data from a monitoring site to represent pollution levels at a different location. Alternatively the data can be modified to reflect the location of interest by using established empirical relationships. In some cases empirical relationships enable the levels of one pollutant to indicate the likely levels of another pollutant. The UK Air Quality Archive internet site provides interactive GIS-based maps of background concentrations of certain pollutants for recent years, and projected background concentrations (or calculation methodologies to predict them) for future years.

Not all sites monitoring pollution are part of a national network. Since 1997, UK local authorities have been assessing air quality in their areas, in order to assist them in carrying out their statutory duty to work towards meeting the national air quality objectives, i.e. in Local Air Quality Management (LAQM) (see Defra 2006). Consequently, local authority Environmental Health Officers may be able to provide information concerning their own pollution monitoring. Many produce annual reports for their local authorities summarising the pollution data collected and assessing its significance in relation to air quality standards. Moreover:

- The AQS requires local authorities to complete a staged "Review and Assessment" of their air quality and the associated reports can be consulted (many are available from the LA web sites); and
- As part of LAQM, if a local authority finds areas where AQS standards are not currently met, and AQS objectives are not likely to be achieved, it must declare an Air Quality Management Area (AQMA) and draw up an Air Quality Action Plan (AQAP) setting out measures by which it proposes to improve air quality within in the AQMA – in which case there is a good likelihood of monitoring data being available. A map of AQMA locations is available on the AQA website.

8.3.3 *On-site pollution monitoring*

If pollution data are not available or are insufficient, then on-site monitoring will be required and should be planned and initiated during the scoping exercise of an EIA (Harrop 1993). A baseline monitoring programme needs to consider (a) what pollutants to monitor, (b) what type of monitor to employ, (c) the number and location of sampling sites, (d) the duration of the survey, and (e) the time resolution of sampling.

Selecting the equipment to measure air pollution concentrations depends upon (a) the intended use of the data, (b) the budget allocated to purchase or hire the equipment, and (c) the expertise of personnel available to set up and maintain the equipment and, in some cases, to undertake laboratory analyses of collected samples. Setting up an automatic pollutant analyzer can be costly, so hiring the equipment may be more appropriate. Environmental Protection UK (www. environmental-protection.org.uk/) holds a list of companies offering consultant expertise, and the UK Air Quality Archive holds a list of air quality monitoring equipment suppliers (at www.airquality.co.uk/archive/laqm/helpline.php). It is important that the equipment selected for monitoring is accredited nationally so that the data collected can be compared with UK and EU air quality standards (Defra 2003). Mooney (2006) provides a guide for local authorities purchasing air quality monitoring equipment.

Local authorities faced with the need to monitor pollution, in order to assess whether air quality objectives, are being attained are turning to relatively simple and inexpensive equipment such as passive diffusion tubes. These absorb the pollutant on to a specially-prepared metal gauze placed at the bottom of a short cylinder open at the other end to the atmosphere. After exposure the tubes are sent for laboratory analyses. They can provide useful information for a range of pollutants including ammonia, benzene, CO, hydrogen sulphide, NO_2, O_3 and SO_2. In areas of high pollution concentrations they can produce results for daily or even three-hourly exposures although in areas with low concentrations they are usually exposed for two weeks at a time. Monthly exposure readings from these tubes can provide estimates of the annual mean concentrations.

When using diffusion tubes, it is always preferable to correct the readings obtained from a specific batch against more sophisticated equipment and it is good practice to "co-locate" some diffusion tubes from the same batch as those exposed in the study area at an automatic pollution analyser. Once exposed, the results recorded by the co-located diffusion tubes can be compared with the results recorded by the automatic analyser for the same period that the tubes were exposed. Provided the automatic analyser is operating correctly, and has been calibrated, any difference between the two data sets is likely to be due to a bias in the measurement of the diffusion tubes and a "bias correction factor" can be calculated from this differential which is then applied to all results obtained from diffusion tubes exposed over the same period from the same batch. The process must be repeated for each set of diffusion tubes exposed as their bias will vary. Further details are provided in Defra 2003.

The duration of baseline monitoring will depend upon the pollutant to be tested and the standard which is to be assessed. Pollution concentrations vary from hour to hour, day to day, and month to month and are influenced by a range of external variables such as wind speed and direction, sunlight, temperature, precipitation, humidity etc. As a result, monitoring for a short period of time is unlikely to provide a satisfactory indication of baseline conditions. LAQM recommends a minimum monitoring period of three months, and six months is preferable for the pollutants set out in the AQS. For this reason, early commencement of monitoring in the EIA process is essential.

Pollution bio-indicators, types of plant that are sensitive to pollution levels (e.g. lichen for SO_2, tobacco plants for O_3) may provide supplementary information on pollution levels (Mulgrew and Williams 2000). Soil and vegetation analyses can also provide long-term levels of pollutants such as metals.

When siting monitoring equipment it is necessary to consider (a) the need to protect against vandalism, (b) access to the site, (c) the avoidance of pollution from indoor and localised sources which may make the data unrepresentative of the wider area, and (d) the availability of a power supply (if needed).

8.3.4 Projecting the baseline forwards: air pollution

Having established current baseline pollution levels, it is then necessary to consider how these levels are expected to change in the future, irrespective of the possible effects of the proposed development. If emission sources and strengths (as well as climate conditions) in the area are not expected to change in the future, then current pollution levels may be considered to approximate pollution levels in the next few years. However, changes in population and activity patterns, new industrial developments or closures, changes in fuels (e.g. decline of coal in favour of gas, the prohibition of leaded petrol in the EU since the start of 2000) and stricter emission standards (e.g. increasing number of vehicles fitted with catalytic converters) can affect emission rates. Weather conditions that favour a build up of pollutants (e.g. periods of calm or light winds, higher temperatures promoting increase evaporative emissions) may alter too, but in practice, these are not usually considered.

The implications of significant changes to emission rates and patterns for future pollution concentrations need to be assessed. Local, district and county authorities can usually supply information on new developments under construction as well as details of likely population and land use changes. A judgement will then have to be made as to how these and other changes (e.g. relevant UK and EU legislation) will alter emissions in the area and consequently alter baseline pollution levels.

If there are insufficient pollution data available in the study area, it may be necessary to compile an **emissions inventory** (Defra 2003). Taking into account the factors that may affect emissions in future years may enable emission sources and rates to be approximated for future years. These emission data then become the input into a suitable numerical dispersion model in order to predict future pollution concentrations in the area. Emission inventories for some pollutants, compiled for the purposes of the AQS, are available from local authorities and can save much time and effort. National 1 × 1km grid maps of current emissions from background sources are available from the UK Air Quality Archive at www.airquality.co.uk/archive/laqm/laqm.php.

8.3.5 Projecting the baseline forwards: climate

Baseline climate conditions can be established using meteorological data readily available from hundreds of sites throughout the UK maintained by the Meteorological Office (MO), local authorities, universities, schools and individual weather enthusiasts. Some national pollution monitoring sites, especially those with multiple automatic analyzers, also monitor meteorological conditions. The MO can supply hourly, daily, monthly, annual and long-term averages of temperature, relative humidity, air pressure, precipitation (including fog), wind speed and wind direction for any of its stations at a small cost, and in a format compatible with a number of the commonly used computational dispersion models. Although the meteorological site for which data are available may be some distance away from the study site, the MO and other meteorological consultants can provide expert advice concerning how local factors such as altitude, topography and proximity to the coast may lead to differences between the two locations, and the MO is now able to offer data which it underwrites to be representative for any geographical location in the UK, based on interpolation from the closest observation stations and mathematical processing to account for relevant conditions a the site in question.

Future climate baseline levels are not usually predicted for the purposes of an EIA, given the major limitations of current models in predicting regional changes, let alone local changes, attributed to say, global warming due to the increase in atmospheric concentrations of greenhouse gases. Improved models may alter this situation in the future (Houghton 2004, Hulme *et al.* 2002, MO 2008).

8.4 Impact prediction

8.4.1 Physical models and expert opinion

There are several types of models available to predict air pollution concentrations. Physical (scale) models using wind tunnels or computer graphics are employed occasionally in situations involving complex hilly terrain or where numerical models suggest uncertainty concerning the possible effects of nearby buildings on dispersion of pollution emissions.

Predictive methods include the use of expert opinion, providing it is backed up with reasons and justification which support that opinion, such as comparison with similar existing developments or planned projects for which prediction has already been undertaken. The use of expert opinion can be justified readily on cost when a number of similar projects are being proposed in different locations.

8.4.2 Numerical dispersion models

The type of model used most frequently in predicting air pollution is the numerical dispersion model. A numerical dispersion model takes the form of a computer program run on a personal computer. It calculates how specified emission rates are transformed by the atmospheric processes of dilution and dispersion (and sometimes chemical and photochemical processes) into ground level pollution concentrations at various distances from the source(s). Models are available for predicting pollution concentrations for emissions from a single point source (e.g. industrial stack or vent) as well as for emissions from a large number of point sources simultaneously. The basic model can be improved in accuracy by taking into account complications, appropriate to the specific location under study, such as type of terrain (e.g. flat or hilly), surface roughness (e.g. urban or rural conditions), coastal influences (e.g. effects of a sea breeze) and the presence of nearby buildings which may cause building wake effects. Models are also available for area sources (e.g. construction sites, car parks, motorway service stations, industrial processes with numerous vents, urban areas, county regions, storage lagoons), line sources (e.g. open roads, street canyons, railways) and volume sources (area sources with a vertical depth e.g. leaking gases from a group of industrial processes, take-off and landing activities at an airport).

Simple and complex (advanced) versions of numerical dispersion models are available. Simple (screening) models are designed to be applied relatively easily and inexpensively as a scoping tool to identify whether or not a problem warrants further investigation. Screening models employ grossly simplified assumptions about the behaviour of pollutants in the atmosphere and are designed to calculate the worst-case pollution concentrations. As such they have pre-set meteorological conditions and the user does not usually have to input any meteorological information. If a screening model predicts that emissions from a proposed development will produce air pollution concentrations far below an air quality standard, this would indicate that it may not be necessary to obtain a more accurate estimate of the predicted concentrations using a complex model. However, if the screening model predicts that pollution concentrations are likely to approach or exceed air quality standards then a more rigorous investigation using a complex model is needed. For major developments, regardless of how small an increase in pollution levels are caused by their emissions, the use of a complex model may be appropriate for an EIA. Additional software may be needed if the results are to be displayed graphically or in map/GIS form.

Some commonly used dispersion models are listed in **Table 8.5** and described below. The free or low-cost models are generally simple screening tools (some simple LAQM tools are also available from the UK Air Quality Archive). The cost of purchasing a model with a user-friendly windows-type computer interface is usually very worthwhile. Some environmental consultancies and other organisations have developed their own models (e.g. box models) or modified the standard ones (Barrowcliffe 1993, Street 1997). Further information on web-based resources for atmospheric dispersion studies is available from the UK Atmospheric Modelling Liaison Committee (ADMLC) at www.admlc.org.uk/

Table 8.5 Some commonly used air pollution numerical dispersion models

Model name	Source type[1]	Met. data needed[2]	Software costs[3]	Time needed[4]	Expertise needed[5]
CALTRANS (California Department of Transportation) (www.dot.ca.gov/hq/env/air/index.htm)					
CALINE 4	L,A	U	Free	M	L
CERC (Cambridge Environmental Research Consultants) (www.cerc.co.uk/software/index.htm)					
ADMS-Screen	P	N	£	M	L
ADMS 4	L,P,A,V	U,S,L	£££	H	L,E
ADMS-Roads	L	U,S,L	£££		
ADMS-Urban	L,P,A,A	U,S,L	££££	H	L,E
Environment Agency (see EA 1998, 2003, 2008)					
Guidance & H1 software tool	P	N	free	M	A
Highways Agency (HA 2007 & search for air quality spreadsheet at www.highways.gov.uk)					
DMRB screening method	L	N	free	M	A
Lakes Environmental (www.weblakes.com/ISCAERMOD/ISCAERFeatures.html)					
ISC-AERMOD View	P,A,V	U,S,L	£££	M/H	L,E
MO (Meteorological Office) (www.metoffice.gov.uk/environment/serv4.html).					
AEOLIUS	L	S	free	M	L
BOXURB	A	S	free	M	L
SMHI (Swedish Meteorological & Hydrologial Institute) (www.indic-airviro.smhi.se/)					
INDIC-Airviro	P,A,L	S,U	££££	M	L,E
USEPA (US Environmental Protection Agency) (www.epa.gov/scram001/dispersionindex.htm)					
AERMOD	P,A,V	U,S,L	££	M/H	L,E
CAL3QHC	L,A	U	££	M	L
ISC	P,A,V	U,S,L	£££	H	L,E
PAL (from www.ntis.gov/)	P,A,L	U	££	M	L
SCREEN 3	P	N	£	M	L

Notes

[1] L = Line, P = point, A = area, V = volume.

[2] Met data needed: N = none required (assumes worst-case scenario), U = user defined, S = sequential hourly, L = long-term statistical.

[3] If purchased commercially, with user-friendly input and output modules, single user prices are aproximately: £ = £50–£500, ££ = £500–£1,500, £££ = £1,500–£10,000, ££££ = > £10,000.

[4] Time for setting up and running a simple scenario such as a single stack or line source: M = minutes, H = hours.

[5] Expertise needed: A = basic maths calculator, L = understanding of air quality issues, E = expert use only.

links.htm, and the European Environment Agency's Topic Centre on Air and Climate Change (ETC/ACC) holds a comparative database of models at http:// pandora.meng.auth.gr/mds/strquery.php?wholedb. Guidance on the application of dispersion models is provided in ADMLC (2004) and Defra (2003).

The most appropriate **model outputs** that should be incorporated in an EIA are predictions of short-term pollution impact (e.g. highest or "worst-case" hourly mean concentration) and long-term impact (e.g. annual mean concentration). Outputs need to be compared with the appropriate air quality standards, objectives and guideline values and any locations which approach or exceed these concentrations must be identified. In some cases a model may not calculate pollution concentration over the averaging period used to define an air quality standard. For example, the UK SO_2 objective refers to a 15-minute averaging period. In this situation it is necessary to use empirical relationships to decide whether the air quality standard is exceeded or not. Air dispersion models are becoming more advanced in being able to predict short term averages, but it is always worth remembering that the smallest unit of time that meteorological data they use is based upon is one hour – so any predictions presented by the model for periods of less than one hour are mathematical calculations performed within the model and will be based on empirical relationships. It may be best, therefore, to set up the model to predict the hourly concentrations and apply further calculations outside the model so that the user has a clear understanding and ownership of what has been done. Guidance on such empirical calculations is provided in Defra (2003). An EIA should seek to specify predicted concentrations at sensitive receptors such as the nearest residential housing, hospital, school etc.

One of the key benefits of using more complex models is that they allow the user to generate graphical outputs such as **isoline plots** which can greatly assist the reader of the EIA in understanding the results being presented (**Figure 8.1**). Many of the latest models will also interface with Geographical Information Systems (GIS) (see Chapter 14). If residential maps and census data are included as GIS datasets, these be overlain with model pollution isolines, etc so that the change in exposure to pollution from a given source can be presented in terms of the number of households or even an estimate of the number of people, affected. Hourly maxima concentrations may be shown as a plot of concentration versus downwind distance for a range of specified meteorological conditions including those conditions which give rise to the highest concentration (see Figure 8.2).

8.4.3 Models assumptions and models for point sources

For many years numerical prediction models have been based on Gaussian assumptions. The **Gaussian model** assumes that the pollutant emissions spread outwards from a source in an expanding plume aligned to the wind direction, in such a way that the distribution of pollution concentration decreases away from the plume axis in horizontal and vertical planes, according to a specific Gaussian mathematical equation, a symmetric bell-shaped distribution. Although a plume may appear irregular at any one moment, its natural tendency to meander results

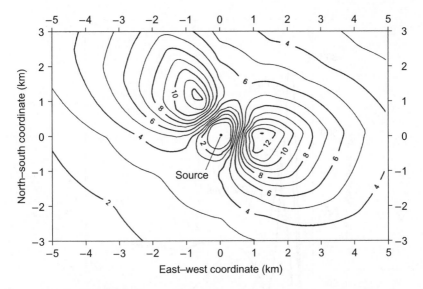

Figure 8.1 Predicted distribution of annual averaged ground level concentrations of sulphur dioxide (μg/m³) due to emissions from a 50-metre-high stack using the US EPA Industrial Source Complex model. As is often the case with UK climate data (in this example, data from Aughton, near Liverpool), the result is a distribution with two distinct peaks (to the northwest and east of the source).

in a smooth cone-shaped Gaussian distribution after ten minutes of averaging time. The horizontal axis of the plume does not normally coincide with the height of the stack or point of emission, as the density and momentum of the emissions quickly carries the plume to a higher elevation, known as the "effective release height" (sometimes many times higher than the stack or point of emission). The maximum ground level concentration experienced from a pollution plume is where the plume touches the ground.

Gaussian models assume the rate of dispersion of the plume, and consequently the pollution concentrations experienced at any location at the surface, are a function of wind speed, wind direction and atmospheric stability (Barrowcliffe 1993, Defra 2003, Middleton 1998). Estimates of atmospheric stability for the simpler versions of the model can be obtained using a table or nomogram involving solar radiation, cloud cover and mean wind speed and expressed in the form of six or seven **Pasquill stability categories**. Stability categories range from class A (very unstable) occurring during hot, sunny conditions with light winds through category 4 (neutral) to class F or G (both very stable) occurring during cold, still nights with clear skies. For the purposes of the model, it is assumed that each stability class is characterised by a specified depth of boundary layer into which the pollutants are mixed. Typical mixing heights are around 1,500m for very unstable conditions through 800m for neutral conditions to only 100m for very stable conditions. When using the model to predict annual average pollution concentrations, the necessary summary of Pasquill stability classes for the

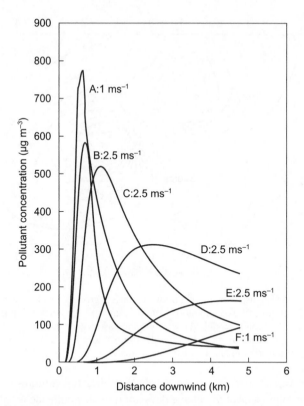

Figure 8.2 Predicted one-hour average sulphur dioxide concentrations (μg/m^3) due to emissions from a 50-metre-high stack using the US EPA Industrial Source Complex model (ISC) for the "worst-case" wind speed in each Pasquill atmospheric stability class.

nearest meteorological station can be obtained from the Meteorological Office Air Pollution Consultancy Group. These tables indicate the annual percentage frequencies of each stability class by 30-degree wind direction sectors in six wind speed bands, averaged over several years of data.

Figure 8.2 highlights that the highest ground level concentrations from an elevated source tend to occur close to the source during light winds when the atmosphere is very unstable with substantial vertical mixing such as happens on hot summer days. It can also be seen that during light winds the peak concentration is found further from the source during conditions of increasing atmospheric stability. Where tall buildings lie adjacent to a tall stack, an occasion of strong winds is another situation that can give rise to high ground-level concentrations. This happens because buildings cause eddies to form that make the plume touch the ground much closer than would be expected otherwise. It is generally considered that building downwash problems may occur if the stack height is less than 2.5 times the height of the building upon which it protrudes. Similarly problems may occur if adjacent buildings are within about five stack heights of the release point. Other situations giving rise to high pollution concentrations may be when plumes impact directly on hillsides under certain meteorological conditions, or when valleys trap emissions during low-level inversions (DETR 2000).

More recently, what are termed second- or new-generation models have been developed which employ atmospheric dispersion assumptions based on recent improvements in the understanding of the behaviour of pollutants released into the atmosphere (DETR 2000, Middleton 1998). In particular they recognise that there are different turbulence and diffusion characteristics within the atmosphere at different heights and so treat the atmosphere in a more realistic way.

The ADMS (Atmospheric Dispersion Modelling System) was introduced by Cambridge Environmental Research Consultants (CERC) in 1993 and has been developed to the current ADMS4 version (see Table 8.5). In addition to predicting long-term concentrations it has the ability to predict short-term concentrations over averaging times of a few seconds, as is needed in the case of odours. It employs boundary layer data such as surface heat flux and boundary layer depth instead of Pasquill stability categories as its meteorological data. In 1998 the US EPA released their new generation model, AERMOD, which is under continued development. It contains improved algorithms for convective and stable boundary layers, and for computing vertical profiles of wind, turbulence and temperature. In 2000 the UK Meteorological Office teamed up with Lakes Environmental to create a more user-friendly interface for this model, ISC-AERMOD View (see Table 8.5) which may prove to be a strong competitor to ADMS in the UK. A fluid dynamics model, *fluiyin* PANACHE, is available (from www.fluidyn.com) which can predict concentrations for industrial (and traffic) sources and offers good treatment of very low wind speeds and wind-flow patterns around uneven terrain and high-rise buildings.

8.4.4 Road traffic models

Several models have been developed specifically to predict pollution concentrations arising from emissions from road vehicles. The simplest is the Department of Transport's nomogram-based *Design manual for roads and bridges* (DMRB) screening model which can be used to indicate those areas, if any, where air pollution is likely to cause concern (HA 2007). An Excel spread sheet version (available from www.highways.gov.uk/business/238.aspx) is very simple to apply, and is used (a) widely by planners as a screening model, and (b) in the DfT's *Transport Analysis Guidance* (TAG) (DfT 2004). A more advanced road model is CALINE4 (the California Line Source Dispersion model, version 4). This Gaussian model can model junctions, street canyons, parking lots, bridges and underpasses and predicts one-hour concentrations of pollutants such as CO and NO_2. The model can handle up to 20 road links and 20 receptors (locations at which the pollution impact of the emissions will be predicted). The USEPA PAL (the Point, Area and Line source model) extends the CALINE algorithms to treat edge effects more accurately which makes it useful for predicting concentrations from car parks and small areas of a city for up to 99 point, area and line sources and 99 receptors.

The USEPA CAL3QHC model (developed by extending the CALINE3 model to take into account Queuing and Highway Capacity considerations) is appropriate for traffic-congested roads and complex intersections, being able to incorporate emissions from both moving and engine-idling vehicles. It is able to predict one-hour means concentrations for up to 120 road links and 120 receptors. Road traffic model outputs can be produced for specified locations or additional software can be used to convert the results into map form to show isolines of various pollution concentrations. The CALINE4 and CAL3QHC models and user guides can be downloaded from the internet.

The AEOLIUS model, developed by the UK Meteorological Office, enables the user to predict one-hour mean concentrations of pollutants from traffic flowing along a canyon-like street such as is found in city centres. Screening and full versions (AEOLIUSF, AEOLIUSQ) of this model can be downloaded free from the MO website (see Table 8.5). ADMS-Urban (Atmospheric Dispersion Modelling System, Urban module) can cope with up to 1,000 road sources and includes a street canyon option.

8.4.5 Emissions data input to models

All numerical dispersion models require emissions data either in the form of a specified emission rate for the source (e.g. the amount of pollutant released per unit of time) or a measure of the level of activity of the source (e.g. amount of fuel consumed) together with the corresponding emission factor (e.g. the quantity of pollutant emitted per unit of activity). Emission rates need not necessarily be exact, as the likely impact of a planned development could be assessed by using the highest likely emissions, such as the maximum emission limits defined for prescribed processes. If the emission rate for a proposed development is not already specified in the plant design then an estimate may be based upon expected fuel consumption and characteristics of the fuel, or by obtaining "surrogate" information from another, similar plant or process elsewhere. Information on emissions and emission factors are available from the UK Emission Factors Database, accessible via www.naei.org.uk/emissions/index.php. Emissions factors (F) are described in terms of, for example, grams of NO_x per km driven for vehicles, grammes of NO_x per kilowatt fired for boilers, and grams of NO_x per tonne of nitric acid product for a nitric acid works. Emissions would then be calculated as $M \times F$ where M is a measure of the level of activity.

Typical emission rates can be used when calculating long-term pollution concentrations but for short-term models a number of worst-case scenarios may be needed (e.g. periods of intensive activity, during start-up, and the operation of emergency release vents). Complex models applied to a point source will require input information about the release conditions of the emissions. This may include the stack height and internal exit diameter as well as the flue-gas exit temperature and exit velocity (or volumetric flow rate).

In the case of road traffic models, vehicle emission rates for a specific section of road are calculated by the model itself from input data such as vehicle flow (e.g. vehicles per day, peak hourly value), average vehicle speed, vehicle mix (e.g. fraction of heavy goods vehicles, fraction of petrol- and diesel-engine cars) and vehicle emission factors (Defra 2003). If the model is being used to predict pollution concentrations for a future year, then input forecast data not only for future traffic flow, speed and mix are needed but also the likely change in emission factors. Emission factors for future years, which take into account the expected effects of phasing in of cleaner technologies and fuels, are available from the UK Air Quality Archive www.airquality.co.uk/archive/laqm/tools.php and are already embedded in some models such as the DMRB and ADMS Roads.

8.4.6 Model limitations

All predictions have an element of uncertainty and it is important to acknowledge this and not treat the model as a "black box" by concentrating only on the results produced. Models are simplifications of reality and their limitations, accuracy and confidence levels should be recognised and explained (ADMLC 2004, Benarie 1987, Defra 2003, RMetS 1995). Some limitations have yet to be resolved such as the availability of detailed and accurate meteorological and emissions input data: the quality of the input data will clearly affect the accuracy of a model. Even if accurate input data were available the algorithms employed in the model to represent the behaviour of pollutants released into the atmosphere contain many uncertainties. Confidence in the accuracy of a model is gained by assessing its ability to predict the current baseline conditions in the study area since the results can be verified using monitored pollution data, and current guidance on modelling local air quality sets out methodologies that can be applied to verify modelled results against monitoring data collected at the same location as the model's predictions. This guidance, and guidance published by the National Society for Clean Air (NSCA 2006) also sets out the importance of understanding systematic and mathematical errors inherent in any modelling results, so that the user is able to make judgements as to the validity of the model outputs.

8.4.7 Assessing significance

The level of significance of the likely pollution impacts of a proposed development is assessed by comparing the predicted changes in the area to air quality standards, objectives or guideline values, and determining whether these are likely to be exceeded at any locations, after taking into account the existing and predicted baseline pollution levels. If the planned development is predicted to increase pollution levels in excess or close to the air quality standard, then mitigation measures need to be proposed. If the changes are well below the standard, it is useful to express the increase in ground level pollution concentrations in a meaningful way. For example, an EIA may conclude that a proposed development is expected to increase the annual average NO_2 concentration at the location worst affected (5km downwind) by only 3 per cent and that this increase is well within the year-to-year variability of annual average concentration produced by meteorological fluctuations. Even when a development is likely to add only small amounts of pollution to the area, it is important that an EIA makes specific assessment of what effect (perhaps negligible) this will have on any nearby sensitive receptors such as residential areas, schools, historical buildings, and ecosystems. A number of organisations have published guidance to assist in the assignation of significance to the results of air dispersion modelling. These include the Environment Agency's Air Quality Modelling and Assessment Unit (AQMAU) (at www.environment-agency.gov.uk/subjects/airquality/?version=1&lang=_e) and the Association of London Government (ALG) (www.alg.gov.uk).

Determining the level of significance of climate changes can be difficult in some cases. A local increase in temperature, wind turbulence, fog or frost may affect people, and wildlife directly or indirectly (e.g. fog causing road accidents), but the level of significance of the changes may require the use of expert opinion.

8.5 Mitigation

8.5.1 *The need for mitigation measures*

Mitigation measures should aim to avoid, reduce, or remedy any significant adverse effects that a proposed development is predicted to produce. At one extreme, the prediction and evaluation of likely impacts may indicate such extreme adverse effects that abandonment or complete redesign of the proposed development is the only effective mitigating measure. More likely, modifications to the development can be suggested in order to avoid or reduce potential impacts (Wood 1989, 1990, Defra 2003/2005). Some mitigation measures may be required by law for new – though not for existing – developments (e.g. fitting of specific types of pollution-control devices) but the use of others depends upon the significance of the predicted impacts. In the case of industrial processes authorised under the IPPC regime, the mitigation of impacts through design is always promoted ahead of the application of "end of pipe" processing to "clean up" emissions which could have been avoided through alternative process design.

Various mitigation measures may be suggested to solve a potential problem and it is important to assess the likely effectiveness of each measure in terms of the extent to which the problem will be reduced, as well as to indicate the costs of implementation. Whatever mitigation measures are proposed, it is important to ensure that they do not create problems of their own. Mitigation feeds back into design, so mitigation measures proposed to minimise adverse impacts of the project can be incorporated as alternatives in the project description. Subsequent proposed developments can make use of the information contained in a previous EIA in order to incorporate appropriate mitigation measures at the outset, rather than wait for its own EIA to identify potential problems.

8.5.2 *Mitigating adverse pollution impacts*

If a planned development is likely to exceed say, maximum hourly pollution standards only during periods of poor atmospheric dispersion, then one possible mitigation measure would to keep a cleaner stand-by fuel for use during those forecasted occasions or to reduce emissions by reducing production output in the case of an industrial process. Improved fuel combustion designs can reduce pollutant emissions, such as by using low nitrogen oxides burners in furnaces. In many cases the type and amount of pollutants emitted are a function of the fuel being burned, so alternative fuels can be proposed, such as fuel oil with a very low sulphur content or natural gas. Traffic-generated pollutants decrease rapidly away from roads, and this process can be enhanced by roadway trenching, embankments, walls and trees, to reduce the pollution concentrations in nearby residential areas. A number of innovative solutions are also becoming available, such as pollutant absorbing paving stones, which are specially treated with catalysts to photo-oxidise certain pollutants, thereby reducing concentrations in roadside urban environments. Such innovations are still in the early stages of development, and their longevity is not fully proven.

The **construction stage** of most projects has the potential to cause localised wind-blown dust problems, either when excavation is taking place or when materials are being transported and stored in stockpiles. Careful design of construction operations including the selection of haulage routes into the site and the location of stockpiles can help to minimise dust problems in nearby residential areas. Mitigation measures can include (a) frequent spraying of stockpiles and haulage roads with water, (b) regular sweeping of access roads, (c) covering of lorries carrying materials, (d) enclosing conveyor-belt delivery systems, and (e) early planting of peripheral tree screens where they are part of the planned development.

The need for mitigation measures may not always be clear. For example, should action be taken to ensure odours from a food processing plant are not experienced by residents of a few isolated houses on several days each year when the wind blows in their direction? In such a situation, consultation with the local planning authority will be needed to agree whether the impacts are sufficiently adverse to justify the cost of mitigation measures. Alternatively the local authority may suggest the developer offers compensation to the affected residents, or offers to purchase the affected properties in order to create a buffer zone around the plant. If potential odour problems are to be tackled at source, solutions include taller stacks to encourage greater dispersion of the emissions, or removal of the pollutant completely by absorption, adsorption, oxidation or chemical conversion.

8.5.3 *Mitigating adverse microclimate impacts*

Adverse microclimatic changes, such as increased wind turbulence around a proposed shopping precinct, can be minimised by the widening of narrow gaps between buildings, roofing of open spaces and changing the height and layout of buildings (Oke 1987). Unwelcome high air temperatures in open shopping precincts during summer can be reduced by the choice of building materials, consideration of building layout in relation to areas of sun and shade, and the planting of trees. Frost pockets affecting agricultural and horticultural crops can be prevented by landscaping and creating openings through road or railway embankments, which allow for the passage of cold air. The frequency of icing of roads can be reduced by landscaping and choice of road surface materials. The frequency of fog forming on cold clear nights along proposed motorways can be lessened by (a) eliminating any nearby areas of standing water, (b) reducing air pollution (suspended particulates) in the vicinity, (c) raising the road onto pillars above the fog-shrouded valley floor, and (d) planting tree belts which help reduce cold-air drainage and scavenge fog droplets. Water vapour plumes from power station cooling towers, which have the potential to increase fog and icing of nearby roads, can be designed so that the banks of towers are oriented along the direction of the prevailing wind, such that the merging of individual plumes enhances buoyancy and reduces the number of occasions when plumes are brought to the ground.

8.6 Monitoring

Numerical prediction models contain uncertainties so monitoring should be continued after completion of the development to compare predictions with those that actually occur. Confirmation of the accuracy of the predictions will provide credibility to the process of EIA, but it is important to provide options within the assessment for action to be taken to address potential problems should monitoring indicate that impacts are not as they were originally predicted to be, whatever the reason. This is particularly appropriate if similar projects are likely to be proposed in the future for other locations. Continued monitoring is also necessary to assess the effectiveness of any mitigation measures proposed in an EIA and to ensure that any potential air and climate problems identified have been minimised or eliminated.

References

ADMLC (UK Atmospheric Dispersion Modelling Liaison Committee) 2004. *Guidelines for the preparation of dispersion modelling assessments for compliance with regulatory requirements*, Version 1.4. Didcot, Oxon: ADMLC, www.admlc.org.uk/model_guidelines/documents/ADMLC-2004-3.pdf.

Barrowcliffe R 1993. The practical use of dispersion models to predict air quality impacts. Paper presented at the IBC Technical Services Conference on Environmental Emissions: Monitoring Impacts and Remediation, London (paper available from Environmental Resources Management).

Benarie MM 1987. The limits of air pollution modelling. *Atmospheric Environment* **21**, 1–5.

Canter LW 1996. *Environmental impact assessment* (Ch. 22). New York: McGraw-Hill.

Colls J 1997. *Air pollution: an introduction*. London: E & FN Spon.

Defra (Department for Environment, Food and Rural Affairs) 2003. *Part IV of the Environment Act 1995: Local Air Quality Management, Technical Guidance LAQM.TG(03)*. London: TSO, www.defra.gov.uk/environment/airquality/local/guidance/index.htm.

Defra 2003/2005. *Part IV of the Environment Act 1995: Local Air Quality Management, Policy Guidance LAQM.PG(03) and Appendum LAQM.PGA(05)*. London: TSO, www.defra.gov.uk/environment/airquality/local/guidance/index.htm.

Defra 2005. *About climate change: UK effects*. London: Defra, www.defra.gov.uk/environment/climatechange/about/ukeffect.htm.

Defra 2006. *Local air quality management (LAQM)*. www.defra.gov.uk/environment/airquality/local/index.htm.

Defra (in partnership with the devolved administrations) 2007a. *The Air Quality Strategy for England, Scotland, Wales and Northern Ireland*. London: TSO, www.defra.gov.uk/environment/airquality/strategy/index.htm.

Defra 2007b. *An economic analysis to inform the review of the Air Quality Strategy*. London: TSO.

Defra 2008. *UK legislation: taking the Climate Change Bill forward – progress*. www.defra.gov.uk/Environment/climatechange/uk/legislation/index.htm.

DETR 2000. *Selection and use of dispersion models*, LAQM.TG3(00). London: HMSO.

DfT (Department for Transport) 2004. *Transport Analysis Guidance (TAG): The Local Air Quality Sub-objective: TAG Unit 3.3.3*. London: DfT, www.webtag.org.uk/webdocuments/3_Expert/3_Environment_Objective/3.3.3.htm.

DH (Department of Health) 2001 (updated 2008). *Health effects of climate change in the UK*. www.dh.gov.uk/en/Publicationsandstatistics/Publications/PublicationsPolicyAndGuidance/DH_4007935.

EA (Environment Agency) 1998. *Guidance for estimating the air quality impact of stationary sources*. National Centre for Risk Analysis & Options Appraisal Report GN 24. London: EA.

EA (Environment Agency) 2003. *Integrated pollution prevention and control (IPPC): environmental assessment and appraisal of BAT*, Version 6 (2003). Bristol: EA, www.environment-agency.gov.uk/commondata/acrobat/h1v6_jul03guidance_608809.pdf.

EA 2008. H1 *Environmental risk assessment: Part 1 – Simple assessment of environmental risk for accidents, odour, noise and fugitive emissions; Part 2 – Assessment of point source releases and cost-benefit analysis; and H1 software tool*. Bristol: EA, www.environmentagency.net/business/1745440/1745496/1906135/1986067/?version=1&lang=_e.

EC (European Commission) 1996a. Council Directive 96/62/EC of 27 September 1996 on ambient air quality assessment and management. *Official Journal L 296, 21/11/1996 P. 0055 – 0063*, http://europa.eu.int/eur-lex/lex/LexUriServ/LexUriServ.do?uri=CELEX:31996L0062:EN:HTML.

EC 1996b. Council Directive 96/61/EC of 24 September 1996 concerning integrated pollution prevention and control. *Official Journal L 257, 10/10/1996 P. 0026 – 0040*, http://eur-lex.europa.eu/LexUriServ/LexUriServ.do?uri=CELEX:31996L0061:EN:HTML.

EC 1996c. Council Directive 96/82/EC of 9 December 1996 on the control of major-accident hazards involving dangerous substances. *Official Journal L 010, 14/01/1997 P. 0013 – 0033*, http://europa.eu/scadplus/leg/en/lvb/l21215.htm.

EC 2001. Directive 2001/81/EC of the European Parliament and of the Council of 23 October 2001 on national emission ceilings for certain atmospheric pollutants. *Official Journal of the European Communities L 309/22, 27.11.2001*, http://eur-lex.europa.eu/LexUriServ/LexUriServ.do?uri=OJ:L:2001:309:0022:0030:EN:PDF.

Elsom DM 1992. *Atmospheric pollution: a global problem*, 2nd edn. Oxford: Blackwell.

Elsom DM 1996. *Smog alert: managing urban air quality*. London: Earthscan.

Elsom DM 2001. Air quality and climate. Ch. 8 in *Methods of environmental impact assessment*, 2nd edn, P Morris and R Therivel (eds). London: Spon Press.

HA (Highways Agency) 2007. *Design manual for roads and bridges (DMRB)*, Vol. 11: *Environmental assessment*, Section 3, Part 1: *Air quality*. London: Highways Agency (Department for Transport), www.standardsforhighways.co.uk/dmrb/vol11/section3.htm.

Harrop DO 1993. Environmental impact assessment and incineration. In *Air quality impact assessment*. RM Harrison (ed.). London: Royal Society of Chemistry.

Houghton JT 2004. *Global warming: the complete briefing*, 3rd edn. Cambridge: Cambridge University Press.

HSE (Health and Safety Executive) 2008. *Control of major accident hazards regulations 1999 (COMAH)*. London: HSE, www.hse.gov.uk/comah/index.htm.

Hulme M, GJ Jenkins, X Lu, JR Turnpenny, TD Mitchell, RG Jones, J Lowe, JM Murphy, D Hassell, P Boorman, R McDonald and S Hill 2002. *Climate change scenarios for the United Kingdom: the UKCIP02 scientific report.* Tyndall Centre for Climate Change Research, School of Environmental Sciences, University of East Anglia, www.ukcip.org.uk/index.php?option=com_content&task=view&id=353.

Juniper T 2007. *Saving planet earth.* London: Collins (by arrangement with the BBC).

Middleton DR 1998. *Manual for modelling: a guide to Local Authorities.* Turbulence and Diffusion Note Number 241. Bracknell, Berks: Meteorological Office.

MO (Meteorological Office) 2008. *Types of climate models.* Exeter: Meteorological Office, www.metoffice.gov.uk/research/hadleycentre/models/modeltypes.html.

Mooney D 2006. *A guide for local authorities purchasing air quality monitoring equipment.* Harwell, Oxon: AEA Technology, www.airquality.co.uk/archive/reports/cat06/0608141644-386_Purchasing_Guide_for_AQ_Monitoring_Equipment_Version2.pdf.

Mulgrew A and P Williams 2000. *Biomonitoring of air quality using plants.* Air Hygiene Report 10. Berlin: WHO Collaborating Centre for Air Quality Management and Air Pollution Control.

Murley L 1995. *Clean air around the world,* 3rd edn. Brighton: IUAPPA/NSCA.

NSCA (National Society for Clean Air) 2006. *Development control: planning for air quality.* Bedford: NSCA, www.airquality.co.uk/archive/laqm/ap_guidance.php.

Oke TR 1987. *Boundary layer climates,* 2nd edn. London: Methuen (Reprinted by Routledge 2003).

ODPM (Office of the Deputy Prime Minister) 2000. *Environmental impact assessment: guide to procedures.* London: ODPM, www.communities.gov.uk/documents/planningandbuilding/pdf/157989.

Ortolano L 1997. *Environmental regulation and impact assessment* (Ch. 6). New York: John Wiley & Sons.

RMetS (Royal Meteorological Society Policy) 1995. *Atmospheric dispersion modelling: guidelines on the justification and use of models, and the communication and reporting of results.* Published in collaboration with DoE. Reading: Royal Meteorological Society.

Street E 1997. EIA and pollution control. In *Planning and environmental impact assessment in practice,* J Weston (ed.), 164–179. London: Longman.

Turco RT 2002. *Earth under siege: from air pollution to global change,* 2nd edn. New York: Oxford University Press Inc.

UKCIP (UK Climate Impacts Programme) 2008. *UKIP02: maps – seasonal changes.* Oxford: UKCIP, www.ukcip.org.uk/index.php?option=com_content&task=view&id=357&Itemid=396.

UNEP (United Nations Environment Programme) 2000. *Montreal Protocol on substances that deplete the ozone layer.* Nairobi: UNEP, www.unep.org/ozone/Montreal-Protocol/Montreal-Protocol2000.shtml.

WHO (World Health Organization) 2000. *Air quality guidelines for Europe,* 2nd edn. Copenhagen: WHO Regional Office for Europe, www.euro.who.int/air/activities/20050223_3.

WHO 2005. *Air quality guidelines – global update for particulate matter, ozone nitrogen oxide and sulphur dioxide,* www.who.int/phe/health_topics/outdoorair_aqg/en/.

Wood CM 1989. *Planning pollution prevention: anticipating controls over air pollution sources.* Oxford: Heinemann Newnes.

Wood CM 1990. Air pollution control by land use planning techniques: a British–American review. *International Journal of Environmental Studies* **35**, 233–243.

9 Soils, geology and geomorphology

Chris Stapleton, Kevin Hawkins and Martin Hodson (based on Hodson, Stapleton and Emberton 2001)

9.1 Introduction

Much has been written about the links between soils, geology and civilisation, but considerably less is known about the impact of human activity on soils and geology. The EU/UK EIA legislation (see §1.3) specifically identifies soil as one of the main environmental *receptors* of development impacts for which assessments must be carried out. The DoE (1989) guidance on the scope of EIAs includes soil, agricultural quality, geology and geomorphology as topics in the checklist that should be included in an EIA. This has recently (June 2006) been updated by DCLG through a consultation paper *Environmental impact assessment: a guide to good practice and procedures,* (DCLG 2006a).

Soil is defined as the top layer of the land surface within the biosphere. It is a component/subsystem of terrestrial ecosystems, providing a growing medium for flora, and a habitat for fauna (see Figures 11.4 and 11.5). From the human perspective, soil is also the basis of agricultural and forestry production for food, wood, and textiles. Avoiding significant development impacts on the soil ultimately protects the whole of the ecosystem from degradation. An understanding of the local environment would be incomplete without reference to the underlying geology, but less emphasis is generally given to impacts on this, because relatively few types of development have significant impacts on geology. This chapter therefore concentrates on the assessment of significant soil impacts, although some important geological and geomorphological aspects are described briefly.

9.2 Definitions and concepts – geology and geomorphology

9.2.1 Geology

Geology is a vast and complex subject, and only a few aspects of relevance to EIA will be mentioned here. Keller (2000) is a good introduction to environmental geology covering the topics of interest in this context. Surface geology concerns superficial deposits (e.g. drift, glacial deposits, river gravel) while solid geology only concerns pre-superficial formations. The three main groups of rock are igneous, sedimentary and metamorphic. Many different igneous rocks have formed as a result of volcanic activity, they are characteristically hard and crystalline, and have crystallised from magma, a silicate melt. Sedimentary rocks are formed from pre-existing rocks by processes of denudation and sedimentation. They are relatively soft and easily eroded and include limestones, coal, *evaporites* and sedimentary iron ores. Sedimentary rock strata are often important as *aquifers*, and many are rich in fossils. Metamorphic rocks are formed as the result of heat, pressure and chemical activity on pre-existing solid rock.

A number of aspects of geology are of direct importance in EIA. *Earth Heritage Sites* or *Geological Conservation Review (GCR) sites* (some of which are Sites of Special Scientific Interest – SSSIs) are important for the conservation, protection and management of their fossils, stratigraphy, minerals or other geological interest. They have scientific and amenity value, and include exposures of value to wildlife (e.g. rocky shores, shingle structures, cliffs, screes, and limestone pavements). The underlying geology also has engineering and construction implications, and affects both geochemistry, and geophysics (Ellison and Smith 1998, Bell 2000).

Some geological aspects are of less direct importance in EIA. For example, both the storage and movement of ground and surface waters, and water geochemistry will be affected by the hard geology of an area (see Chapter 10). In addition, the physical and chemical properties of soils will be determined, as most soils are derived from bedrock or transported rock. The geology and hydrogeology of a site influences the potential for on-site and off-site *pollution* as a result of development, and the extent of any pollution that may have occurred in the past. Finally, competition between mineral extraction and other land uses is also an important topic in some circumstances (Ellison and Smith 1998).

9.2.2 Geomorphology

Geomorphology can be defined as "the study of landforms, and in particular their nature, origin, processes of development and material composition" (Cooke and Doornkamp 1990). 'Material composition' includes both the geology and, where present, the soil. Geomorphology therefore includes the study of topography (the terrain), the factors that have moulded the land to the present form (including the nature of the rock and soils in relation to the *erosion* and deposition caused by glaciers and rivers). Human impacts can include landscape/visual aspects (Chapter 6), but also consequences such as erosion (Cooke and Doornkamp 1990), slope failure and subsidence, and *sedimentation* in aquatic systems. Some aspects of geomorphology, such as soil erosion, overlap with soil studies.

9.3 Definitions and concepts – soils

The productive value of soils is determined by a number of important physical and chemical properties. An appreciation of a development's impacts on soils requires an understanding of basic soil features. The coverage of soil science here is necessarily brief, and the reader is referred to Ashman and Puri (2002), Brady and Weil (2002), and Gerard (2000) for further information.

9.3.1 *Soil composition*

There are two major types of soil: mineral and organic. Typically mineral soils have four major components: mineral particles, usually derived from **weathering** of parent rock (about 45 per cent of the volume); organic matter (about 5 per cent); water (about 25 per cent); and air (about 25 per cent). Organic matter is an important component of the soil that is derived mainly from decomposing vegetation. It combines with inorganic particles and cements like iron oxides and calcium carbonate to create stable structural aggregates. The nature of the organic matter in topsoils varies according to the vegetation cover and environmental conditions. In cool wet areas, the organic matter decomposes at a relatively slower rate and tends to be more acidic. In more temperate areas, the organic matter decomposes more completely to form stable complex compounds that are collectively known as **humus**. Most arable agricultural topsoils contain 2–6 per cent organic matter, and structural stability is impaired at lower organic levels.

The inorganic component of soils consists of particles that are classified into standard size ranges (gravel, clay, silt and sand). There are a number of classifications of these particles, and the following is a simplified version from the British Standards Institution (BSI):

> Gravel – particle size over 2.0mm
> Sand – between 0.06 and 2.0mm
> Silt – between 0.002 and 0.06mm
> Clay – less than 0.002mm

These categories are known as separates, and their proportions in a soil define its **texture**. Sandy soils contain at least 70 per cent sand, and less than 15 per cent clay; clays usually have no less than 40 per cent clay; and loams have more equal proportions of clay, silt and sand. The texture of a soil is of great practical importance. Together with the humus content, it influences **soil structure**, which is the degree of aggregation of the separates, the size and shape of aggregates/structures, and both the range and total volume of pore spaces. Soil structure has a major influence on:

- the soil's aeration properties;
- the capacity of the soil to retain moisture, and its **hydraulic conductivity** (and hence drainage properties); and
- the soil biota and plant root growth.

Texture also affects the behaviour of the soil at different moisture contents (its consistency). Thus clay soils tend to be less well drained than sandy and loamy soils. They may be waterlogged in winter, show poor infiltration (see §10.2.4), and have a plastic consistency for much of the year. They are described as "heavy" as they are difficult to cultivate. Medium to heavy loams tend to have a more friable consistency, and a greater capacity to make moisture available to plants during the summer. Sandy soils are described as "light". They are very friable and easy to work, but prone to drought. Loams are generally thought to have the most favourable textures for agriculture.

Soil textures often vary with depth, as a result of the mixing and redistribution of parent materials during the Ice Ages, and subsequent soil-forming processes.

9.3.2 The soil profile and soil classification

Clearly, it is important to know what type of soil is present in a study area. A pit dug into an undisturbed soil will reveal the topsoil and subsoil layers. Such a vertical section is called a **soil profile**, and each individual layer is called a **horizon**. Two different soil profiles are shown in **Figures 9.1 and 9.2**. Not all of the sub-soil horizons are always present, and the horizons are frequently sub-divided. Pedological classifications of soils are concerned with natural horizons that have formed since the last Ice Age as a result of soil forming processes. Most natural soils have an organic-rich topsoil which contains humus. A and E horizons

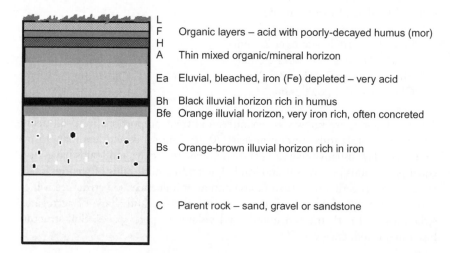

Figure 9.1 Profile of a typical humus–iron podzol.
There are three superficial organic layers (mor) L, F and H which represent litter (leaves or needles), fermentation (where the breakdown of organic material contained in the litter largely occurs) and humus (where breakdown is largely complete). Beneath these are the eluvial A and E horizons (which are bleached and often grey in colour), illuvial B horizons (rich in iron), and the parent material of the C Horizon. These soils and their gleyed variants occur extensively over relatively cold and wet higher ground and some freely drained sandy parent materials in lowland areas. In these areas the main planning issues tend to be the protection of semi-natural habitats and wildlife conservation (redrawn from Bridges 1978).

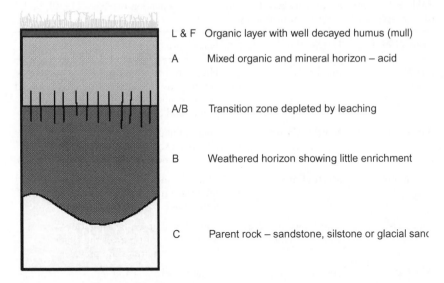

L & F   Organic layer with well decayed humus (mull)

A   Mixed organic and mineral horizon – acid

A/B   Transition zone depleted by leaching

B   Weathered horizon showing little enrichment

C   Parent rock – sandstone, silstone or glacial sanc

Figure 9.2 Profile of a typical acid brown soil.
Here the organic material is of the richer moder or mull type. The soil is leached, but not nearly to the same extent as the podzol. The A and B horizons are far less distinct. These soils and their gleyed variants occur extensively over lowland areas, and the main planning issue is the protection of their productive potential, and the visual amenity of the vegetation cover which they support (redrawn from Bridges 1978).

are **eluvial** upper horizons in which the inorganic particles have become depleted of nutrients as a result of the *leaching* effect of precipitation as it percolates through the profile to groundwater and watercourses. In contrast, **illuvial** B horizons are often enriched with nutrients, iron, clays or organic matter which have been leached from above and deposited in the lower subsoils. The C horizon is the weathering parent material or rock.

The differentiation of horizons within the soil profile is the main criterion used in **soil classifications**. This chapter concentrates on the soils likely to be found in Britain, using the classification system adopted by Avery (1990). Avery's terminology (or similar) is used in many British texts, and certainly seems to be the preferred terminology for British EIAs. There are, however, many other classifications, and two of these: the US *Soil Taxonomy* (USDA-NRCS 1999) which is used in American textbooks such as Brady and Weil (2002); and the *World Reference Base for Soil Resources* (WRB 2006) are gaining ground, even in Britain. **Table 9.1** compares the US terminology with the equivalent British terminology for major soils of the British Isles (Avery 1990). Many EU member states including Belgium, Eire, France, Germany, Italy the Netherlands and Portugal have their own distinctive soil classification systems, which in some cases contain elements of the USDA-NRCS and WRB classifications.

Table 9.1 A comparison between the British soil classification of Avery (1990), and the USDA-NRCS (1999) soil taxonomy

Avery (1990)	USDA-NRCS	Notes
Podzols	Spodosols	Humid to per-humid temperate climates. Acidic soils characterised by grey-coloured A and E horizons, and the deposition of humus and/or iron in the B horizon.
Brown soils	Mostly Alfisols	Humid temperate climates. Leached and elluviated soils, but reasonably fertile. Argillic B horizon. Includes Brown Earths.
Lithomorphic soils	Mostly Entisols	Thin (30cm) soils with no diagnostic subsurface horizon. Includes Rankers and Rendzinas.
Gley soils	Aquic soils of a great variety of types	Soils characterised by saturation with water for at least part of the time. Reducing conditions are prevalent.
Peat soils	Histosols	Organic soils, bog and fen peats, forming in humid climates often in depressions.
Man-made soils	Plaggepts and Arents	Ploughed and disturbed soils.

Almost all of the soils of the British Isles have been influenced by human activity to some extent. Avery (1990) restricts the term **man-made soils** to mineral soils where present or former management of the soil has resulted in distinctive features. Outside of the hills and uplands and smaller patches of lowland *heath* (where the predominant soils are podzols which may be peaty and/or gleyed), most agricultural soils consist of gleyed brown earths, brown earths and gleys. They have topsoils that extend to relatively uniform depths over subsoils, with a gradual transition into weathering parent material. Better quality soils tend to have loamy upper subsoils over lower subsoils that are generally heavier or lighter in texture, depending on the underlying parent material.

Podzols (Figure 9.1) are typical of northern areas of Europe where they are associated with the boreal coniferous forest and heaths, and the climate is characteristically cold and wet. These soils are highly leached and acidic (**pH** often 3.0–4.5). They are little used for agriculture, but are very important for forestry and *heathland* habitats (including British lowland heaths), many of which are protected by statutory designations. Podzols develop best on permeable sands and gravels.

Brown soils are generally associated with areas originally covered by deciduous forest and are the dominant soils of lowland Britain. There are many types of brown soil and Figure 9.2 shows one example, an acid brown soil. Brown earths are the best known and widespread category of this group, and are fairly fertile, with pH 4.5–6.5. They are generally located in warmer and drier climates than podzols, and the precipitation/*evapotranspiration* ratio (see §10.2.3) of the environments in which these soils develop is generally lower than that of the podzols. The amount of water percolating through the soil is sufficient to cause a moderate amount of leaching, but is not enough for podzol formation. Most of the original forest that grew on brown soils has been cleared for agriculture.

In some places, the profiles have distinctive features that have been imposed by the underlying rock, or a geomorphological process. For example, Carboniferous limestone soils tend to have very shallow soil profiles over hard rock, and gravels form impenetrable layers or pans at a range of depths, often in *alluvial* areas or on plateau surfaces. Lithomorphic soils are thin soil types where the parent rock is the dominant feature in soil development, representing an early stage in soil development. The best-known lithomorphic soils are the **rendzinas**, which develop over chalk or limestone. In a typical rendzina, the A horizon, which is generally fairly thin, rests directly on the parent C horizon. The soil is very dark brown or black in colour and is alkaline (pH 7.5–8.4). In contrast, **rankers** are young, acidic soils that develop over non-calcareous rocks such as sandstones. In southern Britain the climax vegetation on rendzinas is deciduous forest (e.g. beech, oak), but the trees have often been cleared and these areas are now mostly used for agriculture.

Gley soils are hydromorphic soils that are waterlogged for at least part of the year. Under these conditions, water saturates the soil, filling most of the pore spaces and driving out air. Any remaining oxygen is soon used up by microorganisms, causing the development of anaerobic conditions in which the process of gleying (reduction of iron compounds from the ferric to the ferrous state) produces a distinctive blue-grey colouration (see §9.3.4).

Peat soils are a major soil type in some parts of the world, but cover a relatively minor fraction of the land surface of the UK (only 3 per cent of England and Wales, but rather more in Scotland and Ireland). Pure peat is partly decayed organic (mainly plant) material that accumulates where lack of oxygen, associated with waterlogging, inhibits the activity of microbial decomposer organisms. *Mires* (peatland ecosystems) occur where there is near-permanent waterlogging and consequent peat accumulation. They provide valuable wildlife habitats, many of which are also protected by statutory designations. They are also important from a global warming perspective because they contain (and hence "lock up") a significant amount of carbon. Mires can be divided into **bogs** and **fens**, which differ largely in relation to their hydrology (see Table C.1). According to MAFF (1988), peats contain at least 20 to 25 per cent organic matter, depending on the clay content. The substratum of bogs is normally almost pure peat, but that in fens can contain high proportions of inorganic material such as marl (calcareous-clay mixtures). Similarly, while the peat in "active" bogs is normally saturated, many peatlands have fairly free drainage, at least near the surface. However, lowering of water tables, e.g. by agricultural drainage schemes and/or water abstraction, can seriously damage peatland ecosystems (see §11.7.2) and lead to soil loss by oxidation and erosion.

9.3.3 Soil structure

In most soils, the soil particles or separates are organized into aggregates. Soil structures called peds, vary in size and shape, and generally recognised standard types of structures are described in Hodgson (1997). Each soil horizon in a soil type usually contains a type of texture and one shape and size of structure, but structure frequently varies with depth. For example, angular and mainly sub-angular blocky structures in loams become coarser (larger) with depth. In clays, there is frequently a transition from coarse angular and subangular blocky to prismatic structures with increasing depth. Sandy soils may have weakly developed angular and subangular structures in the upper subsoils, but sand particles lack cohesion, and such soils are usually devoid of structures (i.e. they are apedal) in the lower subsoil. In addition to drainage channels, soil structure provides air spaces, or pores within the aggregates or peds. These provide the space for plant roots, and the air and water necessary to sustain plants.

9.3.4 Soil colour

Field observations of colour can be a clue to soil composition. A black or grey-brown subsoil is likely to have high humus content. Predominant yellow or red-brown subsoil colours are due to the presence of iron oxides. A white soil may contain abundant silica, aluminium hydroxide, gypsum or calcium carbonate. The colour of subsoil horizons is an important indicator of the drainage status of the soil, and charts (Munsell Color Co. 2000) provide standard examples of the normal range of soil colours. Well-drained soils tend to have uniform brown, yellow-brown or red-brown soil colours. Colour is often inherited from the parent material (e.g. red-brown colours are associated with Triassic lithologies). In poorly drained soils, the drainage channels and pore spaces are saturated and air is largely absent. Under these anaerobic conditions, iron compounds are reduced from the ferric (Fe^{3+}) to the ferrous (Fe^{2+}) state. The ferric compounds are characterised by ochreous colours and the ferrous compounds are characterised by blue-grey colours. Occasional waterlogging gives soils a mottled ochreous and grey appearance, while more permanent waterlogging at greater depths leads to predominantly grey soil colours. These colours are known as gley morphology, and are indicative of impeded soil drainage. This feature is present in many British soils and it occurs at a range of depths. In general, the greater the depth at which gleying occurs, the better the drainage status and quality of the soil.

9.3.5 Soil fertility

This is a vast topic and the reader is referred to Brady and Weil (2002), Cresser *et al.* (1993) and Troeh and Thompson (2005) for more details. Two major soil chemistry problems that are of importance in an EIA are low soil fertility, and toxicity, both of which will lead to poor plant growth. **Low soil fertility** is due either to low levels of nutrients (e.g. nitrogen, phosphorus, potassium and magnesium) in the soil, or their being made unavailable for plant uptake in some way. **Soil toxicity** is caused by high levels of toxic elements or compounds being present in the soil, usually as a result of human activity such as the spraying of pesticides, deposition of industrial waste, fuel spillage and the spreading of farm manure, slurries and sewage sludge. The source of toxic materials may not be on the affected land, and atmospheric deposition and movement in solution in groundwater may be significant. Some elements (e.g. copper and zinc) which are essential *micronutrients* for plant growth can be toxic at high concentrations. Soil toxicity can be a significant limiting factor if levels permitted by the Soil Code (MAFF 1998) are exceeded.

High levels of plant *macronutrients*, especially nitrogen and phosphorus, stimulate plant growth. However, the plant communities of *semi-natural* habitats, such as heathlands and "unimproved" grasslands, are adapted to low nutrient levels – and their value for biodiversity can be degraded by soil *eutrophication* that favours species such as vigorous grasses at the expense of *ericoids* and *forbs*.

Soil pH *per se* rarely affects plant growth, but it strongly influences the availability of plant nutrients. Aluminium and nearly all of the *heavy metals* are much more available for plant uptake and entry to food chains in acid soils than in neutral or alkaline soils.

9.3.6 Land evaluation

The pedological classification of soils considered above is based mainly on the nature of soil parent materials, modified by natural soil-forming processes. Land evaluation methodologies for the assessment of natural land quality (e.g. for agriculture or forestry) concentrate on the physical properties that cannot be altered by land management. For land use planning purposes, it has until recently been necessary to focus on determining the relative productive value of different areas of land for agriculture. The concept of sustainable development has introduced the need to protect the other functions of soils, which are valuable in respect of a wider range of environmental objectives.

Land quality (or capability) classification systems are based on the severity of climatic, topographic and soil limitations to the agricultural or silvicultural use of the land. Climatic limitations have an overriding downgrading effect (irrespective of soil conditions) in areas that are cold and wet for most of the year (i.e. hills and uplands). In the more favourable locations (i.e. most of lowland Britain), soil wetness and liability to drought are the most common limiting factors. These are determined by both soil and climatic influences. The severity of a soil wetness limitation is determined by interactions between soil texture and structure, and the length of the period when soils are at *field capacity* in the winter. The severity of a soil drought limitation is determined by interactions between soil texture and structure, and summer *soil moisture deficits* (SMDs) in relation to selected crops. Land quality is also determined by soil depth and stone content. Shallow and stony soils are downgraded, as are: sandy soils on sloping ground, which are prone to water erosion; and a relatively narrow range of fine sandy and silty soils, which are susceptible to wind erosion. Topographic limitations include steep slopes that preclude mechanised farm operations, and flood risk on river *floodplains* (see §10.2.7).

The quality of agricultural land in England and Wales is assessed according to a system devised by MAFF (1988), and known as the Agricultural Land Classification (ALC). This is the system utilised for land use planning and development control decisions, and the ALC has five grades (see Table 9.2). Grade 1 is the best quality land that permits flexible land management and crop production and supports the full range of horticultural and arable crops. Grade 5 is so limited by severe climate, flood risk or steep slopes as to be capable of supporting only grass pasture, semi-natural vegetation and extensive grazing. Grade 3 is subject to moderate limitations, and is generally associated with cereal and grass crops. It can be subdivided into an upper category (Subgrade 3a) and a lower category (Subgrade 3b). The proportions (percentage) of the grades in England and Wales are shown in **Table 9.2**. ALC regional maps at the 1:250.000 scale are available at www.magic.gov.uk. If significant soil impacts are anticipated, a detailed field survey and ALC map at a larger scale are necessary to obtain a definitive grade.

In Scotland, a similar Land Capability Classification for Agriculture (LCA), which has seven classes, has been developed by the Macaulay Land Use Research Institute (MLURI 1991). This publication is now out of print, but the

Table 9.2 Agricultural Land Classification (ALC) statistics in England and Wales

Grade or land use	Quality of land, severity of limitation and cropping capability	% in	
		England	Wales
1	Excellent quality. No limitations. Very wide range of horticultural and agricultural crops.	2.7	0.2
2	Very good quality. Minor limitations. Wide range of horticultural and agricultural crops.	14.2	2.0
3a	Good quality. Moderate limitations. Wide range of agricultural crops.	48.2	16.2
3b	Moderate quality. Moderately severe limitations. Mainly cereals and grass.		
4	Poor quality. Severe limitations. Mainly grass.	14.1	39.8
5	Very poor quality. Very severe limitations. Mainly semi-natural grazing and grass pasture.	8.4	30.8
Non-agricultural	Land with largely undisturbed natural soils. Includes woodland, parkland, golf courses etc.	5.0	8.2
Urban	Land largely devoid of soil and covered with houses and industrial development.	7.3	2.8

Sources: England – Defra (2007); Wales – Ian Rugg (RA-TSD Aberystwyth).

LCA is described in Wright *et al.* (2006), and outlined at www.macaulay.ac.uk/explorescotland/lcfa1.html where information on soils and landcover in Scotland is also available. LCA maps and GIS data can be purchased at www.macaulay.ac.uk/MRCS/mrcs.html.

It should be noted that "land quality" has several meanings in current EIA terminology. It relates not only to the natural quality of soils, but also to the degree to which soils have been degraded by disturbance and contamination arising from human activity.

9.4 Legislative background and interest groups

9.4.1 Geology

The DoE (1989) currently being upgraded (DCLG 2006a) suggest that an EIA of impacts on geology should consider the local geomorphology, and the "loss of, and damage to, geological, palaeontological and physiographic features". Other published advice for planners and developers is available (DETR 1999a, 1999b, 1999c). In the UK, sites of geological significance (i.e. sites important for their fossils, minerals or other geological/geomorphological interest) are identified in the Geological Conservation Review (GCR) as GCR /Earth Heritage Sites (see www.jncc.gov.uk/page-2947, from where the GCR site database can be accessed). These are non-statutory sites, but most are protected by their designation as Earth Science SSSIs (see www.jncc.gov.uk/page-2317#download). The selection criteria are fully described in the introduction to the GCR (Ellis *et al.* 1996).

There is also a national network of Regionally Important Geological/geomorphological Sites (RIGs) which are selected on the basis of their local value for education, scientific study, historical significance or aesthetic qualities (see www.ukrigs.org.uk). These do not currently enjoy statutory protection, but consideration of their importance is integral to the planning process. Limestone pavements can be given special protection by Limestone Pavement Orders issued by LAs under the *Wildlife & Countryside Act 1981 & (Amendment) Act 1985*. They are UKBAP priority habitats (see Table C.2) and some are designated as Special Areas for Conservation (SACs) under the Habitats Directive (see www.jncc.gov.uk/protectedsites/sacselection/habitat.asp?FeatureIntCode=H8240).

The statutory consultee for a project likely to affect an Earth Heritage Site is the relevant SNCO (see Appendix B). Other potential consultees or interest groups include the LA, British Geological Survey (BGS) and the local geological society.

9.4.2 Soil protection and restoration

The *UK government sustainable development strategy* (Defra 2005) refers to the need to maintain soil functions; and some aspects are monitored in the "sustainable indicators" programme (see Defra 2004b). However, soil protection tends not to be directly addressed in the legal frameworks of EU states, and until recently, soils in the UK were protected only when they formed part of a habitat or land use valued by the planning system. For example, the conservation of soils in England, Scotland and Wales has been implemented through policies for the protection of agricultural land from urban development, for the restoration of mineral sites to agriculture, forestry and other soil-based land uses, and for ecology within Sites of Special Scientific Interest.

In September 2006 the European Commission proposed the *Soil framework directive* (http://ec.europa.eu/environment/soil/index_en.htm) which is currently under negotiation (Defra 2008a). The UK Government has published a *Draft soil strategy for England* (Defra 2001), followed by *The first soil action plan for England: 2004 to 2006* (Defra 2004a) and, most recently, a new *Consultation on the draft soil strategy for England* (Defra 2008b). To complement Defra's Action Plan, the Environment Agency has published: *The state of soils in England and Wales* (EA 2004a); a strategy consultation paper entitled *Soil, the hidden resource* (EA 2004b); and its final soil strategy entitled *Soil, a precious resource, our strategy for protecting, managing and restoring soil* (EA 2007).

Defra's Draft Soil Strategy and Soil Action Plan set out the Government's approach to the protection of different types of soil for a wide range of environmental functions, and not just the productive potential of the soil for agriculture and forestry. The main soil functions are:

- soil and atmosphere interactions (e.g. the hydrological and carbon cycles);
- food, timber and fibre production;
- foundations for civil engineering;
- supporting habitats and biodiversity;
- providing raw materials (e.g. gravel); and
- protecting archaeological features.

The Soil Action Plan expired in April 2007, and Defra intends to publish a Soil Strategy for England that is integrated with the European Soil Framework Directive. Information on Defra's policy and programmes is available at www.defra.gov.uk/environment/land/soil/index.htm (see also CS2000 and UKNFC in Table 11.3).

In England and Wales, further policies for the protection of land and soils are contained in Planning Policy Statement 7 (PPS7) issued by the DCLG (2004), and Minerals Planning Guidance Note 7 (MPG 7) issued by the DCLG (1996). In accordance with the principles of **sustainable development**, PPS7 advises that in certain circumstances some weight should be given to protecting land from development, because it is a national resource for future generations. On the other hand, outside of the hills and uplands (where lower quality land may still be important), less weight is normally given to the loss of moderate or poor quality land. Because of the national interest in protecting the best and most versatile agricultural land, developers are generally required to consult Local and Mineral Planning Authorities, about any proposed development that does not accord with strategies and policies set out in Local Development Frameworks

(LDFs), and which involves, or is likely to lead to, the irreversible loss of best and most versatile agricultural land. The loss of such land should be taken into account alongside other sustainability considerations, such as biodiversity, landscape character and heritage interest when determining planning applications. Natural England and Government Offices for the regions are consulted on technical matters relating to ALC and land restoration matters, and EIA procedures respectively.

For mineral sites there is the need to restore the land to equivalent quality. However, planning permissions for non-mineral developments almost always lead to the loss of soil resource, and this unsustainable practice has yet to be effectively addressed by the planning system. Additional guidance on the conservation of land and soil resources is given in MPG 7, which states that land restoration schemes should be based upon the careful investigation of the site before it is worked for minerals, to identify the soil resources available for use in land restoration. Such pre-application site investigations are required to provide adequate information on the volumes and physical characteristics of the topsoil, subsoil and soil-forming materials, together with a description of the original landform and drainage. It is also necessary to draw up a programme for the working and restoration of the site to include soil stripping and storage, mineral extraction, back-filling operations, soil replacement and aftercare. This information represents the basis for consultations between the mineral operator and the statutory authorities over development control and land restoration conditions. Further guidance on best practice criteria is available from a number of sources, including DoE (1996b and 1996c), DETR (1999d) and MAFF (1998, 2000).

In Scotland, policies for the protection of agricultural resources from development are contained in a number of Scottish Planning Policies (SPPs), which have to be considered as a whole. These include SPP 3 *Housing* (SE 2003), SPP 4 *Planning for minerals* (SE 2006a) and SPP 15 *Rural development* (SE 2006b). The SPPs are supported by Circular 25/1994 (SO 1994). These guidance documents refer to the protection of agricultural land against irreversible development. Prime quality land is generally defined as Classes 1, 2 and 3.1 (the upper part of Class 3), but the land that is actually protected depends on the overall quality of land in a given location. Furthermore, just as in England and Wales, there has been a general relaxation in the protection of agricultural land.

9.4.3 Contaminated land

Prior to 1990 there were no specific regulations related to the management of contaminated land in the UK. Authorities were restricted to using statutes and policies in related areas. These included: the *Public Health Act 1936*; the *Town and Country Planning Act 1971* and subsequent updates; the *Control of Pollution Act 1974*; and the *Derelict Land Act 1982*. The *Environmental Protection Act 1990* presented a statutory framework for dealing with waste, and section 143 of the Act introduced a requirement for Local Authorities to develop Public Registers of land known to be contaminated, although this was never enacted. Most current legislation in relation to contaminated land was introduced by amendments to the Environmental Protection Act 1990, mainly through Section 57 of the *Environment Act 1995*.

Legislation and guidance on the assessment of contaminated sites are now provided under Part IIA of the Environmental Protection Act 1990 as amended by the Environment Act 1995, the Water Act 2003 and Planning Policy Statement 23 (PPS23) Planning and Pollution Control (ODPM 2004). This legislation endorses the principle of a "suitable for use" approach to contaminated land, whereby remedial action is only required if there are unacceptable risks to health or the environment, taking into account the use of the land and its environmental setting. The legislation places a responsibility on the local authority to determine if the land in its area is contaminated by consideration of whether:

- significant harm is being caused; or
- there is a significant possibility of significant harm being caused; or
- pollution of controlled waters is being caused or there is a significant possibility of such pollution being caused.

The statutory guidance that brought into effect the Environmental Protection Act 1990 was published by DETR (2000) and has been modified in Defra 2006). It describes a risk assessment methodology in terms of "significant pollutants" and "significant pollutant linkages" within a source–pathway–receptor model of the application site. For land to be defined as contaminated there must be a source of contamination, a receptor which can be affected by the contaminant, and a pathway which may connect the two. At the EIA stage the introduction of new receptors, such as occupants of proposed buildings, and the creation and blocking of pathways, such as when soils are removed or placed, has to be considered. The change in use of a site and the works required for this have the potential to change a site from contaminated to uncontaminated land or *vice versa* without changing the chemistry of the ground at depth.

Under Section 161 of the *Water Resources Act 1991*, the Environment Agency can serve a works order on a person or persons who cause or knowingly permit pollution of **controlled waters**. The Water Act 2003 further amends the definition of "contaminated" in relation to controlled waters under the Environmental Protection Act 1990 by changing "pollution of controlled waters" to "significant pollution of controlled waters".

Annex 2 of PPS23 relates to development on land affected by contamination and provides guidance on how the development of contaminated land can be controlled through the planning process. While the planning and pollution control systems are separate, they are complementary in that both are designed to protect the environment from potential harm caused by development and operations. Historic land contamination is a material planning consideration that must be taken into account at various stages in the planning process, including proposals for the future use and redevelopment of a site. PPS23 follows the contaminated land regime set out in the Environmental Protection Act 1990 (as amended), and the accompanying regulations which deal with the existing condition of land. A local authority may require remediation to be undertaken as part of the redevelopment of a site. These works usually encompass site investigation, consultation and remediation works/risk management (see Table 13.1).

The 1990 and 1995 Acts introduced the Source-Pathway-Target concept to the management of contaminated land. The use of risk assessment (Chapter 13) to assess where contamination has significant potential for causing harm has considerably assisted in the management and remediation of contaminated land (Cairney 1995). The Acts also identified those responsible for the remediation of contaminated land. As with other pollution, it is the responsibility of the polluter to decontaminate polluted sites where these are causing significant harm. As stated above, however, a site may not be defined as "contaminated" for its current use, and it is the proposed change in use which may introduce the requirement for investigation, risk assessment and remediation.

Governmental advice on contaminated land can be found at www.defra.gov.uk/environment/land/contaminated/index.htm. This identifies the standards to be used, and the potential for contamination to be present. The most important are those introduced as CLR Reports CLR7 to 11 (Defra and EA 2002a to 2002d and 2004). DoE published a range of industry guides that identify contaminants potentially present on sites that were subject to specified uses, such as the chemical industry, and the iron and steel industry. The findings of these reports are summarised in CLR8 (Defra and EA 2002b). The EPAs (see Appendix B) also publish a range of Pollution Prevention Guides (PPGs) which include advice on site control and remediation see EPAs (undated).

9.5 Scoping and baseline studies

9.5.1 Introduction

Both scoping and subsequent investigations can involve a desk study and consultations. At the scoping stage it is necessary to decide if these will suffice, or if a reconnaissance field survey, a detailed field survey, and laboratory analysis of soils are required. Scoping-stage site visits will normally be brief (e.g. to confirm features identified on maps), but some may involve walkover surveys. Such visits may be best undertaken with other members of the EIA team, so that interactions between subject areas can be identified. For example, information on geology, geomorphology and soils may also be of relevance to other EIA components such as landscape/visual, water, and ecology (Chapters 6, 10, 11 and 12). Coordination at an early stage is important to achieve an integrated approach, and to avoid duplication of effort while ensuring that key aspects are not omitted. If the use of GIS (Chapter 14) is considered appropriate for the EIA, it may be possible to include geology, geomorphology and soil layers and hence facilitate integration with other layers.

The most important scoping considerations are whether the geological or soil resources within a project's impact area are likely to be significantly affected, and if there are any practical measures which can be undertaken to mitigate anticipated impacts. Where a significant impact on soils is anticipated, it is necessary to carry out an ALC/LCA survey to determine the grades or classes of land and the areas of best and most versatile or prime quality land which are likely to be affected. Where it is necessary to conserve the soils for land restoration (i.e. at mineral sites), or where the developer wishes to make beneficial use of this resource on the development itself (e.g. for landscaping), the field survey should also include an assessment of the volumes of topsoil and subsoil available at the site. Where contamination is anticipated an appropriate site investigation will have to be carried out, and this is addressed below.

9.5.2 Desk study

The desk study should make good use of existing information on geology, geomorphology, soils and land quality, associated aspects such as site history and local climate, and consider the potential for there being contaminated land on or adjacent to the site.

Information on geology and geomorphology

Information on Earth Heritage Sites (see §9.4.1) including the 45-volume *Geological Conservation Review Series* and the GCR database of 3,000 sites, is available at www.jncc.gov.uk/page-2947. Geological maps, published by British Geological Survey (BGS) are available for most of the British Isles. "Solid" maps show only Pre-Quaternary rocks, and "drift" maps also show superficial Quaternary deposits that have been laid down principally since the last Ice Age. Lithology has a big influence on soil types through the mineralogical composition and texture of the weathered rock. However, because of the erosion, mixing and redistribution of surface rocks and weathered materials during the Ice Ages, drift maps tend to give the most informative indication of the soil parent materials in a survey area.

BGS paper maps include 1:250,000 regional, 1:63,360 or 1:50,000 scale maps of most areas, and 1:25,000 or 1:10,000 of some areas of special interest to geologists or planners. The latter include some Applied Geological Mapping (AGM) studies (e.g. within coalfields), commissioned by DETR (Ellison and Smith 1998). Digital geological maps at the 1:50,000, 1:250,000 and 1:625,000 scales are available at the DiGMapGB website (www.bgs.ac.uk/products/digital-maps/digmapgb.html). BGS operates a **GeoIndex** (GDI) that is a spatial index of BGS data holdings held in an ArcView GIS (see Chapter 14). It is available online at www.bgs.ac.uk/programmes/infoserv/im/gdi.html, and provides the facility to zoom in on areas or place names, and gives the costs of supplying more specific information.

If examined in conjunction with geological and soil maps, OS topographical maps, (e.g. at 1:50,000, 1:25,000 and 1:10,000), will give a general idea of geomorphology. If a GIS is being used, digitised OS maps (see Table 14.1) should be useful, and it may be possible to produced Digital Terrain Models (DTMs), which may also be able to make use of remotely sensed imagery. DTMs in GIS are explained in §14.2.3, and their use in geomorphology is discussed in Cooke and Doornkamp (1990). The EA holds a Geomorphology Core Survey database. Further information on sources of geological (and related) information is provided in Ellison and Smith (1998).

Information on soils and land quality

Published soil and ALC/LCA maps provide an initial understanding of the soil types and land quality likely to be found at the sites. Soil maps of England and Wales are available from the NSRI (National Soils Research Institute) LanDis (Land Information System) website (see Table 14.1) which also holds other facilities including GIS datasets and a "soils site reporter" service. Paper maps include the National Soil Map in 6 regional sheets at 1:250,000 and, for some areas, maps at 1:50,000 or 1:25,000 with reports. Soil maps of Scotland (from MLURI) include 1:250,000 soil and land capability for agriculture (7 sheets); and soil maps at 1:50,000 or 1:63,360 of most areas, and at 1:25,000 of some areas. These maps, and GISdatasets, are available at www.macaulay.ac.uk/MRCS/gis/gis2.html. In 1997 a series of soil maps covering the whole of Northern Ireland have been published by Queens University, Belfast (www.qub.ac.uk/envres/EarthAirWater/jordan.htm. There are many soil memoirs (describing the soils in specific geographical areas) and monographs (describing relevant soil properties) published by MLURI (see www.macaulaysoils.com/MacaulayMaps.html) and NSRI (website as above). The Environmental Change Network (ECN) holds a database of soil analytical data (mostly inorganic nutrients and physical properties) from 12 regularly monitored terrestrial sites in the UK (www.ecn.ac.uk/).

Information on climate and site history

When a detailed survey of land quality is required in England and Wales, the relevant climatic information is derived from the data set specifically produced by the Meteorological Office (MO 1989) for this purpose. The figures for each of the relevant climatic variables are available for each 5km national OS grid intersection, and these are interpolated for the exact location and altitude of the study area. For projects that are likely to have a significant impact on soils and land quality, local climatic conditions may also have to be assessed in the field for **microclimate** and exposure. This will be carried out during a soil survey of the development site. Projects which have significant air quality and noise implications may be the subject of other specialist studies on microclimate. The history of the site and estimated impact area should be investigated to identify activities or land uses that might have contaminated the land. Sources of historical information are given in Box 7.1.

Information on contaminated land

If the site is contaminated then certain additional procedures will be required. The methodology which has become standard in the UK is set out in The Environment Agency and Defra Report CLR11 *Model procedures for the management of contaminated land* (Defra and EA 2004). The type and extent of any contamination that may be present on a site will depend upon the previous uses that the site has been subject to, and the management practices used to control and maintain those activities. In addition, activities on adjacent sites may also have resulted in pollution of the sub-surface that may then migrate onto the subject site. It is important, therefore, to ascertain the activities and management practices that occurred on site, and on adjacent sites, and the type of chemicals used in the initial phase.

Interviews with site staff, where available, can help to determine past and present site activities that may have caused contamination of the soil or groundwater at the facility. Such staff could include the site manager, site agent, maintenance manager and the caretaker. Regulatory authorities maintain records that are very important in assessments of contaminated land. Information such as the presence of underground and aboveground storage tanks and electrical equipment can be gathered. In addition, data on known past pollution incidents is often available. Data such as **aquifer** location, type and vulnerability should be collected (see §10.2.5 and §10.8.4). Authorities to be contacted should include the EA, and the Local Authority's Environmental Health, Contaminated Land and Petroleum Officers. There is much information on the type of materials and chemicals that were used in a wide range of commercial activities. This can be gathered from published data (HMSO and Governmental guidance documents, e.g. the DoE Industry Profiles and CLR8), and the publications of professional bodies such as the Society of Chemical Industry (SCI). The Construction Industry Research and Information Association (CIRIA) have published 12 volumes covering all aspects of *Remedial treatment for contaminated land* (see www.ciria.org/acatalog/SP164_.html. Although dated, the first of these (CIRIA 1998) is a useful guide and introduction to all aspects of this topic.

9.5.3 Fieldwork

If desk studies and walkover surveys indicate that more detailed data are required then fieldwork will be initiated.

Geological and geomorphological surveys

The locations of Earth Heritage sites and RIGs will have been identified in the desk study, but there may be other rock exposures that are worth investigation and evaluation (e.g. for their fossil content). Where a significant geological impact is anticipated (e.g. for opencast mineral extraction), a more detailed assessment is likely to be required than can be made from existing information alone. This will usually involve field survey, e.g. sampling in **wells** to identify the extent of the mineral resource, and to understand the local hydrogeology (see Chapter 10). A topographic survey can also be carried out, for example to measure the gradients of slopes, and delineate flood risk areas.

Soil surveys

The complex geology of the British Isles and the redistribution of soil parent materials during the Ice Ages have made our soils very variable. This is a major problem for soil surveyors. Field observations are made by using a soil auger to take samples from successive horizons within a soil profile to a depth of 1.2m, where this is possible. As the soils are observed only where the samples are taken, the sample network and density have to be designed to be representative of the variation in soil types within the survey area. Soil survey methods are discussed in Tan (2005), and a detailed statistical account is provided in Webster and Oliver (1990).

Generalised soil surveys of large areas are carried out by the physiographic (or free survey) technique that ensures that samples are representative of the range of geological parent materials and topography within the survey area. The results are shown on maps at intermediate scales (e.g. 1:50,000). For detailed surveys of specific development sites on undisturbed and uncontaminated agricultural land in England and Wales, Defra/Natural England and most practitioners favour a grid sampling pattern (see §11.6.1) and a minimum density of one sample per hectare, with supplementary samples as necessary to accurately delineate soil boundaries. Soil pits are dug to observe the soil structures and extent of crop rooting in each of the main soil types. For mineral sites, topsoil and subsoil resource maps are derived from the information collected during the ALC survey. These indicate the areas, thicknesses and volumes of the topsoils and subsoils. The resulting ALC and soil resource maps are usually shown at a scale of 1:10,000, and are capable of reasonably precise interpretation. It is important to note, however, that land classification is a field survey technique and not an exact science.

During the field survey, some soil properties like soil depth are easily measured, and other properties are either estimated by eye, or assessed using a standard technique, depending on the degree of precision required. For example, stone content can be estimated by eye or measured using a sieve and weighing scales. Some idea of the texture of a soil can be gained in the field by observing it with a lens and by feeling it between the fingers. This requires much experience if an exact identification of the soil texture is needed, and occasional calibration with standard samples. However, even an inexperienced person should be able to classify the soil into the broad categories of clay, silt, sand or loam. Portable field apparatus can be used to obtain estimates of soil strength, pH and mineral status. Small handheld penetrometers consist of a metal probe which is pushed into the soil until it reaches a certain mark. The probe is spring-loaded, and the pressure required to push it into the soil is read off on a scale. Soil test kits produced for horticultural or agricultural purposes may also be used, although they require some practice before reliable results can be obtained.

Surveys of contaminated sites

The desk study and walkover survey should indicate the extent of any intrusive ground investigation which may be required. Such investigations will be essential for design but may not be necessary at EIA/outline planning stage of a project, provided the desk study/walkover report is sufficient for an assessment of risk, as required under Annex 2 of PPS23, to be completed. Where potential for contamination has been identified, investigation targeted at potential sources and extending into other parts of the site will be necessary. PPS23 does demand that the possibility of contamination should always be considered, regardless of past land use, when development including housing with gardens, schools, nurseries or allotments is proposed.

The appropriate layout of exploratory holes locations and depths of sampling and analysis are discussed in *CLR4* (DoE 1994), *CLR11* (Defra and EA 2004), *BS10175* (BSI 2001) and *BS ISO 10381-1* (BSI 2002a). As mentioned above any likely areas of contamination should be targeted. Such areas could include the locations of surface spillage/staining, storage tanks (above ground tanks are easily recognised on plans and visually on site but underground storage tanks are often only identified by the presence of vent pipes or manholes), obvious made-up ground, blighted vegetation, and electrical equipment which could contain PCBs. Apart from these locations exploratory holes are generally set out in a grid arrangement at spacings of 20 to 25m for a proposed residential site which is expected to be contaminated, and to 100m for a commercial development on green-field land. The layout may be modified due to the location of services, buildings and areas of particular environmental sensitivity.

It is not uncommon for a variety of sampling methodologies to be utilised on a single investigation. Trial pits are cheapest and excavate the largest volume of material for sampling, but are restricted to less than 5m depth, and are often used for gathering shallow soil samples for metal analysis. Window samplers are useful in areas where access is difficult, and wells for subsequent gas and groundwater sampling can be installed. Boreholes are the most expensive but are also the most permanent and can normally be installed to considerably greater depth. The types of pollutants present may affect where, when and how samples are taken. Pollutants may be in solid, liquid or gaseous form. Contaminants in solid form and of low solubility will principally be of concern where they are or will be at a depth where normal activity of animals, plants and man could bring them to the surface. Liquid and soluble solid contaminants have to be considered in relation to groundwater and surface water pollution, while gases and volatile substances should be taken into account with respect to migration into buildings, manholes and excavations. It is essential that sampling is carried out in a manner which prevents cross contamination and the loss of volatile contaminants. Guidance on this is given in BS10175 (BSI 2001) and BS ISO 10381-2 (BSI 2002b).

9.5.4 Laboratory work

The ALC/LCA assessments set clear and quantified cut-offs between the grades and classes of land for the selected climatic, topographic and soil variables. In cases where the field observations indicate a marginal classification, it is necessary to analyse samples in the laboratory for greater precision and the definitive grading of land quality. In practice, this applies most frequently to the analysis of soil texture and stone content. It may also be necessary to determine the relationships between moisture contents and the plastic limits of topsoil and subsoil samples in the preparation of soil handling strategies for land restoration schemes.

Laboratory analysis can be expensive, and as a result it is usually undertaken on samples of soils for specific purposes only. Soil samples may be analysed at a number of stages in the EIA process, during baseline studies for land evaluation, and as a guide to possible mitigation measures, including the treatment of contamination. Soils may also be analysed during project construction and operation for monitoring and mitigation purposes. In practice, a very wide range of analyses are selectively undertaken, but only the more common analyses are described in this account.

During baseline studies and the evaluation of undisturbed agricultural land, **topsoil texture** is often analysed in the laboratory for a definitive ALC grading. Basically the methods differentiate between the mineral fractions of soils on the basis of particle size. The usual method involves sedimentation of mineral particles in a water column. The disadvantages are that it takes a long time (several days), and at current (2008) prices each determination will cost about £30. On disturbed land that is largely devoid of natural soils, it is a matter of identifying suitable soil-forming materials for land restoration. *Soil-forming materials – their use in land reclamation* (DETR 1999d) is a useful reference. The British Standards Institute (BSI 1994) issued a specification for topsoil (BS 3882), which also refers to a number of qualifying threshold levels in soil texture and other variables. These include **soil chemistry** variables such as pH, organic matter content, *electrical conductivity*, available phosphorus, potassium, magnesium and total nitrogen. This test costs about £46 to £55, depending on the electrical conductivity result. Rowell (1994) and Tan (2005) provide detailed methods of soil analysis.

Mineral extraction may be preceded by soil stripping and storage, and followed by the reinstatement of the soils. Conditions attached to planning consents by the Mineral Planning Authorities specify the **moisture content** at which soils may be moved. This is related to the **plastic limit** of the soils, and is intended to avoid damage to soil structures during soil handling. It may be determined in the field by hand, but the moisture content may have to be determined with more precision in the laboratory. Most workers use gravimetric analysis, which involves taking a sample of soil from the field and weighing it before and after heating in an oven. For soil surveys on a single site at a given time, the gravimetric method yields good results, giving information on where the wettest parts of the site are, and where soils are too wet to be moved. For other types of work where monitoring over a time period is required, more sophisticated machinery (e.g. neutron probes or time domain reflectometry) can be used (Brady and Weil 2002).

When mineral sites have been restored, a period of aftercare is instituted to recreate favourable soil conditions for a range of beneficial uses, including agriculture, forestry and wildlife and amenity planting. As a part of this rehabilitation process, samples of soil may be taken to determine bulk density and plant nutrient status. **Bulk density** is the mass of dry soil per unit of bulk volume (g/cm^3), including the air space. It can be used indirectly to assess damage to soil structure and reduced porosity caused by inappropriate soil handling for example. It is usually measured directly with the use of a volumetric corer. Essentially a pipe is pushed into the ground to extract a core of soil on which measurements can be made. If the soil texture is known, however, it can be estimated (together with other soil properties such a field capacity and hydraulic conductivity) by means of a soil texture triangle calculator (see www.pedosphere.com/resources/texture/). In EIA, bulk density is a very useful measure if soil compaction is likely to be a problem. The results of these tests can be used to guide subsequent remedial cultivations (like subsoiling) and fertiliser applications.

As a result of the efforts of Defra and the EA there has been a move towards the standardisation of methods of testing, assessment and agreement on generic guideline maximum mean levels (**Soil Guideline Values** or SGVs) of contaminants for particular site uses. For a meaningful assessment it is essential that the soils are analysed for all of the contaminants potentially in the ground below the site. Investigations of contaminated sites are often hindered by an incomplete understanding of the polluting activities that have taken place. There are so many potential contaminants that it would be excessively expensive to test for every possibility. Certain suites of contaminants associated with the main industrial processes and mining operations are provided by the DoE Industry Profiles and CLR8.

Where there are no clearly identified contaminants on a site, or in addition to any "expected" contaminants, it is common to analyse soils for pH, arsenic, cadmium, chromium, lead, mercury, nickel and selenium, as well as cyanide, the 16 most common polycyclic aromatic hydrocarbons (PAH) and total petroleum hydrocarbons (TPH). Often the concentration of phenol in the ground is assessed to determine whether this could permeate plastic water-supply pipes. Other specific analyses will depend upon the history of the site, and may include contaminants such as *pesticides*, PCBs, chloride, mineral oils, elemental sulphur, organic acids, and the components of landfill gas.

9.6 Impact prediction

9.6.1 Geological and geomorphological impacts

Potential impacts on Earth Heritage sites, and other sites of conservation interest, are likely to be direct and hence relatively easy to predict. Quarrying and other forms of mining often have considerable geological impacts because they remove the geological resource and may also affect the local hydrogeological balance. Apart from possible benefits of new rock exposures (e.g. with fossil beds) this may be considered an entirely negative impact, particularly in view of (a) the finite nature of mineral resources, and (b) competition with other land uses such as agriculture or nature conservation. However, an EIA takes place within a statutory context and the Government considers mineral extraction to be a valid component of sustainable development. Minerals Planning Statement 1: *Planning and minerals* (DCLG 2006b) summarises the Government position. It states that minerals are essential to the nation's prosperity and quality of life, and that it is necessary to provide adequate minerals in accordance with the principles of sustainable development, through the long-term conservation of this resource, and the minimisation of consequent environmental impacts. It is also necessary to restore worked-out mineral sites to a beneficial use. However, this often first involves using the site for waste disposal, and, if not carefully managed, this landfill phase can result in groundwater pollution by **leachates**.

In addition to geological and geomorphological impacts mineral extraction usually introduces a number of secondary, but significant, impacts on the local environment. These include noise, air quality (e.g. dust) and traffic impacts, together with landscape amenity and ecological impacts in some cases. These are addressed in other chapters, but useful advice on their assessment is available in *The environmental effects of surface mineral workings* (DoE 1991). Landfill operations may follow in the wake of worked-out opencast mineral extraction, introducing additional potential waste disposal impacts and the need to monitor operational sites for pollution.

Seismic risk is not usually a significant problem in the UK, although there are occasional small earthquakes. In some parts of Europe (e.g. Italy) this can be a serious problem. **Volcanic risk** in the UK is negligible, but in some parts of the world a section of the EIA should be devoted to this topic. Keller (2000) includes chapters on both seismic and volcanic risks. **Subsidence and slope stability** are factors that should be considered in the UK. Subsidence is caused by underground mining and is usually associated with traditional coalfield areas, where the subsidence extends for considerable distances around collieries (Bell 1998). It can also occur as a result of the underground extraction of salt and chalk, and in limestone and chalk areas where natural chemical dissolution has occurred. The risks associated with the development of land that has been disturbed by previous mining activity are addressed in PPG14 *Development on unstable land* (DoE 1990). There are likely to be relatively few proposals for new underground workings that would create a subsidence impact, but avoiding areas of actual or potential subsidence, which are a risk to the development project, itself is an important part of the EIA process. Natural slope stability is a more widespread problem, and the objective of EIA is to avoid the construction of new developments in unstable areas, particularly when the development might make the area even less stable. Information on subsidence and slope stability is available from the BGS, and the Coal Authority at Burton on Trent. The

DETR (1999a, 1999b, 1999c) has published the findings of research projects on environmental geology in land-use planning. The objective is to avoid negative interactions between development and geology. However, there is no overall assessment methodology for geology, and the significance of impacts is determined in consultation with the relevant statutory authorities including the EA, Natural England and the Coal Authority.

The *Design manual for roads and bridges* (Highways Agency 1993) considers the impacts of **road developments** on geology and geomorphology. Such schemes can have a direct impact on geology. For example, in a mining area, they can increase the rate of collapse of underground tunnels. Indirect effects may be felt through alterations to hydrogeology (e.g. diverting streams or affecting the recharge of aquifers). The major impacts of such developments are, however, likely to be damage to geological exposures, fossil beds, stratigraphy and geomorphological systems (PAA 1994). Not all of the impacts will be negative, and it should be remembered that about one-third of geological SSSIs have been created as a result of human activity (Highways Agency 1993). Although road developments can create new exposures that may be of great interest to geologists, care is needed in the design of exposure angle and shape so that rock sequences can be best observed (PAA 1994). It is more difficult to preserve geomorphological features, and the best of these (e.g. stream systems, glacial forms) should be avoided by the proposed development.

9.6.2 Impacts on soils

When a baseline soil survey has been carried out, the various sources of information (e.g. published and new field survey) are compiled, analysed and interpreted. The EIA then has to predict the **magnitude** and **significance** of the main impacts on soil, both temporary and permanent. The DoE (1989) currently being updated (DCLG 2006a) suggest that the following effects of a development should be taken into account: physical (e.g. changes in topography, stability and soil erosion); chemical (emissions and deposits on the soil); and land use/resource changes. The significance of these impacts is determined by the ALC land evaluation methodology in England and Wales, and the relevant legislative guidelines and standards set out in PPS7 (DCLG 2004), and MPG 7 (DCLG 1996). In Scotland the LUCC methodology is used, and the guidelines are to be found in SPP 4 (SE 2006a) and Circular 25/1994 (SO 1994).

There is no recognised evaluation methodology, beyond the ALC and LUCC systems, to reflect the new emphasis on the sustainable protection of soil functions in the wider environmental context. For example, the *Draft Soil Strategy* and *Soil Action Plan* (Defra 2001, 2004a) are less restricted to the protection of the best and most versatile agricultural land for food production, and extend to the other functions of soils that are valuable in respect of wider environmental objectives. In view of this, a new land evaluation methodology is being considered, which will combine agricultural criteria with forestry, biodiversity, landscape character, heritage interest, and an assessment of contamination.

This will encompass the full scope of "land quality", discussed in §9.4.2. It will also seek to unify the forthcoming Defra Soil Strategy for England with the European Soil Framework Directive.

Almost all developments are likely to lead to some **soil erosion** unless suitable mitigation procedures are adopted. There are two major types of erosion, by water and by wind (Bell 1999, Lal 2001, Morgan 2004). The factors that most influence erosion by water are mean annual rainfall, storm frequency and intensity, slope, the soils infiltration capacity and vegetation cover (see §10.2.4). Rain and overland flow cause some natural erosion in most environments, but this is insignificant compared with **accelerated erosion** resulting from human activities such as the disturbance or removal of vegetation, e.g. for agriculture, mineral extraction or development (Cooke and Doornkamp 1990). Only dry soil is subject to wind erosion and so rainfall must be fairly low for it to occur (<250–300mm). Steady prevailing winds are generally found on large fairly level landmasses, and it is these that are most susceptible to wind erosion (e.g. East Anglia). Soil scientists have developed a number of predictive equations, including the Universal Soil Loss Equation (USLE) that can be used in a variety of contexts to predict soils loss due to erosion (Lal 2001).

In the, UK erosion by water is most likely. When it occurs, damage will often not be restricted to the terrestrial environment because the removed soil often causes increases in *turbidity*, siltation and soil nutrient levels in nearby watercourses. It is not uncommon for the levels of certain nutrients (particularly nitrate) to exceed legal limits in steams and rivers as a result (see §10.3.5 & §10.3.6).

Soil erosion by wind and water is considered by many to be a serious threat to the soil resource in the UK, but most soil erosion occurs as a result of agricultural land management practices which are not subject to planning controls, and which are beyond the scope of the EIA process. In relation to development, potential causes of soil erosion include:

- construction phase impacts such as the removal of vegetation, increased *runoff* from impermeable surfaces and creation of unstable slopes;
- increased runoff from impermeable surfaces associated with urbanisation; and
- creation of unstable and unvegetated surfaces that are subject to soil erosion, associated with poor quality land restoration following mineral extraction.

Damage to soil structure can occur during soil stripping, storage and reinstatement operations at land restoration sites. This is due to the use of inappropriate methods and machinery and carrying out soil movements when the soil is too wet. Vehicles driving over soil will compact it, destroying soil structure and increasing bulk density. Topsoils also tend to become mixed with the less favourable subsoils, when they should be stripped, and stored separately to facilitate the restoration of a natural soil profile upon reinstatement. Soils which have been damaged in this way lack the natural drainage channels and porosity which normally absorb precipitation, and transfer it to groundwater reserves. As a result, infiltration is reduced, runoff is increased, and erosion is more likely to occur.

Furthermore, soil compaction inhibits root penetration. Damaged soils also have a reduced capacity to retain moisture and to make it available to plant roots, with the result that plants are prone to severe limitations by drought. A detailed account of the effects of wheel traffic on soils and the plants growing in them is provided by Hamza and Anderson (2005).

In response to this threat to sustainability, the DoE has published *The reclamation of mineral workings to agriculture* (DoE 1996b), *Guidance on good practice for the reclamation of mineral workings to agriculture* (DoE 1996c) and *The good practice guide for handling soils* (MAFF 2000). Proposals for the working and restoration of mineral sites have to conform to this guidance in order to satisfy the requirements of the relevant Mineral Planning Authority (MPA) and Defra concerning the protection of soil structure.

There are two types of situation where **soil pollution** is an important factor in an EIA. In the first, the site is already contaminated, and a clean-up operation is required prior to development. This will be considered in §9.7. In the second, the concern is to predict pollution that may be caused by the project. Most developments pose the threat of some pollution of the local soils during the construction phase (e.g. oil from vehicles, dust from the building materials used). Major developments like ore smelting plants, refineries, chemical works, and power stations also introduce pollution to local soils during the operational phase. Soils beside new roads will receive heavy metals from exhaust fumes, motor oils and salt (from winter de-icing).

During the operational phase, air-borne emissions (Chapter 8) may also begin to impact on the local soils. *Acid deposition/precipitation* arises mainly from sulphur dioxide emitted from power stations, and nitrogen oxides from vehicle exhausts. It has major effects on soil pH in some locations; for example, Hallbäcken and Tamm (1986) observed that soil pH in southwest Sweden had dropped by 0.3–0.5 units between 1927 and 1984, and this decline has continued (Jonsson *et al.* 2003). Lowered soil pH increases available soil aluminium and heavy metal levels, and causes increased leaching of soil nutrients. There are often many sources of acid rain and these create a cumulative and dispersed impact that is felt some distance away. In 1979 the Convention on Long-range Transboundary Air Pollution (LRTAP) began to tackle the problem (Sliggers and Kakebeeke 2004). Further work led to agreement on the 1985 Sulphur Protocol, and there are now 50 countries that are parties to the Convention and a total of eight protocols. The protocols gradually brought in targets to reduce emissions of a number of key pollutants across Europe and North America. In 25 years sulphur emissions across Europe have been decreased by 60 per cent. Nitrogen oxides remain a significant problem, particularly in causing **eutrophication** of terrestrial systems, which can lead to changes in vegetation and biodiversity (Emmett 2007).

The UK NFC (see Table 11.3) holds a **critical loads** database and maps giving estimates of the vulnerability of land to atmospheric pollution (especially acid, nitrogen and sulphur deposition) in relation to receptor soils, geology, freshwaters and vegetation in the UK. Hettelingh *et al.* (2007) state that, in 2000,

8.5 per cent of the ecosystem area of Europe was at risk from acidification, and 28.5 per cent from eutrophication. The same authors have attempted to construct a dynamic model that allows prediction of future acidification. Their results suggest that 95 per cent of the area at risk from acidification will recover by 2030 provided that current pollution legislation is adhered to.

All of the above impacts can have serious effects on soils, but the soil types outlined in §9.3.2 will be affected to different extents by each. Podzolic soils, which occur most frequently in areas of nature conservation interest, are already acidic and have a low buffering capacity (the greater the buffering capacity, the more acid rain will be needed to change the pH of a soil). Consequently, these soils are the most vulnerable to acid precipitation. Podzols also suffer the greatest disruption by disturbance and soil mixing because they have distinctive layers. Gleys are vulnerable to changes in soil hydrology; as are peats which are extremely sensitive soils, especially to erosion and compaction. Susceptibility to erosion is also a feature of many sandy soils. Brown earths are generally less susceptible to any of the above impacts.

9.7 Mitigation

Under the present legislation and planning guidance, it is not possible to mitigate the loss of land and soils arising from most types of non-mineral development. A small proportion of displaced soils may be retained for landscaping purposes, but most are lost to any productive use. Accordingly, it is necessary to ensure that the smallest area of high quality land is lost, consistent with the sustainable functioning of the proposed development. This is a particularly important objective when land is allocated in the Local Development Framework (LDF) process, and where there are a number of competing interests promoting alternative site locations. Site boundaries and linear developments like roads can also be adjusted to avoid better quality land and well structured farm holdings.

Furthermore, development schemes can be designed to locate hard development (e.g. structures, infrastructure, and constructed surfaces) on poorer quality land, with soft development (i.e. where the soil profile remains largely undisturbed) like public open spaces on the better quality land. This is particularly effective where the soft uses are placed adjacent to agricultural land, which is not affected by urban problems like trespass and vandalism, and which remains commercially viable. Under such circumstances the soft uses have the potential to be converted back into productive use, if necessary. Similarly, they can act as recreational **buffer zones** if placed adjacent to nature conservation sites.

The identification and conservation of soil resources and reinstatement of soil profiles (§9.3.2) has the potential to effectively mitigate the impacts of mineral extraction. This, however, applies only to well managed operations that conform with the best practice guidelines published by DoE (1996a–1996c) and MAFF (2000). Essentially, this is a matter of the separate handling of topsoil, subsoil and soil-forming materials using specialist machinery under appropriate weather and soil moisture conditions. If the soils are to be stored for any length of time they may need to be grassed over to prevent erosion and colonisation by weeds. In most circumstances, land evaluation methodologies assume that under normal standards of land management nutrient deficiencies can be remedied by fertiliser applications.

Most mineral extraction occurs in rural areas and urban fringes, and in recent years the wider objectives of sustainable development have prompted a change from restoration for agriculture to a restructuring and diversification of land uses. As a result, Government Offices for the regions and Mineral Planning Authorities require the reinstatement of best and most versatile land to a viable agricultural use, using the best soils available, but poorer soils can be used for other beneficial uses such as amenity and/or nature conservation wetland sites or broadleaved woodlands with enhanced public access. The Forestry Commission and DETR have published some useful guidance on the reinstatement of soils for tree planting over capped wastes at landfill sites (Bending and Moffat 1997). The Landfill Communities Fund (formerly known as The Landfill Tax Credit Scheme), administered by ENTRUST under the Landfill Tax Regulations 1966, provides a mechanism by which landfill operators can fund environmental projects that have been proposed by environmental bodies.

It is not possible to cover here all of the mitigation measures necessary to prevent **erosion and compaction** problems during and after developments, but the following general guidelines are of use.

- Minimise vegetation removal, and re-vegetate bare areas as soon as possible.
- Avoid creating large open expanses of bare soil. These are most susceptible to wind erosion. If such large areas are created then windbreaks may be a useful mitigation procedure.
- Where possible create gentle gradients and avoid steep slopes.
- Install suitable drainage systems to direct water away from slopes.
- If the development is near to a water body, consider installing *siltation traps* to trap sediment, and prevent damage to the freshwater ecosystem.
- Avoid driving over the soil, or use wide tyres to spread the weight of vehicles, thereby avoiding compaction.
- Use a single or few designated tracks to bring vehicles to the working area.
- Cultivate the area after compaction has taken place.

The reclamation of mineral workings to agriculture (DoE 1996b), *Guidance on good practice for the reclamation of mineral workings to agriculture* (DoE 1996c), and *The good practice guide for handling soils* (MAFF 2000) are primary references discussing the above, and erosion control methods are also discussed by Bell (1999). It is important to avoid runoff of pollutants carried in a liquid form, and if this is perceived to be a major problem then procedures for the containment of the pollutants on site must be considered (see Table 10.12). The mitigation of cumulative and dispersed impacts on soil chemistry as a result of air and water-borne pollution from developments is a matter of emission controls (see Chapters 8 and 10).

If the baseline survey shows that the ground below the site contains contaminants a risk assessment based on the source–pathway–receptor model should be carried out. In simple situations, the risk assessment can be undertaken using empirical methods but often some form of numerical modelling will be necessary to quantify the potential for migration/release to occur. The modelling of transport of contaminants to groundwater is considered by Adriano *et al.* (1994). Techniques for modelling presently being used are: hydrogeological flow models such as AQUA3D (SSG 2008), MODFLOW (USGS 2007), ConSim (EA 2003) and the *Remedial targets* worksheet (EA 2006); and air dispersion models such as ADMS (CERC 2008).

If the risk assessment shows that the site is contaminated as defined under a source–pathway–receptor model then remediation may have to be undertaken. There are a number of remediation techniques available, some of which could also be applicable to clearing up pollution caused during and after the development phase. These include:

- **Removal of the contamination for off-site disposal** (so called dig and dump). This is the most commonly used technique, but will result in the transport of hazardous material along the public highway, and the displacement of pollution to a landfill site.
- **Capping of the contamination**. Provision of a suitable thickness of inert materials (ranging from concrete to topsoil) over the contaminated materials will break the pathway to the surface. The capping may have to be of low permeability and, in some cases, may have to be capable of collecting and dissipating gas.
- **Excavation and on site disposal**. This removes the need for off-site transport, but if the material is still defined as contaminated in its new setting it may require a custom designed facility, and a waste management licence. If the material is fit for use elsewhere on the site and on source–pathway–receptor considerations is not contaminated in its new location it is not waste.
- **On-site stabilisation by adding materials such as cement or bentonite**. These techniques remove the ability of a pollutant to move off-site.
- **In situ and *ex-situ* bio-remediation**. These methods use natural microorganisms to break down organic pollutants in soil and groundwater, generally by providing oxygen.
- **Soil washing**. Acid or solvent washing of soils is commonly undertaken in countries such as Holland, and is very effective at removing contaminants and minimising material for disposal. The end product is, however sterile, and has to be modified if it is to be used as a growth medium.
- **Air sparging, vacuum extraction and pump and treat methods** are effective at removing a range of contaminants from groundwater.

For a review of the above techniques and a discussion of how to select the best practicable environmental option see Wood (1997). The choice of technique will depend upon the type of pollutant(s) present, the geology and hydrogeo-logy, the development type, and the sensitivity of the surrounding environment. Even where contamination is found, it does not automatically mean that some form of remediation is required. The most common approach used in the UK at present, and the approach being promoted by the EA, is the use of risk assess-ment techniques to ascertain the potential for impact on the environment (Cairney 1995, Syms 1997). The need for remediation must be proven by carrying out a risk assessment (Chapter 13).

9.8 Monitoring

The loss of soils implicit in the conversion of agricultural land to urban uses is recorded by Defra, and other soil impacts are monitored under the Draft Soil Strategy, and the Soil Action Plan (Defra 2001, 2004a) as indicators of sus-tainable development. These are subject to regular review as part of the British Government's commitment to global sustainability. The DoE (1996c) has pub-lished the results of wide-ranging research into standards of land restoration following mineral extraction, and this forms the technical basis to the best prac-tice guidelines. More recent results (DETR 1997) have been made available on a landfill site restored to agriculture and monitored since 1974, and the results are being used to further elaborate on good restoration practice.

Where baseline studies indicate a potential for groundwater contamination or the generation or migration of gas or vapours, the installation of wells and the monitoring of water levels and chemistry and gas/vapour concentrations, pres-sures and flow rates will be necessary. Guidance on monitoring wells and sampling is provided in BS10175 (BSI 2001), and on the monitoring and assessment of hazardous ground gases by Wilson *et al.* (2007) and NHBC (2007).

References

Adriano DC, AK Iksandar and IP Murarka (eds) 1994. *Contamination of groundwaters.* Boca Raton, FL: CRC Press.

Ashman MR and G Puri 2002. *Essential soil science.* Oxford: Blackwell.

Avery BW 1990. *Soils of the British Isles.* Wallingford, Oxon: C.A.B International.

Bell FG 1998. *Environmental geology; principles and practice.* Oxford: Blackwell Science.

Bell FG 1999. *Geological hazards; their assessment, avoidance and mitigation.* London: E & FN Spon.

Bell FG 2000. *Engineering Properties of Soils and Rock,* 4th edn. Oxford: Blackwell Scientific.

Bending NAD and AJ Moffat 1997. *Tree establishment on landfill sites.* London: Forestry Commission and DETR.

Brady NC and RR Weil 2002. *The nature and properties of soils,* 13th edn. Upper Saddle River, NJ: Prentice-Hall.

Bridges EM 1978. *World soils.* 2nd edn. Cambridge: Cambridge University Press.

BSI (British Standards Institute) 1994. BS3882. *Specification for topsoil.* London: BSI.

BSI 2001. *BS10175. Investigation of potentially contaminated sites – Code of practice.* London: BSI.

BSI 2002a. *BS ISO 10381-1. Soil quality – Sampling – Guidance on the design of sampling programmes.* London: BSI.

BSI 2002b. *BS ISO 10381-2. Soil quality – Sampling – Guidance on sampling techniques.* London: BSI.

Cairney T 1995. *The re-use of contaminated land: a handbook of risk assessment.* Chichester: John Wiley & Sons.

CERC (Cambridge Environmental Research Consultants) 2008. *ADMS air pollution models.* Cambridge: CERC, www.cerc.co.uk/software/index.htm.

CIRIA 1998. *Remedial treatment for contaminated land*, Vol I: *Introduction and guide.* CIRIA special publication 101. London: CIRIA/DETR.

Cooke RU and JC Doornkamp 1990. *Geomorphology in environmental management: a new introduction*, 2nd edn. Oxford: Clarendon Press.

Cresser M, K Killham and T Edwards 1993. *Soil chemistry and its applications.* Cambridge: Cambridge University Press.

DCLG (Department for Communities and Local Government) 1996. Minerals Planning Guidance Note 7 (MPG 7). *The reclamation of mineral workings.* London: HMSO, www.communities.gov.uk/publications/planningandbuilding/mineralsplanningguidance5.

DCLG 2004. Planning Policy Statement 7 (PPS7). *Sustainable Development in Rural Areas.* London. HMSO, www.communities.gov.uk/publications/planningandbuilding/pps7.

DCLG 2006a. *Environmental impact assessment: a guide to good practice and procedures: a consultation paper*, www.communities.gov.uk/archived/publications/planningandbuilding/environmentalimpactassessment.

DCLG 2006b. Minerals Planning Statement 1 (MPS 1): *Planning and minerals.* London: HMSO, www.communities.gov.uk/publications/planningandbuilding/mineralspolicystatement5.

Defra (Department for Environment, Food and Rural Affairs) 2001. *Draft soil strategy for England – a consultation document.* London: Defra.

Defra 2004a. *The First Soil Action Plan for England: 2004 to 2006.* London: Defra, www.defra.gov.uk/environment/land/soil/sap/index.htm.

Defra 2004b. *Quality of life counts. Indicators for a strategy for sustainable development for the United Kingdom 2004; updating the baseline assessments made in 1999.* London: Defra, www.sustainable-development.gov.uk/publications/pdf/qolc04/qolc2004.pdf

Defra 2005. *Securing the future – UK government sustainable development strategy.* London: Defra, www.defra.gov.uk/sustainable/government/publications/uk-strategy/index.htm.

Defra 2006. *Environmental Protection Act 1990: Part 2: Contaminated land.* Circular 01/2006. www.defra.gov.uk/environment/land/contaminated/pdf/circular01-2006.pdf.

Defra 2007. *Agricultural Land Classification (ALC) statistics.* London: Defra, www.defra.gov.uk/rds/lgmt/ALC.htm.

Defra 2008a. EU *Thematic strategy for soil protection, including proposals for a soil framework directive.* www.defra.gov.uk/ENVIRONMENT/land/soil/europe/index.htm.

Defra 2008b. *Consultation on the draft soil strategy for England.* London; Defra, www.defra.gov.uk/corporate/consult/soilstrategy/.

Defra and Environment Agency (EA) 2002a. *Assessment of risks to human health from land contamination; an overview of the development of soil guideline values and related research. Report CLR7.* Bristol: Environment Agency, www.environment-agency.gov.uk/commondata/acrobat/clr7_675334.pdf.

Defra and EA 2002b. *Potential contaminants for the assessment of land. Report CLR8.* Bristol: Environment Agency, www.environment-agency.gov.uk/commondata/acrobat/clr8_675394.pdf.

Defra and EA 2002c. *Contaminants in soil: collation of toxicological data and intake values for humans, Report CLR9*. Bristol: Environment Agency, www.environment-agency.gov.uk/commondata/acrobat/clr9_675402.pdf.

Defra and EA 2002d. *Contaminated land exposure assessment model (CLEA); technical basis and algorithms Report CLR10*. Bristol: Environment Agency, www.environment-agency.gov.uk/subjects/landquality/113813/672771/675330/678753/?version=1&lang=_en.

Defra and EA 2004. *Model procedures for the management of contaminated land. Report CLR11*. Bristol: Environment Agency, www.environment-agency.gov.uk/commondata/105385/model_procedures_881483.pdf.

DETR (Department of the Environment, Transport and the Regions) 1997. *Agricultural quality of restored land at Bush Farm*. London: DETR.

DETR 1999a. *Environmental geology in land use planning; a guide to good practice*. London: DETR.

DETR 1999b. *Environmental geology in land use planning; advice for planners and developers*. London: DETR.

DETR 1999c. *Environmental geology in land use planning; emerging issues*. London: DETR.

DETR 1999d. *Soil-forming materials – their use in land reclamation*. London: DETR.

DETR 2000. *Contaminated Land: Implementation of Part IIA of the Environmental Protection Act 1990*. Circular 02/2000. London: DETR, www.clarinet.at/library/Part2aintro.PDF.

DoE (Department of the Environment) 1989. *Environmental assessment: a guide to the procedures*. London: HMSO.

DoE 1990. Planning Policy Guidance Note 14 (PPG14) *Development on unstable land*. HMSO, www.communities.gov.uk/documents/planningandbuilding/pdf/147471.

DoE 1991. *Environmental effects of surface mineral workings*. London: HMSO.

DoE 1994. *Sampling strategies for contaminated land*. CLR4. London: HMSO.

DoE 1996a. Mineral Planning Policy Guidance Note 1 (MPG 1) *General considerations and the development plan system*. London: HMSO.

DoE 1996b. *The reclamation of mineral workings to agriculture*. London: HMSO.

DoE 1996c. *Guidance on good practice for the reclamation of mineral workings to agriculture*. London: HMSO.

EA (Environment Agency) 2003. *Contamination impacts on groundwater: simulation by Monte Carlo method*, ConSim release 2, Environment Agency R&D Publication 132. Nottingham: Golder Associates (UK) Ltd, www.consim.co.uk/.

EA 2004a. *The state of soils in England and Wales*. Bristol: Environment Agency, www.environment-agency.gov.uk/commondata/acrobat/stateofsoils_1747056_1879364.pdf.

EA 2004b. *Soil, the hidden resource* – a consultation document available at: www.environment-agency.gov.uk/commondata/acrobat/soilsstrat_cons_782297.pdf.

EA 2006. *Remedial targets methodology: hydrological risk assessment for land contamination*. Bristol: Environment Agency, http://publications.environment-agency.gov.uk/pdf/GEHO0706BLEQ-e-e.pdf?lang=_e.

EA 2007. *Soil, a precious resource, our strategy for protecting, managing and restoring soil*. Bristol: EA, http://publications.environment-agency.gov.uk/pdf/GEHO1007BNDB-e-e.pdf

Ellis N, DQ Bowen, S Campbell, J Knill, A McKirdy, C Prosser, M Vincent and R Wilson 1996. *An introduction to the geological conservation review*. Peterborough, Cambs: JNCC, www.jncc.gov.uk/page-2965.

Ellison RA and A Smith 1998. *Environmental geology in land use planning: a guide to sources of earth science information for planning and development*. British Geological Survey Technical Report WA/97/85. London: HMSO, or www.bgs.ac.uk/reference/landuse/landuse.html.

Emmett BA 2007. Nitrogen saturation of terrestrial ecosystems: Some recent findings and their implications for our conceptual framework. *Water, air, and soil pollution: Focus* 7, 99–109.

EPAs (EA, EHS and SEPA) Undated. *General guide to the prevention of pollution: PPG1*, http://publications.environment-agency.gov.uk/pdf/PMHO0501BFOX-e-e.pdf.

Gerard J 2000. *Fundamentals of soils*. London: Routledge.

Hallbäcken L and CO Tamm 1986. Changes in soil acidity from 1927 to 1982–1984 in a forest area in south-west Sweden. *Scandinavian Journal of Forest Research* 1, 219–232.

Hamza MA and WK Anderson 2005. Soil compaction in cropping systems: a review of the nature, causes and possible solutions. *Soil and Tillage Research* 82, 121–145.

Hettelingh J-P, M Posch, J Slootweg, GJ Reinds, T Spranger and L Tarrason 2007. Critical loads and dynamic modelling to assess European areas at risk of acidification and eutrophication. *Water, Air, & Soil Pollution: Focus* 7, 379–384.

Highways Agency 1993. *Design manual for roads and bridges (DMRB)*, Vol. 11: *Environmental assessment*, Section 3, Part 11: *Geology and soils*. London: Highways Agency, www.standardsforhighways.co.uk/dmrb/vol11/section3.htm.

Hodgson JM (ed.) 1997. *Soil survey field handbook*, 3rd edn. Cranfield, Beds: Cranfield University.

Hodson MJ, C Stapleton and R Emberton 2001. Soils, geology and geomorphology. Ch. 9 in *Methods of environmental impact assessment*, 2nd edn, P Morris and R Therivels (eds). London: Spon Press.

Jonsson U, U Rosengren, G Thelin and B Nihlgard 2003. Acidification-induced chemical changes in coniferous forest soils in southern Sweden 1988–1999. *Environmental Pollution* 123, 75–83.

Keller EA 2000. Environmental geology, 8th edn. London: Prentice-Hall.

Lal R 2001. Soil degradation by erosion. *Land Degradation & Development* 12, 519–539.

MAFF (Ministry of Agriculture Fisheries and Food) 1988. *Agricultural land classification of England and Wales: revised guidelines and criteria for grading the quality of agricultural land*. London: MAFF, www.defra.gov.uk/rds/lgmt/ALC.htm.

MAFF 1998. The Soil Code: *Code of good agricultural practice for the protection of soil*. London: MAFF, www.defra.gov.uk/farm/environment/cogap/pdf/soilcode.pdf.

MAFF 2000. *The good practice guide for handling soils*. London: MAFF, www.defra.gov.uk/farm/environment/land-use/soilguid/index.htm.

MLURI (Macauley Land Use Research Institute) 1991. *Land capability classification for agriculture (LCA)*. Aberdeen: Macaulay Institute.

MO (Meteorological Office) 1989. *Climatological data for agricultural land classification*. Bracknell, Berks: Meteorological Office.

Morgan RPC 2004. *Soil erosion and conservation*, 3rd edn. Oxford: Blackwell Science.

Munsell Color Co. 2000. *Soil color charts*. Newburgh, NY: Macbeth Division, Kollmorgen Instruments Group.

NHBC (National House-Building Council) 2007. *Guidance on the evaluation of development proposals where methane and carbon dioxide are present*. Amersham, Bucks: NHBC.

ODPM (Office of the Deputy Prime Minister) 2004. Planning Policy Guidance Statement 23 (PPS23) *Planning and pollution control*. London: TSO, www.communities.gov.uk/publications/planningandbuilding/planningpolicystatement23.

PAA (Penny Anderson Associates) 1994. *Roads and nature conservation: guidance on impacts, mitigation and enhancement*. Peterborough: English Nature.

Rowell DL 1994. *Soils science: methods and applications*. London: Addison Wesley Longman.

SE (Scottish Executive) 2003. Scottish Planning Policy 3 (SPP 3). *Housing.* Edinburgh: Scottish Executive, www.scotland.gov.uk/Publications/2003/02/16499/18894.

SE 2006a. Scottish Planning Policy 4 (SPP 4 *Planning for minerals*). Edinburgh: Scottish Executive, www.scotland.gov.uk/Resource/Doc/146319/0038293.pdf.

SE 2006b. Scottish Planning Policy 15 (SPP 15 *Rural development*). Edinburgh: Scottish Executive, www.scotland.gov.uk/Publications/2005/02/20624/51511.

Sliggers J and W Kakebeeke 2004. *Clearing the air. 25 years of the convention on long-range transboundary air pollution.* New York and Geneva: United Nations.

SO (Scottish Office) 1994. Circular 25/1994. *Agricultural land.* Edinburgh: Scottish Office.

SSG (Science Software Group) 2008. AQUA3D: *3-dimensional Finite-Element Groundwater Flow and Transport Model.* Sandy, UT: SSG, www.scisoftware.com/environmental_software/product_info.php?products_id=31.

Syms P 1997. *Contaminated land. The practice and economics of redevelopment.* Oxford: Blackwell Science.

Tan KH 2005. *Soil sampling, preparation and analysis*, 2nd edn. London: Taylor & Francis.

Troeh FR and LM Thompson 2005. *Soils and soil fertility*, 6th edn. Oxford: Blackwell Publishing.

USDA-NRCS (United States Department of Agriculture-Natural Resources Conservation Service) 1999. *Soil taxonomy: a basic system of soil classification for making and interpreting soil surveys*, 2nd edn. http://soils.usda.gov/technical/classification/taxonomy/.

USGS (US Geological Survey) 2007. *MODFLOW and related programs.* Denver, CO: USGS http://water.usgs.gov/nrp/gwsoftware/modflow.html.

Webster R and MA Oliver 1990. *Statistical methods in soil and land resource survey (Spatial information systems).* Oxford: Oxford University Press.

Wilson S, S Oliver, H Mallett, H Hutchings and G Card 2007. *Assessing risks posed by hazardous ground gases to buildings (revised) CIRIA Report 665.* London: CIRIA

Wood PA 1997. Remediation methods for contaminated sites. In *Contaminated land and its reclamation*, RE Hester and RM Harrison (eds), 47–71. London: Thomas Telford.

WRB (World Reference Base for Soil Resources) 2006. *A framework for international classification, correlation and communication.* Rome: FAO, www.fao.org/landandwater/agll/wrb/default.stm.

Wright IA, RV Birnie, A Malcolm, W Towers and M McKeen 2006. *The potential use of the Land Capability for Agriculture Classification for determining support to disadvantaged areas of Scotland.* Aberdeen: Macaulay Land Use Research Institute, www.macaulay.ac.uk/publications/LFAreport.pdf.

10 Water

Sally-Beth Kelday, Andrew Brookes and Peter Morris (based on Morris, Biggs and Brookes 2001)

10.1 Introduction

Water is a common chemical substance essential to all known forms of life. Water dissolves more substances than any other liquid and, wherever it travels, it carries chemicals, including minerals, and nutrients. Somewhere between 70 and 75 per cent of the earth's surface is covered with water, mostly in oceans and other large water bodies. About 96 per cent of the earth's free water is seawater, and approximately 3 per cent is snow and ice. Liquid fresh water only constitutes about 1 per cent, and is a relatively scarce resource. Considerably more freshwater is stored under the ground in *aquifers* than on the earth's surface.

Within 25 years, half the world's population could experience problems in sourcing enough freshwater for drinking and irrigation. Currently, more than 80 countries, representing some 40 per cent of the world's people, are subject to serious water shortages. While future droughts and water shortages are predicted for parts of Europe, access to clean water is generally taken for granted, and large quantities are used for domestic purposes, for cooling, rinsing and cleaning in industry, and for irrigation in agriculture. Such pressures place a heavy burden on water resources in terms of both quantity and quality.

This chapter concentrates on those elements of surface and ground freshwaters relevant to EIA in the UK. "Water" is a subject of great concern to European and UK Governments, and this is reflected in a large series of laws. The Water Framework Directive (WFD) (EC 2000) is the most substantial piece of EU water legislation to date. It requires all inland and coastal waters to reach "good status" (or "good potential" in the case of Heavily Modified Water Bodies (HMWBs)) by 2015. In 2008, in the UK a **river basin district structure** was set up, within which demanding environmental objectives are set, including ecological targets for surface waters. The full impact of the WFD on the EIA process is yet to evolve but will do so in the life of this edition of the book.

The study of water in land areas is known as **hydrology**. This science is concerned with the movement, distribution and quality of water throughout the Earth's systems. Hydrological systems are highly dynamic, and planning any development that may potentially impact upon them requires an understanding, and some type of assessment (proportional to the issues being considered), of variations in the storage and flow of water (**water quantity**) and of the materials it carries (**water quality**).

Water has a pivotal role in environmental systems, and the water assessment in an EIA typically has implications for other disciplines. For example:

- The water quantity and quality of a specific area is strongly influenced by local climate (Chapter 8), soils, geology and geomorphology (Chapter 9), and the biota (especially vegetation) – and in turn affects them (see Figure 11.4). The link between water and ecology is particularly strong in freshwater ecosystems.
- Surface waters (such as rivers and lakes) typically have high landscape and recreational values (Chapter 6).
- River *floodplains* usually contain valuable agricultural land (which can impact directly on the river itself). Floodplains have historically been some of the first areas to be populated (due to proximity to water and river crossing points with the result that they typically contain archaeological features (Chapter 7).
- The provision of adequate water supply (in terms of both quantity and quality) is a vital socio-economic requirement, and hydrological processes can be highly significant in relation to the siting of developments, e.g. on floodplains.

"Water" is a fundamental and wide-ranging subject. Typically the specialists involved in an EIA include engineers, scientists or hydrological experts with an understanding of flood risk; water quality experts with an understanding of water chemistry, geomorphologists and/or hydromorphologists, and ecologists concerned with preserving or re-creating more natural habitats that can potentially sustain or support an existing or improved ecology (Chapter 11).

Inevitably, with such a vast subject, this chapter can only provide a brief overview of key issues likely to be involved in EIA and to point the reader to other literature sources, of which there are many. Texts covering most aspects include Manning (1996), Shaw (1994), Viessman and Lewis (2003), Viessman and Hammer (2004) and Ward and Robinson (2000). Texts focusing on environmental aspects include Newson (1994), Singh (1995), Thompson (1998), Wanielista *et al.* (1996), Ward and Trimble (2003), and Watson and Burnett (1995). Increased use is being made in EIA of remote sensing and GIS (Chapter 14); publications focusing on hydrological applications of these techniques include Gurnell and Montgomery (2000), Schultz and Engman (2000), Singh and Fiorentino (1996) and WUF (2001).

10.2 Definitions and concepts of water quantity

10.2.1 Introduction

Studies of water quantity are largely concerned with the storage of water in various environmental systems and the flows of water within and between these systems. A major feature of the earth's water system is the **hydrological cycle** in which:

- water evaporates (principally from the oceans) to form atmospheric water vapour;
- water vapour condenses (e.g. forming clouds) and returns to the earth's surface as precipitation (rain, snow and dew);
- water precipitated on land drains into rivers, lakes, soils and aquifers; and either evaporates back to the atmosphere or flows back to the seas and oceans, thereby completing the cycle.

This global circulation of water is a closed system with no significant gains or losses. By contrast, a site, region or land mass has an open system of water flows, with inputs (I) and outputs (O) that control the amount of water stored in it, and hence its **water budget**, which can be expressed as

$$I - O = \Delta S$$
where ΔS = change in storage (increase if $I > O$ *or* decrease if $O > I$)

The only significant input to land masses is precipitation. The outputs are *evapotranspiration*, groundwater seepage and *runoff* (mainly in rivers).

10.2.2 Catchments

A water assessment will normally need to consider the hydrology of a **catchment**. As defined in the *Water Framework Directive* (EC 2000), this can be:

- a **river basin** (main catchment) – defined as "an area of land from which all surface runoff flows through a sequence of streams, rivers, and possibly lakes, into the sea at a single river mouth, estuary or delta"; or
- a **sub-basin** (sub-catchment) – defined as "an area of land from which all surface runoff flows through a series of streams, rivers, and possibly lakes, to a particular point in a watercourse (normally a lake or a river confluence)".

A catchment is a fairly discrete system, and provides an excellent focus for scientific research, water management and EIA. It has a water budget in which:

- the main input is precipitation, although groundwater seepage can occur when a groundwater body underlies more than one catchment;
- the outputs are evapotranspiration, runoff and groundwater leakage.

Within the catchment, various storage components and fluxes can be identified (**Figure 10.1**).

A development or *receptor* site located within a catchment may receive land-phase water (surface water and/or groundwater) from higher in the catchment,

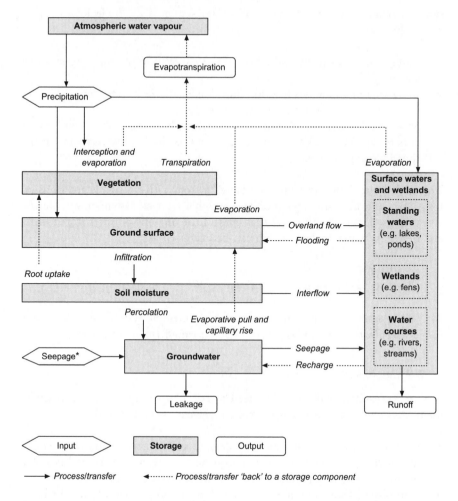

Figure 10.1 Catchment processes and storage components.

and therefore has a **site catchment** and a **site water budget** with several inputs and outputs:

$$(Pn + R_s + R_g) - (ET + Q_s + Q_g) = \Delta S$$

where: Pn = Precipitation   ET = evapotranspiration
           R_s = surface water recharge Q_s = surface water discharge
                (run on)   (runoff)
           R_g = groundwater recharge Q_g = groundwater discharge
                (seepage)   (leakage)
                    ΔS = change in storage

The relative importance of the inputs and outputs will depend on a number of factors including the site's location in the catchment. Sites situated high in a catchment may depend largely on precipitation, and can be particularly vulnerable to water shortages in times of drought. On the other hand, low-lying sites may be susceptible to flood risk, and systems such as lowland rivers that depend on significant and sustained inputs of land-phase water (including groundwater) are vulnerable to impacts that reduce or contaminate this supply.

10.2.3 Precipitation and evapotranspiration

Precipitation (Pn) and evapotranspiration (ET) bring about the interchange of water between the atmospheric and land-phase water (Figure 10.1) and a catchment water budget is markedly influenced by the balance between them. This can be expressed as the **Pn/ET ratio**, or the **meteorological water balance** (Pn − ET). When Pn > ET, there is a **water surplus** which is discharged as runoff; when Pn < ET, there is a **water deficit** which leads to a reduction in storage water and runoff.

In the long term, Pn/ET ratios are a function of the local or regional **climate**. For example, in the UK: (a) they are high in north-western areas and lower in the south and east; and (b) they show a marked seasonal pattern – all areas normally having an appreciable **winter surplus** and a **summer deficit**, which is usually slight in north-western areas and increases to the south and east. The summer deficit normally arises from high evapotranspiration rates rather than low summer rainfall. This is because (a) evaporation increases in response to higher temperatures and lower humidities, and (b) *transpiration* increases when the vegetation is in leaf. However, evapotranspiration is often reduced because *soil moisture deficits* (SMDs) develop, especially during droughts. These inhibit transpiration and plant growth, and explain the frequent need to irrigate many crops in the drier areas.

In addition to the "normal" seasonal patterns, meteorological water balance exhibits marked, unpredictable variation, which has been particularly apparent in recent years, with sustained deviations from normal seasonal patterns in many areas (§10.8.2). This trend is thought to be related to climate change (§8.1.3). Soil moisture levels, groundwater recharge and river flows are all very sensitive to changes in rainfall/evapotranspiration patterns, which therefore have significant knock-on effects in catchments.

Meteorological water balance is also influenced by factors other than climate. These include land cover, particularly the extent of surface waters and the extent and nature of vegetation. The latter is important because:

- **Interception** of precipitation by vegetation, and re-evaporation from the canopy, means that much precipitation water never reaches the ground (Figure 10.1). This **interception loss** (which contributes to evapotranspiration) varies in relation to the **interception capacities** of vegetation types. For instance, it can be up to *c*.25 per cent of precipitation in broadleaved woodland, higher conifer forest and tall grassland, but much lower in short swards or sparse vegetation.

- **Transpiration** can return >50 per cent of rainfall to the atmosphere, although it also varies with vegetation type, e.g. is higher from woodland than from grassland.

The combination of interception and transpiration can therefore account for >75 per cent of rainfall, leaving <25 per cent to become runoff – so vegetation is a major factor affecting runoff (see Baird and Wilby 1999). Both interception and transpiration are markedly reduced when vegetation is replaced by a built environment, and this is a major cause of increased runoff from urban areas. Similarly, while mature crops can have high interception capacities and transpiration rates, cultivated land is usually bare or sparsely vegetated for much of the year.

10.2.4 Infiltration and overland flow

Most rainfall reaching vegetated ground normally infiltrates into the soil (Figure 10.1) where it is stored, re-evaporates, is taken up by plant roots, or percolates downwards in response to gravity. The release of infiltrated water to surface waters is normally slow. However, if precipitation exceeds the soil's **infiltration capacity** (its ability to absorb water) the excess collects in depressions or runs down inclines as **overland (sheet) flow** (Figure 10.1).

Infiltration capacity is most likely to be exceeded under intense or sustained rainfall (especially when soils are already wet) or if heavy winter snowfall is followed by a rapid spring thaw. However, infiltration and associated surface runoff are strongly influenced by:

- **soil depth and texture** (§9.3.1) – in the US, four **hydrologic soil groups** are recognised, ranging from A – soils with good infiltration when wet, and hence low runoff potential (e.g. deep sandy soils) to D – soils with low infiltration when wet, and hence high runoff potential, e.g. heavy clays and shallow soils (see Fangmeier *et al.* 2005);
- **slope and vegetation cover** – overland flow tends to increase on slopes and/or where vegetation (which enhances infiltration) is sparse, and this increases the risk of soil *erosion* and flash floods.

Infiltration is also drastically reduced by factors such as soil compaction, e.g. on construction sites (§9.6.2) and is completely prevented by impervious surfaces. This increases the volume and rate of runoff from built environments, and reduces recharge to groundwater beneath them.

10.2.5 Groundwaters

The subsurface system can be divided into an **unsaturated (vadose) zone** that normally has air-filled spaces, and a **saturated zone** in which all available spaces are filled with **groundwater**. Soil is an important component of the unsaturated zone, and the properties of a soil, especially its texture and structure (§9.3.1) affect both its ability to retain water and its *hydraulic conductivity*.

If percolating water encounters an impermeable layer in the unsaturated zone, it may accumulate or move down inclines as **interflow** (Figure 10.1), but this is usually a minor and intermittent flux compared with percolation to the saturated zone. Within the saturated zone, groundwater is usually held in strata of porous rock called *aquifers*, of which there are two main types – **confined aquifers** and **unconfined aquifers (Figure 10.2)**. Two other types occur in some areas: **"leaky" aquifers** which are partially confined below a semi-pervious layer, above which an unconfined aquifer is also present, and **karst aquifers** which consist of fractured rather than porous rock.

Globally, groundwater constitutes *c.*97 per cent of all liquid fresh water. In the UK, it currently provides *c.*30 per cent of public water demands (>70 per cent in south-east England), and *c.*75 per cent of groundwater abstracted in England is used for drinking water (EA 2000).

UNCONFINED AQUIFER

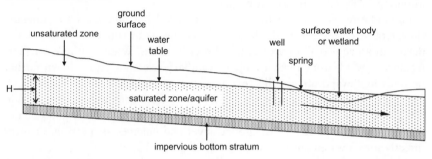

CONFINED AQUIFER

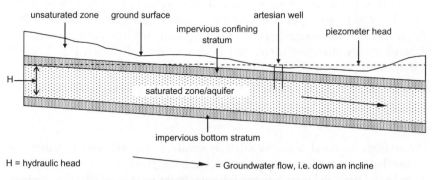

H = hydraulic head   → = Groundwater flow, i.e. down an incline

An **unconfined aquifer** has a free **water table** (groundwater surface) – and a *well* sunk into it will fill to the water table level (WTL). The **hydraulic head** is strictly the height of the groundwater body from the impervious bottom rock to the water table, but is effectively the elevation of the water table – and water will flow down the **groundwater slope** from a point where the WTL is higher to one at lower altitude. A **confined aquifer** lies beneath an impervious confining stratum, although it must fill from one or more un-confined areas. Confined groundwater is **artesian** (i.e. under pressure), and given a break in the impervious layer, e.g. at an artesian well or spring, water will rise to the level of the **piezometer head**. This is a horizontal line drawn from the highest level of hydraulic head in the system.

Figure 10.2 Groundwater relationships in an unconfined aquifer and a confined aquifer.

In Britain, groundwater can be abstracted from most "rocks". However, the **storage capacity** of an aquifer depends largely on its dimensions and porosity – and many strata (e.g. clays and shales) are not usually classed as aquifers because the porous material is thin (<50m), and the groundwater supply tends to be small and unreliable during droughts. The principal aquifers are the sandstones, limestones and chalk that underlie much of southern, eastern and midland areas of England.

Aquifer storage levels (and associated water table levels) normally follow a seasonal cycle. Storage is depleted during the summer, when output to springs and rivers continues, but: input is minimal because there is a meteorological water deficit; and abstraction demands increase. Groundwater recharge occurs mainly during winter, when there is a meteorological water surplus. Consequently, groundwater droughts are mainly caused by a lack of winter rainfall rather than dry summers, and serious droughts occur when (a) a dry summer follows a very dry winter, as in 1975/1976, or (b) winter recharge is below average for several years, as during 1988–1992 in eastern England.

Groundwater flows down inclines (Figure 10.2) but flow rates are generally slow, rarely exceeding 10m/day and sometimes less than 1m/year. Moreover, the deeper in an aquifer the water is, the slower it moves. Water can move a short distance upwards from a water table by **capillary rise** and can be drawn further upwards by **"evaporative pull"** (exerted by evapotranspiration) (Figure 10.1). However, groundwater cannot reach the surface from deep water tables; and in these situations it is not available to vegetation, and abstraction requires pumping. In some places, it reaches ground level and emerges as a spring, or seeps directly into a watercourse or water body (Figure 10.2).

In many catchments, groundwater and surface water levels are intimately linked, and groundwater is responsible for river **baseflows** which continue when there has been little rainfall for some time. In these systems, river **low flows** during droughts can be partly due to over-abstraction of groundwater (Cook 1998). Groundwater is also often important in supporting wetland ecosystems such as fens which are therefore threatened by groundwater depletion (see §11.7.2). Information on groundwater, with particular reference to the UK, is provided in Downing and Wilkinson (1992).

10.2.6 Surface waters

Apart from overland flow, which is normally transitory, surface waters can be divided into **standing waters** (lakes, reservoirs, ponds etc.) in which there is little lateral flow, and **watercourses** (streams, rivers etc.) in which there is appreciable flow (Figure 10.1).

Standing water bodies occur in depressions, or in valleys with natural or artificial dams behind which water accumulates. They range in size from small ponds to large lakes and artificial reservoirs, which are a major water resource in many areas. In spite of having little lateral flow, they are not static systems. Many have inflow and outflow streams, and typically there is movement of water between groundwater and the surface body. Consequently, levels in water bodies may change within a few hours, and affect local groundwater levels and streamflows. Standing waters also receive water by direct precipitation and overland flow, and lose appreciable amounts by evaporation (Figure 10.1).

Watercourses can include slow flowing channel systems such as canals and ditches, but most **streamflow** (the gravitational movement of water in a channel) is in streams and rivers. The rate of streamflow is influenced by channel slope, cross-sectional channel area/shape and the hydraulic roughness of the channel boundary. However, it also responds to the amount of water entering the channel, and is rarely stable for long. Water volumes and levels may rise rapidly in response to **storm rainfalls**, and because channels have a limited capacity, the water may rise above the bankfull level and spill out onto an adjacent floodplain – and **flood risk** is a principal reason for considering channel flow in EIA's. Runoff peaks (**quickflows** or **peak flows**) tend to be short-lived, but more sustained highflows can occur, e.g. in winter.

In recent years, **low flows** have also been the subject of increased attention of some EIAs (Cook 1998). Prolonged dry periods can lead to markedly reduced flow in many rivers (or even drying out, e.g. of chalk rivers including SSSIs) especially when these have a limited natural baseflow, or where there has been significant abstraction. Low flows can potentially have serious consequences for river ecology, and for public water supply, particularly where this relies principally on abstraction from rivers and/or reservoirs. Without some sustained input from rivers, only the largest UK reservoirs have the capacity to meet demands through very dry summers. This applies even if they were full at the start of the summer; so while surface water shortages can follow the failure of winter rainfall to fill reservoirs, they are more commonly associated with low summer flows in rivers (CEH 2008a). For the period 2005 to 2010 (Asset Management Planning Period 4) the EA has identified a number of sites, wetlands and rivers, which may be adversely affected by public water supply abstraction. Water Companies are currently investigating these sites to determine whether or not there is an adverse effect and whether local alterations can be applied to minimise that effect.

10.2.7 *Floodplains*

Floodplains constitute *c.*10 per cent of the land area in England and Wales (EA 2000), and *c.*8 per cent of England is at risk from river flooding (DETR 2000). River floodplains are associated with freshwater while coastal floodplains are areas of low lying land along the coast (e.g. tidal rivers and estuaries) which can be flooded by the sea (see §12.2.2). River channels have a limited capacity for water, and when this is exceeded, flooding of the adjoining land (or floodplain) becomes flooded and then acts to convey and temporarily store this water. In the UK this typically occurs without risk to human life and can reduce flood levels downstream. Flooding and floodplain processes are discussed in Anderson *et al.* (1996), Bailey *et al.* (1998), Bridge (2003), Marriott *et al.* (1999), Petts and Amoros (1997), Philippi (1996) and Smith and& Ward (1998). In addition to their importance in providing natural storage for floodwater, floodplains can also provide fertile *sediments* to agricultural land, help to maintain valuable habitat for wildlife and provide a recreational resource.

Flooding, together with associated processes such as sedimentation, are natural phenomena but can be adversely impacted by human activity. Because of their locations, relatively flat topography and rich *alluvial soils*, floodplains have historically attracted human development such as urbanisation and farming in spite of their natural susceptibility to flooding. Despite regulatory processes through the planning system, the rate of development on floodplains has more than doubled in some areas of the UK in the past 50 years (EA 2000). These activities have reduced floodplain storage, particularly in heavily urbanised areas, resulting in increased incidence of serious flooding, and further human intervention in the form of flood alleviation/defence measures such as channel modification (e.g. widening and deepening) or embankments (Brookes 1988). Such solutions can have adverse impacts on the local environment, cannot eliminate flood risk, and may increase the risk elsewhere, particularly downstream.

The Wise Use of Floodplains Project (WUF 2001) (an EU Life-Environment Project) detailed water and floodplain problems experienced in Europe (including several UK catchments). A series of guidance notes were produced in 2001, providing a starting point for thinking about the wise use of floodplains and floodplain restoration measures. They are relevant to, everyday floodplain management issues as well as policy development and strategic planning.

Defra's Making Space for Water programme (Defra 2008) aims to take forward flood and coastal risk management, and hence to increase resilience to flooding whilst achieving sustainable development, in England.

10.3 Definitions and concepts of water quality

10.3.1 Introduction

Water quality refers to the physical and chemical conditions of surface and groundwaters. Physical conditions include temperature and the presence of particulate matter; chemical conditions depend on the types and concentrations of dissolved chemicals present.

Water in the environment is never pure; natural waters always contain at least some dissolved chemicals (solutes) which originate from the atmosphere, soils or the *weathering* of bedrock. The water chemistry depends largely on the catchment climate and (especially) geology, and there is wide variation in **solute load** – the range and concentrations of solutes, including nutrients.

Natural waters also vary in the amount of particulate material present, which generally depends on the same factors as solute load. The terminology here is somewhat confusing. **Total sediment load** refers to the quantity and quality of *both* bottom *sediments* (sediments in the strict sense) *and* fine organic and inorganic particulates suspended in the water. However, while the latter are sometimes referred to as **suspended solids**, they are more commonly called **suspended "sediments"** – and the quantity present may be called the **suspended sediment load** or just **sediment load**.

Rivers may carry large quantities of particulates. Fine suspended particles will not normally settle in a river unless the flow is slow, and even in standing waters, *silt* particles may remain in suspension for some time before sinking to the bottom to become sediment. River bed particulates are called the **bedload**, and can range in size from silts to coarse sands, gravels and boulders. Bedload materials can move, but only when the flow of water exceeds a particular power, which is related to both the channel slope and the water discharge, and increases in relation to particle size. Although the bedload is a relatively small component of total sediment load, it is a major influence on the form of the channel itself and adjacent floodplain. The movement of bedload materials can be related to the formation and maintenance of natural features such as gravel *riffles* and point bars. These types of morphological features may also provide important habitats for freshwater invertebrates.

Water quality can be affected by *pollution* from a wide range of human activities, including large and small industrial enterprises, the water industry, urban infrastructure, agriculture, transport and deliberate or accidental pollution incidents. In general, pollution sources can be divided into two types: *point source pollution* and *diffuse (non-point) source pollution*. Water pollution can involve changes in the concentrations of naturally occurring chemicals (e.g. nitrates, phosphates, metals); the input of new synthetic substances (e.g. *pesticides*); and changes in sediment loads.

The likely effects of a development on water quality will depend not only on the development type but also on the **type and quality of the receiving waters**. For example, rivers export most of their pollutants downstream; so the effect at any one point may be transitory, although polluted water and silts may be carried considerable distances before they are sufficiently degraded or diluted to have no effect. By contrast, standing waters such as lakes and ponds are sediment sinks, and their water turn-over rate is usually slow; so sediment and pollutants tend to accumulate, and impacts may intensify with time.

Those aspects of water quality that are usually most relevant in EIAs are briefly discussed below. Further information can be found in standard hydrology texts and texts such as Gray (2008), Kiely (1997), Moss (1998), Laws (2000), and Ward and Robinson (2000). Because the problems of groundwater contamination differ somewhat from those of surface water pollution, they are discussed in a separate section (§10.3.9).

10.3.2 Oxygen levels and organic pollution

The concentration of dissolved oxygen in water can have important implications for wildlife and commercial fisheries. Oxygen levels vary naturally both within and between water bodies. Fast flowing streams and rivers normally have constantly high levels because turbulent flow enhances oxygen absorption from the atmosphere. Levels are lower in slower-moving water, especially at night, but should never be very low in most British rivers. Still-waters such as ponds and slow-flowing ditches have highly variable oxygen levels which may range from supersaturated during daylight hours to zero at night. Large water bodies such as lakes and reservoirs frequently stratify during the summer into an upper layer (the **epilimnion**) which is well oxygenated, and a lower layer (the **hypolimnion**) which is isolated from the atmosphere and may suffer oxygen depletion.

Oxygen depletion can occur through pollution, mainly by organic matter from sources such as sewage, soils, and agricultural or industrial *effluents*. High organic levels may be discharged from sewage treatment works, cattle yards, silage clamps, most food processing industries, and the wood and paper industry. Dissolved oxygen is consumed by the respiration of microbes that degrade the organic matter.

Low oxygen levels are particularly damaging in rivers, where fish and invertebrates require consistently high oxygen levels. Lakes may suffer if the bottom waters become *anoxic*, so (a) causing loss of **benthic** biota, and (b) promoting the release of phosphorus from the sediments, and hence enhancing and perpetuating *eutrophication*. Small still-water bodies that have highly variable oxygen levels, and support communities adapted to these conditions, may still be damaged by organic pollution if overloaded.

Reduced oxygen levels can also lead to increased levels of potentially harmful chemicals (e.g. ammonia, methane, hydrogen sulphide, and **heavy metals**) by increasing their production or solubilities.

10.3.3 Thermal pollution

The main source of thermal pollution is power stations which can increase the temperature of aquatic systems above the normal range. The principle damaging effects are:

- It can lead to oxygen starvation because increasing temperature (a) reduces the amount of dissolved oxygen held by water, and (b) promotes oxygen consumption by increasing rates of animal and microbial respiration, thus exacerbating the effects of organic matter pollution.
- Freshwater ecosystems have temperature regimes to which the aquatic life is adapted, and increased temperatures can (a) cause stress to cold-blooded animals by causing above-normal respiration rates and (b) disrupt the life cycle timing of native species.
- It may favour species not normally present in the area, including non-native invasive species (see §11.7.2).

The first two effects may make (particularly organically polluted) waters uninhabitable for much aquatic life; the third may lead to the local extinction of native species.

10.3.4 Acidification

The *pH* of natural waters varies considerably, and can change dramatically both seasonally and through the day. Many freshwater systems have naturally low pHs and should not be regarded as having poor water quality even if, for example, they do not support a commercial activity such as a fishery. However, acidification by **acid deposition** is now widespread, and many naturally acidic water bodies have become more acidified during the last 100–200 years. Low pH affects many freshwater animals directly, but a major effect is that they increase the solubility of toxic pollutants such as aluminium. These conditions are highly injurious to many freshwater animals, and have diverse biological effects including changes in the abundance, biomass and diversity of invertebrates, plants, fish and amphibians. The effects occur wherever there is high rainfall and/or a prevalence of acidic soils, and freshwater ecosystems and fisheries can be seriously affected in these areas.

10.3.5 Eutrophication

Excessive levels of nitrates and phosphates in freshwater systems can cause problems for both environmental and human health. The main source is runoff and **leaching** of fertilisers from farmland, although sewage effluent is thought to contribute *c.*5–10 per cent of the nitrate, and detergents in waste water contribute *c.*10 per cent to the overall phosphorous loading (DETR 1999).

The principal cause of **environmental damage** is *eutrophication* of surface waters. This results in enhanced growth of **macrophytes, phytoplankton** and filamentous **algae**) followed by oxygen depletion of the water when they decay. Enrichment by nitrogen and phosphorus is often accompanied by organic wastes and associated deoxygenation. It can result in considerable loss of conservation value, including loss of species diversity and dominance by a few tolerant plants (particularly algae). **Algal blooms** also increase turbidity and hence light attenuation in water, and macrophytes can clog rivers. Fish community composition may alter, and an initial increase in fish biomass is often followed by high mortality when plant decay causes deoxygenation. Phosphorus is usually considered to be the principal eutrophicating agent in temperate regions; but once a system is rich in phosphorus, nitrates may become the main factor controlling aquatic productivity, and this tends to promote the growth of nitrogen-fixing blue-green "algae" (**cyanobacteria**) which may produce toxins.

Eutrophication may also bring socio-economic problems by causing fish kills, increasing drinking water treatment costs, and (by promoting algal blooms) decreasing the amenity value of water bodies. It is generally perceived as a threat to standing waters, but is increasingly recognised as also having an impact on rivers. Many lowland water bodies, and slow-flowing and highly regulated rivers, are already eutrophicated.

The main **health concern** is methaemoglobinaemia (blue baby syndrome), a condition associated with nitrate. In many areas, nitrate levels in water bodies used for drinking water (particularly rivers and aquifers) are now sufficiently high to cause concern, and have led to protective legislation such as the designation of Nitrate Vulnerable Zones (NVZs) and Sensitive areas (Nitrate) (see Table 10.1).

10.3.6 Sediments

Sediments can be regarded as pollutants when present in unnaturally large quantities and/or when they are contaminated with chemical pollutants. Excessive sediment loads (especially of **silts**) can be derived from a variety of sources including agricultural land, bare urban surfaces and construction sites. Sediments from eroded soils or sewage may have a high organic content (causing deoxygenation), and where the site catchment is urbanised or intensively farmed, they may contain high levels of phosphates, metals, pathogens and pesticides.

Impacts of polluted sediments can be particularly severe in lakes and ponds, where they may become trapped and hence accumulate, with potentially damaging effects on ecosystems. Reduction of light by suspended particulates inhibits macrophyte growth, and may favour algal dominance. On settling, silts change the characteristics of the bottom substrate and hence the habitats of benthic invertebrates. Where deposition rates are high, they may progressively seal water bodies, isolating them from groundwater flows and hence potentially enhancing eutrophication.

Abrasive effects of suspended particulates in rivers may kill fish through gill damage; and in rivers with gravel bottoms used for spawning by fish (especially salmonids), siltation of gravels is of widespread concern as it leads to deoxygenation inside the gravels, starving the eggs and fry of oxygen.

10.3.7 Metals, microorganics, and other harmful chemicals

Many chemicals harm aquatic life, some at levels considerably below those which cause immediate death, e.g. sub-lethal levels may enhance the risk of disease, affect reproductive capacity, or alter competitive or foraging behaviour. Some toxins may **bioamplify** or have **synergistic** effects.

Water pollution by these chemicals is largely due to accidents associated with licensed discharges to rivers, and from various difficult-to-control diffuse sources such as runoff from roads and urban or agricultural areas.

The **metals** of greatest concern in freshwaters include aluminium, chromium and **heavy metals**. They are normally present in the environment in low concentrations or – as in the case of aluminium – are normally not "free". Metals are most toxic when in solution, and metal solubility is influenced by the prevailing conditions – most are more soluble at low pH, and less soluble in hard water (with high calcium levels and normally a high pH). Consequently, different water quality standards are often set for metals in hard and soft waters. Organic compounds often remove dissolved metals from water by binding with them; but they may also release metals which would otherwise have remained insoluble, and this is the reason for concern over some water softeners such as EDTA (ethylene diamine tetraacetic acid) which are added to many detergents. Metal toxicity often varies between different taxa. For example, zinc is relatively non-toxic to humans but very toxic to most fish, so levels of zinc acceptable in drinking water would be much higher than those acceptable for a fishery. Metals may also act synergistically.

In addition to naturally occurring toxins, between 20,000 and 70,000 compounds are estimated to be in common use worldwide (EA 1998a). These chemicals may or may not have toxic effects on organisms, or may be toxic above critical doses. An important group is the **microorganics**, which includes most pesticides. *Environmental Quality Standards* (EQSs) have been set for many of these (see Table 10.1) but adequate toxicity data only exist for a tiny proportion of synthetic compounds, and long-term *ecotoxicology* and environmental fate is known for only 20–30 chemicals. Recent research has shown that many chemicals have detrimental effects on organisms at levels far below those that cause immediate death, and often far below legal limits. Such sublethal effects include changes in physiology (such as hormone disruption), behaviour and reproductive rate.

Oils are commonly washed into freshwater systems from roads and industrial and development sites; and motorised pleasure boats also cause oil pollution. In addition to coating plants and animals, causing injury and death, oils can blanket the water surface, reducing oxygen diffusion. They also deoxygenate water as they are broken down. Oils contain many harmful chemicals, including carcinogens, such as polycyclic aromatics and phenols, which mix with water and poison aquatic life.

10.3.8 Pathogens

There are four broad categories of human pathogens in temperate freshwaters – viruses, bacteria, protozoans (microscopic animals) and helminths (flatworms), although helminths are not normally a problem in Britain. Viral pathogens tend to have a limited host range, so sources are usually limited to waters containing human wastes such as sewage. There are more potential sources of bacterial and protozoal pathogens because these tend to have less specific requirements.

10.3.9 Groundwater pollution

Porous rock has a filtering effect as water moves through it; so groundwater is generally much cleaner than surface water, and often requires little or no treatment before use. Chemicals are not completely removed however, and there is increasing concern about groundwater pollution. Contamination can occur from a range of both urban and rural sources, and can result from point source or non-point source pollution (e.g. see Adriano *et al.* 1994, DETR 2001, Downing and Wilkinson 1992). Diffuse source pollution is difficult to trace and prevent. As there is a direct link between groundwater and surface water, pollution of groundwater can impact surface water supplies, river ecosystems and wetlands.

Because groundwater moves very slowly (§10.2.5) pollutants take a long time to disperse naturally, and deep groundwater can remain contaminated for centuries or even millennia (EA 2000). Remedial measures, such as pollutant removal or degradation, are difficult and expensive; so it is particularly important to focus on pollution prevention. This has lead to specific legislation and policies for groundwater protection.

Approximately 81 per cent of groundwater bodies in England and 35 per cent in Wales are at risk of failing *Water Framework Directive* objectives due to diffuse pollution. The most prevalent pollutant in England is nitrate. Pesticides, oil, solvents and potentially phosphate have also been identified by the Environment Agency as groundwater pollutants (EA 2007a).

10.4 Legislative background and interest groups

10.4.1 Legislation

The main EU Directives relevant to the water component of EIAs are listed in **Table 10.1**. Most of these Directives have traditionally been focused on one of two approaches:

1. **quality objectives for receiving waters** – aiming to limit cumulative pollution by setting *Environmental/Water Quality Objectives* (EQOs/WQOs);
2. **source-based controls** – aiming to minimise pollution by setting *Emission Limit Values* (ELVs) that may be related to *Environmental Quality Standards* (EQSs) for specific pollutants.

Both these approaches are recognised to have deficiencies, and the *Water Framework Directive* (WFD) (EC 2000), which came into force on 22 December 2000, sets out a timetable for both initial transposition into laws of Member States and thereafter for the implementation of requirements. The WFD will move to a "combined approach" in which WQOs and ELVs are used to reinforce each other, with the more rigorous requirements applying in any particular situation. It also aims to (a) provide a framework for integrated management of inland surface waters and groundwaters, transitional waters (e.g. estuaries), and coastal waters, (b) maintain and enhance the status of aquatic ecosystems and dependent terrestrial ecosystems (thus integrating water management and nature conservation), and (c) achieve long-term protection of water resources. It includes provisions for Member States to:

- classify surface waters in terms of their chemical and ecological quality, set standards of "good status", achieve "good status" or "good potential" by 2015 and monitor the water bodies;
- prohibit direct discharges to groundwater, and monitor groundwater bodies;
- limit abstraction from groundwater bodies to the portion of recharge that is not needed to support connected ecosystems such as surface waters;
- produce and periodically update river basin management plans.

The WFD also proposes further laws to protect against water pollution. A "daughter directive" aimed at protecting groundwater has recently (2007) been adopted at European level, and a further daughter directive has been proposed aimed at reducing pollution of surface water (rivers, lakes, estuaries and coastal waters) by pollutants on a list of priority substances.

Table 10.1 Key EU Directives relevant to water assessments

Surface Waters Directive 75/440/EEC[1,3] – Control of the quality of surface waters intended for abstraction of drinking water, using *Water Quality Objectives* (WQOs).

Bathing Waters Directive 76/160/EEC[1] – to protect the health of bathers, and maintain the aesthetic quality of inland and coastal bathing waters. Sets standards for nineteen physical, chemical and microbiological variables, and includes requirements for monitoring and control measures to comply with the standards.

Dangerous Substances in Water Directive (DSWD) 76/464/EEC[2,3] – Control of inputs to water of dangerous substances (toxic, persistent, and likely to **bioaccumulate**). Requires member states to establish a consent system or set emission standards for two prescribed lists: those which should be prevented from entering waters (List I); and those which "should be minimised" (List II). There are several related Directives for specific pollutants.

Freshwater Fish Directive 78/659/EEC and **Shellfish Waters Directive 79/923/EEC**[1,3] – to protect the health of freshwater fish and shellfish populations, by setting WQOs for *designated waters*.

Groundwater Directive 80/68/EEC[1,3] – Related to the DSWD, to protect groundwater against pollution by dangerous substances (itemised in List I and List II). Implemented in the UK under the Water Resources Act.

Drinking Water Directive 80/778/EEC[1] – Control of the quality of water intended for human consumption. Sets limits for total coliforms and substances such as nitrates.

Agricultural Sewage Sludge Directive 86/278/EEC[2] – Sets limits on heavy metal levels in sewage sludge applied on agricultural land.

Urban Waste Water Treatment Directive (UWWTD) 91/271/EEC[2] – Protection of surface waters by regulating the collection and treatment of urban waste water (sewage) and certain industrial waste waters. Requires at least **secondary treatment** for most sewage effluent, e.g. from sewage treatment works (SWTs) which have a **population equivalent** (pe) >2k for inland waters and estuaries, or >10k for coastal waters. Discharges from a STW with a pe >10k to waters in a *Sensitive Area (Eutrophic)* or *Sensitive Area (Nitrate)* must comply with specified standards for removal of phosphorus and/or nitrogen.

Nitrates Directive 91/676/EEC[2] – Requirement to reduce nitrate pollution from agricultural sources (fertiliser and livestock manure) to safeguard drinking water, and protect fresh and marine waters from eutrophication. Sets a 50mg/l limit and, where this is in danger of being exceeded in surface or groundwaters, requires the designation of *Nitrate Vulnerable Zones* (NVZs) within which the use of nitrate is restricted.

Integrated Pollution Prevention and Control Directive (IPPCD) 96/61/EC[2] – Pollution control for prescribed industrial installations and pollutants, using permits based on *Emission Limit Values* (ELVs), *Best Available Techniques* (BATs) and *Environmental Quality Standards* (EQSs) – levels of pollutants that should not be exceeded, based on current knowledge of the their toxicities.

Water Framework Directive (WFD) 2000/60/EC – Reflects a thorough restructuring of EU Water Policy and will be the operational tool, setting the objectives for water protection for the future (see also Table 12.2).

Floods Directive 2007/60/EC – To reduce flood risks to human health, the environment, cultural heritage and economic activity in river basins and associated coastal areas (to be transposed into UK law in 2009).

Notes
[1] Directive focusing on quality objectives for receiving waters.
[2] Directive focusing on source-based controls.
[3] Directive to be incorporated into the Water Framework Directive.

Further information can be found at http://ec.europa.eu/environment/ *or* http://ec.europa.eu/environment/water/index_en.htm.

Defra and the Devolved Administrations have policy responsibility for the implementation of the WFD in the UK. Much of the implementation work is currently (2008) being undertaken by the **competent authorities**, which are the Environment Protection Agencies (EPAs) (see Appendix B).

The main relevant legislation in England and Wales, much of which implements the above EU Directives, is outlined in **Table 10.2**.

In relation to the EU/UK EIA legislation (§1.3), EIA is mandatory for six Annex I water-related project types and discretionary for 12 Annex II project

Table 10.2 Major England and Wales legislation relevant to water assessments

---

Salmon and Freshwater Fisheries Act 1975 – Regulation of inland fisheries, salmon and sea trout.

Environmental Protection Act (EPA) 1990 – *Integrated Pollution Control* (IPC) system for emissions to air, land and water, which requires: EA authorisation for scheduled dangerous processes or pollutants; operators to use *Best Available Techniques Not Entailing Excessive Cost* (BATNEEC) to prevent or minimise releases and make any emissions harmless; and (when more than one medium is threatened) adoption of the *Best Practicable Environmental Option* (BPEO) to minimise environmental damage.

Water Resources Act (WRA) 1991 – Protection of the quantity and quality of water resources and aquatic habitats. Duties and powers of the EA for: inland and coastal flood defences; **discharge consents** and abstraction licences; setting standards for **controlled waters**, *Water Quality Objectives* (WQOs) for inland and coastal waters, and *River Quality Objectives* (RQOs) for stretches of river; protecting groundwater; and monitoring water quality. Offences, e.g. to pollute groundwater.

Water Industry Act (WIA) 1991 – Duties of water companies; standards set for water supplies and wastewater treatment. Consents required for discharge of trade effluents into public sewers.

Land Drainage Acts (LDA) 1991, 1994 – Powers and duties of: the EA, mainly for flood defences and river engineering projects relating to designated '**main rivers**'; LAs, mainly for '**ordinary water-courses**' (not forming part of a main river); and Internal Drainage Boards (IDBs) for general drainage.

Environment Act 1995 – EA and SEPA established and given: (a) further powers relating to flood defence and land drainage, prevention and remediation of water pollution, contaminated land, abandoned mines, and regulation of fisheries for environmental purposes; and (b) duties to promote the conservation of: the natural beauty and amenity of inland and coastal waters and associated land; flora and fauna which depend on an aquatic environment; geological or physiographic features of special interest, and buildings/sites/objects of archaeological, architectural, engineering or historic interest. Regulations on mineral extraction strengthened. Duty of water companies to promote efficient water use.

Groundwater Regulations 1998 – Requirements for authorisation by the EPAs of direct and indirect discharges to groundwater of substances itemised in two lists (as in the Groundwater Directive).

Pollution Prevention and Control Act (PPCA) 1999 – Implements the IPPC Directive. Replaces IPC with *Pollution Prevention and Control* (PPC) which applies to a wider range of installations.

Table 10.2 (*continued*)

Water Act (WA) 2003 – Strengthens the EA's powers for the sustainable management of water resources. Key changes include: time limits for all new abstraction licences; facility to revoke abstraction licences causing serious environmental damage without compensation; greater flexibility to raise or lower licensing thresholds; small and environmentally insignificant abstractions deregulated; licensing extended to abstractors of significant quantities presently outside the licensing system; Water company drought plans and water resource management plans to become a statutory requirement.

The Water Environment (Water Framework Directive) (England and Wales) Regulation 2003 – Transposed the WFD for river basins in England and Wales.

Water Resources (Abstraction and Impounding) Regulations 2006 – Specify new procedural requirements in respect of the licensing of abstraction and impounding of water in England and Wales.

Water Resources (Environmental Impact Assessment) (England and Wales) (Amendment) Regulations 2006 – Amend the Water Resources (EIA) (England and Wales) Regulations 2003 to transpose into law the requirements of the *Public Participation Directive* (see §1.3) insofar as this amends the EIA process. The 2003 regulations apply to certain water management projects for agriculture which are subject to regulation under abstraction and impoundment controls.

Environmental Impact Assessment (Land Drainage Improvement Works) (Amendment) Regulations 2005 – Came into force on 25 June 2005. Strengthens previous SI, defining consultation and public participation (as appropriate)

Details of most of the above legislation, and on Scottish and Northern Ireland legislation, are available at www.opsi.gov.uk. Further information can be found on the EPA websites and www.doeni.gov.uk/index/protect_the_environment/water.htm.

types, some of which only qualify if they are near ***controlled waters***. However, all major projects are likely to have water-related impacts and the DCLG (2006a) guidance prescribes screening for the water component in any EIA. Where river engineering works (including improvements to flood defences) are carried out under a General Development Order (if planning permission is not required), an EIA may still be required under the EIA (Land Drainage Improvement Works) Regulations 1999 (SI 1783) as amended by The Environmental Impact Assessment (Land Drainage Improvement Works) (Amendment) Regulations 2006 (see www.opsi.gov.uk/si/si2006/20060618.htm).

10.4.2 Policies and guidance

Because the water environment is very sensitive to impacts, it is particularly important to apply the central principles of EU/UK environmental policy outlined in §1.3, including the requirement for the polluter to pay for necessary controls (e.g. DETR 1998). UK Government policy on water quality includes the declaration of ***designated waters***, ***controlled waters***, WQOs, RQOs, NVZs and *Sensitive Areas* (*Eutrophic* and *Nitrate*) (Tables 10.1 and 10.2). In addition, the EA's policy on groundwater pollution control (EA 1998b, 2007b) emphasises prevention by:

- controlling discharges;
- protecting vulnerable aquifers by the use of *groundwater vulnerability maps* (see Table 10.4);
- protecting groundwater abstraction sites by the designation of *Groundwater Source Protection Zones* (GSPZs). For each site, three zones are defined, based on estimated groundwater travel times: Zone I (50 days); Zone II (400 days); and Zone III (the whole site catchment).

Overall policy for **land drainage** and **flood defences** is set by the relevant Executive Agencies. MAFF produced guidance on strategies and codes of practice (MAFF/ WO 1993, 1996) and a series of publications on project appraisal (MAFF 2000–2001). Typical promoters of flood defences are *riparian* landowners or the **operating authorities** which, for inland waters, are normally the relevant EPA, LPA and Internal Drainage Board (IDB). The EA:

- is also a developer of flood defence and certain navigation and water resources schemes, and often conducts its own EIAs;
- takes the view that "the principles of EIA should be applied to all activities which impinge on its statutory responsibilities" (EA 1996); and
- often produces or requires informal environmental appraisals.

In Scotland: planning policy guidance is given in SPP7 *Planning and Flooding* (SG 2004); and SEPA's flood risk assessment strategy is described in SEPA (1998).

Generally, the EPAs' powers relate to river channels and flood defences, and LPAs have control over **floodplain development**. However, the EA is a statutory consultee on development plans, and seeks to persuade LPAs to follow its policies which include:

- natural floodplains (including those through settlements) should be safeguarded, and where possible restored;
- development should be resisted where it would be at risk from flooding or may cause flooding elsewhere;
- potential cumulative effects (including setting precedents) should be considered, even if the impact of a single project is small (EA 1997).

Planning Policy Statement 25 (PPS25) sets out government policy on development and flood risk (DCLG 2006b). It aims to ensure that flood risk is taken into account at all stages in the planning process in order to avoid inappropriate development in areas at risk of flooding, and to direct development away from areas of highest risk. This includes the requirement on LPAs to produce Strategic Flood Risk Assessments. Where new development is, exceptionally, necessary in such areas, the policy aims to make it safe, without increasing flood risk elsewhere, and, where possible, reducing flood risk overall. The document replaced Planning Policy Guidance Note 25: *Development and flood risk* (PPG25), published July 2001.

In Wales, *Planning Policy Wales (2002)* (WAG 2002) sets out the land-use planning policies of the Welsh Assembly Government. This is supported by a series of Technical Advisory Notes (TANs), in particular *TAN 15 Development and flood risk* (2004) (WAG 2004) provides advice on assessing flood risk (both fluvial and coastal) and relates to sustainability principles.

The EA's policy on hydroecology (defined as "ensuring relevant ecological considerations are integral to water resource evaluation and management decisions") is set out in EA (2004). It includes taking consideration of the *Habitats Directive*, the WFD, sustainable abstraction, and drought and flood risk management.

The EA's policies for catchments have been set out in *Local Environment Agency Plans* (LEAPS) (see Table 10.4). These are non-statutory and draw together responsibilities into an integrated plan of action subject to review after five years. Another important management tool is *Water Level Management Plans* (WLMPs) (MAFF *et al.* 1994), aimed at balancing and integrating the water-level needs of a range of issues including flood defence, water resources, navigation, archaeology/heritage, landscape/visual amenity, agriculture, forestry, and nature conservation. Priority is given to nationally important wildlife sites (Defra 2006), including European Sites and SSSIs (see Tables D.1 and D.2), and a target has been set by the Government of bringing 95 per cent of these sites to favourable condition by 2010 (see Defra 2005).

The EA has also developed *Catchment Abstraction Management Strategies* (CAMS) (EA 2008a) with the intention of: informing the public on water resources and licensing practice; providing a consistent approach to local water resources management; helping to balance the needs of water users and the environment; and involving the public in managing their local water resources. The EA's *Catchment Flood Management Plans* (CFMPs) (EA 2008b) are currently (2008) the subject of consultation, the aims of which are to:

- understand the factors that contribute to flood risk within a catchment, e.g. how the land is used;
- recommend the best ways of managing the risk of flooding within the catchment over the next 50 to 100 years.

The *Water Framework Directive* recognises that the best model for a single system of water management is management by river basin – the natural geographical and hydrological unit. *River Basin Management Plans* (RBMPs) will be available by 2009.

10.4.3 Regulators, consultees and other interest groups

The principal Statutory Consultees for the water component of a mainland-UK EIA are the EA and SEPA, which are the **competent authorities** in issuing licences and consents such as IPC/IPPC authorisations, water abstraction licences and land drainage consents (Table 10.2). In Northern Ireland, the EHS regulates water quality, abstraction and impoundment, but the Rivers Agency is the regulator for flood risk management and drainage (see Appendix B).

Other interested parties (dependent on the type of development) may include:

- water utilities (see Table 10.4) who have a clear interest in potential impacts on water supply and quality;
- private water companies (who provide water supplies only);
- local authorities (with various powers including flood risk management on non-main rivers, protection against coastal erosion and flooding and regulation of private water supplies);
- British waterways (responsible for inland navigation on certain water bodies);
- the relevant SNCO (see Appendix B);
- Internal Drainage Boards (IDBs);
- port authorities;
- riparian landowners who own land adjoining a watercourse (and usually the river bed) and have "riparian rights", e.g. to receive water in its "natural" state;
- fisheries and angling associations, boat user groups and recreation and water sport bodies;
- NGOs such as Royal Society for the Protection of Birds and the Wetland and Wildfowl Trust.

The above list is not exhaustive and, dependent on the potential impacts, other organisations might need to be informed.

10.5 Scoping

10.5.1 Introduction

Scoping should follow the principles and procedures outlined in §1.2.2. The Environment Agency (EA 1996, 2002) strongly advocates the use of **scoping checklists** such as **Table 10.3** (which is abridged from an EA checklist, e.g. by omitting impacts on components such as traffic, landscape and heritage). The sources and types of impact listed are discussed further in §10.8. Because the water environment is very susceptible to pollution, it is particularly important to make a thorough inventory of materials that will be used (and of how they will be stored and used) during both the construction and operational phases of a project (Atkinson 1999).

The water assessment is almost certain to overlap with other EIA components (§10.1), so early liaison between specialists responsible for assessing the potential impacts of a particular development is important. It is also essential to focus on key impacts and *receptors*, and a competent generalist, together with water quantity and water quality specialists, should be employed at the scoping stage. It is also anticipated that new breed of practitioner, hydromorphologists, will need to be employed in the near future as the WFD takes effect. It is considered that geomorphologists are best placed to take up this relatively new role.

In a few cases, the **impact area** may be confined to the project site and its immediate surroundings, but water-related impacts are likely to be more widespread, particularly in the downstream direction in the case of rivers.

Table 10.3 Scoping checklist for water impacts of construction work, with particular reference to river engineering schemes (adapted, with permission, from an EA checklist)

Issues	*Sources of impact*	*Potential impacts/effects*
Surface water hydrology/ hydraulics	Soil excavation, removal, storage	Changed surface water runoff. Sediment contamination. Riparian drainage affected.
	Soil compaction/laying impervious surfaces (including roads)	Increased: surface runoff and velocities; magnitude, duration and frequency of flooding. Riparian drainage affected.
	Drainage	Changed flow velocities.
	In-channel works/channel diversion	Changed flow velocities.
Channel morphology/ sediments	Riparian soil excavation/ movement/loss of trees	Changed: bank/bed stability (degradation/erosion); planform/ siltation; suspended sediment/bed loads. Sediment pollution.
	In-channel works: piling, piers, bridges, vehicle movements	Degradation/erosion of bed or banks. Disturbance to bed forms (pools, riffles). Changed: channel size; suspended sediment and bed loads.
	Channel realignment/ diversion	Changed bank/bed stability; bed slope; planform/pattern; channel size. Disturbance to bed forms. Deposition/siltation.
	Laying of impervious surfaces	Deposition/siltation. Degradation/ erosion of bed or banks. Changed: bank/bed stability; suspended sediment/bed loads.
Groundwater hydraulics	Excavation	Changed flow.
	Dewatering	Changed flow. Change in water table level (*drawdown*).
	Laying of impervious surfaces	Changed: infiltration; water table level; pressure potential.
	Structure	Changed flow rates and direction.
Surface water quality	Storage and use of chemicals, fuel, oil, cement etc., accidental spillage, vandalism, unauthorised use, site management including sanitation	Changed in quality. Chemical/organic/ microbial pollution. Rubbish/trash. Change in oxygen content. Changed *turbidity*. Changed dilution capacity. Nutrient enrichment. Change in *electrical conductivity* and pH; acidification.
	Earthworks, soil storage/disposal	Changed turbidity. Re-suspension of contaminated sediments.
	Disturbance of contaminated land	Chemical pollution. Organic pollution. Rubbish/trash.
	Laying of impervious surfaces	Changed turbidity.

Table 10.3 (*continued*)

Issues	Sources of impact	Potential impacts/effects
	Vegetation/tree removal	Change in quality and water temperature. Nutrient enrichment.
	In-channel works	Changed turbidity. Organic pollution.
	Channel realignment/ diversion	Changed dilution capacity upstream.
	Dewatering	Changed: dilution capacity; turbidity; in residence/flushing time.
	Balancing ponds	Change in quality. Changed turbidity.
Groundwater quality	Soil excavation, removal, storage	Change in quality.
	Construction below water table	Change in quality. Chemical/organic pollution.
	Storage and use of chemicals etc.	Change in quality. Chemical pollution. Organic pollution.
	Pumping	Chemical pollution. Movement of contaminated water.
	Disturbance of contaminated land	Chemical pollution. Organic pollution.
Human related	In-channel structures	Changed flood risk. Disruption to commercial navigation.
	Dewatering	Changed water resource.
	Channel realignment	Changed flood risk. Changed abstraction rights.
Aquatic and wetland ecology	In-channel and associated works. Channel realignment/culverting/ diversion.	Altered habitat. Loss of habitat. Changes in the composition, *species diversity* and *biomass* of the biota, including loss of sensitive species, fish kill and effects on fish spawning.
	Sources increasing runoff, e.g. soil compaction/ impervious surfaces.	Altered habitat. Changes in the composition, species diversity and biomass of the biota, including loss of sensitive species.
	Dewatering	Altered habitat, including reduced water levels in wetlands.
	Balancing ponds	Altered habitat. Changes in the biota (as above).
	Sources affecting surface and groundwater quality	Altered habitat. Pollution through food chains (§11.2.2, §11.7.2). Changes in the biota (as above).

10.5.2 Methods and levels of study

The precise methods and levels of study need to be proportionate and tailored to the issue in hand. This can range from a basic desk study of existing information, to extremely sophisticated (and costly) modelling, requiring considerable data collection. For some types of development, water-related methods are already well defined in England and Wales. For example, road infrastructure which complies with the *Design manual for roads and bridges* (DMRB), Vol. 11 (HA 2006). The DMRB methodology, which combines water quality and drainage, requires a routine runoff pollution risk assessment to be completed, e.g. for a widening project from two to four lanes on an existing road. This method typically needs collection of the following information:

- Annual Average Daily Traffic (AADT) flow;
- the road length draining to each proposed highway drainage outfall;
- the average road width;
- an assumed runoff coefficient of 0.5 (i.e. assumes half of the rain falling on the road passes into the drainage system and reaches the outfall);
- rainfall data from *DMRB* Vol. 11;
- pollutant build-up rate for total zinc and dissolved copper from *DMRB* Vol. 11;
- background total zinc and dissolved copper concentrations in the receiving watercourses obtained from water quality sampling; *and*
- the 95-percentile flow (flow exceeded 95 per cent of the time) of the receiving watercourse estimated from channel dimensions, approximate velocity of flow, and by comparison with actual flow data.

This is fairly straightforward. For other types of water variable and for more complex projects collection of field data can be more difficult, time consuming, and require sampling over extended periods.

Typical sources of information are given in **Table 10.4**. The organisations referred to hold more information than that shown, and in the case of development types for which EIA is mandatory, it is obligatory for the relevant EPA to provide the developer (on request) with any relevant information in their possession. Other useful sources of information include: LAs, angling clubs, local universities, previous EISs, and scientific papers. Historical information may also be relevant (see Box 7.1) as may information on geology, geomorphology and soils (Chapter 9).

Table 10.4 includes some examples of digital data. These have become increasingly available, and typically involve the use of **GIS** (Chapter 14) and/or **hydrological and hydraulic models**. Numerous models have been developed for simulating, and predicting changes in, systems. Reviews are provided in many hydrology texts, and the use of models in EIA is discussed by Atkinson (1999). Physical models are sometimes used, but most modelling involves the mathematical and statistical analysis of input data. Some calculations can be made using a hand calculator or computer spreadsheet (e.g. see Karvonen 1998, Thompson 1998, Wanielista *et al.* 1996), but more detailed modelling is carried out using software packages, many of which can be run on PCs (**Table 10.5**).

The use of models has limitations, especially in relation to the time and resource restrictions common in EIA. For example:

Table 10.4 Sources of information on water quantity and quality in the UK

BGS (British Geological Survey) (www.bgs.ac.uk/)

Geoscience Data Index (GDI) Online spatial (GIS) index of BGS data (e.g. *well* locations, aquifer properties, streamwater chemistry/sediments, well water chemistry). Gives costings of more specific information.

Hydrogeological Maps Various scales and information, e.g. surface water features/quality, aquifer potential.

CEH (Centre for Ecology and Hydrology) (www.ceh.ac.uk/)

National Water Archive (NWA) Holdings range from catchment scale data, e.g. climate and hydrology in experimental catchments, to national flood event data. Consists principally of:

The **National River Flow Archive (NRFA)** (www.ceh.ac.uk/data/nrfa/index.html) – includes: (a) online data for *c*.200 stations, e.g. catchment area and rainfall, runoff, low/high flows, abstractions/discharges affecting runoff; (b) retrieval service for other stations; (c) regional maps; (d) gauging station summary sheets; (e) UK hydrological conditions (including floods and droughts) and trends;

The **National Groundwater Level Archive (NGLA)** (CEH 2008a) – includes: (a) online data for some observation wells; (b) a register of other sites; (c) a map showing major aquifers and gauging site locations;

Other Archives, e.g. weather station, soil moisture, flood event, and flood peak-over-threshold data; **Spatial data**, e.g. digitised rivers at 1:50k and 1:250k; UK terrain model/map; soil types hydrology map (1km); digital rainfall and evaporation data; flood studies report maps; floodplain/flood risk map of England and Wales.

UK Environmental Data Index (UKEDI) – Searchable database on water quantity and quality variables.

Indicators of Freshwater Quality – Results of the ECN monitoring programme for rivers and lakes.

Critical loads of acidity – Methods and results (database and maps) for rivers and lakes.

EA (Environment Agency) (www.environment-agency.gov.uk/)

Digital terrain models/maps (see §14.5.2), e.g. of flood risk areas.

Databases including: pesticides and trace organics in *controlled waters*; GQA chemistry (§10.7.1); freshwater fish (water quality); reservoirs; chemical releases inventory; user tables and river flow data. **Groundwater Vulnerability maps** – 1:100k paper or digital maps of England and Wales (from TSO). A "map picker" at the EA Website gives information on each map. A 1:250k map of N. Ireland is available from BGS.

Groundwater Source Protection Zones (GSPZs) – A national set, in digital format suitable for use with GIS, will be available soon for downloading from the EA Website.

Local Environment Agency Plans (LEAPS) – (from local EA offices). Assess water resources, abstraction, GQAs, groundwater quality and specific issues, and include management strategies.

Public Registers (at EA Regional Offices) – e.g. IPC; Water Quality and Pollution Control; Water Abstraction.

River Habitat Survey (RHS) database (see Table 11.3). **River Corridor Surveys (RCS)** – reports

---

Table 10.4 (*continued*)

EHS (Environment and Heritage Service Northern Ireland) (www.ehsni.gov.uk/)

Water Quality Unit monitoring data archives – most data are available on request

MO (Meteorological Office) (www.met-office.gov.uk/)

Local climatic data including precipitation, temperature and evapotranspiration (ET).

MORECS (Met Office Rainfall and Evaporation Calculation System) – calculates ET and soil moisture (weekly for a 40km nationwide grid, and at weather recording sites for hindsight data.

SEPA (Scottish Environmental Protection Agency) (www.sepa.org.uk/)

Digital terrain map of Scotland (1:50k) – can show flood envelopes for the 100-year return period.

Public Registers including Integrated pollution Control (IPC), Water quality Pollution Control.

Reports and policies e.g.: State of the Environment; Bathing Waters Report; Flood risk assessment.

Water UK (Association of UK water utilities) (www.water.org.uk/) Information on and links to the: water and sewerage or water-supply-only companies in England and Wales; publicly-owned water operators in Scotland; and Northern Ireland Water Service.

Table 10.5 Some hydrological and hydromorphological modelling software available from UK and US government agencies

CEH Wallingford (Centre for Ecology and Hydrology) (www.ceh.ac.uk/)

FEH CD-ROM Version 2 – A range of UK data including catchment descriptors (e.g. boundaries, drainage paths) for catchments $\geq 0.5 \text{km}^2$; rainfall depth-duration-frequency (DDF) data for catchments and 1km grid points; facility to compute design rainfalls, or estimate rainfall event rarity.

LOWFLOWS 2000 – Estimation of catchment characteristics (e.g. area, rainfall) and lowflow statistics from digitised river network data. Monitoring and water-use data, e.g. abstraction licences.

PC-IHACRES – Catchment rainfall-runoff model. Requires rainfall, streamflow and temperature or evaporation data. Provides hydrographs with dominant, quickflow and slowflow components.

PC-QUASAR – Water quality and flow model for river networks; comparison between present and potential water quality over time and downstream; setting of effluent consent levels.

PSM for PCs (Penman Store Model) – Conceptual rainfall-runoff model that calculates catchment outlet runoff from rainfall and evaporation data, based on subdivision of the basin into different response zones, e.g. runoff from aquifer, watercourse, paved area and sewage effluent sources.

ReFH – Uses rainfall-runoff methods to estimate flood magnitudes at any UK site. Hydrographs can be routed through a storm reservoir/balancing pond to facilitate spillway design and assessment.

RIVPACS – Biological assessment of river quality.

Table 10.5 (*continued*)

WINFAP-FEH – Flood frequency analysis methods of FEH Vol. 3 (CEH 1999). Provides a range of analyses including estimation of probable events (e.g. the magnitude of an event in a give return period, or the return period of a flood of given magnitude; includes input from FEH CD-ROM.

USDA–ARS (Agricultural Research Service) (www.ars.usda.gov)

RUSLE2 (Revised Universal Soil Loss Equation 2) – estimates soil erosion caused by rainfall and associated overland flow (www.ars.usda.gov/research/docs.htm?docid=6010).

USDA-NRCS (Natural Resource Conservation Service) (www.wsi.nrcs.usda.gov/products/W2Q/H&H/Tools_Models/tool_mod.html)

HecRas (River Analysis System) – water surface profiles in rivers (based on channel morphometry etc.), engineering works (e.g. bridges, *culverts* and floodways), and floodplain encroachment.

WinTR-20 – catchment runoff hydrographs which can combined and routed through stream reaches and reservoirs.

WinTR-55 (Urban Hydrology for Small Watersheds) – storm runoff volume, peak rate of discharge, and hydrographs in small (especially urbanised) watersheds.

USEPA (US Environmental Protection Agency) (www.epa.gov/ATHENS/wwqtsc/index.html)

BASINS – GIS/model catchemnt analyis and monitoing, e.g. for pollutants from point and nonpoint rural and urban sources.

QUAL2E – max. daily chemical streamloads in relation to dissolved oxygen.

SWMM (Storm Water Management Model) – rainfall-runoff simulation model for single event or long-term simulation of runoff quantity and quality mainly from urban areas.

WAM (Watershed Assessment Model) – assessment of catchment water quality of surface and groundwaters based on land use, soils, climate etc.

USGS (US Geological Survey) (http://water.usgs.gov/software/)

GSFLOW – Coupled surface and groundwater flow model.

HSPF – quantity and quality processes on pervious/impervious surfaces and in streams etc.

MODFLOW – groundwater flow (and solute transport) in aquifers.

US NCSU Water Quality Group (www.water.ncsu.edu/watershedss/)

WATERSHEDSS – online package to assist in formulating mitigation/management practices for non-point source pollution. Includes information on pollutants and sources.

- some software is expensive, but the most commonly used is typically held under licence by larger consultancies in the UK;
- most models need expert input by a hydrologist/hydraulic engineer, and even simple models should be used only under supervision by a competent specialist;
- the current capabilities of models are often limited by incomplete understanding of hydrological systems, and even complex models "necessarily neglect some factors and make simplifying assumptions about the influence of others" (Fangmeier *et al.* 2005);
- models can only be as good as the input data, and inadequate data can be a major source of error;
- predictions have a degree of uncertainty, and should be validated throughout the life of a project;
- results have to be interpreted by a competent specialist.

However, hydraulic or hydrodynamic modelling is increasingly required to predict impacts on the flow and sediment regimes (e.g. in relation to scour around bridge piers in a watercourse).

While water assessments should make maximum use of existing information and data, this is unlikely to be fully adequate, and it is usually necessary to collect new data by field survey. Limited data are often misleading, and surveys should aim to ensure validity in terms of accuracy of measurements, number of samples, length of sampling period and frequency of sampling.

10.6 Baseline studies on water quantity

10.6.1 Introduction

This section aims to provide a brief overview of methods for obtaining new data on water quantity variables. General survey and modelling methods are described in many hydrology/ hydraulic engineering texts, including those referred to in §10.1. However, in the UK many of the industry-standard approaches are known by the consultancies involved in these types of study.

10.6.2 Catchments

Most of the hydrological variables considered in an EIA will be studied in the context of the relevant catchment, and it is therefore important to obtain information on its characteristics. The *Water Framework Directive* also requires a more holistic "water body" and river basin management approach to be considered. A catchment study should include (a) the main catchment descriptors (its boundary/area and drainage patterns) and (b) other aspects such as geomorphology (especially slopes), geology and soils, and land cover/use (including standing waters, vegetation and developments). A typical geomorphological approach (for example) is a fluvial audit which may (at the least) involve walking lengths of watercourse upstream and downstream of the proposed development, and may require a walkover of the entire catchment upstream to determine channel and sediment characteristics.

General information can be found in sources such as LEAPs and CFMPs (§10.4.2). The main descriptors, and most other features can be determined with reasonable accuracy from OS, geological and soil survey paper or digitised maps (see §9.5.2 and Table 14.1). Digital terrain models/maps (see §14.5.2) are becoming increasingly available (Table 10.4), and the FEH CD-ROM (Table 10.5) contains data on numerous catchments.

10.6.3 Precipitation and evapotranspiration

Precipitation data from the nearest weather station should be adequate for most EIAs, and can be obtained from the MO (Table 10.4). If rainfall-runoff modelling (§10.6.6) is envisaged, it will be necessary either to use a database, such as the FEH CD-ROM, containing rainfall depth-duration-frequency data, or to obtain long-term records from which such information can be extracted.

Occasionally, it may be desirable to obtain short-term site rainfall data, e.g. to correlate variations in streamflows to localised rainfall patterns. In such cases, rainfall can be measured using **rain gauges/recorders**. Information on these and their application can be found in most hydrology texts, and in MO (1982) and Strangeways (2000).

A complication in the estimation of evapotranspiration (ET) is that, in addition to the influence of meteorological conditions, its rate may be limited by shortages of soil water. To allow for this, distinction is drawn between **actual evapotranspiration** (AE) and **potential evapotranspiration** (PE). AE is equal to PE when the soil is saturated, but falls below PE when the soil surface dries out, and more so when SMDs develop and transpiration is inhibited (§10.2.3). Evaporation from a free water surface, and AE or PE from a vegetated surface, can be measured at point sites by using **evaporation pans, lysimeters** and **irrigated lysimeters** respectively (described in Brassington 2006, Strangeways 2000, Ward and Robinson 2000). However, area ET values are usually estimated using models, such as MORECS (Table 10.4), and relevant data obtained from the MO should be adequate for most EIAs.

10.6.4 Infiltration and overland flow

Point measurements of these variables can be made (see Shaw 1994) and may be justified for small areas of particular concern, e.g. on a steep slope. However, it is not practicable to obtain direct field measurements over large areas, and use is often made of approximate indices (based on factors such as slope, soil properties, vegetation cover, and amount of impermeable surfaces) that can indicate runoff potential, and are incorporated in rainfall-runoff models (§10.6.6).

10.6.5 *Water in the ground*

The two most important aspects of water quantity in both the unsaturated (vadose) zone and the saturated zone, are storage and flow (§10.2.5). For example, if a project is likely to affect **soil drainage**, it may be important to consider moisture levels, and water retention and flow properties, of local soils. The **soil moisture** data available from the MO (Table 10.4) should be adequate for most EIAs. If additional data are required, soil moisture contents can be measured. If the texture of a soil is known, its water retention properties (such as **saturation capacity** and **field capacity**), and its saturated **hydraulic conductivity**, can be estimated using a soil texture triangle calculator (see www.pedosphere.com/resources/texture/).

If the project may have a significant impact on **groundwater abstraction** rates, it will be necessary to consider the local aquifer's storage capacity and storage level patterns. It may be important also to know its **specific yield** – which is the volume of water that can be withdrawn under the influence of gravity. This is because an aquifer also has a **specific retention** – which is the proportion of water that is retained by surface tension on the solid particles, and is high in fine-grained materials. Indicative values of specific yield for a range of geological materials are given in Brassington (2006).

General data for UK aquifers is available in the *NGLA*, and the locations of *wells* for which BGS holds data can be found in the *GDI* (Table 10.4). Methods of monitoring groundwater are described in Brassington (2006), Nielson (2006) and Wilson (1995). **Groundwater hydraulics** can be studied using (a) pumping tests in which water is pumped from wells, and groundwater flowrates are calculated from observed recharge rates, and (b) models based on the properties of the aquifers. Groundwater modelling techniques are discussed in Anderson and Woessner (1992) and Kresic (2006), and some programs are listed in Table 10.5. These can be complex, but they often incorporate a simple formula known as Darcy's Law. This can provide an estimate of the flowrate in an aquifer (and the distance that water can be expected to flow in a day) on the basis that the velocity is a function of the aquifers' hydraulic conductivity and the groundwater slope. In its simplest form, Darcy's law is

$$V = K\frac{\Delta H}{L}$$

where: V = velocity (m/day)
K = hydraulic conductivity (m/day)
ΔH = the difference in hydraulic head (Figure 10.2) between two points in the aquifer (m)
L = the distance between the two points (m)
$\Delta H/L$ = the groundwater slope

Typical hydraulic conductivity values are given in Atkinson (1999) and Brassington (2006). The groundwater slope can be determined from aquifer maps or from field measurements of water table levels (as explained below). The simple application of Darcy's law has limitations, e.g. it assumes aquifer homogeneity (with a single hydraulic conductivity throughout) which is rarely the case.

Groundwater storage levels can be monitored by measuring water level changes in wells. Drilling new wells is expensive, but most areas contain existing monitored and/or unmonitored wells. Most of these should be shown in the GDI (Table 10.4) and there will probably be some private wells, which can be found on 1:25k or 1:10k OS maps. In wetland sites where the water table is normally near the surface, tubes (e.g. lengths of plastic waste pipe) can be inserted in the ground to act as mini wells.

Water level measurements can be made using continuous recorders, or more simply by weekly or monthly observations using a "dipper". This consists of an electric probe attached to a graduated cable, and a visual or audible signal that is activated when the probe contacts water. Because of weather-related fluctuations in water levels, monitoring should be continued for at least a year.

Measurements taken at a network of wells can also provide information on **groundwater contours**, and hence on likely flow patterns. Recorded water-level depths are subtracted from the relevant ground level altitudes to calculate the **absolute water table elevations**. A water table contour map can then be produced to show the groundwater slope(s) and hence the likely direction(s) of flow. Such information may be useful for assessing the vulnerability of a wetland to potential impacts such as pollution or water abstraction in its catchment. For example, Cothill Fen SAC (*Special Area of Conservation*) was thought to be threatened by a proposed extension of sand extraction workings (and subsequent landfill) near to its western boundary; but the results of a study suggest that the groundwater flow in the area of the proposal largely by-passes the site, and that this is more vulnerable to water abstraction or pollution (e.g. *eutrophication*) in the catchment area to the north (**Figure 10.3**). It may be beneficial also to estimate the site's water budget, and in particular the relative importance of precipitation, surface water recharge and groundwater recharge. For example, Cothill Fen was found to be largely fed by groundwater (Morris 1988, 2002). However, a site water budget can only be calculated if all but one of the variables in the budget equation (§10.2.2) can be measured or neglected – and requires measurements taken over at least a year.

10.6.6 Surface waters

The main surface-water quantity aspects likely to be important in an EIA are the current conditions of standing waters and watercourses and their vulnerability to changes in runoff, abstraction, and interference with *river corridors* and *floodplains*.

In order to assess the vulnerability of standing **water bodies**, it is desirable to obtain information on their size (area, depth and volume/capacity), elevation, site catchment, recharge and discharge regime, water level ranges and variability,

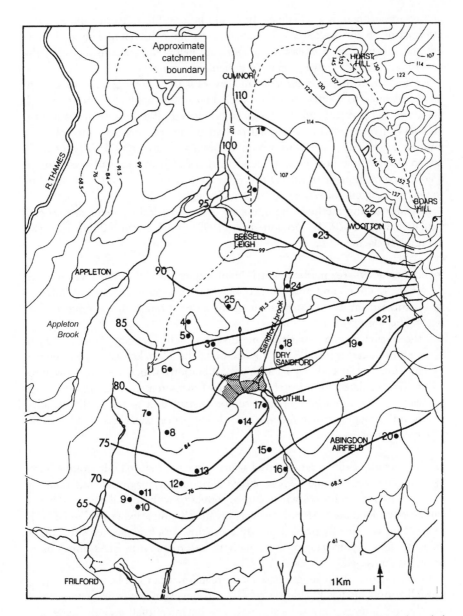

Figure 10.3 Groundwater contours (m) in the catchment of Cothill Fen SAC (stippled area) in Oxfordshire. The contours were drawn from mean absolute water table levels derived from monthly measurements over two years at 25 wells (numbered).
Source: Morris 1988, 2002; data of Morris and Finlayson.

and reservoir operating schedules. It should be possible to gather some of this information in the desk study. If necessary, recharge/discharge data for inflow/outflow streams can be measured as outlined below, but transfer between the water body and groundwater may be difficult to quantify.

An important aspect of **streams and rivers** is their flow regimes, which can have relevance to a range of issues, including water supply, pollution control, flood risk and control, and the design of bridges etc. If an assessment is needed of a length of river, this is normally divided into **reaches** (sections of fairly uniform morphology and flow) which are used as study units. It is particularly important to know how flows respond in times of heavy rainfall (resulting in quickflows) or drought (resulting in lowflows). Streamflows can be measured by stream gauging and/or estimated by rainfall-runoff models.

Stream gauging methods are discussed in most hydrology texts, and in particular in Boiten (2000), Gordon *et al.* (1992) and Herschy (1999). The two main methods are:

- the **velocity–area method**, which involves measuring the cross sectional area of the channel, and flow rates (obtained with a current meter) at different points within it, with measurements repeated throughout the range of flow at the site;
- the **stream gauging structure method** in which a gauging structure (e.g. a weir or flume) is installed in the channel. This has a known stage-discharge relation (often called its rating or calibration) which permits flow rates to be calculated from water-level (**stage**) measurements. Changes in stage can be monitored by a float or sensor located in a stilling well (installed near the gauging structure), and recorded either on paper charts or by a solid state logger.

Stream gauging results can be plotted against time to produce **hydrographs** (plots of streamflow against time). These show the frequency, magnitude and duration of events, such as highflows, which can be correlated with rainfall data, and hence can assist in flood prediction. However, stream gauging is expensive and a fairly long record is normally needed; so while existing data from gauged sites can be valuable, new stream gauging is unlikely to be profitable in EIAs unless monitoring is envisaged.

In the absence of stream gauging data, streamflows can still be estimated using **rainfall-runoff models** (Table 10.5). These assume that the main factors affecting channel flow at a given location are catchment rainfall and characteristics such as area, slope and infiltration – which is affected by slope, vegetation cover, soil type and condition (including wetness), and the presence of impermeable surfaces (§10.2.4). They may include facilities for incorporating sub-catchments, runoff components such as overland flow, and flow retardance by in-channel vegetation. The input data requirements vary, depending on the sophistication of a given model and whether the software includes data for some variables. A major application of rainfall-runoff models is the estimation of flood risk at specific river locations (see §10.8.3) for which they utilise *design events*.

The Lotic-invertebrate Index for Flow Evaluation (LIFE) method has been developed to assess the habitat value of river stretches in relation to flow rates. Like RIVPACS (see §10.7.3) it uses **macro-invertebrates** as biological indicators, and is based on the sensitivity of different taxa to flow rates. Scores for the represented taxa are combined to give a weighted average (the LIFE score) which has been found to decline with reduced flow rates (see Dunbar *et al.* 2006 and EA 2005, 2007c). It can therefore be used to monitor the effects of changes in river flow rates, including the impact of low flows.

10.6.7 Floodplains

The limits of a river floodplain are defined in EA (1997) as the approximate extent of floods with a 1 per cent annual probability of exceedance (1-in-100-year flood) or the highest known level – although these "do not take account of the presence of defences or the likelihood that flood **return intervals** will be reduced by climate change" (DETR 2000). Information on **flood envelopes** (areas of recorded or design floods) is increasingly available in the form of flood studies reports, flood risk maps and digital terrain models (Table 10.4). The EA has a Flood Map website (www.environment-agency.gov.uk/homeandleisure/floods/31656.aspx) that shows areas of the floodplain subject to flooding (without defences), defences in place, and areas of the floodplain benefiting from defences and provides a risk assessment of flooding in specific locations. The frequency and extent of floodplain inundation can also be typically estimated by computer models which utilise design floods (§10.8.3) and indeed for many floodplain developments this may be a requirement of the relevant EPA.

10.7 Baseline studies on water quality

10.7.1 Introduction

Water quality can be assessed by chemical, biological and aesthetic methods. All approaches can involve a wide range of variables and techniques, or a few variables can be selected. The EA use the *General Quality Assessment* (GQA) method, for routine monitoring and assigning quality grades to stretches of rivers and canals according to biological, chemical, nutrient (nitrate and phosphate) status and aesthetic quality. This consistent method can be used to compare the quality of different rivers and canals and to consider changes over time. SEPA has adopted a single classification that incorporates the chemical, biological and aesthetic elements of water quality for ease of interpretation (SEPA 2008).

Chemical methods involve analysing water samples for a range of variables (nitrate, oxygen, pH etc.). They have the advantage of giving estimations of levels that can be compared with statutory standards; and apart from some microbiological techniques, they are the only available method for assessment of groundwaters. There are, however, three major disadvantages in assessing water quality from chemical data alone:

1. there are many possible pollutants in any given situation and each has to be assayed separately;
2. many pollutants (e.g. the hundreds of microorganic compounds) are both difficult and expensive to monitor;
3. the sample will only reflect the chemical conditions at the time of sampling.

Biological methods use living organisms as an indirect way of measuring water quality. A disadvantage of these methods is that it is not possible to determine the exact pollutant impacting a system, but they have three main advantages:

1. impacts on ecosystems are normally the primary concern of EPAs, and surveys of biota are the most direct way of assessing ecosystem status;
2. surveys will often detect the net effects of one or more (often unknown) pollutants;
3. surveys can be used to assess long-term environmental health, e.g. pollution inputs that affect a river only occasionally may be detected, even if the pollutant is not present at the time of survey.

Aesthetic methods use indicators such as litter, oil, and colour and odour of the water. While the assessment is somewhat subjective it provides a semi-quantitative approach, giving an indication of the public view of water quality.

Under the *Water Framework Directive* the emphasis will be on biological monitoring of water quality for a broad assessment of the health of rivers, and the EA intends to replace the GQA with this system (EA 2008c).

10.7.2 Chemical methods of assessment

Variables commonly measured in water quality assessments are listed in **Table 10.6**, which highlights those most used in relation to human health, conservation, and fisheries. The chemical component of the GQA scheme currently includes only **biochemical oxygen demand** (BOD), dissolved oxygen and ammonia, but an additional "nutrient component" is being developed. The EPAs also monitor dangerous substances.

Levels of chemicals often vary considerably seasonally, throughout the day, and within a water body at a given time, sometimes over quite short distances. In addition, many elements occur in a number of different forms, only one of which may be of interest. For example, phosphorus may be measured as soluble reactive phosphorus, soluble unreactive phosphorus, particulate phosphorus, or a combination of these. Metals are often present in numerous forms, including organo-metallic forms, measurement of which is often difficult. Understanding the inherent variability of chemical variables is critical for selecting analysis and sampling programmes, and interpreting the results.

The level at which individual variables are monitored can also markedly influence the cost and extent of the survey, and care is needed to avoid selecting levels that are either too precise or too crude. For example, it would be pointless

Table 10.6 Common variables of water quality surveyed in water quality assessments

Variable	System	C	H	F	Notes
Nutrients					
Phosphorus	R	f	i	i	Several different forms. Much of load transported in sediment.
	L & P	c	i	c	Varies between hypolimnion and epilimnion. Detection often difficult.
Nitrate	R	f	c	f	Usually higher in late autumn/winter.
	L & P	c	c	f	Levels generally increase with amount of flow through system.
Chlorophyll a	AS	f	i	f	Used as a general index of standing crop of **algae**.
Organic matter					
Biochemical oxygen demand (BOD)	R	c	f	c	A main variable in monitoring sewage outfalls and GQAs. Can range from <5 mg/l in clean rivers to 100,000mg/l in industrial waste.
Chemical oxygen demand (COD)	R	c	i	c	Measures total organic matter which *could* use up oxygen. An alternative to BOD, e.g. where **non-labile organics** are suspected.
Metals					
Al, Cu, Cd, Hg, Pb, Zn	AS	f	f	f	Often serious pollutants of freshwaters. Toxicities usually increase with decreasing pH and water hardness.
Ca, Mg, Na, K	AS	c	c	c	Used to assess water type but not quality. Useful in conjunction with other variables to assess likely toxicity of other metals.
Others	AS	f	f	f	Industry-specific surveys may be needed (e.g. silver for electroplating, tin from old mines) but most not routinely covered.
Microorganics	AS	f	f	f	Difficult to identify unless potential source suspected; so although potentially important, rarely included in standard surveys.
Oils					
General effects	AS	c	f	c	Most are easily detected by sight/smell. Not normally a health problem as polluted water unlikely to be imbibed. Tainting can damage fisheries.
Carcinogenic effects	AS	f	f	f	Rarely routinely done as particular carcinogen will vary with type of oil, geographic source and batch.

Table 10.6 (*continued*)

Variable	System	C	H	F	Notes
Others					
Ammonia	R	c	c	c	Organic decay product. Toxic to fish, and toxicity increases at high pHs.
	L & P	f	f	c	In large water bodies, only likely to be high in intensively stocked fisheries. Small stagnant water bodies may naturally have high levels.
Hydrogen	R	f	f	f	Generally as for ammonia.
sulphide	L & P	f	f	c	
Cyanide	AS	f	f	f	Very toxic but occurrence limited to particular industries.
Sediment	R	c	i	c	Part of routine monitoring especially in relation to sewage outfalls.
	L & P	i	i	f	May be of concern in fisheries and reservoirs (may block filters).
Pathogens	AS	i	c	i	Mainly for faecal contamination, especially for water-areas.
Dissolved	R	c	i	c	A routine variable because many river animals need high levels.
oxygen	L	f	i	f	Levels vary with depth, time of day and season.
	P	i	i	f	Levels often highly variable.
pH	AS	c	c	c	Interpretation is very use-related. Used to qualify other data.
Alkalinity	AS	c	c	c	Used to qualify pH data.
Electrical conductivity	AS	c	c	c	Useful as an indication of the levels of other major variables.
Temperature	AS	c	c	c	Assessing thermal pollution, but mainly used to qualify other data.

Systems: L = lakes and reservoirs; P = ponds; R = rivers; AS = all systems (usually including groundwaters).

Purposes: C = conservation; H = human health; F = fisheries. **Measured**: i = infrequently measured (but may be important in specific circumstances); f = fairly frequently; c = commonly/frequently.

to stipulate a detection limit of 5µg/l for monitoring nitrate in lowland rivers, where levels are never likely to fall below 1mg/l. Conversely, there is little point in conducting a survey only to find that the assays have failed to detect the variable under study. Results of water chemistry monitoring around the world are given in Meybeck *et al.* (1989), and may help in formulating a strategy. However, water analysis will usually be carried out by an independent analyst

(a public analyst if the results are to be legally accepted) who should be consulted about suitable procedures.

Assay methods are described in Golterman (1978), Hunt and Wilson (1995),
Mackereth *et al.* (1978) and relevant HMSO standards (Standing Committee
of Analysts). Hunt and Wilson (1995) includes an extensive discussion of sampling strategies. Various samplers exist for taking samples at depth (Hellawell
1986); most other samples can be taken using a suitable bottle.

The EA has developed a predictive technique for assessing the extent to which
lakes are **eutrophicated** and affected by acidification. This method "hindcasts"
the expected chemical status of lakes using equations which predict the chemical composition of runoff based on catchment geology, climate and land-use
variables. Water quality is "predicted" for the period around 1930 (which pre-
dates the widespread use of chemical fertilisers, but post-dates the industrial
revolution), and this is used as a baseline against which the quality of modern
lakes can be judged. Decisions about the appropriateness of attempting to return
a degraded lake to the 1930 conditions are then made on grounds of cost and
practicability (Johnes *et al.* 1996).

10.7.3 Biological indicators of water quality

Hellawell (1986) and Rosenberg and Resh (1992) review the use of **biological
indicators** in assessing water pollution, and Newman *et al.* (1992) gives summary papers describing the various types of biological monitoring of river water
quality throughout Europe. Most groups of freshwater organisms have been used
as indicators of given pollution problems; but **macro-invertebrate** families (not
species) are by far the most widely used taxa in Britain and Europe.

In Britain, the main biological assessment method in streams and rivers is the
Biological Monitoring Working Party (BMWP) index (Hawkes 1997). This awards
points to different invertebrate families according to their perceived tolerances
to low oxygen levels (low points for tolerance, high for intolerance). This and
the associated indices, *Number of Taxa* (TAXA) and *Average Score Per Taxon*
(ASPT), are used as a broad indication of the level of water pollution. BMWP
scores are sometimes used incorrectly in EIAs, e.g. it is often wrongly assumed
that family level macroinvertebrate data can be used to directly assess the conservation value of freshwater invertebrate communities.

The BMWP system is used in conjunction with the *River Invertebrate
Prediction and Classification System* (RIVPACS) computer program (Wright et
al. 1998, 2000, EA 2007c) which is available from CEH. This allows actual BMWP,
TAXA and ASPT values in a river to be compared with those predicted for
an unpolluted site of similar physical characteristics, and includes a facility
for locating high-quality sites within a national classification of sites. The site
evaluation procedure is as follows.

1. Environmental variables (e.g. altitude, slope, channel morphology and **alkalin-
    ity**), are evaluated for the test site, and used to predict the macroinvertebrate

fauna that might be expected in the absence of environmental (water quality) stress, i.e. in high-quality sites.

2. Macroinvertebrate data are obtained at the test site using a standard sampling protocol.

3. Values of biotic indices (based on the number of macroinvertebrate families) are calculated for the observed and expected fauna.

4. The observed and expected biotic index values are compared using observed/expected ratios (also known as EQIs – Environmental Quality Indices).

5. The test site EQI is used to classify it in relation to UK quality grades and *Water Framework Directive* ecological status classes.

Biological monitoring methods are gradually becoming available for still waters (lakes, ponds, canals, ditch systems). For example, the *Predictive System for Multimetrics* (PSYM) software package, developed jointly by the EA and Pond Action (Biggs *et al.* 2000 and www.pondnetwork.org.uk/Main/methods.aspx) assesses the ecological quality of still waters, and has been implemented for ponds and small lakes up to 5ha, which, in Britain, represent about 98 per cent of all discrete standing waters. PSYM operates in a similar way to RIVPACS but is based on a combination of **macrophyte** (mainly **vascular plants**), macroinvertebrate and water quality data (see §D.3.5), and incorporates the concept of multimetric assessment for describing the overall ecological quality of water bodies. It has been designed to fulfil the reporting requirements of the *Water Framework Directive* (§10.4.1) and also has some diagnostic potential, e.g. for identifying eutrophication impacts and poor physical habitat structure.

Many aquatic vascular plants are sensitive to water and sediment nutrient concentrations, and methods for assessing eutrophication in rivers using plants have been developed by the EA. Several other bioindicators are available. Diatoms are widely used to assess river water quality and in palaeoecological studies of long-term changes in lake water quality, particularly of acidification. Fish are sometimes monitored to assess incoming water quality at inlets to reservoirs (Hellawell 1986), and changes in fish populations with time can give information about long-term pollution trends such as acidification and eutrophication (see EA 2007c). Some microorganisms, such as the bioluminescent bacterium *Photobacterium phosophoreum* have been used to assess water quality (Calow 1997).

Various plant and animal species **bioaccumulate** toxins, and some are used in ecotoxicological studies using **bioassay** techniques. These are generally species-specific, however, and do not necessarily indicate the effects of pollutants on whole ecosystems. The EA and SEPA have developed *Direct Toxicity Assessment* (DTA) methods (EA 2000). DTA is a process of measuring the hazard (toxicity) of a complex industrial effluent discharged to controlled waters and then using the data in a risk assessment process to predict the risk to the aquatic environment. DTA determines the overall toxic effect of all contaminants in an effluent sample using a suite of standardised aquatic ecotoxicological assays. It can be used as a biological assessment alone or in conjunction with a chemical specific approach and provides a degree of biological relevance to the risk assessment process. There are accredited laboratories that can undertake this testing in the UK.

Pathogens in waters can be detected by two broad methods; detection of species/strains or detection of indicator groups/species. Detection of individual species would be ideal, but there are several problems:

- there are many different pathogens in freshwater, all of which would need to be assessed;
- many species and strains of bacteria and virus require sophisticated culture and detection methods, often taking long periods of time (for some, techniques have not been developed);
- protozoan parasites are difficult or impossible to grow in culture, so large samples are often needed (e.g. a tonne of water for *Cryptosporidium*).

For these reasons, most routine monitoring involves indicator groups, and relies on two broad assumptions: (a) that the principal concern is with human faecal contamination of water, and (b) that the indicators used will be present in proportion to all pathogenic species of interest. In practice these two conditions are never fulfilled, and there has been much debate over which indicator organisms should be used and how much faith should be placed in such assessments. Nevertheless, in the absence of any other practicable method, human health limits for freshwater are set in terms of the number of indicator organisms per unit volume. The most common organisms used are coliform bacteria, some species of which are a natural (largely non-pathogenic) component of the biota of the human gut. In Britain, assessment is made for (a) total coliforms (which will include many species that are not necessarily of faecal origin), and (b) faecal coliforms (which should correspond more closely to the extent of faecal contamination of the water). Bathing waters, and surface waters used for extraction of water intended for human consumption, are also monitored for faecal streptococci and *Salmonella*.

10.7.4 Aesthetic indicators of water quality

Monitoring the aesthetic quality of water is subjective, and different Environmental Agencies have developed different techniques for assessing aesthetic water quality. Indicators generally include litter, sewage, builders waste, oil, surface scum, sewage fungus and the colour and odour of the water.

The assessment can be descriptive, for example, SEPA consider whether their identified contaminants are not present, have a minor presence, are occasional or widespread. The aesthetic water quality is then graded from excellent to poor accordingly (SEPA 2006).

In contrast the Environment Agency has developed a more complex scoring system. This is based on the number of items of litter and the percentage cover of surface scum, oil, foam, sewage fungus and/or ochre. For colour and odour the assessment is made of the type of colour (blue/green, red/orange or brown/

yellow/straw) and smell (for example earth, chlorine or sewage) and the strength of the colour (colourless to dark) and odour (no smell to strong smell). The aesthetic parameters are then assigned to a class and the points for each parameter summed to give a total score and an overall grade of aesthetic water quality from good to bad (EA undated).

10.8 Impact prediction

10.8.1 Introduction and types of hydrological impact

Because of the complex, dynamic nature of water systems, accurate prediction of impacts is often difficult, and there are bound to be uncertainties, that must be made transparent in the EIA and recorded in any EIS. Predictions can be assisted by the techniques referred to in Table 1.1; they can be qualitative, but should be quantitative if required by the development type and/or the specific local circumstances.

Some projects can have potentially **positive impacts.** For example, reservoirs can provide water-based amenities and both aquatic and wetland habitats, as can mineral workings when extraction is completed – although these benefits must be weighed against construction and operational phase negative impacts.

Many types of potential negative impact have already been mentioned in previous sections. This section aims to summarise the range of impact sources and the range of potential impacts these generate. The impact sources can be roughly divided into those involving direct manipulation or utilisation of water systems (**Table 10.7**), and those with less direct associations (**Table 10.8**). As a specific example, the potential impacts of a road widening scheme on the water environment are outlined in **Table 10.9**.

10.8.2 Changes without the development

It is important to consider a project's potential impacts in the context of environmental changes that may occur in its absence. These can include global and regional issues such as climate change and acid deposition, and national issues such as water resource depletion by abstraction. Such issues can be assessed in relation to past, present and predicted trends. The causes and implications of recent hydrological changes in UK are discussed in Acreman and Law (2000).

In relation to **climate change**, fairly long-term records held by CEH (Table 10.4) suggest that, until recently, in areas not markedly affected by human activity, most river flows and groundwater levels have fluctuated around a fairly stable mean. In recent years, however, rainfall, river flow and groundwater recharge have been notably variable, with sustained deviations from normal patterns in many areas. For example, exceptionally high rainfalls, especially in Scotland, and protracted dry spells in England have lead respectively to a number of serious floods and a series of droughts. In England's drier eastern and southern areas, where water demands are greatest and much of the supply is from

Table 10.7 Impacts from direct manipulation or utilisation of water systems

Sources	*Potential impacts*
River engineering/manipulation	(see also Table 10.3)
Resectioning/channeliSation (widening, deepening, realigning/straightening), e.g. to increase channel capacity for flood defence or drainage, or to facilitate project layout.	Loss of channel and bank habitats. Enhanced erosion and hence silt production (especially during construction, when pollution risks also increase). Increased flood risk and siltation downstream. Lowering of floodplain water table caused by deepening. (See Brooke 1992, Brookes 1988.)
Embanking and bank protection (e.g. with concrete) usually for reasons as above.	Floodplain inundation and siltation prevented, with consequent risk of soil drought and loss of wetlands. Drainage from floodplain inhibited (unless sluices installed) with consequent waterlogging.
Clearing bank vegetation	Loss of wildlife habitats and visual/amenity value.
Fluvial dredging and deposition of dredgings, e.g. to maintain/enhance flood capacity or navigation.	Damage to channel habitats and biota at dredging sites. Increased sediment load and hence turbidity and smothering of downstream benthic and marginal habitats.
Diversion, e.g. to increase water supply to receptor area, or as a flood relief channel.	Decreases supply in donor area. Channelisation and evaporative loss from open channels. Risk to habitats in main river corridor.
Development on river floodplains	(See DETR 2000, EA 1997, Smith & Ward 1998, WUF 2001.)
Use of floodplain area Construction of flood defences Laying impermeable surfaces	Increased flood risk upstream and downstream. Reduced groundwater recharge and river baseflows. Loss of ecological, heritage and visual/amenity features.
Reservoirs and dams:	(See Petts 1984.)
General	Loss of terrestrial habitats/farmland/settlements. Local climate change and rise in water table. Visual impacts of retaining walls. Water-borne pathogens. Earthquake/landslip/failure risks.
On-stream dams: above dam	Loss of river section; changes in flow regime; siltation.
On-stream dams: below dam	Reduced flows, oxygen levels and floodplain siltation.
On-stream dams: barrier effects	Migration of fish and invertebrates blocked.
Off-stream dams (not on a main channel)	Changes in groundwater recharge, levels and flow directions.

Table 10.7 (*continued*)

Sources	Potential impacts
Irrigation	Water abstraction (often from rivers). Increased evapo-transpiration and local runoff. Risk of waterlogging and salination.
Drainage schemes	May involve channelisation. Increased soil drought risk and oxidation of organic soils. Water table lowered and wetlands lost. Increased flood/erosion risk downstream.
Water abstraction	Water resources depleted. Water table lowered. Risks of river lowflows, loss of wetlands, soil droughts and subsidence.
Sewage treatment works	Increases in silts, nutrients (especially if treatment is poor), heavy metals, organics, and pathogens, e.g. faecal coliforms. (See Petts and Eduljee 1994.)

Table 10.8 Impacts not directly associated with manipulation or utilisation of water systems

Sources	Potential impacts
Roads	Changes in drainage systems, e.g. due to gradient changes, bridges, embankments, channel diversion or resectioning. Drawdown by dewatering when deep cutting. Increased runoff from impermeable surfaces, with risks of flash floods and erosion. Increased sediment loads from vehicles, road wear, and erosion of cuttings and embankments. Pollution of watercourses by organic content of silt, other organics (e.g. oils, bitumen, rubber), de-icing salt (and impurities), metals (mainly vehicle corrosion), plant nutrients and pesticides from verge maintenance, and accidental spillages of toxic materials. (See Brookes and Hills 1994, HA 2006.)
Urban and commercial development	Changes in drainage systems due to landscaping. Abstraction. Drawdown/changes in groundwater flow, e.g. when dewatering deep foundations. Reduced groundwater recharge, and increased runoff velocities and volumes (with flood and erosion risks from rapid stormflows) due to impermeable surfaces. Pollution of watercourses and groundwaters by a wide range of pollutants which are rapidly transported to receiving waters by increased runoff. Increased sewage treatment. (See Shaw 1994, Walesh 1989.)

Table 10.8 (*continued*)

Sources	Potential impacts
Industrial development	As above but with: greater runoff effects (from a higher proportion of hard surfaces); higher pollution levels and a wider variety of pollutants including metals and microorganics from heavy industry and refineries, pesticides from wood treatment works, and nutrient-rich or organic effluents from breweries, creameries etc. Thermal pollution from power plants.
Mineral extraction	**Operation phase** – Removal/realignment of watercourses. Loss of floodplain storage/flow capacity. Drawdown and reduced local streamflows caused by dewatering for dry extraction, or increased runoff from process wash water or extraction methods involving water use. Increased siltation and chemical pollution downstream, e.g. from spoil heaps/vehicles/machinery/stores. **Restoration/aftercare phase** – see landfill. (See Rust Consulting 1994.)
Landfill	Increased runoff from raised landforms, especially if clay-capped. Reduced groundwater recharge and river baseflows if clay sealed. Pollution of groundwater and near-surface runoff by **leachates** and by fertilisers and pesticides from restored grassland (Petts and Eduljee 1994).
Forestry and deforestation	Reduced evapotranspiration and infiltration after felling – with consequent (a) decreased groundwater recharge, (b) increases in runoff, soil erosion, stream-sediment loads and siltation. Pollution by pesticides, especially herbicides used to prevent re-growth after clear felling.
Intensive agriculture	Enhanced runoff and erosion from bare soils. Drainage or irrigation impacts. Pollution of surface and groundwaters by: fertilisers; pesticides; organics from soil erosion, silage clamps and muck spreading; heavy metals from slurry runoff, and pathogens in animal wastes.

aquifers, groundwater levels were low for extended periods during the 1990s (CEH 2008b).

This variability is consistent with predicted anthropogenically driven climate changes (§8.1.3), but because of the wide range of natural climatic variation, and the influences of human activities, future hydrological changes cannot be predicted with any certainty. In addition, there is considerable variation in climate, geology, land use, and water use within the UK – so responses to climatic change will vary regionally and even locally. However, given that river flows and aquifer recharge rates are very sensitive to rainfall and evapotranspiration, increased incidence of floods and droughts seems likely in many areas.

Table 10.9 Potential impacts of a road widening scheme

Potential receptor: water	*Activities and potential impacts*		
	Construction phase	*Operational phase/ ongoing site maintenance*	*Decommissioning/ post operation*
Surface water hydrology and channel morphology	**Use of vehicles and machinery** Increase in surface runoff from soil compaction. **Works next to or near watercourses** Change in flow velocities. Increased erosion and subsequent changes in bed and bank stability. Increased flood risk. **Earthworks** Increased sedimentation of watercourses.	**Physical presence of bridge** Upstream potential impediment to flow, decreased water velocity and increased depth; so increased flood risk. Change in deposition regime upstream, caused by changes in flow and potential flood risk and changes to riffle/pools. Downstream potential increased water velocity, turbulence and erosion. **Physical presence of culvert** Loss of pools/riffles, alteration of natural bed slope, decreased water turbulence and oxygenation, increased bank erosion downstream.	**Site drainage** Increase in surface runoff from bank areas during decommissioning due to soil compaction. Possible increased flood risk.
Surface water quality	**Earthworks** Pollution from suspended material. Disturbance of contaminated soil and subsequent pollution of watercourses. **Materials management** Pollution from spills or leaks of fuel, oil and construction materials.	**Physical presence of bridge** Upstream impounded waters will reduce oxygenation. Downstream water quality may be reduced by increased turbidity.	**Materials management** Pollution of surface water by fuel and oil spillages from vehicular activities.
Groundwater hydrology	**Earthworks and site drainage** Reduction in water table. Changes to ground-water distribution and flow.	**Physical presence bridge/culvert** No significant impacts.	

Table 10.9 (*continued*)

Potential receptor: water	Activities and potential impacts		
	Construction phase	Operational phase/ ongoing site maintenance	Decommissioning /post operation
Groundwater quality	**Earthworks** Disturbance of contaminated soil and subsequent groundwater pollution. **Materials management** Pollution from spills or leaks of fuel, oil and building materials.	**Physical presence of bridge/culvert** No significant impacts. **Maintenance work and materials management** Contamination from spills or leaks of fuel and oil from routine maintenance work.	**Materials management** Pollution of groundwater by fuel and oil spillages from the decommissioning vehicular activities.

Source: Environment Agency (2002).

Designing in resilience and adaptability to new schemes can allow for future climate changes that cannot be predicted. EA guidance recommends applying the *precautionary principle* or **managed adaptive approaches**. Following the precautionary principle involves designing a defence structure that is of a higher specification than required currently, but this will reduce to the required standard over the life of the structure. This approach would be appropriate for areas where impacts are understood with a degree of certainty and where modification of structures at a later date would be difficult. A managed adaptive approach does not allow for climate change at the outset but ensures that defences can be adapted at a later date. This would be appropriate where the impacts are less well understood and where additional capacity can be accommodated fairly easily (EA 2007d). Recommended precautionary sensitivity ranges for peak rainfall intensities and peak river flows, as given in PPS25 (DCLG 2006b) are shown in **Table 10.10**. Similar values for offshore wind speeds and wave height, and recommended contingency allowances for net sea level rise, are in Table 12.4.

Table 10.10 Recommended national precautionary sensitivity ranges for peak rainfall intensities and peak river flows over time up to 2115

Parameter	1990–2025	2025–2055	2055–2085	2085–2115
Peak rainfall intensity	+5%	+10%	+20%	+30%
Peak river flow	+10%	+20%		

Source: DCLG (2006b) (PPS25).

Note: Estimated peaks are derived by multiplying current measurement by the percentages shown. So, for example, a 10mm/hour rainfall event would equate to 11mm/hour for the 2025–2055 period, and 12mm/hour for the 2055–2085 period.

10.8.3 Predicting impacts on water quantity

Typical questions that should be considered in relation to water quantity are – is the project likely to significantly:

- affect river channel/corridor, standing water or wetland features because it will (a) cross or impinge on any of these, (b) involve river works, (c) need new flood defences or (d) require that a watercourse is re-routed;
- increase flood risk because it will (a) constrict a river channel, (b) inhibit floodplain storage and conveyance, (c) increase channel flow directly, or (d) increase runoff;
- reduce surface and/or groundwater levels and increase the risk of river lowflows.

Physical, hydraulic and computer modelling are all used to predict the **hydraulic impacts of river works** with a reasonable degree of accuracy. For example, programs such as HecRas (Table 10.5) can be used to assess the impacts of bridges and channel works on river flows and downstream flood levels. However, these require detailed information on aspects such as channel morphometry.

A major tool in the prediction of **flood frequency and magnitude** is the risk analysis technique of *design events* which can be utilised in flood-frequency models and rainfall-runoff models. The latter also require information on various catchment characteristics (§10.6.6). There are some **gauged catchments** for which data on most variables (including streamflows) are available, but most are **ungauged catchments** which lack existing data on many variables.

Most flood prediction in the UK is likely to follow the *Flood estimation handbook* (FEH) methods (CEH 1999). Importantly, this includes methods for estimating flood frequency in ungauged catchments by using techniques such as **pooled analysis** of similar sites. The FEH methods are intended for use with the accompanying software (WINFAP-FEH) and CD-ROM (Table 10.5). These are expensive, however, and since the main concern in the majority of EIAs will be to estimate the increased runoff that a development will generate, an alternative option is to use a relatively simple rainfall-runoff model such as WinTR-55 (Table 10.5).

Impacts of abstraction and dewatering can be estimated from the projected quantities involved and the nature of the sources (river, reservoir, aquifer). If a project is likely to contribute significantly to river lowflows, the LOWFLOWS2000 program (see Table 10.5 and EA 2007b) may be applicable. However, most developments simply add to the overall demands on public water supply, and a project's requirements should be discussed with the relevant EPA. In some cases, an abstraction licence may be needed.

10.8.4 Predicting impacts on water quality

Methods for predicting changes in water quality are discussed in a number of texts including Kiely (1997) and Singh (1995). Computer models are available, but in many EIAs, their application may not be appropriate or feasible.

Point source pollution is relatively easy to predict, and all point source pollutants discharged to **controlled waters** require a consent licence from the relevant EPA. In considering the application, the authority will examine the potential discharges in relation to the relevant WQOs and standards, including those for **designated waters** (Table 10.1). If a proposed development does not require a consent licence, but might still pose a threat, e.g. through accidental spillage, the same criteria can be applied. If adequate data can be obtained, a model such as PC-QUASER (Table 10.5) may be applicable.

Estimating the amount and effect of **diffuse (non-point source) pollution** is generally more difficult. There are relatively few methods, and they tend to have limited capability. Commonly used methods include the *Unit Load Method*, the *Universal Soil Loss Equation*, and *Concentration Times Flow Method*. Walesh (1989) gives a useful overview of the applications and drawbacks of these and other methods, some of which are incorporated in computer models such as RUSLE2 (Table 10.5). To guard against the uncertainty inherent in many of these methods, more than one should be employed where possible. An additional problem is that many projects will not in themselves cause significant impacts, but may contribute to the cumulative impacts, e.g. from an existing urban area.

The relevant EPA must be notified of any potential **groundwater pollution** that may require authorisation. Consideration should also be given to the project's location in relation to *groundwater vulnerability maps* and GSPZs (Table 10.4). If adequate data can be obtained, the vulnerability of other receptor sites can be assessed using Darcy's law (§10.6.5) or a computer model such as MODFLOW (Table 10.5).

10.8.5 Significance of impacts

Impact significance will depend on impact magnitudes and the sensitivity and value of **receptors**. The relatively straight forward example shown in **Tables 10.11a, 10.11b** and **10.11c** refers primarily to road schemes, but can be applied to other projects. It involves an assessment made in line with the following prescribed guidance provided in:

* *Design manual for roads and bridges* (DMRB), Vol. 11: *Environmental Assessment*, Section 3, Part 10: *Road drainage and the water environment.* (HA 2006);
* *Transport Analysis guidance* (TAG): *The water environment sub-objective, TAG Unit 3.3.11* (DfT 2003).

An assessment is first made of the Importance of the Water Feature (using Table 10.11a) and then the Magnitude of the potential impact (by referring to Table 10.11b). The overall significance is then calculated by combining the Importance and Magnitude scores (using Table 10.11c). This is a relatively simple approach for a type of development that admittedly is not typically regarded as having a major impact on watercourses. It provides an opportunity to combine the 'significance' of impacts on various water features for summation in a single EIS chapter concerned with 'Water Quality and Drainage'.

Table 10.11a Assessment of importance of a water feature

Importance	Description
Very High	International designation (e.g. SAC, SPA, Ramsar Site) (see Table D.1) relating to water feature (e.g. estuary, river, lake, wetland); Aquifer providing potable water to a large population; Groundwater Source Protection Zone; EC Designated Salmonid Fishery; and/or Floodplain with many properties present.
High	National designation (e.g. SSSI) (see Table D.2) relating to a water feature; River Ecosystem Class RE1 watercourse; Navigable watercourse or canal with high usage; Aquifer providing potable water to a small population; EC-designated Cyprinid Fishery; and/or Floodplain with a few properties present.
Medium	Water feature of regional value; River Ecosystem Class RE2 or RE3 watercourse; Navigable watercourse or canal with low usage; Aquifer providing abstraction water for agricultural or industrial use; Watercourse or water body used for angling; and/or Floodplain comprising recreational or agricultural land.
Low	Local value; River Ecosystem Class RE4 or RE5; No floodplain; and/or No angling.

Table 10.11b Assessment of magnitude of impact on a water feature

Magnitude	Description
Major	Loss of substantial part of feature; Loss of integrity of feature; Serious pollution resulting in substantial derogation of quality of feature; Major shift away from baseline conditions; and/or Major changes to the flow regime.
Moderate	Loss of noticeable proportion of feature; Contribution of significant proportion of effluent to a receiving watercourse, estuary or aquifer; Reduction in economic value of feature; Moderate shift away from baseline conditions; and/or Moderate and noticeable changes to flow regime.
Minor	Measurable deterioration in feature but of limited proportion, degree or extent; No change in quality classification and/or use potential; Minor shift away from baseline conditions; and/or Minimal though measurable changes to the flow regime.
Negligible	Change in discharges to surface water or groundwater but effects unlikely to be measurable; No change in discharges; Very slight shift away from baseline conditions; and/or Negligible changes to the flow regime.

Table 10.11c Water quality and drainage-impact significance matrix

Magnitude	Importance			
	Very High	**High**	**Medium**	**Low**
Major	Very significant	Highly significant	Significant	Low significance
Moderate	Highly significant	Significant	Low significance	Insignificant
Minor	Significant	Low significance	Insignificant	Insignificant
Negligible	Low significance	Insignificant	Insignificant	Insignificant

10.9 Mitigation and enhancement

The EIA process identifies if a project could have potential significant impacts on environmental receptors. In the water environment, receptors include surface water hydrology and channel morphology, surface water quality, groundwater hydrology and groundwater quality (EA 2002). The assessment will determine the potential significant impacts on these receptors and identify appropriate mitigation for them. The appropriate type of mitigation will depend on the potential impact and the sensitivity of the receptor. Once appropriate mitigation has been taken into account it will be possible to assess the residual impact (that is the impact after mitigation) on the environmental receptors.

The EIA process will establish whether a project could be carried out in a different way to minimise any potential environmental impacts. This may not be possible (e.g. due to social or economic reasons) and even the option with the least potential for environmental impact may still need to be mitigated for and may have residual impacts. For example, in relation to the road widening project referred to in Table 10.9; at a strategic level it may be possible to consider alternatives such as improving public transport in the locality, but the option of considering alternative routes is not available. Consequently, in the context of an EIA the only real alternative to widening the road would be the "do nothing" option which may not be possible for safety reasons. Mitigation can still be achieved by means of options for the design of the widening that can reduce potential environmental impacts. For instance, widening into a central reservation rather than laterally from the outside could minimise the impact on any rivers that cross the route.

Mitigation measures commonly adopted in relation to various water-impact issues are outlined in **Table 10.12**, together with some sources of further information.

Wherever possible, *Sustainable Urban Drainage Systems* (SUDS) should be considered early and become integral to the layout and design of any new development (CIRIA 2007). Proposals for their maintenance should also be considered and recorded in the EIS.

Table 10.12 Some typical mitigation and enhancement measures relating to water-impact issues (see also Table 11.9)

Damage to riparian features, or change in channel morphology, caused by river works

Where possible, maintain natural river depths and courses, bottom sediments, and flood-plain/flood regimes. Use natural materials for bank protection/stabilisation, e.g. vegetation fringes and bankside trees instead of concrete or steel reinforcements. Limit damage by working from one bank and retaining vegetated areas. Make new channels sinuous (not straight) with asymmetrical cross section, and create new features such as pools, *riffles* and islands. Use dredgings positively, e.g. for landscaping or habitat creation. (See Brooke 1992, Brookes 1988, Brookes and Shields 1996, Brookes *et al.* 1998, De Waal *et al.* 1998, USEPA 2007, Maitland and Morgan 1997, Petts and Calow 1996, RRC 2002.)

Increased sediment loads and turbidity caused by river channel works

Select appropriate equipment and timing, e.g. construct new channels in the dry and allow vegetation to establish before water is diverted back in. Store spoil away from water-courses.

Impacts of development on floodplains

If development is permitted: (a) steer away from wetlands and high-flood-risk areas; (b) ensure that new flood defences do not increase flood risk elsewhere; (c) take compensatory measures, e.g. floodways and flood storage areas/reservoirs to provide flood storage and flow capacity; (d) allow for failure/overtopping of defences, e.g. by creating flood routes to assist flood water discharge; (e) take opportunities for enhancement in redevelopment, especially where (as in many urban sites) existing conditions are poor, e.g. use river corridor works to restore floodplain (by removing inappropriate existing structures), enhance amenity and wildlife value, and create new floodplain wetlands. (See EA 1997, Philippi 1996, Smith and Ward 1998, WUF 2001.)

Impacts of mineral workings, especially on floodplains

Operational phase – Carefully manage the use and storage of materials/spoil, and runoff from spoil heaps/earthworks. Use siltation lagoons. Route dewatering water into (a) lagoons, wells or ditches to recharge groundwater, (b) watercourses to augment streamflows.
Restoration phase – Careful backfill and aftercare management. Enhancement, e.g. of amenity/wildlife value (see §9.7) (Rust Consulting 1994).

Impacts of new roads and bridges, or road improvement schemes

Use: careful routing; designs to minimise impacts on river corridors (not just channels); and measures to control runoff, e.g. routed to detention basins or sewage works, and not into high quality still waters. If construction imposes river re-alignment, create new sinuous channel with vegetated banks (HA 2006).

Impacts of dams and reservoirs

Adjust size or location (avoid sensitive areas). Minimise height and slope of embankments, and plant with trees.

Table 10.12 (*continued*)

Water depletion by abstraction

Promote infiltration and hence groundwater recharge, in urban areas (see below). Minimise water use, e.g. metering and the installation of water-efficient equipment/appliances.

Increased runoff and reduced aquifer recharge in urban and industrial developments

Use *Sustainable Urban Drainage Systems* (SUDS) with (a) efficient piped drainage and sewer systems and (b) runoff source control measures, i.e. at or near the point of rainfall – to promote infiltration and/or delay runoff before it reaches piped systems or watercourses – e.g.: porous artificial surfaces (car parks, pavements etc.), soakaways (gravel trenches, vegetated areas); flow detention measures (grass swales, vegetated channels, stepped spillways, detention/balancing ponds/basins/storm reservoirs, and project layout/landscaping to increase runoff route). (See CIRIA 2007, Fangmeier *et al.* 2005, Ferguson 1998, Mansell 2003, Scholz 2006, Shaw 1994, Walesh 1989.)

Chemical pollution from built environments, e.g. roads, urban/industrial areas

Control runoff (as above). Use: oil traps; siltation traps/ponds/lagoons; vegetated *buffer zones* and wetlands, e.g. constructed reed beds (see §11.8.2 and Table 11.9). (See CIRIA 2007, Scholz 2006.)

Increased sewage and/or sewage-pollutant content

Increase capacity and/or *sewage treatment level*, e.g. from primary to secondary or secondary to tertiary

Increased runoff and pollution (including sediments) from construction sites

Minimise soil compaction and erosion (see §9.7). Ensure careful storage and use of chemicals, fuel etc. Install adequate sanitation. Guard against accidental spillage, vandalism and unauthorised use.

Chemical pollution from an accidental spillage

Effective contingency plans. Use booms and dispersants.

Groundwater pollution

Guide development away from GSPZs. Avoid contamination from leaking storage tanks etc. by appropriate bunding of tanks and improved site management. Use buffer zones (EA 1998b).

Inevitably, given the uncertainties surrounding the effectiveness of mitigation measures in a specific location there are potentially residual impacts that should be made transparent in the EIA and recorded in the EIS.

Developments can also provide opportunities for benefit and enhancement. For example, restoration of previously degraded damaged watercourses can offer opportunities for environmental improvement. There are now many examples where artificially straight and deepened river channels have been re-naturalised by introducing a more sinuous course and natural instream features such as pools, riffles and substrate (www.therrc.co.uk/).

10.10 Monitoring

Because of the sensitivity of hydrological systems, and the inevitable uncertainties associated with impact predictions, monitoring is particularly important for the water component of EIAs, and should be prescribed for both the construction and post-development phases. It can utilise baseline survey methods, and may justify the use in the baseline study, of techniques and sampling programmes that would otherwise be excluded by time constraints. Monitoring is frequently hindered by the difficulty of isolating the effects of a project from those of other developments and activities, but aspirations for the success of a project can often be set and monitored (e.g. see **Table 10.13**). Monitoring is also a costly exercise and frequently needs to be justified as part of legislative requirements or the licensing or consenting process.

Table 10.13 Example criteria for the success for pool-riffle reconstruction in lowland Europe (from Brookes *et al.* 1998).

Issue	*Example Criteria*	*How to measure*
Surface-water hydrology	The typographic highs caused by *riffles* should not be so high that they cause overbank flooding of property	Flood monitoring
	The riffles should be of sufficient height to cause divergence of flow	Mapping of flow patterns
	The gravels forming the riffles should remain free of significant silt deposition	Repeat topographic surveys and/or visual checks during and after construction
Channel morphology	The gravels forming the riffles should remain in situ, i.e. should not erode out during moderate to high flows	Repeat topographic surveys and/or visual checks during and after construction
Aquatic ecology	There should be an increase in the diversity of fish, plant and invertebrate species	Repeat ecological surveys before, during and after construction
Visual amenity	The diversity introduced should improve the aesthetic value of the channel	Repeat public perception surveys of the existing and improved channels
Recreation	The addition of pools should improve the angling quality	No standard methods exist at present

References

Acreman MC and F Law (eds) 2000. *Hydrology of the UK: a study of change.* London: Routledge.

Adriano DC, AK Iksandar and IP Murarka (eds) 1994. *Contamination of groundwaters.* Norwood, Essex: Science Reviews.

Anderson MG, DE Walling, and PD Bates (eds) 1996. *Floodplain processes.* Chichester: John Wiley & Sons.

Anderson MP and WW Woessner 1992. *Applied groundwater modelling: simulation of flow and advective transport.* New York: Academic Press.

Atkinson S 1999. Water impact assessment. In *Handbook of environmental impact assessment*, Vol. 1, J Petts (ed.), 273–300. Oxford: Blackwell Science.

Bailey RG, José PV and BR Sherwood (eds) 1998. *UK floodplains.* Otley, W. Yorks: Westbury Academic & Scientific Publishing.

Baird AJ and RL Wilby 1999. *Eco-hydrology: plants and water in terrestrial and aquatic environments.* London: Routledge.

Biggs J, P Williams, M Whitfield, G Fox and P Nicolet 2000. Biological techniques of still water quality assessment. *R&D Technical Report E110.* Bristol: Environment Agency.

Boiten W 2000. *Hydrometry.* Rotterdam: Balkema.

Brassington R 2006. *Field hydrology*, 3rd edn. Chichester: John Wiley & Sons.

Bridge JS 2003. *Rivers and floodplains: forms processes and sedimentary record.* Oxford: Blackwell Scientific.

Brooke JS 1992. River and coastal engineering. In *Environmental assessment: a guide to the identification, evaluation and mitigation of environmental issues in construction schemes*, CIRIA Research Project 424, Ch. 4. Birmingham: CIRIA.

Brookes A 1988. *Channelized rivers: perspectives for environmental management.* Chichester: John Wiley & Sons.

Brookes A and KR Hills 1994. The impact of road developments on river corridors: lessons learnt from south-central England. In *Nature conservation and the management of drainage system habitat*, D Harper (ed.). Chichester: John Wiley & Sons.

Brookes A and FD Shields Jr (eds) 1996. *River channel restoration: guiding principles for sustainable projects.* Chichester: John Wiley & Sons.

Brookes A, P Downs and K Skinner 1998. Engineering of wildlife habitats. *Journal of the Chartered Institute of Water and Environmental Management*, **12**, 25–29.

Calow P (ed.) 1997. *Handbook of ecotoxicology.* Oxford: Blackwell Scientific.

CEH (Centre for Ecology and Hydrology) 1999 (and updates). *Flood estimation handbook: procedures for flood frequency estimation* (FEH): Vol. 1: *Overview*; Vol. 2: *Rainfall frequency estimation*; Vol. 3: *Statistical procedures for flood frequency estimation*; Vol. 4: *Rainfall-runoff method* (2006); Vol. 5: *Catchment descriptors*; FEH CD-ROM. Wallingford, Oxon: CEH, www.nwl.ac.uk/ih/feh/.

CEH 2008a. *The National Groundwater Level Archive (NGLA): about the data.* Wallingford, Oxon: CEH, www.ceh.ac.uk/data/nrfa/groundwater.html.

CEH 2008b. *Hydrological trends-background.* Wallingford, Oxon: CEH, www.ceh.ac.uk/data/nrfa/hydrological_trends.html.

CIRIA (Construction Industry Research and Information Association) 2007. *The Sustainable Urban Drainage Systems (SUDS) manual (C697).* Birmingham: CIRIA, www.ciria.org.uk/suds/publications.htm.

Cook HF 1998. *The protection and conservation of water resources: a British perspective.* Chichester: John Wiley & Sons.

DCLG (Department for Communities and Local Government) 2006a. *Environmental impact assessment: a guide to good practice and procedures: a consultation paper*, London: DCLG, www.communities.gov.uk/archived/publications/planningandbuilding/environmental-impactassessment.

DCLG 2006b. *Planning Policy Statement 25: Development and flood risk*. London: DCLG, www.communities.gov.uk/publications/planningandbuilding/pps25floodrisk.

Defra (Department for Environment, Food and Rural Affairs) 2005. *High level targets*. London: Defra, www.defra.gov.uk/environ/fcd/hltarget/default.htm#target4.

Defra 2006. *Water level management plans*. London: Defra, www.defra.gov.uk/environ/fcd/policy/wlmp.htm.

Defra 2008. *Making Space for Water*. London: Defra, www.defra.gov.uk/environ/fcd/policy/strategy.htm.

DETR (Department of the Environment, Transport and the Regions) 1998. *Economic instruments for water pollution*. London: HMSO, www.defra.gov.uk/Environment/economics/index.htm.

DETR 1999. *Water quality: a guide to water protection in England and Wales*. London: HMSO.

DETR 2000. *Sustainable urban drainage systems: a design manual for England and Wales* London: DETR/CIRIA.

DETR 2001. *Guidance on the Groundwater Regulations 1998*. London: HMSO, www.defra.gov.uk/Environment/water/ground/pdf/groundwater-guidance.pdf.

De Waal LC, ARG Large and PM Wade (eds) 1998. *Rehabilitation of rivers: principles and implementation*. Chichester: John Wiley & Sons.

DfT (Department for Transport) 2003. *Transport Analysis Guidance (TAG): The water environment sub-objective, TAG Unit 3.3.11*. London: DfT, www.webtag.org.uk/webdocuments/3_Expert/3_Environment_Objective/3.3.11.htm.

Downing RA and WB Wilkinson (eds) 1992. *Applied groundwater hydrology: a British perspective*. Oxford: Oxford University Press.

Dunbar MJ, AR Young and V Keller 2006. *Distinguishing the Relative Importance of Environmental Data Underpinning flow Pressure assessment (DRIED-UP)*. EMCAR Research Project EMC/WP05/086 (by CEH for EA). Bristol: Environment Agency, http://nora.nerc.ac.uk/2257/1/DRIED-UP_final_3_small_photos.pdf.

EA (Environment Agency) 1996. *Environmental assessment, scoping handbook for projects*. London: HMSO.

EA 1997. *Our policy and practice for the protection of floodplains*. Bristol: Environment Agency.

EA 1998a. *State of the environment of England and Wales: fresh waters*. London: TSO.

EA 1998b. *Policy and practice for the protection of groundwater*, 2nd edn. Bristol: Environment Agency.

EA 2000. *State of the Environment*. Bristol: Environment Agency

EA 2002. *A handbook for scoping projects*. Bristol: Environment Agency.

EA 2004. *Hydroecology: integration for modern regulation*. Bristol: Environment Agency, www.environment-agency.gov.uk/commondata/105385/hydroecology_879252.pdf.

EA 2005. *Producing generalised LIFE response curves*. Science Report SC990015/SR. Bristol: Environment Agency, http://nora.nerc.ac.uk/2303/1/SCHO0305BIQJ-e-e.pdf.

EA 2007a. *Underground, under threat: the state of groundwater in England and Wales*. Bristol: Environment Agency, http://publications.environment-agency.gov.uk/pdf/GEHO0906BLDB-e-e.pdf

EA 2007b. *Underground, under threat: policy and practice (GP3)*. www.environment-agency.gov.uk/subjects/waterres/groundwater/1463256/?version=1&lang=_e.

EA 2007c. *Understanding water for wildlife. Water resources and conservation: assessing the eco-hydrological requirements of habitats and species.* Bristol: Environment Agency, http://publications.environment-agency.gov.uk/pdf/GEHO0407BMNB-e-e.pdf?lang=_e.

EA 2007d. *Project appraisal technical note for flood risk management projects: economic analysis and climate change.* Bristol Environment Agency,

EA 2008a. *Catchment Abstraction Management Strategies (CAMS).* www.environment-agency.gov.uk/subjects/waterres/564321/309477/?lang=_e.

EA 2008b. *Catchment Flood Management Plans (CFMPs).* www.environment-agency.gov.uk/subjects/flood/1217883/1217968/907676/.

EA 2008c. *River quality (GQA) and the Water Framework Directive.* www.environment-agency.gov.uk/yourenv/eff/1190084/water/213902/880308/?version=1&lang=_e.

EA (undated). *The General Quality Assessment of rivers: aesthetics.* Bristol: Environment Agency, www.environment-agency.gov.uk/commondata/acrobat/aesthetics.pdf.

EC (European Commission) 2000. *Directive 2000/60/EC of the European Parliament and of the Council of 23 October 2000 establishing a framework for community action in the field of water policy.* Brussels: Official Journal of the European Communities L 327/1, http://ec.europa.eu/environment/water/water-framework/index_en.html.

Fangmeier DD, WJ Elliott, SR Workman, RL Huffman and GO Schwab 2005. *Soil and water conservation engineering,* 5th edn. New York: Delmar Cengage Learning.

Ferguson BK 1998. *An introduction to stormwater: concept, purpose, design.* New York: John Wiley & Sons.

Golterman HL 1978. *Methods for chemical analysis of fresh waters,* 2nd edn. Oxford: Blackwell Scientific.

Gordon ND, TA McMahon and BL Finlayson 1992. *Streamflow hydrology: an introduction for ecologists.* Chichester: John Wiley & Sons.

Gray NF 2008. *Drinking water quality: problems and solutions,* 2nd edn. Cambridge: Cambridge University Press.

Gurnell AM and DR Montgomery 2000. *Hydrological applications of GIS.* New York: John Wiley & Sons.

HA (Highways Agency) 2006. *Design manual for roads and bridges (DMRB),* Vol. 11: *Environmental assessment,* Section 3, Part 10: *Road drainage and the water environment.* London: Highways Agency, www.standardsforhighways.co.uk/dmrb/vol11/section3.htm.

Hawkes HA 1997. Origin and development of the Biological Monitoring Working Party score system. *Water Research* **32**, 964–968.

Hellawell JM 1986. *Biological indicators of freshwater pollution and environmental management.* London: Elsevier.

Herschy RW (ed.) 1999. *Hydrometry: principles and practice,* 2nd edn. Chichester: John Wiley & Sons.

Hunt DTE and AL Wilson 1995. *The chemical analysis of water: general principles and techniques,* 2nd rev. edn. London: The Royal Society of Chemistry.

Johnes P, B Moss and G Phillips 1996. The determination of total nitrogen and total phosphorus concentrations in freshwaters from land use, stock headage and population data: testing of a model for use in conservation and water quality management. *Freshwater Biology* **36**, 451–473.

Karvonen T 1998. *Soil and groundwater hydrology: basic theory and application of computer models.* Helsinki: Helsinki University of Technology, www.water.hut.fi/.

Kiely G 1997. *Environmental engineering.* London: McGraw-Hill.

Kresic N 2006. *Quantitative solutions in hydrogeology and groundwater modelling,* 2nd edn. Boca Raton, FL: CRC Press.

Laws EA 2000. *Aquatic pollution: an introductory text.* 3rd edn. Chichester: John Wiley & Sons.

Mackereth FJH, J Heron and JF Talling 1978. *Water analysis: some revised methods for limnologists.* FBA Scientific Publication 36. Ambleside, Cumbria: Freshwater Biological Association.

MAFF *et al.* (Ministry of Agriculture, Fisheries and Food) 1994. *Water Level Management Plans: a procedural guide for operating authorities.* PB 1793. London: MAFF, www.defra.gov.uk/environ/fcd/policy/wlmp.htm.

MAFF/WO (Ministry of Agriculture, Fisheries and Food/Welsh Office) 1993. *Strategy for flood and coastal defence in England and Wales,* PB 1471. London: MAFF.

MAFF/WO 1996. *Code of practice on environmental procedures for flood defence operating authorities,* PB 2906. London: MAFF.

MAFF 2000–2001. *Flood and coastal defence project appraisal guidance* (FCDPAG1–FCD-PAG5). London: MAFF, www.defra.gov.uk/environ/fcd/pubs/pagn/default.htm.

Maitland PS and NC Morgan 1997. *Conservation management of freshwater habitats: lakes, rivers and wetlands.* Dordrecht, The Netherlands: Kluwer Academic.

Manning JC 1996. *Applied principles of hydrology,* 3rd edn. Upper Saddle River, NJ: Prentice-Hall.

Mansell MG 2003. *Rural and urban hydrology.* London: Thomas Telford.

Marriott S, J Alexander and R Hey 1999. *Floodplains: interdisciplinary approaches.* London: Geological Society.

Meybeck M, D Chapman and R Helmer (eds) 1989. *Global freshwater quality – a first assessment.* Oxford: Basil Blackwell (for WHO and UNEP).

MO (Meteorological Office) 1982. *The handbook of meteorological instruments* (7 vols). London: HMSO (see www.metoffice.gov.uk/corporate/library/catalogue.html).

Morris P 1988. *The hydrology of Cothill Fen SSSI.* Unpublished report to Nature Conservancy Council.

Morris P 2002. The hydrology and plant communities of Cothill Fen SSSI. *Fritillary* 3, 20–36.

Morris P, J Biggs and A Brookes 2001. Water. Ch. 10 in *Methods of Environmental Impact Assessment,* 2nd edn, P Morris and R Therivel (eds). London: Spon Press.

Moss B 1998. *Ecology of fresh waters: man and medium, past to future,* 3rd edn. Oxford: Blackwell Science.

Newman PJ, MA Piavaux and RA Sweeting 1992. *River water quality ecological assessment and control.* Luxembourg: Commission of the European Communities.

Newson M 1994. *Hydrology and the river environment.* Oxford: Oxford University Press.

Nielson DM (ed.) 2006. *Practical handbook of environmental site characterization and groundwater monitoring,* 2nd edn. Boca Raton, FL: CRC Press.

Petts GE 1984. *Impounded rivers: perspectives for ecological management.* Chichester: John Wiley & Sons.

Petts GE and C Amoros (eds) 1997. *Fluvial hydrosystems: a holistic approach to river and floodplain ecosystems.* London: Chapman & Hall (Kluwer).

Petts GE and P Calow (eds) 1996. *River restoration.* Oxford: Blackwell Science.

Petts J and G Eduljee 1994. *Environmental impact assessment for waste treatment and disposal facilities.* Chichester: John Wiley & Sons.

Philippi NS 1996. *Floodplain management: ecologic and economic prespectives.* London: Adademic Press.

Rosenberg DM and VH Resh 1992. *Freshwater biomonitoring and benthic macroinvertebrates.* New York: Chapman & Hall.

RRC (River Restoration Centre) 2002. *Manual of river restoration techniques.* Cranfield, Beds: RRC, www.therrc.co.uk/rrc_manual.php.

Rust Consulting 1994. *Hydrology and mineral workings – effects on nature conservation:* *Guidelines; Technical Annex.* English Nature Research Reports 106 and 107. Peterborough, Cambs: English Nature.

Scholz M (ed.) 2006. *Wetland systems to control urban runoff.* Amsterdam: Elsevier.

Schultz GA and ET Engman (eds) 2000. *Remote sensing in hydrology and water management.* Berlin: Springer-Verlag.

SEPA (Scottish Environmental Protection Agency) 1998. *Flood risk assessment strategy.* Edinburgh: SEPA, www.sepa.org.uk/pdf/policies/22.pdf.

SEPA 2006. *National Water Quality Classification.* Edinburgh: SEPA, www.sepa.org.uk/data/classification/index.htm.

SEPA 2008. *River quality classification.* Edinburgh: SEPA, www.sepa.org.uk/data/classification/river_classification.htm.

SG (Scottish Government) 2004. *Scottish Planning Policy SPP7: Planning and flooding.* Edinburgh: Scottish Government, www.scotland.gov.uk/Publications/2004/02/18880/32953.

Shaw EM 1994. *Hydrology in practice*, 3rd edn. London: Chapman & Hall.

Singh VP 1995. *Environmental hydrology.* Dordrecht: Kluwer Academic.

Singh VP and M Fiorentino (eds) 1996. *Geographical information systems in hydrology.* Dordrecht: Kluwer Academic.

Smith K and R Ward 1998. *Floods: physical processes and human impacts.* Chichester: John Wiley & Sons.

Strangeways I 2000. *Measuring the natural environment.* Cambridge: Cambridge University Press.

Thompson SA 1998. *Hydrology for water management.* Rotterdam: Balkema.

USEPA (US Environmental Protection Agency) 2007. *River corridor and wetland restoration.* Washington, DC: Environmental Protection Agency, www.epa.gov/owow/wetlands/restore/.

Viessman W and M Hammer 2004. *Water supply and pollution control.* Upper Sadle River, NJ: Prentice Hall

Viessman W and GL Lewis 2003. *Introduction to hydrology.* London: Prentice Hall.

WAG (Welsh Assembly Government) 2002. *Planning Policy Wales (2002).* http://new.wales.gov.uk/topics/planning/policy/planpolicywales/?lang=en.

WAG 2004. *Technical Advice Note (TAN) 15 Development and flood risk.* http://new.wales.gov.uk/topics/planning/policy/tans/tan15?lang=en.

Walesh SG 1989. *Urban surface water management.* New York: John Wiley & Sons.

Wanielista MP, R Kersten and R Eaglin 1996. *Hydrology: quantity and quality control,* 2nd edn. New York: John Wiley & Sons.

Ward AD and SW Trimble 2003. *Environmental hydrology,* 2nd edn. Boca Raton, FL: Lewis (CRC Press).

Ward RC and M Robinson 2000. *Principles of hydrology,* 4th edn. Maidenhead, Berks: McGraw-Hill.

Watson I and A Burnett 1995. *Hydrology: an environmental approach.* Boca Raton, FL; CRC Press.

Wilson N 1995. *Soil water and ground water sampling.* Boca Raton, FL: Lewis (CRC Press).

Wright JF, MT Furse and D Moss 1998. River classification using invertebrates: RIVPACS applications. *Aquatic Conservation-Marine and Freshwater Ecosystems* 8, 617–631.

Wright JF, DW Sutcliffe and MT Furse (eds) 2000. *Assessing the biological quality of fresh waters: RIVPACS and other techniques.* Ambleside, Cumbria: Freshwater Biological Association, www.ceh.ac.uk/sections/re/RIVPACS.html.

WUF 2001. *The Wise Use of Floodplains Project – overall guidance note: learning from experience.* www.floodplains.org/.

11 Ecology

Peter Morris and Roy Emberton
(based on Morris and Emberton,
Biggs et al., Morris and Thurling 2001)

11.1 Introduction

The EU/UK EIA legislation (§1.3) refers to the ecological component of EIA as the *fauna* and *flora*. In practice, this means the **wildlife** and its environment which together form functional ecological systems – **ecosystems** (§11.2.3). These sustain the wildlife and provide **ecosystem services** that are essential for human well-being (§11.2.4).

This chapter provides an overview of Ecological Impact Assessment (EcIA), and focuses on terrestrial and freshwater ecosystems. Because marine ecosystems differ significantly from those on land, and because there is a close relationship between coastal ecology and geomorphology, these two components are considered together in Chapter 12. Similarly, the major environmental components of terrestrial and freshwater ecosystems are largely dealt with in Chapters 8, 9 and 10. However, while the different components may be investigated by different assessors in an EIA, care must be taken to consider them all in the EcIA, and to integrate the findings in the EIS.

Any development will have some direct or indirect impact on ecosystems; so EcIA should be considered in all EIAs. Ecological systems are complex and dynamic, and this imposes particular difficulties in obtaining adequate baseline data, making accurate impact predictions and formulating dependable mitigation measures (physical or management).

The aim of an EcIA should be to avoid or minimise the adverse impacts of a proposed development on ecosystems, and hence on **biodiversity**, and where possible to foster ecological enhancement.

Biodiversity worldwide is under increasing threat. For example, *The Millennium Ecosystem Assessment* (MA 2005a, 2005b, 2005c) reported that:

- "Over the past 50 years, humans have changed ecosystems more rapidly and extensively than in any comparable period of time in human history", and "approximately 60% of the ecosystem services examined by the MA are being degraded or used unsustainably";

- over the last few hundred years, the size and/or range of many species populations has declined markedly, and species extinction rates have increased by as much as 1,000 times typical Earth history rates; and
- the projected overall future extinction rate is over ten times the current rate.

Similarly:

- the *WWF Living Planet Index*, which tracks trends in the abundance of wild species, fell by about 30 per cent between 1970 and 2003 (WWF 2006);
- within well-studied groups in the IUCN Red List (see §D.2.1) between 12 per cent and 51 per cent of species are currently threatened with extinction (IUCN 2006); and
- the *Global Biodiversity Outlook 2* (CBD 2006) states that "In effect, we are currently responsible for the sixth major extinction event in the history of the Earth, and the greatest since the dinosaurs disappeared, 65 million years ago."

In the UK, there have been serious habitat losses (**Figure 11.1**) and associated declines in many species populations (see EN 2004a, OWWT 2005, PI 2000). In the last century, 170 species became extinct (ZSL 2007); and many native species are under threat, including 12 per cent of lichens and bryophytes, 28 per cent of seed plants and ferns, 6 per cent of invertebrates, 22 per cent freshwater fish, reptiles and amphibians, and 65 per cent of birds and mammals (Defra 2005a). Defra (2007a) has reported some improvements, but continuing declines in: woodland and farmland birds; plant diversity in woodlands, boundary habitats and some grasslands; and substantial numbers of priority species (27 per cent) and habitats (42 per cent) in the UKBAP (§11.3.2).

The most important causes of biodiversity loss and ecosystem degradation worldwide are habitat loss, overexploitation, pollution, climate change, and non-native species (Juniper 2007, MA 2005b). In the UK, major causes include intensive farming and the **cumulative impacts** of land development (EN 2004a, LUC 2005). Climate change is also an issue. For example:

- the MONARCH report (Walmsley *et al.* 2007) predicts that the majority of 32 rare and protected species that were considered in detail, are likely to be adversely affected;
- Huntley *et al.* (2007) predict that, by the end of the century, the average distribution of European breeding birds will shift nearly 550km north east and be reduced by 20 per cent, and the ranges of 75 per cent of Europe's breeding bird species are likely to decline;
- Plantlife International (PI 2005) predict that many UK plant species will need to migrate northwards and/or to higher altitudes, and that, if they manage to do so, the ranges of species currently inhabiting these areas will be "squeezed".

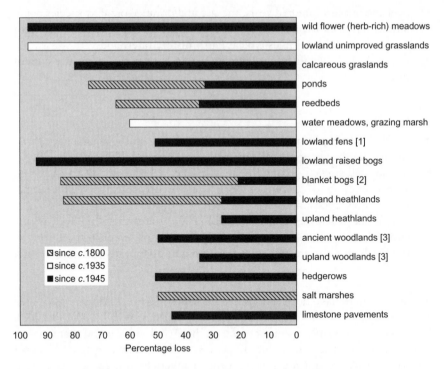

[1] 99.7% of the East Anglian fens existing in 1637 have been drained (EA 2000)

[2] the values for losses since *c.*1800 and *c.*1945 refer to N. Ireland and Scotland respectively

[3] WT is currently fighting >400 cases of woods under threat from development (WT 2008)

Figure 11.1 Some estimated habitat losses in the UK. In some cases, "loss" includes degradation, e.g. by agricultural "improvement", over-grazing or pollution.
Sources include EHS (2004), EN (2001, 2004a), LUC (2005).

11.2 Definitions and concepts

Ecology includes the study of species populations, biological communities, ecosystems and habitats; and it is important to understand what these are and how they are inter-related. This section provides a brief explanation; further information can be found in a wide range of ecology books including introductory texts (e.g. Townsend *et al.* 2007) and more comprehensive texts (e.g. Begon *et al.* 2005, Krebs 2001).

11.2.1 Species populations

In some EISs, the information on species is restricted to lists of those recorded (perhaps by a single sighting) as present locally or on receptor sites. This is inadequate since individuals are members of species populations, and simple presence records of a species give no information about, and rarely reflect: its **abundance**, which may range from a few individuals to a thriving population; or its **distribution**, which may be throughout an area or restricted to a small patch within it. Meaningful predictions about impacts on species frequently require both abundance and distribution data, together with an understanding of the factors that control the current abundance and distribution patterns and how the populations are likely to respond to impacts.

The viability of a species population depends on the presence of a suitable environment with adequate resources, and this involves a complex of biotic and abiotic **environmental factors** that affect its **population dynamics**.

Species can usually tolerate short-term environmental variations, and while populations may undergo marked temporary fluctuations, they subsequently tend to re-stabilise. Species are also capable of responding to slow progressive environmental changes by evolving or changing their geographical ranges; but they may be unable to adjust quickly enough to rapid environmental changes such as those resulting from rapid urbanisation or climate change, especially if their dispersal is inhibited by factors such as habitat fragmentation (§11.7.2). **"Specialists"** (which are adapted to a narrow range of environmental conditions or food sources) are more vulnerable to such changes than **"generalists"** (which have less specific requirements).

11.2.2 Communities

Biological communities are assemblages of species that have evolved in ways that facilitate their coexistence, e.g.: predator–prey relationships normally exhibit long-term equilibrium; inter-specific competition is minimised by **niche separation**; and many species have mutually beneficial relationships.

Communities include all plants, animals and microbes, but investigations usually focus on plants or animals, and comprehensive studies are generally limited to plant communities because these are relatively easy to survey. Community studies focus on **community attributes**, which can be divided into eight categories as outlined below.

1. **Vegetation physiognomy** refers to the physical structure and appearance of vegetation. This includes: **life-form composition**, i.e. the types and proportions of **plant life forms** that form the physical matrix of vegetation types; and **vertical structure**, i.e. the stratification of vegetation types – for example broad-leaved woodland has up to four layers (canopy, under-storey/shrub, field, and ground) while **heathlands** and grasslands rarely have more than two. Both of these features influence the associated animal communities.
2. **Species composition** can refer simply to the species present, e.g. represented by list. However, meaningful studies require quantitative data on **species abundance**. Information on **dominant species**, **keystone species** and **indicator species** is also valuable. Such studies are important in Phase 2 surveys (§11.4.2 and §11.6).

3. **Species richness** and **species diversity** are measures of a community's bio-diversity. They are often used in community or site evaluation, but must be applied with caution (see §D.3.2).

4. **Trophic structure** refers to the flows of energy and nutrients through communities and ecosystems (**Figure 11.2**). A **food chain** is simply a general route of energy and nutrients. In reality, a community's trophic structure

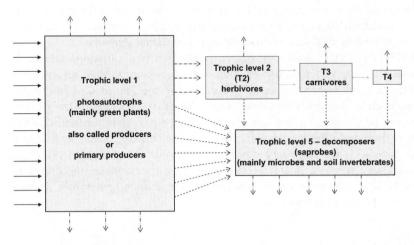

Input of light energy to trophic level 1 (photoautotrophs) by photosynthesis

Transfer of energy (in organic compounds) to higher trophic levels – T2 (herbivores), T3 (carnivores), and T4 (top carnivores) – along the **consumer food chain**

Transfer of energy to trophic level 5 (decomposers) in the form of dead plant and animal remains and animal excretory products. This route is often called the **decomposer food chain**.

Loss, from all trophic levels, of energy (mainly heat) generated by respiration.

The sizes of boxes and numbers of arrows indicate the relative amounts of energy entering, leaving and within the various trophic levels – but are not strictly proportional.

Communities need sustained flows of energy and nutrients, and rely on **autotrophs** which synthesise organic compounds using inorganic nutrients and external sources of energy. These are nearly always **photoautotrophs** in which the primary process is photosynthesis of glucose from CO_2 and H_2O using light energy absorbed by chlorophyll. All **heterotrophs** obtain their energy and nutrients from the organic compounds synthesised by autotrophs.

Energy assimilation by photosynthesis is called **primary production** (PP), and the total amount is **gross primary production** (GPP). Plants use *c.*55% of this; so *c.*45% (**net primary production** (NPP)) is available for heterotrophs, whose utilisation of energy is called **secondary production**. In terrestrial communities, only a small proportion of NPP passes along the consumer food chain – the bulk goes directly to the decomposers as dead plant remains. The decomposers also receive energy in the form of animal remains and excretory products.

All organisms carry out **respiration**, by which organic compounds are broken down to release usable energy (and CO_2). Much of this energy is lost to the environment as heat; so (a) energy flow through the community must be sustained by PP, and (b) less energy is available to higher trophic levels – which is why there is a **pyramid of decreasing *biomass*** from trophic levels 1 to 4, and why top carnivore populations are generally small.

Figure 11.2 Simple model of energy and nutrient flow through a terrestrial community. A similar model can be constructed for aquatic communities in which the photoautotrophs are *phytoplankton*, a much larger proportion of which are consumed by heterotrophs (see §12.2.5).

consists of a **food web**, i.e. a network of feeding relationships between species. Some knowledge of food chains and webs can assist in impact prediction and mitigation. However, food webs are usually complex, and few are fully understood. For example, it took 25 years to document a food web, in a small estuary, that was shown to involve >90 species and *c*.5,500 feeding links (Gorman and Raffaelli 1993). Consequently, monitoring of food webs is rarely appropriate in EcIA.

5. **Community productivity** (rate of production) varies widely, largely in relation to environmental temperature, water, and nutrient regimes. For example, tropical rain forests, swamps, estuaries and beds of marine *algae* normally have high productivities, while deserts, bogs and open oceans have low productivities. Highly productive communities have a large *biomass*. Some also have high species diversities, although low-productivity ecosystems can be more biologically diverse than many with higher productivities.

6. **Spatial pattern** refers to the spatial configuration of communities. While a managed landscape, as in the UK, is generally characterised by sharp boundaries, these are mostly man-made; and the spatial pattern of natural communities tends to consist of **community gradients** rather than discrete entities, with attributes such as species composition adjusting progressively along environmental gradients. Where the environmental gradients are steep, there may be obvious transition zones (**ecotones**) between adjacent communities, and these are often species rich because they contain species of adjacent communities. Mosaics of communities may be readily apparent, but less discernible gradients are common, and *semi-natural* vegetation is rarely homogeneous, even within small areas.

7. **Temporal pattern** refers to community changes through time. **Short-term changes** include seasonal variations, intrinsic vegetation cycles (e.g. associated with forest canopy gaps), and environmental perturbations (e.g. fire, storm, flood, drought, cold). **Ecological succession** is a progressive process that culminates in the development of a climatic climax community (*biome*) (**Figure 11.3**). Precise prediction of succession is difficult because: biomes are broad generalisations, within which there is wide variation in relation to local conditions, and secondary successions are influenced by the "stock" of potential colonisers living in the area and in the soil *seed bank*. In most of Britain, however, abandoned land and unmanaged plagioclimax communities will revert (often quite rapidly) to some form of woodland. Under an unchanging climate, climatic climax communities are relatively stable; but they still undergo (usually slow) **long-term changes** in response to factors such as immigration, emigration, evolution and soil development.

8. **Stability, fragility/sensitivity, resilience/recoverability** and **recreatability** are also attributes of species populations, ecosystems and habitats.

   • *Stability* can refer to: (a) the tendency to undergo little change through time, e.g. the relative stability of climax communities compared with successional communities; or (b) the ability to resist change in the face of environmental pressures. It is normally assisted by *negative feedbacks*

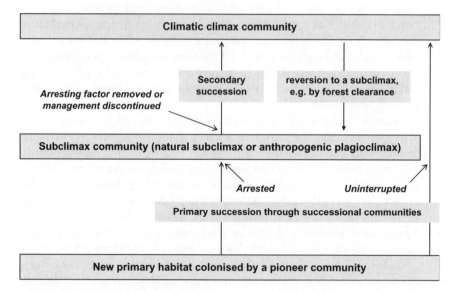

A **primary succession** (or **prisere**) starts from a near-sterile **primary habitat**, e.g. rock (exposed by volcanic activity, glacial retreat, mineral extraction etc.) or new water body (lake, reservoir etc.) which is colonised by a **pioneer community**. This is followed by a series of **successional (seral*) communities** (each replacing the previous one), and ultimately by a **climatic climax community** (**biome**). For example, a lake in lowland Britain is likely to be gradually infilled and undergo the following succession:
open water community → swamp → fen/marsh → carr → broableaved woodland.

Succession can stop at a persistent **subclimax** stage. The arresting factors can be natural, but most "subclimaxes" (including UK heathlands and grasslands) are semi-natural communities maintained by human activity (including management such as grazing); and because these **anthropogenic climaxes** differ from natural subclimaxes, they are often called **plagioclimaxes**. However, they are much more natural than communities such as "improved" grasslands. Removal of an arresting factor results in a **secondary succession** (or sub-sere) which can be rapid because features such as soil already exist.

* The terms sere and seral are often used as a synonyms of succession and successional respectively, but a sere is strictly a particular type or example of primary succession. Recognised types include the lithosere (from rock) and the hydrosere (from open water), both of which may eventually culminate in the same climatic climax.

Figure 11.3 Simple model of ecological succession.

operating within the system. Conversely, *fragility/sensitivity* refers to a system's susceptibility to environmental pressures.

- *Resilience* can refer to the level of disturbance that a system can absorb without crossing a **threshold** to a different (usually degraded) state, in which case it is virtually synonymous with *stability*. More usually, it refers to *recoverability*, i.e. the system's ability to return to a pre-disturbance state (and the speed at which it can do so) if the disturbance is removed. In the context of EcIA, this can be particularly important in relation to short term impacts, e.g. associated with the construction phase of a project.

- *Recreatability* refers to the potential for re-establishing a system of similar richness and complexity as one that has been destroyed.

In general, natural and semi-natural ecological systems are more sensitive, less resilient, and less recreatable than highly modified ones; and this is important in EcIA because it devalues community/habitat creation as a mitigation method, especially for long-established, complex systems (§11.8.4).

11.2.3 Ecosystems

An ecosystem is a self-sustaining, functional system consisting of environmental and biological subsystems. The planet has a global ecosystem and numerous regional and local ecosystems. Like communities, however, while ecosystems are usually considered as entities, in reality they intergrade. Each subsystem of an ecosystem interacts with the others and itself consists of numerous interacting components and processes, often involving delicate balances in relationships. Consequently, a change in even a single component, such as a species population or an environmental variable, can cause unpredictable knock-on effects. The interactions between major subsystems of a terrestrial ecosystem are illustrated in **Figure 11.4**.

Like its community, a whole ecosystem is sustained by fluxes of energy and materials. The principal energy source is nearly always solar radiation, only a small proportion of which (normally <1 per cent) is absorbed by the autotrophs and passes through the community (Figure 11.2). However, solar radiation also controls the ecosystem's temperature regime, both directly and by providing the evaporative energy for ***evapotranspiration*** which consequently has a cooling effect and can also result in the formation of a protective cloud screen, especially over tropical rainforests.

While the flow of energy through the global ecosystem is a minor diversion of the linear flux of solar energy, there is little exchange of matter between the earth and space, and the global flows of materials are essentially cyclical, i.e. involve ***biogeochemical cycles***. A local ecosystem is affected by, and affects, these cycles by means of inputs and outputs across its "boundaries", and thus has a **nutrient budget** (for each nutrient) that depends on the balance between inputs and outputs. It also has "internal" cycles in which nutrients pass along food chains and are returned to the environment (**Figure 11.5**).

Volatile elements (in elemental form or in compounds) can be exchanged between an ecosystem and the atmosphere. The main inputs are: carbon (from CO_2) which is assimilated by photosynthesis and absorbed in precipitation as carbonic acid; and nitrogen (from N_2), which is "fixed" by lightning and nitrogen-fixing bacteria. The main outputs are: CO_2 from respiration; and O_2 from photosynthesis (which normally exceeds CO_2 output from the majority of terrestrial and aquatic ecosystems). N_2 (mainly from nitrates) may also be released by ***denitrification*** in waterlogged soils. Volatile elements can also enter of leave ecosystems as solutes in surface and groundwaters, but the atmospheric inputs normally prevent depletion of these elements over time.

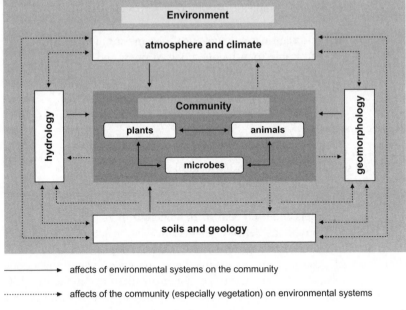

affects of environmental systems on the community

affects of the community (especially vegetation) on environmental systems

interactions between environmental systems

interactions within the community

In any given location, the climate affects the geomorphology, hydrology, soil and all the species of the community. Conversely: *microclimates* and local climates are affected by the other sub-systems; and vegetation and major geomorphological features such as mountain ranges, can affect macroclimates (regional and even global).

The community is also strongly influenced by, and in turn affects, the other sub-systems – particularly the soil, which is an ecosystem in its own right, with a community consisting of plant roots, soil animals, bacteria and fungi.

In addition, there are innumerable interactions within the subsystems, e.g. between abiotic environmental variables and between species.

Figure 11.4 Simple model of interactions between subsystems of a terrestrial ecosystem.

By contrast, **non-volatile elements** normally only enter local ecosystems by **weathering** of bedrock, as airborne particulate matter, or in solution or suspension in water. Water is usually the most important input-output medium; so an ecosystem's nutrient budget is strongly influenced by its water budget (§10.2.2). Thus, a local ecosystem may receive nutrients in drainage water from higher in its *catchment*, but may lose nutrients by *leaching* and *erosion*. Consequently, if the area has a climatic water surplus, as in the UK (§10.2.3) outputs of non-volatile nutrients are likely to exceed inputs, and ecosystems tend to undergo gradual nutrient depletion.

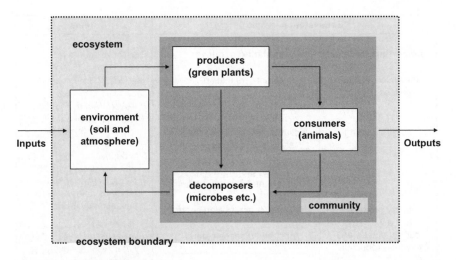

Figure 11.5 Nutrient flows within in a terrestrial ecosystem and across its boundaries. A similar model could be constructed for aquatic ecosystems, the main difference being that the source of nutrients for non-rooted producers is the water body.

Ecosystem nutrient regimes can be markedly affected by human activities, which can result in: excessive inputs, e.g. *acid deposition* and *eutrophication*; or nutrient depletion, e.g. by enhanced leaching or soil erosion. In addition, many toxic pollutants can enter, and circulate within, ecosystems in the same ways as nutrients.

11.2.4 Ecosystem services, fragility and resilience

In addition to their importance for wildlife; ecosystems provide human populations with essential benefits that are called **ecosystem services**. The *Millennium Ecosystem Assessment* (MA 2005a, 2005b, 2005c) divided these into four broad categories, and identified major threats to them that result from anthropogenic *drivers* (**Figure 11.6**). The effects of a development on local ecosystem services have at least some relevance to most of the EIA components discussed in this book.

Like communities, different ecosystems exhibit differing degrees of **stability**, **fragility/sensitivity** and **resilience** (see §11.2.2). In relation to anthropogenic drivers, another important attribute is **inertia**, which refers to the delay (time lag) or slowness in the response of a system to a driver, and in its recovery if the cause is removed. Ecosystem supporting and regulating services generally change more slowly than provisioning services, and this may lead to impacts on them being overlooked or ignored. Similarly, time lags for potential recovery vary considerably in relation to different drivers. For instance, the impact of a driver such as overharvesting may be quickly checked or reduced for some species (provided that a *threshold* has not been exceeded), but much longer time lags apply to

Ecosystem services		Threats
supporting services	**regulating services**	***anthropogenic drivers***
(on which all other services depend)	climate regulation	induced climate change
	air and water quality regulation	pollution from agricultural/ urban/industrial/transport runoff & emissions including:
nutrient cycling	pollution control, detoxification and waste decomposition	acid deposition; toxins, e.g. pesticides, heavy metals; eutrophication, e.g. by fertilizer & animal waste; salination by irrigation
water cycling	river, groundwater, drought and flood regulation	
primary production and associated carbon uptake and oxygen production*	soil/river/coast erosion control	
	pest and disease control	over-exploitation including: water resource overuse; fishery overharvesting; deforestation & farming
soil formation and retention	**provisioning services**	
	food, fibre, wood, paper, fuel, and fresh water	soil erosion
habitat provision	genetic resources	habitat destruction and fragmentation
pollination (of wild plants and crops) and seed dispersal	medicines/pharmaceuticals	species introductions or removals
	cultural services	change in land use/cover, e.g. by urban sprawl
biodiversity maintenance	educational, recreational, aesthetic and spiritual	technology development and use
	sense of place, social relations	

Associated well being
health; access to clean air and water; adequate livelihood with sufficient food and shelter; personal safety, secure resource access and security from environmental disasters; good social relations/cohesion; freedom of choice and action

* There is strong evidence that photosynthesis (see Figure 11.2) is responsible for (a) the initial generation and subsequent maintenance of free atmospheric oxygen, and (b) compensating for the gradual increase in solar energy emission over geological time, by absorbing carbon dioxide and hence reducing the greenhouse effect.

Figure 11.6 Ecosystem services, and threats to them resulting from anthropogenic drivers. *Source:* Based on MA 2005a, 2005b, 2005c.

recovery from the impacts of drivers such as habitat destruction, **nutrient load-ing**, pollution by persistent toxins, severe soil erosion or climate change.

Because of current limitations in the understanding of the dynamic nature of ecosystems, and the complex interactions within them, the potential effects of drivers are often difficult to predict. This explains why often surprisingly large (**nonlinear**) and unexpected changes (**ecological surprises**) occur.

11.2.5 Habitats

An ecosystem is a concept (or model) rather than a percept (that can be seen), and its most perceivable ecological features are habitats. A habitat is tradi-tionally defined as a physical environment in which a species naturally occurs. However, a given environment supports a community of coexisting species, and the plant community (vegetation) is an important component of most terres-trial habitats. Consequently, 'habitat' is commonly used to mean 'community habitat'. In this sense, the terms ecosystem and habitat are often used inter-changeably, and identifiable **habitat types** are designated in **habitat class-ifications** (Appendix C) that are widely used in conservation, environmental legislation and EcIA.

There is increasing use of the term **biotope**, which seeks to distinguish between physical habitats and habitat-community units (biotopes). However, most of the widely used systems are habitat classifications in which the majority of habitat types are at least partly defined by the characteristic vegetation. Consequently, biotope is only used in this book when there are specific reasons to do so (e.g. in §12.4.5 and §C.4).

11.3 Legislative background and interest groups

11.3.1 Legislation and international conventions

The main legal requirements governing EcIA are those in the EIA legislation (§1.3). An important change in the amended Directive 97/11 is the section (in Annex III) on the "location of projects" in relation to the "environmental sensitivity" of areas. However, this concept of "sensitive environments" requires further modification if it is to rectify the widely held perception that only rare and protected habitats need be conserved.

In addition, EcIAs must take account of international conventions, and EU and UK legislation, policies and plans, that seek to protect biodiversity through one or more of the following inter-related aims:

- **protection of species**, especially those with high conservation value (see §D.2), which usually also involves protection of their habitats;
- **protection of communities, habitats, and sites**, especially those with high conservation value (see §D.3);

- **countryside conservation** – which focuses on the protection of landscape and cultural features (Chapters 6 and 7) but can assist nature conservation because: scenic features often are, or host, valuable habitats; and the survival of many species depends on sensitive management of the wider countryside outside protected sites.

The "wider countryside" context is reflected in a recent shift of emphasis towards the conservation of "wider area" biodiversity, especially in relation to ecosystems, ecosystem services, and combinations of habitats in areas such as catchments (MA 2005a, 2005b, 2005c, Defra 2007b). However, high-value species, habitats and sites are still recognised as core elements for biodiversity maintenance, and it remains to be seen how effective the stated change in emphasis will be.

Tables 11.1 and **11.2** list the main international agreements, EC Directives and UK legislation on nature conservation – excluding those specific to coastal and marine systems which are referred to in §12.3.1. UK planning legislation is also relevant, but the level of protection afforded by "non-statutory designation" under planning law falls well short of the legislative protection provided under national and international law.

The *Habitats Directive* (and associated UK Habitats Regulations) is particularly important but, like most legislation, it does have deficiencies. For example –

- "Favourable conservation status" (see §D.1), "significant effect" and "imperative reasons of overriding public interest" are open to interpretation.
- "Compensatory measures" may be inadequate or inappropriate (see §11.8.4).

Table 11.1 International conventions/agreements and EC directives on nature conservation

UNESCO Man and the Biosphere (MAB) programme 1970 – established **Biosphere Reserves** to innovate approaches to conservation and sustainable development (www.unesco.org/mab/).

Ramsar Convention on Wetlands of International Importance 1971 – to conserve wetlands of international importance as **Ramsar sites** (www.ramsar.org).

UNESCO World Heritage Convention 1972 – to protect natural and cultural areas of outstanding value as **World Heritage Sites** (http://whc.unesco.org/en/conventiontext).

Council of Europe (COE) 1973 – Recommendation for the establishment of **Biogenetic Reserves** (www.jncc.gov.uk/page-1527).

Wild Birds Directive (WBD) 1979/409/EEC – to protect wild bird species and their habitats, with particular protection of rare species (in Annex I) in **Special protection Areas (SPAs)**[1] (http://ec.europa.eu/environment/nature/legislation/index_en.htm *and* www.jncc.gov.uk/page-1373).

Table 11.1 (*continued*)

Bonn Convention on the Conservation of Migratory Species of Wild Animals (CMS) 1979 – to protect threatened animals that migrate across seas and/or national boundaries (www.cms.int).

Bern Convention on the Conservation of European Wildlife and Natural Habitats 1979 – to protect endangered species and their habitats. Amended (1989, 1996) to set up the EMERALD network of **Areas of Special Conservation Interest (ASCIs)**. Its provisions underlie the *Habitats Directive* (http://conventions.coe.int/Treaty/EN/Treaties/Html/104.htm).

Convention on Biological Diversity (CBD) – Adopted at the **Rio Earth Summit 1992** to conserve biodiversity (www.cbd.int/convention *and* www.jncc.gov.uk/page-1365) *and*

CBD 2010 Biodivesity Target 2002 – "to achieve by 2010 a significant reduction of the current rate of biodiversity loss" (www.cbd.int/2010-target).

Habitats Directive 1992/43/EEC (and amendments) – (a) to protect **habitats** (some with priority status) listed in **Annex I**, amended in Directive 97/62/EC) and **species**[2] (some with priority status) listed in **Annex II** using measures to maintain or restore their "favourable conservation status", principally by **Special Areas of Conservation (SACs)**[1] but also through land-use and development policies and landscape management outside SACs; (b) to safeguard **species needing strict protection**[3] (listed in **Annex IV**). Two provisions of particular relevance to EcIA are:

1. Any project considered likely (alone or in conjunction with other projects or plans) to have "significant effect" on an SAC must go through an *appropriate assessment*, and will normally be accepted only if shown not to affect the "*integrity* of the site";
2. Harmful development may be allowed if there are "imperative reasons of overriding public interest", but there must be "compensatory measures", and if the site hosts a priority habitat or a priority species, only "human health or public safety" reasons are normally acceptable (http://ec.europa.eu/environment/nature/legislation/index_en.htm *and* www.jncc.gov.uk/page-1374).

Bonn Convention Agreement on the Conservation of Bats in Europe (EUROBATS) 1994 – to promote the conservation of bat species across Europe (www.jncc.gov.uk/page-1385).

Water Framework Directive 2000/60/EC (WFD) – requires that aquatic, wetland and, with regard to their water needs, terrestrial ecosystems meet "good status" by 2015 (www.jncc.gov.uk/page-1375, *and* http://ec.europa.eu/environment/water/water-framework/index_en.html.

UN World Summit on Sustainable Development (Rio' Earth Summit +10) Johannesburg 2002 – reiterates the principles and aims of the Rio' Earth Summit (www.earthsummit2002.org/).

G8 Potsdam Initiative on Biodiversity 2007 – to conserve biodiversity (including the CBD 2010 target) and combat climate change (http://biodiversity-chm.eea.europa.eu/convention/F1125911898/2007-03-18-potsdamer-erklaerung.pdf).

Notes
[1] SPAs and SACs are collectively called "European sites".
[2] Annex II species are called "European species".
[3] Annex IV species are called "European protected species" (EPS).

Table 11.2 Major UK legislation on nature conservation (excluding that for specific taxa)

National Parks and Access to the Countryside Act 1949 (NPACA) – Provisions for creation of *Areas of Outstanding Natural Beauty* (AONBs), *National Parks* (NPs), *National Nature Reserves* (NNRs), *Sites of Special Scientific Interest* (SSSIs) and *Local Nature Reserves* (LNRs).

Countryside Act 1968 – Powers under the 1949 Act strengthened; duty of LAs to have regard to the desirability of conserving the "natural beauty and amenity" of the countryside and wildlife.

Town and Country Planning (Scotland) Act 1972 – Provisions for *National Scenic Areas* (NSAs).

Wildlife and Countryside Act 1981 (WCA) and **Amendment Act 1985** – Increased protection of SSSIs; enactment of the Birds Directive; designation of protected species; provisions for Limestone Pavement Orders, *Marine Nature Reserves* (MNRs) and *Areas of Special Protection* (AOSPs).

Town and Country Planning Act 1990 – Obligation for LAs to take account of nature conservation in **Development Plans**, based on surveys to provide adequate information on species and habitats.

Planning and Compensation Act 1991 – Additions to classes of project requiring EIA. Increased powers of LAs to safeguard conservation and amenity areas. Requirement for structure, local and unitary Development Plans to include policies on conservation of natural beauty and amenity of land.

National Heritage (Scotland) Act 1991 – *Natural Heritage Areas* (NHAs) given special protection.

Conservation (Natural Habitats &c.) Regulations 1994 (Habitats Regulations) – Implement the Habitats Directive. Provisions for protection of European and Ramsar sites (and EPS), including the statutory requirement for **appropriate assessment** if the integrity of a site may be threatened.

Environment Act 1995 – Includes establishment of The EA and SEPA, and provisions on National Parks and hedgerow protection (www.chm.org.uk/detail.asp?m=900) (see also Table 10.2).

Hedgerows Regulations 1997 (England and Wales) – Removal of most hedges of 20m prohibited without notifying LAs which may impose "hedge retention notices" for "important" hedges.

Town and Country Planning (Trees) Regulation 1999 (England and Wales) – Includes provision for LAs to protect woods and trees by means of *Tree Preservation Orders* (TPOs).

Conservation (Natural Habitats &c.) Regulations 2000 – Extend the *Habitats Regulations* (1994) to include full protection to cSACs (see Table D.1) before they are adopted by the EC.

Countryside and Rights of Way Act 2000 (CROW) – Increased SSSI protection, and access to "open countryside"; powers against wildlife crime; improved ANOB management; UKBAP given statutory basis + Gov. duties to further the conservation of listed species and habitats.

National Parks (Scotland) Act 2000 – enabled the establishment of National Parks in Scotland.

Table 11.2 (*continued*)

Water Environment (Water Framework Directive) (England and Wales) Regulations 2003 and **Water Environment (Controlled Activities) (Scotland) Regulations 2005** – Implement the FWD.

Nature Conservation (Scotland) Act 2004 – Provisions for notification and protection of SSSIs; nature conservation and land management orders; wildlife protection measures.

Natural Environment and Rural Communities (NERC) Act 2006 (England and Wales) – Natural England (NA) established; amendments to WCA and CROW; statutory duty of public bodies to have due regard to the conservation of biodiversity and to publish relevant information.

EIA (Agriculture) Regulations 2006 – Implement EU Directive EC 97/11 to protect uncultivated land and semi-natural areas from damage by farm work and rural projects (see Defra 2007c).

Conservation (Natural Habitats, &c.) (Amendment) Regulations 2007– protection of EPS strengthened by removing the "defence" that acts which could constitute an offence were the incidental result of an otherwise lawful activity and could not reasonably have been avoided.

Note
Details of most of the above legislation, and on Northern Ireland legislation are available at www.opsi.gov.uk/. Further information can be found in Cowley and Vivian (2007) and at www.defra.gov.uk/wildlife-countryside/ewd/ewd09.htm *and* www.jncc.gov.uk/page-1359.

- Emphasis on "European" species, habitats and sites, may lead to under-valuation (in member states) of those that do not qualify, usually because they are well represented in the EU as a whole.

The *Water Framework Directive* (WFD), and associated UK Water Environment Regulations, are also of great importance, especially in relation to aquatic and **wetland** ecosystems (see §10.1 and §10.4.1).

Protection of taxa in the UK is primarily provided by the *Wildlife and Countryside Act 1981* as amended, although some additional protection is provided by other acts, such as the *Protection of Badgers Act 1992*, the *Wild Mammals (protection) Act 1996*, the *Deer Act 1991*, and the *Conservation of Seals (Scotland) Order 2002*. Details of these can be found at www.opsi.gov.uk/legislation/about_legislation.htm.

The protection afforded to sites in the UK varies appreciably in relation to their designations (see Table D.2). Sites with international designations have the greatest level of protection. UK statutory sites, including "ordinary" SSSIs (which have no additional designation), are also supposed to enjoy a high degree of protection. The *Countryside and Rights of Way Act 2000* (CROW) strengthens SSSI protection, principally through: a statutory duty for public bodies to further SSSI conservation and enhancement; powers for SNCOs (see Appendix B) to refuse consent for damaging activities and promote positive management; and increased penalties for deliberate or reckless damage by owners/occupiers or any other party.

Non-statutory sites normally have little legal protection other than that provided by local planning legislation. This is imperfect, and often leads those managing such sites (e.g. LAs and NGOs such as LWTs, RSPB and WT)[1] being reliant on the favourable interpretation of Local Development Framework Plan policies during planning applications. A notable example is **ancient woodland** which has no statutory protection *per se*, and 85 per cent of which has no legal protection (WT 2000).

11.3.2 Policies and guidance

The main global policies on biodiversity stem from the Rio Earth Summit (UNCED 1992) which established: the Agenda 21 global action plan for sustainable development; the UN Commission on Sustainable Development (UNCSD); and The Convention on Biological Diversity (CBD) which set The 2010 biodiversity target "to achieve by 2010 a significant reduction of the current rate of biodiversity loss at the global, regional and national level as a contribution to poverty alleviation and to the benefit of all life on Earth". UNCSD's aims were reiterated by The Rio' +10 Summit 2002 (Johannesburg Earth Summit) and The G8 Potsdam Initiative (see Table 11.1).

The principal European policies are:

- The EU Sixth Environmental Action Programme 2002–2012 (http:// ec.europa.eu/environment/newprg/index.htm);
- The EU Biodiversity Strategy (COM(98)42) (www.ec.europa.eu/environment/ docum/9842sm.htm) under which the Commission is required to produce biodiversity action plans (www.ec.europa.eu/environment/nature/index_ en.htm); and
- The Pan European Biological and Landscape Diversity Strategy (PEBLDS), developed by COE, UNEP and ECNC (www.strategyguide.org/). PEBLDS projects include the Pan-European Ecological Network (PEEN), which aims to link European and national protected areas and ecological networks in order to ensure the conservation of Europe's key species, habitats and ecosystems (www.ecnc.nl/).

The UK Government published its strategy for implementing the CBD in the UK Biodiversity Action Plan (UKBAP 1994). This contains:

- Lists of "priority" species and habitat types (designated within a broad habitat classification) that are selected using a set of criteria, and are considered to be priorities for conservation action (see §C.3); and
- Associated Species Action Plans (SAPs) and Habitat Action Plans (HAPs) that include an assessment of current status, actions to be taken, targets and costings (see www.ukbap.org.uk/species.aspx and www.ukbap.org.uk/ habitats.aspx).

Following a recent review (BRIG 2007) the number of priority species and habitats has been increased, and the criteria for selecting them revised (§D2.2 and §D3.3). The new UKBAP contains: 1149 species; 65 habitats (www. ukbap.org.uk/newprioritylist.aspx); 391 SAPs; 11 "grouped" species Action Plans; 45 HAPs; and 28 Broad Habitat Action Plans.

As a means of implementing the national plans, the UKBAP also promotes the development of local biodiversity action plans (LBAPs). These are developed by LBAP Partnerships, often as components of community or sustainability plans (formerly known as Agenda 21 plans). They are usually county-based, and aim to identify local priorities and contribute to the delivery of the national SAPs and HAPs. There are currently 162 LBAPS, which can be accessed via www.ukbap.org.uk/GenPageText.aspx?id=57.

In addition, Governmental Agencies, such as the Highways Agency, have prepared their own BAP (the HABAP) which includes both priority species and habitats (www.highways.gov.uk/aboutus/1153.aspx).

The Environment Agency's (EA's) strategy, for ensuring that ecological considerations are integral to water resource management, is outlined in EA (2004). As indicated in §10.4.2:

- protection of wetlands is sought in Water Level Management Plans and, where available, these are incorporated in the EA's LEAPS, a stated aim of which is to conserve and enhance biodiversity;
- the UK is committed to implementing the Water Framework Directive, largely by means of River Basin Management Plans (RBMPs).

The importance of the wider countryside is recognised in Government policies on **sustainable development**, which include commitments to base decision making on established data such as those from a series of Countryside Surveys. The latest of these to be published is the Countryside Survey 2007 (CS2007) (see Table 11.3); although the associated Land Cover Map is not available until 2009. The wider-countryside approach is also inherent in initiatives such as NE's Natural Areas programme (see Table D.2), and SNH's Natural Heritage Zone programme (www.snh.org.uk/) – which seek to focus conservation priorities within biogeographic areas.

Planning policy guidance on biodiversity/nature conservation is given in PPS9 and associated documents (ODPM 2005a, 2005b, 2005c, 2006). Similar guidance is given in NPPG14 Natural Heritage (Scotland) 1998; Technical Advice Note (Wales) 5 Nature Conservation 1996 – currently being updated (2007); and PPS2 Planning and Nature Conservation (Northern Ireland) 1997. The guidance clearly states that nature conservation issues should be (a) taken into account in **Development Plans**, and (b) included in the relevant surveys to ensure that these are based on adequate ecological information, and take account of local nature conservation strategies. It also specifically refers to aspects such as the conservation of:

- designated sites, including the presumption that an EIA should be undertaken for all proposals (a) within or adjacent to designated sites of national/international importance, or (b) likely to have a significant effect on a SAC, SPA or Ramsar site;
- non-designated sites and the wider countryside, including **linear habitats** and "sites of local conservation importance".

Planning legislation also required the preparation of a sustainability assessment (SA) for Regional Spatial Strategies and Local Development Frameworks and Plans.

11.3.3 Consultees and interest groups

It is advisable to consult widely when planning a survey, and to agree methodologies with the **statutory consultees** who will review the work prior to it being undertaken. For EcIA in the UK, these are the regional SNCOs (see Appendix B). The relevant SNCO has several important roles –

- It must be notified by the relevant authority (usually the local planning authority (LPA)) about a development application and will assist in the screening and scoping procedures.
- The LPA must supply it with a copy of the EIS for comment. This may include (a) an appraisal of the EIS in terms of its scope, technical competence, validity, and proposed mitigation measures, and (b) an indication of whether it would support or oppose planning consent.
- It will hold, and has a duty to provide if requested, non-confidential information on local ecology (and perhaps on previous EIAs undertaken in the local area).
- It will employ and have contacts with experienced ecologists, and will be willing to give advice on all aspects of the EcIA. This will be in concept only, although it will be willing to review mitigation proposals prior to their inclusion in the EIS.

Other GOs likely to have an interest in the EcIA are: the relevant EPA (Appendix B), especially when there are concerns relating to pollution, contaminated land, freshwater ecosystems or coastal ecosystems; CEH; FC; and the LPA(s), who will have specific policies on nature conservation and on the implementation of relevant national legislation.

UK **NGOs** that have interests which may be affected, and/or are potential sources of information and advice, include: BBS, BC, BCT, BENHS, BHS, BLS, BSBI, BTO, CPRE, CPRW, FBA, GWCT, MS, NT, NTS, PI, RSPB, TWT/LWTs, WT, WWF-UK, WWT[1] and local clubs/societies (e.g. bat, birdwatching, natural history). It may be only necessary or possible to consult a few of these organisations, and a "starting list" should be made as part of the scoping process. Ecological concerns may also be relevant in the context of public consultation, e.g. with parish councils, local farmers/landowners, residents and community groups.

11.4 Scoping and baseline studies

11.4.1 Introduction

Scoping should be undertaken at an early stage in the project, and should follow the principles and procedures outlined in §1.2.2. Checklists are an important aid, e.g. see Table 10.3 which includes aquatic and wetland ecology as an issue. Further guidance can be found in IEEM (2006), SNH (2005a) and Treweek (1999).

In a few cases, the **impact area** may be confined to the project site and its immediate surroundings. IEA (1995) recommend that a minimum 2km radius should normally be considered for non-linear projects; and a corridor at least 1km wide should be examined along the proposed route of linear projects such as roads. However, IEEM (2006) recommend that, rather than stipulating any specific radius from the site, an assessment is made of all potential *receptors* within an estimated zone of influence (impact area). This area can be large, especially in relation to impacts that may be transmitted in air or water. Its estimation is bound to involve some educated guesswork and IEEM state that it "should be continually reviewed and, if appropriate, amended as the scheme evolves".

The amount of ecological information that could be collected is potentially enormous, and it is essential to **focus resources** on important aspects. This can be done by identifying *Valued Ecosystem Components* (VECs). These can be species, habitats or sites that qualify in terms of their ecological/conservation value (see §D.1), or other attributes such as socio-economic value (Treweek 1999, Tucker 2005). It is also important to focus on VECs that are receptors, since there is no point in using resources to study species or habitats that will not be impacted (Wathern 1999).

The most obvious VECs are protected species/habitats/sites and UKBAP priority species/habitats. However, the scoping inventory should include all receptors that may warrant further investigation, including (a) those that may have local importance, and (b) small habitat patches and **linear habitats** – which can be valuable in their own right, and may also act as refuges, *stepping stones*, *wildlife corridors* or *buffer zones* – often within an urban or intensively cultivated landscape. By providing refuges for wildlife, allowing small populations to remain viable and facilitating migration in an otherwise low diversity area, even small sites with ruderal communities that are individually of low conservation value, can have a significant role in a "green network" that permeates the area. Ultimately, the baseline survey (and evaluation of baseline conditions) should include all ecological receptors that qualify as VECs in terms of the criteria outlined in Appendix D.

11.4.2 Methods and levels of study

In selecting study methods and levels, compatibility with other surveys is desirable – and there is a strong case for adopting the two-phase strategy employed by JNCC (2007) and recommended by IEA (1995) for baseline surveys. However, some standard methods, such as that prescribed in *Design manual for roads and bridges (DMRB)* (Highways Agency *et al.* 1993), use a different phasing system which is more integrated into the design process.

The two JNCC phases are progressive in terms of information sought, and hence intensity of study. The **Phase 1 survey** (§11.5) aims mainly to provide information on habitats, and should be undertaken in all EcIAs. The **Phase 2 survey** (§11.6) is a more detailed study to evaluate species, communities, and habitats in selected areas, and is also required in the majority of EcIAs.

Resource and time constraints often impose severe limitations on the range and depth of field survey work that can be conducted, and it is important to make maximum use of existing information by means of the **desk study**. Some useful sources of ecological information are given in **Table 11.3**. The organisations listed generally hold more information than that shown, and can usually be approached directly. Some of the NGOs referred to in §11.3.3 may be particularly useful sources of local information, but their limited resources may restrict their ability to respond to enquiries within tight timeframes.

While the desk study is essential, much of the existing information may be sketchy, out of date or inaccurate. For example, the Peak District National Park Authority found 219 species-rich meadows that were not recorded in a previous Phase 1 survey (Parker 1998), and a review of 294 phase 1 surveys carried out by CCW showed that there was only a 74 per cent correspondence between surveyor and reviewer (Stevens *et al.* 2004). Consequently, it is normally essential to undertake new fieldwork.

Table 11.3 Sources of ecological information

Botanical Society of the British Isles (BSBI) www.bsbi.org.uk/ – database of vascular plant species recorded in *vice-counties* or regions; distribution maps (in 10km squares) of taxa.

Biological Records Centre (BRC)[1] www.brc.ac.uk/ – database of species location coordinates, with information on habitat and conservation status (used for many published distribution maps, although the highest available resolution is 1km square).

Countryside Council for Wales (CCW) www.ccw.gov.uk/interactive-maps.aspx – interactive maps: protected sites, GIS boundary downloads, and Landmap.

Countryside Survey 2007 (CS2007)[1] www.countrysidesurvey.org.uk – UK land cover census (from field observations in random samples of 1km squares) for data such as habitat types, hedgerows, plant species and freshwater invertebrates; and associated: Land Cover Map of Great Britain (LCM2007) (see Table 14.1); and Countryside Information System (CIS) www.cis-web.org.uk, which holds a range of data sets including: critical loads; designated sites; land cover and linear features; *Natural Areas*; physical features,

Table 11.3 (*continued*)

e.g. climate, geology, soils, topography); species; and vegetation. It can generate maps/charts and has facilities for data analysis and data input by the user.

Environment Agency (EA) – River Habitats Survey (RHS) database of physical habitat features of many sites. www.environment-agency.gov.uk/subjects/conservation/840884/208785/?lang=_e.

Environment and Heritage Service (EHS) www.ehsni.gov.uk/biodiversity/designated-areas.htm – Designated areas: location maps and descriptions of Ramsar sites, SACs, SPAs, NRs and ASSIs.

European Environment Agency (EEA) and component organisations (EIONET, ETCs and EUNIS) – host a range of databases and maps (see Appendix A and Table 14.1).

Joint Nature Conservation Committee (JNCC) www.jncc.gov.uk – information on: legislation; species rarity, threat, designations and action plans; and protected sites including: site designations, site lists and location maps of Ramsar sites, SACs, and SPAs.

Greenfacts (www.greenfacts.org/glossary/) – provides an extensive glossary and digests (summaries) of consensus documents on environmental issues.

Local sources such as county floras/atlases, and survey data, e.g. for research projects, SSSI notifications, LBAPs, *Development Plans*, or previous EIAs – and held by LRCs (contact list at www.nbn-nfbr.org.uk/nfbr.php), LAs, SNCO offices, NGOs, and academic institutions.

National Biodiversity Network (NBN)[1] **Gateway** www.searchnbn.net/ – datasets for: species and species groups (with a map facility to access species lists for 10km squares); habitats; and areas.

National Ponds Database (NPD) www.pondnetwork.org.uk/PondData/Introduction.aspx – search facility for ponds by name, location or species, and information on their conservation value.

Natural England (NE) – Nature on the Map www.natureonthemap.org.uk/ – locations, maps and information on international sites, NNRs, LNRs, SSSIs, and UKBAP priority habitat sites; GIS digital boundary datasets for designated sites, ancient woodlands and various habitat types; *Natural Areas* (www.english-nature.org.uk/science/natural/role.htm) – maps, profiles etc.

Scottish Natural Heritage (SNH) www.snh.org.uk/about/ab-ourwork.asp – **GIS digital datasets** for species, habitats, and sites/areas; and Sitelink (site information and boundary maps).

UK Biodiversity Action Plan (UKBAP) www.ukbap.org.uk/ – see §11.3.2.

UK Environmental Change Network (ECN)[1] www.ecn.ac.uk/index.html – includes biodiversity indicators of pollution and climate change.

UK National Focal Centre (UKNFC) for critical loads modelling and mapping[1] – *critical loads* and exceedance maps, especially in relation to acid deposition and nitrogen, critloads.ceh.ac.uk/.

UN Environmental Programme-World Conservation Monitoring Centre (UNEP-WCMC) www.unep-wcmc.org/ – worldwide data and maps on species, biodiversity, protected sites etc.

Note
[1] Part of, or affiliated to, CEH (Centre for Hydrology and Ecology).

11.4.3 *Resource requirements and timing*

The resources needed for an EcIA will vary in relation to factors such as the availability of existing information and the need for Phase 2 surveys. Mapping will be essential, and consideration should be given to the use of GIS (Chapter 14). This may be costly, but can be useful in all stages of an EcIA, and can facilitate comparison and integration of ecological information with that on other EIA components.

Ecological expertise is a "resource" of prime importance. It is essential to employ an appropriate number of competent ecologists for scoping and Phase 1 surveys; and Phase 2 surveys require experts (often with appropriate survey licences) in order to ensure accurate species identification and the application of suitable sampling and data analysis methods. In addition, the work undertaken by different specialists must be co-ordinated, and the findings integrated in the EIS.

Under a seasonal climate, as in Britain, the **timing of fieldwork** can be a critical factor because it is difficult or impossible to sample many species or communities during much of the year. Some Phase 1 survey work can be carried out during the winter months, but the optimal sampling season is limited to the period April–September. Similarly, for most taxa, Phase 2 surveys can only obtain appropriate and reliable data during short sampling seasons (**Figure 11.7**). Communities pose additional problems because most contain species that are inconspicuous or absent during part of the normal sampling season, and some have components with distinctly different seasonalities – so failure to carry out repeat surveys on at least two occasions can lead to error.

Provision of sufficient surveying time to accommodate these seasonality constraints requires careful planning. Phase 2 field surveys can be started as soon as the need becomes apparent during scoping or the Phase 1 survey; but decisions on their nature and extent are best made after evaluation of the Phase 1 survey findings. Ideally, therefore, the EcIA should start at least one year before the submission date of the EIS.

Developers' time-scales are often inconsistent with this requirement, especially (a) if the total time-scale (for design and planning application) of a small project is less than a year, or (b) where a developer defers the start of an EIA until late in the development process. Under such circumstances the developers and their agents must be made aware of the potential consequences. These include surveys having to be conducted "out of season" or during inappropriate weather, and (if Phase 1 surveys are not started until late in the survey season) Phase 2 surveys for **notable** species not being undertaken despite appropriate habitats having been identified.

Such failings are often accompanied by the promise to conduct adequate surveys after planning permission is granted. This should be avoided, however, because (a) it provides insufficient information upon which the relevant authorities can base an informed decision, and (b) Local Authorities have difficulties in using the current planning procedures in relation to protected species. As a result, many planning applications have been made conditional (Section 106 agreements) on

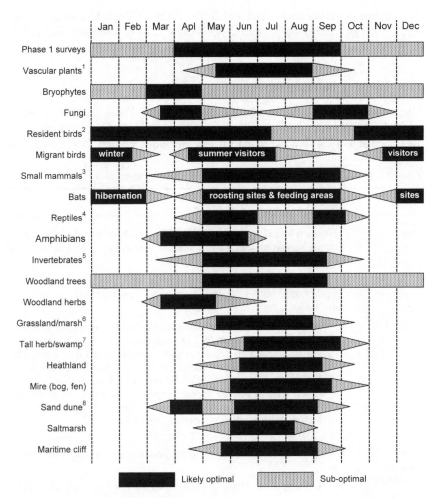

Figure key:
- Likely optimal
- Sub-optimal

[1] There are some exceptions, e.g. see woodland herb layer.
[2] The breeding season is restricted to March–June
[3] The optimal survey period for badgers is November–April
[4] Artificial refuges are best checked in May, June and September–October (Reading 1996)
[5] Preferably with three samples taken during early, mid and late parts of the optimal sampling period. Some aquatic invertebrates are best sampled in early spring.
[6] Hay meadows should not be sampled after cutting (usually in June).
[7] Short vegetation in tall herb and swamp should be sampled in March–April (as woodland herbs).
[8] Sand dune animals and Spring annual plants should be sampled in March–April.

Figure 11.7 Suitable periods for surveys of taxa and habitats in the UK. They may vary locally, e.g. growing seasons in the north generally start later than in the south.

the outcome of further studies (ODPM 2005a, 2005b, 2005c). Moreover, Circular 06/05 (ODPM 2005c) states that all surveys need to be complete and actions for conservation/mitigation in place before planning permission can be granted.

11.5 Phase 1 baseline surveys

The majority of UK EcIAs employ the Extended Phase 1 Habitat survey method. This is basically the method developed by JNCC (2007) which is outlined in **Table 11.4**, but extended (as recommended by IEA 1995) to include

Table 11.4 Outline of the JNCC Phase 1 Habitat survey method

Aspects	Features
Aim	The main aim is "to provide, relatively rapidly, a record of the semi-natural vegetation and wildlife habitat over large areas of countryside" (JNCC 2007).
Scope and form	Applicable to both rural and urban areas. Primarily designed to provide: • **colour maps of vegetation/habitat types** defined in the **JNCC Habitat classification** (§C.2) using standard colour codes and symbols, and with dominant plant species shown where possible; • **additional information** (largely as "target notes"), e.g.: species lists (including partial faunal lists recorded from "casual" observations), *notable* species; vegetation features and condition; topography and substratum conditions (e.g. soils, geology, wetness); protection; ownership and management.
Use of existing information	Information is collected to facilitate and supplement the field survey, e.g. • **OS maps**, e.g. 1:50k (for overviews), 1:25k and 1:10k (for field surveys). • **Geological and soil survey maps** (see §9.5.2) as aids to habitat mapping. • **Historical records and old maps** (see Box 7.1) can provide valuable information on a site's history and past management that may enhance its conservation value. • **Aerial photographs** can be useful for: providing an overview prior to field survey; mapping where access is restricted; identifying the locations, boundaries and areas of some vegetation types or other features (e.g. hedges, roads and undeveloped urban areas) that are unclear or out of date on the OS maps. • **Satellite data** is considered useful, but not adequate for the whole range of habitats mapped (but resolutions are increasing rapidly). • **Information on the site, taxa and habitats** e.g. conservation status; records of species lists and species distributions from previous surveys and research studies.

Table 11.4 (*continued*)

Aspects	Features
Field survey and recording methods	Phase 1 habitat classification types are recorded directly on 1:10k or 1:25k OS maps and/or map record sheets, using standard colour and/or alphanumeric codes, and labelled with dominant species names where possible (using standard abbreviations). **Target note record sheets** can be used for additional information (see above).
Data processing and presentation	Data are transferred from the field maps to **final maps** (usually 1:10k scale for sites). On the maps and/or aerial photographs: (a) plot areas are measured, e.g. using **Romer dot grids**, (b) the proportions (%) of different habitat types are estimated e.g. by the **line-intercept method** using parallel lines such as map grid lines. Alternatively, the maps can be digitised for **GIS** (see Chapter 14 and SNH 1998) and a GIS colour mapping palette is available at www.jncc.gov.uk/page-4258. Target notes are completed, and a written report is usually produced.
Site evaluation	Not primarily intended for site evaluation, but: is considered adequate for classifying sites on a three-point scale: 1 = high conservation value, 2 = lower priority for conservation, 3 = limited wildlife interest; and should provide the information required to determine the need for Phase 2 surveys. Moreover, sites hosting protected or priority taxa and/or habitats will almost certainly have protected status.
Limitations	The maps are not 100% accurate (error estimates should be provided). Small sites may be omitted (<c.0.5ha at 1:25k scale, and <c.0.1ha with 1:10k scale). Sites are normally only visited once, so seasonal variations may be missed. Species lists may not be complete, and rarities may have been overlooked. Changes may have occurred since the survey.

additional information such as evidence for the presence of notable taxa, assessments of the site's context in the area, and assessment of its suitability for notable taxa even if their presence has not been recorded (see §D.3.4).

Advantages of the JNCC (and Extended) Phase 1 Habitat Survey method incude the following.

• It was developed for mapping habitats within SSSIs and nature reserves, *and* for larger scale surveys, and hence is suitable for surveying small or large sites and impact areas.

- The "extended" method was recommended by IEA (1995) as a standard method for preparing EISs under the Environmental Impact Assessment Regulations 1988, and has been endorsed by IEEM (IEEM 2006).
- It has been used extensively, and there is no lack of qualified staff who can undertake it.
- Existing surveys are widely used by SNCOs and LPAs in formulating conservation policies and considering planning applications.
- It is relatively rapid, and provides information that is easily understood by non-experts.

The standard survey procedure involves ecologists walking over a site and recording areas occupied by the **habitat types** defined in the JNCC habitat classification (§C.2) directly onto maps, using prescribed colours and/or alphanumeric codes. However, it is important to relate the results to other classifications such as UKBAP habitats (§C.3) and Habitats Directive Annex I habitats (§C.5) and, for this purpose, the Integrated Habitat System (IHS) can be useful (§C.7).

The relative importance of the habitat types on a site should be assessed in terms of the proportion-of-site covered by each, which can be determined using the **line-intercept method**. This can be applied, as recommended by JNCC, in relation to parallel lines on the maps or aerial photographs. The length occupied by each habitat type along each line is measured; the values are summed; and the cumulative length, expressed as the percentage of the total length of all lines, provides a measure of the proportion (percentage) of the site covered by each habitat.

If time and recourses permit, however, the line intercept method can be applied as an integral part of the field survey. In this case, a base line is established from which observers walk along parallel transects, e.g. using the same compass bearing, that traverse a study area. The lengths of each transect occupied by each habitat type can by determined by means of a measuring tape, but pacing normally provides adequate distance measurements. If the transects are equidistant from each other, this procedure also provides a systematic survey of the study area, which facilitates the recording of target notes and the identification and mapping of habitat mosaics. Alternatively, rather than producing and then digitising paper maps, the data can be entered directly into a GIS, which can facilitate the delineation of habitats, and allow habitat and species distributions to be overlaid on similar distributional representations of other EIA-component data held in the same GIS.

Although the Phase 1 survey method focuses on habitats, it is desirable to record the presence of species that are noticed during the survey. Faunal lists compiled in this way are bound to be limited, but the Extended Phase 1 habitat methodology (IEA 1995) may require species lists as evidence of the presence on the site, or its use by, notable faunal species and/or its suitability for these. It may also be useful to collect some semi-quantitative data on the abundance of plant species, e.g. using DAFOR ratings (see Table 11.5).

Linear habitats, such as hedgerows and ditches, can usually be surveyed by simply walking along the feature, making notes, and recording the species seen (perhaps using DAFOR ratings). Hedgerows can be surveyed quite rapidly in this way, but their evaluation may require a more thorough Phase 2 study.

It may be necessary also to check the presence and distributions of some species within the impact area as a whole, especially when these have "wider-countryside" distributions, and are hence unlikely to be concentrated in specific sites. Again, however, Phase 2 methods may be needed to determine distributions, especially of animals.

11.6 Phase 2 surveys and evaluation of baseline conditions

11.6.1 Introduction and sampling options

The purpose of Phase 2 ecological surveys is to supplement the findings of Phase 1 surveys, the main limitation of which is usually lack of quantitative data. Consequently, Phase 2 surveys generally need to focus on collecting quantitative information. Some of this may be obtained by the desk study, but new field surveys will almost certainly be needed, and these can require intensive sampling of vegetation, a number of taxa and environmental variables. Phase 2 field surveys require a range of expertise, and are time consuming, expensive, and subject to seasonal constraints. Consequently, it is important to focus on carefully selected priority objectives. It is also vital that the work on different aspects is co-ordinated, and that the findings are integrated and clearly presented.

IEA (1995) recommend criteria (based on the findings of the desk study and Extended Phase 1 survey) for triggering Phase 2 surveys. They are largely habitat/site evaluation criteria in terms of evident importance or potential importance/suitability for *notable* species (see §D.3.4). IEEM (2006) recommend a somewhat different approach that focuses on the evaluation of taxa, communities, habitats and sites in terms of VECs (§11.4.1), and hence of most the criteria outlined in Appendix D, including biodiversity value, potential value, secondary or supporting value (e.g. as buffers or stepping stones), and socio-economic value.

This section outlines survey methods for terrestrial, *wetland* and *freshwater ecosystems*; methods for coastal systems are dealt with in §12.4. Further information is available in texts such as Hill *et al.* (2005) and Sutherland (2006); and a bibliography of identification books and keys is available in IEEM (2007). However, it must be stressed that both surveys and identification should be carried out by experienced personnel who already have the necessary skills, and that specialists are likely to be needed for many taxa, especially invertebrates.

Whether surveying individual species or whole habitats, it is important to remember the following.

- Species conservation value, distributions and habitat requirements should be checked.

- Many species (and some habitats) are legally protected, and this imposes restrictions, e.g. any activity likely to involve handling or disturbance may require a licence from the relevant EPA or SNCO (see IEEM 2007).
- Periods during which species can be readily observed and/or identified are usually seasonally restricted (Figure 11.7), and can vary widely between species living in the same habitat. Consequently, unless sites are visited at least twice (e.g. in spring/early summer and late summer/early autumn) many species may be underestimated or even missed. In many cases, weather conditions are also important.
- Where possible, quantitative data such as species abundances should be obtained. The main options for estimating abundances are outlined in **Table 11.5**.

Care should be taken to ensure that selected **sampling methods** are appropriate, and will provide results that are compatible with proposed data analysis procedures. Data collection methods include the following.

- Plot sampling involves taking observations within defined plots, usually *quadrats*.
- Plotless sampling is any method in which sampling is not conducted within defined areas. Simple methods include transect walking, or using the line intercept method, which can be applied (a) as a habitat-measurement method (§11.5) or (b) for estimation of plant species cover in sparse vegetation. Most other plotless methods involve distance measurements from sampling points. These include methods for estimating: tree densities in woodlands (e.g. see Kent and Coker 1992); and animal populations (e.g. see Buckland *et al.* 2001). Some plotless techniques, e.g. for bats, involve a combination of habitat and activity surveys.
- Specialised collecting equipment is often needed in faunal sampling.

The choice of **spatial sampling patterns** involves the questions *where to sample* and *what pattern of sampling locations is appropriate?* The main options (illustrated in **Figure 11.8**) are as follows.

- **Systematic sampling** is conducted at regular intervals, e.g. along transects or in relation to a grid system. **Transects** are useful for walkover surveys (transect walking) or studying gradients. Their placement can be random, systematic (at regular intervals) or selective, e.g. along linear habitats. A **grid** can be sampled at intersections (stations) or within the squares, e.g. using random sampling. Other options include: (a) inserting sub-stations between intersections or within squares; (b) sampling a sub-set only, e.g. randomly selected, or alternate, stations or squares; (c) analysing the full data-set or sub-sets. If time and resources permit, grid sampling is the best way to obtain representative data showing the patterns of variation within a study area.
- **Random sampling** is conducted at randomised points within a study area. This is regarded as the most statistically acceptable method. However, (a)

Table 11.5 Species abundance measures

Semi-quantitative abundance ratings are visually estimated using systems such as DAFOR in which: D = dominant; A = abundant; F = frequent; O = occasional; R = rare; with the prefix l (locally) added to any category if required. They are quick to record, but are subjective, approximate, and have limited potential for analysis and presentation. Consequently, they are generally more suited to Phase 1 rather than Phase 2 studies.

Number of individuals is a suitable measure for species which have readily discernible individuals that can be counted. It is not usually applicable in community studies because it has little meaning when comparing species of widely differing size. When measured in defined areas, numbers can be expressed as **density** (number per unit area) and/or as **population size** (in the study area). There are two counting methods:

- **Direct counting** is only generally valid for plants, near-sedentary animals or small populations of animals within defined areas. Occasionally, whole populations (e.g. of trees or nesting birds) can be counted in small areas. More usually, population estimates are derived from samples, e.g. in *quadrats* or by plotless sampling.
- **Indirect Counting Methods** can provide estimates of fairly small populations (e.g. of small mammals in a study area), although certain assumptions must apply, at least approximately. **Mark-recapture methods** (see Krebs 1998, Hill *et al.* 2005, Sutherland 2006) involve capturing and marking a number of individuals, releasing them, and re-sampling after a suitable time interval. Formulae are used to derive the population estimate from the proportion of marked individuals in the recapture sample.

Cover (%) is the percentage of ground occupied by the aerial parts of a species. It is usually measured in quadrats by visual estimation along a vertical projection below (and if necessary above) the observer; but there are alternative methods such as the line intercept method or "point quadratting" (see Kent and Coker 1992, Hill *et al.* 2005, Sutherland 2006). It is suitable for studies of communities which include species of differing size. Visual estimates are prone to observer error (accuracy greater than the nearest 5% is not feasible) and species present as small scattered individuals tend to be under-estimated. The **Domin cover-abundance** scale (see Table C.4) aims to minimise these errors by grouping % cover values in designated bands and assessing abundance (in the strict sense of numbers) for cover values of less than 4%.

Frequency (%) is the percentage of observations in a sample that contain the species, and is derived from presence/absence observations, e.g. in quadrats. Limitations are: (a) it is strictly a measure of distribution rather than abundance and does not discriminate between high density and density that is just sufficient for a species to be present in a large proportion of quadrats; (b) it tends to over-represent small species; (c) it increases in value with increasing quadrat size, so results using different-sized quadrats are not strictly comparable and it is best obtained from a large number (≥ 0) of observations using small quadrats. However, frequency can be a cost-effective method for obtaining large representative samples of communities because it is relatively rapid and free from observer error.

---

spatial distributions of variables are rarely random; (b) the random location of points inhibits the detection of gradients and requires large samples to ensure that the whole of a large area is represented. Consequently, random sampling is often employed in fairly small areas, e.g. within selected grid

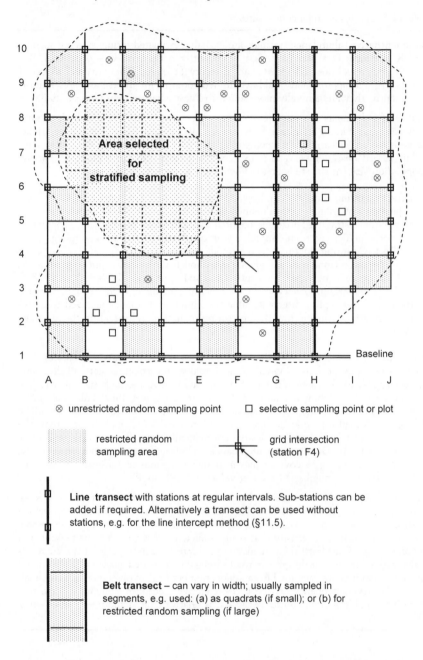

The study area can be a site, a wider area, or a within-site aea such as a habitat patch selected for stratified sampling. Similarly, the size of grid square can vary widely, e.g. from 100m^2 squares to hectads.

Figure 11.8 Spatial sampling pattern options in relation to hypothetical study areas.

squares or habitat patches (when it is called restricted or stratified random sampling).

- **Stratified sampling** involves the selection of fairly small areas of similar character (the "strata") such as fairly homogeneous patches of a habitat type on a site, or on different sites. The areas can be sampled systematically or by stratified random sampling; and can be of equal or varying size (in which case the number of samples is adjusted accordingly). It is widely used where whole-area sampling is unnecessary or impracticable.
- **Selective sampling** is conducted at chosen points because: (a) access to other points is difficult; (b) a variable only occurs in scattered locations; or (c) they are judged to be within homogeneous patches of vegetation that will provide representative samples for comparison with designated types in classifications such as the *National Vegetation Classification* (§C.8). The method is generally considered to be too subjective for other purposes.

The design of **temporal sampling patterns** can be related to aspects such as the selection of sampling intervals during long-term monitoring; but the commonest reason for considering timing in EcIA is seasonal constraints (see §11.4.3).

Sample size is critical because data obtained from small samples are generally unreliable, and cannot be "improved" by the application of sophisticated analytical procedures. For instance, there is little chance that a few randomly or subjectively placed quadrats will provide representative data for a site. There is no completely objective way of determining the minimum requirement, and the number of observations taken is usually a compromise between the need for precision and the cost in terms of labour and time (Krebs 1998). A percentage-of-area target is sometimes applied in vegetation surveys, e.g. to sample 5 per cent of a study area (Mueller-Dombois and Ellenberg 1974). However, this is rarely achieved (especially on large sites) and Greig-Smith (1983) emphasised that sample accuracy is more dependent on the number of observations taken.

11.6.2 Plant surveys

Guidance on surveying and evaluating plant taxa is provided in Hill *et al.* (2005) and Bullock (2006). In general, **vascular plants** are relatively easy to sample during appropriate sampling seasons. Consequently, it should be possible to record all species, and where necessary, to conduct a vegetation survey (§11.6.4) by measuring their abundances.

Sampling **bryophytes** (mosses and liverworts), **lichens** and **fungi** can be more problematical because many species are inconspicuous and/or difficult to identify. However, they are often important components of communities, and bryophytes and lichens should be included in vegetation surveys. In addition, lichens in particular can be useful **indicator species**. Freshwater **macrophytes** and **algae** (including **phytoplankton**) can also pose sampling problems, but should not be ignored. Indeed, macrophytes are important for evaluating many **freshwater habitats** (see §D.3.5).

11.6.3 Animal surveys

Thorough faunal surveys are generally difficult, time-consuming, and require careful planning if successful surveying (and monitoring) is to be achieved. There are six main problems:

1. While the number of vertebrate species may be small, invertebrate species are usually numerous (there are over 22,000 insect species in Britain).
2. Surveys of different taxa often require very different methods and associated expertise in sampling and identification, especially of invertebrates.
3. Many animals are inconspicuous, fugitive or nocturnal, and during parts of the year, many hibernate or have inaccessible life-cycle stages (e.g. most invertebrates).
4. While some site-resident species may only need a particular habitat patch, others may utilise different parts of a site (or wider area) for different purposes such as roosting/shelter, feeding and breeding;
5. Many animals are very mobile, and periodically move between habitat patches, sites or wider areas. Consequently, a species present at a given time may be a casual or regular (e.g. seasonal) visitor; but even transitory migrants are dependent on the site, especially if it is on a regular migration route.
6. Determination of distribution and abundance can be difficult, time consuming and imprecise; and most species vary in abundance from year to year at any site.

The problems inevitably impose limitations on what can be achieved in Phase 2 field surveys, especially when time is limited by developer timescales. Consequently, surveys must be carefully targeted on key and feasible objectives. For example, it is essential to focus on *notable* species, and on the importance (or potential importance) of a site for these species and for animal taxa in general. It may also be important to consider aspects such as potential indirect impacts that might ensue from impacts on particular animal species, especially *keystone species*.

In any case, faunal surveys will be restricted to partial species lists (certainly of invertebrates) and limited quantitative data. Distribution and abundance data may be vital in assessing a species' dependence on a site and the likely viability of the population in the face of impacts; but fully quantitative studies are rarely feasible in EcIA. Similarly, animal *species richness/diversity* estimates are inevitably limited to partial community data, and often to high-profile and/or easily identified taxa such as butterflies.

Vertebrates

Freshwater fish are often important indicators of ecosystem integrity, and are of great interest to anglers and the public. They are rarely important in terms of nature conservation, since most British native species are widespread and common. However, survey data on salmonids may be important (populations are generally declining) and more general surveys of fish may also be relevant because of their economic and recreational importance, and their significance in ecosystem function.

Fish can be surveyed by a variety of methods (e.g. see Côté and Perrow 2006, EA 2007, Giles *et al.* 2005). The main techniques are netting, trapping, electro-fishing, hydro-acoustics, and direct observations of breeding habitats (mainly for salmonids). Surveys usually focus on estimating general fish populations or species diversity in order to provide data for habitat evaluation, management or restoration; and fish are one of the elements employed for assessing the ecological status of rivers (see §10.7.3). Specific surveys and measures may be undertaken to maintain populations of the few rare species (e.g. vendace and powan). Measures for the conservation of rare species are reviewed in Maitland and Lyle (1993).

Amphibians are usually surveyed at their breeding sites (usually ponds) during the breeding season. This varies between species and in different areas, e.g. the common frog typically spawns in late January in Cornwall but not until early April in parts of the Pennines (Swan and Oldham 1993a). Juveniles and some adults remain in or near water during the summer, so summer surveys of ponds and surrounding areas can provide additional data.

The main methods used are: (a) pond netting for individuals in the water; (b) "torching" at night; (c) bottle trapping; and (d) searches for frog and toad egg masses during the breeding season. Egg searches have proved to be a quick and effective means of locating the specially protected great crested newt. Using a combination of survey methods generally proves more effective than one alone e.g. searches for egg masses in spring, followed by summer netting for juveniles and any remaining adults. However, these methods cannot give more than a crude idea of population numbers, and collecting accurate population data can be time consuming and expensive. The most frequently used method involves ring-fencing the breeding site to intercept animals moving to or from the surrounding area. Further details about amphibian survey methods can be found in Halliday 2006 and Latham *et al.* 2005a).

Two of Britain's six native species (great crested newt and natterjack toad) are protected by law, so it is an offence to net or handle them without a licence from the relevant SNCO. It is also illegal to damage their habitat, including the terrestrial areas around the breeding site that they inhabit for most of the year. Great crested newts are relatively widespread in England, and so frequently feature in EcIAs. Gent and Gibson (2003) and Gibb and Foster (2000) provide information on amphibian conservation in the UK.

Reptiles should be considered whenever a *receptor* site is likely to host any British species, which are all protected (EN 2004b). A national survey of reptile sites was produced by Swan and Oldham (1993b). Sampling is seasonally restricted (Figure 11.7), and very hot/dry or cold/wet weather is generally unfavourable. It usually involves transect walking and/or arrays of artificial refuges (Reading 1996). Guidance is provided in Blomberg and Shine (2006), Gent (1996), Gent and Gibson (2003), and Latham *et al.* (2005b).

Birds figure to some extent in the majority of EcIAs. The main aims of a bird survey should be: (a) to evaluate sites and habitats (including small and linear habitats) for birds in general, and for notable species in particular, bearing in mind that habitats may be utilised for various purposes and that most species need to move between them; and (b) to record the presence of species, and where possible to estimate the sizes of populations and their vulnerability to potential impacts.

Bird surveys require expertise in both visual identification and the recognition of bird calls/song. They are time consuming and require repeat sampling, which is seasonally restricted (Figure 11.7) and affected by weather conditions (birds may be less active and conspicuous in wet and windy weather).

Guidance on bird census techniques is provided in Bibby *et al.* (2000), Gibbons and Gregory (2006), Gilbert *et al.* (1998), and Mustoe *et al.* (2005). On land, the most suitable method for EcIA is likely to be transect walking, which can be used to estimate breeding territories and densities. However, its value may be limited in small and/or heterogeneous sites, when the point count method (using randomly located observation points) may be more appropriate. Other options include flightline surveys, radio tracking and collision mortality monitoring.

Regional, national and supra-national population data are available for many bird species (e.g. Gibbons *et al.* 1993); so if the local populations can be quantified, both they and the sites that support them can also be evaluated in terms of their representation. Significant overwintering populations of wildfowl and waders are likely to be already monitored by the Wildfowl and Wetlands Trust (WWT).

Mammal surveys are likely to focus on notable species, a number of which are protected, and for some of which a surveyor must be licensed. For survey purposes, mammals can be divided into three groups – bats, small mammals and larger mammals – each requiring different survey techniques. General guidance is provided by Bennett *et al.* (2005), Corbet and Harris (1991) and Krebs (2006).

All British **bats** and their roosts are protected, and a licence is needed for any survey method that involves catching bats, or may disturb them in their roosts or hibernation sites. Bat survey techniques are described in Altringham (2003), Mitchell-Jones and McLeish (2004) and Stebbings *et al.* (2005), and advice on methods and personnel can be sought from the Bat Conservation Trust (BCT), local bat group, LA Conservation officer or SNCO. Methods include the detection of roosts, foraging bats, and flight pathways, or a combination, e.g. of emergence/foraging surveys in conjunction with earlier surveys of roosts. Roosts may be found in places such as buildings, trees, caves, mines and tunnels. They may be detected by the presence of staining, droppings and insect remains, although it may be necessary to confirm their presence by an ultrasonic or visual search. Flying bats may be observed (visually and by ultrasonic detectors) from fixed points or along transects. Suitable sampling periods are indicated in Figure 11.7.

Small mammals include the shrews, voles and mice. Survey methods are reviewed in Sibbald *et al.* (2006). They include the use of hair tubes (sections of plastic pipe containing sticky pads to which hairs adhere) or nest tubes (e.g. for dormice); but identification and enumeration is best achieved by live trapping and mark-recapture (Table 11.5) using Longworth traps (Gurnell and Flowerdew 2006). A licence is required for trapping shrews. Somewhat different methods are needed for aquatic species, i.e. water vole (Strachan and Moorhouse 2006) and water shrew (Carter and Churchfield 2006a, 2006b), and for species which spend much of the time above ground, e.g. the dormouse (Bright *et al.* 1996, Bright and Morris 2005, Chanin and Woods 2003) fat dormouse (Hoodless and Morris 1993) and harvest mouse.

Larger mammals include the badger (Harris *et al.* 1989), brown hare (GWCT Undated, Langbein *et al.* 1999), deer (Mayle *et al.* 1999), fox, hedgehog, mole, mountain hare, pine marten (Strachan *et al.* 1996), otter (EA 2008, EN 2003) polecat, rabbit, squirrels (Bryce *et al.* 1997, Ayrshire Red Squirrel Group 2004), stoat, weasel and wildcat. Although these can be identified by direct observation, many are fugitive or nocturnal, and survey methods often utilise: (a) hair tubes and live traps (for smaller species); (b) identification of tracks, droppings, excavations, feeding damage, and habitations such as burrows, setts, holts or dreys. Within the scope of an EcIA survey it is rarely possible to determine population sizes, but communal groups such as badgers can be counted when emerging from a sett (bearing in mind that, under the *Protection of Badgers Act 1992*, it is an offence to disturb a badger sett). A major problem with larger mammals is that individuals are often wide ranging and may use a site on a seasonal basis; so time-limited recording may miss important species or misrepresent the importance of a site to a species.

Invertebrates

Sampling invertebrates can be difficult and time consuming. Even a limited survey will produce a large number of individuals and species; and specimens from a day's sampling may require several days for sorting and identification, usually by specialists.

Terrestrial vertebrate surveys are seasonally restricted and should ideally involve repeat sampling (Figure 11.7). Species can be easily missed if they are in a concealed phase when the survey is conducted, e.g. soil dwelling and stem boring larvae, and the egg phase of many species. In addition, the activity of many species is restricted to particular times of day or weather conditions.

Consequently, surveys must be carefully targeted, e.g. on **notable** species, target groups and **indicator species** (which can sometimes attest the general suitability of habitats for invertebrates). Target groups suggested by IEA (1995) include Carabidae (ground beetles), Lepidoptera (butterflies and moths), Orthoptera (crickets and grasshoppers) and Syrphidae (hoverflies).

The question of where to sample is critical. Habitats likely to be important for invertebrates are fairly easy to recognise (see §D.3.4), but target species and groups will vary with habitat type (Brooks 1993). Moreover, different species, and even different life stages of the same species, may utilise different micro-habitats, e.g. ranging from ground level to the vegetation canopy, or on different plant species or even different parts of the same plant.

Survey methods for terrestrial invertebrates can be divided into observer dependent methods, which are carried out by the investigator in the field, and observer independent methods, which employing traps of various types. Commonly used methods are outlined in **Table 11.6**. Most of these can also be employed for sampling *wetland* and semi-aquatic species (associated with the margins of water bodies). Further information is given in Ausden and Drake (2006), Brooks (1993), Hill *et al.* (2005), New (1998) and Southwood and Henderson (2000).

Aquatic invertebrates make up a large proportion of the diversity of most freshwater habitats and often contribute significantly to the conservation value of a site. They are also used as biotic indicators of water quality in freshwater ecosystems, and for this purpose the preferred group is widely considered to be benthic *macroinvertebrates* (see §10.7.3).

Table 11.6 Methods for sampling terrestrial invertebrates

Observer dependent methods

Direct searching and recording in selected habitat/vegetation patches. It is not normally quantitative, can lead to misidentification, only records species that are active at the time, and tends to be limited to species that are conspicuous and/or common in the study area.

Transect walking involves the observation, identification and enumeration of species (usually only of butterflies and day-flying moths) along a set route, within prescribed time and weather conditions.

Sweep netting involves a hand held net swept through vegetation (that is not woody, thorny or wet) up to 1m in height. It collects most species from the vegetation (except the basal parts), but flying insects often escape. It can be quantitative if a standard number of sweeps is taken, but sweeps in different vegetation types are not directly comparable because of differing resistance to the net.

Swish netting is like sweep netting but is restricted to the air boundary immediately above vegetation. It is especially good at collecting Diptera (flies) and Hymenoptera (bees and wasps).

Suction sampling uses a portable vacuum to collect invertebrates from the ground layer and/or basal parts of vegetation. It can be efficient in dry conditions and where there is little vegetation litter, and can provide quantitative data if a set number of samples are obtained.

Soil samples can be taken for identification and enumeration of soil invertebrates. A variety of physical or chemical extraction methods are used to extract the organisms from the soil samples.

Beating uses a stout stick to knock invertebrates off vegetation onto a sheet, from which they are collected. It is usually used to sample the fauna of individual tree species. With care, it can be used to obtain quantitative data, but is not practical in wet conditions.

Subsidiary methods are used by many experts for particular groups. They include observing flower visitors, hand searching vegetation for plant grazers (especially molluscs), stone turning especially for beetles, molluscs and millipedes, and investigating litter and dead wood for decomposers.

Table 11.6 (*continued*)

Observer independent methods

Pitfall traps are placed on a regular grid within selected areas, and provide quantitative data, mainly for ground dwelling beetles, which fall into the traps. They usually contain a killing/preserving fluid.

Malaise traps intercept flying insects by a net, and funnel them into a collection vessel. They can collect large numbers of insects (especially Diptera and Hymenoptera) and obtain quantitative and comparative data, but do not discriminate between insects resident in or flying through the area.

Sticky traps usually consist of a mesh screen on which a viscous oil is applied. They can be used like malaise traps or placed within vegetation. Fragile species may become damaged in trying to escape from the trap, and samples have to be removed using a solvent.

Water traps rely on the fact that a variety of flying insects (especially flower visitors) are attracted to coloured surfaces. They are simple to use but selective.

Light traps attract night flying insects, especially if they emit ultra-violet wavelengths. They are useful but require a power source, are not easily transported, and may sample species that are flying over a site rather associated with it.

Emergence traps usually consist of a closed mesh canopy (placed over vegetation) and a collecting vessel, and are designed to collect adult flying insects that were in a developmental stage when the trap was erected. They can be used quantitatively, but must be in place for long periods.

Ideally surveys should allow the assessment of the value of a whole site, and of habitats (e.g. mud or submerged plants) within it; so samples from different habitats should be kept separate, and should be replicated to assess whether perceived differences between habitats are likely to be real. At least two seasonal surveys should be carried out, and should include an early spring visit to record mayfly and caddisfly fauna. Identification to species level should be undertaken, at least in the case of notable species and taxa for which keys are available (see IEEM 2007).

The most commonly used sampling method for aquatic macro-invertebrates is the use of pond nets. However, there are many different techniques, including "kick sampling" and the use of dredges, grabs and traps, which may be appropriate under certain circumstances (see Ausden and Drake 2006, EA 1999, Kerrison *et al.* 2005, New 1998, Pond Action 1998, and Southwood and Henderson 2000). For small standing water sites, standardised survey methods have been developed which use a three-minute hand-net sample from all significant habitats, and form the basis of the PSYM system for assessing the ecological quality of ponds and small lakes (see §D.3.5 and §10.7.3). A three-minute hand-net method is also widely used in river surveys (see EA 1999). Additional surveys are often conducted for adult dragonflies, either as they emerge or on the wing (Plant *et al.* 2005).

11.6.4 Habitat surveys

Phase 2 habitat surveys normally focus on establishing the conservation status, and susceptibility to impacts, of whole "community habitats" (§11.2.5). However, they may also supplement Phase 1 findings on aspects such as habitat suitability for **notable** animal species (see §D.3.4). Habitat survey methods are reviewed in Hill *et al.* (2005).

Terrestrial and wetland habitat surveys can consist largely of vegetation surveys, together with data on relevant environmental factors (§11.6.5). In the UK, they generally utilise the *National Vegetation Classification* (NVC) (§C.8) which is recommended by IEA (1995) as the main phase 2 vegetation survey method for EcIA. All NVC community descriptions include information on environmental factors that relate to the community's habitat requirements. Surveys may also include studies on particular aspects such as **species diversity**, which is usually calculated from species abundance data using numerical indices (see Hawksworth 1995, Kent and Coker 1992, Krebs 1998). However, species diversity values must be interpreted with caution (see §D.3.2).

Occasionally, there may be a need to conduct an "extended Phase 2" site survey using a systematic sampling pattern rather than the selective sampling procedure employed for NVC studies. For example, if potential changes in ground water level or quality may affect the **integrity** of a high-value **wetland** site, it may be important to quantify the community-environment patterns and relationships in order to assess the threats and formulate mitigation measures (e.g. Morris 2002). The results from this type of survey can be analysed by GIS (Chapter 14) and/or by **multivariate analysis**.

Freshwater habitat surveys can utilise the NVC. However, survey and classification methods designed specifically for standing waters, rivers or ditches, are generally more appropriate. These are outlined in §C.9, §D.3.5 and §10.7.3.

11.6.5 Environmental variables and site history

Information on a range of environmental factors may be important e.g.: to understand environmental relationships of species or communities; to assist in evaluating a site's conservation value and/or its potential for habitat creation; or to facilitate impact prediction. Relevant factors may include: topography/aspect; local climate; soil conditions, water quality; river morphology; pollution; and land/habitat management.

Existing data may be available (e.g. from sources listed in Table 11.3), and new data may be collected for other components of the EIA, e.g. climate, soils and water. If necessary, additional data can be obtained using the methods described in Chapters 8, 9 and 10 of this book, and in reviews such as Jones *et al.* (2006). Some variables, such as pH, conductivity and dissolved oxygen, can be readily measured in the field. However, detailed chemical analysis is time consuming; and if relationships between the results and biological data are required, it may be important to employ a sampling pattern whereby one sample can be associated with the mean of several biological observations.

An understanding of current ecological systems can often be facilitated by knowledge of past conditions. Historical and archaeological information may be available (see Box 7.1); and evidence on ecological conditions may be obtainable using palaeo-ecological techniques such as dendroclimatology and analysis of sediment (including peat) cores (e.g. see Birks and Birks 2004, Fritts 2001, Moore 1986). Such evidence can provide valuable information on changes that have occurred in a range of aspects, e.g., land cover/use, climate, hydrology and the biota. However, the required techniques are time-consuming and expensive, and existing data for specific receptor sites are rarely available. Past conditions can also be inferred from current ecological features such as floristic richness and *indicator species*.

11.6.6 Description and evaluation of the baseline conditions

It is essential that the work on different ecological aspects is coordinated, and that the findings are integrated to produce a clear description and evaluation of the baseline conditions. This should include the following.

- The aims and scope of the investigations.
- The findings of the desk study, indicating sources of the information obtained.
- Clear descriptions of the methods employed in the field surveys, with information on where and when they were carried out (and weather conditions where pertinent).
- Clear presentation of the results including species lists, tables of quantitative data, clear descriptions and maps of sites and habitats and, where relevant, charts/graphs and GIS presentations.
- Indications of limitations (e.g. time restrictions and data accuracy) and uncertainties.
- An assessment of the environmental factors (including management) controlling the current ecological systems, and of existing trends.
- An evaluation of all key receptors including: conservation value and status; aspects such as habitat suitability and potential; and susceptibility to impacts.

11.7 Impact prediction

11.7.1 Changes without the development

In order to make valid assessments about the ecological impacts of a project, it is important to consider what ecosystem changes may occur in its absence. Such changes can result from intrinsic ecosystem processes, or from "external" factors, whether or not these are caused by human activities.

The most significant intrinsic changes over the relevant time scales are likely to be associated with ecological succession (Figure 11.3). Precise outcomes of this are difficult to foresee, but general predictions can be made, e.g. that unmanaged grasslands and **heathlands** will give way to scrub and eventually a climax community such as woodland.

External influences that may cause changes in the absence of the project include: climate change; changes in farming practices/policy and countryside access (e.g. under CROW); biodiversity management (e.g. HAPs); water resource depletion caused by abstraction; and cumulative impacts of land development, including other local projects.

These influences may have differing implications in relation to a project, e.g. that:

- the project's impacts would/would not contribute significantly to cumulative impacts;
- the project's impacts on a habitat/site would not be important because its ecological value will decline anyway;
- although a habitat/site may not be considered worthy of protection in its current condition, its value will increase if impacts from the project are avoided.

11.7.2 Types of ecological impact

In relation to the various types of impact referred to in the EIA legislation (§1.2.3), it is important to remember that, because of the interactive nature of ecosystems, almost any direct impact will have secondary (knock-on) effects. It may be useful to consider the duration and reversibility of ecological impacts in terms of three types of disturbance: pulse (temporary); press (sustained); and catastrophic (highly destructive/irreversible). These are explained further in §12.5.3).

Developments can have **positive ecological impacts** including habitat creation, especially where adequate management is also provided. For example:

- sensitive and sustainable redevelopment on "brownfield" sites can improve their ecological value, e.g. by incorporating features such as "green networks" (e.g. see Angold *et al.* 2006, Barker 1997, Harrison *et al.* 1995), or providing new habitats and space for locally indigenous species, e.g. by using local seed initiatives.
- new roadside verges can become valuable wildlife corridors and habitats, especially for grassland communities, although a net positive impact is only likely in urban or intensive agriculture areas – not where the road crosses valuable *semi-natural* habitats.

Examples of **negative ecological impacts** generated by major impact sources are shown in **Figure 11.9** and discussed below. Publications on impacts associated with particular development types include: major civil engineering projects (Carpenter 2001); cross-country pipelines (DTI 1992); roads (Bignall *et al.* 2004, ERM 1996, Highways Agency *et al.* 1993, PAA 1994); railways (Carpenter 1994); and waste treatment facilities (Petts and Eduljee 1994).

	Linear projects, e.g. roads	Heavy industry and power	Light industry and urban	Mineral extraction	Landfill / waste disposal	Recreation and tourism	Agriculture and forestry
Habitat loss and fragmentation	⬤	⬤	⬤	⬤	?	•	⬤
Habitat damage	⬤	⬤	⬤	⬤	•	⬤	•
Wildlife disturbance	⬤	⬤	⬤	•	•	⬤	•
Direct mortality	⬤	•	•	•	•	•	•
Pollution	⬤	⬤	⬤	•	⬤	•	⬤
Hydrological impacts	⬤	⬤	⬤	⬤	⬤	•	⬤

• impacts usually minor and/or localised

⬤ impacts often major and/or extensive

? depends if the land has already been taken, e.g. for mineral extraction

The indicated magnitudes are for illustrative purposes only, and will vary in relation to specific developments and receptors.

Figure 11.9 Examples and approximate relative magnitudes of negative ecological impacts associated with various types of impact source.

Habitat destruction and fragmentation

This is probably the greatest single threat to biodiversity from development in the UK. The amount of semi-natural habitat destruction that is caused directly by a new development will depend largely on how much exists within the project's "red line" (construction and final landtake areas). Some loss, if only of habitats such as hedgerows, is usually inevitable. The significance of habitat loss depends on a range of factors including:

- the ecological/conservation value of the habitat, and the degree to which notable species depend on it;
- the degree to which displaced species can migrate to, and survive in, other suitable sites/habitat patches (which will depend on the availability of such

sites, and on factors such as the existing density of the species in them, and hence the potential severity of competition);

- the quantity off habitat lost, and the degree to which its loss will affect the fragmentation and integrity of remaining habitats;
- indirect impacts such as increased flood risk downstream resulting from development on floodplains (in addition to the loss of valuable wetland habitats by landtake).

Fragmentation has two primary effects: (a) it splits a habitat patch into two or more smaller patches; and (b) it creates barriers between the remaining habitat patches, resulting in (or increasing) their isolation, and making them unavailable to some species. Habitat fragmentation is one of the indicators or sustainable development in the UKBAP, and is specified as a particular threat in a number of SAPs.

When they are part of a close-knit mosaic, **small habitat patches** can promote biodiversity (see §D.3.4); but when they are "islands" in a fragmented landscape, they generally support fewer species, and smaller populations, than large patches of the same habitat type. Moreover, their biodiversity tends to decline over time (Joshi *et al.* 2006). One reason is that a small patch may not contain sufficient resources, such as food, water, cover or habitation sites, to support viable populations of some species (Teitje and Berlund 2000). However, there are additional factors including the following.

- Resident species populations are more susceptible to local catastrophic events such as severe drought or fire, and some species need several habitat patches within a given area, e.g. over time, the marsh fritillary butterfly tends be lost from some patches (in response to parasite pressure) and colonise others (EN 2004a).
- Small patches are less likely to be colonised, especially by habitat "specialists" (Joshi *et al.* 2006), and are susceptible to edge effects and isolation.

Edge effects are associated with the increased length of habitat edge relative to its area, i.e. of the boundary/area ratio. As a result, small habitat patches are susceptible to (a) "external" impacts such as pollution, physical damage and disturbance – which may be more important for some species than reductions in patch size *per se* (Kirby 1995), and (b) invasion by "foreign" species from neighbouring areas. In addition, habitat edges have different environmental conditions from their interiors, and a large edge/area ratio favours edge-living species at the expense of core species (Bender *et al.* 1998), which are usually more characteristic of, and dependent on, the core habitat type. On the other hand, edge communities are ecotones (§11.2.2) that can be species rich, and may host notable species.

An important aspect of **isolation** is the ability (or not) of species to move between habitat patches. According to the theory of ***metapopulations*** a "sink" sub-population in a small habitat patch (with insufficient resources to sustain it) may be augmented by immigration from a "source" (reservoir) population living in a larger habitat patch – but only so long as the two populations are not isolated. Consequently, the viability of many species populations in fragmented landscapes may be affected by (a) their dispersal capabilities, which vary considerably (see below), and (b) the degree of isolation between habitat patches – and hence the distances (and likely number and severity of barriers) between them. In the longer term, lack of genetic exchange may also lead to the decline of isolated sub-populations. Some migrant species (e.g. birds) are less affected (Bender *et al.* 1998), and small isolated patches can still act as *stepping stone habitats* for these species.

New barriers are created by fragmentation, the removal of interconnecting habitats, or the interposition of a "hostile" feature (e.g. a road, fence, building or cultivated field) between habitat patches. A barrier may be *physical* (a species cannot cross it), *behavioural* (a species is capable but unwilling to cross it), or *hazardous* (a species may suffer high mortality in attempting to cross it – and the importance of barriers varies between species (Eycott *et al.* 2007). For example:

- some species have efficient dispersal mechanisms that are not seriously effected by most local barriers;
- some species have very limited dispersal ability, and such "low-mobility" species (a) are restricted to remaining habitat patches, and (b) are unlikely to re-colonise isolated habitat patches;
- animals such as badgers, deer and otters have wide habitat-area requirements that may exceed the areas of remaining patches (or of patches to which they have been displaced by development) and must risk crossing hazardous barriers;
- animals such as amphibians may have to cross barriers in order to reach their breeding habitats.

An additional problem that may follow from the isolation of small habitat patches is that conservation management practices, such as low-intensity grazing, may be prevented because the remaining areas are too small or are not accessible.

The Dorset heaths provide a good example of fragmentation effects. In 1759, the heaths consisted of ten large blocks, separated only by rivers; by 1978 they were divided into 768 fragments (Webb and Haskins 1980) and the trend has continued since then. Webb and Rose (1994) provide evidence of associated losses of heathland species (especially from small, isolated patches) since 1962. Much of the heathland loss has been through forestry and changes in management, including cessation of low-intensity grazing (EN 1997), but a major factor, especially in the south-east of the county, has been urban development. The effects of this are reviewed by Haskins (2000) and summarised in **Figure 11.10**.

There is increasing evidence that habitat fragmentation inhibits regional dispersal for many species, especially when the remaining habitat patches are small (e.g. Collingham and Huntley 2000); and this has serious implications in

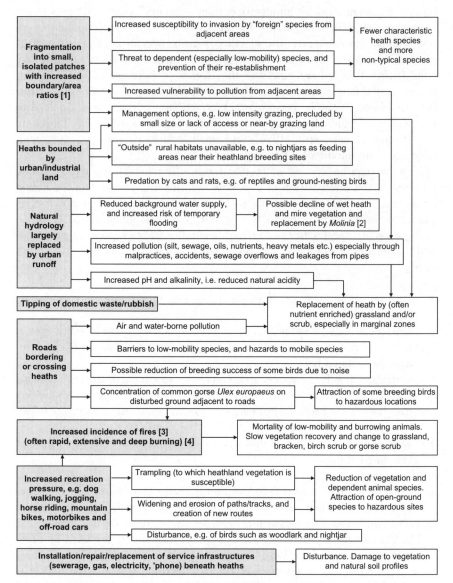

[1] Very few heaths in or around the urban areas are over 100ha, and most are no more than 5ha.
[2] *Molinia caerulea* (purple moor grass) is relatively tolerant of fire, grazing, fairly dry conditions and both low and high soil pHs (Grime *et al.* 1988).
[3] For example, since 1990: 179 fires on Canford heath (urban); 2 on Hartland Moor (rural).
[4] Controlled fire has long been used as a management tool on heathlands, but in conditions (e.g. in winter) when it will not be rapid, extensive or deep burning.

Figure 11.10 Impacts of urban spread on the heathlands of south-east Dorset.
Source: Adapted from Haskins (2000).

relation to climate change. The MONARCH report (Walmsley *et al.* 2007), and PI (2005) predict that the survival of many species will depend on their ability to disperse, and that many (including notable species) will find this very difficult unless action is taken. The need to address these issues in spatial planning is presented in Piper *et al.* (2006), and the MONARCH report suggests that action should include: (a) conserving all semi-natural habitats, and creating **buffer zones/ strips** to protect them from negative effects of adjoining land use; and (b) extend-ing the area of semi-natural habitats and increasing connectivity by "making intervening agricultural, forestry or urban areas more permeable and less hostile to wildlife rather than simply linking fragmented semi-natural habitats through slim green corridors".

Habitat damage, wildlife disturbance and direct mortality

Habitat damage (e.g. by vegetation trampling or removal, and soil compaction or erosion (§9.6.2)) may be associated particularly with the construction phase of projects; but it does not follow that this is temporary or reversible, especially when the receptors are long established semi-natural habitats. Chronic and pro-gressive habitat damage can also result from many forms of increased human activ-ity that a development may generate, e.g. traffic and recreation/visitor pressure.

Habitat damage can also involve the destruction of **microhabitats**, and this can affect the whole ecosystem. Such damage can be caused by simplifying hab-itats. For example, river straightening often gives more uniform flow regimes, water depths, and bank profiles, all of which reduce habitat complexity and associated plant and invertebrate diversity (see Table 10.7). Similarly, many species live in (or need) different habitats at various stages of their lifecycle. For example fish fry benefit from backwaters or bays in which they can develop, and the adults of some aquatic animals need terrestrial habitats. Removing any one of these habitats, or blocking the migration route between them, can therefore elimin-ate those species from the community.

Wildlife disturbance can result from a variety of sources, e.g. construction, traffic, or visitor pressure, and can involve a number of factors, including visual impacts, noise, trampling, and night-time light pollution. The susceptibility of animals to disturbance often varies seasonally, e.g. in relation to breeding periods **(Figure 11.11)**. However, vulnerable periods may not be immediately obvious. For instance, invertebrates with mobile adult phases (e.g. butterflies and other flying insects) may be most vulnerable when in developmental stages (eggs, lar-vae and pupae) because of damage to their foodplants and pupal sites. Most inver-tebrates are also vulnerable in winter because they are dormant and hence cannot escape. Permanent vertebrate residents are most sensitive to disturbance during the breeding season, but some species may be also vulnerable in overwintering periods, and the risk to migrant birds is during their visit period. All British bats are dependent on buildings or trees for their roost sites, and if a development is likely to affect these the appropriate SNCO must be consulted and allowed time to advise.

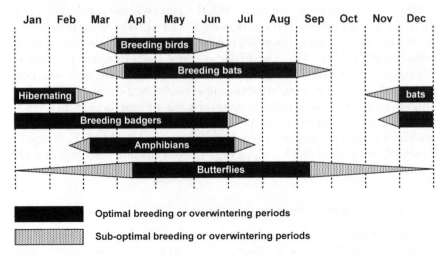

Figure 11.11 Seasonal periods in which some animal taxa are particularly sensitive to impacts.

Direct mortality can result from factors such as vegetation destruction, trampling and fire. Roads present serious long-term threats, especially to animals that need to cross them. During a 12-month survey of road deaths throughout Britain, 5,675 mammal casualties and 142 bird of prey casualties were recorded (Mammal Society 2002); and the Wildlife Trusts have reported that road casualties account for 60 per cent of recorded otter deaths in the UK (TWT 2001).

Pollution

Any development is bound to generate some regular or accidental pollution. Industrial, urban and road developments are regular sources of a wide range of atmospheric pollutants and water-borne pollutants (Chapters 8 and 10). It is important to remember that:

- pollutants can enter and circulate in **biogeochemical cycles**, and that those carried in air or water can affect ecosystems far from their source;
- some pollutants **bioaccumulate**, and **bioamplification** in food chains can have serious consequences, especially for top carnivores;
- some pollutants can undergo **biotransformation** in the environment or within the bodies of individuals (Connell *et al.* 1999).

Most pollution is chronic, but accidental pollution can be a major threat, especially from heavy industry and transport, and developers should be asked to provide a **risk assessment** (including a worst case scenario) for this type of impact (see Chapter 13).

Atmospheric pollution can affect vegetation and animals directly, or indirectly through environmental changes such as those in the chemistry of soils and waters (§8.1.2 and §9.6.2). **Water pollution** can affect terrestrial ecosystems wherever polluted water periodically inundates the ground surface or soil, e.g. as *leachates* from landfill sites, mine workings or surface deposits, or as runoff from urban and road surfaces. In addition, salt-rich spray regularly falls in the "splash zones" of road verges during winter months, and influences species composition within these zones. However, water pollution is particularly detrimental in wetland and aquatic ecosystems (see below).

Hydrological impacts: changes in water quantity and water quality

In addition to changes in precipitation associated with climate change, the **water quantity** features of hydrological systems are affected by a range of impacts from a variety of sources (see §10.8). The principle concerns in relation to ecosystems are changes in water level and water flow regimes.

Changes in **water level and stability** can affect most ecosystems and are often critical for *wetland* and *freshwater ecosystems*, and the seasonal water regime can be particularly important, e.g. in marshes and wet grasslands during the breeding season of wetland birds, many of which need a mosaic of varying water levels (EA 2007). Some water level fluctuation is natural in all open water ecosystems, but they are damaged when this exceeds what is normal for the system (especially if it is erratic) or if water level changes are permanent.

Lowered water levels can be particularly damaging to rivers and wetlands. For example, many fens have been lost or degraded as a result land drainage or water abstraction (Fojt 1992), and a recent report (BCG 2007) highlights 101 rivers affected, and 201 wetland SSSIs in danger of drying out, due to abstraction for agricultural irrigation or public water supply. Lowering of water table levels can also increase the incidence of soil drought in terrestrial ecosystems.

Raised water levels can include the increased incidence and duration of inundation and waterlogging of *floodplains* outside the winter flood-risk period, which may adversely affect invertebrate diversiy (EA 2007); and can be particularly damaging to temporary water habitats, such as seasonal ponds and streams, which may host specialised animals and plants of high conservation interest (Bratton 1990).

Changes in **water flow** are particularly important to watercourses, but also affect standing water bodies and *minerotrophic* wetlands such as fens. The effects of flow go far beyond increases in water velocity, because this is inevitably accompanied by changes in other variables such as dissolved oxygen concentration, nutrient fluxes and sediment type and volume. An increase or decrease, can indirectly damage communities adapted to the prevailing flow, and may irreversibly modify the physical and biological environment.

Water quality varies naturally in relation to local climate and (especially) geology. It makes a major contribution to the diversity of wetland and freshwater systems, which is reflected in associated habitat classifications (Appendix C).

Thus each type is dependent on a narrow range of water quality, and its integrity is threatened by any deviation beyond this range; and since the majority of freshwater and wetland systems are intimately linked to the surrounding land, any change in their **catchments** may influence their water quality.

The main types of pollutant and pollution affecting freshwater ecosystems are: organic matter; thermal pollution; acidification; **eutrophication**; sediments; metals, micro-organics, and other harmful chemicals; and oils. The main sources and effects of these are discussed in §10.3 and §10.8.

Contamination of freshwater systems by non-mobile elements (e.g. phosphorus) or non-biodegradable toxins, must be minimised since their effect may be permanent and effectively irreversible. Such impacts are most likely to have significant effects on standing water systems, such as lakes, which act as cumulative sinks for sediment; but watrcourses can also be affected, and while new pollution events may have little effect in an already polluted reach of a river, they may progressively damage downstream sections.

Changes in the competitive balance between species

Changes in the species composition of a community often occur because the competitive balance is altered in favour of species that are more tolerant of new conditions. This frequently favours "generalists" at the expense of "specialists" (§11.2.1) which are often notable species or species confined to high-value habitats. For example, as indicated in Figure 11.10, changes in environmental conditions can lead to the replacement of heathland species by bracken, gorse and tolerant grass species. Native UK species, such as bracken, have also gained competitive edge and become **invasive species** because they are unpalatable and/or toxic. However, a more serious problem throughout the UK is that caused by non-native ("alien", "exotic") species that have been introduced (sometimes accidentally) and lack natural competitors or predators. They replace native species, are difficult to control or remove, and are having detrimental effects in many terrestrial and freshwater habitats. Indeed, PI (2005 and Undated) state that non-native invasive plant species pose one of the most serious threats to native UK plants, and predict that climate change is likely to favour these species. Developers should avoid the inappropriate use of alien species in landscape schemes, which can lead to invasion of adjacent semi-natural areas.

11.7.3 Methods of impact prediction

It is relatively easy to identify primary ecological impacts such as habitat loss or fragmentation, but much more difficult predict their effects, or even to itemise the numerous potential secondary (knock-on) impacts that may be generated. **Cumulative impacts** are particularly difficult to assess, partly because virtually all negative ecological impacts are bound to add to general pressures on biodiversity. Guidance on the assessment of indirect and cumulative impacts is provided in CEAA (1999), EC (1999) and LUC (2006).

The techniques outlined in Table 1.1 can assist in ecological impact prediction. GIS can be particularly useful, especially if used in conjunction with a system for analysing quantitative data (Chapter 14). Mathematical and statistical models have been used as research tools in ecology for many years, and are increasing employed in relation to aspects such as: risk assessment (Chapter 13) including estimation of minimum critical areas and viable populations (e.g. Burgman *et al.* 1993); **ecotoxicology** (e.g. Connell *et al.* 1999); **critical loads** (see UKNFC in Table 11.3); and hydrological processes (see Table 10.5). However, their use in EcIA is limited by:

- the current lack of knowledge and understanding of ecosystems' complex interactive processes, and hence of how species and communities will respond to impacts;
- the unsuitability of many models for "off the peg" use;
- expense and time constraints; *and*
- the difficulty of obtaining sufficient quantitative data on impacts and/or baseline conditions.

The problems outlined above mean that impact predictions often have to be qualitative, but every effort should be made to make precise, and where possible quantitative, predictions. The procedures recommended by IEEM (2006) and the *Design manual for roads and bridges* (DMRB) (Highways Agency *et al.* 1993) aim to increase the transparency and rigour ecological impact assessment, and EA (2007) provides guidance on identifying source–pathway–receptor links for impacts on freshwater and wetland sites. However, these methodologies still require a large input of professional judgement; and a degree of uncertainty is inevitable, and should be acceptable provided that it is clearly stated in the EIS. Two important aspects of impact prediction are the assessment of magnitude and significance.

Impact magnitude (severity) is relatively easy to predict for direct impacts that can be quantified. For example, landtake and extents of physical damage (and associated impacts such as habitat loss and fragmentation) can be measured and/or mapped; and if the distributions of species populations, habitats and communities are known, the proportionate direct losses from these can be estimated (although it is important to avoid over-reliance on simple measures such as percentage-of-site affected, which can be misleading because the loss of even a small area may affect the *integrity* of a site). However, the majority of impacts are difficult or impossible to quantify; and even when some quantification is possible, final assessments of impact magnitude will usually be restricted to qualitative estimates such as *slight, moderate* or *large*.

Impact significance is a function of impact magnitude and the conservation value, sensitivity, and resilience of ecological receptors. Conservation value can normally be assessed in relation to the criteria outlined in Appendix D, but care is needed: to avoid under-valuing non-designated and small sites/habitats; and to consider the integrity of whole sites. Some ecosystem types are known to be more sensitive or resilient than others, but assessing impact significance in relation to these attributes can be can be one of the most difficult aspects of ecological impact prediction. One approach is to consider each potential impact in turn and assess whether any changes are likely to lie within the natural range of perturbation for the ecosystem, or for any significant element of it. For example, it may help to consider the most sensitive species and its position in the food chain. Such potential changes should be considered both in the short and long term, and for all phases of the development. As a rule, where predicted impacts are within the normal range of the system, the level of change is likely to be acceptable. However, where a normal range is exceeded, assessment of impact significance will still have to rely on expert judgement.

Guidance on determining ecological impact significance is provided in EN (1999) and IEEM (2006); and several structured procedures have been developed. These include the *Transport Analysis Guidance* (TAG) (DfT 2003, 2004) which incorporates the *Guidance on the New Approach to Appraisal* (NATA) (DETR 1998) and is related to the *DMRB* (Highways Agency *et al.* 1993). It is designed primarily for assessment of options in road schemes (see §5.6.2) but can be applied to other projects. Assessment of ecological impact significance is mainly provided in the biodiversity sub-objective, TAG Unit 3.3.10 (DfT 2004) which recommends a four-stage process.

1. describe the characteristic biodiversity features;
2. assess the overall biodiversity/nature conservation values of sites;
3. assess the magnitude of potential impacts of proposed options on biodiversity features;
4. derive overall assessment scores (impact significance levels) from the biodiversity/nature conservation evaluation and impact magnitude categories.

Stages one and two employ a set of **appraisal indicators** of nature conservation/biodiversity value based on the criteria described in Appendix D, with emphasis on site evaluation, and including the concept of environmental capital which incorporates attributes such as cultural value (DfT 2003). The appraisal indicators, overall biodiversity values, and impact magnitude categories are entered on a worksheet, the contents of which are summarised in **Table 11.7**.

The final column of the worksheet contains **overall assessment scores** (impact significance levels) that are derived from the nature conservation/biodiversity evaluation and impact magnitude categories, as shown in **Table 11.8**.

When more than one feature is affected, three rules (describe in DfT 2004) are applied.

1. **Most adverse category** – if an option affects more than one feature, the assessment score should be based on the most adverse effect.
2. **Cumulative adverse effects** – if an option affects several sites/resources it should be scored in a higher category than the score(s) determined for individual resources.

Table 11.7 Appraisal indicators, overall nature conservation/biodiversity values, and impact magnitude categories used in the TAG biodiversity worksheet

Column 1: Area

A list of all biodiversity features (including designated and non-designated sites) affected by each option, preferably with reference to EN's *Natural Area* profiles (and LBAP objectives) so that the appraisal is set in the context of the objectives of the area. Consequently, each area listed may relate to a specific site, or to a wider area relating to an important habitat type.

Column 2: Features/attributes

A description of each area/site in terms of Phase 1 habitat types and notable taxa, perhaps with separate assessments of biodiversity and cultural/recreational attributes.

Column 3: Scale (at which each attribute matters)

International, national, regional, local.

Column 4: Importance (of each attribute)

Description, including designations, and (where appropriate) reasons for designation. Where the feature is not designated, the importance should be considered by judgement in relation to factors such as rarity, representativeness, distinctiveness and quality (see §D.3.2).

Column 5: Trend (in relation to target)

Information on the abundance of the habitat or species relative to its trend (if known) and (if appropriate) its UKBAP target level (as specified in HAPs and SAPs)

Column 6: Substitution possibilities

Assessment of whether: habitats are technically replaceable to sufficient quality; species can be successfully relocated; or ecosystem services can be fully substituted. This relates to the fact that the loss of an irreplaceable feature is often considered to be more significant than one that is replaceable.

Column 7: Overall appraisal of biodiversity value (based on the previous indicators)

Very high – International scale and limited potential for substitution, e.g. Internationally designated;
High – Nationally designated, or regionally important with limited potential for substitution;
Medium – Regionally important, or locally designated with limited potential for substitution;
Lower – Undesignated sites of some local biodiversity interest;
Negligible – Local sites with little or no biodiversity interest.

Column 8: Appraisal of impact magnitude (on a seven-point textual scale)

1. Major negative – "The proposal (on its own or together with other proposals) may adversely affect the integrity of the site . . . across its whole area".

Table 11.7 (*continued*)

2. Intermediate negative – "The site's integrity will not be adversely affected, but the effect is likely to be significant in terms of its ecological objectives".
3. Minor negative – "Neither of the above apply, but some minor negative impact is evident". (Further assessment may be needed for a "European" site if detailed plans are not yet available).
4. Neutral – "No observable impact in either direction".
5. Minor positive – "There is a small net positive wildlife gain".
6. Intermediate positive – "There is a significant gain in biodiversity within the Natural Area"
7. Major positive – "The net gain is of national importance".

Note
The impact categories take account of mitigation and enhancement and are therefore assessments of **net (residual) impacts**. They do not include compensation proposals such as habitat replacement, although the interpretation of some overall assessment scores (**Table 11.8**) include possible compensation in terms of net gain or loss in *Natural Areas* (see Table D.2).

Table 11.8 Derivation of TAG overall assessment scores (impact significance levels) from biodiversity/nature conservation evaluation and impact magnitude categories

Impact	*Nature conservation/biodiversity value/importance*				
Magnitude	**Very High**	**High**	**Medium**	**Lower**	**Negligible**
Major negative	Very large adverse	Very large adverse	Moderate adverse	Slight adverse	Neutral
Intermediate negative	Large adverse	Large adverse	Moderate adverse	Slight adverse	Neutral
Minor negative	Slight adverse	Slight adverse	Slight adverse	Slight adverse	Neutral
Neutral	Neutral	Neutral	Neutral	Neutral	Neutral
Positive	Large beneficial	Large beneficial	Moderate beneficial	Slight beneficial	Neutral

Notes
Prescriptive advice in relation to impact significance levels:

Very large adverse – The proposal option is likely to be unacceptable on nature conservation grounds alone (even with compensation proposals).
Large adverse – There should be a strong presumption against the option, and greater than 1:1 compensation (net gain within the Natural Area) for the very occasional case where development is allowed as a last resort.
Moderate adverse – The option should have at least 1:1 compensation (no net loss in the Natural Area) if development is allowed.
Positive impacts – should be: (a) classed as "moderate beneficial" if they provide significant gains to UKBAP objectives in the Natural Area, and as "large beneficial" if they provide positive gains of national or international importance; (b) considered to be of lower value if the gains are not significant in terms of the conservation objectives of the Natural Area.

3. **Balancing adverse and beneficial effects** – if an option has negative impacts on some resources but positive impacts on others, it may be legitimate to make an overall net assessment. However, this requires careful ecological judgement rather than a simple area or number-of-sites approach, and "balancing should err on the side of caution" and "should be restricted to 'slight' or, exceptionally, 'moderate' impacts".

The results are subsequently entered (together with those for other EIA components such as noise, landscape, air quality and water) in an Appraisal Summary Table (see Table 5.1).

The IEEM (2006) impact prediction method differs from TAG in three important respects as follows.

1. It pays more attention to impact attributes such as timing, frequency, extent, duration, and reversibility; and it recommends the application of a confidence/probability scale to predictions of residual impacts.
2. It places more emphasis on aspects of ecological structure and function on which a feature depends. These may include: available resources; ecological processes, functions, roles and relationships; ecosystem properties; environmental processes; human influences; and historical context.
3. To assess impact significance, it focuses on assessing whether (and how) impacts are likely to affect the *integrity* of high-value ecological receptors (see also Table 12.6). IEEM believe that this provides a better link between value and impact magnitude than the TAG {value × magnitude = significance} method and similar "matrix" methods (e.g. SNH 2005b). IEEM criticise these methods on the grounds that the resulting "significance" levels are open to subjective interpretation, and in particular, that this can lead to decision makers awarding "low" rather than "moderate" significance to impacts on locally important receptors.

11.8 Mitigation

11.8.1 Introduction

There is a growing opinion that new developments should aim to deliver enhancement (net ecological gain) rather than just damage limitation (e.g. Defra 2005b, IEEM 2006). Developments can have positive ecological impacts, especially on "brownfield" sites (§11.7.2); but where a project impacts semi-natural habits, provision of net ecological gain is likely to be both difficult and costly.

The first priority should be to avoid or minimise impacts at source, and this may require modification of a project's location, alignment, design, or construction and operating procedures (IEEM 2006). When the destruction of, or serious damage to, a valuable habitat or species population is deemed to be unavoidable, remedial or compensatory options are often proposed. These can appear attractive to developers, who often assume that they are easy, and readily provide like-for-like compensation – neither of which is true. In addition, the costs of these measures (including provisions for management and monitoring) may significantly exceed those of impact avoidance measures.

11.8.2 Measures to avoid or minimise impacts

The **location** of a project can be a key factor. It is usually determined largely by socio-economic and technical criteria rather than environmental considerations, and the choice of sites is often restricted. However, if the proposed siting will clearly cause significant impacts on high-value habitats and/or species, the relocation, rezoning or no action options should be considered. EcIA scoping reports can be a useful tool for making such decisions. For example, some developers own or have options on "landbanks" of sites, and ecological information about these can influence decisions on which sites to bring forward. Similarly, *Local Development Frameworks* (LDFs) will be subject to Sustainability Appraisal (including potential impacts on biodiversity); so the early identification of important habitats should help to protect them by influencing the classification of land in or adjacent to them.

The **alignment** of linear projects such as pipelines, roads and railways can be relatively amenable to modification, and the TAG method is designed to identify the least ecologically damaging option. However, this may be precluded by technical and financial constraints, or by conflicting interests, e.g. with other EIA components.

Project design may be modified in various ways including the following:

- re-align site boundaries, e.g. to reduce landtake.
- modify the within-site layout to retain semi-natural habitats and/or create on-site habitats such as ponds (see SEPA 2000), which may result in enhancement if the development is in an urban or intensively farmed location;
- incorporate features to minimise pollution, soil erosion and runoff;
- create site-boundary *buffer zones*;
- provide features to reduce barrier effects, e.g. road underpasses for large mammals such as badgers (EN 2002) and small tunnels under roads for amphibians.

Much of the ecological damage caused by developments occurs during the **construction phase**, and all associated mitigation measures should be incorporated in a *Construction Environmental Management Plan* (see §1.2.4).

Construction phase impacts are often considered "temporary", but full recovery may take many years, and it is important to ensure that adequate mitigation measures are proposed and carried out. These can include the following.

- Minimise storage of construction materials, excavated soils etc, e.g. by off-site pre-assembly, just-in-time deliveries, and phasing of works.
- Restrict the extent of access roads, access and service areas, constructors compounds, temporary buildings and materials stores, and exercise care in the routing/siting of these.

- Apply appropriate storage, handling and management of soils (see §9.7).
- Minimise waste and employ pollution-prevention measures.
- Minimise damage to vegetation and soils, e.g. by using wide tyres on vehicles, and restricting the size of vehicles and plant.
- Create seed banks by collecting seed before vegetation is damaged, and/or use a local seed initiative for re-sowing after construction.
- Where possible, avoid major construction-phase operations during periods when taxa are particularly vulnerable to disturbance (§11.7.2).
- Designate protection zones, e.g. along river banks and around semi-natural habitats, trees, badger setts and bat roosts (see Mitchell-Jones 2004).
- Protect adjacent habitats by erecting boundary fences (although it should be remembered that these may act as barriers to animal movements).

While mitigation during the **operational phase** will depend largely on the project design, it may also involve aspects such as maintenance procedures and the management of amenity areas. Measures to avoid or minimise public pressure can include restricting access to valuable wildlife areas, and providing other focuses of attention.

It is important to remember that *freshwater ecosystems* are almost always profoundly influenced by adjacent terrestrial ecosystems; that they are particularly susceptible to water-borne pollution; and hence that particular care should be taken in the selection of impact avoidance measures such as those outlined in **Table 11.9** (see also Table 10.12).

Deciding which methods will be most effective in any situation may be difficult, since there has been little monitoring of the long-term effectiveness of different techniques. As a general rule: *point source pollutants* should be dealt with at source; while *diffuse source pollution* is best dealt with by a combination of measures, including biological techniques such as *buffer zones* and/or natural and artificial/constructed wetlands (especially reedbeds or ponds). However, these techniques are not a panacea in the log term. For example, a reedbed used to intercept road runoff may effectively deal with degradable pollutants such as nitrates, but have only a limited capacity to store non-degradable pollutants such as phosphates and heavy metals. Thus, unless suitable maintenance is undertaken, it may eventually become saturated and then export most of the non-degradable pollutants subsequently received. The nature conservation benefits of biological mitigation techniques have also often been over-emphasised and used to justify other forms of damage. For example, ponds created to intercept urban runoff are unlikely to be optimal wildlife habitats. Further information on the use and value of natural and constructed wetlands for pollution control can be found in CIRIA (2007), Cooper and Findlater (1991), Crites *et al.* (2006), and Nuttall *et al.* (1998).

Finally it is important to consider whether mitigation measures may themselves have an adverse impact on freshwater habitats. For example, the creation of an on-stream lake to create a landscape feature or intercept sediment may have downstream implications for the flow regime, and ecology of the stream.

Table 11.9 Mitigation measures relating to pollution of freshwater ecosystems

Pollutants	*Mitigation measures*
Sediments/ silt	Avoid major construction during wet seasons. Minimise soil disturbance, erosion and vegetation removal (or re-vegetate rapidly). Use: (a) *siltation traps*, *french drains*, or siltation basins/ponds/ lagoons (regular maintenance by dredging is essential); and (b) vegetated *buffer zones* (30–100m) or wetlands, as filters.
Organic matter and nutrients	Reduce silt inputs as above. Encourage formation of wet organic soils (e.g. create wetlands and wet woodland) to promote *denitrification*. In sewage treatment use nutrient stripping, tertiary treatments, separation of effluents, storm overflows.
Heavy metals, micro- organics, and other toxic materials	Treat or recycle industrial pollutants at source, and monitor effluents. Reduce silt inputs (as above). Use buffer zones (30–100m) and constructed wetlands such as reed beds, which may remove many industrial and domestic effluents, although they require proper design and maintenance, and can lead to long-term accumulation and/or release of non-degradable pollutants. Minimise surface drainage from polluted areas. Reduce use where possible (e.g. of *pesticides*). Ensure isolation of waste-storage facilities and landfill sites from surface and groundwater bodies, and monitor for *leachates*. Discharge vehicle and other wash waters to foul sewers rather than surface water drains. Guard against accidental pollution by: effective safety systems (with back-up), security systems against fire or vandalism where potential pollutants are stored or delivered; contingency plans; and education/training of personnel.
Oils	Install silt/petrol traps (gully traps) in road or parking areas and ensure a proper maintenance (replacement of filters). Bund, dike or create vegetated buffer zones around fuel/oil storage areas during construction. Guard against accidental pollution.
Acidification	Strip power station flue gases. Modify forestry practices. Avoid use of liming to increase the pH of water bodies because of adverse effects on the ecosystem.
Heat	Re-circulate and/or use to heat local buildings.

11.8.3 Remedial measures

The main remedial measures are **translocation** and **habitat restoration**. Translocation involves "rescuing" a species or habitat from a donor site (that will be destroyed) and moving it to a receptor site that already contains a suitable *semi- natural* habitat or (in the case of habitat translocation) is environmentally suitable, e.g. it has similar soil type, hydrology and climate. Restoration is the repair of a habitat that has been damaged or has declined in "value" in the absence of appropriate management. To have any chance of success, these methods require a thorough understanding of the ecology of the species or habitat in question.

Species translocations have usually been attempted when a project threatens a site hosting a protected or priority species, and have included the bee orchid, marsh fritillary, great crested newt, red squirrel and most UK reptiles. They should only be attempted as a last resort because: (a) the threatened habitat may be valuable even if no other notable species are present; (b) there may be adverse impacts on the recipient habitat; and (c) the chances of success are low, either because the recipient habitat is unsuitable or because adding to the existing population increases the severity of competition. For example, attempts to transfer the great crested newt into existing ponds have often proved unsuccessful because the recipient ponds were unsuitable or were already at their maximum *carrying capacity* for the species.

A JNCC policy document (JNCC 2003a) provides guidance on evaluating and undertaking species translocations for conservation purposes. However, it concludes that "relocation of species is not an acceptable alternative to in situ conservation, but where a development has been given planning approval, relocation should be considered as a means of partially compensating for the loss of the populations affected".

Habitat translocation involves moving vegetation (and some substratum) together with incidentally associated animals. It is usually attempted for high-value habitats that are threatened with destruction by projects. Attempts have occasionally involved ancient woodland, but most have been undertaken for semi-natural grassland. This is usually done by lifting turves, although transfer of roto-vated topsoil and turf fragments has sometimes been used.

Some successes have been claimed, but a review by Gault (1997) concluded that success could not be assumed in any of the cases examined because: there had been insufficient post-translocation time for adequate assessment; most were poorly documented; and there had been a general lack of monitoring. In a translocated grassland case in which monitoring was conducted (Jefferson *et al.* 1999) significant deterioration occurred over a period of nine years. The report also warned that short-term monitoring might have suggested that the translocation was a success; and the case was used by EN to successfully argue that a developer's new proposal to translocate an adjacent grassland SSSI should be refused.

Anderson and Groutage (2003) provides and extensive review of habitat translocation projects, and a best practice guide that sets out minimum standards. However, it does not promote habitat translocation, and concludes that it "should be regarded a last resort for all sites of high nature conservation value". Similarly, a JNCC policy document (JNCC 2003b) concludes that habitat translocation is not an acceptable alternative to in situ conservation, and states that "The statutory conservation agencies will continue to make the strongest possible case against translocating habitats from within SSSIs and from ancient habitats or other areas with significant biodiversity interest".

Habitat restoration should be undertaken whenever damage by a project to semi-natural habitats is unavoidable. For example, where a project necessitates re-routing a watercourse, steps should be taken to ensure that the channel and *river corridor* of new section has high environmental quality (see Table 10.12). Similarly, gravel pits can be successfully restored for wildlife (Andrews and Kinsman 1990). Guidance on the restoration of wetland habitats is provided in Acreman *et al.* (2007), Crofts *et al.* (2005), EPA (2007), and Treweek *et al.* (1997).

Severely damaged habitats may be difficult to restore, especially if they are long-established complex ecosystems (such as ancient woodland and high quality freshwater systems) that would take a very a long time to recover naturally. In these cases, one option is to effect some basic restoration and rely on time and management to "do the rest" (the more complex the "design" of a restoration scheme, the more likely it is to fail or at least not meet expectations). If this is not considered feasible, the last resort may have to be compensation.

11.8.4 Compensation and enhancement

Compensation and enhancement usually involve some form of **habitat creation**. This can include activities such as the creation of *buffer zones* (e.g. adjacent to remaining habitat patches) or the establishment of vegetation cover, e.g. by tree planting and landscaping within a development site. However, while these can have some protective and/or enhancement value, they cannot compensate for the loss of high-value semi-natural habitats.

More usually, habitat creation is proposed in off-site locations with the aim of providing like-for-like compensation for the loss of a valuable habitat. Like translocation, this should only be undertaken as a last resort because, while a successful programme may create communities that are superficially similar to those lost, it "will never fully compensate for the destruction of high quality natural communities" (Wathern 1999). This view is endorsed in the UKBAP (1994), which states:

> While some simple habitats, particularly those populated by mobile species which are good colonisers, have some potential for re-creation, the majority of terrestrial habitats are the result of complex events spanning many centuries which defy recreation over decades. Therefore, the priority must be to sustain the best examples of native habitats where they have survived rather than attempting to move or recreate them elsewhere when their present location is inconvenient because of immediate development proposals.

Similarly, while the creation of new *linear habitats* may be a valuable mitigation measure, Andrews (1993) stresses that "maintaining the continuity of existing links is more important than establishing new ones".

Any attempted habitat creation requires careful planning, which PAA (1994) suggest should involve several basic questions.

- Is it suited to the local geography, climate, soil type and fertility, and geology?
- Is it consistent with (or will complement) the local ecology and landscape?
- What management will it require, and will this be feasible?
- Should it be patches and/or linkages?

Appropriate methods of habitat creation vary according to the proposed habitat type (see Gilbert and Anderson 1998, Parker 1995). For example, new ponds and reedbeds are relatively easy to create and maintain (see EN 2005, SEPA 2000, Williams *et al.* 1999), and river works can sometimes be used as an opportunity to repair damage caused by earlier insensitive schemes (see Table 10.12). Grasslands may be sown using seed mixes of native species that are tolerant of local climatic and soil conditions (see Crofts 1994, Crofts and Jefferson 1999, SNH Undated). A similar approach can be adopted for woodlands and hedges, but tree and shrub planting will normally be required, again using suitable native species, and stock grown from native (preferably local) seed (see CCW 1996, Ferris-Kaan 1995, Rodwell and Petersen 1994, and WT 2001).

New habitat patches should normally be as large as possible, although it is worth bearing in mind that several small patches, with the same overall area as a single large patch, may: have a better chance of hosting more species if they contain a wider range of habitat conditions; and may increase connectivity between existing patches. An alternative strategy which may also promote colonisation of a new patch, is to locate new patches adjacent to existing patches (Buckley and Fraser 1998) as this may promote colonisation of the former and increase the viability of the latter.

Successful habitat creation requires expertise, and the new habitats will need long-term management. Consequently, if habitat creation is deemed necessary as a compensatory measure, an option is for the developer to contribute funding towards the purchase of new reserves by NGOs such at RSPB and WT, who have experience in both the creation and management of semi-natural habitats.

11.9 Monitoring

As explained in §1.2.6 and §12.7, monitoring fulfils a number of purposes. It is an important aspect of EcIA, and should be undertaken whenever there are uncertainties concerning the significance of impacts or the effectiveness of proposed mitigation measures, including on-going management procedures associated with these measures.

Monitoring can normally be achieved by periodic repeat sampling, using the same or similar methods as those employed in baseline surveys (see Spellerberg 2005). Photo-sites and permanent quadrats can be useful to record changes (Goldsmith 1991). A difficult aspect is allowing for changes that may occur without the development, e.g. as a result of natural trends or other developments and activities. The only way to assess this with reasonable certainty is to compare changes in receptor or compensatory sites with those in control/reference sites (Bisset and Tomlinson 1990). The latter is effectively baseline monitoring.

Monitoring should be conducted by experts and in consultation with the statutory consultees and relevant NGOs (§11.3.3). The procedures are time-consuming and expensive; so the monitoring programme should be carefully targeted, e.g. on selected variables. A completion date will probably be imposed, at which time a final audit and report should be produced.

11.10 Conclusions

The following conclusions can be drawn about how EcIAs should be carried out.

- Experienced ecologists must always be employed, and (together with the statutory consultees) should be consulted early.
- It is vital to identify key impacts and receptors (if possible during scoping) and to target resources on these.
- The baseline studies should make maximum use of existing information, but new field surveys (at suitable times of year) will almost always be required.
- While qualitative information is useful, quantitative data is often vital.
- The baseline ecological conditions and features should be evaluated.
- Impact predictions and mitigation proposals should be as precise and quantitative as possible, although a degree of uncertainty must be accepted.
- Monitoring should be prescribed wherever necessary.
- The EIS should include clear explanations of survey methods, results, limitations, uncertainties, and relationships with other components.

Note

1 Full names of acronyms, and organisations' internet addresses, are given in Appendix A.

References

Acreman MC, Fisher J, Stratford CJ, Mould DJ, and Mountford JO 2007. Hydrological science and wetland restoration: some case studies from Europe. *Hydrology and Earth System Sciences* **11**(1), 158–169.

Altringham JD 2003. *British bats*. London: HarperCollins.

Anderson P and P Groutage 2003. *Habitat translocation – a best practice guide*. London: CIRIA.

Andrews J 1993. The reality and management of wildlife corridors. *British Wildlife* **5**, 1–7.

Andrews J and D Kinsman 1990. *Gravel pit restoration for wildlife. A practical manual*. Sandy, Beds: RSPB.

Angold PG, JP Sadler, MO Hill, A Pullin, S Rushton, K Austin, E Small, B Wood, R Wadsworth, R Sanderson and K Thompson 2006. Biodiversity in urban habitat patches. *Science of the Total Environment* **360**, 196–204 (www.nora.nerc.ac.uk/240/ or www.dx.doi.org/10.1016/j.scitotenv.2005.08.035).

Ausden M and M Drake 2006. *Invertebrates*. In *Ecological census techniques: a handbook*, 2nd edn. WJ Sutherland (ed.), 214–249. Cambridge: Cambridge University Press.

Ayreshire Red Squirrel Group 2004. *Walked transect surveys – instructions for surveys*. www.Ayreshireredsquirrels.org.uk.

Barker G 1997. A framework for the future: green networks with multiple uses in and around towns and cities. *English Nature Research Report No. 256*. Peterborough, Cambs: English Nature.

BCG (Biodiversity Challenge Group) 2007. *High and Dry*. Sandy: RSPB Policy Operations Dept.

Begon M, C Townsend and JL Harper 2005. *Ecology:from individuals to ecosystems*, 4th edn. Oxford: Blackwell Publishing.

Bender DJ, TA Contreras and L Fahrig 1998. Habitat loss and population decline: a meta-analysis of the patch size effect. *Ecology* **79**(2), 517–533.

Bennett A, P Ratcliffe, E Jones, H Mansfield and R Sands 2005. *Other mammals*. In *Handbook of biodiversity methods: survey, evaluation and monitoring*, D Hill, M Fasham, G Tucker, M Shewry and P Shaw (eds), 450–472. Cambridge: Cambridge University Press.

Bibby CJ, ND Burgess, DA Hill and SH Mustoe 2000. *Bird census techniques*, 2nd edn. London: Academic Press.

Biggs J, G Fox, P Nicolet, M Whitfield and P Williams 2001. Freshwater ecology. Ch. 12 in *Methods of environmental impact assessment*, 2nd edn. P Morris and R Therivel (eds). London: Spon Press.

Bignall K, M Ashmore1 and S Power 2004. The ecological effects of diffuse air pollution from road transport. *English Nature Research Report No. 580*. Peterborough, Cambs: English Nature. www.naturalengland.communisis.com/NaturalEnglandShop/.

Birks HJB and HH Birks 2004. *Quaternary palaeoecology*. Caldwell, NJ: The Blackburn Press.

Bisset R and P Tomlinson 1990. Monitoring and auditing of impacts. In *Environmental impact assessment: theory and practice*, P Wathern (ed.), 117–128. London: Routledge.

Blomberg S and R Shine 2006. *Reptiles*. In *Ecological census techniques: a handbook*, 2nd edn. W.J. Sutherland (ed.), 297–307. Cambridge: Cambridge University Press.

Bratton JH 1990. Seasonal pools – an overlooked invertebrate habitat. *British Wildlife* **2**, 22–31.

BRIG (Biodiversity Reporting and Information Group) 2007. *Report on the species and habitat review; Report to the UK Biodiversity Partnership*. www.ukbap.org.uk/bapgrouppage.aspx?id=112.

Bright P and P Morris 2005. *The Dormouse*, 2nd edn. London: The Mammal Society.

Bright P, P Morris and A Mitchell-Jones 1996. *Dormouse Conservation Handbook*. Peterborough, Cambs: English Nature.

Brooks SJ 1993. Guidelines for invertebrate site surveys. *British Wildlife* **4**(5), 283–286.

Bryce J, JS Pritchard, NK Waran and RJ Young 1997. Comparison of methods for obtaining population estimates for red squirrels in relation to damage due to bark stripping. *Mammal Review* **27**(4), 165–170.

Buckland ST, DR Anderson, KP Burnham, JL Laake, DL Borchers and L Thomas 2001. *Distance sampling: estimating abundance of biological populations*. Oxford: Oxford University Press.

Buckley GP and S Fraser 1998. Locating new lowland woods. *English Nature Research Report No. 283*. Peterborough, Cambs: English Nature. www.naturalengland.communisis.com/NaturalEnglandShop/.

Bullock JM 2006. Plants. In *Ecological census techniques: a handbook*, 2nd edn. WJ Sutherland (ed.), 186–213. Cambridge: Cambridge University Press.

Burgman MA, S Ferson and HR Akçakaya 1993. *Risk assessment in conservation biology*. London: Chapman & Hall.

Carpenter TG 1994. *The environmental impact of railways*. Chichester: John Wiley & Sons.

Carpenter TG (ed.) 2001. *Environment, construction and sustainable development*. Volume 2: Sustainable civil engineering. Chichester: John Wiley & Sons.

Carter P and Churchfield S (2006a). *The Water Shrew Handbook*. London: Mammal Society Publication.

Carter P and Churchfield S (2006b). *Distribution and habitat occurrence of water shrews in Great Britain*. Environment Agency Science Report SC010073/SR, The Environment Agency, Bristol and The Mammal Society Research Report No. 7. London: The Mammal Society, www.abdn.ac.uk/mammal/report7.pdf.

CBD (Convention on Biological Diversity) 2006. *Global Biodiversity Outlook 2*. www.cbd.int/GBO2 *or* www.biodiv.org/GBO2.

CCW (Countryside Council for Wales) 1996. *Hedgerow management and recreation: a guide for land managers in the hedgerow restoration scheme*. Bangor: CCW.

CEAA (Canadian Environmental Assessment Agency) 1999. *Cumulative Effects Assessment Practitioners Guide*, Hull, Quebec: CEAA. www.ceaa-acee.gc.ca/013/0001/0004/index_e.htm.

Chanin P and M Woods 2003. Surveying dormice using nest tubes; results and experiences from the South West Dormouse Project. *English Nature Research Report No. 524*. http://naturalengland.communisis.com/naturalenglandshop/docs/R524.pdf.

CIRIA (Construction Industry Research and Information Association) 2007. *The Sustainable Urban Drainage Systems (SUDS) manual (C697)*. Birmingham: CIRIA, www.ciria.org.uk/suds/publications.htm.

Collingham YC and B Huntley 2000. Impacts of habitat fragmentation and patch size upon migration rates. *Ecologial Applications* 10(1), 131–144.

Connell DW, P Lam, B Richardson and R Wu 1999. *Introduction to ecotoxicology*. Oxford: Blackwell Science.

Cooper PF and BC Findlater (eds) 1991. *Constructed wetlands in water pollution*. Oxford: Pergamon.

Corbet GB and S Harris (eds) 1991. *The handbook of British mammals*, 3rd edn. Oxford: Blackwell Science.

Côté IM and MR Perrow 2006. *Fish*. In *Ecological census techniques: a handbook*, WJ Sutherland (ed.), 2nd edn, 250–277. Cambridge: Cambridge University Press.

Cowley M and B Vivian 2007. *The business of biodiversity: a guide to its management in organisations*. Lincoln: Institute of Environmental Management and Assessment (IEMA). www.defra.gov.uk/wildlife-countryside/pdfs/biodiversity/bbpg2007.pdf.

Crites RW, EJ Middlebrooks and SC Reed 2006. *Natural wastewater treatment systems*. Boca Raton, FL: CRC Press.

Crofts A 1994. *How to create and care for wildflower meadows*. Lincoln: The Wildlife Trusts.

Crofts A and RG Jefferson (eds) 1999. *The lowland grassland management handbook*, 2nd edn., Ch. 11: *Grassland creation*. English Nature and The Wildlife Trusts. www.naturalengland.communisis.com/naturalenglandshop/docs/low11.pdf.

Crofts A, L Bardsley and N Giles 2005. *The wetland restoration manual*. Newark: TWT.

Defra (Department for Environment Food and Rural Affairs) 2005a. *Key facts about: wildlife: scarce and threatened native species (2005)*. London: Defra, www.defra.gov.uk/environment/statistics/wildlife/kf/wdkf02.htm.

Defra 2005b. *New high level targets for flood and coastal erosion risk management*. London: Defra, www.defra.gov.uk/environ/fcd/hltarget/default.htm.

Defra 2007a. *Biodiversity Indices in your Pocket. Measuring our progress towards halting biodiversity loss*, PB12626. London: Defra, www.jncc.gov.uk/pdf/2010-BIYP2007.pdf.

Defra 2007b. *Conserving biodiversity – The UK approach.* PB12772. London: Defra. www.defra.gov.uk/wildlife-countryside/pdfs/biodiversity/ConBioUK-Oct2007.pdf.

Defra 2007c. *Guidance on the EIA (Agriculture) (England) (No. 2) Regulations 2006,* www.defra.gov.uk/farm/environment/land-use/eia/pdf/eia-guidance2007.pdf.

DETR 1998. *Guidance on the New Approach to Appraisal.* London: DETR.

DfT (Department for Transport) 2003. *Transport Analysis Guidance (TAG): The Environment Capital Approach,* TAG Unit 3.3.6. London: DfT, www.webtag.org.uk/webdocuments/3_Expert/3_Environment_Objective/3.3.6.htm.

DfT 2004. *Transport Analysis Guidance (TAG): The biodiversity sub-objective,* TAG Unit 3.3.10. London: DfT, www.webtag.org.uk/webdocuments/3_Expert/3_Environment_Objective/3.3.10.htm.

DTI (Department of Trade and Industry) 1992. *Guidelines for the environmental assessment of cross-country pipelines.* London: HMSO.

EA (Environment Agency) 1999. *Procedures for collecting and analysing river macro invertebrate samples,* Report no. BT001, Issue 2.0. Bristol: Environment Agency.

EA 2000. *State of the Environment of England and Wales: the land.* Bristol: Environment Agency.

EA 2004. *Hydroecology; integration for modern regulation.* www.environment-agency.gov.uk/commondata/105385/hydroecology_879252.pdf.

EA 2007. *Understanding water for wildlife. Water resources and conservation: assessing the eco-hydrological requirements of habitats and species.* Bristol: Environment Agency, http://publications.environment-agency.gov.uk/pdf/GEHO0407BMNB-e-e.pdf?lang=_e.

EA 2008. *Otters.* Bristol: Environment Agency, www.environment-agency.gov.uk/subjects/conservation/483249/?version=1&lang=_e.

EC (European Commission) 1999. *Guidelines for the assessment of indirect and cumulative impacts as well as impact interactions.* Brussels: EC, http://ec.europa.eu/environment/eia/eia-support.htm.

EHS (Environment and Heritage Service) 2004. *Northern Ireland Peatlands.* Belfast: EHS. www.peatlandsni.gov.uk/formation/nipeatlnds.htm.

EN (English Nature) 1997. *Dorset heaths Natural Area profile.* Peterborough, Cambs: English Nature, www.english-nature.org.uk/science/natural/profiles/naProfile81.pdf.

EN 1999. *Habitats Regulations Guidance Note 3: The determination of likely significant effect under The Conservation (Natural Habitats &c.) Regulations 1994,* www.mceu.gov.uk/MCEU_LOCAL/Ref-Docs/EN-HabsRegs-SigEffect.pdf.

EN 2001. *State of nature. The upland challenge.* Peterborough, Cambs: English Nature, http://naturalengland.communisis.com/NaturalEnglandShop/browse.aspx.

EN 2002. *Badgers and development.* Peterborough, Cambs: English Nature, www.badger.org.uk/_Attachments/Resources/48_S4.pdf.

EN 2003. *Conserving Natura 2000 Rivers. The Eurasian Otter (Lutra lutra).* Peterborough, Cambs: English Nature, www.english-nature.org.uk/lifeinukrivers/species/otter.html.

EN 2004a. *State of nature. Lowlands – future landscapes for wildlife.* Peterborough, Cambs: English Nature, http://naturalengland.communisis.com/NaturalEnglandShop/browse.aspx.

EN 2004b. *Reptiles: guidelines for developers.* Peterborough, Cambs: English Nature, http://naturalengland.communisis.com/naturalenglandshop/docs/IN15.1.pdf.

EN 2005. *Getting wetter for wildlife. Guidance on habitat restoration and creation by the Wetland HAP Steering Group.* Peterborough, Cambs: English Nature, http://naturalengland.communisis.com/naturalenglandshop/docs/IN17.3.pdf.

EPA (US Enironmental Protection Agency) 2007. *River corridor and wetland restoration.* Washington, DC: Enironmental Protection Agency, www.epa.gov/owow/wetlands/restore/.

ERM (Environmental Resources Management) 1996. The significance of secondary effects from roads and road transport on nature conservation. *English Nature Research Report No. 178.* http://naturalengland.communisis.com/NaturalEnglandShop/browse.aspx.

Eycott A, K Watts, D Mosely and D Ray 2007. *Evaluating biodiversity in fragmented landscapes: the use of focal species.* Edinburgh: Forestry Commission, www.forestry.gov.uk/PDF/FCIN089.pdf/$FILE/FCIN089.pdf.

Ferris-Kaan R (ed.) 1995. *The ecology of woodland creation.* Chichester: John Wiley and Sons.

Fojt W 1992. East Anglian fens and ground water abstraction. *English Nature Research Report No. 30.* Peterborough, Cambs: English Nature, http://naturalengland.communisis.com/naturalenglandshop/docs/R030.pdf.

Fritts HC 2001. *Tree rings and climate.* Caldwell, NJ: The Blackburn Press.

Gault C 1997. *A moving story: species and community translocation in the UK – a review of policy, principle, planning and practice.* Godalming, Surrey: WWF-UK.

Gent T 1996. *Evaluation of reptile survey methodogies. Final Report (R200).* Peterborough, Cambs: English Nature, http://naturalengland.communisis.com/NaturalEnglandShop/browse.aspx.

Gent T and S Gibson (eds) 2003. *Herpetofauna workers manual.* Peterborough, Cambs: JNCC.

Gibb R and J Foster 2000. *The herpetofauna workers guide.* Halesworth, Suffolk: Froglife.

Gibbons DW and RD Gregory 2006. Birds. In *Ecological census techniques: a handbook,* WJ Sutherland (ed.), 2nd edn, 308–350. Cambridge: Cambridge University Press.

Gibbons DW, JB Reid and RA Chapman (eds) 1993. *The new atlas of breeding birds in Britain and Ireland.* Carlton, Staffs: T & AD Poyser.

Gilbert G, DW Gibbons and J Evans 1998. *Bird monitoring methods: a manual of techniques for key UK species.* Sandy, Beds: RSPB.

Gilbert OL and P Anderson 1998. *Habitat creation and repair.* Oxford: Oxford University Press.

Giles N, R Sands and M Fasham 2005. Fish. In *Handbook of biodiversity methods: survey, evaluation and monitoring,* D Hill, M Fasham, G Tucker, M Shewry and P Shaw (eds), 368–386. Cambridge: Cambridge University Press.

Goldsmith FB (ed.) 1991. *Monitoring for conservation and ecology.* London: Chapman & Hall.

Gorman M and D Raffaelli 1993. The Ythan estuary. *Biologist* **40**(1), 10–13.

Greig-Smith P 1983. *Quantitative plant ecology,* 3rd edn. Oxford: Blackwell Science.

Grime JP, JG Hodgson, and R Hunt 1988. *Comparative plant ecology.* London: Unwin Hyman.

Gurnell J and JR Flowerdew 2006. *Live Trapping Small Mammals, a practical guide,* 4th edn. London: The Mammal Society, www.abdn.ac.uk/mammal/live_trapping.shtml.

GWCT (Game and Wildlife Conservation Trust) Undated. The Brown Hare: a practical guide for farmers, landowners and LBAP groups. Fordingbridge, Hants: GWCT, www.gct.org.uk/brownhare.

Halliday TR 2006. Amphibians. In *Ecological census techniques: a handbook,* W.J. Sutherland (ed.), 2nd edn, 277–296. Cambridge: Cambridge University Press.

Harris S, P Cresswell and DJ Jefferies 1989. *Surveying badgers.* London: The Mammal Society.

Harrison C, J Burgess, A Millward and G Dawe 1995. Accessible natural greenspace in towns and cities. A review of appropriate size and distance criteria. *English Nature Research Report No. 153,* http://naturalengland.communisis.com/NaturalEnglandShop/.

Haskins L 2000. Heathlands in an urban setting – effects of urban development on heathlands in south-east Dorset. *British Wildlife* **11**(4), 229–237.

Hawksworth DL (ed.) 1995. *Biodiversity: measurement and estimation*. London: Chapman & Hall.

Highways Agency, Scottish Office, Welsh Office & Department of the Environment Northern Ireland 1993. *Design manual for roads and bridges (DMRB)*, Vol. 11: *Environmental assessment*, Section 3, Part 4: *Ecology and nature conservation*. London: Highways Agency, www.standardsforhighways.co.uk/dmrb/vol11/section3.htm.

Hill D, M Fasham, G Tucker, M Shewry and P Shaw 2005. *Handbook of biodiversity methods: survey, evaluation and monitoring*. Cambridge: Cambridge University Press.

Hoodless A and PA Morris 1993. An estimation of the population density of the fat doormouse (*Glis glis*). *Journal of Zoology* **230**, 337–340.

Huntley B, RE Green, YC Collingham and SG Willis 2007. *A climate atlas of European breeding birds*. Barcelona: Lynx Editions.

IEA (Institute of Environmental Assessment) 1995. *Guidelines for baseline ecological assessment*. London: E & F N Spon.

IEEM (Institute of Ecology and Environmental Management) 2006. Guidelines for ecological impact assessment in the United Kingdom (version 7, July 2006). Winchester: IEEM. www.ieem.net/ecia/.

IEEM 2007. *Sources of survey methods (Guidelines for survey methodology)*. Winchester: IEEM, www.ieem.net/survey-sources/.

IUCN (World Conservation Union) 2006. *The IUCN Red List of threatened species*, www.iucnredlist.org.

Jefferson RG, CWD Gibson, SL Leach, CM Pulteney, R Wolton and HJ Robertson 1999. Grassland habitat translocation: the case of Brocks Farm, Devon. *English Nature Research report No. 304*. http://naturalengland.communisis.com/NaturalEnglandShop/.

Jones JC, JD Reynolds and D Raffaelli 2006. *Environmental variables*. In *Ecological census techniques: a handbook*, WJ Sutherland (ed.), 2nd edn, 370–408. Cambridge: Cambridge University Press.

Joshi J, P Stoll, HP Rusterholz, B Schmid, C Dolt and B Baur 2006. Small-scale experimental habitat fragmentation reduces colonization rates in species-rich grasslands. *Oecologia* **148**(1), 144-152.

JNCC (Joint Nature Conservation Committee) 2003a. *A policy for conservation translocations of species in Britain*. Peterborough, Cambs: JNCC. www.jncc.gov.uk/pdf/species_policy.pdf.

JNCC 2003b. *A habitat translocation policy for Britain*. Peterborough, Cambs: JNCC. www.jncc.gov.uk/pdf/habitats_policy.pdf.

JNCC 2007. *Handbook for phase 1 habitat survey – a technique for environmental audit*. Peterborough, Cambs: JNCC, www.jncc.gov.uk/page-4258.

Juniper T 2007. *Saving planet earth*. London: Collins (by arrangement with the BBC).

Kent M and P Coker 1992. *Vegetation description and analysis: a practical approach*. London: Belhaven Press.

Kerrison P, T Norman and M Fasham 2005. *Aquatic invertebrates*. In *Handbook of biodiversity methods: survey, evaluation and monitoring*. D Hill, M Fasham, G Tucker, M Shewry and P Shaw (eds), 359–367. Cambridge: Cambridge University Press.

Kirby KJ 1995. *Rebuilding the English countryside: habitat fragmentation and wildlife corridors as issues in practical conservation*. English Nature Science No. 10. Peterborough, Cambs: English Nature.

Krebs CJ 1998. *Ecological Methodology*, 2nd edn. New York: Harper & Row.

Krebs CJ 2001. *Ecology: the experimental analysis of distribution and abundance*, 5th edn. New York: Benjamin Cummings.

Krebs C 2006. Mammals. In *Ecological census techniques: a handbook*, WJ Sutherland (ed.), 2nd edn, 351–369. Cambridge: Cambridge University Press.

Langbein J, MR Hutchings, S Harris, C Stoate, SC Tapper and S Wray 1999. Techniques for assessing the abundance of brown hares, *Lepus europaeus*. *Mammal Review* **29**(2), 93–116.

Latham D, E Jones and M Fasham 2005a. *Amphibians*. In *Handbook of biodiversity methods: survey, evaluation and monitoring*, D Hill, M Fasham, G Tucker, M Shewry and P Shaw (eds), 387–403. Cambridge: Cambridge University Press.

Latham D, E Jones and M Fasham 2005b. *Reptiles*. In *Handbook of biodiversity methods: survey, evaluation and monitoring*, D Hill, M Fasham, G Tucker, M Shewry and P Shaw (eds), 404–411. Cambridge: Cambridge University Press.

LUC (Land Use Consultants) 2005. Going, going, gone? The cumulative impact of land development on biodiversity in England. *English Nature Research report No. 626*. Peterborough, Cambs: English Nature, http://naturalengland.communisis.com/NaturalEnglandShop/browse.aspx.

LUC 2006. A practical toolkit for assessing cumulative effects of spatial plans and development projects on biodiversity in England. *English Nature Research report No. 673*, Peterborough, Cambs: English Nature, http://naturalengland.communisis.com/NaturalEnglandShop/browse.aspx.

MA (Millennium Ecosystem Assessment) 2005a. *Living beyond our means: natural assets and human well-being – Statement of the MA Board*, www.maweb.org/en/Reports.aspx.

MA 2005b. *Ecosystems & human well-being: synthesis*. Washington, DC: Island Press, www.maweb.org/en/Reports.aspx.

MA 2005c. *Ecosystems & human well-being; biodiversity synthesis*. Washington, DC: World Resources Institute, www.maweb.org/en/Reports.aspx.

Maitland PS and AA Lyle 1993. Freshwater fish conservation in the British Isles. *British Wildlife*, **5**, 8–15.

Mammal Society 2002. National survey of road deaths. London: The Mammal Society, www.abdn.ac.uk/~nhi775/road_deaths.htm.

Mayle BA, AJ Pearce and RMA Gill 1999. *How Many Deer?: a guide to Estimating Deer Population Size*. Forestry Commission Field Book 18. Edinburgh, Forestry Commission.

Mitchell-Jones AJ 2004. *Bat Mitigation Guidelines*. Peterborough, Cambs: English Nature, http://naturalengland.communisis.com/naturalenglandshop/docs/IN13.6.pdf.

Mitchell-Jones AJ and AP McLeish (eds) 2004. *The Bat Workers Manual*, 3rd edn. Peterborough, Cambs: JNCC, www.jncc.gov.uk/page-2861.

Moore PD 1986. Site history. In *Methods in plant ecology*, 2nd edn. PD Moore and SB Chapman (eds), 525–556. Oxford: Blackwell Scientific.

Morris P 2002. The hydrology and plant communities of Cothill Fen SSSI. *Fritillary* **3**, 20–36.

Morris P and R Emberton 2001. Ecology – overview and terrestrial systems. Ch. 11 in *Methods of environmental impact assessment*, 2nd edn. P Morris and R Therivel (eds). London: Spon Press.

Morris P and D Thurling 2001. Phase 2–3 ecological sampling methods. Appendix G in *Methods of environmental impact assessment*, 2nd edn. P Morris and R Therivel (eds). London: Spon Press.

Mueller-Dombois D and H Ellenberg 1974. *Aims and methods of vegetation ecology*. Chichester: John Wiley.

Mustoe S, D Hill, D Frost and G Tucker 2005. *Birds*. In *Handbook of biodiversity methods: survey, evaluation and monitoring*, D Hill, M Fasham, G Tucker, M Shewry and P Shaw (eds), 412–432. Cambridge: Cambridge University Press.

New TR 1998. *Invertebrate surveys for conservation*. Oxford: Oxford University Press.

Nuttall PM, AG Boon and MR Rowell 1998. *Review of the design and management of constructed wetlands*. London: CIRIA.

ODPM (Office of the Deputy Prime Minister) 2005a. *Planning Policy Statement 9 (PPS9): Biodiversity and geological conservation*. London: ODPM, www.communities.gov.uk/publications/planningandbuilding/planningpolicystatement9.

ODPM 2005b. Circular 05/05. *Planning obligations*. London: ODPM, www.communities.gov.uk/publications/planningandbuilding/circularplanningobligations.

ODPM 2005c. Circular 06/05. *Biodiversity and geological conservation – statutory obligations and their impact within the planning system*. London: ODPM, www.communities.gov.uk/publications/planningandbuilding/circularbiodiversity.

ODPM 2006. *Planning for biodiversity and geological conservation – a guide to good practice*. London: ODPM, www.communities.gov.uk/publications/planningandbuilding/planningbiodiversity.

OWWT (Offwell Woodland and Wildlife Trust) 2005. *Habitats*. Honiton, Devon: OWWT, www.countrysideinfo.co.uk/habitats.htm.

PAA (Penny Anderson Associates) 1994. *Roads and nature conservation: guidance on impacts, mitigation and enhancement*. Peterborough, Cambs: English Nature.

Parker DM 1995. *Habitat creation – a critical guide*. English Nature Science No. 21, Peterborough, Cambs: English Nature.

Parker K 1998. Meadows still in decline. *British Wildlife* 10(2), 144.

Petts J and G Eduljee 1994. *Environmental impact assessment for waste treatment and disposal facilities*. Chichester: John Wiley & Sons.

PI (Plantlife International) 2000. *Where have all the flowers gone? A study of local extinctions as recorded in the county floras*. Salisbury, Wilts: Plantlife, www.plantlife.org.uk/uk/assets/saving-species/saving-species-publications/where-have-all-the-flowers-gone-2000.pdf.

PI 2005. *Under pressure: climate change and the UK's wild plants*. Salisbury, Wilts: Plantlife, www.plantlife.org.uk/uk/assets/saving-species/saving-species-publications/Under-pressure-climate-change-and-wild-plants.pdf.

PI (Undated). *Non-native invasive plants*. Salisbury, Wilts: Plantlife, www.plantlife.org.uk/uk/plantlife-campaigning-change-invasive-plants.html.

Piper JM, EB Wilson, J Weston, S Thompson and J Glasson 2006. Spatial planning for biodiversity in our changing climate. *English Nature Research report No. 677*. http://naturalengland.communisis.com/NaturalEnglandShop/browse.aspx.

Plant C, R Sands and M Fasham 2005. Dragonflies and damselflies. In *Handbook of biodiversity methods: survey, evaluation and monitoring*, D Hill, M Fasham, G Tucker, M Shewry and P Shaw (eds), 322–327. Cambridge: Cambridge University Press.

Pond Action 1998. *A guide to the methods of the National Pond Survey*. Oxford: Pond Action, www.pondnetwork.org.uk/Downloads/NPSMethods.pdf.

Reading CJ 1996. Evaluation of reptile survey methodologies: Final report. *English Nature Research Report No. 200*, http://naturalengland.communisis.com/NaturalEnglandShop/.

Rodwell JS and Petersden GS 1994. Creating new nature woodlands. *Forestry Commission Bulletin No. 112*. London: HMSO (see also current FC publications on woodland establishment and regeneration at www.forestry.gov.uk/fr/INFD-6XCHBT).

SEPA (Scottish Environmental Protection Agency) 2000. *Ponds, pools and lochans: guidance on good practice in the management and creation of small waterbodies in Scotland.* Edinburgh: SEPA, www.sepa.org.uk/pdf/guidance/hei/ponds.pdf.

Sibbald S, P Carter and S Poulton 2006. Proposal for a national monitoring scheme for small mammals in the United Kingdom and the Republic of Eire. *The Mammal Society Research Report No. 6.* London: The Mammal Society, www.abdn.ac.uk/mammal/report6.pdf.

SNH (Scottish Natural Heritage) 1998. *Handling Phase 1 habitat survey within a GIS environment.* Information and Advsiory Note 62. Edinburgh: SNH, www.snh.org.uk/publications/on-line/advisorynotes/62/62.html.

SNH 2005a. *Environmental assessment handbook: guidance on the Environmental Impact Assessment process, D4: scoping the environmental statement.* Edinburgh: SNH, www.snh.org.uk/publications/on-line/heritagemanagement/EIA/d.4.shtml.

SNH 2005b. *Environmental assessment handbook: guidance on the Environmental Impact Assessment process, D8: assessing the significance of impacts.* Edinburgh: SNH, www.snh.org.uk/publications/on-line/heritagemanagement/EIA/d.8.shtml.

SNH Undated. *Using wildflower seed mixtures for grassland creation.* Information and Advisory Note 106. Edinburgh: SNH. www.snh.org.uk/publications/on-line/advisorynotes/106/106.htm.

Southwood TRE and PA Henderson 2000. *Ecological methods*, 3rd edn. Oxford: Blackwell Science.

Spellerberg IF 2005. *Monitoring ecological change*, 2nd edn. Cambridge: Cambridge University Press.

Stebbings R, H Mansfield and M Fasham 2005. Bats. In *Handbook of biodiversity methods: survey, evaluation and monitoring*, D Hill, M Fasham, G Tucker, M Shewry and P Shaw (eds), 433–449. Cambridge: Cambridge University Press.

Stevens JP, TH Blackstock, EA Howe and DP Stevens 2004. Repeatability of Phase 1 Habitat Survey. *Journal of Environmental Management* **73**(1), 53–59.

Strachan R and T Moorhouse 2006. *Water vole conservation handbook.* Oxford: Wildlife Conservation Research Unit (WildCRU), Oxford University.

Strachan R, DJ Jefferies and PFR Chanin 1996. *Pine marten survey of England and Wales 1987–1988.* Peterborough, Cambs: JNCC.

Sutherland WJ (ed.) 2006. *Ecological census techniques: a handbook*, 2nd edn. Cambridge: Cambridge University Press.

Swan MJS and RS Oldham 1993a. Herptile sites Vol. 1: National amphibian survey, final report and appendices. *English Nature Research Report No. 38.* Peterborough, Cambs: English Nature (pdf available from http://naturalengland.communisis.com/NaturalEnglandShop/browse.aspx).

Swan MJS and RS Oldham 1993b. Herptile sites, Vol. 2: National reptile survey, final report and appendices. *English Nature Research Report No. 39.* Peterborough, Cambs: English Nature (pdf available from http://naturalengland.communisis.com/NaturalEnglandShop/browse.aspx).

Teitje W and Berlund T 2000. *Land-use planning in oak woodland: applying the concepts of landscape ecology using GIS technology and the CDF oak woodland maps.* IHRMP Oak Fact Sheets No. 52, http://danr.ucop.edu/ihrmp/oak52.htm.

Townsend CR, M Begon and JL Harper 2007. *Essentials of ecology*, 3rd edn. Oxford: Blackwell Publishing.

Treweek J 1999. *Ecological impact assessment.* Oxford: Blackwell Science.

Treweek J, M Drake, O Mountford, C Newbold, C Hawke, P José, M Self and P Benstead (eds) 1997. *The wet grassland guide: managing floodplain and coastal wet grasslands for wildlife*. Sandy, Beds: RSPB.

Tucker G 2005. *Biodiversity evaluation methods*. In *Handbook of biodiversity methods: survey, evaluation and monitoring*, D Hill, M Fasham, G Tucker, M Shewry and P Shaw (eds), 65–104. Cambridge: Cambridge University Press.

TWT (The Wildlife Trusts) 2001. *Severe weather warning for otters* (News Archive 4th June, 2001), www.wildlifetrusts.org/index.php?section=news:archive&id=192.

UKBAP 1994. *Biodiversity: the UK Biodiversity Action Plan (UKBAP)*. Cm2428. London: HMSO, www.ukbap.org.uk/GenPageText.aspx?id=53.

UNCED 1992. *United Nations Conference on Environment and Development* (UNCED), Rio de Janeiro, 3–14 June 1992, www.un.org/geninfo/bp/enviro.html.

Walmsley CA, RJ Smithers, PM Berry, M Harley, MJ Stephenson and R Catchpole (eds) 2007. MONARCH – *Modelling Natural Resource Responses to Climate Change; a synthesis for biodiversity conservation*. Oxford: UKCIP (UK Climate Impacts Programme), www.ukcip.org.uk/resources/publications.

Wathern P 1999. *Ecological impact assessment*. In *Handbook of environmental impact assessment*, Vol. 1, J Petts (ed.), 327–346. Oxford: Blackwell Science.

Webb NR and I Haskins 1980. An ecological survey of heathland in the Poole Basin, Dorset, England in 1978. *Biological Conservation* 17, 281–296.

Webb NR and RJ Rose 1994. Habitat fragmentation and heathland species. *English Nature Research Report No. 95*. Peterborough, Cambs: English Nature.

Williams P, J Biggs, M Whitfield, A Thorne, S Bryant, G Fox and P Nicolet 1999. *The pond book: a guide to the management and creation of ponds*. Oxford: Ponds Conservation Trust.

WT (Woodland Trust) 2000. *Why the UK's ancient woodland is still under threat*. Grantham, Lincs: Woodland Trust, www.woodland-trust.org.uk/publications/publicationsmore/ancientreport.PDF.

WT 2001. *New woods for people*. Grantham, Lincs: Woodland Trust. www.woodland-trust.org.uk/publications/publicationsmore/newwoodsforpeople.pdf.

WT 2008. Road to nowhere. *Broadleaf No. 69*, Autumn 2008. Grantham, Lincs: Woodland Trust.

WWF 2006. *The living planet report*, www.wwfindia.org/news_facts/lpr2006.

ZSL (Zoological Society of London) 2007. *UK native species conservation*. www.zsl.org/field-conservation/uk-native-species.

12 Coastal ecology and geomorphology

Richard Cottle and Sian John
(based on Thompson and Lee 2001)

12.1 Introduction

The coastal zone of the UK, with 15,000km of coastline and more than one-third of a million km² of territorial waters (Gubbay 1990), is one of the most diverse and spectacular in the world. The variety of aspects, coastal landforms, processes, geology and substrates present, as well as the influence of man, has given rise to a wide array of complex ecosystems and a valued environment. However, this value has led to the coast being subjected to a considerable number of different pressures. Consequently its management is often complex, due to the need to balance potentially conflicting requirements, such as meeting the demands of economic development and recreation; protecting vulnerable settlements from flooding and *erosion*; and protecting important scenic, geological and ecological systems.

These pressures are well illustrated at both a UK and European level. For example, in 2000 the proportion of land area covered by artificial surfaces was 25 per cent higher at the coast than inland (EEA 2006). Between 1990 and 2000, trends in the European coastal zone showed that the growth rate of artificial surfaces was about ⅓ faster than inland. It was also projected that by 2004 the 1990 levels of urban spread at the coast would have been exceeded by 12 per cent. In several coastal regions of Italy, France and Spain the coverage of built-up areas in the first kilometre of the coastal strip exceeds 45 per cent. Population densities are also higher on the coast than inland. In Europe, they are on average 10 per cent higher (EEA 2006). However, in some countries, this figure can be more than 50 per cent (e.g. Belgium). One of the consequences of this coastal development and population pressure is the loss of semi-natural and natural habitats, with an estimated loss of between 1 and 4 per cent of the area of wetlands, grasslands, pasture and mixed farmland having occurred in the EU between 1990 and 2000 (EEA 2006).

An additional and pressing issue facing coastal areas is the predicted sea level rise associated with climate change. Mean global sea level has risen during the twentieth century by an average rate of 1.7mm/yr and a further rise of 20–50cm is predicted by 2100 (IPCC 2007). In England, Defra has produced sea level rise estimates (up to 2115) for use in flood defence planning (see §12.3.2).

In addition to the risks to human life, settlements and agricultural land, rising sea levels threaten the integrity of significant areas of coastal habitats. For example, it has been estimated that, given existing coastal management policies, there could be a net loss of around 4,000ha of freshwater habitats and a net gain of around 700ha of mudflat and saltmarsh habitats (Lee 2001). However, the predicted figure for intertidal habitats depends on at least 60ha of new habitat being created each year from 1998 onwards. Moreover, saltmarshes that are "trapped" between rising sea-levels and fixed seawalls are being lost rapidly by *coastal squeeze*, and saltmarsh loss nationally is estimated to be 100ha per year (Covey and Laffoley 2002). This also threatens the integrity of seawalls (defending low-lying areas) that rely on the wave absorbing power of saltmarshes.

12.2 Definitions and concepts

12.2.1 The coastal zone

What precisely is meant by the term coastal zone is problematic. In terms of geomorphology (land forms and associated processes) it can be defined as the zone between the land and sea that includes the shallow waters in which waves transport **sediment**, and the zone of beaches, cliffs and dunes that are affected by the movement of this sediment (Summerfield 1991). Ecologically, its inland extent can be determined approximately as the limit of influence by salt spray, which is rarely further than about 0.5km inland (UKBG 1999). However, the Environment Agency's definition of the coastal zone includes land within 10km of the coast. The marine extent of the zone is usually taken to be "inshore waters", although it can be interpreted to include "offshore waters" which extend to the edge of the continental shelf (see §12.2.5).

All of these systems are sometimes collectively referred to as "maritime". More usually they are subdivided, in relation to the land–sea axis, into three zones: the **littoral** (intertidal or shore) **zone**, the **supralittoral** (or maritime) **zone**, and the **sublittoral** (or marine) **zone**. These zones are commonly used in classifications such as the UKBAP *Broad Habitats Classification* (see §C.3) and the JNCC *Marine Habitat Classification for Britain and Ireland* (MHCBI) (Conner *et al.* 2004) (see §C.4). The habitats and communities within all three zones are profoundly influenced by the substratum type, i.e. rock or sediment type (see **Figure 12.1**). In a given location, the substratum, and other habitat features, depend on the prevalent geology and geomorphological processes in the area.

12.2.2 Coastal geomorphology

Coastal geomorphology is important in EIA for two main reasons: it has direct relevance with respect to erosion and flooding; and geomorphological formations and processes are integral components of coastal ecosystems. Hence a change in, for example, the hydraulic and sedimentary regime of an estuarine system is likely to result in indirect effects on intertidal habitats throughout the system

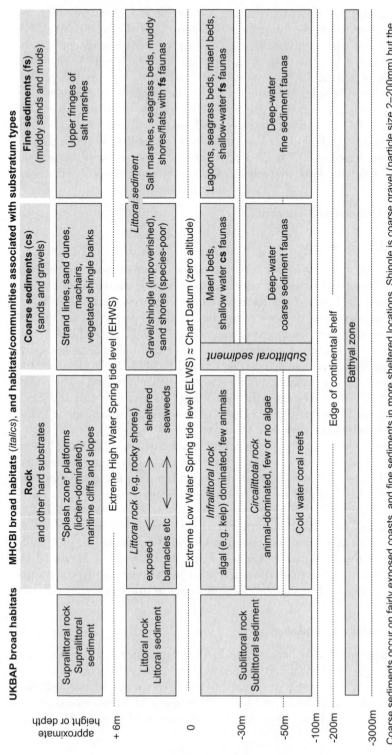

Figure 12.1 Outline of maritime (supralittoral) and marine (littoral and sublittoral) broad habitats defined in the UKBAP Classification and the Marine Habitats Classification of Britain and Ireland (MHCBI), both of which focus on **benthic** marine habitats.

Coarse sediments occur on fairly exposed coasts, and fine sediments in more sheltered locations. Shingle is coarse gravel (particle size 2–200mm) but the term is most commonly used for supralittoral banks which become at least partially vegetated.

(such as changes in exposure due to a change in the tidal range, and effects on the rate of intertidal erosion). This is a complex area and, consequently, only a brief outline of some important aspects can be given here. Further information can be found in many texts including Bird (2008), Carter (1988), Cooke and Doornkamp (1990), Masselink and Hughes (2003), Pethick (1984), Trenhaile (1997) and Woodroffe (2002).

Coastal geomorphology involves interactions between many components, but the principal factors are waves, tidal regimes and currents.

Waves are a major erosive force, and an important ecological factor, especially in the littoral zone. Most waves are wind generated, and vary in size and force largely in relation to wind velocity, duration and *fetch* (the distance of open water). Wave action is, therefore, greatest on coasts exposed to strong on-shore winds over extensive areas of sea. Wave effects are modified by tidal regimes.

The two main components of **tidal regimes** are rhythm and range. In most locations around Europe, the **tidal rhythm** consists of approximately two tides per day. The **tidal range** (rise and fall) varies daily, with a two-weekly cycle of large **spring tides** that advance and retreat much further than the small **neap tides** of the alternate weeks. In addition, there are larger seasonal cycles, with the largest spring tides near the Spring and Autumn equinoxes (in March and September). These are the extreme high-water spring-tide levels (EHWS), and extreme low-water spring-tide (ELWS) levels. The EHWS level can be extended by waves, especially on exposed shores and during storms.

The **mean tidal range** (taken as the distance between the mean high water spring tide (MHWS) and mean low water spring tide (MLWS) levels) varies considerably between different locations. It can be *macrotidal* (as much as 12m in the UK), although most of the coastline has a tidal range of much less than this, and some locations have a *microtidal* regime, with a range of only 1–2m. The tidal range affects coastal geomorphology by controlling the vertical distance over which waves and currents are effective. For instance, tidal sand ridges develop in macrotidal environments (Reading and Collinson 1998). The tidal rhythm also affects the intensity of currents.

Coastal currents are important, both as a means of sediment transport and as agents of erosion. They result from the interaction of climate, tides, wave regime and coastal morphology. Two important types are:

- **longshore currents**, which are commonly caused by oblique waves, tend to run parallel to the shore line, and result in lateral movement of sediment (**longshore drift**) along the coast (Carter 1988);
- **tidal currents**, which are important where coastal morphology funnels tides, e.g. in narrow straights and inlets, and in extreme cases may produce **tidal rapids**.

Under certain conditions (usually a combination of low atmospheric pressure and high winds) funnelling of shallow coastal seas by coastlines can cause **storm surges** or, when combined with high tides, **tidal surges**. These surges may pose serious flooding risk. For example, at the southern end of the North Sea, surges can raise predicted tide levels by over 2m. Bathymetric (sea floor) topography is also important in influencing the pattern of currents.

The complex interaction of tides, currents and waves create either an erosive or depositional (and hence constructive) regime in a given area.

Erosive processes are widespread, e.g. it has been estimated that 70 per cent of the world's sandy coastline is being eroded (Bird 1985), with waves being the most important agent. The predominant erosional landform types are sea cliffs and shore platforms. Cliffs suffer minimal destruction in deeper water but are subject to severe erosional processes at their base when water is sufficiently shallow for waves to break. As a cliff retreats a shore platform is left which protects the cliff base by dissipating wave energy. The stability of cliffs may also be affected by groundwater seepage and frost action above sea level, and by cliff geology. Soft cliffs, consisting of unconsolidated materials such as boulder clay, are often subject to quite rapid erosion, as along many stretches of the east coast of England.

Processes of sediment deposition lead to a variety of landforms, the most important of which are:

- **beaches**, which hold the greatest amounts of deposited coastal material, usually sand or pebbles;
- **spits**, which are formed by longshore drift of sediments (usually shingle) along fairly exposed coastlines;
- **dunes**, which are formed by wind-blown sand, usually from beaches and sand banks exposed at low tide, although their development and maintenance depends, to a large extent, on vegetation, which facilitates accretion and stabilisation of the sand (see Carter *et al.* 1992, Nordstrom and Carter 1991);
- **tidal flats**, which occur in estuaries and sheltered inlets, and consist largely of muddy sediments. In estuaries, accretion is enhanced by the mixing of freshwater and seawater, which causes flocculation and hence settling of water-borne sediments (see Dyer 1998). Further accretion occurs if mudflats are colonised and stabilised by saltmarsh plants.

All of these systems depend on a continued supply of sediment (from rivers, coastal erosion etc.), which can be interrupted by activities such as coastal protection works and dredging (§12.5.2). Changes in sediment supply are the commonest cause of **downdrift effects** (impacts on the lee side of coastal activities) including downdrift erosion.

Along the coastline of England and Wales, 11 major **coastal sediment cells** have been identified, which are evidently largely self-contained in terms of the movement of coarse sediments (HR Wallingford 1993). Consequently, these cells (or smaller sub-cells which have also been identified) are considered to be suitable units for study, and for the development of *Shoreline Management Plans* (§12.3.2).

The upper sections of estuaries and coastal inlets can be regarded as parts of coastal *floodplains*, which provide protection to more inland areas against flooding resulting from storm and tidal surges and sea-level rise. However, the seaward sections of many areas of former coastal floodplain are now protected by man-made flood defences, and support a variety of land uses ranging from grazing marsh to urban and industrial development. These areas are susceptible to flooding due to poor drainage, or breaching or overtopping of coastal defences. Estuarine floodplains can be flooded from raised sea levels, river floodwaters, or a combination of both (EA 1997).

12.2.3 Littoral habitats

The **littoral zone** can be very narrow (where the slope of the land is steep) or quite extensive, e.g. on mud flats. The approximate boundaries of this zone are the EHWS and ELWS tide levels (Figure 12.1). In most littoral habitats the resident species are essentially marine, but adapted to the regime of immersion and emersion associated with tidal cycles. Organisms living near the EHWS or ELWS levels are only submerged or emersed (respectively) for short periods during the year. Between these extremes, the communities usually exhibit clear zonation along the land–sea axis, although this is controlled by elevation in relation to the tidal frame rather than distance from EHWS or ELWS.

The substrata characteristics of littoral habitats vary depending on local geology, landform type, and exposure to wave action and currents, e.g. mud only accumulates in sheltered locations, and rocky shores occur where exposure prevents any sediment deposition (see **Table 12.1**).

Rocky shores provide a generally impenetrable substratum that precludes burrowing or penetration by all but a few organisms, but supports seaweeds and animals that adhere to rock surfaces (**epibiota**). The wide variation in wave exposure and rock types leads to a wide variety of associated community types. Sheltered

Table 12.1 Typical locations of, and relationships between, littoral and supralittoral habitats in relation wave exposure and currents.

Locations	Littoral zone	Supralittoral zone
Exposed coastlines and headlands	Rocky shores	Sea cliffs and slopes
Fairly exposed coastlines, usually where lateral currents drag the material (longshore drift) to the deposition locations	Shingle beaches	Vegetated shingle banks
Exposed or fairly exposed coastlines, often in bays or at the mouths of esturaries	Sandy shores	Sand dunes and machairs
Estuaries and sheltered inlets (sometimes behind sand dunes or shingle banks)	Mudflats	Saltmarshes[1]
Depressions partially cut off from seawater, usually by barriers of sand or shingle	Saline lagoons	

Note
[1] Saltmarshes are littoral habitats, but are sometimes classed as "maritime"

shores are normally dominated by seaweeds such as fucoids (species of *Fucus* and similar "shrubby" brown algae) and support a diverse fauna including gastropods (e.g. topshells, whelks and winkles). By contrast, most seaweeds and animal species are excluded from very exposed rocky shores, which are usually dominated by barnacles, mussels and limpets. Further information on rocky shore ecology can be obtained from Moore and Seed (1985), Raffaelli and Hawkins (1996) and Little and Kitching (1996).

Shingle beaches, as a result of the constant movement and grinding action of sediment, are a hostile environment in which few resident species can survive. However, supralittoral shingle is a valuable habitat (§12.2.4).

Sand and mud are soft, unstable substrates that do not provide adequate anchorage for epibiota, but are suitable for burrowing molluscs and marine worms that live in the substratum (**infauna**). Sandy shores are a relatively hostile environment (see Brown and McLachlan 2006) and most are too unstable for plant growth. However, *Zostera* (seagrass) beds occur on some muddy sands in the lower littoral and sublittoral (see UKBG 1999). Mudflats are usually coated with a film of microscopic *algae* (Coles 1979) and normally contain a diverse and abundant invertebrate infauna, principally of bivalves (e.g. cockles), and *marine annelids* (polychaetes, and oligochaetes), especially in estuaries.

Saltmarshes develop on mudflats where there is sufficient shelter, and the mud is sufficiently stable, to permit colonisation by *vascular plants*, the growth of which facilitate further sediment accretion and stabilisation of the substrate. Saltmarshes are largely restricted to the zone between mean high water neap tides and mean high water spring tides, so only the lower fringes are submerged by the daily tidal cycle throughout the year, and the upper levels are only subject to inundation at EHWS tides. Although dominated by essentially terrestrial vegetation, the plants are halophytic (i.e. adapted to live in saline conditions). The communities usually exhibit zonation, along the land-sea axis, in relation to the frequency and duration of inundation. Saltmarshes are often located in **estuaries**, which are unique ecosystems in which the mixing of fresh and salt water is a fundamental component of their ecology. Information on saltmarsh and estuarine systems is provided in texts such as Adam (1993), McLusky and Elliott (2004), Little (2000) and Packham and Willis (1997).

Coastal lagoons are bodies of saline or brackish water that are partially separated from the sea, but retain some seawater at low tide (see Downie 1996, UKBG 1999). They often support unusual communities that include algae, vascular plants, and invertebrates that rarely occur elsewhere (see Barnes 1994).

12.2.4 Supralittoral (maritime) habitats

Supralittoral habitats lie above the limits of the EHWS tides, and support terrestrial vegetation. In near-littoral locations which are affected by wave splash and spray, salt tolerant plant species often dominate the vegetation communities. The zone includes several important habitats (Figure 12.1). As in littoral habitats, an important controlling factor is substratum type; indeed, the different types of littoral habitat are usually backed by supralittoral habitats on similar substrates (Table 12.1).

Maritime cliffs and slopes vary widely in character, reflecting local geology and land forms, and may possess faces ranging from vertical to gently sloping. These features support a variety of habitats such as rock crevices and ledges, seepages, coastal grasslands, *heathlands* and scrub (see Table C.1). These habitats are considered to extend inland to at least the limit of salt spray deposition, and hence sometime encompass whole headlands or islands (UKBG 1999).

Vegetated shingle banks sometimes support scrubby vegetation or a grass sward, but more exposed areas have open vegetation with scattered vascular plants and lichens (see Packham and Willis 1997, Packham *et al.* 2001). This habitat is particularly sensitive to human disturbance, and "nearly 50 per cent of designated shingle habitat is in unfavourable condition as a result of poor coastal management and from activities that damage the fragile plant communities" (Covey and Laffoley 2002). Moreover, once damaged, recovery can be slow.

Sand dune systems usually principally consist of several dunes (aligned approximately parallel to the coastline and increasing in age along the sea-land axis) interspersed with depressions (dune slacks). They are complex systems that include a range of habitats (see Table C.1) that are sensitive to disturbance. Information on sand dune ecology is provided in Crawford (1998), Gimmingham *et al.* (1989), Packham and Willis (1997) and Martinez and Psuty (2004).

Machairs are distinctive habitats that occur on wind-blown calcareous sand, and are confined to north west Scotland and western Ireland where strong onshore winds prevail. The vegetation is usually predominantly seasonally waterlogged short grassland, but can include dunes, fen and swamp (see Bassett and Curtis 1985, Owen *et al.* 1996, UKBG 1999). Machairs have a long history of traditional management, e.g. by seasonal grazing and rotational cropping (Kent *et al.* 2003).

In Britain, these maritime habitats are usually backed by land in agricultural production or land that has been developed (e.g. residential properties, industry, recreation and communication infrastructure). In the absence of these human landuses, these habitats would grade into fully terrestrial habitats such as woodland. Consequently, from an ecological perspective the landward extension of the coastal zone may not be clearly definable for these maritime habitats.

12.2.5 Sublittoral habitats

The upper limit of the **sublittoral zone** is the ELWS tide level at any given location, which is a fairly discrete boundary. The seaward limit less is clear, but can be taken to include all the shallow seas which extend to the edge of the **continental shelf** of the European land mass. The extent of this area varies, but it includes the English Channel, the Irish Sea, and most of the North Sea. It also varies in depth, but generally slopes gently to a depth of about 200m before the **continental shelf slope** falls steeply to the bathyal zone and deep ocean floor.

Most EIAs are likely to focus on the **benthic** communities of **inshore waters**. These are defined as within six nautical miles of the shoreline, where the UK has authority to exercise unilateral protection of fish stocks (although UK territorial waters extend to 12 nautical miles offshore). However, environmental impacts such as **pollution** of the entire North Sea, demonstrate that land-based developments can have significant impacts on the whole continental shelf area.

The ecology of the sublitoral is discussed in Earle and Erwin (1983), Hiscock (1998) and Gray and Elliot (2008). The environment is less widely fluctuating than that of the littoral zone, and the seabed is usually dominated by soft sediments – rocky substrates being normally restricted to narrow zones adjacent to coastlines, and isolated features such as reefs (UKBG 1999). However, benthic communities exhibit appreciable variation due to:

- substrate type – which largely controls the range and types of organisms present in an area (e.g. soft sediment, burrowing fauna or cobble/boulder attached fauna), and to a lesser degree those in the water above (which include organisms that depend on the sea floor for food, shelter or reproduction);
- the considerable variation in water movement, including turbulence, currents and tidal movement; *and*
- differences in salinity and **turbidity**. Near the mouths of rivers and in estuaries, salinity may be reduced by fresh water inputs, and turbidity increased by suspended sediments, especially in wet weather. Turbidity tends to be high also in areas with a muddy or sandy seabed, especially when sediments are disturbed during storms.

Under the *Marine Habitat Classification for Britain and Ireland*, the sublittoral zone includes three broad habitat types: infralittoral rock (to *c*.30m); circlittoral rock (to *c*.50m); and sublittoral sediment (to *c*.100m) (Figure 12.1), with the latter subdivided into infralittoral and circalittoral habitat complexes (see §C.4). It therefore typically extends from the extreme lower shore, covers much of the continental shelf, and includes benthic habitats and communities ranging from near shore algal or seagrass dominated communities (where light levels permit photosynthesis) to deeper water animal-dominated communities on a variety of sediment types (boulders and cobbles, through pebbles and shingle, coarse sands, sands, fine sands, muds and mixed sediments). Sublittoral sediment communities generally have high proportions of polychaetes, bivalves and **echinoderms**, and can include biogenic reefs built by polychaetes, bivalves or cold-water corals (which can extend down to *c*.2,000m).

As in all ecosystems, sublittoral and open sea communities depend on flows of energy and nutrients along **food chains** (see §11.2.2) that are based on **photoautotrophs** (except for deep ocean hydrothermal vents where the food chains rely on chemoautotrophs that utilize chemical energy). However, apart from infralittoral algal and seagrass beds, the primary producers are **phytoplankton** which form the basis of food chains in both **pelagic** (free floating and swimming) and **benthic** (sea bed) communities. A difference from terrestrial communities is that a much larger proportion (up to 80 per cent) of the "primary pasturage" (the phytoplankton) is consumed by **zooplankton**, and passes along grazing food chains.

12.2.6 The ecological value of British coastal ecosystems

The coast and seas around north west Europe are among the most productive wildlife habitats in the world. They are home to a high diversity and abundance of flora and fauna, partly as a result of the high nutrient status of nearshore coastal waters and shallow seas. High nutrient availability allows primary producers (e.g. phytoplankton) to flourish, and these form the basis of large and often complex **food webs** (see §11.2.2).

The British coastal zone is particularly special because of the location of the Islands on a broad and extensive continental shelf that is also heavily influenced by the Atlantic Ocean. Temperate, warm temperate, and Arctic species are all found around the shores as a result of the interplay of various water currents derived from water masses many kilometres to the north and south. The coastline is geologically and topographically varied, heavily indented, and subject to a wide range of wave activity and tidal regimes. These processes and features provide for the development of a wide variety of habitats, that often occur within relatively small stretches of coastline.

The UK's coastal areas are of particular importance for birds, and provide habitats for many rare species; and British seabird colonies are of global importance. Of the 287 internationally important bird areas in the UK, 67 are noted for the populations of breeding seabirds that they support, with many holding over 1 per cent of the world population of a seabird species (Heath and Evans 2000).

Two particularly valuable UK habitats are **maritime cliffs**, which often support internationally important populations of breeding seabirds, and **estuaries**, which are internationally important for the migratory waterbird populations that they support. Because of the indented coastline and large tidal ranges, Britain has the highest proportion of estuarine habitats in Europe (Davidson *et al.* 1991). In addition – because factors such as the relatively warm seas, mild winters, and nutrient inputs from the land provide suitable conditions for the development of abundant and species-rich invertebrate communities in intertidal areas – they are among the most biologically productive ecosystems in the world (Rothwell and Housden 1990). Consequently, estuaries provide rich feeding grounds for birds and, in particular, form vital links between the breeding and overwintering grounds of migratory waders and wildfowl. Britain hosts about 20 per cent of migratory waterbird populations each spring and autumn, and over 33 per cent of the populations of over-wintering waders on the European Atlantic coast (EA 1999).

The importance and threatened nature of UK coastal habitats is reflected by the facts that (a) a total of 25 marine habitats and four supralittoral habitats are identified as BAP priority habitats (see Table C.2), and (b) the coastal zone hosts many BAP priority species, and the 2007 review of the UKBAP identified 88 marine species to be included in the UK Priority List of Species (BRIG 2007). In addition, many species, habitats and sites are afforded legislative protection.

12.3 Legislative background and interest groups

12.3.1 Legislation

Coastal zone legislation in the UK is very complex, with no overall authority responsible for its management. Hence responsibility is divided between a large number of central and local agencies with varying responsibilities and limits of jurisdiction. However, there have been, and continue to be, moves towards greater unification of responsibility. For instance, Defra, NAW and SG (see Appendix B) now set the overall policy for **coastal defence** (against erosion or flooding) in England, Wales and Scotland respectively; while the EA, SEPA and Maritime District Councils (MDCs) are the **operating authorities**, responsible for policy implementation. However, other organisations also have coastal management responsibilities and may have powers to pass bylaws for specific purposes. These include the SNCOs, LPAs, harbour authorities, and landowners (including NGOs such as the RSPB and National Trust).

Pertinent international agreements, EU Directives and UK legislation containing specific references to the coast are listed in **Tables 12.2 and 12.3**. Much of this legislation refers to both inland and coastal waters. Recently implemented, the *Water Framework Directive* (WFD) is one of the most substantial pieces of EC water legislation thus far. It requires all inland, estuarine and coastal waters to reach "good status" by 2015. It will do this by establishing a river basin district structure within which demanding environmental objectives will be set, including ecological targets for surface waters (see also §10.4.1). In addition, EU directives such as the DSWD and IPPCD (Table 10.1) and related UK legislation such as the EPA and PPCA (Table 10.2) aim to control pollution of all surface waters, including coastal waters. Similarly, while most legislation on nature conservation (§11.3.1) is not specific to the coast, it is highly important and relevant to the coastal zone. For instance, Annex I of the *Habitats Directive* lists 24 coastal habitats (including 5 with priority status) that occur in the UK (see §C.5).

The only specifically marine sites with statutory nature conservation protection in the UK are those designated as Marine Nature Reserves (MNR) (Table D.2), of which there are currently only three. This situation is likely to change with the designation of marine SACs (see Table D.1) in UK offshore waters. The JNCC has recently launched consultation on proposals to designate seven SACs in offshore waters that support important Annex 1 habitats listed in the *Habitats Directive*. This has been enabled through the coming into force of the *Offshore Marine Conservation Regulations* in August 2007, which means that the scientific justification for these sites and their boundaries can now be consulted upon.

There are also a number of coastal sites that have non-statutory designations, e.g. Heritage Coasts, and SMAs/MCAs (see Table D.2); and much of the coastal zone is afforded some degree of protection under the general designations listed in this table. As always, the greatest protection is afforded to "international" sites, with which the zone is well endowed. For example, there are 76 SACs and

Table 12.2 International agreements and EU legislation relevant to the coastal zone

---

Bathing Water Directive (BWD) (76/160/EEC) revised in **06/7/EC*** – see Table 10.1

Wild Birds Directive (WBD) 79/409/EEC – see Table 11.1.

Shellfish Waters Directive (SWD) (79/923/EC) revised in **06/113/EC*** – to protect coastal and brackish shellfish waters by setting water quality standards and requiring member states to reduce pollution where necessary. Standards are set for a number of parameters including salinity, dissolved oxygen and nine metals in *designated waters* (see §10.4.2). Will be repealed by the Water Framework Directive in 2013 (see http:// rod.eionet.europa.eu/show.jsv?id=214andmode=S)

Urban Waste Water Treatment Directive (UWWTD) (91/271/EEC)* – see Table 10.1.

Agreement on the Conservation of Small Cetaceans of the Baltic and North Seas (ASCOBANS) 1991 (www.cms.int/species/ascobans/asc_bkrd.htm, www.ascobans.org/ index0101.html).

Convention on Biological Diversity (CBD) 1992 – see Table 11.1 and §11.3.2.

The Habitats Directive 1992/43/EEC (and amendments) – see §11.3.1 and Table 11.1.

Oslo and Paris Convention for the Protection of the Marine Environment of the North-East Atlantic (OSPAR) 1992 accepted in EU Council Decision 98/249/EC – signatories agreed to continually reduce emissions of hazardous substances, with the aim of achieving near background levels of naturally occurring substances and near zero concentrations of synthetic substances by 2020 (see www.ospar.org/eng/html/welcome.html and EA 1999).

Agreement for the Conservation of Cetaceans (whales and dolphins) **in the Black Sea, Mediterranean Sea and Contiguous in the North and Baltic Seas (ACCOBAMS) 1996** (www.cms.int/species/accobams/acc_bkrd.htm, www.jncc.gov.uk/page-1382).

EIA Directive 97/11/EC (see §1.3) – includes (a) in Schedule 1: large ports and piers (except ferry piers), and (b) in Schedule 2: coast protection works (other than maintenance or reconstruction); large fish farms; reclamation; shipyards; marinas > 0.5ha; and construction of harbours and ports > 1ha (unless included in Schedule 1). Other particularly relevant projects include oil or gas extraction plants and pipelines, and extraction of minerals by fluvial dredging (but not marine dredging).

North Sea Conference 2006 – to protect and improve the marine environment of the North Sea (see www.northsea.org/nsc/news/index.htm).

Strategic Environmental Assessment (SEA) 2001/42/EC – see §1.6.

Water Framework Directive 2000/60/EC* (http://ec.europa.eu/environment/water/water-framework/iep/circa_structure_en.htm) – Imposes a requirement on Member States to work towards and achieve at least "Good Ecological Status" in all bodies of surface water (including rivers, transitional waters (estuaries), coastal waters, and artificial (man-made)), and also to prevent deterioration in the status of those water bodies by 2015. Some water bodies (artificial water bodies and heavily modified water bodies) will only be required to achieve "Good Ecological Potential" (i.e. a slight deviation in ecological status from the relevant reference condition, represented by the maximum level which could reasonably be achieved for a water body of that type). The Directive is primarily concerned with the ecological status of aquatic ecosystems (i.e. biological elements, hydromorphological elements supporting the biological elements, and chemical and physico-chemical elements supporting the biological elements.

Note
* See also www.defra.gov.uk/environment/water/quality/index.htm *and* www.environment-agency. gov.uk/business/1745440/.

Table 12.3 UK legislation relevant to the coastal zone

Coast Protection Act 1949 – To make provision for the law relating to the protection of the coast against encroachment by the sea and to make provision for the safety of navigation.

Harbours Act 1964 – To give financial assistance for the improvement of harbours and to make other provisions respecting their construction and maintenance. Section 14 of the Harbours Act allows a Harbour Revision Order (HRO) for works to an existing facility beyond its operational boundary or a Harbour Empowerment Order (HEO) for works to create a new facility.

Sea Fisheries Regulation Act 1966 – Sea Fisheries Committees are responsible for managing and policing sea fisheries and may set byelaws in respect of them.

Salmon and Freshwater Fisheries Act 1975 – Regulations for inland fisheries and for salmon and sea trout within a six-mile zone.

Deposits in the Sea (Exemptions) Order 1985 (www.mceu.gov.uk/) – Lists activities that are exempt from licensing. These exemptions include the return of some matter removed during dredging or deposited for coastal protection or harbour works.

Food and Environment Protection Act (FEPA) 1985 (www.opsi.gov.uk/acts/acts1985a) – Pollution control in coastal waters. Licences required for construction works, dumping at sea (including dredged materials); use of herbicides affecting tidal waters.

Protection of Military Remains 1986 – Protects military remains (War Graves) from ships or aircraft lost in UK waters since 4th August 1914. Aircraft are automatically covered; ships must be designated.

Water Act 1989 – Defines coastal waters as those which are within the area which extends landwards from baselines from which the breadth of the territorial sea is measured as far as the limit of the highest tide or tidal limit of the river.

Town and Country Planning Act 1990 – see Table 11.2.

Environmental Protection Act 1990 – Part I sets out the framework for controlling releases to air, land and water from prescribed process (listed under the Environmental Protection (Prescribed Processes and Substances) Regulations 1991) and include some port and harbour operations.

Land Drainage Act (LDA) 1991 – includes provisions for coastal (as well as inland) flood defences.

Water Resources Act (WRA) 1991 – see Table 10.2.

Conservation (Natural Habitats, andc.) Regulations 1994 – see Table 11.2.

Environment Act 1995 – see Table 10.2.

Natural Environment and Rural Communities (NERC) Act 2006 – see Table 11.2.

Marine Works (Environmental Impact Assessment) Regulations 2007 – make provision of EIA to be carried out prior to the granting of consent for certain regulated activities in UK water and controlled waters, including deposits in the sea, works to ensure safe navigation and harbour works.

Offshore Marine Conservation (Natural Habitats, andc.) Regulations 2007 – provisions for the potential designation of marine SACs (see Table D.1).

Marine Bill 2008 – Defra has launched a Bill to put in place a better system for delivering sustainable development of the marine and coastal environment. This is aimed at addressing both the use and protection of UK marine resources.

Note
Details of most of the original legislation and/or revised statutes are available from www.opsi.gov.uk/.

72 SPAs (see Table D.1) with marine components already present in UK coastal and inshore waters (i.e. within 12 nautical miles of the coast). Many other coastal sites have national (e.g. "ordinary" SSSI) designations, or are non-statutory sites, and significant stretches of coastline are owned or managed by NGOs such as RSPB, NT or NTS.

The geological/geomorphological importance of the coast is also recognised by a large number of *GCR/Earth Heritage Sites* and *Regionally Important Geological Sites* (RIGS) (see §9.4.1 and May and Hansom 2003), and in the case of the internationally important East Devon and West Dorset coast (the "Jurassic Coast"), by designation as a World Heritage site.

In spite of the stringent obligations often imposed by designation, however, many UK estuaries and sections of coastline, recognised as internationally important wildlife sites, are still subject to significant development pressures.

12.3.2 Policies and guidance

The EC *Fifth Environmental Action Programme* (EC 1993) called for **sustainable development** of coastal zones in accordance with the **carrying capacity** of the coastal environments. To this end the development of *Integrated Coastal Zone Management* (ICZM) has been called for by several UN and international conferences, including the *Rio' Earth Summit* (see §11.3.2) and the *World Coastal Conference* (WCC) 1993.

In Britain, the general policies on nature conservation, outlined in §11.3.2, apply to the coastal zone. The planning and policy situation with regard to the coastal zone is set out in Planning and Policy Guidance Note 20 (DoE 1992), although material in this document is now out of date and needs updating in light of recent and planned changes to legislation.

Following a period of limited consideration by relevant authorities, specific coastal zone planning and management issues have received significant attention in the past decade. Particular focus has been placed on improved and integrated coastal management in order to deal with the historically complex, sectoral management arrangements and also to reflect increased awareness of the pressures facing the coastal zone (e.g. climate change, coastal erosion and recreational development). This was initially achieved through the development of *Shoreline Management Plans* (SMPs) (MAFF/WO 1995), *Estuary Management Plans* and, subsequently, *Coastal Habitat Management Plans* (CHaMPs) (EN *et al.* 2003) in certain relevant locations.

In addition to providing a framework of conditions for coastal management (including environmental assessment), these were and are intended to identify (among other things) the flood and coastal defence works likely to be needed to conserve key coastal assets, including the nature conservation interest of SACs, SPAs and Ramsar sites. This is particularly important where the current defence line may be unsustainable or could cause substantial losses, either by preventing intertidal habitats from migrating inland (*coastal squeeze*) or, as a result of retreat, threatening freshwater habitats located behind the current defence line. Second generation *Shoreline Management Plans* (SMP2s) are currently being developed (Defra 2006 and, for example, the North East SMP2 (www.northeastsmp2.org.uk).

In 2002, the European Community also recognised the need for an improved approach in this area and adopted a Recommendation concerning the implementation of *Integrated Coastal Zone Management* (ICZM). In the same year the first marine stewardship report, published jointly by UK Government and the Devolved Administrations, outlined an intention to develop "a new, shared vision for the future of our coastal areas" which would be underpinned by ICZM. In 2003 Defra and the devolved administrations joined together to commission a study which set out to undertake a stocktake of ICZM in the UK. Workshops were held during the extensive consultation with key UK coastal organisations to test gaps between the theory of ICZM and its practical implementation, and a report was produced in 2004 (Defra 2004). Following the UK Stocktake, the UK Government and the Devolved Administrations have been preparing separate draft national strategies on either ICZM or more generally on marine and coastal management (see Defra 2008 and SCF 2004).

In order to deal with the implications of sea level rise, Defra and the Environment Agency (EA) are promoting a long term, adaptive and **precautionary principle** approach to future coastal and flood defence planning, and have produced "recommended contingency allowances" for net sea level rise (up to 2115) for different regions around the English coast (Defra 2006). These have been incorporated in *Planning Policy Statement 25: Development and Flood Risk* (DCLG 2006) together with "recommended national precautionary sensitivity ranges" for offshore wind speed and wave height (**Table 12.4**). PPS25 also states that Regional Spatial Strategies (RSSs) should be consistent with SMPs.

Table 12.4 Recommended: A. regional contingency allowances for net sea level rise; and B. national precautionary sensitivity ranges for offshore wind speed and wave height

A. *Administrative region*	*Net sea level rise (mm/yr) relative to 1990*			
	1990–2025	*2025–2055*	*2055–2085*	*2085–2115*
East of England, East Midlands, London, SE England (south of Flamborough Head)	4.0	8.5	12.0	15.0
South West	3.5	8.0	11.5	14.5
NW England, NE England (north of Flamborough Head)	2.5	7.0	10.0	13.0

B. *Parameter*	*Increase (%) relative to 1990*	
Offshore wind speed	5%	10%
Extreme wave height	5%	10%

Source: DCLG (2006) (PPS25).

Most significantly, the UK Government is currently consulting on new legislation for the marine environment, known as the *Marine Bill*. This new legislation will enable a strategic approach to marine management (Marine Spatial Planning), that integrates effectively with what is already happening on land. The Marine Bill, when it is adopted (which is expected in 2009) will also provide measures for the streamlining and simplification of marine licensing systems, legislation for the delivery of an effective network of Marine Protected Areas (MPAs) and the potential set up of a new organization with the remit to manage marine issues.

The European Union is also considering producing legislation that would require member states to manage marine areas in an integrated manner. This *Marine Strategy Directive* will provide for the environmental protection of Europe's seas and oceans and once in force will oblige Member States to ensure that EU marine waters are in a healthy state by 2020.

12.3.3 Consultees and interest groups

In Britain, the statutory consultees for coastal zone ecology and geomorphology are the relevant SNCO and EPA (Appendix B). Other potential consultees and interested parties will include those referred to in §11.3.3 for ecological impact assessment (EcIA) in general, as well as organisations such as the Centre for Environment Fisheries and Aquaculture Science (CEFAS), the Marine Conservation Society (MCS), port and harbour authorities, boating and sailing clubs, Sea Fisheries Committees, sea angling clubs, and commercial fishing firms, among others.

12.4 Scoping and baseline studies

12.4.1 Introduction and scoping

Much of the ecological interest of the coastal zone is linked to its geomorphology, and ecological studies must take this into account. Moreover, geomorphological processes and changes can have important implications for coastal defence policy and practice. Given this, establishment of an **impact area** may be difficult because of the difficulty of determining both the potential extent of influence associated with a change (e.g. in the tidal range or current speeds) and in determining boundaries in the coastal zone, especially of the sublittoral zone. It is, therefore, sensible for initial geomorphological predictions to be made early in the assessment in order to inform the potential extent of ecological influence. Original estimates may also have to be revised in the light of information that emerges during the study. Consideration of the lateral extent of most geomorphological processes should be confined to **coastal sediment cells** (§12.2.2) and Defra (2006) suggests that, where available, *Shoreline Management Plans* and *Estuary Management Plans* (§12.3.2) should be the starting points for project design and appraisal.

The coastal zone is also affected by developments in associated **catchments** (§12.5.2); so another important aspect may be catchment hydrology (Chapter 10). Furthermore, since many of a project's impacts are likely to be cumulative, it is important to seek information on other predicted developments and trends (e.g. in recreational use). Time and resources permitting, the use of GIS (Chapter 14) should be beneficial, e.g. for facilitating integration between different aspects.

Coastal EcIAs should employ the scoping procedures outlined in §11.4, including the strategy of phases (study levels) for baseline surveys. As for all ecological surveys, planning coastal surveys should also critically accommodate the seasonal windows of key species (see §12.4.4). An EcIA may be deemed to be insufficient by the Regulators if surveys have not been undertaken during key periods of use (or potential use) by notable taxa. The scoping phase can, therefore, play an important role in determining both the key species likely to be affected and the periods during which they may be present (in turn determining the required timing of surveys).

12.4.2 Use of existing information

Much of the information required for a coastal assessment can be compiled in the form of a desk study. General sources of ecological information are given in Table 11.3. Aerial photographs and satellite data, topographic maps, and bathymetric charts, can provide information on the current and recent morphology of the coast, and may reveal substantial changes such as coastal erosion. In some cases, it may be beneficial to consult old maps or other historical information (see Box 7.1) although historic records of coastal erosion are often scarce.

An increasing amount of information is available in the form of inventories and databases (**Table 12.5**). Although many of the data are unlikely to refer to

Table 12.5 Inventories and databases on the coastal zone

British Geological Survey (BGS) National Geosience Data Centre (NGDC) (www.bgs.ac.uk). Online spatial index of BGS data holdings (e.g. seabed datasets sediment particle size and geochemistry (including contaminants), saline intrusion of aquifers). It is held in a GIS format, can be zoomed to small areas and gives costings for the supply of more specific information.

British Oceanographic Data Centre (BODC) (www.bodc.ac.uk) (housed at POL)
United Kingdom digital marine atlas (UKDMAP) 3rd edn (1998) – CD ROM free on request containing maps and databases, e.g. geomorphology, protected areas, JNCC coastal and marine data, species distributions (including seabirds and mammals), plankton, benthos, fisheries, currents, tides, waves, weather, chemical distributions.
UK Directory of Marine Environmental data (UKDMED) and **European Directory for Marine Environmental Data (EDMED)** – online searchable directories of data sets.

Table 12.5 (*continued*)

Coastal Zone Management Centre (CZMC) NetCoast (www.netcoast.nl/) – online access to information on International Coastal Zone Management (ICZM); links to relevant websites.

Environment Agency (EA) www.environment-agency.gov.uk
Bathing Waters Directive database for 464 coastal sites.

Centre for Environment, Fisheries and Aquaculture Science (CEFAS) (www.cefas.co.uk/)
National Marine Monitoring Programme (NMMP) database of significant contaminants, benthic biology and biological effects in estuarine and coastal waters for 87 sites.

Environment and Heritage Service Northern Ireland (EHS) (www.ehsni.gov.uk/)

Water Quality Unit monitoring data archives – most data is available on request.

European Union for Coastal Conservation (EUCC) (www.coastalguide.org/)
Coastal Guide – information on topics such as coastal typology, tidal ranges, threats and management.

Joint Nature Conservancy Committee (JNCC) (www.jncc.gov.uk)
National inventories of UK coastal systems – saltmarshes (JNCC 1989), vegetated shingle (JNCC 1993–94), sand dunes (JNCC 1993–1995) and estuaries (JNCC 1993–1997). **Marine Nature Conservation Review (MNCR) Series** (JNCC 1996–1999) – focus on benthic habitats. **Coastal Directory Series** (JNCC 1995–1998) – focus on environmental and human-use information. **Other Online information** (www.jncc.gov.uk/page-3) including: advice, habitats (e.g. classification, mapping, monitoring and protected); species (e.g. lists, protected species and seabirds).

Mapping European Seabed Habitats (MESH) (www.searchmesh.net) – A range of facilities including guidance on mapping, interactive GIS maps and a metadata catalogue of survey data.

National Biodiversity Network (NBN) (www.searchnbn.net/ – species/habitats/areas datasets)

Marine Biological Association (MBA) (www.mba.ac.uk)
Marine Life Information Network for Britain and Ireland (MarLIN) (www.marlin.ac.uk) – includes: (a) species listed in Conventions and EU/UK legislation: (b) information on species' identification, biology, habitat preferences, distributions, sensitivity (to a range of factors) recoverability, and importance; (c) information on MHCBI biotopes; (d) links to other UK datasets.

Proudman Oceanographic Laboratoty (POL) (www.pol.ac.uk)
Tidal prediction Service and software (see Table 13.4); **Archived data** on physicochemical variables, bathymetry, waves, currents, sea levels, extreme tide estimates, storm surges etc.

Scottish Environmental Protection Agency (SEPA) (www.sepa.org.uk)
Public Registers e.g. Integrated pollution Control (IPC), Water quality Pollution Control; **Reports and policies** e.g. State of the Environment; Bathing Waters Report; **Flood risk assessment**.

---

the immediate vicinity of a project, they can still be useful. For example, tidal regimes can be calculated from data for the nearest ports, available from the National Tidal and Sea Level Facility at the Proudman Oceanographic Laboratory (POL). In addition, some of the websites listed also provide links to other sites, often worldwide, and the organisations may hold, and be willing to supply, information other than that available on the websites. For example, the EPAs have a duty to supply relevant information, on request, for EIAs (although there may be a charge for the provision of this information).

In spite of the increasing range and extent of existing information, much of it may be out of date or inadequate in terms of quality or resolution, and new surveys should be conducted wherever necessary. For example, the SNCOs will normally require more than two years of overwintering (or other relevant) water-bird data for projects that may influence the intertidal zone.

12.4.3 Geomorphological surveys

Geomorphological parameters can be measured by a variety of methods, using in-situ recording instruments and remote sensing techniques, see Andrews *et al.* (2002), Cooper *et al.* (2000), Miller *et al.* (2005) and Woodroffe (2002). However, the methods are generally time consuming and expensive. Moreover, although coastal geomorphology is very dynamic, changes occur relatively slowly; so many methods require repeat measurements over extended periods. Consequently (a) assessment of trends will normally have to rely on existing information, and (b) new surveys for EIA are likely to be restricted to large projects and post-development monitoring programmes (in which case it may be beneficial to initiate appropriate studies at the baseline survey stage). In making decisions about the need for new data, and the selection of appropriate methods, advice should be sought from agencies such as the EPAs (see Appendix B), POL and CEFAS (see Table 12.5).

12.4.4 Problems of ecological field surveys

The coastal zone presents special problems for ecological sampling, especially of the sublittoral zone. However, this is not a good reason to exclude new field-work. Baseline surveys should be undertaken to cover all habitat types and specific taxa that occur within the potential impact area and/or are also identified as particularly sensitive to potential changes in coastal processes. As in all EcIAs, sampling and identification of many taxa can be difficult, time consuming and expensive, so surveys may need to be targeted, e.g. on **notable** species. A bibliography of identification books and keys is available in IEEM (2007) but experts in both sampling methods and identification will usually be needed.

The timing of field surveys and (where possible) repeat sampling, is particularly important in coastal zone assessment because many of the ecosystems have a high degree of seasonality. While some animals may be present all year round, the presence and abundance of many fish and bird populations vary in relation to breeding and overwintering strategies. In particular, many waders and other migratory seabirds are resident on coasts and in estuaries only during the winter months, and some species undertake shorter "stop overs" on spring and autumn migrations. Saltmarsh vegetation grows and flowers relatively late in the summer, and sand dune fauna (and some annual plants) should generally be sampled earlier than the most suitable period for a general vegetation survey (Figure 11.7). Resident shore communities can be sampled at most times of year, but neap tides do not expose the lower shore, and sampling is best conducted during the large spring tide periods in March or September.

12.4.5 Phase 1 ecological field surveys

Phase 1 surveys of maritime and littoral habitats can employ the JNCC phase 1 habitat survey method (§11.5) and, for highly developed coastlines, it may be beneficial to include additional land use categories (see Tables C.1 and C.6). However, The JNCC classification does not cover the sublittoral zone and surveys of both sublittoral and littoral habitats should follow the *Marine Habitat Classification for Britain and Ireland* (MHCBI), which includes habitats from the supralittoral out to the UK 200 nautical mile limit (Connor *et al.* 2004).

The **biotope** was chosen as a fundamental unit in the MHCBI because: (a) there is a strong relationship between benthic marine communities and abiotic habitat factors such as substratum type, water depth and exposure to waves or currents; (b) many marine habitats, especially in deeper water, lack **macrophytes**. Consequently "more significant use of the habitat is made than for many terrestrial classifications, where vegetation is often the prime determinant of the classification's structure" (Connor *et al.* 2004).

The classification is outlined in §C.4. Levels 1 to 3 are readily applicable to Phase 1 surveys because information can usually be obtained by a desk study, and *biotope complexes* can be identified by non-experts or use of subtidal video. Because they involve species identification, *biotopes* and *sub-biotopes* may be considered to require surveys at the Phase 2 level. However, dominant and conspicuous species are not usually difficult to identify; and guidance on Phase 1 survey and mapping (Bunker and Foster-Smith 1996, Wyn *et al.* 2000) suggests that phase 1 surveys should include biotopes except in cases of uncertainty.

12.4.6 Phase 2 surveys of maritime and benthic species and communities

In general, Phase 2 fauna and flora surveys of maritime (supralittoral) habitats can follow the procedures described in §11.6 for terrestrial or freshwater systems.

Coastal birds are included here because they are most frequently surveyed from the land. However, in addition to the general census techniques referred to in §11.6.3, a number of specific methods have been developed for seabirds, e.g. see Tasker *et al.* (1984) and Camphuysen *et al.* (2004) for seabirds at sea; Lloyd *et al.* (1991) and Walsh *et al.* (1995) for seabird breeding colonies; Bibby *et al.*

(2000) for breeding waders; and the British Trust for Ornithology for low tide counts (www.bto.org/webs/). Information on seabird distributions and numbers is available in a number of publications, including Gibbons *et al.* (1993), JNCC (1992–2007), Lloyd *et al.* (1991), and Stone *et al.* (1995). Consequently, data will already exist for many sites and species, enabling the importance of an area for coastal birds to be determined. If it is suspected that information is out of date or that more specific data on assemblages of local or regional importance is required then surveys should be undertaken.

Vegetation surveys can employ the *National Vegetation Classification* (see §C.8). Rodwell (2000) contains the relevant maritime communities, and those of the two vegetated littoral habitats – saltmarshes and seagrass beds; and techniques for shingle and sand dune habitats are described in Hill *et al.* (2005). Saltmarsh and seagrass beds are also included in the MHCBI (see §C.4), levels 4 and 5 of which are suitable for Phase 2 surveys of other littoral and sublittoral biotopes. The system for measuring *species abundances* is SACFOR ratings (Superabundant, Abundant, Common, Frequent, Occasional, Rare) which are based on ranges of per cent cover *or* density (see Table 11.5 and www.jncc. gov.uk/page-2684) depending on the species being sampled. This is because some species, such as seaweeds and encrusting animals, are best sampled by per cent cover, while most animals are best sampled as density. Details of the system, and guidance on survey and mapping methods is given in Connor *et al.* (2004).

Quadrat sampling can be employed on **rocky shores** because seaweeds and most animal residents are immobile and easily visible at low tide (see Baker and Crothers 1987, Davies *et al.* 2001). Rocky shore communities normally show clear zonations along the land-sea axis, so the use of transects along this axis is usually a suitable sampling pattern (Figure 11.8).

A similar sampling pattern may be suitable for **sandy and muddy shores and mudflats**, but sampling the infauna of these requires different techniques. Subsurface *macroinvertebrates* are an important group in these habitats because they are at the base of the food chain. They can be surveyed by a number of methods ranging from a simple inspection of the sediment (e.g. to estimate the densities of lugworms from their castes) to methods which employ the use of corers and grabs to estimate densities and *biomass* (see New 1998, Wolff 1987 and Davies *et al.* 2001).

A problem affecting **sublittoral benthic** surveys is the need for specialist equipment and personnel (e.g. boats and/or divers), and EcIA baseline studies may have to rely on existing information, unless it is identified that these habitats are of particular interest and may potentially be adversely affected by a proposed development or activity. Techniques for survey and monitoring of sublittoral habitats are described in Davies *et al.* (2001).

In both Phase 1 and Phase 2 surveys, attention should also be paid to the presence of UKBAP priority habitats and *Habitats Directive* Annex I habitats. Correspondences of these with JNCC Phase 1 habitats, NVC communities and MHCBI categories are available from several sources (see §C.1).

12.4.7 *Phase 2 surveys of pelagic species and communities*

Like those of sublittoral benthic habitats, pelagic (free swimming or floating) species and communities are relatively inaccessible and can be difficult to survey.

The survey of **plankton** presents problems because (a) they are very small and diverse, (b) they are widespread over large areas of sea, and (c) abundance may undergo rapid fluctuation in time and space (e.g. in relation to currents). Satellite and airborne sensors that respond to chlorophyll-a fluorescence may provide detailed distribution maps for phytoplankton, and are used in **eutrophication** studies, e.g. by the EA. However, the method is very expensive and therefore generally unrealistic for EcIA, and most plankton sampling employs nets and samplers that can be filled with seawater at prescribed depths. These methods, and techniques for analysing the samples, are explained in Newell and Newell (2006) and Tett (1987) who suggests that for survey purposes it is convenient to adopt categories based mainly on ecological rather than taxonomic criteria. Baseline data may be available from the Sir Alister Hardy Foundation for Ocean Science (www.sahfos.ac.uk/) which operates the Continuous Plankton Recorder (CPR) survey in the North Sea and North Atlantic.

Fish survey techniques are numerous and variable in their level of complexity. They are influenced by various characteristics of the fish populations and communities, including: distribution (vertical and horizontal); size and mobility; and population and community dynamics, e.g. single or mixed species shoals, and seasonal migration and breeding patterns. Reviews of methods are provided in Blower *et al.* (1981), Côté and Perrow (2006), Davies *et al.* (2001), Jennings *et al.* (2001), Pitcher and Hart (1982), and Potts and Reay (1987). They can be grouped under two broad headings:

- observation, e.g. aerial, direct underwater, underwater photography and acoustic surveys;
- capture, e.g. by traps, hook and line, hand nets, set nets, seines, trawls, lift, drop and push nets – most of which can provide specimens for mark-recapture programmes (Table 11.5).

The samples obtained by these methods can be analysed to provide information on species abundance, age structure, fish health, dietary requirements and site productivity (see Potts and Reay 1987). This information can indicate the relative worth of a site to fish stocks and hence the significance of a development's potential impact.

Marine mammals can prove difficult to survey. It is relatively easy to estimate numbers in colonies of common seal and grey seal because these are easily recognised, are faithful to particular stretches of coast, and come ashore (especially at pupping time and during the seals' moult) – when aerial and boat surveys can be conducted (Hiby *et al.* 1988, Thompson and Harwood 1990, Ward *et al.* 1988). Numbers of Cetaceans (whales, dolphins and porpoises) can be estimated by aerial, ship and land-based sightings (Hammond 1987, Hammond and Thompson 1991,

Hiby and Hammond 1989). However, precise estimations of marine mammal populations involves the use of time consuming and often expensive field techniques such as mark-recapture and radio telemetry, and are therefore unlikely to be considered in EcIA.

12.4.8 Evaluation of the baseline conditions

When evaluating the baseline conditions, particular attention should be paid to sensitive geomorphological systems and high-value species, habitats and sites. UK government guidelines tend to focus on SACs, SPAs, Ramsar sites and priority UK BAP species and habitats, but this should not preclude the thorough evaluation of "less important" and small sites, especially if these support *notable* species or habitats.

In evaluating habitats, consideration should also be given to "secondary" attributes (e.g. ecological function). For example, in addition to their ecological value, sand dunes and saltmarshes act as natural defence systems. Guidance on determining the value of biodiversity interests (i.e. habitats and species) in the context of EcIA is provided by the Institute of Ecology and Environmental Management (IEEM 2006).

12.5 Impact prediction

12.5.1 Introduction

The difficulty of accurately predicting impacts, imposed by ecosystem complexity (Chapter 11), particularly applies to the coastal zone because of its dynamic nature and the diversity of the habitats and species that occur there. In addition, each type of development brings with it a suite of potential impacts and issues and there can be significant variability between and within individual development types. For example, the potential impacts of a salmon farm on an inshore sea loch are likely to be very different from those of a nuclear power station or barrage scheme on the open coast. However, while activities and development types may differ, some effects may impact in similar ways upon sensitive *receptors*. Thus, both a barrage scheme and a salmon farm may have similar implications for water quality and productivity, but via different impact pathways. It is therefore important in impact prediction to determine and understand both the nature of the effects of the development or activity under consideration and the likely response of the receptors to the potential effects. Because of the value and fragility of many coastal ecosystems, any development which has the potential to disrupt the fine balance of interacting processes and the habitats and species that these processes influence should be viewed with concern.

Significantly, coastal ecosystems are dynamic, hence a combination of natural trends and human influences will inevitably lead to changes even in the absence of development or coastal management. For example, some soft cliffs are currently suffering rapid erosion; some estuaries are changing through progressive sedimentation; and systems such as sand dunes are intrinsically unstable and can be significantly altered by severe storms. A new project must be considered in this context of dynamic natural change and also in the knowledge that many of its potential impacts may be cumulative (i.e. contributing to the impacts of other developments and pressures). It is important to note, however, that the fact that a coastal system is changing will not necessarily make an anthropogenic contribution to the change acceptable.

Within this potential complexity it is important to adopt a structured approach to EIA at the coast, i.e. the assessment of impacts should involve four distinct phases, discussed below:

1. impact identification;
2. description of impact;
3. impact assessment; and
4. derivation of significance.

12.5.2 Sources and types and of impact

The identification of project-related impacts is a key stage within any EIA and should be based on:

- inputs from consultation with the public, key marine users and regulatory authorities;
- a review of existing survey data;
- a review of impacts associated with similar schemes;
- the findings of specialist studies undertaken in relation to the eia (e.g. modelling); and
- the expertise and judgement of the assessors.

Following the identification of site-specific impacts, each impact should be described fully. Ideally, all potential impacts should be identified, quantified and expressed as testable hypotheses, based on the results of earlier studies, where these are available. In the coastal zone, as elsewhere, these hypotheses should then be tested through the use of well-designed monitoring programmes.

Major causes and associated types of impact in the coastal zone are shown in **Figure 12.2** and discussed below. However, this does not represent a complete list or indicate relationships between development types or all of the possible relationships of these with impacts. As in all ecosystems, primary impacts inevitably lead to secondary, tertiary and, potentially, cumulative impacts. Impacts will also vary from development to development.

Urban, industrial and commercial development is considerable, and is the greatest source of impacts, in the coastal zone. In England and Wales: about 31 per cent of the coastline (and 11 per cent of land within 10km) is developed; and the 10km zone is heavily populated, with about 33 per cent of the total population (EA 1999 and Defra 2002). About 40 per cent of UK industry is also

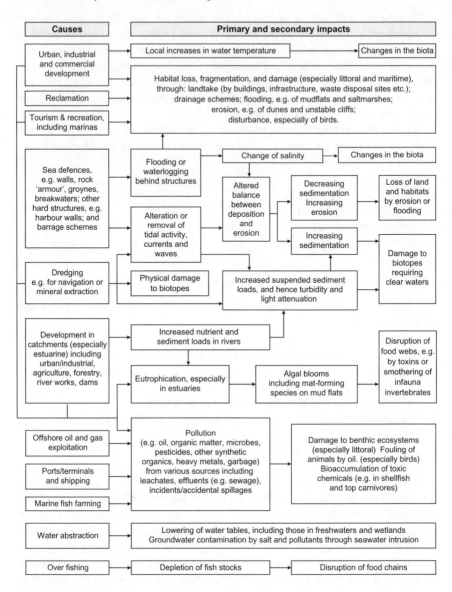

Figure 12.2 Causes and types of impact in the coastal zone.

situated at or near the coast. Much of this is *heavy* (including chemical) *industry*, and many of the developments are very large. As indicated in Figure 12.2, major impacts include habitat loss and fragmentation, and pollution.

A principal reason for industrial siting at the coast is for the transport of goods via ports, but historically another has been the need for the use of large quantities of water in industrial processes and the ease of disposal of unwanted by-products through discharge into coastal and estuarine waters. Industrial dis-charges are now under tighter control through the implementation of various national and European legislative requirements and the introduction of the *Water Framework Directive* (Table 12.2), the ongoing implementation of which will be likely to have a significant beneficial impact upon the coastal environment.

Point source pollution from urban and industrial developments (particularly via sewage effluent) is still the main source of coastal and estuarine water pol-lution, closely followed by *diffuse pollution* from urban areas and land under agricultural production. *Bioaccumulation* of toxic pollutants by coastal and marine organisms can have significant adverse physiological and ecological impacts, espe-cially in shellfish and top carnivores and may also have serious implications for human health (see Brouwer *et al*. 1990, Davies and McKie 1987 and Walker *et al*. 2006). *Eutrophication* (particularly from sewage effluent, urban areas and farmland) can also have various consequences (especially in estuarine and nearshore coastal waters) including contamination of shellfish by toxins from *algal blooms*.

In Scotland, over the last decade, coastal water quality has improved dramatically as a result of the application of full treatment to sewage discharges, improved treatment of industrial effluents, and work to reduce diffuse pollution (SEPA 2006a).

Coastal waters also suffer from pollution by **garbage** from land-based sources, ships and pleasure craft. It is estimated that every seabird in the world has waste plastic inside it. The stomachs of fulmars in the North Sea, storm petrels in the Antarctic and albatrosses in Hawaii have all been found to contain plastic dis-carded by consumers or industry. Some birds may consume hundreds of plastic fragments and many have died as a result. In a study, 19 out of every 20 dead fulmars analysed from around the North Sea had plastic in them. Each bird had swallowed an average of 44 pieces, weighing a total of 0.33 grammes (Save the North Sea 2005).

Tourism and recreation pressures are increasing both on the coast and in estuaries. Direct impacts include visitor pressure on sensitive coastal ecosystems such as sand dunes, very few of which are not impacted by development, leisure facilities or artificial sea defences (Covey and Laffoley 2002). Once dune vege-tation cover becomes damaged, wind can severely erode young frontal dunes and cause large *blowouts* even in mature dunes. A major affect of developments such as marinas is the associated increase in disturbance pressure on wildlife, espe-cially birds, which are heavily reliant upon undisturbed feeding sites.

Reclamation of intertidal areas has a very long history; re-configuring the morphology of the coastline, and hence potentially altering sedimentation and erosion patterns (Cooke and Doornkamp 1990). It is estimated that about one-third of all British intertidal estuarine habitat and half the saltmarsh area has been reclaimed since Roman times, largely for agricultural use (Thornton and Kite 1990). As an example, the intertidal area of the Tees estuary has been reduced by around 90 per cent in the last 100 years (Rothwell and Housden 1990). Today, the large-scale reclamation of intertidal area for agricultural purposes no longer occurs. However, small-scale reclaim for maritime infrastructure projects (e.g. ports, marinas and associated developments) is still on-going, although such schemes are now subject to stringent regulatory controls. Estuarine habitat loss has also been widespread in other countries.

Barrage schemes fall into two basic categories: permeable and impermeable. Some *impermeable barrages*, such as the Thames Barrier, are flood defences against high tides and tidal surges, but many are intended for total exclusion of tides, primarily for amenity purposes such as water sports or providing pleasing views for waterside developments (Therivel *et al.* 1992). The immediate impacts of the latter include the replacement of marine habitats, such as mudflats, by freshwater bodies. The implications of such changes on marine/coastal fauna and flora can be profound, as demonstrated by the numerous studies of ecological impacts associated with the Cardiff Bay Barrage which was completed in 1999. Here, monitoring has revealed significant declines in the populations of waders and waterfowl associated with intertidal mudflats and a rise in the populations of species of terrestrial open water habitat such as mute swan and coot, as well as several species of gull (Burton *et al.* 2003). Barrages are known to have profound effects on sedimentation regimes for many kilometres along the coastline, often enhancing erosion at susceptible sites.

Permeable barrages are intended to harness tidal power for generating hydro-electricity. These may also change sedimentation patterns and enhance eutrophication by inhibiting tidal activity "upstream". By 1990, 22 estuarine sites had been subject to preliminary investigation for this type of barrage scheme (Rothwell and Housden 1990), although none of these schemes have subsequently been advanced. The potential importance of tidal barrages for electricity generation has come to the fore again in recent years as a result of UK Government commitments to produce energy from renewable sources and cut CO_2 emissions as part of a response to tackling the impacts of potential climate change. Leading the way is the proposal to construct a 16km barrage across the Severn Estuary. This ambitious scheme would have the potential to generate 4.4 per cent of the UK electricity needs, but the impacts of a barrage on the existing environment would be immense with the loss of up to 14,500ha of intertidal area (SDC 2007). Further information on the design and environmental impacts of barriers are discussed in Burt and Watts (1996).

Coastal and flood defences are essential to protect many settlements and agricultural land from flooding and coastal erosion. However, "hard" defences and structures (such as harbour walls) can result in disruption to physical processes, leading to geomorphological change. Such structures fail to dissipate wave energy and, by deflecting waves and currents, affect deposition and erosion processes (Carter 1988). For example, sea walls can cause erosion of the protecting beach, and deprive a coastal system of sediment which may be vital in the replenishment of beaches further along the coast, thus causing *downdrift erosion* (Komar 1983). On the other hand, changes in *longshore drift* (§12.2.2) can lead to enhanced sedimentation in calmer waters. Historically, such problems have arisen as a result of the management of coastal defences in relation to administrative rather than geomorphological boundaries when, for example, erosion from within one frontage led to deposition within the frontage of another district (Clayton 1993). Although the legacy of this management approach is still with us, the current management of coastal defences at the level of the coastal sediment cell, in conjunction with SMP reviews as to whether to hold, advance or retreat the line of defence, will help to minimise such impacts in the future. An additional problem associated with hard sea defences is *coastal squeeze* causing the loss of intertidal habitats due to rising sea levels, especially since realignment (retreating the line) can threaten freshwater habitats that have developed behind seawalls (see §12.1 and §12.3.2).

Dredging is carried out for various purposes including: (a) maintenance of navigable waterways, e.g. to ports; (b) harbour and marina creation; and (c) the provision of sand and gravel, e.g. for *beach renourishment* (replacement of eroded material), other coastal defence work, or use by the construction industry. In 2006, 24.3 million tonnes of aggregates were dredged from the sea around Britain (Highley *et al.* 2007). Conversely, it is estimated that 26 million tonnes of dredged waste material was deposited at licensed English marine disposal sites in 2004 (Defra 2007). Impacts associated with dredging include:

- physical damage to the dredge/disposal site, and associated habitat loss or disruption (Posford Haskoning 2004);
- deepening of inshore waters, increasing shoreface slopes and allowing larger waves to break closer to the shore, thus increasing the risk of shoreline erosion (Carter 1988);
- an increase in turbidity during the activity, which may reduce light penetration, and hence primary production and visibility and cause acute physiological responses in some organisms;
- the settlement of material released into suspension by the dredging process, potentially affecting habitats and species outside the immediate dredge area;
- changes in coastal and estuarine bathymetry which may in turn affect local hydrodynamic conditions and sedimentary processes;
- possible release of toxins and nutrients which normally remain locked up in the sediment, thus creating toxic pollution or eutrophication problems;
- landtake at land-based disposal sites which, partly because of the high water content and poor settling qualities of dredged material, can require large areas (ICE 1995).

Land use within river catchments is important because most sections of the coastline from an integral component of river catchments (§10.2.2); so river flow, groundwater levels, and water quality (including nutrient, sediment and toxic pollutant loadings) at the coast can be affected by land use and infrastructure development anywhere in the catchment – often many kilometres inland. Water abstraction, and developments such as dams and irrigation schemes, can reduce (a) groundwater levels, and (b) river flows and sediment loads, leading, for example, to lower sediment accretion rates in estuaries.

Conversely, urban development, river works and agro-forestry (including defor-estation) can increase:

- **runoff** (including flash floods during storm periods);
- soil erosion and consequent suspended sediment loads, which can lead to increased sedimentation in estuary systems and associated consequences such as the need for dredging to maintain navigation; and
- nutrient and toxic pollutant loadings in estuarine and marine waters, e.g. nitrogen inputs to the seas around Britain have increased by c.20 per cent since 1984, and pollutants in many industrial estuaries have reached levels which may harm plankton (Covey and Laffoley 2002).

Most runoff is transported to the coast by rivers, so estuaries are particularly affected by upstream land management. For example, diffuse pollution from agriculture adversely affects 83 per cent of polluted lochs in Scotland (SEPA 2007). Eutrophication can be particularly problematic in small estuaries or those in which tidal flushing has been reduced by other activities. In the River Ythan in Scotland, water quality deteriorated during the 1980s and 1990s, with the estu-ary in particular showing signs of eutrophication. High levels of nitrates (and phosphates) in the river and estuary waters have been the most prominent prob-lem and are believed to have contributed to the increase in algal blooms observed within the estuary (SEPA 2006b). Algal blooms can have a negative effect on bird populations as they reduce the quantity and availability of infau-nal invertebrates which are a prime food source for birds. Studies during the 1990s indicated a decrease in the number of birds in the Ythan Estuary related to an increase in macro-algal biomass in the Ythan (Gorman and Raffaelli 1993). The eutrophication effects observed in the estuary resulted in the designation in 2000 of the entire catchment area of the Ythan as a *Nitrate Vulnerable Zone* (NVZ) (see Table 10.1). The estuary was also designated a "Sensitive Area (Eutrophic)" under the *Urban Waste Water Treatment Directive* (UWWTD) in 2000, and has been identified as a "Problem Area" under the *Oslo and Paris (OSPAR) Convention* (Table 12.2).

Oil and gas exploitation involves exploration, laying of pipelines, construc-tion of offshore rigs and onshore terminals, and eventual decommissioning. All of these activities cause at least local disturbance of marine species and ecosys-tems. However, the greatest hazard related to this activity is probably the accid-ental release of oil and the consequent chronic and acute effects that this may have on the marine environment. The transport of oil by ocean-going tankers is probably the most prominent and visible source of oil pollution events, largely through accidental spillage. However, shipping as a whole inputs significant amounts of oil and oily waste products to the sea as a result of routine opera-tional discharges, illegal discharges and accidental spills (GESAMP 2007).

Marine fish farming (e.g. salmon farms) in the UK is usually undertaken in the sheltered waters of sea lochs. Fish farms have a high potential to lower water quality in and around the rearing cages as there is often a heavy reliance upon chemicals to control pest outbreaks. Further pollution of the water column and seabed can also result from the high loadings of organic and nitrogenous compounds present in faecal material and uneaten food (Thompson *et al.* 1995). This may reduce the environmental quality of the sea lochs, and hence their ability to support viable populations of characteristic wild species. A further issue is the noted rise of parasitic lice infections associated with salmon farming and the role that these infections may have in observed declines of wild salmonid stocks (Krkošek *et al.* 2005). Additional concerns include disturbance caused by fish farm operational activities, the excessive use of wild stocks of fish to feed captive fish, and the genetic decline of wild salmon stocks as a result of interbreeding with escaped captive stock.

Water abstraction within the coastal zone is an important issue because many coastal communities rely on groundwater for their drinking water supply, and by depleting the groundwater in **aquifers**, abstraction can lead to intrusion by seawater. The main result is *saline intrusion*, but the groundwater can also be contaminated by pollutants present in the seawater. Removal or alteration of certain habitat types such as sand dunes can have a similar effect, as dune formations act as small-scale aquifers and may maintain the water table at an elevated level in relation to surrounding areas. Saline intrusion can also affect the biota of maritime fresh or brackish water habitats. In some areas, the combination of abstraction and infrastructure development has caused the land to sink relative to sea level (IAH 2006).

Over-fishing represents a significant problem for marine ecosystems around the world. Although there are some well-known instances of the collapse of fish stocks, such as the loss of the once prolific cod fishery of the Grand Banks off Newfoundland and the demise of the North Sea cod fishery, the scale of the loss of ocean and coastal fish stocks has only recently been determined. Worm *et al.* (2006) calculate that fish stocks have collapsed in nearly one-third of sea fisheries, and the rate of decline is accelerating. Catch records from the open sea give a picture of declining fish stocks. In 2003, 29 per cent of open sea fisheries were in a state of collapse, defined as a decline to less than 10 per cent of their original yield. Bigger vessels, better nets, and new technology for spotting fish are not bringing the world's fleets bigger returns – in fact, the global catch fell by 13 per cent between 1994 and 2003. Historical records from coastal zones in North America, Europe and Australia show extensive loss of biodiversity along coasts since 1800, with the collapse of about 40 per cent of species. About one-third of once viable coastal fisheries are now considered useless. Although there are many factors that are likely to have contributed to these recorded collapses, over-fishing is considered to be the prime driver behind the observed declines. In particular, the continued capture of small species of fish for use in the animal feed or fertiliser industries, can disrupt food chains, with particularly serious consequences for top carnivores, including large fish, birds and marine mammals.

12.5.3 Methods of impact prediction

The impact assessment phase should follow the identification and subsequent description of impacts. An *impact* arises when a particular *effect* interacts with a receptor to cause a *change* to the environment (adverse or beneficial). Therefore, during the impact assessment stage of a coastal or marine EIA, any site-specific impacts identified should be assessed fully, taking account of both: the nature of the effect; and the nature of the receptor.

Without information relating to these two aspects, it will not be possible to confidently assess potential impacts. It will also not be possible to derive the significance of any impact on the receptor in question, as the derivation of significance is a function of the nature of the effect and the nature of the receptor.

The following aspects of the effect should be defined, as far as possible:

- **Spatial extent** – The spatial extent over which the predicted effect will arise (e.g. regional or national, local (say within 5km of a dredge zone) or at the site of impact).
- **Magnitude** – The scale of change that the effect may cause compared to the baseline.
- **Duration** – The length of time over which the effect occurs.
- **Frequency** – The number of times that the effect occurs within the duration of the activity.

In addition to defining the nature of the effect, it is important to identify and describe the receptors that might be affected by the proposed activity or development. The key aspects of coastal and marine receptors that would require such description are (Posford Haskoning 2004):

- **Vulnerability** – The likelihood (or risk) of an effect interacting with (or affecting) the receptor.
- **Sensitivity/intolerance** – The sensitivity (level of intolerance) of the receptor to the effect being considered – is the species/population or some of the species/population likely to be killed/destroyed and how will viability be affected?. MarLIN (Table 12.5) provides detailed information on the sensitivity of many key features of the marine environment, although the data should be critically appraised, as they may be extrapolated from other similar species).
- **Recoverability** – How long/quickly does it takes for the receptor to recover to its pre-impact state following exposure to an effect (distinguishing between partial and full recovery)?
- **Importance** – Is the receptor "Important" based on a number of criteria, including its occurrence and value on a local, regional, national and international basis, i.e. is it rare or unique, does it have a conservation or commercial value, what is its ecosystem function? (see Appendix D).

Given this context, potential changes (with or without a development) to geomorphological processes and coastal ecological interests should be assessed in relation to baseline conditions, known linkages and interactions, and information on past, current and predicted trends. Due to the highly dynamic nature of the coastal environment and the complexity of relationships between geomorphological processes and the habitats that these processes support and modify, prediction of outcomes as a result of human activity at the coast is uncertain and often difficult to define. Assessment effectively needs to consider the likely changes in processes that an action may cause and then the result of any process change on coastal and marine habitats, species and other environmental parameters (e.g. navigation). Assessing impacts may, therefore, require several steps and need to consider both the primary impacts of an action (e.g. landtake) and also secondary impacts that result from the effects of any process change (e.g. the modification of a sediment transport pathway and the effect that this may have on a habitat).

Where good historical data exists, predicting change in coastal and estuarine processes and morphological features can be undertaken using observed trends. However, because aspects such as coastal sedimentation and erosion are very dynamic processes, even where good historical records are available it cannot be assumed that the same conditions will continue to apply in the future (MAFF 2000). Relying purely on previous trends in forecasting system responses is not, therefore, advisable. It is also important to utilise best available knowledge of the processes and interactions likely to be affected, in order to determine with greater certainty, likely outcomes that may result from changes to one or more of the processes.

To this end a large number of **computer models** have been developed for predicting changes in coastal and estuarine systems and/or for coastal management. But, as discussed above, due to the complexity of the systems and interactions involved, accurately modelling these processes and systems, and determining responses, is difficult. The results from such work should, therefore, be considered in light of limitations of knowledge about the processes, the ability of models to accurately replicate "natural" dynamics and also other relevant contextual information (i.e. modelling results should not be used in isolation for predictive purposes). However, where it is apparent, or likely, that potential changes to coastal processes may result from works in the coastal zone, the use of predictive models in determining potential changes is advisable. Advice on available models, and on the feasibility of utilising them in an EIA, can be sought from a number of organisations, such as CZMC (Coastal Zone Management Centre, www.netcoast.nl/), HR Wallingford (www.hrwallingford.co.uk), ABPmer (www.abpmer.co.uk), Delft Hydraulics (www.wldelft.nl), and Proudman Oceanographic Laboratory (POL, www.pol.ac.uk). A range of relevant predictive approaches were assessed in detail as part of EMPHASYS, a MAFF funded research project which looked at morphological change in estuary systems, how such changes could be modelled and the use of models and outputs in estuary management (EMPHASYS 2000).

In many cases, for example where knowledge or resources are limited, predictions will have to rely on relatively simple methods, such as those outlined in §11.7.3. The implications of some geomorphological changes can be predicted, for example, using standard risk assessment methods (Chater 13) such as the calculation of **return periods** (MAFF 2000; Penning-Rowsell *et al.* 1988). Background information on assessing flood and coastal erosion risks is provided in Thorne *et al.* (2007).

In terms of assessing environmental risk, guidelines have been produced that provide a framework for the development of functional risk assessment (DETR 2000). This document emphasises the establishment of risk assessment, risk management and risk communication as essential elements of a structured decision-making processes across Government.

Usually, within EIA, the derivation of significance for individual impacts has been based on:

Significance of Impact = Magnitude of Effect × Value and Sensitivity of the Receptor

With respect to the magnitude of the effect, this has traditionally been ascribed a value of high, medium or low, based on the scope and nature of the effect, while the value and sensitivity of the receptor has been based on, among other things, the relative geographic importance of the receptor, e.g. is it important on a national, regional, local or site-specific level? Following assessment of these two factors, it is then possible to assign a level of significance to the impact, perhaps using a simple "major/moderate/minor" type matrix (see Table 10.11c and Table 11.8).

However, although this method does enable the significance of an impact to be described, it *does not* take into account a range of other important factors related to both the effect and the receptor which will influence the overall significance of the effect. Therefore, in order to ensure that the impact is fully described, it is recommended that all of the information related to the nature of the effect and the receptor is utilized (e.g. see **Table 12.6**).

It may, for example, be useful to differentiate between pulse, press and catastrophic disturbance types in assessing impact significance (Glasby and Underwood 1996).

A **pulse disturbance** is a short-term disturbance, of potential high intensity, which may result in a temporary response in a population or process. Examples might be (a) the short-term impacts associated with the construction of a building near a coastal waterway which results in disposal of spoil to that waterway, or (b) the temporary changes in beach profile and extent associated with a beach recharge scheme. An important point to consider in determining the significance of pulse disturbances is that many coastal and shallow marine habitats and species groups are adapted to natural pulse disturbances such as fluctuations in sediment transport or high energy storm events.

A **press disturbance** is a sustained or chronic disturbance to the environment which may cause a long-term response. For example, any permanent development

Table 12.6 Example summary table of key aspects of impact and receptor

Nature of Effect	
Description	Intensive deposition of sediment from overflowing and screening
Spatial Extent	This is judged to be **LOCAL** (within 5km of the dredge zone).
Magnitude	**HIGH** – based on the large amount of deposition compared to baseline deposition levels.
Duration	**SHORT-TERM** (six months to five years), i.e. the effect will persist for the duration of the initial five-year dredging licence.
Frequency	**VERY FREQUENT** – deposition is predicted to occur for a period of more than 50% of the life of the activity or will be intermittent.
Nature of Receptor	
Description (example)	**Herring spawning ground (identified through baseline studies).**
Is the receptor vulnerable to the impact being assessed?	**YES** – spatial analysis using GIS indicates that the deposition footprint and the herring spawning ground overlap.
Sensitivity (intolerance) of receptor to impact being assessed	**HIGH** – the predicted depth of deposition is higher than values of smothering that would create adverse effects on herring spawning. Therefore, it is predicted that the deposition of sediment will change the substrate composition to a degree that makes the ground unsuitable for herring spawning.
Recoverability of receptor to the impact being assessed	**HIGH** – the receptor has a rapid recovery rate. The impact is judged to be temporary, as following the cessation of dredging (and deposition), excess sediment would be removed by natural processes and depths of sediment would return to baseline levels within five years. Therefore, the ground would once again be suitable for herring spawning.
Importance of the receptor	**HIGH** – it is the only known spawning ground for this species within the wider study area for this project. In addition, the pre-spawning aggregation of herring in this area also represents an important component of the local commercial fishery (i.e. it has economic value).

Note
The judgement as to both the sensitivity and recoverability of the receptor should be based on the specific aspects of the impact being assessed, i.e. sensitivity and recoverability will vary based on impacts with differing spatial extents, magnitude, duration and frequency.

such as a coastal defence scheme may cause long-term changes to the sediment balance, perhaps enhancing erosion or sediment accretion (which may have positive or negative consequences). Other examples could be (a) the long-term discharge of a thermal plume from a nuclear power station, causing changes in the distribution of littoral biota, or (b) the increased presence of fish near the intake screens of a water cooling system, and their subsequently entrapment on the sieve system.

A **catastrophic disturbance** is a major habitat destruction from which populations are unlikely to recover or that may lead to a complete change in habitat type. An example is the permanent flooding of inter-tidal mudflats by a static barrage scheme. Similarly, cliff collapse caused by the construction of buildings on unstable cliffs might result in the permanent loss of valuable geological or geomorphological features (Baird 1994).

Although these definitions are clear, in practice, a project may generate combinations of the disturbance types and responses to them may vary between organisms (Glasby and Underwood 1996). For example, a pulse disturbance to a population of very long-lived organisms may be a press disturbance to a population of organisms with a short life span. Similarly, a local geomorphological pulse disturbance, such as dredging a channel, may upset the sediment balance and lead to catastrophic disturbances elsewhere in the coastal sediment cell.

A potential framework for integrating information on vulnerability, sensitivity (intolerance), recoverability and the importance of receptors in the assignment of significance criteria to impacts is provided in **Figure 12.3**. This framework is relevant to the assessment of impacts on the following environmental parameters:

- marine ecology,
- nature conservation,
- fish and shellfish resources,
- commercial fisheries, and
- archaeology.

It is not relevant to the assessment of impacts related to changes in physical processes (waves, tidal currents and sediment transport) or navigation (where navigational risk assessments are more useful). With respect to the hydrodynamic regime, extensive information is often available but may be difficult to categorise in the fashion described above. This is because the relevant components (e.g. currents) represent forcing parameters that, if altered, can result in a *change* arising which may or may not directly translate into an *impact* (e.g. a change in current speed). However, its indirect influence on other parameters (such as the benthic resource) could cause an impact to arise, but this would be considered as part of the assessment of impacts on marine ecology (for example). Therefore, discussions concerning the hydrodynamic regime tend to focus on describing change rather than defining impact.

Clearly, the assessment of potential impacts and derivation of significance is heavily reliant on our level of understanding, and also on the quantity and quality of data on potential effects and the sensitivity and recoverability of certain species/habitats to those effects, e.g. smothering and habitat removal. The complexities inherent in coastal ecosystems illustrate how inadequate data and/or understanding of the coastal system hamper impact prediction, and explain why scientists are often loath to make concrete statements regarding changes or losses

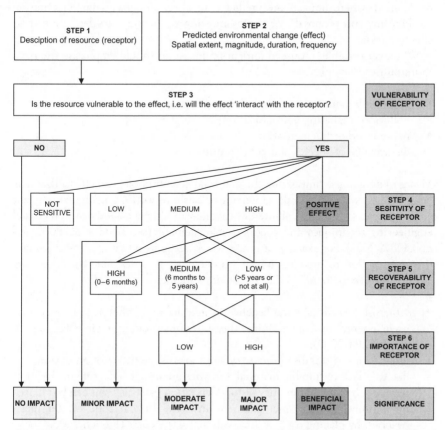

Figure 12.3 Potential decision framework for assigning signficance to impacts on marine ecology, nature conservation, fish and shellfish, and archaeology.
Source: Redrawn from Posford Haskoning (2004).

that a project may generate (i.e. impact prediction is an inexact science). Given that data gaps often exist and that knowledge is incomplete with respect to base-line conditions and certain effects or impacts then, as a mater of good practice, the *precautionary principle* should be applied when such situations are faced in the assessment process.

12.6 Mitigation

Ecologists and geomorphologists involved in the environmental assessment of coastal developments should have the formulation of appropriate mitigation mea-sures as one of their main objectives. Descriptions of proposed measures should be detailed, where impacts are predicted to arise, along with implementation mechanisms and proposals for the monitoring of measures to determine their effectiveness.

Wherever possible, proposed mitigation measures should emphasise the need to minimise or avoid:

- potentially harmful geomorphological changes;
- pollution, including eutrophication;
- habitat loss or fragmentation;
- disturbance of species and communities.

Means of avoiding or mitigating the potential geomorphological effects that may be associated with coastal development or offshore works, and the consequent adverse impacts on ecological interests that may result, are based largely on **coastal engineering** techniques and good site management (see Budd *et al.* 2003 and ENCORA 2007). For example, it is now widely recognised that if a project requires the construction or modification of sea defences, it is desirable that these are "soft" rather than "hard" (§12.5.2). Options include:

- replenish shallow sloping beaches, which are more effective at dissipating wave energy and maintaining the erosion/deposition regime (Brampton 1992, SNH 2000);
- use groynes to stabilise beaches where replenishment is not an option, e.g. due to a lack of suitable material. Groynes are usually effective in the short term, but by their nature they disrupt deposition patterns. This can be reduced by minimising their encroachment into the littoral zone or, for many beaches, by placing them at intervals along the coast (French 2000, Cooke and Doornkamp 1990);
- encourage the maintenance and development of natural barriers such as saltmarshes and sand dunes, which also have positive ecological impacts (e.g. see RH 2005);
- use *Managed realignment* to replace the loss of intertidal habitat (saltmarsh and mudflats) that may be associated with coastal development either directly, through land take, or indirectly, through the disruption of sediment supply (where this may be erosion due to a reduction in supply or smothering due to the presence of a barrier) (see Defra/EA 2002, Leggett *et al.* 2004).

Mitigation measures can also involve "sensitive" construction methods. For example, during the construction phase of projects such as barrage schemes, impacts on sediment balance can be minimised by conducting the work on the leeward side of existing structures, and/or by the use of floating platforms for construction machinery. Further guidance on good construction practice in the coastal and marine environment is provided in the CIRIA guide C584 (Budd *et al.* 2003).

The impacts of **dredging** in estuaries and on the open coast can be reduced by carefully planned extraction programmes and controlled techniques (see Simpson and John 2005). In estuaries, operations can be confined to defined tidal periods in order to facilitate the transport and distribution of sediment disturbed during the dredging process to specific parts of the estuary. Through this approach sediment can either be maintained in the system, so as to promote accretion, or sediment can be taken out of the system in order to minimise potential increases in nutrient loadings, high turbidities and sedimentation rates in sites where biota may be sensitive to these changes. For the dredging of fine sediments, appropriate hydrodynamic techniques can be utilised to minimise impacts (see ABP 1999). Such techniques enable sediment to be redistributed in nearshore and estuarine systems and significantly reduce or avoid the need for the disposal of dredged sediments. In situations where dredged sediments require disposal, this is undertaken at a licensed (normally offshore) site, where environmental characterisation has demonstrated that the likely impacts of disposal will be minimal. It is also a requirement of any dredging programme to consider the beneficial use of any material arising from the dredging process. If undertaken and planned with regard to environmental sensitivities, the beneficial use of dredged material can provide the opportunity to offset adverse impacts associated with the dredging activity. Guidance on the beneficial use of dredged material is provided in Burt (1996).

In addition to maintaining and enhancing natural features, such as sand dunes, that maintain water table levels, mitigation against groundwater contamination by seawater intrusion can be achieved by methods such as **artificial recharge** of the aquifer, e.g. by importing fresh water from outside the catchment or by re-routing streams or storm run-off into infiltration pits, which reduce *evapotranspiration* (Carter 1988). However, care is needed to ensure that such measures do not generate other impacts on the freshwater systems involved.

Is important to avoid or minimise **habitat loss or fragmentation** on both the landward and seaward sides of a project. Together with disturbance of wildlife, these impacts depend largely on project location and design, including the siting of associated infrastructure such as new roads; so mitigation measures must focus on sensitive siting and design. If loss of valuable habitat is unavoidable, compensation may be considered as an alternative, but this should be seen as a last resort since it can be difficult and expensive to recreate many ecological processes and habitat types (see §11.8.4). An example of the creation of compensatory habitat (defining needs and demonstrating success) associated with port developed and the loss of intertidal habitat is provided in John *et al.* (2007).

Apart from protection in reserves that are closed to the public, **damage to fragile habitats** (such as sand dunes) by visitor pressure can be limited by measures such as the exclusion of vehicles, provision of board walks and management procedures to control or repair wind erosion. These may include the use of netting or brushwood fencing or, more effectively, replanting and protecting vegetation, especially marram grass (see EN *et al.* 2003, Doody 1985, 2001 and Houston 1997).

12.7 Monitoring

Monitoring should be undertaken by experts and in consultation with the statutory/regulatory authorities and relevant NGOs (§12.3.3). It forms an integral component of environmental assessment and fulfils a number of purposes, as set out below:

- to test impact hypotheses and thus further understand and improve predictive capabilities for the future;
- to verify the effectiveness of mitigation measures;
- to modify mitigation measures if there are unpredicted harmful effects on the environment;
- to assess performance and monitor compliance with any agreed conditions;
- to provide early warning of undesirable change so that corrective measures can be implemented;
- to provide evidence to refute or support claims for damage compensation; *and*
- to further the knowledge base relating to the actual effects of a particular activity.

The first step in devising a monitoring plan is to define the relevant objectives. The objectives of monitoring must be realistic and measurable. It is important to ensure that the scale of monitoring relates to the scheme or project and that the results will be meaningful and provide effective guidance within the context of the assessment process.

It is important that an effective baseline against which future monitoring can be compared is available. However, it should be recognised that other factors could influence the parameters that are being measured. In this respect, the baseline conditions used for monitoring should take account of other activities that occur or could occur within the EIA study area. The natural variability within a system will need to be determined, as far as possible, in order to predict possible changes in factors such as species abundance and composition in benthic communities, seabed mobility and changes in suspended sediment concentrations (e.g. due to storm activity). Control sites selected for monitoring will also need to take account of these factors to ensure that results are not biased.

In the coastal environment, dealing with variability in the natural system and therefore developing a baseline against which to compare monitoring data may be difficult, particularly for small schemes or projects. To combat this issue, particularly in relation to coastal defense schemes, large-scale regional monitoring programmes are being set up in England. The co-ordination of data gathering at this scale enables resources to be combined, better characterisation of wider coastal dynamics to be gained and the provision of data to enable sound and sustainable management decisions to be made.

Monitoring criteria should effectively be defined by the predicted impacts and proposed mitigation measures. Requirements for monitoring should be site-specific and based on the findings of the baseline surveys and subsequent interpretation. The methodology used for monitoring environmental effects should be the same as that used for determining the characteristics of the relevant parameter during the baseline survey. The frequency of sampling during monitoring will need to be based on the objectives and the criteria for the monitoring as changes in different parameters may occur over a variety of timescales and the frequency of monitoring will need to take this into account (i.e. it cannot be standardized for all parameters).

Dependent on the objective of and criteria for monitoring, it is important to define a level above or below which an effect is considered to be unacceptable, i.e. an "environmental threshold". This is the point beyond which changes in environmental conditions become unacceptable (e.g. for the maintenance of the affected habitat or species). Without this knowledge, monitoring for many parameters is only justified on the basis of improving the knowledge base of the particular effect. Certain parameters, however, do not require this level of information as they are measured just to record changes or reactions to a certain effect (e.g. recovery of benthos).

Defining thresholds can be problematical due to the difficulty of accurately determining the level above or below which an effect becomes sufficiently adverse to warrant action being taken. It often requires detailed knowledge on the sensitivity of various receptors to environmental change. Where knowledge is lacking, there may be a need to apply the precautionary principle. However, this should be applied appropriately to the specific situation under investigation and be based on a realistic scenario and the latest information. The results of monitoring should be analysed and interpreted using the same techniques as applied to the baseline data in order to provide valid comparison over time.

Some geomorphological parameters can be monitored using fairly simple techniques. For example:

- On rocky coasts, cliff recession can be measured with pegs driven into the rock, and beach profiles can be measured using conventional field surveying techniques. Other methods of measuring processes such as coastal erosion are reviewed in Dugdale (1990).
- At a defended coast, Chorley *et al.* (1984) suggest that rates of deposition can be monitored by indicators such as accumulation/erosion at breakwaters and groynes, dilution rates of particles in sediment of known source, or the use of sediment traps or tracers such as dyes.
- Rates of mud accretion (e.g. on saltmarsh) can be measured using standard levelling techniques or sediment traps (Thayer *et al.* 2005).
- Sediment transport can be monitored (a) directly by sampling water, or (b) indirectly by beach profile and groyne height exposure measurements, benthic sampling, or remote sensing.
- Photographic or video records can be made, e.g. of beach profiles and sand dune erosion or recovery (see SNH 2000 or Thayer *et al.* 2005 for techniques and guidance).

Advice on the use of other methods, e.g. for sublittoral monitoring and the use of models, can be sought from a variety of published sources (e.g. Davies *et al.* 2001) and relevant organisations such as CEFAS (see Table 12.5).

12.8 Conclusions

Over the past decade, there have been significant improvements in the approaches and methodologies applied to undertaking EIA in the coastal zone. In particular there has been a move towards greater consideration of cumulative impacts and a shift to looking at ecosystem function and the assessment of changes in interactions between geomorphological and physical processes, and ecological interests. Much of this has been driven by changes in legislation, notably the implementation of the Habitats Regulations and the designation of European sites covering coastal and marine habitats. However, there are still some issues that development proposals and the associated EIA process need to consider further if EIA is to act as a tool that drives sustainability.

One area of particular note is the need for all involved in the process to recognise that the coastal zone is often very dynamic, with significant fluctuations in physical and biological processes occurring over a variety of timescales. To adequately assess potential impacts in relation to this dynamic behaviour requires that data are collected over timescales that reflect the range of environmental conditions and that, sufficient effort is then expended in the monitoring and documentation of impacts and success, or otherwise, of mitigation measures. This issue also requires an element of risk to be accepted in the development of mitigation measures, since it will be almost impossible to know with complete certainty how a coastal system will respond to an effect. Best estimates and predictions must therefore be used in making management decisions. Activities must then be fully monitored and a system put in place to allow appropriate response to the findings (i.e. active management).

While there is clearly still a focus on EIA at the project level, the wider aspects and content that EIA needs to consider is now provided by planning and policy objectives set at the regional and strategic level. On the coast, the context provided by studies at the strategic level has been driven, in part, by the adoption of process driven SMPs (§12.3.2) and the implementation of the SEA *Directive* (see §1.6), e.g. in relation to the exploitation of marine and coastal areas for the production of offshore energy.

The long-running need for a national strategic planning framework for the coast may finally be answered through the measures that will be set out in the *Marine Bill*. This legislation should provide for the development of a strategic planning system that takes on board many of the advantages of ICZM and also leads to better protection for the valuable habitats and species that occur at the UK coast. Adoption of a more strategic planning system for the coastal zone will hopefully lead to the removal of piecemeal development and provide an arena in which to bring together conflicting and overlapping interests. Strategic assessment, planning and management will not remove the need for project-based EIAs, but it should facilitate their execution and effectiveness.

The coastal zone is an outstanding area for wildlife in the UK, and EIA provides a means of providing checks on development activities which could undermine its ecological worth. Both ecological and geomorphological science have an obvious role in the process. While there has been significant progress in describing and determining ecological and geomorphological processes on the coast, there is still much work to do in understanding the linkages between the physical and biological environment and how, in particular, habitats and species respond to changes in coastal processes. If coastal EIA is to develop as a tool for environmental management, which helps to realize the goals of conservation and sustainability, it is important that ecologists and geomorphologists have a greater input to the process.

References

ABP (Associated British Ports) Research and Consultancy Ltd 1999. *Good practice guidelines for ports and harbours operating within or near UK European marine sites.* English Nature, UK Marine SACs Project Report, www.ukmarinesac.org.uk/pdfs/guidelines.pdf.

Adam P 1993. *Saltmarsh ecology.* Cambridge: Cambridge University Press.

Andrews BD, Gare PA and Colby JD 2002. Techniques for GIS modelling of coastal dunes. *Geomorphology* **48**, 289–308.

Baird WJ 1994. Naked rock and the fear of exposure. In *Geological and landscape conservation.* D O'Halloran, C Green, M Harley, M Stanley and J Knill (eds), 335–336. London: The Geological Society.

Baker JM and JH Crothers 1987. Intertidal rock. In *Biological surveys of estuaries and coasts,* JM Baker and WJ Wolff (eds), 157–197. Cambridge: Cambridge University Press.

Barnes RSK 1994. *The brackish-water fauna of Northwest Europe. An identification guide to brackish-water habitats, ecology and macrofauna for field workers, naturalists and students.* Cambridge: Cambridge University Press.

Bassett JA and TGF Curtis 1985. The nature and occurrence of sand dune machair in Ireland. *Proceedings of the Royal Irish Academy* **85B**, 1–20.

Bibby CJ, ND Burgess, DA Hill and S Mustoe 2000. *Bird census techniques.* 2nd edn. London: Academic Press.

Bird ECF 1985. *Coastal changes: a global review.* Chichester: Wiley.

Bird ECF 2008. *Coastal geomorphology: an introduction,* 2nd edn. Chichester: John Wiley & Sons.

Blower JG, LM Cook and JA Bishop 1981. *Estimating the size of animal populations.* London: Allen & Unwin.

Brampton AH 1992. Beaches – the natural way to coastal defence. In *Coastal zone planning and management,* MG Barrett (ed.), 221–229. London: Thomas Telford.

BRIG (Biodiversity Reporting and Information Group) 2007. *Report on the species and habitat review; Report to the UK Biodiversity Partnership.* www.ukbap.org.uk/bapgrouppage.aspx?id=112.

Brouwer A, AJ Murk and JH Koeman 1990. Biochemical and physiological approaches in ecotoxicology. *Functional Ecology* **4**, 275–281.

Brown AC and A McLachlan 2006. *Ecology of sandy shores*, 2nd edn. London: Academic Press.

Budd M, S John, J Simm and M Wilkinson 2003. *Coastal and marine environmental site guide* (C584). London: CIRIA.

Bunker F and RL Foster-Smith 1996. *A Field guide for seashore mapping*. Peterborough, Cambs: EN/SNH/CCW/JNCC.

Burt N 1996. *Guidelines for the beneficial use of dredged material*. Report SR 488. HR Wallingford report published on behalf of DoE. London: DfT (Department for Transport), www.dft.gov.uk/pgr/shippingports/ports/environment/issues/dredging/guidelinesforbeneficialuseof4932?page=1#a1000.

Burt N and J Watts 1996. *Barrages: engineering, designs and environmental impacts*. Chichester: John Wiley & Sons.

Burton HHK, MM Rehfisch and NA Clark 2003. *The effect of the Cardiff Bay Barrage on waterbird populations. Final report*. British Trust for Ornithology. Research Report No. 343. Thetford, Cambs: British Trust for Ornthology (BTO).

Camphuysen CJ, AD Fox, MF Leopold and LBK Petersen 2004. *Towards standardised seabirds at sea census techniques in connection with environmental impact assessments for offshore wind farms in the U.K. A comparison of ship and aerial sampling methods for marine birds, and their applicability to offshore wind farm assessments*. Published for the Collaborative Offshore Wind Research Into the Environment (COWRIE), www.offshorewindfarms.co.uk/.

Carter RWG 1988 (reissued 1991). *Coastal environments: an introduction to the physical, ecological and cultural systems of coastlines*. London: Academic Press.

Carter RWG, TGF Curtis and MJ Sheehy-Skeffington (eds) 1992. *Coastal dunes: geomorphology, ecology and management for conservation*. Proceedings of the 3rd European Dune Congress. Galway June 1992. Rotterdam: Balkema.

Chorley RJ, SA Schumm and DE Sugden 1984. *Geomorphology*. London: Methuen.

Clayton KM 1993. *Coastal processes and coastal management*. Cheltenham, Glos: Countryside Commission.

Coles SM 1979. Benthic microalgal populations on intertidal sediments and their role as precursors to salt marsh development. In: *Ecological processes in coastal environments*, RL Jefferies and AJ Davy (eds), 25–42. Oxford: Blackwell Science.

Connor DW, JH Allen, N Golding, KL Howell, LM Leiberknecht, KO Northen and JB Reker 2004. *The Marine Habitat Classification for Britain and Ireland, Version 04.05* Peterborough, Cambs: JNCC, www.jncc.gov.uk/Default.aspx?page=1584.

Cooke RU and JC Doornkamp 1990. *Geomorphology in environmental management*, 2nd edn. Oxford: Oxford University Press.

Cooper NJ, DJ Leggett and JP Lowe 2000. Beach-profile measurement, theory and analysis: practical guidance and applied case studies. *Water and Environment Journal* 14(2), 79–88.

Côté IM and MR Perrow 2006. Fish. In *Ecological census techniques: a handbook*, WJ Sutherland (ed.), 2nd edn, 250–277. Cambridge: Cambridge University Press.

Covey R and D.d'A Laffoley 2002. *Maritime state of nature report for England: getting onto an even keel*. Peterborough, Cambs: English Nature, http://naturalengland.communisis.com/naturalenglandshop/docs/CORP1.26.pdf.

Crawford RMM 1998. Shifting sands: plant survival in the dunes. *Biologist* 45 (1), 27–32.

Davidson NC, D d'A Loffoley, JP Doody, LS Way, J Gordon, R Key, CM Drake, MW Pienkowski R Mitchell and KL Duff 1991. *Nature conservation and estuaries in Great Britain*. Peterborough, Cambs: Nature Conservancy Council.

Davies J, J Baxter, M Bradley, D Connor, J Khan, E Murray, W Sanderson, C Turnbull C, and M Vincent 2001. *Marine monitoring handbook*. Peterborough, Cambs: JNCC, www.jncc.gov.uk/page-2430.

Davies IM and JC McKie 1987. Accumulation of total tin and tributyl tin in muscle tissue of farmed Atlantic salmon. *Marine Pollution Bulletin* 18(7), 405–407.

DCLG 2006 *Planning Policy Statement 25: Development and flood risk*. London: DCLG, www.communities.gov.uk/documents/planningandbuilding/pdf/planningpolicystatement25.pdf.

Defra (Department for Environment Food and Rural Affairs) 2002. *Safeguarding our seas: a strategy for the conservation and sustainable development of our marine environment*, www.defra.gov.uk/Environment/water/marine/uk/stewardship/index.htm.

Defra 2004. *ICZM in the UK: a stocktake*. Report by WS Atkins for Defra, London, www.defra.gov.uk/environment/water/marine/uk/iczm/stocktake/index.htm.

Defra 2006. *Shoreline Management Plan guidance*, Vol. 1: *Aims and requirements*. HMSO, www.defra.gov.uk/environ/fcd/policy/smp.htm.

Defra 2007. *Waste strategy for England 2007*. London: HMSO, www.defra.gov.uk/ENVIRONMENT/waste/strategy/strategy07/pdf/waste07-strategy.pdf.

Defra 2008. *Marine: Integrated Coastal Zone Management (ICZM)*. London: Defra, www.defra.gov.uk/environment/water/marine/uk/iczm/index.htm.

Defra/EA 2002. *Managed realignment review: project report*. Defra/Environment Agency Flood and Coastal Defence R&D Programme, Policy Research Project FD 2008, www.defra.gov.uk/science/project_data/DocumentLibrary/FD2008/FD2008_537_FRP.pdf.

DETR 2000. *Guidelines for environmental risk assessment and management*. London: DETR, www.defra.gov.uk/environment/risk/eramguide/.

DoE (Department of Environment) 1992. *Planning and Policy Guidance note 20. Coastal planning* (PPG 20). London: HMSO.

Doody JP (ed.) 1985. *Sand dunes and their management*. Focus on Nature Conservation No. 13. Peterborough, Cambs: JNCC.

Doody JP 2001. *Coastal Conservation and management: an ecological perspective*. Conservation Biology Series, 13. Boston, MA: Kluwer Academic.

Downie AJ 1996. *Saline lagoons and lagoon-like saline ponds in England*. English Nature Science No. 29. Peterborough, Cambs: English Nature.

Dugdale R 1990. Coastal processes. In *Geomorphological techniques*, 2nd edn, A Gougie, M Anderson, T Burt, J Lewin, K Richards, B Whalley and P Worsley (eds), 351–364. London: Unwin Hyman.

Dyer KR 1998. *Estuaries: a physical introduction*, 2nd edn. Chichester: John Wiley & Sons.

EA (Environment Agency) 1997. *Our policy and practice for the protection of floodplains*. Bristol: Environment Agency (www.environment-agency.gov.uk/).

EA 1999. *State of the environment in England and Wales: Coasts*. London: TSO (extracts available from www.environment-agency.gov.uk/).

Earle R and DG Erwin (eds) 1983. *Sublittoral ecology, the ecology of the shallow sublittoral benthos*. Oxford: Oxford University Press.

EC (European Commission) 1993. *Towards sustainability: The Fifth EC Environmental Action Programme*. Brussels: EC, http://ec.europa.eu/environment/actionpr.htm.

EEA (European Environment Agency) 2006. *The changing faces of Europe's coastal areas*. EEA Report 6/2006, http://reports.eea.europa.eu/eea_report_2006_6/en.

EMPHASYS 2000. *A guide to prediction of morphological change within estuarine. systems*: Version 1B. EMPHASYS Consortium for MAFF Project FD1401, http://books.hrwallingford.co.uk/acatalog/free_downloads/tr114.pdf.

EN *et al.* (English Nature, Environment Agency, Defra, LIFE and NERC) 2003. *Living with the sea: good practice guide.* Peterborough, Cambs: English Nature, www.english-nature. org.uk/livingwiththesea/project_details/good_practice_guide/habitatCRR/enrestore/ home.htm.

ENCORA 2007. *European platform for sharing knowledge and experience in coastal science, policy and practice,* http://encora.eu.

French PW 2000. *Coastal Protection: Processes, problems and solutions.* London: Routledge.

GESAMP (Group of Experts on the Scientific Aspects of Marine Environmental Protection) 2007. *Estimates of oil entering the marine environment from sea-based activities.* International Marine Organisation. Report No. 75. London: GESCAMP, http://gesamp.net/page.php?page=3.

Gibbons DW, JB Reid and RA Chapman (eds) 1993. *The new atlas of breeding birds in Britain and Ireland.* Carlton, Staffs: T & AD Poyser.

Gimmingham CH, W Ritchie, BB Wiletts and AJ Willis (eds) 1989. *Coastal sand dunes.* Edinburgh: Royal Society of Edinburgh.

Glasby TM and AJ Underwood 1996. Sampling to differentiate between press and pulse disturbances. *Environmental Monitoring and Assessment* **42**, 241–252.

Gorman M and D Raffaelli 1993. The Ythan estuary. *Biologist* **40**(1), 10–13.

Gray JS and M Elliot 2008. *The ecology of marine sediments,* 2nd edn. Oxford: Oxford University Press.

Gubbay S 1990. *A future for the coast: Proposals for a UK Coastal Zone Management Plan.* Ross-on-Wye, Herefordshire: Marine Conservation Society.

Hammond PS 1987. Techniques for estimating the size of whale populations. *Symposium of the Zoological Society of London* **58**, 225–245.

Hammond PS and PM Thompson 1991. Minimum estimation of the number of bottlenose dolphins *Tursiops truncatus* in the Moray Firth, N.E. Scotland. *Biological Conservation* **56**, 79–87.

Heath, MF and MI Evans (eds) 2000. *Important bird areas in Europe: priority sites for conservation.* Vol. 1: *Northern Europe.* Cambridge: Birdlife.

Hiby AR and PS Hammond 1989. Survey techniques for estimating abundance of cetaceans. *Report to the International Whaling Commision (Special Issue No. 11),* 47–80.

Hiby AR, D Thompson and AJ Ward 1988. Census of grey seals by aerial photography. *Photogrammetric Record* **12**, 589–594.

Highley DE, LE Hetherington, TJ Brown, DJ Harrison and GO Jenkins 2007. *The strategic importance of the marine aggregate industry to the UK.* BGS Report (OR/07/019). Keyworth, Notts: British Geological Survey, http://nora.nerc.ac.uk/1763/.

Hill D, M Fasham, G Tucker, M Shewry and P Shaw 2005. *Handbook of biodiversity methods: survey, evaluation and monitoring.* Cambridge: Cambridge University Press.

Hiscock K (ed.) 1998. *Benthic marine ecosystems of Great Britain and the north-east Atlantic.* Peterborough, Cambs: JNCC.

Houston J 1997. Conservation and management on British dune systems. *British Wildlife* **8**, 297–307.

HR (Hydraulics Research) Wallingford 1993. *Coastal management: mapping of littoral cells.* Report SR 328. Wallingford, Oxon: Hydraulics Research.

IAH (International Association of Hydrogeologists) 2006. *4th World Water Forum. Groundwater for life and livelihoods – the framework for sustainable use.* Kenilworth, Warks: International Association of Hydrogeologists.

ICE (Institution of Civil Engineers) 1995. *Dredging: ICE design and practice guide.* London: Thomas Telford.

IEEM (Institute of Ecology and Environmental Management) 2006. *Guidelines for Ecological Impact Assessment in the United Kingdom* (version 7 July 2006). www.ieem.org.uk/ecia/index.html.

IEEM 2007. *Sources of survey methods (Guidelines for survey methodology)*. Winchester: IEEM, www.ieem.net/survey-sources/.

IPCC (Intergovernmental Panel on Climate Change) 2007. *Climate change 2007: the physical science basis* (Contribution of working group I to the Fourth Assessment Report of the IPCC). Cambridge and New York: Cambridge University Press. (Summary available at www.aaas.org/news/press_room/climate_change/media/4th_spm2feb07.pdf.)

Jennings S, MJ Kaiser and JD Reynolds 2001. *Marine fisheries ecology*. Oxford: Blackwell Science.

JNCC (Joint Nature Conservation Committee) (Burd F) 1989. *The saltmarsh survey of Great Britain: an inventory of British saltmarshes*. Peterborough, Cambs: JNCC.

JNCC (various authors) 1992–2007. *Seabird numbers and breeding success in Britain and Ireland*. Peterborough, Cambs: JNCC, www.jncc.gov.uk/page-1530.

JNCC (Sneddon P and RE Randall) 1993–1994. *The coastal vegetated shingle structures of Great Britain*: Main Report (1993); Appendix 1 *Shingle sites in Wales* (1993); Appendix 2 *Shingle sites in Scotland* (1994); Appendix 3 *Shingle sites in England* (1994). Peterborough: JNCC.

JNCC 1993–1995. *Sand dune vegetation survey of Great Britain: Part 1 England* (GP Radley, 1994); *Part 2 Scotland* (TCD Dargie, 1993); *Part 3 Wales* (TCD Dargie, 1995). Peterborough, Cambs: JNCC.

JNCC (Buck et al.) 1993–1997. *An inventory of UK estuaries*: Vol. 1: *Introduction and methodology* (1997); Vol. 2: *South-west Britain* (1993); Vol. 3: *North-west Britain* (1993); Vol. 4: *North and east Scotland* (1993); Vol. 5: *Eastern England* (1997); Vol. 6: *Southern England* (1997); Vol. 7: *Northern Ireland* (1996). Peterborough, Cambs: JNCC.

JNCC (Barne et al.) 1995–1998. *Coasts and seas of the United Kingdom – Coastal directory series* (16 regional vols). Peterborough, Cambs: JNCC, www.jncc.gov.uk/default.aspx?page=2157 (also available (1999) on CD ROM from CIRIA).

JNCC 1996–1999. *Marine Nature Conservation Review (MNCR) series*. Rationale and methods, Hiscock K (ed.) 1996; 15 regional sectors, various authors 1996–1998 (see also Hiscock 1998). Peterborough, Cambs: JNCC, www.jncc.gov.uk/page-1596.

John SA, M Simpson and T Gray 2007. Compensatory habitats: defining needs and demonstrating success. In *International conference on coastal management*, Institution of Civil Engineers, 183–192. London: Thomas Telford Publishing.

Kent M, TC Dargie and C Reid 2003. The management and conservation of machair vegetation. *Botanical Journal of Scotland* **55**, 161–176.

Komar PD 1983. Coastal erosion in response to the construction of jetties and breakwaters. In: *Handbook of coastal process and erosion*. PD Komar (ed.), 191–204. Boco Raton, FL: CRC Press.

Krkovek M, MA Lewis and JP Volpe 2005. Transmission dynamics of parasitic sea lice from farm to wild salmon. *Proceedings of the Royal Society B*. **272**: 689–696.

Lee M 2001. Coastal defence and the Habitats Directive: predictions of habitat change in England and Wales. *Geographical Journal* **167**, 57–71.

Leggett DJ, N Cooper and R Harvey 2004. *Coastal and estuarine managed realignment – design issues* (CIRIA 628). London: CIRIA, www.ciria.org/acatalog/c628.pdf.

Little C 2000. *The biology of soft shores and estuaries*. Oxford: Oxford University Press.

Little C and JA Kitching 1996. *The biology of rocky shores*. Oxford: Oxford University Press.

Lloyd CS, ML Tasker and KE Partridge 1991. *The status of seabirds in Britain and Ireland.* London: T & A Poyser.

MAFF 2000. *Flood and coastal defence project appraisal guidance: approaches to risk,* FCD-PAG4. London: MAFF, www.defra.gov.uk/environ/fcd/pubs/pagn/default.htm.

MAFF/WO (Welsh Office) 1995. *Shoreline management plans: a guide for coastal defence authorities,* PB 2197. London: MAFF.

McLusky DS and M Elliott 2004. *The estuarine ecosystem: ecology, threats and management,* 3rd edn. Oxford: Oxford University Press.

Martinez ML and NP Psuty (eds) 2004. *Coastal dunes: ecology and conservation.* Berlin and Heidelberg: Springer-Verlag.

Masselink G and MG Hughes 2003. *An introduction to coastal processes and geomorphology.* London: Hodder Arnold.

May VJ and JD Hansom 2003. *Coastal geomorphology of Grea Britain.* Geological Conservation Review Series (GCR) No.28). Peterborough, Cambs: JNCC, www.jncc.gov.uk/default.aspx?page=3012.

Miller RL, CE Del Castillo and BA McKee 2005. *Remote sensing of coastal aquatic environments: technologies, techniques and applications.* Berlin: Springer-Verlag.

Moore PG and R Seed (eds) 1985. *The ecology of rocky coasts.* London: Hodder & Stoughton.

New TR 1998. *Invertebrate surveys for conservation.* Oxford: Oxford University Press.

Newell GE and RC Newell 2006. *Marine plankton: a practical guide* (CD or paperback). Lymington, Hants: Pisces Conservation.

Nordstrom K and W Carter 1991. *Coatsal dunes: form and process.* Chichester: John Wiley & Sons.

Owen N, M Kent and P Dale 1996. The machair vegetation of the Outer Hebrides: a review. In *The Outer Hebrides: the last 14,000 years,* D Gilbertson, M Kent and J Grattan (eds), 123–131. Sheffield: Sheffield University Press.

Packham JR and AJ Willis 1997. *Ecology of dunes, saltmarsh and shingle.* London: Chapman & Hall (Kluwer Academic).

Packham JR, RE Randall, RSK Barnes and A Neal 2001. *Ecology and geomorphology of coastal shingle.* Otley, W. Yorks: Westbury Academic and Scientific Publishing.

Penning-Rowsell E, P Thompson and D Parker 1988. Coastal erosion and flood control: changing institutions, policies and research needs. In: *Geomorphology in environmental planning,* JM Hooke (ed.), 211–230. Chichester: John Wiley & Sons.

Pethick J 1984. *An introduction to coastal geomorphology.* London: Edward Arnold.

Pitcher TJ and PJB Hart 1982. *Fisheries ecology.* London: Croom Helm.

Posford Haskoning 2004. *Marine aggregate environmental impact assessment: approaching good practice* (SAMP1.03). London: DCLG, www.dclgaggregatefund.co.uk/docs/final_reports/samp_1_031.pdf

Potts GW and PJ Reay 1987. Fish. In *Biological surveys of estuaries and coastal habitats,* JM Baker and WJ Wolff (eds), 342–373. Cambridge: Cambridge University Press.

Raffaelli D and S Hawkins 1996. *Intertidal ecology.* Chapman & Hall, London.

Reading HG and JD Collinson 1998. Clastic coats. In *Sedimentary environments: processes, facies and stratigraphy,* 3rd edn, HH Reading (ed.), 154–231. Oxford: Blackwell Science.

RH (Royal Haskoning) 2005. *Saltmarsh management manual.* Electronic Publication (EP), funded by Defra/EA, www.saltmarshmanagementmanual.co.uk/.

Rodwell JS (ed.) 2000. *British plant communities,* Vol. 5: *Maritime communities and vegetation of open habitats.* Cambridge: Cambridge University Press.

Rothwell PI and SD Housden 1990. *Turning the tide: a future for estuaries.* Sandy, Beds: RSPB.

Save the North Sea 2005. *Save the North Sea – Final Report. A project targeting change of attitudes and behaviour towards marine litter in the North Sea.* Interreg IIIb North Sea Programme.

SCF (Scottish Coastal Forum) 2004. *A strategy for Scotland's coast and inshore waters.* Edinburgh: SCF, www.scotland.gov.uk/Publications/2004/07/19639/40165.

SDC (Sustainable Development Commission) 2007. *Turning the tide – tidal power in the UK.* London: SDC, www.sd-commission.org.uk/publications.php?id=607.

SEPA (Scottish Environment Protection Agency) 2006a. *State of Scotland's environment 2006.* Edinburgh: SEPA, www.sepa.org.uk/publications/state_of/2006/main/index.html.

SEPA 2006b. *Nutrient enrichment in the Ythan River and estuary. State of Scotland's environment – supplementary material.* Edinburgh: SEPA, www.sepa.org.uk/publications/state_of/2006/supplemental/pdf/SN3.pdf.

SEPA 2007. *Significant water management issues in the Scotland river basin district.* www.sepa.org.uk/pdf/consultation/current/swmi/swmi_scotland_main.pdf.

Simpson M and SA John 2005. *Port development and estuarine stewardship.* Proceedings of the 3rd International Conference on Marine Science and Technology for Environmental Sustainability. Newcastle-upon-Tyne, April.

SNH (Scottish Natural Heritage) 2000. *A guide to managing coastal erosion in beach/dune systems.* Prepared by HR Wallingford, www.snh.org.uk/publications/on-line/heritage-management/erosion/1.shtml.

Stone CJ, A Webb, C Barton, N Ratcliffe, TC Reed, ML Tasker and MW Pienkowski 1995. *An atlas of seabird distribution in north-west European waters.* Peterborough, Cambs: JNCC.

Summerfield M 1991. *Global geomorphology.* Harlow, Essex: Longman.

Tasker ML, PH Jones, TJ Dixon, BF Blake 1984. Counting seabirds from ships: a review of methods employed and a suggestion for a standardised approach. *AUK* **101**, 567–577.

Tett PB 1987. Plankton. In *Biological surveys of estuaries and coastal habitats*, JM Baker and WJ Wolff (eds), 280–341. Cambridge: Cambridge University Press.

Thayer GW, TA McTigue, RJ Salz, DH Merkey, FM Burrows and PF Gayaldo 2005. *Science-based restoration monitoring of coastal habitats.* Vol. 2: *Tools for monitoring coastal habitats.* NOAA Coastal Ocean Program. Decision Analysis Series No. 23, Vol. 2. Silver Spring, MD: NOAA/CCMA, http://coastalscience.noaa.gov/ecosystems/estuaries/restoration_monitoring.html.

Therivel R, E Wilson, S Thompson, D Heaney and D Pritchard 1992. *Strategic environmental assessment.* London: Earthscan.

Thompson PM and J Harwood 1990. Methods for estimating the population size of common seals, *Phoca vitulina. Journal of Applied Ecology* **27**, 924–938.

Thompson S and J Lee 2001. Coastal ecology and geomorphology. Ch. 13 in *Methods of environmental impact assessment*, 2nd edn, P Morris and R Therivel (eds). London: Spon Press.

Thompson S, JR Treweek and DJ Thurling 1995. The potential application of Strategic Environmental Assessment (SEA) to the farming of Atlantic Salmon (*Salmo salar* L.) in Scotland. *Journal of Environmental Management* **45**, 219–229.

Thorne CR, EP Evans and EC Penning-Rowsell 2007. *Future flooding and coastal erosion risks.* London: Thomas Telford.

Thornton D and DJ Kite 1990. *Changes in the extent of the Thames estuary grazing marshes.* Peterborough, Cambs: Nature Conservancy Council.

Trenhaile AS 1997. *Coastal dynamics and landforms.* Oxford: Clarendon Press.

UKBG (UK Biodiversity Group) 1999. *Tranche 2 Action Plans*: Vol. V: *Maritime species and habitats*. Peterborough, Cambs: English Nature (the plans are available at www.ukbap.org.uk).

Walker CH, SP Hopkin, RM Sibly and DB Peakall 2006. *Principles of ecotoxicology*, 3rd edn. London: Taylor & Francis.

Walsh PM *et al.* 1995. *Seabird monitoring handbook for Britain and Ireland: a compendium of methods for survey and monitoring of breeding seabirds*. Peterborough, Cambs: JNCC.

Ward AJ, D Thompson and AR Hiby 1988. Census techniques for grey seal populations. *Symposia of the Zoological Society of London* **58**, 181–191.

Wolff WJ 1987. Identification. In *Biological surveys of estuaries and coastal habitats*, JM Baker and WJ Wolff (eds), 404–423. Cambridge: Cambridge University Press.

Woodroffe CD 2002. *Coasts: form, process and evolution*. Cambridge: Cambridge University Press.

Worm B, EB Barbier, N Beaumont, J Emmett Duffy, C Folke, BS Halpern, JBC Jackson, HK Lotze, F Micheli, SR Palumbi, N Sala, KA Selkoe, JJ Stachowicz and R Watson 2006. Impacts of Biodiversity Loss on Ocean Ecosystem Services. *Science* 3 November: Vol. 314, no. 5800, 787–790.

Wyn G, P Brazier and M McMath 2000. *CCW's Handbook for Marine Intertidal Phase 1 Survey and Mapping*. Countryside Council for Wales Marine Science Report: 00/06/91. Bangor: CCW.

Part II

Shared and integrative methods

13 Environmental risk assessment and risk management

Andrew Brookes

13.1 Introduction

Risk provides the answer to three key questions: *what can go wrong; how likely is it; and what are the consequences?* (Kaplan and Garrick 1981). To this can be added the question: *what can be done to manage any risks identified and who should be involved?* Environmental Risk Assessment and Management concerns environmental, ecological and human issues and has been an area of rapid growth over the last two decades.

There is now a wealth of publications ranging from provision of guiding principles set by governments for public domain risk analyses (e.g. USEPA 1992, DoE 1995, DETR 2000) to handbooks prescribing more detailed approaches to particular aspects of risk assessment (e.g. Carpenter 1995, Calow 1998, Royal Society 1992). In the last ten years there have been several seminal textbooks, summarising a wealth of scientific papers on all aspects of ecological and human risk assessment (e.g. Burgman 2005, Paustenbach 2002/2007, Suter *et al.* 2000). Decisions are increasingly being made on a risk footing and some government agencies, for example, have acquired specialist expertise in risk analysis (e.g. EA 1997a). EIA practitioners are also increasingly familiarising themselves with risk assessment as a complementary and powerful tool for analysis (e.g. Carpenter 1995, Petts and Eduljee 1994). However, Environmental Risk Assessments (ERAs) are typically undertaken by a separate specialist (trained, for example, in software application) in the relevant discipline (e.g. air quality, flood risk or contaminated land assessment).

Despite Government guidance (e.g. DETR 2000) there are still some issues, not least the need for clarification of terminology. There are still instances where the term "impact" is used, rightly or wrongly, in an interchangeable way with "risk". This chapter is written with the needs of the EIA practitioner in mind, rather than a risk specialist, and seeks to demonstrate the considerable benefits of following a risk-based approach. From an EIA perspective, risk assessment has conventionally been used as a tool for prediction and evaluation, but this chapter also seeks to explore its role as a complementary approach in its own right.

13.2 Definitions and concepts

13.2.1 Overview

Risk assessment is well established in the fields of banking, insurance, and engineering as a management tool for dealing with uncertainty. It is also well used as a tool for improving occupational safety and setting priorities for the allocation of resources. This experience stretches back several decades. Individuals use risk assessment, either consciously or sub-consciously, in their everyday lives such as in negotiating a busy road as a pedestrian or placing a bet on a horse. However it is only relatively recently that risk assessment techniques have been extended to wider environmental considerations.

Environmental Risk Assessment (ERA) is a generic term for a series of tools and techniques concerned with the structured gathering of available information about environmental risks and then the formation of a judgement about them (DoE 1995, DETR 2000). **Risk management** involves reaching decisions on a range of options that balance these risks against the costs and benefits (specifically including the environmental costs and benefits). Communicating the nature and scale of risk and the options is also a key part of the process. **Figure 13.1** sketches out the basic elements of a framework within which ERA may be carried out, including the options of generic and tailored **Quantitative Risk Assessment** (QRA).

13.2.2 Environmental Risk Assessment in the context of EIA

Uncertainty is an inherent and unavoidable aspect of EIA and is a characteristic of all natural systems (see Holling 1978). Uncertainties arise from a variety of sources, including the available data and in the decision-making process itself. Previous literature has largely failed to address this issue with a consequence that EIAs have often included sweeping statements about impacts and the effectiveness of untried mitigation measures (see Brookes 1999, Brookes *et al.* 1998). Where numerical values are used in EIA, a single representative number is chosen that is typically either an average value or the worst-case scenario. This can be very misleading, particularly where there are considerable uncertainties about an outcome and it may be totally inappropriate to use a single number (Harrop and Pollard 1998). By contrast, approaches for managing uncertainty have been developed in parallel with risk assessment techniques (De Jongh 1988) and as a consequence uncertainty is explicit. ERA is a practical tool that can be used to express the likelihood of an outcome.

EIA and ERA are very similar concepts in that they broadly have the same goals and are tools that can inform decision-makers about the frequency and magnitude of adverse environmental consequences arising from activities or planned interventions. A response to such predictions might be that the manager wishes to mitigate or eliminate a particular impact or reduce the risk. Alternative sites or technology options or risk management may be desirable (Figure 13.1).

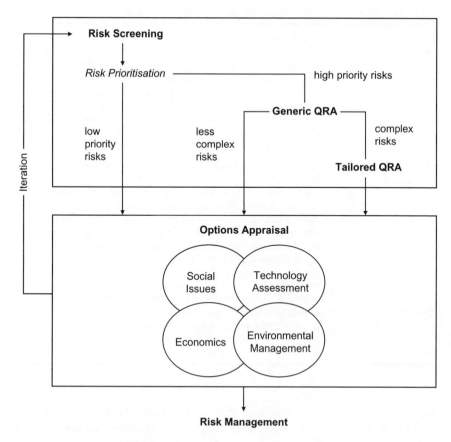

Figure 13.1 A framework for environmental risk assessment.

A major additional aspect provided by ERA is that it can give probabilities to predicted impacts (Suter 1993). EIA and ERA often overlap and are mutually supportive of each other: they both deal with uncertainty, are essentially multi-functional in approach and seek to predict impacts to improve policy, programme, plan and project decisions.

Where potentially negative impacts on the environment and human health must be considered prior to the commencement of a project, they are typically examined through the use of an ERA, ensuring acceptability of site-specific risks and hazards. ERAs are a legal requirement for activities that potentially cause damage to the environment or to human health (and are described in more detail in other relevant chapters in this book). However the question arises as to when in the planning process ERAs should be carried out. Increasingly LPAs have stipulated that they should be submitted at the same time as an EIA, and indeed the results integrated to the EIA, with the details of the method appended. Examples are detailed in **Table 13.1**. ERAs can be applied to air quality (for

Table 13.1 Examples of risk assessment typically covered in EIA in the UK

Type	Description
Flood Risk Assessment	The procedure, set out by the Government in PPS25 (DCLG 2006), aims to avoid inappropriate development in areas at risk from flooding, and to direct development away from areas of highest risk. A Flood Risk Assessment (FRA) needs to assess the risk from all forms of flooding, to and from, the development and demonstrate how these flood risks will be managed taking climate change into account.
Land Contamination Assessment	PPS23 – Annex 2 (DCLG 2004) expands on the policy considerations the Government expects Local Planning Authorities (LPA) to have in regard to preparing policies for development plans and in making decisions on individual planning applications relating to land affected by contamination (see §9.3.4). PPS23 states that the assessment of risks arising from contamination and remediation requirements should be considered on the basis of the current environmental setting, the current land use, and the circumstances of its proposed new use. The underlying approach to identifying and dealing with risk, and the overall policy objective of safeguarding human health and the environment, are similar to that outlined in Part IIA of the Environmental Protection Act (EPA) 1990: "Contaminated Land".

example, waste to energy plants), brownfield site redevelopment and contaminated land issues, as well as ecological risks and health risks from new incinerators and industrial processes. Potentially there are considerable cost-saving and time advantages of combining approaches such as EIA and ERA.

Trained specialists are typically required to assess risks using a range of software packages, including (in the UK):

- CLEA (Defra and EA 2002) and SNIFFER (1999, 2003) to model the effects on human health from contaminated soil;
- ConSim (EA 2003a), and the *Remedial Targets Methodology* (EA 2006) for simulating contamination to groundwaters; *and*
- RBCA (EA 2003b) to calculate risk levels and/or clean-up standards for soil and groundwater for the purposes of protecting human health and the environment.

Staff within regulatory bodies such as the EPAs (see Appendix B) may invoke the **precautionary principle** when there is good reason to believe that harmful effects may occur to human, animal or plant health or to the environment; and the level of scientific uncertainty about the consequences or likelihood of the risk is such that the best available scientific advice cannot assess the risk with sufficient confidence to inform decision-making. This could subsequently put a stop to a particular development proposal. It can therefore be important for the developer to have undertaken the risk assessment prior to submission of a planning application (and accompanying EIA). While there may be reluctance on cost grounds to undertake ERA (particularly if quantitative risk assessment is prescribed rather a more rapid desk study) it can make sense to have completed the ERA early on before, for example, a commitment is made to land purchase.

13.2.3 Problems with the terminology

One of the difficulties with the concept of risk is that it has been developed and applied across a broad range of disciplines and activities, leading to different terminologies. In the UK, the Government-led Interdepartmental Liaison Group on Risk Assessment (ILGRA) has helped to standardise and embed accepted terms over the past decade. The following definitions employed in this chapter:

- **Hazard**: a property or situation with the potential to cause harm;
- **Risk**: a combination of the probability, or frequency of the occurrence of a particular hazard and the magnitude of the adverse effects or harm arising to the quality of human health or the environment;
- **Probability**: the occurrence of a particular event in a given period of time or as one among a number of possible events;
- **Risk Management**: the process of implementing decisions about accepting or altering risks.

In addition, ERA is taken to be a comprehensive term including both human health and wider ecological aspects (see Calow 1998); and ecological risk assessment is seen as a sub-component of ERA.

A particular issue for ERA is the lack of a definable measure of harm to the environment. In dealing with ecosystems (§11.2.3) there are no equivalent endpoints to the premature death of a human used in health risk assessment. For example, a species extinction is a definable endpoint but outcomes of impacts on whole communities and their habitats are much more difficult to quantify (Carpenter 1995). Although there are some definitions laid down in law, appropriate criteria will need to be chosen in other circumstances to reflect both scientific information and social judgements.

13.3 Legislative and policy background and interest groups

13.3.1 Legislative and policy background

While EIA has been evolving for more than two decades in the UK, it is only in the last decade that policies for consistent approaches to risk assessment have been developed for environmental protection. Many regulations and proposed legislation require human health risk assessment. The Environment Act of 1995 specifically requests local authorities to carry out risk assessment and maintain registers of contaminated land (King 1998). MAFF's (now DETR) Control of Pesticides Regulations (1986) requires environmental risks to be assessed and to some extent the Health and Safety Executive, which is responsible for enforcing legislation on workplace safety, includes elements of environmental protection (e.g. Control of Substances Hazardous to Health (COSHH) Regulations, 1994). Generally, however, risk assessment concerned with ecosystems is still not specifically defined in legislation and, unlike EIA, it is not a process that has been tied to the planning system. Nevertheless, risk terminology has crept into the ecological chapters of many Environmental Statements in the UK over the past decade, prompted by the acceptance of uncertainty about impacts and effectiveness of mitigations. Furthermore the Habitats Directive (brought into force in the UK by the Conservation (Natural Habitats) Regulations 1994 (Habitat Regulations)) has led to licence applications which have referred to risk and uncertainty for species afforded the status European Protected Species (EPS).

13.3.2 Interest groups and sources of information

In recent years in the UK there has been progress towards harmonising the approaches to risk assessment advocated or used by Government (e.g. DoE 1995, DETR 2000), and considerable efforts have been made to extend the use and acceptability of ERA. Much has been done to promote it as a best practice tool; and a principal reason for undertaking risk assessment and risk management is a commitment to **sustainable development**. The Environment Agency, through its National Centre for Risk Analysis and Options Appraisal (EA 1997a) is an example of a specific group that was tasked with the development of tools and techniques. Surprisingly, however, there are still relatively few *"how to do it"* manuals for ERA. While it is beneficial to refer to examples of practice, such as previous EIAs with risk assessments of incinerators or landfill sites, at the prescriptive level of EIA for a particular specialism it may be wise to employ a risk specialist.

13.4 Key steps in performing an ERA

ERA attempts to analyse the risks to human health and ecosystems from human activities and natural phenomena. There are several basic steps (outlined below) which should be followed in a process that is iterative.

13.4.1 Hazard identification and analysis

The set of hazards to be identified needs to be clearly defined. For a hazard to result in harm there must be a way in which it can affect a **receptor**. If this is not the case then a risk is non-existent. Some risk specialists use the term source–pathway–receptor to describe the process. An example for a flood defence scheme might be:

- How likely is it that the scheme will be over-topped with flood water? (Hazard);
- How might people living on the neighbouring floodplain be exposed? (Pathway); *and*
- What effects might be experienced by an exposed individual? (Receptor).

For a sewage treatment works the hazard might be the likelihood per year of the exceedance of Environmental Quality Standards (EQSs) to an adjacent river; a pathway would be how fauna and flora are exposed; and a receptor might be a single exposed organism.

Identification of the routes by which a hazardous event may occur is exemplified by the example of a lined landfill site with a **leachate** collection system and an associated treatment plant. Since the concern is the escape of leachate to groundwater then it is not adequate to consider only the possibility of the liner being punctured. It is equally important to look at the possibility of failure of the leachate treatment plant. Techniques are available for the identification of hazards. However, **event tree analysis** is an accepted means of undertaking hazard analysis. **Figure 13.2** shows a typical *event tree* for an accidental spillage. Event trees (also called *decision trees*) can be relatively simple as in the example shown and it is important not to make them too detailed.

Hazard analysis also involves estimating the probability or chance of occurrence of a particular hazard. This involves the collection and analysis of data. The more data that are available, the better, particularly those that are relevant to the local circumstances under consideration. For example, data on actual crashes of road tankers on British roads would be far more relevant to analysis of the risk of a chemical spill from a motorway in Britain than would be worldwide data on past road accidents. In putting numbers or scores on event trees it is important not to be too precise. Precision to one decimal place may have little credibility.

13.4.2 Exposure assessment

The next step is to examine the potential consequences associated with exposure to a hazardous event. A chemical spill, for example, could have a wide range of impacts on the built and natural environment. Factors to take into account would include:

- A clear definition of the nature of the hazard (e.g. quantity and rate of spill). This should be relatively straightforward.
- The characteristics of the local environment (e.g. sensitivity, presence of rare species). Determining this can be problematic, and a detailed site survey over a considerable area could be costly.
- Behaviour of the hazard (e.g. infiltration rates, stream dilution, air dispersion).
- Specific "dose-response" relationships that might be known for particular species or environmental features being considered.

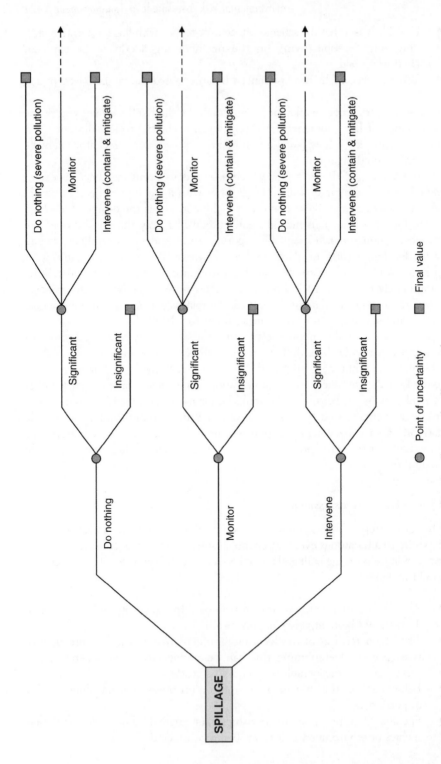

Figure 13.2 An event or decision tree for accidental spillages and pollution risk.

Table 13.2 Examples of risk consequences

Type of consequence	Description
Very high risk	Ecosystem irreversibly altered; no recovery. Over 100km^2 affected.
High risk	Ecosystem altered, but not irreversibly; recovery may take as long as 50 years. 50–100km^2 affected.
Moderate risk	Only one component of the ecosystem affected; 10 year recovery period.
Low risk	Temporary alteration; effects confined to less than 0.5 km^2; recovery in less than five years.
Very low risk	Temporary alteration; very localised and minor consequences.

Determining the first factor is a relatively straightforward process, but the remaining three are much more difficult and complex, and demonstrate some of the difficulties surrounding environmental risk assessment. **Table 13.2** lists some descriptors that might be used to indicate various levels of consequence.

13.4.3 Risk estimation

Risk can be determined by combining the results of hazard and consequence analyses and the simplest form of risk estimation is a matrix (**Table 13.3**).

Such matrices can be designed to be as simple or as complex as appropriate. Approaches to completing a matrix can be qualitative, quantitative, or a combination of both. More complex (and perhaps more controversial) approaches include the use of multi-criteria analysis (MCA) which can involve ranking, scoring and weighting methods to attain an overall risk score. Such methods have now been successfully used to examine risks due to genetically modified organisms (see DoE 1995) and road transport (EA 1997b).

Finally, it is possible to present risk results in numerical terms e.g. that there is a 20 per cent chance that the use of pesticides will lead to the loss of 50 per cent of butterflies.

Table 13.3 Simplified risk matrix

Probability or likelihood	Magnitude		
	High	Medium	Low
High	Very high risk	High risk	Moderate risk
Medium	High risk	Moderate risk	Low risk
Low	Moderate risk	Low risk	Very low risk

13.4.4 Risk evaluation/options appraisal

The importance of this step is in the judgement of the acceptability of the risk. In terms of human health this risk might be expressed in terms of the number of additional deaths per million people arising from a lifetime of exposure or the probability of the frequency of events causing fatalities. From an environmental perspective the preferred option is likely to be the one with the lowest risk. However risk acceptability depends on a complex set of psychological factors.

The communication of the ERA results can take the form of an *Options Appraisal*, i.e. for each option what are the risks, costs and benefits? This can also be useful in authoring the "Alternatives" chapter in an Environmental Impact Statement (EIS). Effective communication can change a layperson's pre-conceived assessment of risks. This leads to more rational decision-making based less on emotions.

13.4.5 Risk management

Since all risk assessments systematically examine the causes and consequences of potential failures then it is usually possible to pinpoint where improvements could be made. Risk Management uses the results of ERA to mitigate or eliminate unacceptable risks. It is, however, important to consider whether or not a particular Risk Management measure leads to a secondary consequence. It is also important to ensure that the appropriate level of resource is directed to the level of risk reduction warranted in a particular circumstance. It is clearly not sensible to direct huge funds at a minor risk. There is a clear need to iterate between Risk Management and Hazard Analysis. Table 13.4 lists the types of options that could be evaluated in relation to road transport and the environment (EA 1997b).

13.5 Different levels of ERA

One way of describing the application of ERA is "different horses for different courses". A traditionally held perception is that risk assessment, perhaps as applied to an operational failure, is a very complex, involved and hence costly process. This may very well be the case where the circumstances warrant such a detailed level of analysis. There are various levels of sophistication for ERA (see Pollard *et al.* 1995).

It is important to recognise the value of different stages in the ERA process. It may be that in many circumstances there is no justification to progress beyond the initial stages (perhaps involving just a desk appraisal) that may be relatively low cost. The degree of sophistication should be determined by the magnitude and significance of risks being studied; the sensitivities of receptors; the quality of available data; and the means by which risks are to be communicated and the outputs utilised (Pollard *et al.* 1995).

Table 13.4 Risk Management options that might be addressed in consideration of road transport impacts on the environment

Type of option	Examples of Risk Management
Policy level	Developing a multi-modal approach to transport, e.g. consideration of investment in forms of transport other than roads
Programme	Consideration of the roads programme for the whole country: rejecting schemes at an early stage with the potential for significant environment impact
Plan	Integrating land use and transport plans, e.g. to consider options for reducing traffic congestion in urban areas
Project level	Improved road design for minimising environmental impact: noise reduction using newer types of road surface; improved safety
Technology	New technology fitted to cars to reduce emissions; using techniques for the secondary treatment of road runoff to remove sediments and other pollutants
Economic	Mechanisms for charging for road use (e.g. in selected city areas; increased taxation on fuel etc.
Education	Improved driver training to minimise accidents but also to instruct the relevant services of what to do in an emergency situation to minimise pollution to the environment

The different levels of risk assessment can be described as follows (see EA 1997a):

- **Risk Screening** – the process used to determine the range of risks, and the factors that control whether they will result in environmental damage. It can be based on available data and substantially on professional judgement.
- **Risk Prioritisation** – a step used to describe the most important risks. If it is decided to progress further with analysis, then monies can be invested in these key risks rather than looking in detail at all risks.
- **Generic Quantitative Risk Assessment** – the use of generally available and tested models to provide simple quantification of the risks.
- **Tailored Quantitative Risk Assessment** – the development of specific models to meet a particular purpose. This is usually complex and costly (e.g. for disposal of radioactive waste).

Figure 13.3 shows the different levels of sophistication that might be used with increasing risk and cost. It is important to adopt the most appropriate techniques to suit the issue under consideration. A global problem such as the depletion of the ozone layer is likely to require a different approach to remediation of an old gas works site for housing development.

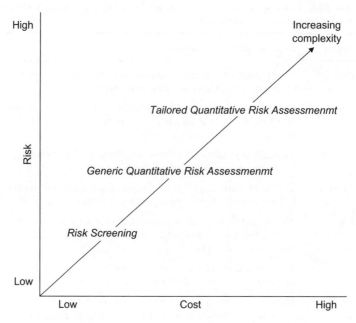

Figure 13.3 Levels of sophistication that might be used with increasing risk and cost.

13.6 Parallels between EIA and ERA

This section attempts to draw some of the parallels between EIA and ERA and also to demonstrate the value of ERA as a tool in its own right (see **Table 13.5**).

Both EIA and ERA are structured tools leading to recommendations concerning the environment that can assist decision-makers. While there are clear parallels to be drawn there are also fundamental differences: for example EIA typically involves consideration of development alternatives while ERA does not. Both are essentially iterative processes and it is important that, as a final stage after implementation of a project, monitoring and audit be considered (Table 13.5). It is only through learning by experiences and mistakes that decisions can be improved "next time". Both EIA and ERA have been developed initially for application at the project level but the processes have been extended to strategic levels of decision-making during the past decade.

13.7 Opportunities and challenges for ERA

ERA should be regarded as a tool allowing the *"what if"* question to be systematically addressed. It is far better to base decisions on the available evidence and in a structured way, rather than relying simply on the "gut feel" of an individual. However there should not be a preoccupation with precision and a quantitative

Table 13.5 Comparison between EIA and ERA

Framework for EIA	*Framework for ERA*
Screening of the project or proposal and preliminary assessment of the existing environment to decide whether to carry out a full-blown EIA followed by *Scoping* of the key environmental issues likely to be affected by the project or proposal.	Screening to determine the range of risks, and the factors that control whether they are likely to result in damage to the environment. When all risks have been identified **prioritisation** or ranking is conducted to ensure that resources for further work are targeted at the highest priority risks. Defining the problem is also known as **hazard identification**.
Baseline Studies – collection of existing information	
Impact Prediction – determining the magnitude, spatial extent and probability of impacts, including direct and indirect effects.	**Hazard Analysis** involves identification of the routes by which hazardous events could occur and estimation of the probability or chance of occurrence. **Consequence Analysis** involves determining the potential consequences of a hazard. **Risk Determination** combines the results of hazard and consequence analysis.
Assessment of the relative importance of the predicted effects, taking into account the present condition and the future condition that would result, as well as any measures of mitigation.	Judging the significance of the estimated risk is known as **Risk Evaluation**, i.e. whether the environment is likely to withstand the effects.
Evaluation of the overall acceptability of the proposal or project and each of its alternatives, leading to selection of one or more preferred options.	It may well be right for decisions to be taken partly in response to pressures generated by risk perceptions. **Risk management** options may be concerned with tolerating or altering risks.
Monitoring and audit e.g. leading to confirmation or rejection of predicted effects.	**Monitoring and audit**. Confirmation or rejection of predicted effects.

output. Rather the process should be seen as tool for assisting decision-makers; it should be transparent, recording the assumptions made and uncertainties in the estimates; and it should be regarded as an iterative process, leading to future refinement. It is important to recognise that ERA and Risk Management are necessarily affected by considerable uncertainties. In established areas of risk assessment such as occupational health and safety evaluations there is a common denominator, namely human exposure. However, ERA is much wider in scope and therefore complex with far greater uncertainty (see Wright 1993). Some factors leading to uncertainty in ERA are:

- Ecosystems are open, dynamic and complex systems with "built-in" variability and recoverability (see §11.2.2–§11.2.4).
- Individual sub-systems may be interdependent.
- Adjustment to, or recovery from, particular impacts may be over a time span longer than a human life.
- It is inherently difficult to measure causal relationships.
- Release of certain persistent materials may cause irreversible change.
- Synergistic effects may arise, e.g. when two chemical pollutants interact and the combined effect is greater than the sum of their separate effects.
- Perceived risk may be just as important (if not more so) than real risk.

However, if the best available information at the time is used, and erroneous data discounted, then gross errors can be avoided.

The relationship of risk assessment with UK Government guidelines on the **precautionary principle** is discussed in ILGRA (2002). One of the key issues in this paper is that application of the precautionary principle "is essentially a matter of making assumptions about consequences and likelihoods to establish credible scenarios, and then using standard procedures of risk assessment and management to inform decisions on how to address the hazard or threat".

Possible uncertainty scenarios are illustrated in Figure 13.4. Increasing uncertainty in the consequences of a hazard is represented by the horizontal axis; while increasing uncertainty in the likelihood that the hazard will be realised is depicted by the vertical axis. Within the "conventional risk assessment" box:

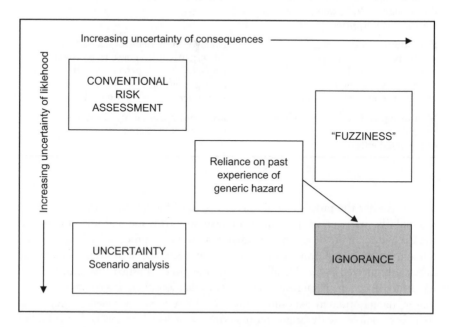

Figure 13.4 Risk, uncertainty and ignorance (adapted from ILGRA 2002).

consequences and likelihoods can largely be established and their robustness checked; the risks are in the main accepted as valid by the stakeholders; and the precautionary principle is not relevant. However, along the axes there is increasing uncertainty, and the precautionary principle has to be invoked and applied to move to a decision. This does not necessarily mean that a development or activity cannot progress provided that, in these circumstances, reasonable assumptions can be made about consequences and likelihoods. For example by moving towards the far right of the horizontal axis more credible consequences can be assigned. Migrating towards the bottom of the vertical axis the assumption is made that the assumed consequences will occur (i.e. the risk will be realised). A credible scenario is established by each set of assumptions.

An ERA completed in this way will not be as full as that resulting from conventional risk assessment but this will not be a serious disadvantage if good judgement is applied on a case-by-case basis in establishing the scenarios. Once the scenarios have been established, conventional means can be used to identify and evaluate, as far as possible, the benefits and costs (advantages and disadvantages) of risk management actions to inform, but not determine, decision-making.

Since risk predictions can be based more on subjectivity rather than on objectivity (Kaplan and Garrick 1981) it is essential that, for the purposes of transparency, gross assumptions and limitations are recorded. It is also a misconception to think that more prescriptive and detailed/quantitative forms of risk assessment will make decisions clearer; difficult choices and trade-offs will still have to be made.

13.8 Risk communication

Communication of risks is of fundamental importance. Decision-making should bring together all relevant social, political, economic, and ethical factors in selecting an appropriate risk management option. Carried out effectively, communication allows people to participate in, or be effectively represented in, decisions concerning management of risks. Guidance on this effective communication is provided in *Risk communication – a guide to regulatory practice* (ILGRA 1998). This publication is of particular general value as it provides some simple guidance, illustrations and pointers to developing good practice on the support principles, e.g. "listening to stakeholders, tailoring the messages and managing the process". Common pitfalls include unrealistic levels of precision in estimates of risk and the portrayal of a zero-risk option. Risk information has often required interpretation by middle management before use by senior decision-makers. It is important that communication between risk experts and decision-makers is appropriate: there needs to be a common understanding of the precise meaning in a particular situation of terms such as significance and inference.

Just as there have been good examples of closer public involvement in the EIA process (not simply through the mandatory steps of consultation) there are those who advocate communication between the risk expert and the public. It is easy to fall into the trap that public consultation exercises to inform (after decisions have already been made on Risk Management options) will suffice. Over the past decade or so, practitioners have moved away from the misconception that "the expert is right" and have increasingly entered into dialogue to ascertain the public's risk perceptions. A more open approach is to create a dialogue that ascertains what the public already knows about a risk and to take on board the public's insight and views on particular Risk Management options. In communicating risk it is important for risk experts to convey that there is no such thing as a risk-free world and that there are considerable uncertainties in scientific knowledge.

13.9 Concluding issues

> Risk assessment can avoid giving wrong answers, but it cannot give uniquely right answers.
>
> (Hrudey 1996)

ERA and EIA are similar forms of impact assessment. While EIA currently remains the predominantly used tool for assessing the potential impacts of projects and proposals, not least because of its definition in legislation, it is clear that ERA has much to offer both in a supportive capacity (e.g. as part of a specialist EIS chapter or annex) and as a complementary technique. ERA is often better at attempting to estimate the certainty, timing and magnitude of potential impacts than EIA. There are now many examples of ERA being used as part of an EIA (and vice versa) to provide information that is combined with information from other sources to contribute to an overall decision. There may be good cost-saving and efficiency reasons for incorporating ERA in the EISs submitted as part of a planning application. Indeed many local planning authorities now prescribe the types of assessment required for determining a planning application (including, for example, Flood Risk Assessment (FRA) and contaminated land assessment).

This chapter has sought to demonstrate that, as long as the assumptions and limitations of ERA are made transparent, then it can be a very useful and credible tool to assist the decision-maker. As practice has increased and the benefits realised, ERA has begun to become more widely accepted. Traditionally, risk assessment has been regarded as a highly quantitative tool that is costly and fraught with uncertainties (see Thomas 1996). However this chapter demonstrated that ERA tools range from relatively simple checklists and matrices to more complex models tailored to specific problems. It is therefore important not to disregard the application of ERA on grounds of cost: it is a highly adaptive and flexible tool and a simple desk study alone can yield valuable information.

Perhaps spawned from specialist chapters based on ERA, the general language in Environmental Statements is increasingly adopting risk terminology, including: the logical source–pathways–receptor concept; consideration of potential impacts in terms of a combination of probability and consequence; risk management (without and with mitigation); and residual risk.

It is also important to appreciate that ERA and EIA have developed largely in parallel and isolation. There is greater scope for cross-fertilisation of experience and procedures between the two processes (Petts and Eduljee 1994) (Table 13.6). Since the concepts are so similar there is still much that EIA practitioners can learn from ERA and risk assessment in general, including a wider acceptance that uncertainty is a fact of life and that risks perceived by the public may be just as important as "real risks". There are now many collaborative and individual initiatives that will strengthen ERA. For example, the UK Interdepartmental Liaison Group on Risk Assessment (ILGRA, now subsumed within HM Treasury) had a sub-group looking at toxicological risk assessment (yielding better estimates of risks and improving assessment procedures). It also set up a study to develop benchmark principles for risk communication and methodology for evaluation and undertook research into the exercise of expert judgement in decision-making.

Table 13.6 Some issues for EIA/ERA cross-fertilisation

Issue	EIA	ERA
Objective process	*Development needed:* EIS reviews often give a high score to grammatical and procedural elements of a report rather than objectively assessing technical credibility	*Considerable experience:* although not professing to be a very objective process, scientific information is considered systematically
Recognition of uncertainties	*Further development needed:* many EISs profess that "all will be well" and/or contain unqualified statements about the effectiveness of new technologies for mitigation	*Considerable experience:* consideration of uncertainty is fundamental to risk assessment
Consideration of alternatives	*Considerable experience:* implicit that development alternatives are considered early in the process	*Further development needed:* more emphasis could be given to consideration of alternatives early in the process
Public involvement	*Further development needed:* calls for public participation in the EIA process	*Considerable experience:* much literature on the value of, and procedures for, evaluating risk perception and communicating risk
Strategic levels of appraisal	*Considerable experience:* theory and now considerable practice of the Strategic Environmental Assessment (SEA) process at policy, programme and plan levels	*Development needed:* much potential to translate what has been learned in SEA to Strategic ERA, e.g. in recent years, Strategic Flood Risk Assessments (SFRAs) have been undertaken

References

Brookes A 1999. Environmental impact assessment for water projects. In *Handbook of environmental impacts assessment*, Vol. 2, J Petts (ed.), 404–430. Oxford: Blackwell Science.

Brookes A, P Downs and K Skinner 1998. Uncertainty in the engineering of wildlife habitats, water and environmental management. *Journal of the Chartered Institute of Water and Environmental Management* 12(1), 25–29.

Burgman M 2005. *Risks and decisions for conservation and environmental management (ecology, biodiversity and conservation)*. Cambridge: Cambridge University Press.

Calow P (ed.) 1998. *Handbook of environmental risk assessment and management*. Oxford: Blackwell Science.

Carpenter RA 1995. Risk Assessment. In *Environmental and social impact assessment*, F Vanclay and DA Bronstein (eds), 193–219. Chichester: John Wiley & Sons.

DCLG (Department for Communities and Local Government) 2004. Planning Policy Statement 23 (PPS23): *Planning and pollution control – Annex 2: development on land affected by contamination*. London: DCLG, www.communities.gov.uk/planningan building/planning/planningpolicyguidance/planningpolicystatements/planningpolicystatements/pps23/.

DCLG 2006. Planning Policy Statement 25 (PPS25): *Development and flood risk*. London: DCLG, www.communities.gov.uk/planningandbuilding/planning/planningpolicyguidance/planningpolicystatements/planningpolicystatements/pps25/.

De Jongh P 1988. Uncertainty in EIA. In *Environmental impact assessment: theory and practice*, P Wathern (ed.). London: Routledge.

Defra (Department for Environment, Food and Rural Affairs) and EA (Environment Agency) 2002. *Contaminated land exposure assessment model (CLEA); Technical basis and algorithms Report CLR10*. Bristol: Environment Agency, www.environment-agency.gov.uk/subjects/landquality/113813/672771/675330/678753/?version=1&lang=_e.

DETR (Department of the Environment, Transport and the Regions) 2000. *Guidelines for environmental risk assessment and management*. London: TSO, www.defra.gov.uk/ENVIRONMENT/risk/eramguide/index.htm.

DoE 1995. *A guide to risk assessment and risk management for environmental protection*. London: HMSO.

EA (Environment Agency) 1997a. *A guide to the National Centre for Risk Analysis and Options Appraisal*. Bristol: Environment Agency.

EA 1997b. *Road transport and the environment, risk profile no. 1*. Bristol: Environment Agency.

EA 2003a. *Contamination impacts on groundwater: simulation by Monte Carlo method*, ConSim release 2, Environment Agency R&D Publication 132. Nottingham: Golder Associates (UK) Ltd, www.consim.co.uk/.

EA 2003b. *Fact sheet for the Risk-Based Corrective Action (RBCA) tool kit for chemical releases* (FS-02). Bristol: Environment Agency, www.environment-agency.gov.uk/commondata/acrobat/ep_123_fact_sheet_rbca.pdf.

EA 2006. *Remedial targets methodology: hydrological risk assessment for land contamination*. Bristol: Environment Agency, http://publications.environment-agency.gov.uk/pdf/GEHO0706BLEQ-e-e.pdf?lang=_e.

Harrop DO and SJT Pollard 1998. Quantitative risk assessment for incineration: is it appropriate for the UK? *Water and Environmental Management, Journal of the Chartered Institution of Water and Environmental Management* 12(1), 48–53.

Holling CS 1978. *Adaptive environmental assessment and management*. Chichester: John Wiley & Sons.

Hrudey SE 1996. *A critical review of current issues in risk assessment and management*, Eco Research Chair in Environmental Risk Management, published as a paper by Environmental Health Program, Department of Public Health Sciences, University of Alberta, Canada, 16pp.

ILGRA (Interdepartmental Liaison Group on Risk Assessment) 1998. *Risk communication – a guide to regulatory practice.* London: Health & Safety Executive (HSE), www.hse.gov.uk/aboutus/meetings/ilgra/risk.pdf.

ILGRA 2002. *The precautionary principle: policy and application.* London: Health & Safety Executive (HSE), www.hse.gov.uk/aboutus/meetings/ilgra/pppa.htm.

Kaplan S and B Garrick 1981. On the quantitative definition of risk. *Risk Analysis* **1**, 1–27.

King NJ 1998. Application of risk assessment in policy and legislation in the European Union and in the United Kingdom. In *Handbook of environmental risk assessment and management*, P Calow (ed.), 249–260. Oxford: Blackwell Science.

Paustenbach DJ (ed.) 2002/2007. *Human and ecological risk assessment: theory and practice.* New York: John Wiley & Sons.

Petts J and G Eduljee 1994. *Environmental impacts assessment for waste treatment and disposal facilities.* Chichester: John Wiley & Sons.

Pollard SJ, DO Harrop, P Crowcroft, SH Mallett, SR Jeffries and PJ Young 1995. Risk assessment for environmental management: approaches and applications. *Journal of the Chartered Institute of Water and Environmental Management* **9**, 621–628.

Royal Society 1992. *Risk analysis, perception and management.* London: Royal Society.

SNIFFER (Scotland and Northern Ireland Forum for Environmental Research) 1999. *Communicating understanding of contaminated land risks.* SNIFFER Project SR97(11)F. Stirling: SEPA, www.sniffer.org.uk.

SNIFFER 2003. *Method for deriving site-specific human health assessment criteria for contaminants in soils*, LQ01. Edinburgh: SNIFFER, http://www.sniffer.org.uk/exe/download.asp?sniffer_news/LQ01.pdf.

Suter GW (ed.) 1993. *Ecological risk assessment*, Boca Raton, FL: Lewis Publishers.

Suter GW, RA Efroymson, BE Sample and DS Jones 2000. *Ecological risk assessment for contaminated sites.* Boca Raton, FL: Lewis Publishers.

Thomas I 1996. *Environmental impacts assessment in Australia: theory and practice.* Sydney: The Federation Press.

USEPA (US Environmental Protection Agency) 1992. *Framework for ecological risk assessment*, Risk Assessment Forum, Report EPA/630/R-92/001. Washington, DC: EPA (online access available at www.epa.gov/nscep/).

Wright NH 1993. *Development of environmental risk assessment (ERA) in Norway.* Tananger, Norway: Norske Shell Exploration and Production.

14 Geographical Information Systems and EIA

Agustin Rodriguez-Bachiller and Graham Wood

14.1 Introduction

Geographical Information Systems (GIS) are databases with powerful mapping capabilities and, for this reason among others, they are becoming increasingly associated with environmental studies of all kinds, including EIA. The definition of GIS has been the subject of some debate (Maguire 1991), and although GIS can be simply described as databases where the information is spatially referenced, what has made GIS so popular is the fact that the spatial referencing of information is related to "maps". It is the manipulation and analysis of the spatial database and the display of maps with relative speed and ease that is the trademark of GIS.

The conceptual and technical origins of GIS can be traced back to the late 1960s and early 1970s, but developing that ease and speed of map combination and display beyond the research environment into commercially viable off-the-shelf systems has taken 20 years of development of computer technology. Today there are thousands of commercial firms world-wide engaged in GIS, in a market worth an estimated $3.6 billion dollars in 2006 (Daratech Inc. 2006) and which is experiencing a rapid rate of year-on-year growth.

The main benefits of GIS seem to be associated with long-term cost-savings in map-production, as well as with extending the use of the GIS to other areas that improve the overall performance of organisations. When GIS technology started to be widely available in the late 1980s, the costs of GIS map-production were initially about twice those of traditional mapping. With time the two tended to converge so that after about seven to eight years the costs of GIS mapping started to be less than those of traditional mapping and the returns of the (sometimes considerable) initial investment in the new system could begin to materialise.

Today, the comparison must be made not with traditional "manual" mapping, but with the production of maps using other (non-GIS) mapping technologies now available, but the question about the time lapse between any investment in GIS technology and the returns it generates still remains. More generally, the problems associated with GIS have changed over the years, and so have the costs associated with these issues. After initial technical problems with the

development of GIS in the 1970s, the lack of available *expertise* to use the systems became the greatest issue in the 1980s, and in the 1990s and into the new
millennium it is mainly the availability of *data* at affordable prices that has become
the greatest bottleneck in GIS use.

In this chapter we shall first introduce and discuss some basic technical
aspects of GIS, and then go on to discuss its potential and applications in EIA.
The literature on GIS is vast, but there are two benchmark publications
(Maguire *et al.* 1991, Longley *et al.* 1999)[1] which summarise most of the
research and development issues in this field. Also, a good introduction to the
concepts and issues behind GIS technology can be found in Longley *et al.* (2005)
while, for the novice, Davis (2001) provides a very useful introduction to the
basics of GIS. On environment-related GIS, the 1990s also provided some key
reference texts. For example, Melli and Zanetti (1992) report on an IBM-
sponsored meeting on computer assisted environmental modelling in 1990 with
many references to GIS, and Goodchild *et al.* (1993, 1996a, 1996b) contain papers
from three subsequent seminal conferences on environmental modelling and GIS
in the US in 1991, 1993 and 1996 respectively. Overviews of GIS in ecology
are provided by Johnston (1998) and Wadsworth and Treweek (1999). The best
known journal on GIS is the *International Journal of Geographical Information Science*
(formerly called *International Journal of Geographical Information Systems*), and useful magazines containing up-to-date information about the GIS industry and its
applications are *GeoWorld* (formerly "GIS World"), *Geo:Connexion*, and *Directions
Magazine* (an online resource available at www.directionsmag.com/).

14.2 GIS concepts and techniques

To understand the potential and limitations of GIS, it is important to remember
that in essence these systems are just a combination of a computer-cartography
system that stores map-data, and a database-management system that stores
attribute-data (an attribute being a characteristic of a map-feature, like the land
use of an area, or the length of a stretch of road). Hence, GIS share the issues
and problems these two types of system (or any information system) have, namely:
data capture and storage; data manipulation and analysis; and presentation of
results.

14.2.1 Data capture

The technology for GIS map-data capture is quite varied, and changing rapidly,
but the techniques can be divided into three categories that can be called
primary, *secondary* and *tertiary* data capture.

Primary data capture techniques (from the real world) include: (a) ground surveys based on sampling, the traditional source of cartographic data; (b) "passive"
remote-sensing based on classifying the "pixels" in a satellite infra-red picture,
and "active" remote-sensing using data from radar; and (c) Global Positioning
Systems (GPS) that use a network of satellites to determine the coordinates of

a point with errors of less than 1 metre for the most sophisticated systems. GPS is used today for all kinds of cartographic and navigation applications, and is probably the most important advance of recent times in the field of cartographic data input.

Secondary data capture techniques, use paper-maps or aerial photographs by: (a) digitising (tracing) on a wired "tablet" the points on the source-map as well as "caricatures" of its lines (lines broken down into straight segments) – labour-intensive and expensive; or (b) scanning maps, using refined versions of the type of technology used in fax machines (much cheaper than tablet-digitising) and converting the scans into digital maps by "heads-up digitizing" on the screen using the mouse as a digitiser.

Tertiary data capture is based on "importing" data from existing sources already in digital form. That this is currently an area of fast growth is not surprising, given the cost and difficulty associated with obtaining primary data, and the labour-intensive nature of secondary data capture. Digital data from airborne and satellite sensors is becoming increasingly available and many national cartographic and environmental agencies are now providing digital cartographic information which is GIS-compatible, even if issues of compatibility of formats sometimes arise when combining several sources. Some examples of sources of digital spatial data are provided in **Table 14.1**.

14.2.2 Data storage

Raw map-data become information when interpreted by conceptual *data-models*, and the type of model used to store GIS maps is one of the clearest dividing lines between different types of GIS maps and, sometimes, even between entire GIS systems (see **Figure 14.1**).

Regular-tessellation "raster" models store maps using more or less simplified versions of a matrix-file, where the different square cells (*rasters*) are stored with the value of their attributes. The advantage of a file of this kind is that it simultaneously defines the map (*where* features are) and the *values* of particular attributes (one for each map) for every feature. First-generation GIS belonged to this kind because they were easier to program and simpler in terms of file-structure. However, they are wasteful of space (they repeat the same information many times, once for every cell) and their greatest drawback is that their accuracy is ultimately determined by the size of the cells they use. Well-known raster-based GIS are:

- GRASS (Geographic Resources Analysis Support System) – free, by the US Army (www.tec.army.mil/TD/tvd/survey/GRASS.html); *and*
- IDRISI Andes – by Clark University (www.clarklabs.org/).

Irregular-tessellation "vector" models represent map-features (points, lines, polygons) by the precise coordinates of their defining points and segment-ends. This greatly increases precision but has the problem of requiring *two* sets of files for

Table 14.1 Selected digital products and sources of digital data

Ordnance Survey (OS) (www.ordnancesurvey.co.uk)

Master Map – an object-based system (based on "objects" like buildings, land-plots, roads etc. instead of "layers" of points, lines and polygons) that supersedes previous OS data sets. It is organised into nine "themes": Administrative boundaries; Buildings; Heritage and antiquities; Land; Rail; Roads, tracks and paths; Structures; Terrain and height; and Water. Each of these themes is divided into detailed sub-classes (e.g. "water" includes sub-classes such as canals, rivers, springs and swimming pools) and each sub-class contains maps that cover the whole country "seamlessly" i.e. in a continuous way, instead of being subdivided into "tiles". Map-features are cross-referenced with postal addresses, and data can be downloaded by geographical or postcode area.

Land-Form PROFILE – topographic contour information at the 1:10,000 scale.

Raster data – largely for use as background maps, available at 1:10,000, 1:25,000, 1:50,000 and 1:250,000 scales.

Historical maps (also in raster form) – national cover dating back to the mid-nineteenth century.

Multi-Agency Geographic Information for the Countryside (MAGIC) (www.magic.gov.uk)

A very useful resource based upon a web-based interactive map that brings together information on key environmental schemes and designations in one place. (MAGIC) hosts a wide range of spatial data including land cover and boundary maps of designated conservation sites (see Tables D.1 and D.2) such as WHSs, Ramsar sites, SACs, SPAs, SSSIs, ESAs, ancient woodland, and greenbelts.

Centre for Ecology and Hydrology (CEH) (www.ceh.ac.uk)

Land Cover Map of Great Britain (LCM2007) – provides a complete map of the land cover of Great Britain derived from satellite information, accurate to the field scale, and also validated using ground surveys. The data set is available either as a vector database containing 26 target/subclasses or as a raster data set available at 25m and 1km resolutions.

British Geological Survey (BGS) (www.bgs.ac.uk)

Digital Geological map data sets for England, Wales and Scotland at 1:625,000, 1:250,000 and 1:50,000 scale, and work continues to extend coverage to the most-detailed 1:10,000 scale.

National Soil Resources Institute (NSRI) Land Information System (www.landis.org.uk)

A range of digital soils information including **NATMAP** (National Soil Map) which is a vector data set that covers 300 mapped soil associations in England and Wales at a scale of 1:250,000. Reclassifications of NATMAP vector in 1, 2, and 5km^2 "gridded-vector" form are available. Data can be obtained for regions, catchments or other user-specified areas.

European Environment Agency (EEA) (www.eea.europa.eu)

Hosts a range of European-wide spatial data sets including: the **CORINE land cover** database and digital map (using 44 land cover classes) at 1:100,0000 and minimum mapable units of 25ha; the **CORINE biotopes** database and map of >7,500 sites significant for nature conservation; the **EUNIS biodiversity** database which has a search facility and GIS tool for habitats, and designated sites.

Other sources

Data provided by GOs and IGOs, e.g. ECNC, ETCs, FAO, UNEP-WCMC, USGS

Base maps etc. from **GIS software vendors** and other **commercial firms**

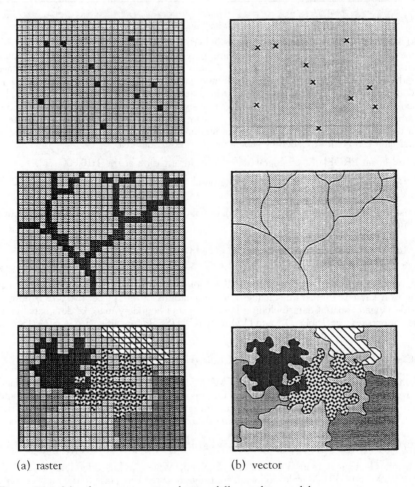

(a) raster   (b) vector

Figure 14.1 Map-features represented using different data-models.
Source: ESRI, Arc-Info reference manual for GRID.

each map: one to store the position and shape of the map-features, and another to store the attributes associated with those features. Vector data can be stored by "layers" (each containing one or several features), or by "objects" (the latest approach) where the attention is on individual cartographic objects, their properties and their membership of different "classes" and sub-classes, with the possibility of "inheritance" of properties between them. Well-known vector-based GIS include:

- Arc-Info, ArcView, building up to ArcGIS (the latest) – the family of packages by ESRI (www.esri.com/);
- GeoMedia – by INTEGRAPH (www.intergraph.com/);
- MapInfo Professional by MapInfo (www.mapinfo.com/).

Today it is quite common to see the most sophisticated of these packages (like the ESRI family above) belonging to a type that could be called "integrated", i.e. capable of combining vector and raster data. Simple mapping programs, with only limited GIS functionality, are also now available for use on PCs. Examples of these include:

- Map Maker pro (www.mapmaker.com/);
- MapPoint (www.microsoft.com/mappoint/);
- AGIS (www.agismap.com/);
- Map Sheets Express (http://gi.leica-geosystems.com/).

14.2.3 Data manipulation and analysis

Despite the cartographic sophistication of GIS, the tasks they can perform in terms of *spatial analysis* are quite limited, and can be summarised in a fairly typical short-list:

1. In two dimensions:

- map "overlay", superimposing maps to produce simple composite-maps, probably one of the most frequently used GIS operations;
- "clipping" one map with the polygons of another to include (or exclude) parts of them, for instance to identify how much of the area of a proposed project overlaps with a sensitive area;
- producing "partial" maps containing only those features from another map that satisfy certain criteria;
- calculating the size (length, area) of the features of a map;
- calculating descriptive statistics for the features of a map (frequency distributions, mean size, maximum and minimum values, etc.);
- doing some form of multivariate analysis (e.g. standard correlation and regression) of the values of different attributes for different features in a map, or between several raster maps covering the same area;
- calculating minimum distances between features (some systems only use straight-line distances, others can also measure distances along "networks");
- using minimum distances to identify the features on one map nearest to particular features on another map;
- using distances to construct "buffer" zones around features, which can then be used to "clip" other maps to include/exclude certain areas;
- using distances to define "proximity areas" closest to certain features (e.g. "catchment areas" relating to a development proposal).

2. With a third dimension:

- interpolating unknown attribute-values for new points between known values for the sample points, using Triangulated Irregular Networks (TINs) to maximise the efficiency of interpolation, or surface interpolation (e.g. spline, inverse distance weighted, etc.) to increase smoothness;

- drawing contour-lines using the interpolated values of an attribute (a "third dimension") e.g. terrain-height or other types of variables like temperature, air pollution, population or income levels, etc.;
- constructing Digital Elevation Models (DEMs), otherwise known as Digital Terrain Models (DTMs) which can then be displayed or further analysed;
- calculating topographic characteristics of the terrain from a DTM, e.g. slope and orientation ("aspect") of different parts, their concavity and convexity;
- calculating volumes in a DTM, for instance the volumes above/below certain heights, which can be used, for example, to calculate water-volumes in lakes or reservoirs;
- identifying "areas of visibility" or the "viewshed" of certain features of one map from the features of another, for instance to define the area from which the tallest building in a proposed project will be visible;
- so-called "modelling", identifying geographical objects from maps, like the existence of valleys or streams, river networks, river-basins, etc.

3. Hybrid:

- combining several maps (2D or 3D) each weighted differently, into more sophisticated composite maps, using "map-algebra" – also referred to as "cartographic modelling" (Tomlin 1990, 1991) – used for instance to do multi-criteria evaluation of possible locations for a particular activity, or calculating the composite effect of a set of factors on an area (see in **Figure 14.2** an example of application to EIA).

The limited range of analytical tasks available in a GIS used to be a classic areas of criticism. Openshaw (1991) argued sometime ago, somewhat ironically, that of the 1,000+ operations that a sophisticated GIS can perform, virtually none relate to true spatial analysis, and functions like those listed above really correspond to what he called "data description". The GIS industry has reacted to these criticisms, and today many of the more sophisticated operations of spatial analysis (e.g. spatial sampling, nearest-neighbour analysis, spatial autocorrelation, trend-surface analysis, centres of gravity, cluster analysis, even some interaction modelling) can be found in more recent releases of many GIS software products, or in "add-on" modules to them.

14.2.3 Presentation of results

The output of GIS is probably the best developed and most appealing aspect of these systems. Output can be produced for a variety of devices (the computer screen, plotters, and printers) and can be classified by its dimensional level as:

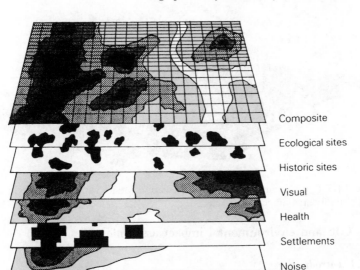

Figure 14.2 The use of overlays to show environmental impacts.
Source: Wathern (1988).

- 2-D displays (maps), which are most common;
- so-called "2.5-D" representations of Digital Terrain Models (DTMs) which use a third (z) dimension over an x-y map. Other maps can be superimposed ("draped") on them so that they *appear* to be in 3D; also, the slopes and aspects of the different raster-cells in these models can be used to calculate sunlight-reflection and produce "shaded" representations of the terrain (see **Figure 14.3**);
- 3-D models, the object of recent research looking at the possibility of representing 3D objects as collections of "sheets" using the standard functions of GIS (which are essentially two-dimensional), or maybe incorporating into GIS some of the features of Computer Aided Design (CAD) or Virtual Reality (VR).

A dominant current trend in GIS output when produced for the computer screen is towards interactive "multimedia" output which combines maps, photographs, moving video-images, and even sound, as part of the emerging approach of "hypermedia", in which the user can move between all these outputs by just "zooming in and out" between them.

Figure 14.3 Representation of a Digital Elevation Model with some sunlight shading and a visibility area draped on it.

14.3 GIS and environmental impact assessment

14.3.1 Introduction

Bibliographical reviews show that by far the most common application of GIS is concerned with environmental issues. Rodriguez-Bachiller (2000) and Rodriguez-Bachiller with Glasson (2004, Chs. 3 and 4) contain extensive bibliographical searches of GIS work since the 1980s, and show that more than half of all GIS applications worldwide (more than all other applications put together) are related to environmental/rural issues, including EIA. Indeed, GIS should be well suited to EIA because it can answer questions that are central in the EIA process. As stated in ESRI (1995) these questions include:

- **What is where?** – which is central in screening, scoping and baseline studies;
- **What spatial patterns exist?** – which can help in understanding the baseline conditions, and in impact prediction and mitigation;
- **What has changed since . . . ?** – which can be relevant to impact prediction, prediction of changes in the absence of the project, and impact monitoring;
- **What if?** – which is the aim of impact prediction and may be important in exploring alternatives and in formulating mitigation measures.

As we shall see, however, the level of sophistication at which GIS are used in practice can vary considerably.

14.3.2 Possible approaches

A review of GIS experience suggests that possible relationships between GIS and EIA can take place at different levels of sophistication as follows:

1.   At the simplest level, GIS can be used for *basic mapping* of the environment or the project or particular impacts from it, to provide visual aids to con-

sultants or managers; the impact assessment is done totally outside the system, and the only use of GIS is the production of maps (pre- or post-impact assessment).

2. In more advanced applications, GIS can itself be involved in technical analytical tasks, with elements of the EIA carried out using the *internal functionality* of the GIS as described in §14.2.3, e.g. buffering, overlay, map-algebra, visibility-analysis etc.

3. At the next level, the GIS can be linked to *external models* programmed outside the GIS and "coupled" to it. This can involve the GIS being used to provide or "pre-process" data (e.g. calculations of slopes, distances and ratios of various kinds) that are then supplied to the external model, followed by using the GIS to "post-process" and display outputs from the model, e.g. drawing contour maps of predicted ground-pollution levels.

4. Finally, in the most sophisticated applications GIS, may be *integrated with a fully interactive system* (an Expert System for example), so that the operation of the GIS and its links with other tools (if any) are guided by the user's "dialogue" with the system, which becomes a fully fledged Decision Support System.

Rodriguez-Bachiller (2000) and Rodriguez-Bachiller with Glasson (2004) found that, in practice, the use of GIS' internal functionality was the approach most frequently employed, accounting for 31 per cent of applications (see **Figure 14.4**) although, surprisingly, the use of GIS as a tool for basic mapping accounted for as much as 27 per cent of recorded applications. At the other end of the spectrum, the most sophisticated (and expensive) use of GIS embedded in an interactive decision-support environment was found in as much as 24 per cent of GIS applications[2].

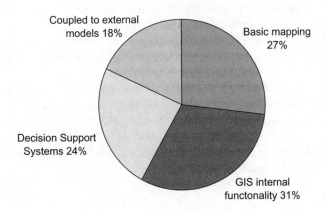

Figure 14.4 GIS use in practice by levels of sophistication.

14.3.3 Resource implications

In EIA, the assessment and reporting of the likely environmental impacts of a development proposal is typically carried out by environmental consultancies working to tight deadlines within limited budgets. The resource implications of using GIS technology within an EIA (e.g. hardware and software costs, skilled staff, and the costs of acquiring or inputting data) indicate that its potential role must be carefully considered, preferably in the early stages of an EIA when the overall environmental assessment methodology is formulated. Project managers need to identify the ways in which GIS could be useful within a particular EIA and must then decide whether the outputs and analysis which GIS can facilitate will justify the resources required.

One of the crucial and most resource-intensive tasks – and one that may determine the feasibility of one or another of the approaches mentioned in §14.3.2 – is the setting up of the appropriate **map-base** (in digital form) for the GIS, including suitable maps of the area, and maps of policy-areas (conservation areas, etc.) that may need to be taken into consideration, as well as maps of the project itself. GIS technology can provide a useful framework in which an **integrated spatial inventory** of environmental information can be developed, analysed and fed into EIA decisions. Typical layers of information may relate to biophysical, socio-economic, historical/cultural features and policy designations, and can include themes such as land use, habitats, soils, geology, hydrology, topography, pollution-monitoring data, census information, transport networks, archaeological resources and conservation areas (including SSSIs and other designated sites). Although digitised forms of these maps or "layers" of information are becoming increasingly available, many will typically be available only in paper form.

Given the potential high cost associated with purchasing or capturing these data sources, two important questions arise. First, whether or not the data set developed can be used again (either for ongoing project-related environmental management, or perhaps in locations where several EIA developments are proposed) to enhance the cost-effectiveness of the GIS by spreading the costs among more than one project/initiative. Second, and crucially in terms of added value, *what can GIS offer the EIA process beyond the provision of high quality cartographic output* (which can also be produced using cheaper and less sophisticated software packages)?

The remainder of this chapter tries to help answer this latter question by focussing on the practical application of GIS technology at various stages in the EIA process. The intention is not only to highlight the different ways in which GIS *can* be used to good effect in EIA, but also to reflect pragmatically upon the limitations and restrictions to its application which can arise given the constraints facing EIA practitioners.

14.4 GIS in screening, scoping and baseline studies

14.4.1 Screening

Screening (deciding whether a project requires EIA) is usually based on: (a) *characteristics of the project* itself, e.g. the type of activity or construction it involves, the size or level of such activities and whether they exceed certain thresholds, and the significance of the impacts it is likely to have; and (b) the project's *location* and the sensitivity of this and the area nearby. Examples of how GIS can facilitate screening include:

- Certain types of projects (like industrial estates in the UK, for instance, or certain infrastructure projects) will require an impact assessment if they *reach or exceed a certain area*, and a GIS will be able to calculate this automatically from a map of the project.
- Often it has to be established if a project lies *within an environmentally sensitive area* – in which case an EIS would be required. Although simple visual inspection of a map (GIS-produced or not) will often suffice, using GIS to overlay a map of the project and a map of the relevant sensitive areas will achieve the same result with increased accuracy, and with the additional advantage that the GIS may be programmed to do it *automatically* and report back (e.g. Rodriguez-Bachiller with Glasson 2004).
- In some cases an EIA will be required if a project is within a certain *distance from a certain type of feature* such as a road or a residential area. The "buffering" capabilities of GIS can be used to good effect to answer such a query. A buffer-zone at the critical distance around the project can be generated by the GIS, and then used to "clip" a map containing all the roads or relevant features. If the clipped area contains any roads or features it means they *are* within the critical distance.

The fact that GIS has technical capabilities to contribute to project-screening does not necessarily mean that it is the best way to do it. As mentioned before, whether it is cost-effective to use GIS for screening will depend largely on how central the GIS is to the whole information environment of the organisation doing this work, and how much of the preparatory work needed (setting up the map-base etc.) if the information is (or not) already contained within the system.

14.4.2 Scoping

The logic here is similar to that of the last section, because the types of considerations involved in scoping are quite similar to those affecting screening. While it is the characteristics of the project that will determine many of the impacts to consider, the setting of the project will also determine impacts that need to be studied. For example:

- a project located on good-quality agricultural land will require a study of potential impacts on the soil and on the agricultural resources of the area;
- a project which involves the discharge of effluent to a nearby river will require a study of water pollution;
- a project located upwind from a nature reserve and producing emissions to the atmosphere will require an air-pollution study and an ecological study.

Placing a development proposal within its **geographical context** will help inform the scoping process through defining the project location, describing its environmental setting, and helping identify potential conflicts or impacts which will require detailed assessment in an EIA; and GIS can be used for this in ways not too different from those applicable to screening. For instance, in the EIA of a road scheme, GIS might be used to inform a scoping decision regarding the consideration of archaeology as follows:

1. The GIS could be used to create a 500m buffer around the proposed route which could then be combined with a map of known archaeological sites using GIS overlay.
2. From this analysis, a map could be generated showing all the relevant features (road, 500m buffer, and archaeological sites) for visual analysis. Alternatively, the query could be structured so that only areas of archaeological interest falling within the buffer zone are identified and "clipped".

In this way, GIS analysis can be used not only to scope the EIA in terms of identifying impact themes which require further investigation, but can also help to clarify the **spatial scope of the study,** i.e. the areas or receptor locations which will require detailed consideration in the assessment of a particular impact. To be effective, however, this requires that the criteria used (for instance, the distance used as a search radius for locating sensitive archaeological sites) be defined in an unequivocal way. This may present problems when such criteria have been defined in the law or in the practice-guidelines in "fuzzy" terms, using expressions such as "near" or "close". Issues arising from "fuzziness" in EIA are discussed in Wood *et al.* (2007).

Haklay *et al.* (1998) provide a useful case-study example and evaluation of the potential of GIS for scoping in relation to the Israeli EIA system, including consideration of both the technical factors and the institutional infrastructure required to make such an approach operate effectively.

Ultimately it should be recognised that GIS is only one of a number of methods which can be used for scoping an EIA (e.g. expert judgement, checklists, matrices, expert systems, public consultation) and that to be most effective it should be used to supplement and complement these techniques. It is probably fair to say that both screening and scoping can be done just as effectively *without* a GIS, and the potential for using a GIS really lies in the possibility of *programming* these activities so that they are carried out *automatically* in the system: finding the right maps, applying the right distances, identifying overlaps and buffers etc., and then reporting back to the user.

14.4.3 Baseline studies

Building on the information generated as part of the scoping process, further data will be required in an EIA to describe and analyse the baseline environmental conditions for specific impact themes. In turn, reflecting the iterative nature of the EIA process, this information may influence and further refine the scope of the assessment as more data are gathered and the EIA progresses.

Once the data have been collected and input, GIS can be a powerful tool for displaying and visualising trends and patterns in spatial data sets.

Point-type data that relate to a specific sampling location (e.g. a pollution-monitoring station) can be displayed in the form of a proportional-symbol map or, where time series data are available, perhaps as a series of maps at various intervals to reflect the dynamic nature of the environmental baseline.

"Spatially continuous" data (e.g. noise, rainfall, topography, groundwater, air pollution) can be used (given a sufficient spatial sample) to produce a contour (isoline) map or, in the case of topography, as a DTM to describe the baseline terrain.

"Linear" data describing features such as rivers or roads can be represented using colour-coding, or perhaps with variations of line width in proportion to the data values e.g. to illustrate traffic-flow data along roads.

Area data which relate to discrete spatial units (e.g. census data, designated sites and habitat patches) can be displayed as choropleth maps, where the intensity of shading is used to reflect the data values.

While these types of graphical output can be produced using simpler software systems, GIS is ideally suited to organising and storing multi-disciplinary monitoring data sets into a framework which can be analysed, queried and displayed interactively in order to support and inform the EIA process. For instance, where comprehensive spatial data sets are available, the spatial query capabilities intrinsic to GIS can be used to highlight potential "hotspots" (e.g. locations with pollution levels above specified thresholds) that may require particular attention in terms of impact prediction and assessment of significance, hence serving to refine the scope and focus of the EIA as more information becomes available. GIS are also ideal for determining the extent to which hotspots and sensitive locations are spatially concentrated across a variety of different environmental parameters.

While GIS technology has some clear strengths that make it appropriate for baseline studies, *its use is limited by the availability of data with a good spatial coverage* (§14.2.1). It should be recognised that reliable data are costly to collect and that, in many EIAs, resources will be targeted towards a small number of receptor locations (which are likely to be most seriously affected by a project) rather than achieving a broad spatial sample which would satisfy the ideal requirements of GIS. Also, some of the information used for the scoping and baseline studies is often presented in numeric form (e.g. socio-economic information about the area, levels of unemployment) without any need for a map to show it.

In recent years, commercial services based upon spatial databases of environmental information which are of potential relevance to EIA scoping and baseline studies have appeared, e.g. "Envirocheck" from Landmark Information Group (www.envirocheck.co.uk/) which, although not a fully fledged GIS, provides (in addition to a written report) maps of environmental data including historical land use centred on user-specified coordinates, all of which is dispatched to a client within two days.

14.5 GIS in impact prediction

14.5.1 Introduction

Impact prediction lies at the core of EIA and is intended to identify the magnitude and other dimensions of likely changes to the environment which can be attributed to a development proposal (Glasson *et al.* 2005). A detailed study of the potential contribution of GIS to impact assessment can be found in Rodriguez-Bachiller with Glasson (2004) which discusses a range of impact assessment approaches (from the quantitative to the qualitative, from the visual to the socio-economic) end examines the potential contribution of GIS to them.

GIS is obviously most suited to dealing with the spatial dimension of impacts, and at the simplest level of analysis they can be used to make quantitative estimates of aspects such as:

- the "land take" caused by development (e.g. the total area of agricultural land, grassland or wetland habitat which may be lost);
- the length of road or pipeline which passes through a designated landscape area such as an Area of Outstanding Natural Beauty (AONB);
- the number/importance of features such as archaeological finds or ancient monuments that would be lost to the development.

More sophisticated predictions will require some form of modelling to represent or simulate the behaviour of the environment. Two broad ways (that correspond to some of the "levels of sophistication" identified in §14.3.2) in which GIS may be used for modelling in impact prediction can be identified:

1. The entire process of developing and implementing a model takes place *within* the GIS software, i.e. GIS is used for data input and preparation, modelling, and finally for the display and spatial analysis of model output;
2. While GIS may be used in data preparation, the actual modelling is undertaken outside the GIS software using an independent computer model, the output from which is imported back into the GIS for purposes of display and further spatial analysis.

14.5.2 *Modelling within the GIS*

Modelling "internal" to the GIS can vary in its level of sophistication. At its simplest, **GIS mapping** is arguably a form of modelling, essentially the same as conventional mapping but with the advantages provided by the overlay and buffering capabilities discussed in §14.2.3. To illustrate this level of GIS involvement in EIA, the case of terrestrial ecology impacts can be used.

Because of their complexity, responses of ecosystems to impacts are notoriously difficult to predict (Chapter 11). Consequently, ecological assessment requires a high level of expertise and judgement. However, it can involve a substantial amount of mapping, and the facilities available in GIS can be very valuable. This can be illustrated in relation to the basic questions referred to in §14.3.1, plus an additional question – *Why is it there?* (Treweek 1999). To have a reasonable chance of understanding an ecosystem's current and likely behaviour it is important to have:

- a knowledge of the spatial relationships of its components (species populations, communities and environmental systems), i.e. to know *what is where* and *what spatial patterns exist*;
- an understanding of the factors that explain these relationships, i.e. *why is it there?* This will depend on a combination of present and past factors, and so may require –
- a knowledge of at least recent trends, i.e. *what has changed?*

Given adequate data, GIS overlay mapping can help to provide answers to these questions. For example:

- layers showing distributions and ranges of species, locations and extents of habitats and sites, and patterns of environmental parameters such as geology, soils, hydrology, or land use can clearly demonstrate spatial relationships;
- spatial relationships, e.g. between species and habitats or habitats and environmental patterns, often go a long way in explaining *why it is there*;
- layers created from past maps or records can illustrate *what has changed*, and help to explain the present patterns and relationships (Veitch *et al.* 1995).

Similarly, GIS mapping can be useful in attempting to answer some impact prediction (*what happens if?*) questions. For example, it can demonstrate locations and dimensions of:

- predicted impact areas, including "buffer" zones along linear projects;
- direct "land take" in relation to habitats and species, e.g.:
  - what parts and proportions of sites or habitat patches will be lost?
  - what will be the overall area loss of habitat types and what proportion of the current stock will this represent?
  - what parts and proportion of a species' habitat will be lost;

- habitat fragmentation, including sizes and isolation (as distances) of remaining habitat patches;
- new barriers to species dispersal, including the project itself (buildings, roads etc.) and barriers created by habitat fragmentation;
- new pollution sources and likely dispersion patterns;
- environmental impacts such as changes in drainage patterns, soil moisture levels or sediment loads in aquatic ecosystems.

Moreover, GIS make it possible to answer "what if" questions about alternative prediction scenarios, project characteristics, or locations, with relative speed and ease.

Of course, while such GIS mapping can provide information on the magnitude of impacts, it cannot provide precise predictions about their significance, assessment of which must rely on ecological interpretation.

At a higher level of sophistication, **Digital terrain models** (DTMs) can be used in various ways, a good example being the prediction of the project's "viewshed" or Zone of Visual Influence (e.g. see Howes and Gatrell 1993, Fels 1992, Davidson *et al.* 1992, Hebert and Argence 1996). The main steps are:

- topographic data are digitised manually from a contour map, or purchased in digital form;
- these data are then used to create a DTM of the land surface within the GIS;
- using the DTM and information describing the height of project structures and other elements in the landscape which could act as visual barriers, the "viewshed" function commonly found within GIS software can be used to delimit the area over which the project will be visible;
- finally the output from the visibility analysis can be mapped (or draped over the DTM) within the GIS, and further spatial analysis performed if required, e.g. the use of overlays to identify residential properties which lie within the viewshed.

A variety of refinements to the basic binary (yes–no) viewshed function have been developed in order to increase the information content of the output. At the simplest level these include: the use of options which serve to indicate how much of a development proposal is visible (e.g. how many turbines in a windfarm are visible from a given location); and weighting schemes to simulate the decline in visual impacts which occurs with increasing distance from the source. Other advances from the research domain include the use of fuzzy logic and probability to simulate project visibility under different atmospheric conditions (Fisher 1994).

Cartographic modelling (equivalent to what in GIS is called "map algebra") is a more generic approach to impact-prediction modelling within GIS (see §14.1.2). It involves the use of raster-based GIS overlay to combine individual layers of data in order to arrive at some form of composite. For example, as part of an EIA of a 1,140km electricity transmission line in the United States, Jensen and Gault (1992) developed a GIS model to assess the ground disturbance impacts associated with construction activities. The model used GIS overlay analysis to combine layers of information describing land cover, slope and the transportation network in order to quantify the impacts into five levels of magnitude and create a map showing the spatial distribution of the disturbance. More recently, Antunes *et al.* (2001) describe a Spatial Impact Assessment Methodology that employs GIS and a series of impact indices in order to evaluate and compare highway route alternatives and impact significance.

Viewshed analysis and cartographic modelling represent relatively basic approaches to impact prediction modelling which are highly deterministic and can incorporate a strong degree of subjectivity, notably when determining weightings or classifications to be used to combine data layers. GIS typically lack the capabilities to undertake more powerful process-driven modelling, but have been used to good effect when combined with environmental models operating external to the GIS.

14.5.3 Modelling external to the GIS

In this section, the example of air quality impact prediction is used to demonstrate how GIS may be used in combination with spatially distributed environmental models which operate outside the GIS software. The discussion then broadens out to identify other impact themes where this approach is appropriate and briefly considers recent developments in environmental software which incorporate elements of GIS technology.

Air pollution impacts in EIA are typically predicted using Gaussian dispersion models (see Chapter 8) for which GIS has the potential to be used as a pre-processor or data preparation tool. For instance, many Gaussian models employ algorithms designed to simulate the dispersion of pollution in either urban or rural settings, and in most cases the criteria used to decide which option to adopt are based upon land use data. With the Industrial Source Complex (ISC) model (see Table 8.5) urban dispersion coefficients should be used if more than 50 per cent of the land use within a 3km radius of a project is classified as industrial, commercial or residential (Maitin and Klaber 1993). A GIS which holds land-use data (collected perhaps during the scoping stage of an EIA) is well placed to answer such a query accurately and efficiently. Air quality models also require terrain data for the receptor co-ordinates to be incorporated in the modelling and, again, GIS could be used to supply this information.

Once the calculation of air pollution impacts has been completed using the external model, GIS can be used effectively as a post-processor, particularly for purposes of presentation and display. Thus, output from the model could be fed into the GIS software, where a contour map of impacts could be developed and perhaps combined with land use data to assist in the interpretation of impacts. GIS can also facilitate further spatial analysis of the predicted impacts which might include overlaying contours on a proportional-symbol map of baseline levels, or querying the GIS to identify residential properties which lie within a certain threshold level of pollution.

In recent years a number of research prototypes and commercial products have been developed which provide an integrated approach to combining air quality models and GIS. The software features "user-friendly" interfaces which enable data to be transferred between the GIS and the model in a seamless fashion, e.g. the ADMS range of models from CERC Ltd. (www.cerc.co.uk) incorporate links to the GIS packages ArcView and MapInfo so that model output can be visualised and analysed spatially. Such approaches are very useful in that they facilitate the rapid simulation of alternative scenarios or mitigation strategies.

In the research domain, GIS have been used in combination with quantitative models for predicting ecological impacts (Hunsaker *et al.* 1993), and commercial systems are starting to become available, for example Land Change Modeller from Clark Labs (www.clarklabs.org) presents an integrated GIS modelling tool and decision support system for predicting and assessing the impacts of land use change upon habitats and biodiversity.

Other impact themes in EIA for which GIS has been linked with environmental models include: (a) hydrology, for instance to calculate runoff and flood risk (e.g. Mattikalli and Richards 1996, Brun and Band 2000), surface and groundwater quality (Bennett and Vitale 2001, Bhaduri *et al.* 2000); and (b) noise (e.g. Schaller 1992, Lam *et al.* 1999). As with air quality, commercial products are now available which combine environmental models and some elements of GIS (particularly in terms of mapping and overlaying data) within a single seamless software package. Examples include: LIMA environmental noise calculation and mapping software (www.bksv.com/2413.asp); MIKE 21 for hydrology (www.dhi-uk.com/); and Visual MODFLOW Pro (www.visual-modflow.com), a groundwater flow and contaminant transport simulation package. The main limitation in the application of these models is likely to be the lack of adequate input data that are specific to the study area.

14.5.4 Reflections on GIS in impact prediction

From the examples cited above it can be seen that the way in which GIS can be used for impact prediction varies according to the extent to which the analysis requires a comprehensive spatial database of information. In the case of ecological analysis, expert information about habitats and species will have to be put into GIS maps and, once created, these maps can be manipulated to produce much information relevant to impact prediction. In the case of viewshed analysis, GIS can be brought into use for a clearly defined "one off" task within an EIA and, to be effective, the analysis does not require the development of a full GIS database, but can be conducted at the most basic level using only topographic data. Where GIS is used in combination with an external model, a limited number of data layers will be required, depending upon the requirements of a particular model and the degree of spatial analysis to be undertaken during post-processing of model outputs. In contrast, the use of cartographic modelling often relies on the "integrating" capabilities of GIS and can sometimes require an extensive and comprehensive spatial database to be effective.

In terms of the use of models for prediction in EIA, the impacts suited to a spatial assessment using GIS appear to be those which exhibit continuous or semi-continuous variability over space and those which undergo diffusion or propagation through space, as opposed to through a functional structure such as the economy. However, the extent to which GIS is likely to be used for impact prediction in EIA will depend upon scoping decisions regarding the level of spatial disaggregation and precision required for decision making and environmental management. As with baseline studies, it may be that impact predictions are only deemed necessary for a limited number of receptor locations, and that a broad spatial assessment is surplus to requirement. To reiterate, the implication is that there is a strong *need for early planning and careful consideration over the extent to which GIS will be useful in EIA.* Finally, it must be stressed that however impressive the results from GIS may appear, they can only be as good as the data and models on which they are based.

14.6 GIS in mitigation

One of the most effective uses of GIS technology in terms of mitigation in the broadest sense relates to the identification and evaluation of **alternative locations** for a development project. Given a comprehensive spatial database and a series of clearly defined constraints or preferences, GIS overlay analysis can be used to good effect to identify and compare potential sites (or route alignments for linear developments). Two classic examples of practical EIA-related applications that have been documented in the literature include the work of Schaller (1995) who used GIS for the ecological assessment of alternative corridors for a Federal Motorway in Southern Bavaria, and Siegel and Moreno (1993) who applied GIS for identifying and assessing potential highway routes across the Tonto National Forest, near Phoenix, Arizona.

Beyond the application of basic overlay analysis, more sophisticated approaches to the identification and evaluation of siting alternatives from the research domain include the use of GIS technology in combination with multi-criteria analysis (Carver 1991, Klungboonkrong and Taylor 1998) including more recently attempts at improving and incorporating stakeholder participation (Bailey 2006, Higgs 2006); fuzzy logic (Bonham-Carter 1994, Bojórquez-Tapia *et al.* 2002); genetic algorithms (Pereira and Antunes 1996); and optimisation methods using Monte Carlo simulation (Sfakianaki and Stovin 2002).

As the focus of an EIA narrows to consider a specific site or route, the strengths of GIS in visualising and displaying the spatial distribution of impacts can be exploited to help identify and **target possible mitigation measures**. In particular, using criteria to define impact significance (determined by the EIA team or using published guidance), a GIS could be queried to identify locations which exceed thresholds and hence may require mitigation.

GIS can also be appropriate for simulating the effects of **alternative mitigation strategies** for individual impact themes (Brown 1994). For instance, the effects on project visibility of planting screening vegetation could be investigated or, in combination with environmental models, the implications of different project design characteristics or operational procedures could be looked at, e.g. the effects upon pollution dispersion of increasing the height of a stack or the velocity of exhaust gases.

In other situations, mitigation requirements may draw upon GIS analysis already conducted at an earlier stage in the EIA. For example, the maps produced for the baseline and impact assessment stages in an ecological assessment could be used to investigate:

- the potential for minimising impacts on nature conservation sites or habitat patches by project design modifications such as minor road realignments;
- the potential for species translocation (to suitable sites) or habitat creation, including the creation of stepping-stone or corridor habitats between fragmented habitat patches;
- the suitability of options in particular localities, e.g. of new woodland planting in relation to existing woodland cover (Purdy and Ferris 1999);
- the optimum locations and dimensions of buffer zones to protect sensitive habitats.

14.7 GIS in monitoring

For large-scale development projects where a GIS system has been developed for use in EIA, it makes sense for the system to be used in the post-development phase as an integrative tool to store, analyse and display monitoring data. In this way the GIS becomes a tool for use in the actual operational environmental management, perhaps as part of an Environmental Management Plan. Using GIS in this way will also serve to recoup some of the costs of setting up a system for use in EIA.

Where monitoring data sets have a good spatial coverage, GIS can be used productively in identifying patterns in the data and for examining change over time. It is worth mentioning here "Monitor-Pro" (www.ehsdata.com/) as an example of a software product which, although not marketed as a GIS, does have some elements of this technology in terms of data mapping and visualisation (contouring, using proportional symbols etc.), in addition to facilities for the automatic generation of reports.

Wood (1999a, 1999b, 2000) has shown – using visibility, noise and air quality impact assessment – how GIS can be used in a spatial approach to audit predictive techniques in EIA, where spatial patterns in the differences between predicted and actual impacts provided useful insights into the possible underlying causes of errors in impact assessment. Such "prediction monitoring" is invaluable in terms of helping the EIA process to learn from experience.

14.8 Conclusions

It is probably fair to say that the development and diffusion of GIS has been supply-led, particularly in Europe, with developers and vendors of GIS and associated technologies (like remote sensing or digital cartography) "sensing" a latent market for good-quality computerised mapping products, and investing in it long before the potential users were even aware of its existence. In this context, it is not surprising to find that the "tone" of discussions about GIS applications (much of it in magazines which rely on advertising) tends to veer towards the positive side, often chanting the praise of this technology and its growing potential.

EIA as an area of application for GIS has been no exception, and articles like those quoted earlier in this chapter tend to present the use of GIS as a step forward, usually pointing in the direction of more – rather than less – involvement with GIS. In contrast, there is a severe shortage of literature which serves to critically discuss the limitations of applying GIS technology within the context of "real world" EIA. This is why in this chapter we have attempted a more pragmatic evaluation of what GIS can realistically be used for given the restrictions of time, money and data facing practitioners involved in carrying out an EIA.

It should be clear from the previous discussion that the technical potential of GIS for EIA is enormous: GIS is able to combine individual maps and databases and perform spatial analysis (overlay, buffering, viewshed analysis etc.) which would be difficult and time consuming to achieve by hand, and which are not part of the armoury of standard mapping packages. In addition, all this can be achieved with maximum accuracy, and with the flexibility to combine data collected from a variety of sources and at a variety of scales.

However, the time and cost required to develop a full GIS database must be recognised, although suitable digital environmental information which can be imported directly into a GIS may be available commercially, at a price. Consequently, the use of GIS to do complex EIA is likely to be restricted to larger, well funded projects for which the development of a full map-base is a viable option, and for which project managers have recognised the potential of the technology for use in several stages and for several aspects of the EIA.

On the other hand, the same argument can be turned around when applied to "simple" EIA: when only a very limited amount of (simple) impact analysis is needed (like viewshed analysis, or contouring ground pollution levels) the map-base required is very simple and easy to acquire, while the results can be quite impressive and considerably improve the overall quality of the final report. Also, an organisation, such as a local authority, may be engaged in a number of reports covering the same area. While an individual project may not justify the expense of setting up a GIS, in situations where a number of projects are proposed in an area, the use of GIS clearly becomes more viable. This also applies to cumulative impact assessment and particularly in relation to Strategic Environmental Assessment (Therivel and Wood 2004).

Looking forwards to the future, we can see current developments pointing in the direction of greater use of this technology via the Internet, as well as greater user-friendliness based on the notion of "hypermedia" already mentioned, both opening the door to ever more *interactive* use of GIS, be it for EIA or for other areas of application. In addition to welcoming improvements in GIS technology to suit the needs of EIA, what is crucial is that all considerations about the potential role and limitations of GIS be an integral part of the planning of EIA work from its early stages. We need EIA managers who are aware of the potential of GIS, as much as we need the GIS industry to have a more thorough understanding of practical EIA issues.

Notes

1 Although Longley *et al.* (1999) is presented as a "second edition" of Maguire *et al.* (1991), it is an entirely new publication, with different authors and chapters, so the two should really be taken *together* as a quite complete and excellent source on GIS.
2 For discussion of specific cases the reader is referred back to Rodriguez-Bachiller (2000) and Rodriguez-Bachiller with Glasson (2004, Chs. 3 and 4).

References

Antunes P, R Santos and L Jordao 2001. The application of Geographical Information Systems to determine environmental impact significance. *Environmental Impact Assessment Review* **21**(6), 511–535.

Bailey K 2006. Principles of the EP-AMIS GIS/Multicriteria methdology for participatory electric power transmission line routing, *Power systems Conference and Exposition, 2006* Atlanta, 29 October, 385–388.

Bennett DA and AJ Vitale 2001. Evaluating nonpoint pollution policy using a tightly coupled spatial decision support system, *Environmental Management* **27**(6), 825–836.

Bhaduri B, J Harbor, B Engel and M Grove 2000. Assessing watershed-scale, long-term hydrologic impacts of land-use change using a GIS-NPS model, *Environmental Management* **26**(6), 643–658.

Bojórquez-Tapia LA, L Juárez and G Cruz-Bello 2002. Integrating fuzzy logic, optimization, and GIS for Ecological Impact Assessments. *Environmental Management* **30**(3), 418–433.

Bonham-Carter GF 1994. Geographic Information Systems for geoscientists: modelling with GIS. Oxford: Pergamon Press.

Brown CR 1994. Toward no net loss: a methodology for identifying potential wetland mitigation sites using a GIS, *Proceedings of the Urban and Regional Information Systems Association (URISA) Conference*, Milwaukee (Wisconsin), 7–11 August, Vol. I, 594–607.

Brun SE and LE Band 2000. Simulating runoff behavior in an urbanizing watershed. *Computers, Environment and Urban Systems* **24**(1), 5–22.

Carver SJ 1991. Integrating multi-criteria evaluation with Geographical Information Systems. *International Journal of Geographical Information Systems* **5**, 321–329.

Daratech Inc. 2006. *GIS/Geospatial market grew 17% in 2005 to top $3.3 billion; Sales led by growth in data products.* Press release 06 July 2006, www.directionsmag.com/press.releases/index.php?duty=Show&id=14697.

Davidson DA, PH Selman and AI Watson 1992. The evaluation of a GIS for rural environmental planning, *Proceedings of the EGIS '92 Conference*, Munich (23–26 March), Vol. 1, 135–144.

Davis BE 2001. GIS: a visual approach, 2nd edn. Santa Fe, NM: On Word Press.

ESRI (Environmental Research Systems Institute) 1995. *Understanding GIS: the ARC/INFO method.* Redlands, CA: ESRI, www.ciesin.org/docs/005-331/005-331.html.

Fels JE 1992. Viewshed simulation and analysis: An interactive approach. *GIS World*, July, 54–59.

Fisher P 1994. Probable and fuzzy models of the viewshed operation. In *Innovations in GIS 1*, MF Worboys (ed.), 161–175. London: Taylor & Francis.

Glasson J, R Therivel and A Chadwick 2005. *An introduction to Environmental Impact Assessment*, 3rd edn. London: Routledge.

Goodchild MF, BO Parks and LT Steyaert (eds) 1993. *Environmental modelling with GIS*. Oxford: Oxford University Press.

Goodchild MF, BO Parks and LT Steyaert (eds) 1996. Third International Conference/ Workshop on Integrating GIS and Environmental Modelling, Santa Fe (New Mexico), 21–25 January. Santa Barbara (California): the National Center for Geographical Information and Analysis (in compact-disk format), www.ncgia.ucsb.edu/conf/SANTA_ FE_CD-ROM/santa_fe.html.

Goodchild MF, LT Steyaert, BO Parks, C Johnston, D Maidment, M Crane and S Glendinning (eds) 1996. *GIS and environmental modelling*. Fort Collins, CO: GIS World Books.

Haklay M, E Feitelson and Y Doytsher 1998. The potential of a GIS-based scoping system: An Israeli proposal and case study, *Environmental Impact Assessment Review* 18(5), 439–459.

Hebert MP and J Argence 1996. Virtual pylons into geographic reality, *GIS Europe* (August), 28–30.

Higgs G 2006. Integrating multi-criteria techniques with Geographical Information Systems in waste facility location to enhance public participation. *Waste Management & Research* 24(2), 105–117.

Howes D and T Gatrell 1993. Visibility analysis in GIS: Issues in the environmental impact assessment of windfarm developments, *Proceedings of the EGIS '93 Conference*, Genoa (Italy), 29 March–1 April, Vol. 2, 861–870.

Hunsaker CT, RA Nisbet, DCL Lam, JA Browder, WL Baker, MG Turner and DB Botkin 1993. Spatial models of ecological systems and processes: the role of GIS. In *Environmental modelling with GIS*, MF Goodchild, BO Parks and LT Steyaert (eds), 248–264. Oxford: Oxford University Press.

Jensen J and G Gault 1992. Electrifying the impact assessment process. *The Environmental Professional* 14, 50–59.

Johnston CA 1998. *Geographic Information Systems in ecology*. Methods in Ecology Series. Malden, MA: Blackwell Science.

Klungboonkrong P and MAP Taylor 1998. A microcomputer-based system for multicriteria environmental impacts evaluation of urban road networks, *Computers, Environment and Urban Systems* 22(5), 425–446.

Lam KC, B Li, W Ma and S Yu 1999. GIS-Based road traffic noise assessment system, paper presented at the conference *Forecasting the Future: IA for a New Century*, IAIA '99, 19th Annual Meeting (15–19 June), The University of Strathclyde (John Anderson Campus), Glasgow.

Longley PA, MF Goodchild, DJ Maguire and DW Rhind (eds) 1999. *Geographical Information Systems*, 2nd edn (2 vols). Chichester: John Wiley & Sons.

Longley PA, MF Goodchild, DJ Maguire and DW Rhind (eds) 2005. *Geographic Information Systems and Science*, 2nd edn. Chichester: John Wiley & Sons.

Maguire DJ 1991. An overview and definition of GIS. In *Geographical Information Systems: Principles and Applications*, DJ Maguire, MF Goodchild and DW Rhind (eds), Vol. 1 (Principles), Ch. 1, 9–20. Harlow, Essex: Longman Scientific and Technical.

Maguire DJ, MF Goodchild and DW Rhind (eds) 1991. *Geographical Information Systems: principles and applications*. Harlow, Essex: Longman Scientific and Technical.

458 *Shared and integrative methods*

Maitin IJ and KZ Klaber 1993. Geographic Information Systems as a tool for integrated air dispersion modeling. *Proceedings of the GIS/LIS Conference* 2, 466–474.

Mattikalli NM and KS Richards 1996. Estimation of surface water quality changes in response to land use change: application of the export coefficient model using Remote Sensing and Geographical Information Systems, *Journal of Environmental Management* 47(3), 263–282.

Melli P and P Zannetti (eds) 1992. *Environmental modelling.* Southampton and Boston, MA: Computational Mechanics Publications.

Openshaw S 1991. Developing appropriate spatial analysis methods for GIS. In *Geographical Information Systems: principles and applications,* DJ Maguire, MF Goodchild and DW Rhind (eds), Vol. 1 (Principles), Ch. 25, 389–402. Harlow, Essex: Longman Scientific and Technical.

Pereira A and P Antunes 1996. Extending the EIA process generation and evaluation of alternative sites for facilities within a GIS. *Proceedings of the International Conference for Impact Assessment* (IAIA '96), 479–484.

Purdy KM and R Ferris 1999. *A pilot study to examine the potential linkage between and application of multiple woodland databases: a GIS based analysis.* JNCC Report N. 298. Peterborough, Cambs: JNCC.

Rodriguez-Bachiller A 2000. Geographical Information Systems and Expert Systems for Impact Assessment. Part I: GIS, *Journal of Environmental Assessment Policy and Management* 2(3), 369–414.

Rodriguez-Bachiller A with J Glasson 2004. *Expert Systems and Geographic Information Systems for Impact Assessment.* London: Taylor & Francis.

Schaller J 1992. GIS helps measure impact of new Munich II Airport, *GIS Europe* (June), 20–21.

Schaller J 1995. Landscape analysis modelling for an environmental impact study of the Danube river construction, *Proceedings of the Joint European Conference and Exhibition on Geographic Information JEC-GI '95,* The Hague (26–31 March), Vol. 1, 279–284.

Sfakianaki E and VR Stovin 2002. A spatial framework for Environmental Impact Assessment and route optimisation. *Proceedings of the Institution of Civil Engineers, Transport,* Vol. 153 (1), February, 43–52.

Siegel MS and DD Moreno 1993. Geographical Information Systems: effective tools for siting and Environmental impact Assessment. In *Environmental Analysis: The NEPA Experience,* SG Hildebrand and JB Cannon (eds), 178–186. Boca Raton, FL, CRC Press.

Therivel R and G Wood 2004. Methodological approaches and techniques for Strategic Environmental Assessment. In M Schmidt, E João and L Knopp (eds), *Implementing Strategic Environmental Assessment.* Berlin: Springer-Verlag.

Tomlin CD 1990. *Geographic Information Systems and Cartographic Modeling.* London: Prentice Hall International.

Tomlin CD 1991. Cartographic modelling. In *Geographical Information Systems: principles and applications,* DJ Maguire, MF Goodchild and DW Rhind (eds), Vol. 1 (Principles), Ch. 23, 361–374. Harlow, Essex: Longman Scientific and Technical.

Treweek J 1999. *Ecological impact assessment.* Oxford: Blackwell Science.

Veitch N, NR Webb and BK Wyatt 1995. The application of geographical information systems and remotely sensed data to the conservation of heathland fragments, *Biological Conservation* 72, 91–97.

Wadsworth R and J Treweek 1999. *Geographical Information Systems for ecology: an introduction.* Harlow, Essex: Addison Wesley Longman.

Wathern P 1988. An introductory guide to EIA. In *Environmental Impact Assessment – theory and practice*, P Wathern (ed.). London and New York: Routledge.

Wood G 1999a. Assessing techniques of assessment: post-development auditing of noise predictive schemas in environmental impact assessment, *Impact Assessment and Project Appraisal* **17**(3), 217–226.

Wood G 1999b. Post-development auditing of EIA predictive techniques: A spatial analysis approach, *Journal of Environmental Planning and Management* **42**(5), 671–689.

Wood G 2000. Is what you see what you get? Post-development auditing of methods used for predicting the zone of visual influence in EIA, *Environmental Impact Assessment Review* **20**(5), 537–556.

Wood G, A Rodriguez-Bachiller and J Becker 2007. Fuzzy sets and simulated environmental change: evaluating and communicating impact significance in environmental impact assessment, *Environment and Planning A* **39**, 810–829.

15 Quality of life capital

Riki Therivel

15.1 Introduction

The concept of environmental "capital" has been widely used by environmental managers and economists to describe the benefits that the environment accrues to humans, particularly in monetary terms. In theory, the idea that the environment consists of assets that can provide a stream of benefits or services so long as the capital is not damaged embodies the principle of sustainable development. However in practice this approach has proven to be difficult and contentious to apply.

An integrated approach to identifying, analysing and managing all aspects of environmental capital was developed in 1997 by CAG Consultants and Land Use Consultants for the (then) Countryside Commission, English Heritage, English Nature and Environment Agency. Eighteen pilot studies were run in 1998/1999 to test the application of this approach. The pilots not only showed that the technique could be useful in a wide range of circumstances, but also suggested that it can be used to consider social and economic as well as environmental capital. As a result, a range of guidance on the approach was prepared (Countryside Agency 1997), and parts of the approach are incorporated in the Government's New Approach to Appraisal (§5.1).

The Quality of Life Capital approach – also called Quality of Life Assessment – has never been actively taken up, probably because there is no legal requirement to do so. However it is a useful approach to EIA scoping, and the original clients recently noted that, although they would no longer be actively supporting the approach, "the core concept underlying QoLA was sound and remains relevant . . . we encourage others to apply or adapt the tool where they believe it may be useful" (Environment Agency *et al.* 2008).

This chapter summarises the approach and gives an example of its use. It then discusses the benefits and limitations of the approach, and how it relates to EIA. It concentrates on those benefits for human quality of life that come from the environment, because the method has been most thoroughly piloted and tested on these, and because planners and practitioners often need a tool for this specific purpose. However the same method can also embrace social and economic capital.

15.2 The quality of life capital approach

All applications of the approach involve the same six basic steps:

A. **Purpose** The first step is to be clear about the purpose of the study, since the details of what needs to be done vary greatly with the purpose. In the context of EIA, the purpose would normally be to compare the suitability of various sites for a given development proposal, to compare different proposals for the same site, and/or to optimally manage the development of a certain site.

B. **Area/features** This stage essentially involves collecting baseline information on the relevant area and/or features, as is done in the EIA baseline environmental description stage. The purpose will determine the area or features that need to be studied. As in EIA, this area is likely to extend beyond the site boundary. For comparing potential development sites already identified, Quality of Life Capital could concentrate on the *differences* between them, whereas an exercise carried out to identify possible sites would need to consider the whole area. Where an area is diverse, this stage may involve classifying and describing areas of common character, as in landscape characterisation. In other cases – particularly for historical and cultural resources – it may involve determining why the resource matters, as a lead-in to Stage C.

C. **Benefits and services** This stage identifies what benefits and services the area or features provides. For instance a woodland (feature) could provide recreation, visual amenity, biodiversity and carbon fixing (benefits). Disbenefits are also identified at this stage.

D. **Evaluation** This stage examines the benefits/services systematically, using a series of questions (the last two of which do not apply to disbenefits):

   • *whom do the benefits/services matter to, why, and at what spatial scale?* For example habitat quality may matter for biodiversity at a regional or national scale, while recreational access may matter for quite specific groups of people from a small local area;
   • *how important are the benefits/services?* A benefit that matters at national level is not necessarily more important than one that matters only locally;
   • *is there enough of them?* It is more important to maintain benefits which are in short supply than ones that are plentiful. Where there is not enough, the aim should be to increase the level;
   • *what (if anything) could make up for any loss or damage to the benefit?* Examples include other places where local people could go equally readily for the same type of recreation, or other areas that could be managed to support displaced bird populations.

This step needs to reflect the views of both experts (for internationally, nationally and regionally important benefits) and the local community (for locally important benefits). It thus draws on public consultation and involvement processes as well as technical appraisal methods such as characterisation studies.

E. **Management implications** This stage draws from the evaluation messages about the policies or "rules" that would be needed to ensure that quality of life capital is enhanced rather than damaged. In the EIA context, this step would aim to develop conditions (possibly couched as planning conditions) that any future development on the proposed site should fulfil. Where several sites for development are being compared, the number and complexity of the conditions for each site can give an indication of how appropriate the sites are for development, and can help to rank sites in terms of ease of development and the likely sustainability benefits that development could provide.

F. **Monitoring** The benefits and services identified as important in the process are the aspects of the environment which should be monitored. Quality of Life Capital thus provides its own performance indicators.

15.3 An example of the approach

Table 15.1 shows partial and simplified results from a Quality of Life Capital exercise that aimed to determine whether an existing stone quarry in Gloucestershire should be extended and, if so, how. The example focuses on those benefits for human quality of life that come from the environment, but similar principles apply to social and economic capital.

The proposed extension site was an agricultural field of about 4ha bounded by hedges and crossed by a footpath. A road, Rock Road, ran between the existing quarry and the proposed extension. The proposal involved re-routing the footpath and road around the extension. Nearby residential properties had already been affected for many years by the noise and disruption of quarrying operations. The developers proposed to relinquish their existing planning permission for quarrying at a nearby site in return for permission to extract from the field.

As shown in Table 15.1, the Quality of Life Capital approach suggested innovative ideas for hedgerow management which went beyond the "replace like for like" approach initially proposed in the developer's EIA. It suggested enhancements to the footpath network, and acknowledged that some benefits – for instance footpath access between Rock Road and other footpaths – would not need to be replaced. It highlighted the importance of maintaining a small, rural scale for any realignment of Rock Road, in contrast to traditional "engineering" design solutions that emphasise safety and speed. It addressed the local residents' wish to gain certainty about the end of the quarrying operations. It also suggested importance rankings for the management implications. It showed that, in terms of virtually all benefits – recreation, biodiversity, visual amenity, and badger habitat – the site with the existing planning permission was superior to the field, so that the developer's proposed "trade" of planning permissions would be environmentally beneficial.

Overall the Quality of Life Capital approach seemed to formalise, and make more transparent and objective, the planning officers' existing good practice

Table 15.1 Example of Quality of Life Capital exercise applied to a stone quarry and its potential for extension

Feature	Benefit	Scale/ importance	Trend/target	Substitutability	Management implications
footpath across the site, from Rock Road to (other) footpath X	recreation	of very local importance, possibly of greater than very local importance if part of walking loop or network of footpaths; *ask footpath officer to comment*	unlikely to be a problem, but ask footpath officer to comment	any reasonably direct footpath linking Rock Road (either existing or diverted) to footpath X.	The new road would provide an adequate replacement *if* it is not more built-up than the existing road. The new footpath currently proposed by the applicants is likely to be too indirect, and walkers would probably use the road anyway. Possible enhancement: changing any of the permissive footpaths in the area into formal footpaths, and provision of a continuous footpath from Rock Road to the A100.
Rock Road	access from A to B for drivers and horseback riders	local/ of limited importance, but would cause outcry if lost	?	road access from A to B that does not significantly increase journey times or accident risk for drivers or horseback riders	Diversion of Rock Road around the extension site, provided that the new road is not more built-up than the existing one
field	agriculture/ grazing	local/ of very limited importance	going down, but not at all close to target	none needed	none needed
site as a whole	symbolic end to the quarry, lack of encroachment	local, very important	there have been about a dozen extensions over the years, well above "target" for nearby residents	– definite end date to quarrying – shorten total *time* of future extraction – removal of existing unused permissions (i.e. reduce *area* of future extraction)	The following are **very important** implications: Definite end date and shortening time of future extraction could be done through planning conditions and Section 106 agreements, but could be subject to future renegotiations, and thus do not offer complete certainty to local residents. Relinquishing planning permission for the site with existing permission would give such certainty.

approaches to dealing with such sites. It also provided more flexible, less onerous "rules" for the developers, and focused on enhancement as well as maintenance of environmental benefits.

15.4 Advantages of the approach

A key aspect of the approach is that it changes the focus of analysis from *things* to the *benefits* that they provide. By doing so, it can suggest more flexible, more creative solutions that focus on compensatory action rather than on trying to prove that an area simply cannot accommodate any more development. The emphasis on benefits and services suggests management measures that may not normally be addressed, for instance replacing the benefits of a footpath with a lightly used road.

By concentrating on the end-result, the benefits provided by an area, the approach effectively considers secondary and indirect impacts, which may well be more significant than the primary impact. Essentially, it sets the primary impact into their social/quality of life context. For instance, it may identify that closing a small segment of footpath would preclude people from being able to complete a well-loved, longer circular walk. The switch from things to benefits also recognises the interrelations between many impacts that are normally considered separately in EIA, for instance air, water and ecology (LUC/CAG 2000).

Through its focus on trends and targets/"enoughness", the approach inherently also considers cumulative impacts. For instance, while individual development projects may have no significant impact on climate (and their EIAs would say so), cumulatively they would, especially when past and likely future development trends are taken into account. The approach would help to identify these changes, relevant targets (e.g. Government targets for reducing CO_2 emissions), and necessary actions (e.g. replacing each unit of carbon fixing lost as a part of a development projects with several units, but this could be anywhere in the world) (LUC/CAG 2000).

The approach also provides a systematic and transparent framework for considering the views of experts and local residents in a complementary manner. Its focus on enhancement could bring forward development that people actively want, rather than proposals with pasted-on mitigation measures to minimise negative impacts. Similarly, the approach focuses on understanding what is important to a given area, rather than on designating and protecting a limited number of "best" areas. It thus helps to promote uniqueness, representativeness and diversity, not just quality.

The approach suggests that there is no fixed capacity for development, but instead a rising "sustainability tariff". The technique gives an indication of the quality of life benefits that a development would have to provide before it was considered acceptable and, as a corollary, indicates where development may not be appropriate. The more benefits the site has (and thus the more attractive to developers it normally is), the more requirements – sometimes complex and expensive ones – the developer would need to fulfil under a Quality of Life Capital approach. Faced with the many demands that are likely to be linked to greenfield sites, developers might conclude that brownfield sites are rather good for development after all. The approach would thus help to most effectively protect those sites that provide the most benefits, possibly reversing the current perverse incentive on developers to develop out-of-town sites (LGA 1999).

The approach also suggests a more rational approach to betterment or planning gain by identifying desirable and relevant improvements, and guiding development to achieve them. Whereas the existing system charges developers based on their economic gain (with the private realm essentially penalising the public realm), the Quality of Life Capital approach highlights how developers could be charged for the removal of environmental benefits (i.e. the private realm "refunds" the public realm) (LGA 1999).

15.5 Links between EIA and quality of life capital

Table 15.2 shows that EIA and Quality of Life Capital are complementary approaches to identifying and managing the impacts of proposed development

Table 15.2 Complementary role of EIA and Quality of Life Capital approaches

FG	EIA	Quality of Life Capital
carried out by	the developer	the competent authority as part of development/design brief, or the developer
considers	impact of a project on the environment	constraints by the environment on projects
deals well with	"things", technical issues, "objective" impacts, primary impacts	benefits that things provide, perceived impacts, secondary/ indirect/ cumulative impacts
public participation	seen as a safeguard to ensure that EIA findings are comprehensive and accurate	seen as a key component in identifying and analysing locally-important benefits, complementary to expert views on regionally, nationally and internationally important benefits
mitigation	minimisation and remediation of all significant impacts sought; protects designated areas	maintenance and enhancement of all important benefits sought; promotes the uniqueness and diversity of all areas
relation to decision-making	can stop environmentally-harmful development, but is seen as restrictive by developers	encourages environmentally-beneficial development, and may be viewed more positively by developers, but this has not yet been tested in practice

projects. Quality of Life Capital is a particularly useful input to the pre-application scoping stage of EIA, where the project context, alternatives and constraints are identified and analysed. It can be used to evaluate potential development sites, compare alternative sites, or establish whether or not there are opportunity sites within the area of search. As project planning evolves, another Quality of Life Capital "check" can be carried out to ensure that the final project really does maintain or enhance the quality of life benefits of the site. This can be used to set a management framework (e.g. Section 106 obligations, planning conditions, etc.) for any development on a given site.

Quality of Life Capital has the potential to merge into the EIA process so that it takes a minimum of additional time and effort. Stages A and B (purpose, area/features) of Quality of Life Capital are already virtually identical to the early stages of EIA. Stages C and D (benefits/services, evaluation) are different: however, by considering public views at this stage, it may be possible to minimise public opposition at the later phases of project planning. In a minimal form, the Quality of Life Capital approach could also easily be incorporated into the development of design briefs and/or the appraisal of different sites as part of a sustainability appraisal of a local development plan/document.

On the other hand, even using both processes in tandem can still have limitations. Neither technique effectively determines the area to be analysed: although both recommend analysing "higher" or "appropriate" scales, the focus is still clearly on the site under consideration. Although Quality of Life Capital in theory is based on (sustainability) targets, in practice few such targets are known and agreed, and EIA generally does not consider "targets" beyond those enshrined in Government policy or legislation (e.g. air and water quality criteria). Both techniques are perceived by local authorities and developers as being expensive and time-consuming.

References

Countryside Agency 1997. *Quality of Life Assessment – What matters and why*, http://www.countryside.gov.uk/LAR/archive/Quality/index.asp.

Environment Agency, English Heritage, Natural England 2008. *Joint Statement by Natural England, Environment Agency and English Heritage on Quality of Life Assessment*, http://www.environment-agency.gov.uk/commondata/acrobat/statement_on_qola_1979914.pdf.

LGA (Local Government Association) 1999. *Environmental capital, sustainability and housing growth: a report to the LGA by CAG Consultants*. London: LGA.

LUC/CAG (Land Use Consultants/CAG Consultants) 2000. *Environmental capital application guide: managing change on individual sites*. London: CAG.

16 Sustainable development and sustainability appraisal

Roy Emberton and Riki Therivel

16.1 Introduction

Sustainability, like climate change, has become one of the most recognised scientific concepts by the public. The concept is increasingly being adopted within the planning system to assess the value of developments, and data on the sustainability of a project is increasingly being requested by planning authorities as part of planning application documentation. This chapter considers the use of EIA to promote sustainable development, and the methods available for measuring the sustainability of projects.

Sustainable development can be defined as "development that meets the needs of the present without compromising the ability of future generations to meet their own needs" (World Commission on Environment and Development 1987). This definition has several components:

- intra-generational equity: present generations have an ethical duty to retain sufficient resources for future generations to prosper, or at least survive;
- inter-generational equity: the "needs of the present" includes the needs of all people, including those in other countries and the disadvantaged people in our own societies; and
- efficient resource use and maintenance of environmental quality: in the absence of a clear understanding of what future generations require, we should minimise the depletion of finite resources and promote the use of renewable alternatives; protect the earth's systems, especially those which serve to replenish resources; and protect ecosystems as they provide resource for future generations to utilise.

Sustainable development is often said to have a "triple bottom line", namely a balanced approach which equally respects economic and social development with environmental protection. Many planners would argue that they have been doing this for years. However, as Stevens (2005) points out, sustainable development involves "complex synergies and trade-offs" among the three elements, and planners need to go beyond a "three silo" mentality. Levett (1997) challenges the traditional view of sustainable development being the overlapping part of three interlocking circles:

> there is no economy – or society – without environment. . . . Furthermore "the economy" is not an end in itself or a force of nature. It's a social construct – it only works as it does because human societies have created the institutions, and inculcated the assumptions, expectations and behaviours which make it so. The only reason for keeping it thus . . . is if we think it will be good at meeting our needs. So the picture is really three concentric circles: economy within society within environment. This says sustainability is about ensuring that human society lives within the environment's limits – and that the economy meets society's needs.

Gibson (2005) has proposed sustainability decision criteria and trade-off rules that also aim to avoid the "three silo" compartmentalisation. These are shown at **Box 16.1**.

In the context of individual development projects, sustainable development could include concerns such as:

- minimal use and effective management of new materials/resources and maximal reuse/recycling of materials (to minimise environmental and economic costs);
- energy management and supply of energy from "green" or renewable sources;
- location of the development near to where people live and work (to minimise the environmental, social and economic costs of travelling);
- future-proofing of buildings to make them usable in a variety of situations and by a variety of people (to avoid the social disruption of people needing to move, and the environmental costs of redevelopment);
- provision of social and green infrastructure such as community centres, local health centres, parks and playing fields (for social and economic benefit);
- taking climate change into account in development, for instance by including sustainable urban drainage systems and shaded areas (to prevent the later economic and social costs of retrofitting these measures); and
- community engagement in planning and possibly building the development (to ensure that the development improves people's quality of life).

In particular, sustainable development needs to ensure that the human race lives within the capacity of the earth's resources and systems. The Global Footprint Network (2006) has estimated that humanity's current ecological footprint is 23 per cent larger than what the planet can regenerate. In the developed world this is largely due to the maintenance of an unsustainable and resource intensive way of living. In the developing nations, it is due to increasing population, a trend towards urbanisation, and the desire of those populations to attain the same level of living as their counterparts in the developed world, with all of the

Box 16.1 *Integrated sustainability decision criteria and general trade-off rules* (*Gibson 2005*)

The following *sustainability decision criteria* avoid compartmentalising sustainability into separate environmental, social and economic parameters:

1. socio-ecological integrity – recognition of the life support functions on which human and ecological well-being depends;
2. livelihood sufficiency and opportunity – ensuring a decent life for all people without compromising the same possibilities for future generations;
3. intra-generational equity – ensuring equity of sufficiency and opportunity for all people;
4. intergenerational equity – favouring options most likely to preserve or enhance opportunities for future generations to live sustainably;
5. resource maintenance and efficiency – reducing extractive damage, avoiding waste and reducing overall material and energy use per unit of benefit;
6. socio-ecological and democratic governance – delivering sustainability requirements through open and better informed deliberations, reciprocal awareness, collective responsibility and other decision-making practices;
7. precaution and adaptation – respect for uncertainty, avoidance of poorly understood adverse risks, planning to learn, designing for surprise and managing for adaptation; and
8. immediate and long term integration – applying all principles of sustainability at once, seeking mutually supportive benefits and multiple gains.

To avoid inappropriate trade-offs and to demonstrate that a sustainable outcome will be achieved, the following *trade-off rules* can be used:

• maximum net gains – deliver net progress towards meeting sustainability requirements (i.e. seek mutually reinforcing, cumulative and lasting contributions that favour the most positive feasible overall result while avoiding significant adverse effects);
• burden of argument on trade-off proponent – the burden of justification (especially where adverse effects in sustainability parameters will result) falls on the proponent of the trade-off;
• avoidance of significant adverse effects – no trade-off that involves a significant adverse effect on any sustainability parameter can be justified unless the alternative is acceptance of an even more significant adverse effect;
• protection of the future – no displacement of a significant adverse effect from the present to the future can be justified unless the alternative is displacement of an even more significant negative effect from the present to the future;
• explicit justification – all trade-offs must be openly identified in an explicit justification in light of the sustainability decision criteria and general trade-off rules; and
• open process – proposed compromises and trade-offs must be addressed and justified through open processes with effective involvement of all stakeholders.

resource depletion this brings. Globally we cannot continue with existing trends in resource use, never mind meet the needs of future generations.

16.2 The UK Government's sustainable development agenda

The UK Government's *Sustainable development strategy* (Defra 2005) promotes five principles of sustainable development:

- Living within environmental limits;
- Achieving a strong healthy and just society;
- Using sound science responsibly;
- Promoting good governance; and
- Achieving a sustainable economy.

It also concentrates on four main priority areas:

- Sustainable consumption and production;
- Climate change and energy;
- Natural resource protection and environmental enhancement; and
- Sustainable communities.

The Government's sustainable development agenda influences the planning system both directly and indirectly. The *Planning and Compulsory Purchase Act 2004* requires regional and local spatial plans to be subject to sustainability appraisal, and in practice these appraisals have included the requirements for strategic environmental assessment. The (Department for) Communities and Local Government is also bringing in a range of Planning Policy Statements to replace its old-style planning policy guidance. These statements more actively promote sustainable development. For instance Planning Policy Statement 1 is entitled "Delivering Sustainable Development" and states:

> Sustainable development is the core principle underpinning planning. . . . Planning should facilitate and promote sustainable and inclusive patterns of urban and rural development by:
>
> - making suitable land available for development in line with economic, social and environmental objectives to improve people's quality of life;
> - contributing to sustainable economic development;
> - protecting and enhancing the natural and historic environment, the quality and character of the countryside, and existing communities;
> - ensuring high quality development through good and inclusive design, and the efficient use of resources; and,
> - ensuring that development supports existing communities and contributes to the creation of safe, sustainable, liveable and mixed communities with good access to jobs and key services for all members of the community.
>
> (ODPM 2005)

In response to the Government's sustainable development agenda, most Regional Assemblies have established regional sustainable development frameworks, which some are now converting into "integrated regional frameworks". These have been used as a basis for the sustainability appraisal of Regional Spatial Strategies and Regional Economic Strategies, and in many cases have been the starting point for local authorities' sustainability appraisal frameworks. These RSSs are starting to influence the next round of local development planning, the Local Development Frameworks, and inter authority planning documents, such as regional waste management plans. These will, when complete, provide direct tests against which developments are assessed. Many authorities have also developed "Agenda 21" checklists, sustainable design guidance, sustainability checklists, Supplementary Planning Guidance on sustainability etc. These aim to both inform developers of the authority's thoughts on best practice and/or minimum standards that should apply; and provide the authority with a clear set of principles or standards against which to test planning applications.

16.3 Sustainable development and EIA

It is clear, therefore, that Government intends the development industry to improve the design and layout of developments along sustainable lines; and that a developer submitting a planning application will need to demonstrate they have integrated sustainability into the development, and have a mechanism for clearly demonstrating this. Can EIA assist in implementing sustainable development and does sustainability have a place in EIA?

EIA has traditionally not included a test for sustainable development, and the UK EIA regulations do not mention sustainability (Geneletti 2001). However, elements of EIA go beyond the narrow confines of "pure" environmental issues to cover wider sustainability issues (e.g. Wahaab 2004). Some authors believe that sustainability is a principal aim of EIA (Glasson *et al.* 2005, Petts 1999, Sadler 1996), and that EIA is a key mechanism for promoting sustainable development (Geneletti 2001). EIA acts throughout the project development process to improve the environmental performance of development projects and it can, if used correctly, help to drive social and economic issues in the same way. However, although EIA has improved the environmental performance of developments to date, it has been less successful at meeting wider sustainability goals (Caldwell 1993).

Some commentators (e.g. Lawrence 1997) have called for sustainability to be formally integrated into EIA regulations. Certainly EIA is sufficiently flexible and robust to be able to include additional elements within the assessment framework while still meeting legislative requirements. Many EIAs currently consider social and economic issues either directly in the ES or as complementary volumes, for instance on social impact assessment, health impact assessment, economic and social inclusion, and employment studies (e.g. retail analyses). Other commentators, instead, are concerned that broadening out EIA to also include social and economic parameters could water down the original purpose of EIA, which was to prevent significant environmental degradation. **Table 16.1** summarises the two sides' arguments.

Table 16.1 Arguments for and against broadening out EIA to cover the full range of sustainability issues

Arguments in favour of integration	Arguments against integration
Improves coherence and efficiency; reduces duplication of reports.	Given that time and resources are limited for any assessment, there will necessarily be a loss of depth in consideration of the environment if social and economic objectives and criteria are considered simultaneously.
Separating social, economic and environmental issues into assessment ghettoes can make it harder to integrate environmental issues in decision-making, as they come to be seen as a special interest subject which constrains other aspirations. Environmental, social and economic "pillars" become "warring houses".	
Helps to identify win-win-win solutions that integrate all three.	EIA was prompted by concerns that environmental consequences of decisions were being given insufficient weight compared to social and economic ones. If the point of EIA is to redress this balance, then expanding it to include social and economic parameters would be unnecessary and self-defeating.
The environment matters because it affects human well-being. The apparently ecocentric idea of "environmental protection" always comes back to anthropocentric judgements about what matters for human quality of life. There is no list of environmental imperatives that can be "read off" purely from science without the intervention of any normative judgements about what matters to humankind.	Removes questions of an essentially political nature from the realm of democratically accountable decision-making and presents them as reconcilable by technical and rational methodologies or procedures.
Allows better identification and documentation of indirect and synergistic effects which result from linkages between environmental, social and economic impacts which otherwise might be overlooked in separate, more specialised assessments.	Increases the risk that environmental concerns continue to be marginalised under a rhetoric of "sustainability"; keeping environmental arguments separate allows a clear environmental case to be made and environmental constraints to be clearly stated.
Avoids developing purely environmental options which preclude, or minimise, opportunities in economic or social development.	Carrying out the assessment in aggregate allows trade-offs between individual aspects or components to be hidden. A deterioration in quality of life for some social groups may not become apparent, and potentially unsustainable environmental effects may go undetected.
Allows a more integrated assessment against the criteria which will be used in the future to assess the value of projects.	

Source: Adapted from Morrison-Saunders and Therivel (2005).

16.4 Sustainability appraisal

16.4.1 Principles of sustainability appraisal

The appraisal/assessment of sustainability is notoriously difficult, especially at the project level. Some authors (e.g. Fricker 1998) have suggested that sustainability is something more than "a thing to be measured" and suggest that "rather than how we can measure sustainability, it may be more appropriate to ask how we measure up to sustainability". In the UK, strategic-level sustainability appraisal has traditionally been "**objectives-led**" – it tests whether a plan or programme achieves sustainability objectives such as the decision criteria listed in Box 16.1 – in contrast to EIA-inspired strategic environmental assessment which may be more "baseline-led" (Smith and Sheate 2001).

Because of the very wide range of issues associated with sustainability, sustainability appraisal generally focuses on a limited number of characteristics that are used to measure change – "**indicators**". These can be used throughout the project planning process to measure, describe, assess and monitor impacts. Examples of project-level sustainability indicators are whether a development is built on previously developed land or not (indicator of land use, resource efficiency, biodiversity); how far the nearest bus stop is where buses to the nearest city centre run at least every 30 minutes (indicator of accessibility, equity, air quality); and the level of energy efficiency of the building (indicator of climate change).

Choosing the right indicators involves a balancing process. Indicators should be "SMART":

- *Specific*: clear, understandable, and appropriate for the project level and for the type of project being assessed.
- *Measurable*: to allow alternatives to be compared, improvements to be detected etc. The provenance and accuracy of data is important to understand if benchmarking is to be successful and accurate.
- *Achievable*: available from existing sources, or able to be collected at reasonable cost and within a reasonable timeframe. Caratti *et al.* (2006) have reviewed the availability of data on the internet and identify suitable sources for information. Data may be required not only for the proposed development but also for other developments or targets to benchmark the development.
- *Relevant* to the decision being made. For instance a mineral extraction project would not be expected to improve educational standards. What indicators are "relevant" is particularly affected by scale. A range of countries, international organisations and research bodies have developed national-level sustainability indicators. Although these can provide a very useful framework for local-level action towards sustainability, and are tempting to use off the peg, they will almost certainly need to be "translated" to the project level to be useful in EIA. For instance, global-scale problems of resource

depletion are not specific enough for project-level EIA. However they manifest themselves at the project level in terms of the materials used in project construction, whether the project includes space for recycling, and the energy-efficiency of the development. It is these indicators that should be used as EIA-level sustainability indicators.

- *Time-bound*: they should allow change over time to be determined. Particular care is needed in areas subject to rapid change, for instance new towns; or where conditions change according to the season, such as tourism developments.

Indicators can be described using the OECD's (1993) pressure–state–response model. The "pressure" is first identified, for instance CO^2 emissions from transport. The "state" would be the concentrations of greenhouse gas. At a national level, the "response" would be fiscal or policy initiatives; at a project scale it could be improved public transport or improved space heating and insulation. A variant of this approach is the "DPSIR" model: "driving forces" such as transport and housing produce "pressures" which degrade the "state" of the environment; this "impacts" on human health and ecosystems, requiring "responses".

16.4.2 Methodologies for sustainability appraisal

A range of methodologies for assessing the sustainability of development projects is presented below. However, this is a rapidly developing field, especially in the use of specialist software models and interlinked databases, and the reader is advised to check the latest methodologies available when choosing one for their EIA.

The simplest approach is the use of **checklists**. These assess the performance of individual indicators against predetermined targets and tend to identify if the development meets or fails the test/target. These are un-integrated and unsophisticated.

Possibly the most common approach to sustainability appraisal is through **individual or linked databases of sustainability indicators.** These use nationally or locally available data in a series of spreadsheets which are used to benchmark the proposed development. Many countries (e.g. Defra 2008) and some international organisations (e.g. UNDESA 2007) have devised such databases. Other sustainability indicators lists at the national or continent level include WWF's (2006) Living Planet Index, Global Reporting Initiative's "G3 Guidelines" (GRI 2006), YCELP/CIESIN's (2005) Environmental Sustainability Index and IISD's (2007) Dashboard of Sustainability. Although these give a helpful indication of national-level sustainability issues and can act as comparators or benchmarks, they are typically too broad-brush to be relevant at the project level.

Several environmental consultancies have developed software or checklists comprising more local-level indicators, for instance Arup's (no date) SPeAR spider diagram, AtKisson's (2005) Accelerator model, Gibberd's (2003) Sustainable Building Assessment Tool, and WSP's *Sustainability Assessment Tool (SAT)* (2007). In addition, specific indicators have been developed for certain industries or development types, e.g. Warhurst (2002) for mining and USDA (1999/2007) for agriculture.

The assessments typically start with a scoping study to identify those sustainability issues which could be influenced by the proposed development and for which data are already available, or could be gained during the duration of the project. "Optimum performance levels" for indicators related to these issues are then displayed, for instance on a histogram or spider diagram. The actual performance of the project is then overlaid onto the same diagram. This allows ready identification of where the project is scoring well, and not so well. It also allows the potential effects of design changes (e.g. site location, chosen technology or site layout changes) and changes in investment decisions (e.g. investment levels, phasing of development) to be easily identified and assessed.

A development of the linked dataset mechanism is in the use of existing tools such as Geographical Information Systems (see Chapter 14) to spatially overlay predicted environmental, social and economic impacts and decision support systems to assess the effectiveness of different options (Geneletti 2001).

A range of **composite or aggregated indices** have also been defined, which aim to summarise sustainability in a single figure: money, efficiency, land etc. They include (Pinter *et al.* 2005):

- the Genuine Progress Indicator (Redefining Progress 2006), which adjusts gross domestic product to account for factors such as income distribution, the value of household and volunteer work, and the costs of crime and pollution;
- the Genuine Savings Indicator (Hamilton *et al.* 1997, Pearce 2000) which aims to encompass resource depletion, environmental degradation, technological change, human resources, exhaustible resource exports, resource discoveries and critical natural capital in a national financial accounting framework;
- Total Material Requirement (EEA 2001), which focuses on the extraction, import and productivity (GDP/input) of materials;
- the World Business Council for Sustainable Development's (WBCSD 2006) eco-efficiency approach, which promotes "the delivery of competitively priced goods and services that satisfy human needs and bring quality of life, while progressively reducing ecological impacts and resource intensity throughout the life-cycle to a level at least in line with the Earth's estimated carrying capacity"; and
- Ecological Footprinting (Global Footprint Network 2006, EEA 2005) which assesses what resources are required (inputs) and how much waste, byproducts and emissions are produced by an area, and expresses the results in terms of the equivalent land area of an average productive hectare, or Global Hectare.

All of these approaches suffer from shortfalls, particularly at the project level: they over-simplify a complex problem, include large uncertainties, and don't necessarily lead to useful avoidance or mitigation measures. For instance, ecological footprinting data are currently available down to the level of many local authorities, but the methods of calculation and the data requirements of the method make it unusable for all but the largest projects. As such, these approaches may be most useful "for internal and temporal reference" (Fricker 1998). Nevertheless, footprinting in particular gives an indication of the scale of the problem, and a useful comparison of the impacts of developed v. developing countries.

At the project scale, the aggregated index most regularly used in the UK is the Building Research Establishment Environmental Assessment Method (BREEAM) (BRE 2007). This measures the performance of different building types based on nine criteria: management, health and wellbeing, energy, transport, water, materials, land-use, pollution and biodiversity. Each assessment requires the design and site layout to be scored quantitatively against a number of questions. The aggregate score is then rated into classes: pass, good, very good and excellent. BRE have developed individual scoring systems for court buildings, residential developments, sustainable homes, multi-residential (halls of residence, sheltered housing etc), industrial buildings, offices, prisons, retail and schools. "BREEAM Bespoke" can be applied to other buildings (e.g. hotels, leisure centres), and "BREEAM for Developments" assesses the sustainability credentials of larger-scale mixed-use developments and communities.

The DCLG's (2007) Code for Sustainable Homes uses a similar approach: assessment against pre-identified criteria then aggregation into a single rating. Minimum levels of performance are expected in six areas: energy efficiency/CO_2, water efficiency, surface water management, site waste management, household waste management and use of materials. The assessment is carried out in two phases, following design and construction. New South Wales's (2006) BASIX sustainability index takes a similar approach.

Although EIA emerged out of a need to define the potential impacts of a development where these could not be assessed merely by using financial accounting techniques, interest has continued in using **cost benefit analysis** (CBA) as a basis to measure the performance of projects across environmental, social and economic criteria (Turner 2006). In its simplest form, this involves measuring environmental criteria in economic terms. Natural Capitalism is one such technique: it seeks to measure ecosystem processes in economic terms, considering them as means of production (e.g. oxygen, crops, soil) and system stabilisation (e.g. erosion control) (Hawken *et al.* 2006). The Genuine Performance Indicator and Genuine Savings Indicator described above also use forms of CBA.

At the project level, traditional CBA can be extended into *whole life costing*. This considers the cost of a development from procurement and construction through to decommissioning. It helps to avoid developers' traditional over-emphasis on reducing capital costs at the expense of increasing running costs (for instance stinting on insulation but paying more for heating), often with associated environmental benefits. The technique's advantage is that it arises from a commonly used business development technique; its main disadvantage lies with the difficulties in predicting social and environmental costs over the lifetime of the project. Organisations such as the Commission of the European

Communities (EC 2001), Office of Government Commerce (OGC 2007), Scottish Procurement Directorate (no date) and Ministry of Defence (MOD 2007) promote the use of whole life costing in developing the business case for procurement of new developments. Others, such as the Whole Life Cost Forum (WLCF 2007), see whole life costing as a wider tool to be used to improve the sustainability of developments. Their approach uses spreadsheets to calculate discounted cash flows; these are then tested against environmental, social and non-financial business related objectives to identify the sustainability performance of the development.

Input–output analysis (or material flow accounting/analysis) seeks to identify all inputs and outputs from a system, for instance light, nutrients, water, biomass (e.g. migrating species); as well as sinks and movements webs within the system. The technique is usually applied at the national or regional scale, for instance to identify the impacts of changes in investment in particular industries or the effect of legislation on particular regions. Similar models exist for economic analysis, and have been used for years to assess company, industry, regional and national accounts.

At a project level, input–output analysis can be used to measure or predict materials flows into and out from a development, and identify the consequent environmental, economic and social effects. It is often used with other techniques such as ecological footprints. For instance the Stockholm Environment Institute uses environmental and economic input–output tables and the Resource and Energy Analysis Programme (REAP) to identify the material flows and ecological footprints of projects (SEI 2007). REAP considers consumption by households and public as well as commercial services, wherever the consumed products may come from and wherever environmental impacts may occur.

Life cycle assessment combines the whole-life approach and input–output analysis. It involves (1) taking an inventory of the raw materials that will be used during the life of a product/project and the emissions that will occur, and (2) assessing what the impacts of these emissions and raw material depletions are.

The **Quality of Life Capital approach**, discussed in Chapter 15, can also be used to promote sustainable development. It "converts" assets such as buildings and woodlands into the benefits that people receive from these assets, and then aims to maximise these benefits. It emphasises the value that local communities and businesses place on assets, rather than only the value judgements of professionals (CA 1999).

A recent and novel method for sustainability monitoring and assessment is the use of **Mind Maps**. These are typically used to order and assess available technology choice against such elements as energy use/supply, materials choice, legislation building performance. They aim to classify environmental benefit and legislative compliance of technology solutions against financial criteria. The mind map's role is to assist the reader to consider the choices made by developers when considering technology options against known and likely legislative and product development in the future. They are based on a temporal scale, allowing developers to identify compliance and "upgradability" in the future against calculated investment levels. They can be used on individual buildings to consider aspects such as natural ventilation and materials choice, or at a site level for issues such as renewable energy and green roof/water management issues.

16.5 Conclusion

The planning system is increasingly being used to ensure that developments achieve Governmental sustainable development objectives, as well as minimise their environmental impacts. The trend to provide greater information on the sustainability credentials of a project is unlikely to reduce in the foreseeable future. Therefore a mechanism for providing this information in a structured, logical and impartial form is urgently required. EIA already considers many aspects of sustainability, and can be broadened out to include wider sustainability issues. Integrated sustainability criteria can help to avoid a silo mentality which trades off environmental versus social and economic benefits. However, until the EIA Regulations are replaced by legislation requiring project-level sustainability appraisal, there will be a gap between the legally required documentation for planning, and the documentation desired by planning authorities.

Methods already exist for considering sustainability in project development, and some of these can be used in EIAs. However, this is a quickly developing field, and new techniques, and models to support them, will undoubtedly be developed in the near future.

References

Arup (no date) *SPeAR: product overview*. London: Ove Arup Consulting Engineers, www.arup.com/environment/feature.cfm?pageid=1685.

AtKisson 2005. *Accelerator: a comprehensive toolkit for sustainable development*. Boston, MA: AtKisson Group, www.atkisson.com/accelerator/AtKissonAccelerator2005.pdf.

BRE (Building Research Establishment) 2007. *BREEAM: BRE environmental assessment methods*. Watford, Herts: BRE, www.breeam.org.

CA (Countryside Agency) 1999. *Quality of Life Capital and Environmental Impact Assessment*. Cheltenham, Glos: Countryside Agency (now Peterborough, Cambs: Natural England).

Caldwell LK 1993. Achieving the NEPA Intent: new directions in politics, science and law. In *Environmental Analysis, the NEPA experience.*, SG Hildebrand SG and JB Cannon. London: Lewis Publishers.

Caratti P, L Ferraguto and C Riboldi 2006. Sustainable development data availability on the internet (October). *FEEM Working Paper No. 125.06*. RePEc, Orebro University, Sweden. Italy, http://ssrn.com/abstract=936927.

DCLG (Department for Communities and Local Government) 2007. *Code for sustainable homes technical guide*. London: DCLG, www.planningportal.gov.uk/uploads/code_for_sustainable_homes_techguide.pdf.

Defra 2005. *Securing the future – UK Government sustainable development strategy*. London: Defra, www.defra.gov.uk/sustainable/government/publications/uk-strategy/index.htm.

Defra 2008. *Sustainable development indicators in your pocket 2008*. London: Defra, www.defra.gov.uk/sustainable/government/.

EC (European Commission) 2001. *Commission interpretative communication on the community law applicable to public procurement and the possibilities for integrating environmental considerations into public procurement*, COM(2001) 274 (final). Brussels: EC, http://eur-lex.europa.eu/LexUriServ/LexUriServ.do?uri=COM:2001:0274:FIN:EN:PDF.

EEA (European Environment Agency) 2001. Total material requirement of the European Union. *EEA technical report No: 55*. Copenhagen: EEA, http://reports.eea.europa.eu/Technical_report_No_56/en.

EEA 2005. *The European Environment Agency in coordination with Global Footprint Network presents: The National Ecological Footprint and Biocapacity Accounts 2005 Edition*. Copenhagen: EEA, www.org.eea.eu.int/news/Ann1132753060.

Fricker A 1998. Measuring up to sustainability. *Futures Journal* **30**(4), 367–375.

Geneletti D 2001. *Promoting sustainability through environmental impact assessment: a case study combining GIS and decision making support systems*. International Workshop on Geo-Spatial Knowledge Processing for Natural Resource Management. 28–29 June, Vargese, Italy: University of Insubria.

Gibberd J 2003. *Sustainable building assessment tool*. Pretoria, South Africa: University of Pretoria, http://upetd.up.ac.za/thesis/available/etd-06142004-144252/unrestricted/22SBAT-PercentagesA.pdf.

Gibson R 2005. *Sustainability assessment: criteria and processes*. London: Earthscan.

Glasson J, R Therivel and A Chadwick 2005. *Introduction to Environmental Impact Assessment*, 3rd edn. London: Routledge.

Global Footprint Network 2006. *Ecological footprint: overview*. Oakland, CA: Global Footprint Network, www.footprintnetwork.org.

GRI (Global Reporting Initiative) 2006. *G3 reporting framework*. Amsterdam: GRI, www.globalreporting.org.

Hamilton K, A Giles and D Pearce 1997. Genuine savings as an indicator of sustainability, *GSERGE Working Paper GEC 97-03*. London: Centre for Social and Economic Research and the World Bank.

Hawken P, A Lovins and L Hunter Lovins 2006. *Natural capitalism: creating the next industrial revolution*. Boulder, CO: Rocky Mountain Institute.

IISD (International Institute for Sustainable Development) 2007. *Dashboard of sustainability*. New York: IISD, www.iisd.org/cgsdi/dashboard.asp.

Lawrence D 1997. Integrating sustainability and environmental impact assessment. *Environmental Management* **21**(1), 23–42.

Levett L 1997. Indicators for a civilised city, contribution to ERIC seminar, London, 7 October.

MOD (Ministry of Defence) 2007. *UK MOD defence acquisition community works*, version 1.1.2: *Defence values for acquisition*. London: MOD www.aof.mod.uk/aofcontent/operational/people/dvfa.htm.

Morrison-Saunders A and R Therivel 2005. Sustainability integration and assessment. *Journal of Environmental Assessment Policy and Management* **8**(3), 281–298.

New South Wales Government 2006. *BASIX, the building sustainability index*. Sydney: NSW Government, www.basix.nsw.gov.au/information/about.jsp.

OECD (Organisation for Economic Co-operation and Development) 1993. OECD core set of indicators for environmental performance reviews. *OECD Environment Monographs No. 83*. Paris: OECD.

ODPM (Office of the Deputy Prime Minister) 2005. *Planning Policy Statement 1: Delivering sustainable development*. London: OPDM, www.communities.gov.uk/documents/planningandbuilding/pdf/147393.

OGC (Office of Government Commerce) 2007. *Whole-life costing and cost management, achieving excellence in construction procurement guide 7.* London: OGC, www.ogc.gov.uk/documents/CP0067AEGuide7.pdf.

Pearce D 2000. The policy relevance and use of aggregate indicators: genuine savings. *OECD Proceedings. Frameworks to Measure Sustainable Development.* Paris: OECD.

Petts J (ed.) 1999. *Handbook of Environmental Impact Assessment:* Vol. 1. *Environmental Impact Assessment: Process, methods and potential.* Oxford: Blackwell Science.

Pinter L, P Hardi and P Bartelmus 2005. *Indicators of sustainable development: proposals for a way forward.* United Nations Division for Sustainable Development. Expert Group Meeting on Indicators of Sustainable Development. New York. 13–15 December.

Redefining Progress 2006. *The genuine progress indicator 2006.* San Francisco: Redefining Progress.. www.rprogress.org/publications/2007/GPI%202006.pdf.

Sadler B 1996. *International study of the effectiveness of environmental assessment (final report). Environmental assessment in a changing world: evaluating practice to improve performance.* Ottowa: Canadian Environment Assessment Agency (CEAA), www.ceaa.gc.ca/017/012/iaia8_e.pdf.

Scottish Procurement Directorate (no date) Procurement instruction toolkit. Glasgow: Scottish Procurement Directorate, www.eprocurementscotland.com/toolkit/Textfiles/Bid_Evaluation.htm,

SEI (Stockholm Environment Institute) 2007. *Environmental input-output analysis.* York: University of York, SEI, www.york.ac.uk/inst/sei/IS/in_out_anal.html.

Smith S and WR Sheate 2001. Sustainability appraisal of English regional plans: incorporating the requirements of the EU Strategic Environmental Assessment Directive, *Impact Assessment and Project Appraisal* 19(4), 263–276.

Stevens C 2005. *Measuring sustainable development.* OECD Statistics Brief. No: 10. Paris: OECD, www.oecd.org/dataoecd/60/41/35407580.pdf.

Turner RK 2006. Limits to CBA and European Environmental Policy: retrospectives & future prospects. *CSERGE Working Paper EDM 06-17.* Norwich: Centre for Social and Economic Research on the Global Environment (CSERGE) School of Environmental Sciences, University of East Anglia.

UNDESA (United Nations Department of Economic and Social Affairs) 2007. *Indicators of sustainable development, guidelines and methodologies,* October 2007, 3rd edn. New York: UNDESA, www.un.org/esa/sustdev/natlinfo/indicators/guidelines.pdf.

USDA (United States Department of Agriculture) 1999/2007. *Sustainable agriculture.* Washington, DC: USDA, www.nal.usda.gov/afsic/pubs/terms/srb9902.shtml.

Wahaab RA 2004. Sustainable development and environmental impact assessment in Egypt: Historical Assessment. *The Environmentalist* 23(1), 49–70.

Warhurst A 2002. Sustainability Indicators and Sustainability Performance. *Management. Report No: 43.* Warwick Business School, University of Warwick. International Institute for Environment and Development and the World Business Council for Sustainable Development.

WBCSD (World Business Council for Sustainable Development) 2006. *Eco-efficiency learning module.* Conches-Geneva: WBCSD, www.wbcsd.org/web/publications/ee_module.pdf.

WLCF (Whole Life Cost Forum) 2007. *About Whole Life Costs.* London: WLCF, www.wlcf.co.uk/whatAreWLCs.htm.

World Commission on Environment and Development 1987. *Our Common Future.* Oxford: Oxford University Press.

WSP 2007. *Sustainability Assessment Tool (SAT)*. London: WSP, www.wspgroup.com.

WWF (World Wide Fund for Nature) 2006. *Living planet report*. Gland: WWF International, www.panda.org/livingplanet.

YCELP/CIESIN (Yale Center for Environmental Law and Policy and Center for International Earth Science Information Network) 2005. *Environmental sustainability index*. New York, Socioeconomic Data and Applications Center, Columbia University, http://sedac.ciesin.columbia.edu/es/esi/.

Appendix A

Acronyms, internet addresses, chemical symbols, and quantitative units

A.1 Acronyms and internet addresses

Acronyms and internet addresses may not be included here when they are given in a chapter or another appendix.

AES	The Amateur Entomologists' Society, www.amentsoc.org/
ALGAO	Association of Local Government Archaeological Officers, www.algao.org.uk/
	Ancient Monuments Society, www.ancientmonumentssociety.org.uk/
BBS	British Bryological Society, www.britishbryologicalsociety.org.uk/
BC	Butterfly Conservation, www.butterfly-conservation.org/
BCT	Bat Conservation Trust, www.bats.org.uk/
BENHS	British Entomological and Natural History Society, www.benhs.org.uk/
BGS	British Geological Survey, www.bgs.ac.uk/
BHS	British Herpetological Society www.thebhs.org
BI	Birdlife International, www.birdlife.org
BLS	British Lichen Society, www.thebls.org.uk/
BSBI	Botanical Society of the British Isles, www.bsbi.org.uk/
BSI	British Standards Institution, www.bsi-global.com/
BTO	British Trust for Ornithology, www.bto.org/
CA	Countryside Agency (incorporated in NE in 2006).
Cadw	Historic environment service of the Welsh Assembly Government, www.cadw.wales.gov.uk/
CBA	Council for British Archaeology, www.britarch.ac.uk/
CBD	Convention on Biological Diversity (adopted at the 1992 Rio Earth Summit), www.cbd.int/convention
CC	Countryside Commission (replaced by CA and subsequently by NE)
CCW	Countryside Council for Wales, www.ccw.gov.uk
CEAA	Canadian Environment Assessment Agency, www.ceaa.gc.ca/
CEFAS	Centre for Environment, Fisheries and Aquaculture Science, www.cefas.co.uk/

CEH	Centre for Ecology and Hydrology, www.ceh.ac.uk/
CIPFA	Chartered Institute of Public Finance and Accountancy, www.cipfa.org.uk/
CIRIA	Construction Industry Research and Information Association, www.ciria.org.uk/
COE	Council of Europe, www.coe.int/
CPRE	Campaign to Protect Rural England, www.cpre.org.uk/
CPRW	Campaign for the Protection of Rural Wales, www.cprw.org.uk/
DARDNI	Department of Agriculture and Rural Development, NI, www.dardni.gov.uk/
DCLG	Department for Communities and Local Government, www.communities.gov.uk
DCMS	Department for Culture, Media and Sport, www.culture.gov.uk/
Defra	Department for Environment, Food and Rural Affairs, www.defra.gov.uk
DETR	Department of the Environment, Transport and the Regions (replaced by Defra and DfT, 2003)
DfT	Department for Transport, www.dft.gov.uk/
DoE	Department of the Environment (merged with DoT to form DETR, 1997)
DOENI	Department of the Environment for Northern Ireland, www.doeni.gov.uk/
DoT	Department of Transport (merged with DoE to form DETR, 1997)
DRA	Department for Rural Affairs (Environment, Planning & Countryside) Wales, www.countryside.wales.gov.uk/
EA	Environment Agency, www.environment-agency.gov.uk/
EA-W	Environment Agency Wales, www.environment-agency.wales.gov.uk/
EC	European Commission, http://ec.europa.eu/
EC-EDG	EC Environment Directorate General, http://ec.europa.eu/environment/index_en.htm
ECN	Environmental Change Network, www.ecn.ac.uk/
ECNC	European Centre for Nature Conservation, www.ecnc.nl/
EEA	European Environment Agency, www.eea.europa.eu/ (see also EIONET, ETCs and EUNIS)
EH	English Heritage, www.english-heritage.org.uk/
EHS	Environment and Heritage Service, Northern Ireland, www.ehsni.gov.uk/
EIONET	European Environment Information and Observation Network, http://eionet.europa.eu/
EIS	Environmental Impact Statement (often called ES – Environmental Statement)
EN	English Nature. Replaced by Natural England (NE) in 2006

ENTRUST	The Environmental Trust Scheme Regulatory Body Ltd, www.entrust.org.uk/
EPAs	environmental protection agencies (see Appendix B and USEPA)
ETCs	European Topic Centres (contracted by EEA): Air & Climate, http://air-climate.eionet.europa.eu/); Biodiversity, http://biodiversity.eionet.europa.eu/; Land Use and Spatial Information, http://terrestrial.eionet.europa.eu/; Resource and Waste Management, http://waste.eionet.europa.eu/; & Water, http://water.eionet.europa.eu/
EUNIS	European Union Nature Information System, http://eunis.eea.europa.eu
FAO	Food and Agriculture Organisation of the UN, www.fao.org/
FBA	Freshwater Biological Association, www.fba.org.uk/
FC	Forestry Commission, www.forestry.gov.uk/
FTE	Full Time Equivalent
	Georgian Group, www.georgiangroup.org.uk/
GO	government organisation (e.g. department, agency)
GRO	General Register Office (Scotland), www.gro-scotland.gov.uk/
GWCT	Game & Wildlife Conservation Trust, www.gct.org.uk
HA	Highways Agency, Executive Agency of DfT, www.highways.gov.uk/
HMIP	Her Majesty's Inspectorate of Pollution (now incorporated in EA)
HMSO	Her Majesty's Stationery Office, now incorporated in OPSI (see also TSO)
HS	Historic Scotland, www.historic-scotland.gov.uk/
HSE	Health and Safety Executive, www.hse.gov.uk/
IAIA	International Association for Impact Assessment, www.iaia.org/
IAU	Impacts Assessment Unit, Oxford Brookes University, www.brookes.ac.uk/iau/
IEA	Institute of Environmental Assessment (now incorporated in IEMA)
IEEM	Institute of Ecology and Environmental Management, www.ieem.org.uk
IEMA	Institute of Environmental Management and Assessment, www.iema.net
IFA	Institute of Field Archaeologists, www.archaeologists.net/
IGO	Intergovernmental organisation (including the UN)
IHBC	Institute of Historic Building Conservation, www.ihbc.org.uk/
IHT	Institution of Highways and Transportation, www.iht.org.uk/
IUCN	International Union for the Conservation of Nature, www.iucn.org/
JNCC	Joint Nature Conservation Committee, www.jncc.gov.uk/

LA/LPA	local authority/local planning authority (UK) Landscape Institute, www.landscapeinstitute.org/
LDF	Local Development Framework, www.planningportal.gov.uk/ uploads/ldf/ldfguide.html
LGA	Local Government Association, www.lga.gov.uk/
LIFE	the EU's financial instrument supporting environmental and nature conservation projects, http://ec.europa.eu/environment/ life/
LRCs	Local Biological Record Centres, www.nbn-nfbr.org.uk/ nfbr.php (see also NFBR)
LWTs	local Wildlife Trusts (affiliated to TWT)
MA	Millennium Ecosystem Assessment Organisation, www. maweb.org
MAFF	Ministry of Agriculture, Fisheries and Food (replaced by Defra in 2001)
MarLIN	Marine Life Information Network for Britain and Ireland, www.marlin.ac.uk
MBR	Monuments and Buildings Record, www.ehsni.gov.uk/built/ mbr_intro.htm
MCS	Marine Conservation Society, www.mcsuk.org/
MLURI	Macaulay Land Use Research Institute, www.mluri.sari.ac.uk/
MO	Meteorological Office, www.met-office.gov.uk/
MPA	mineral planning authority (county or unitary LPA, or National Park Board)
MS	Mammal Society: www.abdn.ac.uk/mammal/
NAW	National Assembly for Wales, www.wales.gov.uk/
NBN	National Biodiversity Network, www.nbn.org.uk
NE	Natural England, www.naturalengland.org.uk
NERC	Natural Environment Research Council www.nerc.ac.uk
NFBR	National Federation for Biological Recording, www.nfbr. org.uk/index.html
NGOs	non-government organisations such as LWTs, RSPB and WT
NICS	Northern Ireland Executive, www.nics.gov.uk
NLUD	National Land Use Database, www.nlud.org.uk/index.htm
NOMIS	National On-Line Manpower Information System, www. nomisweb.co.uk/
NPMN	National Pond Monitoring Network, www.pondnetwork.org.uk
NRA	National Rivers Authority (now incorporated in the EA)
NSCA	National Society for Clean Air and Environmental Protection (now Environmental Protection UK), www. environmental-protection.org.uk/
NSRI	National Soil Resources Institute, www.cranfield.ac.uk/sas/ nsri/index.jsp
NT	National Trust, www.nationaltrust.org.uk/
NTS	National Trust for Scotland, www.nts.org.uk/
ODPM	Office of the Deputy Prime Minister (now succeeded by DCLG)

ONS	Office for National Statistics (and UK Statistics Authority), www.statistics.gov.uk/
OOPEC	Office for Official Publications of the European Communities, http://publications.europa.eu/
OPCS	Office of Population Censuses & Surveys (now incorporated in ONS)
OPSI	Office of Public Sector Information, www.opsi.gov.uk
OS	Ordnance Survey, www.ordsvy.gov.uk/
PI	Plantlife International. The Wild Plant Conservation Charity, www.plantlife.org.uk/
POL	Proudman Oceanographic Laboratory (NERC), www.pol.ac.uk/ Pond Conservation, www.pondconservation.org.uk/
POST	Parliamentary Office of Science and Techology, www.parliament.uk/parliamentary_offices/post.cfm
RANI	Rivers Authority, Northern Ireland, www.riversagencyni.gov.uk/
RCAHMS	Royal Commission on the Ancient and Historical Monuments of Scotland, www.rcahms.gov.uk/
RCAHMW	Royal Commission on the Ancient and Historical Monuments of Wales, www.rcahmw.org.uk/
RCEP	Royal Commission on Environmental Pollution, www.rcep.org.uk/
RCHME	Royal Commission on the Historical Monuments of England (now in EH)
RDS	Rural Development Service (incorporated in NE in 2006)
RMetS	Royal Meteorological Society, www.rmets.org/
RSPB	Royal Society for the Protection of Birds, www.rspb.org.uk/
SCI	Society of Chemical Industry, www.soci.org/SCI/index.jsp
SE	Scottish Executive (became SG in 2007)
SEPA	Scottish Environment Protection Agency, www.sepa.org.uk/
SG	Scottish (or Scotland) Government, www.scotland.gov.uk/
SI	Statutory Instrument (of UK legislation/regulations)
SNCOs	Statutory Nature (and countryside) Conservation Organisations (see Appendix B)
SNH	Scottish Natural Heritage, www.snh.org.uk
SNIFFER	Scotland and Northern Ireland Forum for Environmental Research, www.sniffer.org.uk/
SO	Scottish Office (became SE in 1999, and SG in 2007)
SPAB	Society for the Protection of Ancient Buildings, www.spab.org.uk/
TSO	The Stationery Office, www.tsoshop.co.uk/ Twentieth Century Society, www.c20society.org.uk/
TWT	The Wildlife Trusts, www.wildlifetrusts.org
UKBAP	UK Biodiversity Action Plan, www.ukbap.org.uk
UKBG	UK Biodiversity Group (now replaced by UKBP)

UKBP	UK Biodiversity Partnership, www.ukbap.org.uk
UKCIP	UK Climate Impacts Programme, www.ukcip.org.uk/
UNCED	United Nations Conference on Environment and Development, Rio de Janeiro, 3–14 June 1992. www.un.org/geninfo/bp/enviro.html
UNCSD	United Nations Commission on Sustainable Development (CSD), www.un.org/esa/sustdev/csd/review.htm
UNECE	United Nations Economic Commission for Europe, www.unece.org/
UNEP	United Nations Environment Programme, www.unep.org/
UNEP-WCMC	UNEP-World Conservation Monitoring Centre, www.unep-wcmc.org
UNESCO	United Nations Educational Scientific and Cultural Organisation, www.unesco.org/. Includes the Man and Biosphere Programme, www.unesco.org/mab, and the World Heritage Centre, www.unesco.org/whc
USDA-NRCS	US Department of Agriculture, Natural Resources Conservation Service, www.nrcs.usda.gov/. Includes various sections/centres, e.g. Soils, Water and climate, Watersheds and wetlands, Ecology, and Habitat Management.
USEPA	US Environmental Protection Agency, www.epa.gov/
USFWS	US Fish and Wildlife Service, Division of Ecological Services, www.fws.gov/
USGS	US Geological Survey, www.usgs.gov/. Includes various divisions, e.g.: Biology, http://biology.usgs.gov/; and Water, http://water.usgs.gov/
USNTIS	US National Technical Information Service, www.ntis.gov/ Victorian Society, www.victorian-society.org.uk/
WAG	Welsh Assembly Government, http://new.wales.gov.uk/splash
WCU	World Conservation Union (see IUCN)
WHO	World Health Organization, www.who.org/
WO	Welsh Office (now Welsh Assembly Government (WAG) World Bank, www.worldbank.org/
WT	Woodland Trust, www.woodland-trust.org.uk/
WWF	Worldwide Fund for Nature, www.panda.org/ WWF-UK, www.wwf-uk.org/
WWT	Wildfowl and Wetlands Trust, www.wwt.org.uk/
ZSL	Zoological Society of London, www.zsl.org

A.2 Chemical symbols and acronyms

Al	aluminium	Na	sodium
Ca	calcium	NH_3	ammonia
Cd	cadmium	N_2O	nitrous oxide
CFC	chlorofluorocarbon	NO_2	nitrogen dioxide

CH_4	methane	NO_x	nitrogen oxides
CO	carbon monoxide	O or O_2	oxygen
CO_2	carbon dioxide	O_3	ozone
Cu	copper	P	phosphorus
EDTA	ethylene diamine tetra-acetic acid	Pb	lead
F^-	fluoride	PAH	polycyclic aromatic hydrocarbon
HCFC	hydrochlorofluorocarbon	PCB	polychlorinated biphenyl
Hg	mercury	SO_2	sulphur dioxide
K	potassium	TOMPS	toxic organic micro-pollutants
Mg	magnesium	VOC	volatile organic compound
N_2	nitrogen	Zn	zinc

A.3 Quantitative units and symbols

c.	*circa*/about/approximately	mg	milligram $(g \times 10^{-3})$
cm	centimetre	min	minute
cumec	cubic metres per second	mm	millimetre
dB	decibel	ng	nanogram $(g \times 10^{-9})$
g	gram	MW	megawatt
ha	hectare $(10,000m^2 = 2.471$ acres)	ppb	parts per billion
hectad	$10 \times 10km$ square	ppm	parts per million
hr	hour	s	second
Hz	hertz	tetrad	$2 \times 2km$ square
k	thousand, e.g. $25k = 25,000$	yr	year
kg	kilogram	μg	microgram $(g \times 10^{-6})$
km	kilometre	μm	micrometre $(m \times 10^{-6})$
kJ	kilojoule	<	below/less than
J	Joule	≤	equal to or less than
/ l	per litre	>	above/greater than
m	metre	≥	equal to or greater than

Appendix B

UK environment, conservation and heritage organisations (*and their main roles*)

UK / England	Wales	Scotland	Northern Ireland (NI)
Executive Authorities			
UK Government	National Assembly for Wales (NAW)	Scottish Government (SG)	Northern Ireland Executive (NICS)
Departments			
Department for Environment, Food and Rural Affairs (Defra)	Department for Environment, Planning & Countryside (EPC)		Department of the Environment for Northern Ireland (DOENI)
Environmental policies and strategies, and their implementation through delivery bodies such as the statutory EPAs & SNCOs			
Statutory Environmental Protection Agencies (EPAs)			
Environment Agency (EA)	Environment Agency Wales (EAW) (branch of EA but also under NAW)	Scottish Environmental Protection Agency (SEPA)	Environment & Heritage Service (EHS)
Environmental protection including pollution control, water resources, watercourse management, land drainage and flood defence (In Northern Ireland, the Rivers Agency (RANI) is responsible for land drainage and flood defence)			
Statutory Nature (and countryside) Conservation Organisations (SNCOs)			
Natural England (NE)	Countryside Council for Wales (CCW)	Scottish Natural Heritage (SNH)	Environment & Heritage Service
Nature and countryside conservation, and land management to conserve and enhance biodiversity, landscapes and wildlife in rural, urban, coastal and marine areas; countryside access and recreation			
Joint Nature Conservation Committee (JNCC)			
Statutory adviser to Government on UK and international nature conservation. Delivers the responsibilities of CNCC*, CCW, NE & SNH.			
Heritage Organisations			
English Heritage (EH)	Historic Environment Service (Cadw)	Historic Scotland (HS)	Environment & Heritage Service
Protection and promotion of historic buildings, historic parks, gardens and landscapes, ancient monuments and archaeological sites			

* CNCC (Council for Nature Conservation and the Countryside) is a Statutory Advisory Council to DOENI & EHS.

Appendix C
Habitat, vegetation and land classifications

Peter Morris

C.1 Introduction

A major purpose of classifications is to provide a mechanism by which records from different investigations can be compared in terms of accepted categories that are meaningful to all users, and they are widely employed in EcIA. However, there are two significant problems: ecological variability; and non-conformity between classifications.

Ecological variability

No classification can fully accommodate the variability of ecological systems. For example:

- a community or habitat is the product of past and present local factors, and is therefore unique, so no two examples of a designated type will be precisely the same;
- rather than existing as discrete entities, natural communities and habitats tend to intergrade, even within small areas (§11.2.2), so examples found in given locations may represent points on gradients of variation within or between designated types.

Consequently, while samples from local communities/habitats can usually be fitted fairly readily to designated types of broad classifications, they may not provide a close match with any type described in more precise classifications. Failure to appreciate this can lead to errors such as under-valuation of habitats that do not closely match designated types; and it is essential that this is made clear in EcIAs, so avoiding misinterpretation by developers and decision makers.

Non-conformity between classifications

The ability to "translate" between classifications can be very important. Unlike species classification, however, habitat classification has no widely agreed "taxonomy", and many different systems have been developed, often with different purposes. Consequent lack of compatibility often hinders translation (Gibson 1998), and this can lead to misinterpretation, especially by non-experts. This appendix provides some information on relationships between the main classifications used in the UK. The *National Biodiversity Network* (NBN) *Habitats Dictionary* (NBNHD) (www.nbn.org.uk/habitats/index.htm) holds information on these (and other) classifications, and the NBN Habitat Correspondences interactive spreadsheet (NBNHC) (available at www.jncc.gov.uk/page-4258) provides detailed translations. Translation facilities are also provided in EUNIS (§C.6), the IHS (§C.7).

The following classifications are outlined in this Appendix:

C.2   The JNCC Phase 1 Habitat Classification;
C.3   UKBAP Broad habitats and Priority habitats;
C.4   The JNCC Marine Habitat Classification of Britain and Ireland (MHCBI);
C.5   The Habitats Directive Annex I, CORINE and Palaearctic habitat classifications;
C.6   The EUNIS Habitat Classification;
C.7   The Integrated Habitat System (IHS);
C.8   The National Vegetation Classification (NVC);
C.9   UK Freshwater Vegetation Classifications;
C.10   The Countryside Vegetation System (CVS);
C.11   Land classifications.

C.2 The JNCC Phase 1 Habitat Classification

The JNCC Phase 1 Habitat Classification is an integral part of the JNCC Phase 1 survey method (§11.5). It is a hierarchical, system, with broad (top level) habitat types divided into sub-types (**Table C.1**). The habitats are defined in relation to: (a) vegetation physiognomy (e.g. woodland, grassland); (b) environmental features of vegetated habitats (e.g. saltmarsh, sand dune, calcareous grassland) *or* substratum of non-vegetated habitats (e.g. rock, mud); (c) characteristic plant species; and (d) land use (e.g. improved grasslands and most category J types).

Surveyed habitats may not precisely match any designated type, or may be variants within a type such as broadleaved woodland, which includes a range of variants dominated by different tree species. The problem can be alleviated by using target notes, mapping codes and labels (e.g. for dominant species). It is also permissible to assign a name under "J5 other habitats". Addition of such categories should be normally kept to a minimum, but an exception in EcIA may be to increase the number of some J-class types (e.g. urban, commercial and industrial buildings), thus extending the land use component of the classification (see §C.11).

Table C.1 Outline of the JNCC Phase 1 habitat classification

A Woodland and Scrub – Dominated by trees or shrubs

A1 Woodland – Dominated by trees >5m tall when mature, forming a definite canopy

A1.1 Broadleaved – Dominated by broadleaved deciduous trees with ≤10% confers in the canopy

A1.1.1 semi-natural – Includes: canopy of <30% planted trees; planted standards in semi-natural coppice; mature plantations (> *c.*120 years old) of native species; self-sown stands of exotics, e.g. sycamore; sweet-chestnut coppice >25 yrs old; >5m tall alder/willow *carr* (except *Salix cinerea*)

A1.1.2 plantation – >30% of the canopy obviously planted (regardless of age). Often even-aged stands, with poorly developed and species poor sub-canopy layers

A1.2 Coniferous – Dominated by conifers, with ≤10% broadleaved species in the canopy

A1.2.1 semi-natural – Equivalent to A.1.1.1. The only native coniferous trees are *Pinus sylvestris* (Scots pine) (native in Scotland but re-introduced elsewhere) and *Taxus baccata* (yew)

A1.2.2 plantation – Equivalent to A.1.1.2. Usually commercial plantations (e.g. of non-native larches, firs, pines and spruces) with little or no sub-canopy vegetation

A1.3 Mixed – 10–90% of either broadleaved or conifer species in the canopy

A1.3.1 semi-natural – as above; **A1.3.2 plantation** – as above

A2 Scrub – Dominated by native shrubs <5m. Includes montane willow scrub, willow carr <5m and all *Salix cinerea* carr (even if >5m). Lowland scrub is seral and will be replaced by woodland, but some upland scrub is climax vegetation (see Figure 11.3). Can be: **A.2.1 continuous** or **A.2.2 scattered**

A3 Parkland & scattered trees – Tree cover <30%. Includes historically managed wood-pasture and parkland on grassland or heath. Can be: **A3.1 broadleaved, A3.2 coniferous** or **A3.3 mixed**

A4 Recently felled woodland – Only used when future land use is uncertain, e.g. may be replanted or used for agriculture. Can be: **A4.1 broadleaved, A4.2 coniferous** or **A4.3 mixed**

B Grassland and marsh – Dominated by grasses and/or by sedges, rushes & marsh *forbs*. May be **unimproved** (little affected by intensive farming practices); **improved** (see B4) or **semi-improved**

B1 Acid grassland – On acid soils (pH <5.5) in the uplands or lowlands; often unenclosed; relatively species-poor; often grades into D.1 or D.2. Can be **B1.1 unimproved** or **B1.2 semi-improved**

B2 Neutral grassland – On neutral soils (pH 5.5–7.0); usually lowland and enclosed or roadside verges etc.; may be moist and periodically waterlogged or inundated; often species-rich in grasses and forbs, e.g. *meadows*; can be **B2.1 unimproved** or **B2.2 semi-improved**

B3 Calcareous grassland – On calcareous soils (pH >7.0) over chalk orlimestone; sward short and usually species-rich when close-grazed, but taller (dominated by coarse grasses) and less species-rich when under-grazed; can be **B3.1 unimproved** or **B3.2 semi-improved**

Table C.1 (*continued*)

B4 Improved grassland – Markedly affected by practices such as drainage, grazing, fertilisers, herbicides; usually species-poor, often with >50% of sown species, e.g. rye-grass & clovers

B5 Marsh/marshy grassland – Not normally waterlogged in summer, so peat accumulation restricted and substratum mainly mineral soil or peat <0.5m deep; dominated by grasses, sedges, rushes or marsh forbs; often used as *pasture* (grazing marsh) or *meadow* (water/wet meadow)

C Tall Herb and Fern

C1 Bracken – bracken dominant; may be continuous **(C.1.1)** or in scattered patches **(C1.2)**

C2 Upland species-rich ledges – Mainly dominated by forbs and ferns

C3 Other tall herb and fern – Stands of tall forbs and ferns; ruderal **(C3.1)** or non-ruderal **(C3.2)**

D *Heathland* – Usually: dominated by dwarf shrubs (but see D3/D4); on acid soils (often *podsols*) or thin peats (<0.5m deep); upland heaths over siliceous rock and lowland heaths over sands or gravels

D1 Dry dwarf shrub heath – Mostly **acid heaths (D1.1)** on well-drained sands or gravels; with ≥25% cover of *ericoids* and dwarf gorses and a ground flora of mosses and lichens

D2 Wet dwarf shrub heath – On wetter, peatier substrates than D1, with more-hyrdophilous ericoids, grasses (e.g. *Molinia*), sedges and *Sphagna*; may intergrade with poor-fen valley mire

D3 Lichen/bryophyte heath – Largely montane, but with variants on sandy soils in some lowland areas, e.g. the Brecklands; dominated by bryophytes and lichens, with <30% *vascular plant* cover

D4 Montane heath/dwarf forb – Montane communities of sedges, rushes or dwarf forbs

D5 Dry heath/acid grassland mosaic – Mixture of D1 and B1; common in upland areas

D6 Wet heath/acid grassland mosaic – Similar to D5, but a mixture of D2 and B1

E Mires – Peatlands, normally with peat >0.5m deep, and the water table at or just below the surface

E1 Bog – *Ombrotrophic*, *oligotrophic* and acid; dominated by Sphagna, ericoids and cotton sedges

E1.6.1 Blanket bog – Under N & W cool, wet climates; covers the surface except on steep slopes; often has a hummock-hollow complex with heath vegetation on hummocks and *Sphagna*-rich pools

E1.6.2 Raised bog – In lowland floodplains and to moderate altitudes (where it may grade with blanket bog); typically has a central dome (vegetation like blanket bog) and a marginal *lagg* stream or fen

Table C.1 (*continued*)

E1.7 Wet modified bog – Mainly on degraded (e.g. drained or cut) blanket or raised bog; Sphagna replaced by *Molinia* (purple moor grass), *Tricophorum* (deer grass), or ericoids, with bare patches

E1.8 Dry modified bog – Areas subject to heavy draining, burning or grazing; Sphagna replaced by *Eriophorum vaginatum* (hare's tail cotton sedge) or ericoids (e.g. *Calluna*) with mosses & lichens.

E2 Flush and Spring – *Minerotrophic* and *soligenous*; on sloping ground where groundwater seeps to the surface; peat depth often <0.5m; usually rich in bryophytes, sedges and rushes

E2.1 Acid/neutral flush – Typically species-poor, with Sphagna, rushes and/or cotton sedges.

E2.2 Basic flush – Typically have a carpet of mosses with sedges.

E2.3 Bryophyte-dominated spring – At up-welling points; vegetation usually mainly mats of mosses

E3 Fen – *Minerotrophic*: range *from* **Rich-fen** that is fed by calcareous waters (pH ≥ 5) and has species-rich vegetation with sedges, rushes, forbs and bryophytes *to* **Poor-fen** that is fed by acid, oligotrophic waters (pH < 5) and has species-poor vegetation with a high proportion of Sphagna

E3.1 Valley mire – On the lower slopes and floor of small valleys (e.g. in heathlands); soligenous, so the vegetation can be rich-fen or poor-fen (depending on the catchment geology)

E3.2 Basin mire – In basins with little through-flow of water (*topogenous*) or hence nutrients; vegetation usually poor-fen with swamp or woodland, often on a floating raft over a lens of water

E3.3 Flood-plain mire – On mineral and/or peat substrate; usually inundated periodically, e.g. in winter; generally topogenous, with vegetation similar to E.3.2

F Swamp, marginal and inundation – Have standing water permanently or for most of the year

F1 Swamp – In shallow standing water; vegetation mainly tall, emergent *graminoids*, e.g. reeds

F2 Marginal & Inundation: **F2.1 Marginal** – Narrow (<5m) strips of emergent vegetation at margins of watercourses; may include swamp species, but also large "aquatic" forbs; **F2.2 Inundation** – Open, unstable communities, periodically submerged, e.g. on river gravels and lake margins

G Open water – Beyond the limit of swamp or other emergent vegetation

G1 Standing (still) **waters** – ponds (<2ha in area), lakes, meres, water-filled extraction pits etc.

G1.1 Eutrophic – nutrient-rich; pH > 7; water often turbid/green (due to algae); substrate often mud

G1.2 Mesotrophic – fairly nutrient-rich; pH *c.*7; water sometimes turbid due to phytoplankton

Table C.1 (*continued*)

G1.3 Oligotrophic – nutrient-poor pH 5.5–7; water clear (plankton sparse); substrate rock/sand/peat

G1.4 Dystrophic – very nutrient-poor, pH 3.5–5.5; water often peat-stained; plankton/plants sparse

G1.5 Marl – usually meso-eutrophic; pH > 7.4; water clear, calcium rich; calcareous deposits (tufa)

G1.6 Brackish – Mostly coastal, e.g. lagoons (see §12.2.3); water salty; often host unusual communities that include algae, vascular plants, and invertebrates that rarely occur elsewhere

G2 Running waters – streams, rivers; divided (as standing waters) into G2.1–G2.6

H Coastlands – includes littoral (H1, H2) and supralittoral (H3–H8) but not sublittoral habitats

H1 Intertidal (littoral) – habitats located between the extreme high-water spring-tide (EHWS) and extreme low-water spring-tide (ELWS) levels

H1.1 Sand and mud – host animals in the substratum (infauna) but generally lack surface dwelling organisms (epibiota) (see §12.2.3), but *Zostera* (seagrass) beds occur on some muddy sands.

H1.2 shingle/cobbles – in the littoral zone are an unstable, hostile environment

H1.3 boulders/rocks – Rocky shores (see §12.2.3), including brown and green algal beds

H2 Saltmarsh – develops where terrestrial vegetation can colonise sheltered mudflats

H2.3 Saltmarsh/dune interface – vegetation usually shrubby

H2.4 Scattered plants – usually lower marsh dominated by *Salicornia* (glasswort) spp.

H2.6 Dense/continuous – dense stands of *Spartina anglica* (cord grass), or more species-rich swards with *Puccinellia maritima* (sea poa) and forbs

H3 Shingle/gravel above high tide – Shingle banks sometimes support scrubby vegetation or a grass sward, but more exposed areas have open vegetation with scattered vascular plants and lichens

H4 Rock above high tide (EHWS) **mark** – Mainly lichen dominated platforms in the "splash zone"

H5 Strandline vegetation – at high tide level on sandy/shingly shores.

H6 Sand dunes – Various habitats; usually several dunes (aligned approximately parallel to the coastline and increasing in age along the sea-land axis) interspersed with depressions (dune slacks)

H6.4 Dune slacks – depressions between dunes; usually wet with swamp, marsh or carr vegetation

H6.5–H.6.7 Consolidated and flattened dunes: H6.5 Dune grassland – dominated by grasses such as *Festuca rubra* (includes **machairs** – see §12.2.4); **H6.6 Dune heath** – similar to inland dry heaths (D1) with *Calluna* usually dominant; **H6.7 Dune scrub** – dominated by inland and/or coastal scrubs

Table C.1 (*continued*)

H6.8 Open dune – Semi-consolidated: embryo dunes; mobile dunes dominated by *Ammophila arenaria* (marram grass); and grey dunes (more stabilised, often dominated by mosses and lichens)

H8 Maritime cliffs & slopes – vary in relation to their geology and local land forms

H8.1 Hard cliff (rock including chalk) and **H8.2 Soft cliff** (e.g. clay) – with <10% vascular plant cover

H8.3 Crevice & ledge vegetation – with ≥10% vegetation cover; on cliffs or in the "splash zone" (H4)

H8.4 Coastal grassland – often on cliff tops; contains maritime species, e.g. *Armeria maritima*

H8.5 Coastal heathland – like inland dry heath (D1) but with maritime species

I Rock exposure and waste – exposed inland surfaces with <10% vegetation cover

I1 Natural exposures – **I1.1 Inland cliff, I1.2 Scree/boulder scree, 11.3 Limestone pavement;**

I1.4 Other exposure (**I1.4.1 acid/neutral, I1.4.2 basic**); **I1.5 Caves.**

I2 Artificial exposures – **I2.1 Quarry** (gravel, sand and chalk pits and stone quarries);

I2.2 Spoil (abandoned industrial areas, coal spoil/slag), **I2.3 Mine**; **I2.4 Refuse tip**

J Miscellaneous

J1 Cultivated/disturbed land: J1.1 Arable – croplands, leys, horticultural land; **J1.2 Amenity** – short-mown grassland, e.g. lawn, park, fairway; **J1.3 Ephemeral** – short patchy vegetation on freely drained, usually thin, soils of derelict land; **J1.4 Introduced shrub** – dominated by non-native shrubs

J2 Boundaries: J2.1 Intact hedge (species-rich, species-poor); **J2.2 Defunct hedge** (with gaps); **J2.4 Fence; J2.5 Wall; J2.6 Dry ditch; J2.8 Earth bank**

J3 Built-up areas: J3.4 caravan site; J3.5 Sea wall (artificial material); **J3.6 Buildings**

J4 Bare ground – Any bare soil or other substrate not included elsewhere in the classification

J5 Other habitat – Any habitat not covered by the classification, and justifies mapping as a unit

C.3 UKBAP Broad habitats and Priority habitats

A major aim of the UKBAP (§11.3.2) is to identify **priority habitats** (in special need of conservation) within a framework of **broad habitat types** The resulting system is effectively a two-level habitat classification, except that priority habitats are only a selection of the types that may occur within broad habitats. A recent revision (BRIG 2007) has included some changes of habitat names and the addition of 17 new priority habitats (giving a total of 65). The revised broad and priority habitats, and their approximate correspondences with Phase 1 habitats, are listed in **Table C.2**. Guidance on the Broad Habitat

Table C.2 UKBAP Broad Habitats, Priority Habitats, and related Phase 1 habitats

Broad habitats	Priority habitats	Phase 1
Broadleaved, mixed and yew woodland[1] (>20% of total cover composed of broad-leaved trees, or these and yew)	Lowland beech and yew woodland, Lowland mixed deciduous woodland, Traditional orchards[2], Wood-*pasture* and parkland[3], Wet woodland, Upland mixed ash woods, Upland oak-wood, Upland birchwoods,	A1.1 A1.3 A2.1 A3.1 A4.1
Coniferous woodland[4]	Native pine woodlands	A1.2 A3 A4
Acid grassland	Lowland dry acid grassland	B1.1 B1.2; part of D5 & D6
Neutral grassland	Lowland *meadows*, Upland hay meadows	B2.1 B2.2
Calcareous grassland	Lowland calcareous grassland, Upland calcareous grassland	B3.1 B3.2
Improved grassland	Coastal and floodplain grazing marsh[5]	B4 B5
Bracken (>0.25ha continuous)		C.1.1
Dwarf shrub heath	Lowland heathland, Upland heathland	D1 D2; part of D5 & D6
Fen, marsh and swamp (*minerotrophic* wetlands)	Reedbeds, Lowland fens[3], Purple moor grass and rush pastures, Upland flushes, fens and swamps[2]	B5 E2 E3 F1
Bogs (*ombrotrophic* mires)	Blanket bog, Lowland raised bog	E1.6–E1.8
Standing open water and canals (including open water and fringe vegetation)	*Eutrophic* standing waters, *Mesotrophic* lakes, *Oligotrophic* and *dystrophic* lakes[2], Aquifer fed naturally fluctuating water bodies, Ponds[2]	F2 G1.1–G1.5
Rivers and streams	Rivers[2] (incorporates existing chalk rivers)	F2 G2.1–G2.5
Montane habitats	Mountain heaths and willow scrub[2]	A2 D3 D4
Inland rock (natural or man-made exposures with little vegetation)	Limestone pavements, *Calaminarian grasslands*[2], Inland Rock Outcrop and Scree Habitats[2], Open mosaic habitats on previously developed land[2]	I1 I2 J4

Table C.2 (continued)

Broad habitats	Priority habitats	Phase 1
Arable and horticulture	Arable field margins[3]	J1
Boundary & linear features	Hedgerows[3]	J2
Built-up areas and gardens		J3
Supralittoral rock	Maritime cliff and slopes	H4 H8
Supralittoral sediment	Coastal sand dunes, Machair, Coastal vegetated shingle	H3 H5 H6
Littoral rock (e.g. rocky shores)	Intertidal chalk[3], Intertidal boulder communities[2], *Sabellaria alveolata* reefs	H1.3
Littoral sediment (gravels, sands and muds)	Coastal saltmarsh, Intertidal mudflats, Seagrass beds[6] Sheltered muddy gravels, Peat and clay exposures[2]	H1.1 H1.2
Sublittoral rock[7] (mainly reefs and near-shore rock e.g. sub-tidal zones of rocky shores)	Subtidal chalk[3], Tidal-swept channels[3], Fragile sponge and anthozoan communities on subtidal rocky habitats[2], Estuarine rocky habitats[2], Seamount communities[2], Carbonate mounds[2], Cold-water coral reefs[3], Deep-sea sponge communities[2], *Sabellaria spinulosa* reefs	
Sublittoral sediment[7] (gravels, sands and muds)	Subtidal sands & gravels[3], Horse mussel beds[3], Mud habitats in deep water, Fine shell beds[2], **Maerl beds**, Serpulid reefs, Blue mussel beds[3], Saline lagoons (part of Phase 1 G1.6)	

Notes

[1] Includes recently felled stands, *carr*, and scrub >0.25 ha with continuous canopy.
[2] New habitat.
[3] Revised name and/or scope.
[4] >80% of the total cover composed of conifers (except yew).
[5] May be semi-improved.
[6] Several marine priority habitats occur in more than one broad habitat, e.g. seagrass beds are also sublittoral.
[7] Previously subdivided into "inshore sublittoral" and "offshore shelf" zones.

Classification is provided by Jackson (2000), and relationships of woodland broad and priority habitat types with other woodland classifications are discussed in Hall and Kirby (1998).

C.4 The Marine Habitat Classification of Britain and Ireland (MHCBI)

The JNCC *Marine Habitat Classification for Britain and Ireland, Version 04.05* (JNCCv04.05 or MHCBIv0405) has been developed from, and replaces, the *Marine Nature Conservation Review* (MNCR97.06) BioMar benthic marine *biotopes* classification (Connor *et al.* 1997a, 1997b, Picton and Costello 1997). The re-structured classification (Connor *et al.* 2004) has resulted from improved understanding of inter-relationships between habitat types and the need to increase compatability with the EUNIS classification (§C.6) within which it is now incorporated.

The full classification consists of a six-level hierarchy. However, the top level is a single category – **Environment *(marine)*** – defined, as in EUNIS, to distinguish the marine environment from terrestrial and freshwater habitats; and in practice, the hierarchy is commonly reduced to five levels as follows.

Level 1. Broad habitats – five broad types based on littoral/sublittoral zones and substratum types: Littoral rock (LR); Littoral sediment (LS): Infralittoral rock (IR); Circalittoral rock (CR); and Sublittoral sediment (SS) (see Figure 12.1).

Level 2. Habitat complexes (Main habitats) – 24 divisions of the broad habitat types, defined: by exposure of rock to wave action (high energy, moderate energy, low energy); by sediment type (coarse sediment, sands, muds, mixed); or as biogenic reefs (on rock or sediment). These reflect major differences in ecological character; are equivalent to the intertidal Sites of Special Scientific Interest (SSSI) selection units (for designation of shores in the UK); and can be used as national mapping units.

Level 3. Biotope complexes – 75 groups of biotopes with similar physical and biological character that can be recognised by the dominant *life forms* or above-species-level taxa. Where biotopes consistently occur together and are relatively restricted in their extent (e.g. on rocky shores and very near-shore subtidal rocky habitats) these complexes are more suitable than individual biotopes for mapping, management and assessing sensitivity. They are also relatively easy to identify, either by non-specialists or by coarser methods of survey (such as video or rapid shore surveys), and are therefore readily applicable in Phase 1 ecological surveys (§12.4.5).

Level 4. Biotopes – 265 units, typically characterised by *dominant species* or assemblages of conspicuous species. On rocky substrata, most should be readily recognised by workers with a basic knowledge of marine species, although quantitative sampling will be necessary in many of the sediment types, and both intertidal and subtidal sediment biotopes may cover very extensive areas. The vast majority of available biological sample data are attributable to this (or the sub-biotope) level, which is equivalent to the communities defined in terrestrial classifications such as the *National Vegetation Classification* (§C.8).

Level 5. Sub-biotopes – 105 units, typically characterised by "less obvious differences in species composition, minor geographical and temporal variations, more subtle variations in the habitat or disturbed and polluted variations of a natural biotope" (Connor *et al.* 1997a). They often require greater expertise or survey effort to identify.

The full MHCBI hierarchy, together with further information, is available online (see Connor *et al.* 2004), correspondence with other classifications are given in the NBNHC, as are correspondences with the OSPAR (see Table 12.2) list of threatened or declining habitats (OSPAR Commission 2003).

C.5 The Annex I, CORINE and Palaearctic habitat classifications

The *Habitats Directive* Annex I habitats are not strictly a classification because they are only a small sub-set (selected on the basis of their conservation value) of the European habitat types defined in the *CORINE Habitat Classification*. This is similar to the Phase 1 Classification in that it is hierarchical and uses similar criteria; but it is more complex, with some broad habitats progressively sub-divided into five subsidiary levels.

The Annex I habitats in the original Directive 92/43/EEC were selected from draft versions of the CORINE Habitat Classification (EC 1991). Problems arose because the final CORINE classification contained numerous revisions which caused ambiguities in the interpretation of Annex I. Moreover: (a) it was subsequently revised and extended to include the whole of the Palaearctic region; and (b) while CORINE broad habitats are still widely used (e.g. for the CORINE Land Cover and Biotopes databases and maps (see Table 14.1), the detailed classification was largely superseded by the *Palaearctic Habitat Classification* (Devilliers and Devilliers-Terschuren 1996). This has been developed by the Royal Belgian Institute of Natural Sciences, and most of its designated habitats are now incorporated in the EUNIS Habitat Classification (§C.6).

To rectify the problems in the 1992 Annex I, the *Interpretation manual of European Union habitats* was developed. Its final version, EUR15 (EC 1996), included three codes: the original Annex I code; the Palaearctic Classification code, and a four-digit Natura 2000 code. This was adopted by EU Directive 97/62/EC (EC 1997), although a few EUR15 codes and/or habitat names were amended for the new Annex I, in which the habitats were given Natura 2000 codes.

The full list of Annex I habitats and priority habitats, is available online (see EC 1997), and a list of those that occur in the UK (together with descriptions and location maps of associated SACs) is available at www.jncc.gov.uk/page-1523. Information on Annex 1 wetland and freshwater habitats is also given in EA (2007). Correspondences with other classifications can be found in the

NBNHC, and at the EUNIS website (see below). However, because of the broad nature of some Annex 1 habitat types, and because they were selected on the basis of their pan-European importance, correspondences with habitats and communities defined in UK classifications are sometimes imprecise.

C.6 The EUNIS Habitat Classification

The European Nature Information System (EUNIS) habitat classification (current version: 200611) has been developed by the European Environment Agency (EEA). It aims: to provide a comprehensive pan-European classification covering all terrestrial, freshwater and marine habitats (both natural and artificial); and hence to address the problem of non-compatibility between different European classifications. It incorporates the MHCBI and Palaearctic classifications, and seems likely to be increasing used throughout Europe.

The classification is a hierarchical system comprising three levels (4 for marine habitats) below which it draws on units from other classifications. The website (http://eunis.eea.europa.eu/habitats.jsp) provides a number of facilities including:

- access to the full hierarchies of the EUNIS and Annex 1 classifications, including habitat descriptions and relationships with other classifications;
- an interactive key for identifying EUNIS habitat types that match surveyed habitats; and
- search engines for using names or descriptions to find EUNIS and Annex 1 habitat types, *or* for relating these types to coded habitat types of other classifications.

C.7 The Integrated Habitat System (IHS)

The IHS has been developed by Somerset Environmental Records Centre (SERC) with the aim of providing an integrated approach to the collection, management and analysis of UK habitat data. It has the advantage of being largely derived from (and hence compatible with) other classifications, principally Phase 1, UKBAP and Annex 1 – thus facilitating translation between them.

The classification is hierarchical with up to four levels. It is outlined in the *NBN Habitats Dictionary* which includes relationships of IHS categories with other classifications.

An IHS package is available on CD-ROM (www.somerc.com/cdrom.php) which requires a licence fee and annual update fee. It includes: the integrated classification; a translation tool; field survey and air photo interpretation manuals; and GIS guidance.

C.8 The National Vegetation Classification (NVC)

The NVC focuses on semi-natural vegetation, most of which has high conservation status; and is used as the main classification for terrestrial habitats in the selection of Biological SSSIs (JNCC 1998). It is published as a five-volume series entitled *British Plant Communities* (Rodwell 1991–2000). Related publications . include an illustrated guide to British upland vegetation (Averis *et al.* 2004); and field guides or summary descriptions for grassland and montane communities (Cooper 1998), mires and heaths (Elkington *et al.* 2002), and woodlands (Hall *et al.* 2004).

The major NVC categories are characterised (as in habitat classifications) by vegetation physiognomy and environmental criteria (**Table C.3**). Each category contains a number of coded communities, most of which are further subdivided into two or more sub-communities. Definition of communities and sub-communities is phytosociological, i.e. they are characterised by plant species composition. Each community, and its sub-communities, is described in a chapter of the relevant volume, which includes information on associated aspects such as climate, soils, succession, and distribution. A full list of NVC communities, with descriptions is provided in the NBNHD (§C.1) and correspondence with other classifications are given in the NBNHC.

Field surveys aimed at collecting data for comparison with NVC communities should be conducted using the recommended NVC method, perhaps with minor modifications, as follows:

Table C.3 Outline of the National Vegetation Classification (NVC)

Volume number and title	Major categories (volume sections)	Community codes
1 Woodlands and scrub	Woodlands and scrub	W1–W25
2 Mires and Heaths	Mires (including wet heaths) Heaths (dry)	M1–M38 H1–H22
3 Grasslands and montane communities	Mesotrophic grasslands Calcicolous grasslands Calcifugous grasslands and montane communities	MG1–MG13 CG1–CG14 U1–U21
4 Aquatic communities, swamps, and tall-herb fens	Aquatic communities Swamps and tall-herb fens	A1–A24 S1–S28
5 Maritime communities and vegetation of open habitats	Salt-marsh communities Shingle, strandline and sand-dune communities Maritime cliff communities Vegetation of open habitats	SM1–SM28 SD1–SD19 MC1–MC12 OV1–OV42

Source: Rodwell (1991–2000).

1. Use selective sampling (§11.6.1) within apparently homogeneous stands of vegetation with the aim of ensuring that the results (often called relevés) are representative of a specific community type;

2. Within each stand record the floristic data in **quadrats** of suitable size (aimed at including most of the community's species within each) in relation to the vegetation type. NVC recommended sizes range from 2m × 2m for short herbaceous vegetation to 50m × 50m for woodland. However, for the calculation of Braun-Blanquet constancy classes (which provide the simplest method of matching survey data with NVC community types – see below) it is important to collect ≥10 quadrat samples. Consequently, when sampling within fairly small stands it may be preferable to use smaller quadrats (e.g. 10m × 10m for woodland), from which an average cover-abundance value (for the relevé) can be calculated for each species.

3. Within each quadrat, visually estimate the Domin cover-abundance values (Table 11.5 and **Table C.4**) of all vascular plants, and as many bryophytes and macrolichens as possible. If previously recorded data are in the form of percentage cover values, these can be converted to Domin values (allotting an arbitrary Domni value (e.g. 2) to percentage cover values of <4 per cent), and even percentage frequency values (Table 11.5) can be used to calculate Braun-Blanquet constancy classes.

Data analysis can be achieved by reference to the floristic/diagnostic tables, provided in Rodwell (1991–2000), which characterise the communities and sub-communities in terms of:

- species composition, with an expected Domin-value range for each species;
- a constancy profile, which lists the constancy (frequency) with which each species is expected to occur, expressed as Braun-Blanquet constancy classes

Table C.4 Domin cover-abundance values and Braun-Blanquet constancies

Domin scale of cover-abundance			*Braun-Blanquet constancy classes for grouped quadrats or relevés*	
% cover	Category when cover is <4%	Domin value	% of quadrats or relevés in which a species is present	Species' constancy class
<4%	few individuals	1	1–20%	I
<4%	several individuals	2	21–40%	II
<4%	many individuals	3	41–60%	III
4–10%		4	61–80%	IV
11–25%		5	81–100%	V
26–33%		6		
34–50%		7		
51–75%		8		
76–90%		9		
91–100%		10		

(**Table C.4**). These are a good comparative measure, but require calculation of the proportion (percentage) of the overall sample quadrats/plots in which each species occurred. Species with high constancies (IV and V) contribute most to the diagnosis.

Analysis is greatly facilitated by the use of a computer program such as TABL-EFIT/TABLCORN (Hill 1996), MATCH (Malloch 2000) or MAVIS (Smart 2000). These calculate the goodness-of-fit between survey data and NVC expected Domin range values and Braun-Blanquet constancy values for NVC community types. The goodness-of-fit results are expressed on a scale of 0–100, from which approximate similarity ratings can be assigned as follows: 0–49 = very poor; 50–59 = poor; 60–69 = fair; 70–79 = good; and 80–100 = very good. TABLEFIT/TABLCORN also identifies habitat types according to the CORINE system, but has the limitation of being a FORTRAN/DOS program. MAVIS can also analyse vegetation data in relation to the CVS (§C.10).

While good matches with NVC communities are generally indicative of high conservation status value, potential sampling errors and community variability (§C.1) dictate that the findings should be interpreted with care. For example:

- Apparently good floristic matches can be erroneous. This may be evinced by lack of correspondence with the habitat requirements and distributions of the relevant NVC communities; so it is essential to check the information given in the appropriate chapters of *British plant communities*.
- Genuine similarities >80 are uncommon, and all values ≥60 are generally acceptable. Similarities <60 should rarely be considered significant, but they may result from sampling error or the community being an unusual variant (the NVC does not claim to be a totally comprehensive and precise classification of all British plant communities).
- Survey data may show (usually poor or fair) similarity to more than one NVC type, probably because of community variability within the sampled area (see §C.1).
- While similarity to an NVC type is a good measure of naturalness, a poor match should not necessarily be taken to mean that a community has low ecological or conservation value. In addition, the NVC is not really appropriate for evaluating more disturbed vegetation in the wider countryside (see §C.10) or vegetation that may be of value for "non-ecological" reasons, especially in urban environments.

C.9 UK Freshwater vegetation classifications

Reference to the Phase 1, UKBAP and Annex I classifications should be adequate for Phase 1 surveys, and the NVC can be used for Phase 2 surveys of freshwater plant communities. However, there are UK classifications, designed specifically for freshwater habitats that are generally more appropriate for Phase

2 surveys of these systems, partly because they can facilitate relatively rapid evaluation of whole sites (which may contain a number of different NVC communities). They are partly based on water quality (especially nutrient status, **alkalinity** and **pH**), which vary naturally in UK systems, largely in relation to the local climate and (especially) geology. In areas of siliceous (and often hard) geological materials, especially in the uplands of the north and west, the waters are generally **oligotrophic** or even **dystrophic**. In areas of base-rich (and usually soft) materials (mainly in the lowlands) the waters are more **eutrophic**; and in areas of chalk or limestone, they can be highly calcareous.

The three main UK freshwater classifications are:

1. The *Botanical classification of standing waters* (Palmer 1992, Palmer *et al.* 1992) identifies ten main site types, with associated environmental factors such as alkalinity, pH and nutrient status. Surveys using this method should analyse open water and marginal species separately.
2. The *Vegetation communities of British lakes: a revised classification* (Duigan *et al.* 2006) defines eleven British lake types in terms of their distribution, nutrient status, pH, and vegetation. The NBNHD (§C.1) provides descriptions of these types, and indicates their relationships with other classifications including the NVC, UKBAP and Annex I.
3. The *Vegetation of British Rivers* classification (Holmes *et al.* 1999) includes a comprehensive, three-level system for UK rivers. It can be viewed in the NBNHD. Surveys using this system should include bryophytes.

C.10 The Countryside Vegetation System (CVS)

The CVS (Bunce *et al.* 1999) is based on the data collected for the *Countryside Survey 1990* (CS90), and has been used in the analysis of data collected for CS2000 (www.cs2000.org.uk and CS2007 (see §11.3.2 and Table 11.3). The purpose of the surveys is to provide periodic nationwide censuses of British vegetation in the "wider countryside" as a basis for monitoring vegetation change.

The *Countryside Surveys*, and CVS, employ a random sampling system of: 1km squares located within designated land types (based on UKBAP Broad Habitats); and plots (some permanently marked) located within each 1km square. Consequently, the CVS differs from the NVC in two respects: (a) the sampling plots are placed at random whereas NVC relevés are selectively placed in homogeneous vegetation; and (b) while the NVC is primarily concerned with semi-natural vegetation, the CVS focuses on the more disturbed wider countryside and on monitoring vegetation change. Consequently, correspondence between CVS and NVC types is generally poor.

The CVS consists of 100 vegetation classes (including linear features such as hedgerows and roadside verges) and eight large aggregate classes, both of which were created by **multivariate analysis** of the survey data. The system also incorporates floristic data on species' responses to environmental conditions, principally: (a) average scores (for each CVS class) of Ellenberg's indicators of

Table C.5 CVS aggregate vegetation classes and species-environment criteria

Aggregate vegetation classes			
I	Crops/weeds	V	Lowland wooded
II	Tall grassland/herb	VI	Upland wooded
III	Fertile grassland	VII	Moorland grass/mosaic
IV	Infertile grassland	VIII	Heath/bog

Scales used for Ellenberg scores (Ellenberg 1974, Ellenberg *et al.* 1991, Hill *et al.* 2000)

Light	1 (shaded) – 9 (open)
Moisture	1 (dry) – 12 (wet)
pH	1 (acid) – 9 (basic)
Fertility	1 (infertile) – 9 (fertile)
Continentality	1 (least continental) – 9 (most continental)

Grime's C-S-R species survival strategies (Grime *et al.* 1988)

Competitors (C)	In high productivity (and biomass), low disturbance habitats
Stress-tolerators (S)	In low productivity habitats with high light, moisture or nutrient stress
Ruderals (R)	Exploiting severely disturbed, productive habitats

tolerance to environmental factors; and (b) the percentage of plots characterised in terms of Grime's classification into functional types by means of a triangular ordination model (C–S–R) of competitor, stress-tolerator and ruderal strategies (**Table C.5**).

The CVS Plot Allocation Program (www.ceh.ac.uk/products/software/CEHSoftware_CVS.htm) allows a user to match survey plot data with the 100 CVS vegetation classes, as does MAVIS (Smart 2000). MAVIS can also analyse survey data in terms of NVC communities, Ellenberg scores, Grime's C–V–R strategies, and Preston and Hill's (1997) biogeographic classification of the British flora.

To a large extent, the CVS (especially the aggregate classes) is effectively a land classification (see below), and its main application is likely to be at the strategic level. However, it may be useful in local EcIA surveys, e.g. to check if hedgerow data conform to CVS "diverse lowland hedges" or if grassland or roadside data match CVS *eutrophic* or *mesotophic* types.

C.11 Land classifications

For the purpose of land classification, the concept of "land" usually includes inland and coastal waters. Land classifications are generally intended mainly for application on a regional scale, and they frequently involve data capture by remote sensing, usually with verification by ground-level observations. Associated maps often provide digitised data for mapping and GIS applications that can be useful for EcIAs of large-scale or linear projects. However, limitations for EcIAs of smaller developments are that mapping resolutions are generally low, and only broad habitat types may be represented. The three main attributes employed are land quality (or capability), land cover, or land use.

Land quality (or capability) classifications are mainly concerned with the suitability of land for agriculture or forestry (see §9.3.6). **Land cover classifications** focus on physical cover including water, ice, bare ground (rock etc.), vegetation (natural or planted) and human constructions (built-up areas etc.). They are primarily of value in landscape and ecological assessments. Land use is partially incorporated in land cover, but **land use classifications** focus on the purposes for which land areas are being used, i.e. their socio-economic functions. Consequently, they include more human-activity categories, e.g. agriculture, forestry, amenity and recreation, residential, commerce and industry, traffic and infrastructure – and hence provide a basis for both environmental and socio-economic impact analysis.

Some land cover and land use classifications are outlined in **Table C.6**.

Table C.6 Some UK, EU and UN land cover and land use classifications

UK	**The Land Cover Map of Great Britain (LCM2000)** classification (see Tables 11.3 and 14.1). Its relationship to UKBAP broad habitats is described in Fuller *et al.* 2002 LCM2007 will be available in 2009.
	The NLUD Land Use and Land Cover Classification (ODPM 2006) consists of parallel land use and land cover classifications, within each of which it has a two level hierarchy consisting of a series of main categories (Orders) and subdivisions (Groups). It includes tables of relationships with LCM2000, UKBAP Broad Habitats and LUCAS (see below).
EU	**The CORINE Land Cover Database** (see §C.5 and Table 14.1).
	The Eurostat Land Use/Land Cover Area Frame Statistical Survey (LUCAS) Classification (Eurostat 2003). The land use component has a two-tier hierarchy with 14 classes at the second level, and the land cover component has a three-tier hierarchy with 57 classes at the third level. Cross-reference tables for land use and land cover are included.
UN	**The FAO Land Cover Classification System (LCCS)** (Di Gregorio 2005) is a flexible system for worldwide use. It consists of two phases: a dichotomous phase in which eight major land cover classes are distinguished; and a modular-hierarchical phase in which each major class is sub-divided using a pre-defined set of attributes (classifiers) that are specific to that class.

References

Averis A, B Averis, J Birks, D Horsfield, D Thompson and M Yeo 2004. *An illustrated guide to British upland vegetation*. Peterborough, Cambs: JNCC.

BRIG (Biodiversity Reporting & Information Group) 2007. *Report on the species and habitat review; Report to the UK Biodiversity Partnership*, www.ukbap.org.uk/bapgrouppage. aspx?id=112.

Bunce RGH, CJ Barr, MK Gillespie, DC Howard, WA Scott, SM Smart, HM van de Poll and JW Watkins 1999. *ECOFACT 1: Vegetation of the British countryside – the Countryside Vegetation System*, www.ceh.ac.uk/products/publications/ECOFACT1-VegetationoftheBritishCountryside.html.

Connor DW, JH Allen, N Golding, KL Howell, LM Leiberknecht, KO Northen and JB Reker 2004. *The Marine Habitat Classification for Britain and Ireland, Version 04.05*. Peterborough, Cambs: JNCC, www.jncc.gov.uk/Default.aspx?page=1584.

Connor DW, DP Brazier, TO Hill and KO Northern 1997a. *MNCR marine biotope classification for Britain and Ireland*. Vol.1. *Littoral biotopes*, Version 97.06. JNCC Research Report No. 229. Peterborough, Cambs: JNCC.

Connor DW, MJ Dalkin, TO Hill, RHF Holt and WG Sanderson 1997b. *MNCR marine biotope classification for Britain and Ireland*, Vol.2: *Sublittoral biotopes*, Version 97.06. JNCC Research Report No. 230. Peterborough, Cambs: JNCC.

Cooper EA 1998. *Summary descriptions of National Vegetation Classification grassland and montane communities (UK nature conservation, No. 14)*. Peterborough, Cambs: JNCC.

Devilliers P and J Devilliers-Terschuren 1996. *A classification of Palaearctic habitats*. (Nature and Environment No. 78). Strasbourg: Council of Europe.

Di Gregorio A 2005. *Land Cover Classification System: Classification concepts and user manual; Software version 2* (rev. by A Di Gregorio, based on the original version by A Di Gregorio and LJM Jansen 1996). Rome: Food and Agriculture Organization of the United Nations (FAO), www.fao.org/docrep/008/y7220e/y7220e00.htm.

Duigan C, W Kovach, and M Palmer 2006. *Vegetation communities of British lakes: a revised classification*. Peterborough, Cambs: JNCC.

EA (Environment Agency) 2007. *Water for wildlife. Water resources and conservation: assessing the eco-hydrological requirements of habitats and species*. Bristol: Environment Agency, http://publications.environment-agency.gov.uk/pdf/GEHO0407BMNB-e-e.pdf?lang=_e.

EC (European Commission) 1991. *CORINE biotopes manual*. Vol. 3: *Habitats of the European Community*. Luxembourg: Office for Official Publications of the European Communities.

EC 1996. *Interpretation manual of European Union habitats, Version EUR 15*. Brussels: European Commission, DG XI.

EC 1997. Council Directive 97/62/EC adapting to technical and scientific progress Directive 92/43/EEC on the conservation of natural habitats and of wild fauna and flora. Brussels: *Official Journal of the European Commission* L305/42-65. http://ec.europa.eu/environment/nature/legislation/habitatsdirective/index_en.htm.

Elkington T, N Dayton, DL Jackson and IM Strachan 2002. *National Vegetation Classification field guide to mires and heaths*. Peterborough, Cambs: JNCC (pdf at www.jncc.gov.uk/page-2628).

Ellenberg H 1974. Zeigerwerte der Gefasspflanzen Mitteleuropas. *Scripta Geobotanica*, **9**, 1–97.

Ellenberg H, HE Weber, R Dull, V Wirth, W Werner and D Paulissen 1991. Zeigerwerte von Pflanzen in Mitteleuropa. *Scripta Geobotanica* **18**, 1–248.

Eurostat (Statistical Office of the European Communities) 2003. *The LUCAS Survey: European statisticians monitor territory*. Luxembourg: Office for Official Publications of the European Communities, http://epp.eurostat.cec.eu. int/cache/ITY_OFFPUB/KS-AZ-03-001/EN/KS-AZ-03-001-EN.PDF.

Fuller RM, GM Smith, JR Sanderson, RA Hill, AG Thomson, R Cox, NJ Brown, RT Clarke, P Rothery and FF Gerard 2002. *Countryside Survey 2000 Module 7: LAND COVER MAP 2000*, Final Report. Huntingdon, Cambs: CEH Monks Wood, www.cs2000.org.uk/Final_reports/M07_final_report.htm.

Gibson CWD 1998. *Harmonisation of habitat classifications*. JNCC Reports No. 279. Peterborough, Cambs: JNCC.

Grime JP, JG Hodson and R Hunt 1988. Comparative plant ecology: a functional approach to common British species. London: Unwin Hyman.

Hall JE and KJ Kirby 1998. *The relationship between Biodiversity Action Plan Priority and Broad habitat types, and other woodland classifications*. (JNCC Report No. 288). Peterborough, Cambs: JNCC, www.jncc.gov.uk/page-2191#download.

Hall JE, KJ Kirby and AM Whitbread 2004. *National Vegetation Classification: field guide to woodland*. Rev. edn. Peterborough, Cambs: JNCC (pdf at www.jncc.gov.uk/page-2656).

Hill MO 1996. *TABLEFIT/TABLECORN*. Huntingdon, Cambs: CEH Monks Wood, www.ceh.ac.uk/products/software/CEHSoftware-TABLEFITTABLCORN.htm.

Hill MO, DB Roy, JO Mountford and RGH Bunce 2000. Extending Ellenberg's indicator values to a new area: an algorithmic approach. *Journal of Applied Ecology* **37**, 3–15.

Holmes NTH, PJ Boon and TA Rowell 1999. *Vegetation communities of British rivers – a revised classification*. Peterborough, Cambs: JNCC.

Jackson DL 2000. *Guidance on the interpretation of the Biodiversity Broad Habitat Classification (terrestrial and freshwater types): Definitions and the relationship with other classifications*, Report 307. Peterborough, Cambs: JNCC, www.jncc.gov.uk/page-2433.

JNCC (Joint Nature Conservation Committee) 1998. *Guidelines for the selection of biological SSSIs* – rev. edn of NCC (1989). Peterborough, Cambs: JNCC, www.jncc.gov.uk/page-2303.

Malloch AJC 2000. *MATCH II: A computer program to aid the assignment of vegetation data to the communities and subcommunities of the National Vegetation Classification*. Version 2.15 for Windows NT/95/98. Unit of Vegetation Science, University of Lancaster.

ODPM 2006. *National Land Use Database (NLUD): Land Use and Land Cover Classification* Version 4.4. London: Office of the Deputy Prime Minister, www.communities.gov.uk/publications/planningandbuilding/nationallanduse.

OSPAR Commission 2003. *Initial OSPAR List of Threatened and/or Declining Species and Habitats*, http://jncc.gov.uk/PDF/p00188_InitialListofspeciesandhabitats.pdf.

Palmer M 1992. *A botanical classification of standing waters in Great Britain and a method for the use of macrophyte flora in assessing changes in water quality* (2nd edn), Research & survey in nature conservation, No. 19. Peterborough, Cambs: JNCC.

Palmer MA, SL Bell and I Butterfield 1992. A botanical classification of standing waters in Britain: applications for conservation and monitoring. *Aquatic Conservation: Marine and Freshwater ecosystems* **2**, 125–143.

Picton BE and MJ Costello (eds) 1997. *BioMar biotope viewer: a guide to marine habitats, fauna and flora of Britain and Ireland* (CD-ROM). Dublin: Environmental Sciences Unit, Trinity College.

Preston CD and MO Hill 1997. The geographical relationships of British and Irish vascular plants. *Botanical Journal of the Linnean Society* 124: 1–120.

Rodwell JS (ed.) 1991, 1998*. *British plant communities*, Vol. 1: *Woodlands and scrub*. Cambridge: Cambridge University Press (*current paperback edn).

Rodwell JS (ed.) 1991, 1998*. *British plant communities*, Vol. 2: *Mires and heaths*. Cambridge: Cambridge University Press (*current paperback edn).

Rodwell JS (ed.) 1993, 1998*. *British plant communities*, Vol. 3: *Grasslands and montane communities*. Cambridge: Cambridge University Press (*current paperback edn).

Rodwell JS (ed.) 1995. *British plant communities*, Vol. 4: *Aquatic communities, swamps and tall-herb fens*. Cambridge: Cambridge University Press.

Rodwell JS (ed.) 2000. *British plant communities*, Vol. 5: *Maritime communities and vegetation of open habitats*. Cambridge: Cambridge University Press.

Smart S 2000. *MAVIS (Modular Analysis of Vegetation Information System)*. CEH Lancaster, www.ceh.ac.uk/products/software/CEHSoftware-MAVIS.htm.

Appendix D
Evaluating species, communities, habitats and sites

Peter Morris

D.1 Introduction

Two important concepts in ecological evaluation are conservation value and conservation status.

The **conservation value** of a species, community, or habitat is usually taken to mean the need to protect it, principally in because of its importance as a VEC (see §11.4.1) or unfavourable conservation status (see below). In EcIA, this translates to the imperative to avoid negative impacts on these "high-value/important/**notable**" species and habitats by a proposed development.

The **conservation status** of species and habitats usually refers to the definitions given in the *Habitats Directive*. These definitions, slightly modified, are:

- The *conservation status of a species* is the sum of the influences acting on it that may affect the long-term distribution and abundance of its populations within the EU;
- The *conservation status of a natural habitat* is the sum of the influences acting on the habitat, and its typical species that may affect its long-term natural distribution, structure and functions as well as the long-term survival of its typical species within the EU.

In this context, the Directive also defines when the conservation status of species and habitats can be considered as "*favourable*". The definitions of this, slightly modified, are as follows.

The conservation of a species is favourable when:

- Its population dynamics data indicate that it is maintaining itself on a long-term basis as a viable component of its natural habitats;
- Its natural range is not declining and is not likely to decline in the foreseeable future; and
- There is, and will probably continue to be, sufficient habitat to maintain its populations on a long-term basis.

The conservation of a habitat is favourable when:

- its natural range and areas it covers within that range are stable or increasing;
- the specific structure and functions which are necessary for its long-term maintenance exist and are likely to continue to exist for the foreseeable future; and
- the conservation status of its typical species is favourable.

The *Water Framework Directive* (FWD) takes a similar approach in that the current freshwater ecosystem status is assessed in relation to pristine (reference) conditions.

As suggested by IEEM (2006), conservation status can be a valuable criterion (a) when assessing likely ecological changes in the absence of a proposal, and (b) when assessing the potential significance of impacts generated by a proposal. However, current conservation status may have different implications. For instance:

- Unfavourable status of a species normally means that it is threatened or rare (at least locally), and therefore needs protection.
- Favourable status of a habitat suggests that, in the absence of new impacts, its conservation value is likely to remain high – as will the need to protect it.
- Unfavourable status of a habitat may be taken to mean that it can be "written off", *or* that measures are needed to improve it. The latter applies particularly to designated and priority types.

This appendix outlines ecological evaluation methods and criteria under the following headings.

D.2 Evaluation of taxa
D.3 Evaluation of communities, habitats, ecosystems and sites
D.4 Evaluation in terms of socio-economic resources

D.2 Evaluation of taxa

Taxa usually means species, although a few cases such as the Bern Convention, protection is afforded to higher taxonomic units. The three main categories under which high conservation value (important/**notable**) species are designated in the UK are:

1. legally protected species designated in the annexes and schedules of international conventions, European Directives and UK legislation (see Tables 11.1 and 11.2);
2. Red List (and Red Book) species that have low conservation status because they are internationally or nationally threatened, rare or scarce (§D.2.1);
3. UKBAP priority species (§D.2.2).

The categories overlap, e.g. many Red List and UKBAP priority species are also legally protected; and species may also be designated as regionally or locally notable.

Designated species lists are updated periodically, and JNCC maintains a collated database (currently >6,000 species), is available at www.jncc.gov.uk/page-3408. Information on designations associated with international lists is also available at www.jncc.gov.uk/page-3424.

D.2.1 Red Lists and Red Data Books

The IUCN (International Union for Nature Conservation *or* World Conservation Union) is an internationally accredited organisation that periodically produces **IUCN Red Lists** of globally threatened species based on a set of categories and associated criteria that were revised in 2001 (version 3.1). There are three categories of threatened species: Critically endangered (CR); Endangered (EN); and Vulnerable (VU). The criteria used to assign species to one of these categories are outlined below.

A. Decline in population size, e.g. over the last ten years.
B. Restricted geographical range in terms of extent of occurrence and/or area of occupancy, especially if continuing to decline.
C. Small population size, especially if continuing to decline.
D. Population very small or geographically restricted.
E. Probability of extinction in the wild within 100 years or less.

The other IUCN categories are: Extinct (EX); Extinct in the wild (EW); Near threatened (NT); Least concern (LC); Data deficient (DD); and Not evaluated (NE). Details of all the categories and criteria are available at www.iucnredlist.org/static/categories_criteria_3_1, and the 2007 IUCN Red List can be found at www.iucnredlist.org/.

The IUCN categories, criteria and Red List data are widely used by national (including UK) governments and organisations in assessing species' conservation status, compiling Red Lists and conferring protection designations. Some additional (non-IUCN) categories and criteria are used for UK national Red Listed and rare species (see www.jncc.gov.uk/page-3425). They include: nationally rare *or* scarce species – present in ≤15 *or* 16–100 hectads in the UK; and nationally rare *or* scarce marine species – present in ≤8 *or* 9–55 hectads within Britain's three-mile territorial limit. Account may also be taken of criteria such as species' local importance and the status of UK populations in relation to global and regional contexts, e.g. if the UK population ≥1 per cent of the global or European population.

Rarity is usually evaluated in relation to geographical range (e.g. local, regional, national, international) and in general its conservation value increases accordingly. However, the perception of rarity varies in both space and time (see Gaston 1994, 2003, Kunin and Gaston 1997). For instance, a species may (a) have a wide geographical range, but exist only as small localised populations, or

(b) have large populations but a small geographical range. Similarly, rarity within local areas varies in relation to different types of species distribution, e.g. restricted to, but abundant in, a few habitats, or widespread but infrequent; and for this reason, simple presence records in hectads, or even tetrads, may be of limited value for assessing impacts on local populations. Finally, rarity varies in time, e.g. by temporary population fluctuations or longer-term trends; and much attention is now paid to rates of decline, e.g. during the past 25 years. However, a further complication is that populations of a species may be declining in one area, but increasing in another.

In general, there is normally little point in highlighting the local rarity of a species that is common elsewhere unless there is some other reason to justify its importance locally (see LBAP criteria in §D2.2). One reason for local or national rarity is that the area is near the normal limit of the species' range; and differences between national and international contexts can explain discrepancies between the rarity of some species and habitats in the UK and their status in the Habitats Directive. This is because Annex I habitats and Annex II species are selected in the European context, and consequently (a) include some examples that are locally common in the UK, but rare in the EU as a whole, and (b) exclude others that are rare in the UK but not threatened in the European context (e.g. see Palmer 1995).

Red Data Books (RDBs), which are now published in many countries, usually deal with specific groups of plants or animals, e.g. vascular plants, mosses, reptiles, or insect groups. RDBs of Britain are published by JNCC (see www.jncc.gov.uk/page-2133) who, as part of the *Species Status Assessment Project*, now produce downloadable versions, including *The Vascular Plant Red Data List for Great Britain* (2005) (www.jncc.gov.uk/page-5). UK RDBs usually employ local and national rare/scarce categories togther with three categories that equate to IUCN categories as follows: RDB1 = EN/CR; RDB2 = VU, and RDB3 = NT/LC.

D.2.2 UKBAP Priority Species and LBAP species

Currently, there are 1,149 UKBAP **priority species** (§11.3.2), all of which can be considered to have high conservation value (see www.ukbap.org.uk/NewPriorityList.aspx). The criteria for selecting priority species (recently revised in BRIG 2007) are:

1. International threat (indicated by the IUCN Red List, Red Lists from individual European countries, or other reliable sources).
2. International responsibility (e.g. if the UK supports ≥25 per cent of the global or European population) + moderate decline (by ≥25 per cent over the past 25 years) in the UK.
3. Marked decline (by ≥50 per cent over the last 25 years) in the UK.
4. Other important factors, e.g. geographic range restricted + evidence of decline (for further details, see BRIG 2007).

LBAP species (§11.3.2), automatically include UKBAP priority species, but species lacking UKBAP value may also be selected on the basis of local conservation importance. Guideline criteria for selecting the latter were provided by the UK Local Issues Advisory Group (ULIAG 1997) in Guidance note 4, and are outlined below:

1. Declining *or* rapidly declining locally – Decline of 25–49 per cent *or* ≥50 per cent in numbers or range in the LBAP area in the last 25 years;
2. Locally rare *or* scarce – Occurs in <0.6 per cent *or* 0.6–4.0 per cent of tetrads in the LBAP area;
3. Directly *or* indirectly threatened – Habitat requirements threatened by lack of or inappropriate management; *or* indirectly threatened by human activities such as recreation or pollution;
4. Historically *or* currently "endemic" – Believed to have always been "endemic" to the LBAP area; *or* previously occurred elsewhere but is now the only UK population;
5. Localised *or* highly localised – Comprises 10–19 per cent *or* ≥20 per cent of the UK population;
6. Isolated: from other populations, and may enhance the species' genetic diversity;
7. Outlying – Is at the edge of its range in the LBAP area;
8. Flagship (high profile) – Has popular appeal that can influence other issues such as habitat protection;
9. Typical – Not necessarily identified as being of conservation concern, but is particularly associated with, or characteristic of, the area;
10. *Keystone* or *indicator species*.

Species meeting some of these criteria are highly likely to have qualified for UKBAP priority status, and LBAPS often employ other criteria that the LBAP Partnership considers to be appropriate to the specific locality. However, the guideline criteria are still useful for consideration in EcIAs.

D.3 Evaluation of communities, habitats and sites

To a large extent, the conservation value of a site depends on those of the communities and habitats within it; and that of a habitat on those of its constituent communities, especially the vegetation. Not surprisingly, therefore, (a) there is considerable overlap between the criteria employed to evaluate communities, habitats and sites. Appropriate methods and criteria are described below under the following headings.

D.3.1 Sites with protected status or hosting protected habitats or species;
D.3.2 Nature Conservation Review (NCR) criteria;
D.3.3 UKBAP and LBAP criteria;
D.3.4 Habitat suitability for animal taxa;
D.3.5 Freshwater habitat evaluation using environmental and biological indicators.

D.3.1 Sites with protected status or hosting protected habitats or species

Sites hosting protected species or habitats are highly likely to have designated protection. Types of protected site/area in the UK include international designations (listed in **Table D.1**) and national or local designations (listed in **Table D.2**). A site may have more than one designation. For example, a wetland may have Ramsar/SAC/NNR status, and all high status sites are also notified as SSSIs. Sites with international designations have the highest

Table D.1 International sites designated under international conventions and EC Directives

---

Areas of Special Conservation Interest (ASCIs) – designated under the Bern Convention to protect habitats in a pan-European EMERALD network, equivalent to and encompassing Natura 2000* (www.coe.int/t/e/Cultural_Co-operation/Environment/Nature_and_biological_diversity/)

Biogenetic Reserves – designated by the Council of Europe (COE) to protect, as "living laboratories", representative examples of European wildlife and natural areas. In the UK, all are SSSIs and most are NNRs (http://ims.wcmc.org.uk/IPIECA2/conven/conven_biogen.html)

Biosphere Reserves – designated under MAB (Table 11.1) to promote conservation with sustainable use in terrestrial and coastal ecosystems (www.unesco.org/mab/BRs.shtml)

European Diploma Sites (EDSs) – awarded by COE to areas of particular European interest for natural heritage importance and protection; can be awarded to national parks, nature reserves, natural areas, sites or features (http://ims.wcmc.org.uk/IPIECA2/conven/conven_dip.html)

Ramsar Sites – designated under the *Ramsar Convention* to protect internationally important wetlands; damage to any part of which requires an equivalent designation (www.ramsar.org/index_list.htm)

Special Areas of Conservation (SACs) & **Sites of Community Importance (SCIs)** * – designated under the Habitats Directive to protect Annex I habitats and Annex II species. Stipulated requirements include: "conservation measures involving, if need be, management plans"; measures to avoid habitat deterioration or disturbance of species; and application of EIA (www.jncc.gov.uk/page-23)

Special Protection Areas (SPAs) * – designated under the Wild Birds Directive to protect the most important habitats for rare and migratory birds within the EU (www.jncc.gov.uk/page-162)

World Heritage Sites (WHSs) – designated under the World Heritage Convention for their globally important cultural or natural interest (http://whc.unesco.org/en/convention/)

Note
* SACs and SPAs are sites that have been adopted by the EC and formally designated by the government of country in which they are located. Sites that have been adopted by the EC but not yet designated by the relevant government are **Sites of Community Importance** (SCIs). Sites that have been submitted to, but not yet adopted by, the EC are **Candidate SACs/SPAs** (**cSACs/cSPAs**). The UK also has **Possible SACs** (**pSACs**) which have been formally advised to UK Government, but not yet submitted to the EC, and **Draft SACs** (**dSACs**) which have benn advised to, but not yet approved by, the UK government. SACs and SPAs form the **Natura 2000** network of "**European Sites**" (http://ec.europa.eu/environment/nature/index_en.htm).

Table D.2 UK national and local designated sites and countryside areas

Sites and countryside areas designated under UK national statute

Areas of Outstanding Natural Beauty (AONBs) – designated under the NPACA (Table 11.2) to conserve natural scenic beauty (www.jncc.gov.uk/page-1527)

Areas of Special Protection (AOSPs) – designated under the Wildlife & Countryside Act (WCA) for the special protection of birds (www.jncc.gov.uk/page-1527)

Country Parks – declared and managed by LAs under the Countryside Act 1968. Primarily intended for recreation and leisure (www.jncc.gov.uk/page-1527)

Historic Gardens and Designed Landscapes – identified by SNH and Historic Scotland for their natural heritage and cultural importance (www.jncc.gov.uk/page-1527)

Limestone Pavement Order sites – created by the relevant LA under the WCA; limestone removal or damage prohibited (www.jncc.gov.uk/page-1527)

Local Nature Reserves (LNRs) *or* **Local Authority Nature Reserves (LANRs)** in N. Ireland – designated under the NPACA; declared and managed by LAs (www.jncc.gov.uk/page-1527)

Marine Nature Reserves (MNRs) – designated under the WCA *or* Nature Conservation and Amenity Lands (N. Ireland) Order 1985; to protect marine wildlife and geological features of special interest (www.jncc.gov.uk/page-1527)

Natural Heritage Areas (NHAs) & **National Scenic Areas (NSAs)** – designated for wildlife and landscape conservation (www.snh.org.uk/scripts-snh/ab-pa03.asp)

National Nature Reserves (NNRs) – designated under the NPACA and WCA for very important communities & habitats. Most are managed by the SNCOs (www.jncc.gov.uk/page-1527)

National Parks (NPs) – designated under NPACA *or* National Parks (Scotland) Act for outstanding countryside areas, and their amenity & socio-economic value (www.jncc.gov.uk/page-1527)

Regional Parks (in Scotland) – large areas of attractive countryside close to large towns and cities, managed by agreement with landowners (http://nnr-scotland.org/about/regionalparks/ab-rp00.asp)

Sites of Special Scientific Interest (SSSIs) *or* **Areas of Special Scientific Interest (ASSIs)** in N. Ireland – The main UK site protection category; notified by SNCOs and protected by agreements with landowners/occupiers (www.jncc.gov.uk/page-1527)

Non-statutory sites and countryside areas

Ancient Woodland Sites – NE inventory (www.english-nature.org.uk/pubs/gis/tech_aw.htm)

Environmentally Sensitive Areas (ESAs) – Areas of agricultural land within which NE can provide financial incentives (e.g. Environmental Stewardship) to farmers and land managers for protectiig and enhancing the natural environment (www.defra.gov.uk/erdp/schemes/esas/default.htm)

Forest Nature Reserves & Forest/Woodland Parks – identified and managed by the Forestry Commission primarily for recreation purposes (www.forestry.gov.uk/)

Heritage Coasts (England & Wales) – designated for scenic value by LAs in conjunction with NE or CCW (www.countryside.gov.uk/LAR/Landscape/DL/heritage_coasts/index.asp)

Table D.2 (*continued*)

National Trust / NT for Scotland properties – include areas of scenic and nature conservation value (www.nationaltrust.org.uk/; www.nts.org.uk/)

Natural Areas – 97 terrestrial and 23 maritime areas of England defined by NE to provide a more effective framework for conservation than administrative boundaries (www.english-nature.org.uk/Science/natural/role.htm)

NGO reserves – usually owned and managed by NGOs (www.jncc.gov.uk/page-1527)

Sensitive Marine Areas (SMAs) *or* **Marine Consultation Areas (MCAs)** (in Scotland) – identified by their quality & sensitivity or their support for adjacent statutory sites (www.jncc.gov.uk/page-1527)

Wildlife Sites – variously named areas designated by LAs, as being of local conservation importance, in local and structure plans under the Town and Country Planning system and considered in planning applications (www.jncc.gov.uk/page-1527)

Note
Maps and information for sites and areas is available at www.magic.gov.uk.

protection status, followed by sites designated under UK statute. The relevant legislation is outlined in Tables 11.1 and 11.2, and sources of information (e.g. lists, locations and maps) on designated sites is given in Table 11.3.

Protected sites are clearly of prime importance in EcIA, but this must not lead to undervaluation of non-designated sites, especially if these meet any of the criteria outlined below.

D.3.2 Nature Conservation Review (NCR) criteria

The NCR criteria (Ratcliffe 1977) have been widely used for evaluating sites in the UK, and are still employed, together with the *National Vegetation Classification* (NVC) (§C.8) in the selection of NNRs and SSSIs (JNCC 1998). While primarily intended for site selection, they inevitably evaluate the constituent communities and habitats. There are two levels of criteria, primary and secondary.

Primary criteria

Large size generally enhances habitat/site value. However:

- Minimum viable size varies for different species and communities, e.g. (a) in a farmland area, a 100ha fen may dry out while a 1ha meadow may retain its floristic composition if well managed (JNCC 1998), (b) small habitats can support some important species.
- The edge habitats of sites with small area/edge ratios can host species-rich communities and important species (§11.7.2).
- Small sites may provide valuable *stepping stone habitats*.

Diversity (biodiversity) can be assessed in terms of: (a) **habitat diversity**, which is the variety of habitats/communities in an area, and/or (b) *species richness/ diversity*, perhaps giving weightings to notable species. High habitat diversity and/or species diversity is generally considered valuable. However, caution is needed in interpreting species diversity values because:

- they are area dependent (normally increase with increasing area) so data are strictly compatible only when obtained from sampling areas of similar size;
- they should be derived from all the species of a community, which is not normally possible for animal communities (see §11.6.3);
- they vary intrinsically between different communities (e.g. plant species diversity is normally high in meadows and ancient woodlands, but low in heaths and bogs), and should therefore only be used to compare like with like;
- animal species diversity is not necessarily correlated with plant species diversity, e.g. invertebrate species diversity is usually high in lowland heaths.

Rarity, naturalness and **typicalness** can be assessed by comparison with types defined in habitat or vegetation classifications such as the NVC (§C.8). Naturalness is the degree to which a habitat or community approximates to a natural state, and typicalness is the degree to which it is a good example of those that are, or have been, characteristic of an area.

Sensitivity/fragility is the susceptibility of a community/habitat/ecosystem to environmental changes including project impacts. Assessment, which can include consideration of **resilience/recoverability** (see §11.2.2) requires and understanding of the ecology of the ecosystems in question, and will be related to other criteria such as size.

Non-recreatability is usually related to naturalness because "the more natural an ecosystem, the greater the difficulty of re-creating it in original richness and complexity once it has been destroyed" (JNCC 1998). It applies particularly to long-established habitats with a complex community structure (e.g. *ancient woodlands*).

Secondary criteria

Recorded history can enhance a site's potential for education and research, and as a model for management, e.g. sites with a long history can contribute to ecological understanding.

Position in an ecological unit is when a site (perhaps with fairly low intrinsic value) may be an important component of a larger ecological unit, e.g. part of a network. This can also apply to *linear habitats* and *stepping stone habitats* which may increase the *connectivity* between larger sites/habitats or provide "green networks" in urban areas.

Potential value acknowledges that a site's current ecological value may increase or decrease by intrinsic changes such as ecological succession (§11.2.2) or in response to environmental changes, e.g. associated with management, human pressures, or climate change.

Intrinsic appeal takes account of public perception and economic benefit, including the generation of funds for conservation. It can include criteria such as visual/landscape, amenity, education, accessibility to residents, and presence in an area of deficiency. These are often highly valued, especially in urban environments (e.g. see Collis and Tyldesley 1993).

D.3.3 UKBAP and LBAP criteria

The **UKBAP priority habitat criteria** are designed primarily for the selection of priority habitats within the framework of the **UKBAP broad habitat classification** (§C.3). The current criteria (recently revised in BRIG 2007) are:

1. Habitats for which the UK has international obligations, e.g. Habitats Directive Annex I habitats.
2. Natural and semi-natural habitats at risk, such as those with a high rate of decline in extent and/or quality, especially over the last 20 years, or which are rare.
3. Habitats important for assemblages of key species, e.g. UKBAP priority species, Red List species and Habitats Directive Annex II species.
4. Other important factors such as habitats being "functionally critical", i.e. essential for organisms inhabiting wider ecosystems (for further details, and additional criteria adopted for marine habitats, see BRIG 2007).

ULIAG 1997 (Guidance note 4) suggested the following criteria for selecting **LBAP key habitats** other than those already having UKBAP priority status:

1. Declining *or* rapidly declining – Decline in extent of 25–49 per cent *or* ≥50 per cent in the LBAP area over the last 25 years;
2. Endemic – Comprises 100 per cent of total UK resource of the same habitat;
3. Significant *or* highly significant – Comprises 10–19 per cent *or* 20–99 per cent of the total UK resource of the same habitat;
4. Rare *or* scarce – Covers <0.6 per cent *or* 0.6-4.0 per cent of the total LBAP area;
5. Directly *or* indirectly threatened – Threatened directly by lack of or inappropriate management *or* indirectly by human activities such as recreation or pollution;
6. Potential value – Having potential for increase in area and/or linking fragments;

7. Viability in terms of size – Viable or potentially viable, e.g. by increase in area;

8. Local distinctiveness – e.g. characteristic of the local area, or of special historical/cultural importance;

9. Important for key species – e.g. UKBAP species including keystone or "flagship" species.

UKBAP criteria are bound to be increasingly applied, and LBAP criteria should be useful in EcIA because of their local context. The "functionally critical" criterion can be interpreted more widely to incorporate the need for sensitive management outside protected areas, e.g. by consideration of small and linear habitats that may be important in their own right, may function as refuges, or may increase *connectivity*. The principal linear UKBAP priority habitat is hedgerows.

The priority definition for **hedgerows** has been recently expanded (BRIG 2007) and the current main criteria are: comprising ≥80 per cent cover of native trees/shrubs, and UKBAP criteria: 2 (risk/decline); and 3 (key species). A standard method for surveying and evaluating hedgerows has been developed (Defra 2007a). It uses a number of criteria including: hedgerow type (shrubby/with trees/line of trees); shape, dimensions and integrity; connections with other hedgerows; adjacent land use and width of undisturbed ground; associated features, e.g. bank, ditch, fence; proportions of native and non-native species; species diversity, especially of woody species; and presence of nutrient enrichment *indicator species*.

There is a link between the ecological and historical interest of hedgerows because the number of woody species present is usually related to hedgerow age (Pollard *et al.* 1974). A simple "rule of thumb" is that the average number of woody species per 30m length of hedgerow indicates its approximate age in 100-year increments, e.g. five species per 30m ≈ 500 years. However, the relationship does not always hold. For example, hedges that are relics of woodland tend to have more woody species than planted hedges, regardless of age (Wolton 1999); so estimates should be checked against historical evidence where possible (see Box 7.1). It is also worth bearing in mind that straight field boundaries are often associated with the enclosure acts of the 1700–1800s, and are unlikely to pre-date this period. Further information on the history and ecology of hedges can be found in Dowdeswell (1987), Muir and Muir (1987), and Rackham (1989, 2000).

Ancient woodland is an important habitat that: (a) is not a UKBAP or Habitats Directive priority habitat (although most examples are similar to one or more of the designated woodland types); and (b) has no statutory protection, although Planning Policy Statement 9 (PPS9) states that local authorities should "identify any areas of ancient woodland in their areas that do not have statutory protection" and normally "not grant planning permission for any development which would result in its loss or deterioration". NE holds an inventory of ancient woodlands of ≥2ha (see Table 11.3) but many remaining fragments are smaller.

Ancient woodland can usually be identified by the features outlined in **Table D.3**. Further guidance is given in Kirby and Goldberg (2002/2003), Marren (1990, 1992), Rackham (2000, 2001, 2003) and Reid (1997). The most reliable *indicator species* are considered to be Ancient Woodland Vascular Plants (AWVPs), which are often taken to be species having ≥55 per cent of their locations in ancient woods (Peterken 2000). However:

- Although they are generally indicative of woodland age (Peterken 1993): (a) many can occur in recent woodlands, especially when these are located near ancient woods; (b) because of variations in climate, soils and past management, few are consistently associated with ancient woodland throughout the UK. Marren (1992) provides guidance on regional variations, and local lists are given in some county floras.
- Rose (1999) and Peterken (2000) stress that: (a) the presence of one or a few AWVPs may have little or no significance; (b) the number of AWVPs tends to increase with woodland size; and (c) AWVPs cannot be taken alone as proof of a wood's antiquity, and reference should always made to historical information where this is available.

Table D.3 Ancient woodland indicators

Documentary evidence

- It is shown on old maps (e.g. since c.1820 available from OS or www.old-maps.co.uk), or is mentioned in historical documents such as estate records, tithe and enclosure surveys.
- Its name includes: the name of a nearby settlement; an old name for "wood" (e.g. grove, hanger, frith); reference to an old industry (e.g. kiln, tanner); or tree names (e.g. oak, ash, beech, hazel).

Location, form and historical features

- It has sinuous or irregular external boundaries with boundary ditches and banks (unless the wood has been fragmented), lacks straight internal boundaries, and does not fit a field enclosure pattern.
- It is sited along parish boundaries, adjacent to common land or heath, on a steep slope, or in a deep valley.
- It shows evidence coppicing, pollarding or other traditional uses, e.g. charcoal hearths, kilns.

Vegetation structure and composition

- It has a well-developed vertical structure (canopy, shrub, field and ground layers), old/large coppice stools or veteran trees.
- It has a rich flora of mainly native species including ancient woodland indicator species.
- It contains rare species or species that are local to the area.
- The trees vary in age, and are not evenly distributed (as in plantations). A simple method for estimating the approximate age of trees is described in Mitchell (1974) and Agate (2003).

D.3.4 *Habitat suitability for animal taxa*

Most animals depend directly or indirectly on particular types of vegetation. Important features include the structure of vegetation/habitats and the presence of mosaics (such as small-scale patchworks of scrub, tall and short grassland and open/bare ground) that are likely to benefit notable invertebrates and reptiles (Key 2000). Fry and Lonsdale (1991) and Kirby (2001) provide information on invertebrate habitat requirements.

Consequently, it can be argued that the value of a site for animal taxa can be inferred from a habitat/vegetation study that provides an assessment of habitat suitability. However, while this can indicate where sampling is likely to be profitable, the presence of animal species cannot be assumed from apparent habitat suitability alone because their distributions depend on other factors such as local climate, past site conditions, and degree of isolation from other suitable habitat patches.

On the other hand, if a species is absent because of factors such as past management, the habitat conditions and vegetation should give a good indication of the potential for re-colonisation. This is why it is included in IEAs (1995) criteria for triggering Phase 2 surveys, which can be regarded as evaluation criteria. The main examples are:

- The habitat is in an area that contains a nationally or internationally important number (≥1 per cent of the UK, European or world population) of a bird species, as a resident or regular visitor, e.g. seasonal or during migration.
- The habitat is evidently suitable for a notable species even if this is not now present, e.g. (a) it includes a suitable breeding habitat near to a known population of a protected bird species; or (b) it is suitable for a threatened amphibian, reptile or invertebrate species, and has previously hosted this or is within its geographical range – especially if it occurs in similar habitats nearby.
- The habitat is on the Invertebrate Site Register (see www.searchnbn.net/) or is of high value for invertebrates (Kirby 2001).

In most cases, however, the relevant habitats will already have high conservation value in terms of other criteria.

Habitat suitability can also be assessed by means of the *Habitat Suitability Index* (HSI), which was developed by the US Fish and Wildlife Service for use in their *Habitat Evaluation Procedure* (HEP) which is a habitat-based approach for assessing environmental impacts of proposed development projects (USFWS 1980/1981). HEP evaluates a habitat in terms its **carrying capacity** for selected animal species (evaluation species) when compared with optimum habitats for these species – using measurable habitat "quality" criteria such as vegetation composition. For each evaluation species, this is expressed as the HSI which is the ratio of the study-habitat conditions to optimum-habitat conditions (habitat quality ratio), and ranges from zero (totally unsuitable) to one (**Table D.4**).

Table D.4 Construction of a descriptive HSI (as ratings) and conversion of this to a numerical HSI (as scores) using ranking and the ratio of study-habitat rank to optimal rank

Descriptive HSI (ratings)	Rank	Ratio	Numerical HSI (scores)
Optimal	4	4/4	1.0
Good	3	3/4	0.75
Fair	2	2/4	0.5
Poor	1	1/4	0.25
Unsuitable	0	0/4	0

Source: Based on USFWS (1980/1981).

Thus, given adequate information on a species' habitat requirements, a simple model can be constructed using descriptive terms and ranking these to derive numerical values.

Once this has been achieved the HSI score is multiplied by the area of available habitat to obtain the habitat units (HUs). For EcIA, HUs can be calculated for the habitat with and without the proposed development and can thus be used (a) to predict the potential loss of suitable habitat for the evaluation species, and (b) to formulate mitigation measure to avoid or minimise this loss. They are increasingly being employed with a GIS (Chapter 14) which facilitates comparison of the various scenarios.

Limitations of the method include:

- HEP only evaluates habitats in relation to evaluation species, selection of which is inevitably limited, and does not necessarily imply suitability for other species;
- HSIs assume a linear relationship between HSI values and carrying capacities, which may not always apply (Treweek 1999);
- as with all models, the output can only be as good as the input information (on the species' habitat requirements and the relationship between these and the habitat variables measured), and should be validated, e.g. against measured populations, before being widely applied;
- HSI models have been produced for many US species, but are largely restricted to these.

D.3.5 Freshwater habitat evaluation using environmental and biological indicators

Freshwater ecosystems are strongly dependent on water quality (see §10.3); so this can be used as an environmental indicator of the conservation value of sites. The method involves taking measurements of selected variables (e.g. dissolved oxygen, pH, nutrients and turbidity) and comparing the results with reference conditions for the relevant habitat type (see §10.7).

The advantages of this approach are: (a) it is usually relatively quick and inexpensive, because less time is spent sampling and identifying species – although it becomes much more problematical if any attempt is made to assess pollution; and (b) it treats the system as a whole, rather than perhaps focusing attention on a few notable species. The main drawbacks of adopting this approach alone are: (a) it only reflects conditions at the time of sampling; (b) it gives no indication about the species and communities present; and (c) habitats with low water quality may be "written off" as having little conservation value when valuable species may be present.

The majority of methods that have been developed for assessing freshwater habitats use both environmental and biological indicator data (often combined to produce a numerical index) that can be compared with reference conditions such as those defined in the *Water Framework Directive* (WFD). Methods using bioindicators are discussed in §10.7.3. They include:

- the *River Invertebrate Prediction and Classification System* (RIVPACS) is designed to assess the ecological quality of streams and rivers in the UK (see §10.7.3);
- the *National Pond Survey Method* (NPS) (Pond Action 1998) categorises the conservation values of ponds into four classes (low, moderate, high, very high) on the basis of surveys of water quality and aquatic **macrophytes** and **macroinvertbrates**. The biological results are used to calculate either: (a) the value of the species assemblages in terms of species richness; or (b) numerical species rarity scores based on national/local rarity and RDB criteria (§D.2.1) and hence an average rarity value (Species Rarity Index (SRI) score) for the site (see SEPA 2000). In addition, the water quality and biological data can be collectively analysed, by means of the *Predictive System for Multimetrics* (PSYM) software package (see §10.7.3) to provide a site quality value that can be compared with ponds nationally via the National Ponds Database (see Table 11.3); and
- the *Common Standards Monitoring Guidance for Ditches* (JNCC 2005) assesses features such as water level and availability, water quality, habitat structure, aquatic vegetation composition and species richness, presence of rare and quality-indicator species, and indicators of negative change (e.g. non-native species).

D.4 Evaluation in terms of socio-economic resources

A growing number of methods aim to evaluate biodiversity and ecosystem services (§11.2.4) as socio-economic resources. In these terms they may be depleted, enhanced and in some cases replaced or "traded". Criteria used include notional monetary value, socio-economic benefits, and replacement value. An overview of economic ecosystem evaluation methods (and links to relevant organisations) can be found at www.ecosystemvaluation.org/. Various approaches, including assessment in relation to ecosystem services and *Total Economic Value* (TEV), are also reviewed in Defra (2007b).

Direct contribution to the local economy – e.g. in terms of income and employment generated by activities such as tourism, recreation (including bird watching) and sport (including fishing and hunting) – is included by IEEM (2006) as an evaluation criterion for habitats and sites. Another example of the "monetary value" approach in the UK is the *Habitat Replacement Cost Method* advocated by MAFF (1999, 2000) in relation to *Coastal Habitat Management Plans* (see §12.3.2). This suggests that high-status protected sites can be considered to have a "national economic value" based on the cost of protecting them *in situ*, or (if lower) the cost of replacing them. Other designated sites would have a lower "local value". Given the difficulties of satisfactory habitat creation (§11.8.4) this approach may be viewed with concern. Indeed, MAFF accepted that:

- it tends to favour habitats that are the most expensive to create, regardless of their ecological value;
- it should not be taken to imply that habitat replacement is the most appropriate option and, particularly for *European sites*, there should normally be a presumption in favour of *in situ* habitat protection (with habitat replacement undertaken only as a last resort);
- it cannot strictly apply to technically irreplaceable habitats such as ancient woodland.

Replaceable (or "tradable") and irreplaceable criteria are: (a) included in the concept of *environmental capital*, which: was adopted by EN (1994) for application in *Natural Areas* (Table D.2); and is an element in the Highways Agency's *Transport Analysis Guidance* (TAG) (see §11.7.3) in which some assessment scores refer to "compensation" in terms of net gain, or no net loss, in a *Natural Area*. The *Quality of Life Capital* approach (Chapter 15) considers social and economic as well as environmental capital.

References

Agate E 2003. *Woodlands: a practical handbook.* Doncaster: BTCV, http://handbooks.btcv.org.uk/handbooks/content/section/3730.

BRIG (Biodiversity Reporting & Information Group) 2007. *Report on the species and habitat review; Report to the UK Biodiversity Partnership,* www.ukbap.org.uk/bapgrouppage.aspx?id=112.

Collis I and D Tyldesley 1993. *Natural assets: non-statutory sites of importance for nature conservation.* The Local Government Nature Conservation Initiative, Hampshire County Council.

Defra 2007a. *Hedgerow Survey Handbook: a standard procedure for local surveys in the UK: prepared on behalf of the Steering Group for the UK Biodiversity Action Plan for Hedgerows,* 2nd edn. London: Defra, www.defra.gov.uk/farm/environment/landscape/hedgerows.htm.

Defra 2007b. *Valuing the benefits of biodiversity.* London: Defra, www.defra.gov.uk/wildlife-countryside/pdfs/biodiversity/econ-bene-biodiversity.pdf.

Dowdeswell WH 1987. *Hedgerows and verges.* London: Allen & Unwin.

EN (English Nature) 1994. *Sustainability in practice.* Peterborough, Cambs: English Nature.

Fry R and D Lonsdale (eds) 1991. *Habitat conservation for insects – a neglected green issue.* The Amateur Entomologists' Society, www.amentsoc.org/vol21.htm.

IEA (Institute of Environmental Assessment) 1995. *Guidelines for baseline ecological assessment.* London: E & FN Spon.

IEEM (Institute of Ecology and Environmental Management) 2006. *Guidelines for ecological impact assessment in the United Kingdom* (version 7, July). Winchester: IEEM, www.ieem.net/ecia/.

Gaston KJ 1994. *Rarity.* London: Chapman & Hall.

Gaston KJ 2003. *The structure and dynamics of geographic ranges.* Oxford: Oxford University Press.

JNCC (Joint Nature Conservation Committee) 1998. *Guidelines for the selection of biological SSSIs.* Peterborough, Cambs: JNCC, www.jncc.gov.uk/page-2303.

JNCC 2005. *Common standards monitoring guidance for ditches.* Peterborough, Cambs: JNCC, www.jncc.gov.uk/pdf/CSM_ditches_Mar05.pdf.

Key R 2000. Bare ground and the conservation of invertebrates. *British Wildlife* 11(3), 183–191.

Kirby P 2001. *Habitat management for invertebrates: a practical manual.* Sandy, Beds: RSPB.

Kirby K and E Goldberg 2002/3. *Ancient woodland: guidance material for local authorities.* Peterborough, Cambs: English Nature, www.english-nature.org.uk/pubs/publication/pdf/AWoodlandGuidance.pdf.

Kunin WE and KJ Gaston (eds) 1997. *The biology of rarity: causes and consequences of rare-common differences.* London: Chapman & Hall.

MAFF 1999. *Flood and coastal defence project appraisal guidance: economic appraisal, FCD-PAG3.* London: MAFF.

MAFF 2000. *Flood and coastal defence project appraisal guidance: Environmental appraisal, FCDPAG5.* London: MAFF.

Marren P 1990. *Britain's ancient woodland: woodland heritage.* Newton Abbot, Devon: David and Charles Ltd.

Marren P 1992. *The wild woods: a regional guide to Britain's ancient woodland.* Newton Abbot, Devon: David and Charles Ltd.

Mitchell A 1974. *A field guide to the trees of Britain and Northern Europe.* London: Collins.

Muir R and N Muir 1987. *Hedgerows: their history and wildlife.* London: Michael Joseph.

Palmer M 1995. *A UK plant conservation strategy: a strategic framework for the conservation of the native flora of Great Britain and Northern Ireland,* 2nd edn. Peterborough, Cambs: JNCC.

Peterken GF 1993. *Woodland conservation and management,* 2nd edn. London: Chapman & Hall.

Peterken GF 2000. Identifying ancient woodland using vascular plant indicators. *British Wildlife* 11(3), 153–158.

Pollard E, MD Hooper, NW Moore 1974. *Hedges.* New Naturalist No. 58. London: Collins.

Pond Action 1998. *A guide to the methods of the National Pond Survey.* Oxford: Pond Action.

Rackham O 1989. *Hedges and hedgerow trees in Britain: A thousand years of agroforestry.* Download available from www.odi.org.uk/fpeg/publications/rdfn/8/c.html

Rackham O 2000. *The history of the countryside.* London: Orion.

Rackham O 2001. *Trees and woodland in the British landscape.* London: Orion.

Rackham O 2003. *Ancient woodland: its history, vegetation and uses in England* (revised edition). Dalbeattie, Scotland: Castlepoint Press.

Ratcliffe DA (ed.) 1977. *A nature conservation review* (2 vols). Cambridge: Cambridge University Press.

Reid CM 1997. *Guidelines for identifying ancient woodland.* Peterborough, Cambs: English Nature.

Rose F 1999. Indicators of ancient woodland – the use of vascular plants in evaluating ancient woods for nature conservation. *British Wildlife* 10(4), 241–251.

SEPA (Scottish Environmental Protection Agency) 2000. *Ponds, pools and lochans: guidance on good practice in the management and creation of small waterbodies in Scotland.* Edinburgh: SEPA, www.sepa.org.uk/pdf/guidance/hei/ponds.pdf.

Treweek J 1999. *Ecological impact assessment.* Oxford: Blackwell Science.

ULIAG (UK Local Issues Advisory Group) 1997. *Guidance for local biodiversity action plans: Guidance notes 1–5.* Bristol: UKBG.

USFWS (US Fish and Wildlife Service) 1980. *Habitat evaluation procedures (HEP)*, and 1981 *Standards for the development of habitat sustainability index models for use in HEP.* Washington, DC: Division of Ecological Services, Department of the Interior. Outline available at www.fws.gov/policy/870FW1.html, and *Habitat evaluation procedures handbook* downloadable from www.fws.gov/policy/ESMindex.html.

Wolton R 1999. Do we need hedges any more? *Biologist* 46(3), 118–122.

Glossary

The terms defined are highlighted in **bold italics** at least the first time they appear in a chapter or appendix. Terms similarly highlighted within definitions are defined elsewhere in the glossary.

abundance   see **species abundance**

acid deposition   Dry deposition (gravitational settling, impact with vegetation) and wet deposition (in precipitation) of acidic substances such as sulphates and nitrates. It is often called **acid precipitation** or "acid rain", but these terms strictly refer to wet deposition only.

air quality standard   The concentration of a pollutant, over a specified period, above which adverse effects on health (or the environment) may occur, and which should not be exceeded.

algae   Mainly aquatic, unicelled or multicelled plants that lack true stems, roots or leaves. They include *phytoplankton*, filamentous "pond scum" species and seaweeds.

algal blooms   Rapid growth of *algae* in water bodies, facilitated by high nutrient levels and/or other physical and chemical conditions. They increase water *turbidity* (which inhibits light penetration and hence photosynthesis) and reduce dissolved oxygen levels at night and when the algae decay. Blooms of some algae and *cyanobacteria* also produce toxins that can affect fish and other wildlife, and present a hazard to human health.

alkalinity   (a) the state when the *pH* of a solution is >7; (b) more strictly the concentration of carbonates in water (its carbonate hardness) and hence its ability to resist (buffer) changes in pH – in which terms it is possible for water with pH < 7 to have high alkalinity and for water with pH > 7 to have low alkalinity. Values are often quoted in mg/l calcium carbonate but are better quoted in milli-equivalents of acid per litre, i.e. the amount of acid needed to change the pH.

alluvial soil   A soil that has accumulated by deposition of water-borne *sediments* from a water course (e.g. river or stream) as the current slows, or by successive floods in a *floodplain*.

ancient woodland   Woodland that has existed continuously since at least 1600 AD (often much longer). It normally supports a rich native fauna and flora, and has usually been managed for centuries, so potentially providing a record of early settlements and of traditional practices such as coppicing, pollarding and charcoal burning.

anoxia/anoxic   Complete lack, or a pathological deficiency, of oxygen.

anthropogenic   Generated and maintained by human activities.

appropriate assessment   An assessment that must be carried out (under the EU Habitats Directive and UK Habitat Regulations) by a *competent authority* when a project is considered likely (alone or in conjunction with other projects or plans) to have a significant effect on a European site (SAC or SPA) or Ramsar site (see Table 11.1). Its conclusions must be based only on the scientific considerations, and not influenced by wider planning or other considerations (see EN 1997, ODPM 2005).

aquifer   A stratum of porous or fractured rock that contains groundwater and allows this to flow through.

audit trail   A record of all analyses, decisions etc. during a process such as EIA, to assist in (a) explaining how options were considered, and why decisions were made, and (b) reviewing the study, e.g. if conditions change.

benthic (zone)   The lowest ecological level of a water body, including the sediment surface and some sub-surface layers. Benthic organisms (the benthos, "bottom dwellers") generally live in close relationship with the substrate, and may tolerate low oxygen levels.

bioaccumulation   The process by which some pollutants accumulate in the tissues of living organisms.

bioamplification (biomagnification)   The increase in concentration of bioaccumulating pollutants along food chains, culminating in high concentrations in top carnivores. It is associated with the trend of decreasing *biomass* along food chains (see Figure 11.2).

bioassay   A method using the biological response of a species to test the toxicity of a pollutant.

biochemical oxygen demand (BOD)   The quantity of dissolved oxygen in water (mg/l) consumed (under test conditions) by microbial degradation of organic matter during a given period (five days). It is one of the standard tests used to characterise *effluent* quality and measure organic pollution in surface waters, e.g. in the Environment Agency's General Quality Assessment (GQA).

biodiversity   The variety of life, globally or within any area – defined in the UN Convention on Biological Diversity (1992) as "The variability among living organisms from all sources, including terrestrial, marine and other aquatic ecosystems and the ecological complexes of which they are part; this includes diversity within species, between species and of ecosystems" (see also Gaston and Spicer 2004).

biogeochemical cycles   Cyclical flows of materials within the global ecosystem (ecosphere). There are two principal types: (a) **volatile element cycles** (notably the carbon and nitrogen cycles) – of elements that can exist in gaseous form or as constituents of atmospheric gases, and therefore have efficient global circulations. These are hydrogen, oxygen, carbon, nitrogen, and sulphur, which are all *macronutrients*; and (b) **non-volatile element cycles** – of elements that do not have an atmospheric phase, and therefore have much less efficient cycling. They include important macronutrients (calcium, iron, magnesium, phosphorus, potassium) and *micronutrients*.

biomass   The amount of organic matter in a community's living organisms at a given time, usually measured as dry weight per unit area (e.g. g m^2) or (in aquatic systems) volume (e.g. g m^3).

biomes   The major climatic climax communities (Figure 11.3) on a given continent, characterised largely by the vegetation and the governing climate. Similar biomes on different continents belong to global **biome types**, e.g. tropical rainforest, tundra. The principal biome types in the British Isles are: temperate deciduous forest (now represented by semi-natural broadleaved woodland); boreal (conifer and birch) forest (now represented mainly by the Caledonian pine forest); blanket bog; and alpine communities (on mountains above *c*.650m).

biotope   Usually defined as area of uniform environmental conditions providing living place for a distinctive assemblage of species, i.e. a physical habitat with its biological community. Thus "biotope" is almost synonymous with "habitat" as used in habitat classifications (see §11.2.5) but with emphasis on the whole biota (not just vegetation).

biotransformation   The conversion by organisms (usually bacteria) of chemical pollutants to more toxic forms/compounds, e.g. of inorganic mercury to methyl mercury.

buffer zones/strips   Vegetated strips of land designed to manage various environmental concerns, e.g. (a) to intercept water-borne pollutants and hence protect groundwaters and surface waters; (b) to slow *runoff* and enhance infiltration (within the buffer), so stabilising streamflows; (c) to reduce soil and streambank erosion; (d) to provide visual/noise/odour screens and landscape features (e) to protect wildlife habitats/sites from pollution and/or disturbance, e.g. as "recreational buffer zones"; and (e) to provide *wildlife corridors* and habitats/refuges. Buffer types include: wellhead protection zones, *riparian* buffers, grassed waterways, shelterbelts/windbreaks/snowbreaks, contour strips, roadside verges and field borders. Further information, and an interactive program for selecting and sizing buffers, can be found at www.sd.nrcs.usda.gov/technical/Technical_Tools.html.

calaminarion grasslands   Open grasslands on soils with high levels of heavy metals (e.g. lead, zinc, chromium and copper) that are toxic to most plant species. In the UK, some are found on serpentine rock and mineral vein outcrops, but most are associated with past mining activities, e.g. spoil heaps.

carr   Very wet woodland dominated by *hydrophilous* trees such as alders and willows. It is usually transitional between herbaceous wetland and terrestrial woodland.

carrying capacity   Can have various meanings, e.g.: the population size of a species (including man) which a given environment can support; the ability of a habitat to support one or more given species; or the capacity of an ecosystem to tolerate a given stress such as a pollution level.

catchment   A drainage area/river basin within which precipitation drains into a river system (and associated lakes and wetlands) and eventually to the sea. Catchment boundaries are generally formed by ridges, on different sides of which rainfall drains into different catchments. In the UK, these are usually called watersheds; but in the US, the term watershed is used in place of catchment.

chasmophytic vegetation   Communities of plants (chasmophytes) that colonise the cracks and fissures of rock faces. They vary in relation to rock type; siliceous communities develop on acid rocks, and more calcareous types develop on lime-rich rocks.

climate   The behaviour of the atmosphere (and hence the totality of the *weather* experienced) at a given place over long periods, e.g. months, years, decades or millennia. It is not simply "average weather" since climate includes the extremes or deviations from the mean state of the atmosphere, e.g. the occurrence of fogs, frosts and storms. The "current" climate of a location is usually characterised using long-term records of, say 30 years.

competent authority   A UK decision making organisation or individual responsible (with regard to EIA) for determining a consent application for a project. For projects requiring planning permission this will usually be the Local Planning Authority (LPA), but in some cases (e.g. under the Habitats Regulations) it may involve other authorities such as a Minister, government department or statutory organisation.

connectivity   The degree to which habitat patches in an urban or agricultural matrix are interconnected by *linear habitats* and/or *stepping stone habitats* between the main patches.

controlled waters   Surface waters, groundwaters, and coastal waters (to three nautical miles out to sea) to which UK pollution legislation applies. They include virtually all freshwaters except small ponds and reservoirs (not used for public supply) that do not supply other waters. It is an offence, with certain exceptions, to cause or knowingly permit trade or sewage effluent, toxic pollutants, or solid matter to enter controlled waters without a *discharge consent* (see *designated waters*).

critical load/level   Defined by UK NFC (see Table 11.3) as "a quantitative estimate of an exposure to one or more pollutants below which significant harmful effects on specified sensitive elements of the environment do not occur according to present knowledge". Critical load strictly refers to deposited pollutants (e.g. in soils or waters), while critical level refers to atmospheric concentrations. Exceedance of critical loads/levels may affect organisms directly, or indirectly, e.g. through increased dissolved aluminium concentrations associated with acidity.

culvert   A pipe or box-type conduit through which water is carried under a structure such as a road.

cumulative impacts Combined effects on the environment that are caused by (a) a range of human activities, (b) activities of a given type such as land development, or (c) a new development in conjunction with other (past, present and future) developments and/or other activities. They can result from direct or indirect impacts, or a combination these; can be temporary or long-term; and can be effective over small or large areas. This complexity makes it difficult to assess them and attribute responsibility for them.

cyanobacteria Photosynthetic bacteria that have features similar to free-floating algae and are often called **blue-green algae**. They can be a problem in *algal blooms*.

denitrification The process of nitrogen removal from waterlogged soils by the action of denitrifying bacteria which utilise nitrate and release nitrogen gas (to the atmosphere).

designated waters Water bodies or sections of river that are designated under one or more EU Directives, and must comply with the relevant water quality objectives (WQOs).

design event An event such as a rainstorm or flood of given magnitude and probability, derived from past records. A **design rainfall/storm** can be formulated from depth-duration-frequency (DDF) data of past rainstorms, e.g. can be the maximum rainfall (mm) likely to occur at a location during a given period (e.g. 1hr or 24hrs) within a specified *return period* – so a 50-year, 1-hour design storm is the maximum rainfall probable in a 1hr period within any 50-year interval. Similar models can be constructed for maritime storms and storm surges.

Development Plans Statutory documents produced by LPAs (under the *Town and Country Planning Act 1990*) outlining their strategies for development over a 10–15-year period. They include County Structure Plans, Unitary Development Plans (UDPs) and Local Plans.

dewatering Pumping of water to reduce the flow of groundwater into an excavation, or to reduce its pressure, e.g. to allow dry working for mineral extraction or deep foundations.

diffuse (non-point) source pollution Pollution that cannot be attributed to discharges at specific locations. Typical causes are *runoff* to surface waters, or percolation to groundwater, from farmland, roads, urban and industrial areas, or many minor point sources (e.g. land drains, leakages from sewers etc.). It is generally more difficult to control than *point source pollution*.

discharge consent Statutory document issued by the EA (under schedule 10 of the *Water Resources Act 1991*) setting limits and conditions on the discharge of an *effluent* into a *controlled water*.

dominant species The species of highest *abundance* or *biomass* in a community. It usually has a major influence, but is not necessarily a *keystone species*, e.g. may be replaceable by a similar species without significantly affecting the community organisation. A community may have two or more co-dominant species.

drawdown   Lowering of the water table or piezometric surface (Figure 10.2) usually caused by ***dewatering***, e.g. adjacent to mineral workings.

drivers (of ecosystem change)   Independent variables (factors) that directly or indirectly cause changes in ecosystem components or processes. **Direct drivers** are relatively easy to identify and measure. They may be natural (e.g. volcanic activity, intrinsic climate change, and evolution) or ***anthropogenic*** (e.g. habitat destruction, pollution, induced climate change, overexploitation, and species introductions or removals). **Indirect drivers** operate by altering the level or rate of change of direct drivers. They include demographic, socio-economic, political, cultural and technological factors.

dystrophic   Very nutrient-poor (more so than ***oligotrophic***) soils, waters, or ecosystems; these also have low ***pH*** (<5.5).

echinoderms   "Spiny-skinned" marine invertebrates with radially symmetrical bodies. Most are ***benthic*** (live on the sea floor). They include starfish, sea urchins and brittle stars.

ecological surprises   Unexpected, and often surprisingly large (***nonlinear***) changes in a species population, community or ecosystem in response to environmental change. They are unpredictable because of current limitations in the understanding of the complex interactions within, and dynamic nature of, ecosystems. Surprises to-date include ***bioamplification***, the ability of pests to develop resistance to biocides, the vulnerability of ecosystems to ***eutrophication***, effects of species introductions or removals, and the rapidity of global warming and its consequences (MA 2005).

ecotoxicology   (strictly the study of) The effects on living organisms of toxic chemicals released into the environment.

effluent   Treated or untreated liquid waste material that is discharged into the environment from a point source such as a wastewater treatment plant or an industrial facility.

electrical conductivity (of an aqueous solution)   The "ease" with which an electrical current passes through the solution. Conductivity increases with total ion concentration, and provides a measure of overall amount of solutes present – but gives no indication of the relative amounts of different solutes.

emissions inventory   An organised collection of data relating to the characteristics of processes or activities which release pollutants to the atmosphere across a study area.

environmental components   Aspects of the natural or man-made environment (e.g. population, landscape, heritage, air, soils, water, ecosystems) that are individually assessed in an EIA because they may be significantly affected by a proposed project, i.e. are ***receptors*** and include sub-components that are also receptors, e.g. species or buildings.

environmental factors   Environmental variables (or systems of variables) that affect living organisms, and hence species populations. They can be divided into: **abiotic factors** which are physicochemical systems (climate, soil etc.) and individual variables (e.g. water, temperature, light, oxygen, nutrients, *p*H and toxins); and **biotic factors** which involve interactions between species, e.g. competition, predation, parasitism and ***mutualism***.

environmental impact statement (EIS) (or environmental statement (ES)) The document that presents the findings of an EIA, including proposed mitigation measures, and is submitted (with the planning application) to the ***competent authority*** responsible for deciding if the proposal may proceed.

ericoids Shrubby plants mainly belonging to the heath family (*Ericaceae*), e.g. heather, heaths, bilberry, cranberry – typically major constituents of ***heathland*** vegetation.

erosion The wearing away of rock or soil by water, ice, wind, or chemical processes such as solution. Natural (geologic) erosion is caused by natural factors and is usually a gradual process. Accelerated erosion exceeds estimated naturally occurring rates as a result of human activities.

eutrophic Nutrient-rich soils, waters, or ecosystems; usually having high ***p*Hs** (>7) (see ***dystrophic, mesotrophic, oligotrophic***).

eutrophicated Refers to an ecosystem that contains excessive nutrient levels.

eutrophication The process or trend of soil or water enrichment by plant nutrients – especially nitrogen and phosphorus. It can occur naturally, but usually refers to ***anthropogenic*** enrichment (sometimes called enhanced eutrophication) which can lead to excessive **nutrient loading** and consequent ecosystem degradation.

evaporites Water-soluble mineral sediments, such as salt and carbonates, that are deposited as a result of the evaporation of surface water. They are considered sedimentary rocks.

evapotranspiration Total evaporative loss from a land area, including evaporation from soils and surface waters, and ***transpiration*** (which is the major component in well vegetated terrestrial ecosystems).

field capacity (of a soil) The moisture content of a soil when water percolating downwards under gravity has drained out; usually expressed as cm^3 water per cm^3 soil (see also ***saturation capacity***).

floodplain (a) A **river floodplain** is the land adjacent to a water course over which water naturally spills and flows (unless prevented by flood defences) when floodwaters exceed the capacity of the channel, (b) a **coastal floodplain** is land adjacent to a coastline or estuary that is naturally inundated (unless prevented by coastal defences) by very high tides or (in the case of estuaries) by a combination of high tides and river flows.

forbs Generally broadleaved (non grass-like) herbaceous flowering plants, usually having conspicuous flowers; often called "herbs" or "flowers" (see ***graminoids***).

french drain A trench over a drainage line, backfilled with layers of material (coarse at the bottom and grading to fine-grained at the top) to act as a ***sediment*** filter; usually with a vegetated surface.

freshwater ecosystems/habitats Open freshwater systems in which the primary producers are ***phytoplankton***, filamentous ***algae*** and (in shallow water) submerged or floating-leaved ***macrophytes***. (Marginal emergent vegetation such as swamp is usually classed as **wetland**). The two principal types are: (a) **standing water bodies**, such as lakes and ponds, which have lentic (near-still) water which tends to become stratified (with lower temperatures and oxygen levels in lower layers), and which usually accumulate sediments; and (b) **water courses**, such a streams and rivers, which have lotic (running) water which is generally unstratified and oxygen-rich, and which do not accumulate sediments except in slow reaches. Water quality varies considerably (in relation to local climate and local geology) and is a principle criterion in classifications of both types (see Appendix C).

fungi   Heterotrophic organisms (see Figure 11.2) that are more closely related to animals than to plants, although their study (mycology) is traditionally included as a branch of botany, and they are normally included in floral rather than faunal surveys. The majority of species grow as filaments (hyphae) that are normally hidden, e.g. in soil or rotting wood, and their "fruiting bodies" (e.g. toadstools) provide the only ready means of identification. Most fungi feed on, and degrade, dead organic matter, but many exhibit **mutualism**, e.g. with plants such as conifers, beeches and orchids; and both these roles make them essential ecosystem components. A few species are pathogens.

graminoids   Grasses and grass-like plants, i.e. rushes and sedges (see **forbs**).

heath/heathland   A habitat/vegetation type usually dominated by dwarf shrubs such as **ericoids**. European heathland is an **anthropogenic** community that was created by forest clearance (often in the bronze age) and maintained by grazing, fire, and the use of materials for fuel etc. If unmanaged, it may quickly revert to **woodland**.

heavy metals   Metals with atomic weight >63.5 and specific gravity >4.0. Some (e.g. cobalt, copper, iron, manganese, molybdenum, zinc) are essential nutrients, although more than trace amounts of most are toxic, especially to some taxa. Others, which have an atomic weight >100 (e.g. silver, cadmium, mercury, lead) are highly toxic, and the term heavy metals is often restricted to these.

hydraulic conductivity   The permeability of soil or rock, and hence the ease, and potential rate, of water flow through it, usually expressed as cm/hr.

hydraulics   Processes and regimes of water flow (velocities, volumes, duration, frequency etc.) in hydrological systems such as surface waters and groundwaters.

hydrophilous   "Water-loving"; tolerant of wet conditions.

indicator species   Species that can be used as biological indicators: (a) to define and identify community or habitat types, e.g. **ancient woodland** indicator species (§D.3.3) and high-constancy species of NVC communities (§C.8); (b) to assess the conservation value of habitats, e.g. protected species; or (c) to assess environmental quality and monitor change in this, e.g. **lichens** as atmospheric pollution (especially **acid deposition**) indicators (see Richardson 1992), nettles as nutrient-enrichment indicators, and invertebrate families in relation to river water quality (§10.7.3). Lichens can also be used as indicators of "ecological continuity", e.g. in relation to old woodlands, parklands and heathlands (Gilbert 2000, Hill *et al.* 2005, Hodgetts 1992).

integrity (ecological)   The ability of a species population, habitat or site to maintain its ecological structure and function, e.g. of a site to sustain the important habitat(s) and species populations it hosts.

keystone species   A species having an important or vital influence on the structure and functioning of a community/ecosystem (e.g. with a key role in a food web), and/or can be used (a) to identify genetic issues or (b) as an *indicator species* of habitat health/quality (with fluctuations in abundance indicating habitat change).

leachates   Solutes, including pollutants, in water (or a non-aqueous liquid) that has leached from a "solid" matrix such as a soil or landfill (see *leaching*).

leaching   The removal of soluble nutrients and other chemicals from a "solid" matrix – such as a soil horizon, whole soil or landfill – by water percolating through it.

leakages (economic)   The flows of money out of a national, regional or local economy, following from an initial injection of money into that economy. The most significant leakages are for taxation (direct and indirect), savings and improved goods and services.

lichens   plant-like organisms consisting of an association between an alga and a fungus, on which they both depend (see *mutualism*)

linear habitats   Linear (much longer than wide) features that support biological communities. They can be valuable habitats in their own right, and may also act as *buffer zones* and *wildlife corridors*. Examples are hedgerows, field margins/linear set-aside, road/railway verges, habitat edges, woodland rides/fire breaks, transmission line routes, urban green belts, avenues of trees, ditches, streams, *river corridors*, and lake/coastal shorelines (see Beier and Noss 1998, Church 2008, Dawson 1994, Kirby 1995, Spellerberg and Gaywood 1993, Tattersall *et al.* 2002).

macroinvertebrates   Invertebrate animals that are large enough to be seen by eye or can be captured using a sieve of mesh 0.5–1.0mm.

macronutrients   Nutrient elements needed by organisms in relatively large amounts. They are: carbon, hydrogen, and oxygen – which plants obtain by photosynthesis; and calcium, iron, magnesium, nitrogen, phosphorus, potassium and sulphur – which plants absorb in solution from soil or a water body (although some have root nodules in which nitrogen-fixing bacteria assimilate gaseous nitrogen) (see *micronutrients*).

macrophytes   Plants large enough to be seen by eye. The term is most commonly applied to aquatic (freshwater and marine) species including *vascular plants* and seaweeds.

maerl beds   Calcareous encrustations on the sea bed formed by calcium fixing red algae (maerls).

marine annelids   Marine segmented worms belonging to two main classes: polychaetes, which have parapodia (paired lateral outgrowths) and many chaetae (brisltes); and oligochaetes (which lack parapodia and have few chaetae). Most burrow in sediment, but some polychaetes build tubes on the substratum.

meadow   Grassland maintained primarily for hay, often on poorly-drained land. Meadows are usually species-rich, partly as a result of traditional management which involves taking one late hay crop and then introducing grazing stock until winter or early spring, with no use of artificial fertilisers or *pesticides* (see *pasture*).

mesotrophic   Refers to soils/peats, waters, or ecosystems with nutrient levels intermediate between *eutrophic* and *oligotrophic*, and usually near-neutral *pH* (see also *dystrophic*).

metapopulation   A group of sub-populations that exist in separate habitat patches, but are linked by dispersal between them (Gilpin and Hanski 1991).

microclimate   The climate associated with very localised factors such as topography, aspect, soils, water bodies, vegetation and buildings. Microclimates may differ quite markedly from meso- (small-area/region) and macro- (large-region) climates.

microhabitat   A small habitat, with localised environmental conditions and resources, within a larger habitat. Examples include vegetation strata, and small patches of: distinctive vegetation; open ground; or substratum type (sand, mud or gravel) in aquatic habitats. Microhabitats can be important for animal species and can often support whole invertebrate communities.

micronutrients (trace elements)   Nutrient elements needed by organisms in small quantities, e.g. boron, chlorine, copper, manganese, molybdenum, and zinc. Some (e.g. copper) are toxic if present in more than small amounts (see *macronutrients*).

minerotrophic   The nutrient regimes of *mires* such as fens that, unlike *ombrotrophic* mires (bogs), are fed largely by surface and/or groundwater from mineral ground in their *catchments*, rather than by direct precipitation. Consequently, the nutrient status and *pH* of minerotrophic mires varies in relation to the local geology and hydrology (e.g. whether they are *soligenous* or *topogenous*). They are also less dependent on climate than are bogs, and tend to undergo succession, e.g. to *carr* and eventually to terrestrial woodland.

mires/peatlands   *Wetland ecosystems* in which the water table is normally at or near the surface, and the resulting near-permanent waterlogging (and associated anaerobic conditions) permit peat accumulation. They include *ombrotrophic* mires (bogs) and *minerotrophic* mires (fens, flushes and springs). The peat is typically >0.5m deep, although flushes and springs occur on shallow, incipient peat (see Table C.1).

multiplier   A measure of the scale of the increase in income or employment in a local, regional or national economy resulting from an initial injection of an amount of money into that economy.

multivariate analysis   The simultaneous analysis of a number of variables that have the same set of observations (e.g. community and/or environment data).

There are two main approaches, classification and ordination. **Classificatory methods** seek to identify groups of similar units (e.g. samples or species) that represent communities. **Ordination methods** seek to plot units along axes of variation that represent community, or environmental, gradients (see texts such as Jongman *et al.* 1995, Kent and Coker 1992, Krebs 1998). Suitable computer programs include TWINSPAN for classification, DECORANA for ordination (Hill 1994, Hill and Šmilauer 2005) and CAP (Seaby and Henderson 2007) which contains a suite of programs.

mutualism   A relationship between two species from which both benefit. It may be obligate (essential for survival) or facultative (useful but not vital) for one or both species. Some biologists use mutualism and **symbiosis** as synonyms, but others use symbiosis to include relationships that are only beneficial to one "partner", e.g. parasitism. There are numerous examples of mutualism in ecosystems worldwide.

negative feedbacks   Homeostatic regulatory mechanisms that tend to maintain equilibrium in ecological (and other) systems by dampening the effects of perturbations. For example, factors such as predation and food supply normally prevent the growth of species populations beyond the *carrying capacity* of their habitats (see *positive feedbacks*).

niche separation   The mechanism by which competition between cohabiting species in a community is reduced by the divergence of ecological niches. Each species has a niche that determines how it utilises the habitat resources and its role in the community. The niches of all species evidently differ at least slightly in one or more ways, e.g. trophic (eating different foods), spatial (e.g. in different *microhabitats*) and temporal (e.g. active during the day or night).

non-labile organics   Organic compounds that are resistant to decay, as opposed to labile organics that are easily degraded in the aquatic environment.

nonlinear ecological changes   Changes that do not conform to a simple proportional relationship between cause and effect, usually because a *threshold* is exceeded and *positive feedbacks* come into play. Consequently, they are often abrupt, unexpected (see *ecological surprises*), rapid, large and difficult or impossible to reverse.

notable (species/taxa and habitats)   A general term, denoting some designation of high conservation value, that can include legally protected, UKBAP priority, and internationally, nationally, regionally or locally threatened, rare or scarce (see Appendix D). It can also be applied to *keystone species*.

nutrient loading   see *eutrophication*

oligotrophic (nutrient-poor)   Refers to soils/peats, waters, or ecosystems with low nutrient levels, and usually low *pH* (5.5–7) (see *dystrophic*, *eutrophic*, *mesotrophic*).

ombrotrophic   The nutrient regime of bog ecosystems, which depends almost entirely on precipitation rather than groundwater. Consequently, unlike fens (which are *minerotrophic*), bogs are always *oligotrophic* and acid, and are climatic climax systems that should have long-term stability unless the climate changes.

pasture   Grassland maintained primarily for and by grazing, and on which grazing stock is kept for a large part of they year (see **meadow**).

pesticide   Defined under the Food and Environment Protection Act 1985 as "any substance, preparation or organism used for destroying any pest". This includes herbicides, fungicides, insecticides, molluscicides, rodenticides, growth regulators and masonry and timber preservatives.

pH   Scale of 0–14 defining the acidity/**alkalinity** of solutions including those in soils and water bodies; 0 = extremely acid, 14 = extremely alkaline, and 7 = neutral (although soils and waters with pHs between *c*.6.5 and *c*.7.5 are often referred to as neutral).

phytoplankton   The "plant" component of **plankton**. They are the primary producers of open water communities (with water too deep for **macrophytes**).

plankton   The small (often microscopic) freshwater or marine "plants" (**phytoplankton**) and animals (**zooplankton**) that are suspended in, and drift with, a water body.

plant life forms   Types of plants characterised by their morphology (body form) rather than taxonomy, e.g. herbaceous plants (sub-divided into **graminoids** and **forbs**), and woody plants (sub-divided into trees, shrubs and climbers).

podsols or **podzols**   Soils with highly leached and acidic (**pH** often 3.0–4.5) upper (eluvial) layers above re-deposition (illuvial) humus-rich (black) and iron rich (orange) layers, the later often becoming concreted to form an impermeable "iron pan" (see Figure 9.1).

point source pollution   Pollution from specific locations, e.g. into surface waters from sewage outfalls and industrial **effluent** discharge points; or into groundwaters from underground pipelines, **wells** or the bases of quarries and disposal sites. It is generally easier to control than **diffuse pollution**.

pollutant   see **pollution**

pollution   Any increase of matter or energy to a level that is harmful to living organisms or their environment (when it becomes a **pollutant**). It thus includes **physical pollution** (e.g. thermal, noise and visual) and **biological pollution** (e.g. microbial or by non-native plants and animals), but most commonly refers to **chemical pollution**. Chemical pollutants can be: (a) man-made compounds such as **pesticides**; (b) toxic chemicals, such as **heavy metals**, harmful levels of which are not normally present in ecosystems; or (c) normally benign or even essential substances such as nutrients, either because these are **micronutrients** that are toxic in more than trace amounts, or because of excessive nutrient loading (**eutrophication**).

population dynamics   The variations in time and space in the size and density of a species population which, for a given area, depend on the relationships between natality, mortality, immigration and emigration.

population equivalent   Unit used to quantify populations served by sewage treatment works (STWs). A single population equivalent (pe) is the organic biodegradable load having a five day **biochemical oxygen demand** of 60g per day (approximately the load from a single person's domestic waste).

positive feedbacks   Mechanisms that, in contrast to *negative feedbacks*, amplify the affects of perturbations on ecological (and other) systems and promote *nonlinear changes* (runaway deviation from equilibrium). For example, removal of tropical forest usually leads to decreased rainfall, which in turn inhibits forest growth and hence a positive feedback that promotes progressive loss of forest cover (MA 2005).

precautionary principle   An approach that advocates taking avoiding action notwithstanding scientific uncertainty about the nature and extent of a risk, e.g. to respond to the possibility of a significant environmental impact without conclusive evidence that it will occur. It is included in the 1992 Rio Declaration on Environment and Development (see §1.3) and advocated in EU and UK environmental policy.

project options/alternatives   Options that should be considered in a project proposal, including: location/siting; alignment of linear projects; design (scales, layouts etc.); processes; procedures employed during the construction, operational and decommissioning phases; and the "no action" option that the project should not go ahead. Assessment may result in the selection of **preferred options**.

quadrat   Strictly a four-sided, usually square, sampling plot; but can include shapes such as circles or rectangles, e.g. for sampling linear features. Quadrats can be any size, e.g. from portable frame quadrats (usually $\leq m^2$) to national grid squares.

receptor   Any component of the natural or man made environment that is potentially significantly affected by a development.

return period/interval   A period within which there is a given probability/risk of a *design event* occurring. For instance, a 1-in-100-year event is likely to occur once in any 100-year period. Return periods are based on long-term average time intervals between past (recorded) events, and it is statistically possible for a 1-in-100-year event to occur more than once within a year (or shorter period) or not for several hundred years – so they are often expressed as "per cent chance", e.g. a 1-in-50-year event has a 2 per cent chance of occurring in any one year, a 45 per cent chance of occurring within any 30-year period, and a 76 per cent chance of occurring within any 70-year period.

riffle   An area of a stream/river with a rocky or gravel substrate and shallow, turbulent, fast-moving water.

riparian   Relating to the banks of streams/rivers (sometimes also used to refer to the shorelines/fringes of standing water bodies such as lakes).

river corridor   A river and the adjacent land (that has physical, ecological and visual links to the water course) considered together as a linear feature of conservation importance, e.g. as a *wildlife corridor*. It can be taken to include the river *floodplain*, but is often restricted to the channel, banks and narrow strips of adjacent floodplain land (see *riparian*).

runoff   The part of precipitation that flows as surface water from a site, *catchment* or region and eventually reaches the sea. It is effectively the excess of precipitation over *evapotranspiration*, making allowance for storage in surface, soil and ground waters, and excluding groundwater seepage. Most runoff occurs in streams/rivers, and the term is often restricted to this.

saturation capacity (of a soil) The amount of water held by a soil when it is saturated, usually expressed as cm³ water per cm³ soil (see also *field capacity*).

screening (in the EIA process) Examination of a development proposal to determine if, under the EIA regulations, it: (a) is a Schedule 1 project requiring mandatory EIA; (b) is a Schedule 2 project and hence qualifies for a discretionary EIA; or (c) does not require a formal EIA but should be subject to an informal environmental assessment.

secondary treatment see *sewage treatment levels*

sediments Organic or inorganic material that has settled after deposition from suspension in water, ice, or air, usually as the water current or wind speed decreases. Aquatic sediments include those that accumulate on the floor of a water body (e.g. lake or ocean), water course or trap, or by deposition on a *floodplain* (see *alluvial soil*). Sediment commonly consists of *silt*, but can include coarser particulates and material such as calcium carbonate that has precipitated through chemical reaction. Suspended particulates that have not yet undergone *sedimentation*, are usually called suspended solids or (incorrectly) suspended "sediments" (see §10.3.1).

sedimentation The act or process of depositing *sediments*.

seed bank The accumulation of viable seeds in a soil (mainly the top 40cm) which may germinate if conditions become suitable – often when the soil is disturbed.

semi-natural (ecological system) A habitat, ecosystem, community, vegetation type or landscape that has been modified by human activity – but largely consists of, or supports, native species (and/or has relatively undisturbed soils, waters and geomorphological features) – and appears to have a similar structure and functioning to a natural type. Very few completely natural systems now exist, so conservation is largely concerned with protecting semi-natural systems.

sewage treatment levels (in the UK) **Primary** – usually physical treatment to remove gross solids; and to reduce suspended solids by *c.*50 per cent and **Biochemical Oxygen Demand** (BOD) by *c.*20 per cent. **Secondary** – biological treatment to significantly reduce suspended solids, BOD and ammonia. **Tertiary** – additional treatment, e.g. nutrient removal/stripping or ultra-violet treatment to kill pathogenic bacteria.

silt Fine particulate organic and inorganic material; strictly with an average particle size intermediate between sands and clays (see §9.3.1) but often taken to include all material finer than sands.

siltation trap A hard-lined stilling well/basin with inflow and outflow pipes for drainage water; designed to slow the flow sufficiently for collection of fine suspended solids by sedimentation.

soil moisture deficit (SMD) State when the soil moisture content is below *field capacity*, usually expressed in mm (rainfall equivalent) to indicate the amount of rain needed to cancel the deficit. SMDs develop during periods when *evapotranspiration* (ET) exceeds precipitation (Pn) and can be estimated by simple accounting based on ET – Pn values (mm) for weekly periods. Increasing SMDs result in decreasing availability of soil water to plants and hence an increasing treat of wilting.

soligenous The water regime of a *mire/peatland* in which there is appreciable groundwater flow and hence potential for nutrient replenishment (see *topogenous*).

species abundance The "amount" of a species in an area or community, expressed by a quantitative measure such as number, density or cover (see Table 11.5).

species diversity A measure of both the number of species (*species richness*) and their relative abundance (proportion of the sum of the abundances of all the species) in a community. It is more informative than species richness because a community with a given number of species has higher diversity if the overall abundance is fairly evenly distributed between them rather than being concentrated in one or a few *dominant species*.

species richness The number of species in a biological community. Communities consisting of few or many species are often referred to as "species-poor" and "species-rich" repectively.

sphagna Species of moss belonging to the genus Sphagnum ("bog moss"). They are often common on wet heaths and "poor-fens", and dominant on bogs (see Table C.1).

stepping stone habitats Small habitats that may be scattered and apparently isolated in a landscape, but which may assist in the dispersal of species by providing staging posts between larger habitats. Staging post habitats are also needed by long distance migrants such as migratory birds, especially along their regular migration routes.

sustainable development Defined in the 1987 Report of the World Commission on Environment and Development as "*Development that meets the needs of the present without compromising the ability of future generations to meet their own needs*".

synergism The mechanism by which the combined effect of two agencies, such as pollutants, is greater than the sum of their separate effects, i.e. the effect of one is enhanced by the other.

threshold A point at which an increase or decrease in the level of a *driver* changes the relationships that normally apply between it and dependent variables (such as species populations and ecosystem processes) in a way that usually triggers sudden, and sometimes irreversible, *nonlinear changes*. For instance: an over-harvested species population may decline steadily and then suddenly crash, as in the collapse of the Atlantic cod stocks off the coast of Newfoundland in 1992 (MA 2005); or biodiversity in an area may decline steadily with progressive habitat degradation, and then fall rapidly when a critical threshold is reached (see also *critical load*).

topogenious The water regime of a *mire/peatland* in which there is little or no groundwater flow and hence little potential for nutrient replenishment (see *soligenous*).

transpiration   Evaporative loss of water from plants. When the plants are "in leaf", it is normally the largest component of *evapotranspiration* from well vegetated terrestrial ecosystems, and can return >50 per cent of precipitation water to the atmosphere.

turbidity   The opacity of (and hence the degree of light attenuation in) water, due to the presence of suspended matter and *plankton*. High turbidities are harmful to aquatic life.

vascular plants   "Higher" plants which transport water and nutrients in a specialised structural system that is not present in simple (non-vascular) plants such as bryophytes (mosses and liverworts), *algae* and *lichens*. They include angiosperms (flowering plants), gymnosperms (mainly conifers) and pteridophytes (ferns, horsetails and clubmosses).

vice-counties   A system of county-like areas, covering the British Isles, which are often used for biological recording. Many have boundaries similar to those of the administrative counties.

weather (in a given place)   The condition of the atmosphere at a given time with respect to the various elements, e.g. temperature, sunshine, wind, precipitation. Refers to the behaviour of the atmosphere over a few hours or at most over a few days (see *climate*).

weathering   The physical and chemical breakdown of geological materials which contributes to *erosion* and soil formation.

well   Strictly a hand-dug shaft to a groundwater body, but used in the text to include **boreholes**, which are constructed by machinery, and are usually deeper but smaller in diameter than traditional wells. Both are used for abstraction and for observation of groundwater features including water table levels and water quality.

wetland ecosystems/habitats   Sometimes taken to include *freshwater habitats*, but usually (as in this book) restricted to habitats dominated by essentially terrestrial (or emergent) vegetation that is adapted to live in (at least periodically) waterlogged conditions. In this sense, they are intermediate between, and intergrade with, aquatic and terrestrial habitats. UK wetlands include swamps, *mires/peatlands*, wet heath, marshes (including saltmarshes), marshy grasslands, and *carr* (see Table C.1). The hydrology, ecology and conservation of wetlands are discussed in Gilman (1994), Keddy (2000), Mitsch and Gosselink (2007) and Raeymaekers (2000).

wildlife   Sometimes restricted to "wild animals", but can (as in this book) be taken to include all non-domesticate/cultivated organisms, i.e. the **biota**.

wildlife corridors   Linear habitats/landscape features, such as *river corridors*, hedgerows, field margins and roadside verges, that may increase *connectivity* by acting as routes between habitat patches, and hence: increasing the overall extent of habitat for animals with large range requirements; facilitating migration or dispersal of species between habitats; and facilitating access to, and hence colonisation of, new habitats. Together with *stepping stone habitats* they can be particularly important in areas in which there is severe habitat fragmentation, and may be the only remaining wildlife habitats in urban or intensively cultivated areas.

woodland Vegetation dominated by trees (>5m tall when mature) that form a distinct, although sometimes open, canopy. "Woodland" rather than "forest" is generally used in the UK because "forest" originally meant an area (wooded or not) reserved for hunting (Rackham 2000).

zooplankton The animal component of *plankton*, many of which graze on *phytoplankton* and are thus equivalent to the herbivores of terrestrial communities.

References

Beier P and RF Noss 1998. Do habitat corridors provide connectivity? *Conservation Biology* **12**(6), 1241–1252, http://forest.mtu.edu/info/ecologyseries/Beier-Noss_1998.pdf.

Church C 2008. *Environmental corridors: "lifelines for living"*. University of Illinois Extension, www.urbanext.uiuc.edu/lcr/LGIEN2001-0013.html.

Dawson D 1994. Are habitat corridors conduits for animals and plants in a fragmented landscape? A review of the scientific evidence. *English Nature Research Reports No. 94*, http://naturalengland.communisis.com/NaturalEnglandShop/.

EN (English Nature) 1997. *Habitat Regulations guidance note: The Appropriate Assessment (Regulation 48); The Conservation (Natural Habitats &c) Regulations, 1994*. Peterborough, Cambs: English Nature, www.mceu.gov.uk/MCEU_LOCAL/Ref-Docs/EN-HabsRegs-AA.pdf.

Gaston KJ and JI Spicer 2004. *Biodiversity: an introduction*. 2nd edn. Oxford: Blackwell Science.

Gilbert O 2000. *Lichens* (New Naturalist Series). London. HarperCollins.

Gilman K 1994. *Hydrology and wetland conservation*. Chichester: John Wiley & Sons.

Gilpin M and I Hanski 1991. *Metapopulation dynamics; empirical and theoretical investigations*. London: Academic Press.

Hill D, M Fasham, G Tucker, M Shewry and P Shaw 2005. *Handbook of biodiversity methods: survey, evaluation and monitoring*. Cambridge: Cambridge University Press.

Hill MO 1994. *DECORANA and TWINSPAN for ordination and classification of multivariate species data*. Huntingdon, Cambs: CEH, Monks Wood, www.ceh.ac.uk/products/software/land.html.

Hill MO and P Šmilauer 2005. *TWINSPAN for Windows version 2.3*. Huntingdon, Cambs and České Budějovice, Czech Republic: Centre for Ecology and Hydrology and University of South Bohemia, www.ceh.ac.uk/products/software/wintwins.html.

Hodgetts NG 1992. *Guidelines for selection of biological SSSIs: non-vascular plants*. Peterborough, Cambs: JNCC, www.jncc.gov.uk/page-2303.

Jongman RHG, CJF Ter Braak and OFR van Tongeren (eds) 1995. *Data analysis in community and landscape ecology*. Cambridge: Cambridge University Press.

Keddy PA 2000. *Wetland ecology: principles and conservation*. Cambridge: Cambridge University Press.

Kent M and P Coker 1992. *Vegetation description and analysis: a practical approach*. London: Belhaven Press.

Kirby KJ 1995. *Rebuilding the English countryside: habitat fragmentation and wildlife corridors as issues in practical conservation*. English Nature Science No. 10. Peterborough, Cambs: English Nature, http://naturalengland.communisis.com/NaturalEnglandShop/browse.aspx.

Krebs CJ 1998. *Ecological Methodology*, 2nd edn. New York: Harper & Row.

MA (Millennium Ecosystem Assessment) 2005. *Ecosystems & human well-being: synthesis*. Washington, DC: Island Press. www.maweb.org/en/Reports.aspx.

Mitsch WJ and JG Gosselink 2007. *Wetlands*, 4th edn. Hoboken, NJ: John Wiley & Sons.

ODPM 2005. *Government circular: biodiversity and geological conservation – statutory obligations and their impact within the planning system (Circular 06/2005)*. London: ODPM, www.communities.gov.uk/documents/planningandbuilding/pdf/147570.

Rackham O 2000. *The history of the countryside*. London: Orion.

Raeymaekers G 2000. *Conserving mires in the European Union*. Luxembourg: Office for Official Publications of the European Communities, http://bookshop.europa.eu/.

Richardson DHS 1992. *Pollution monitoring with lichens*. Slough, Berks: Richmond Publishing.

Seaby R and P Henderson 2007. *Community Analysis Package (CAP) 4.0: Searching for structure in community data*. PISCES Conservation Ltd, www.pisces-conservation.com/pdf/capinstructions.pdf.

Spellerberg IF and MJ Gaywood 1993. Linear features: linear habitats and wildlife corridors. *English Nature Research Report No. 60*. Peterborough, Cambs: English Nature, http://naturalengland.communisis.com/NaturalEnglandShop/.

Tattersall FH, DW Macdonald, BJ Hart, P Johnson, W Manley and R Feber 2002. Is habitat linearity important for small mammal communities on farmland? *Journal of Applied Ecology* 39(4), 643–652.

Index

Many topics are listed, or referred to, under the most relevant environmental component impact assessment (IA) or other large topics.

Two forms of cross-referencing may apply to a topic:
and: refers to pages on which it is mentioned in other topics, usually environmental components;
see: refers to topics that are related to it, or under which it is listed.

Bold page numbers indicate where terms and concepts are defined/explained.